RESEARCH AND INFORMATION
GUIDES IN BUSINESS, INDUSTRY,
AND ECONOMIC INSTITUTIONS

T0298406

THE FEDERAL TRADE COMMISSION

RESEARCH AND INFORMATION GUIDES IN BUSINESS, INDUSTRY AND ECONOMIC INSTITUTIONS

WAHIB NASRALLAH
General Editor

THE FEDERAL TRADE COMMISSION

A GUIDE TO SOURCES

ROBERT V. LABAREE

Routledge
Taylor & Francis Group

LONDON AND NEW YORK

First published 2000 by Garland Publishing Inc.

Published 2020 by Routledge
2 Park Square, Milton Park, Abingdon, Oxon, OX14 4RN
52 Vanderbilt Avenue, New York, NY 10017

First issued in paperback 2020

Routledge is an imprint of the Taylor & Francis Group, an informa business

Copyright © 2000 by Robert V. Labaree

All rights reserved. No part of this book may be reprinted or reproduced or utilised in any form or by any electronic, mechanical, or other means, now known or hereafter invented, including photocopying and recording, or in any information storage or retrieval system, without permission in writing from the publishers.

Notice:
Product or corporate names may be trademarks or registered trademarks, and are used only for identification and explanation without intent to infringe.

Library of Congress Cataloging-in-Publication Data
Labaree, Robert V.
    The Federal Trade Commission : a guide to sources / Robert V. Labaree.
        p. cm. — (Research and information guides in business, industry, and economic institutions)
    ISBN 0-8153-1296-2 (alk. paper)
    1. United States. Federal Trade Commission—Bibliography. 2. Trade regulation—United States—Bibliography. I. Title. II. Series.
    KF1611.L32 2000
    016.34373'08—dc21   00-060035

ISBN 13: 978-1-138-96965-0 (pbk)
ISBN 13: 978-0-8153-1296-3 (hbk)

Contents

Series Foreword

The new information society has exceeded everyone's expectations in providing new and exciting media for the collection and dissemination of data. Such proliferation has been matched by a similar increase in the number of providers of business literature. Furthermore, many emerging technologies, financial fields, and management processes have amassed an amazing body of knowledge in a short period of time. Indicators are that packaging of information will continue its trend of diversification, confounding even the experienced researcher. How then will information seekers identify and assess the adequacy and relevancy of various packages to their research needs?

It is my hope that Garland's *Research and Information Guides in Business, Industry, and Economic Institutions* series will bridge the gap between classical forms of literature and new alternative formats. Each guide will be devoted to an industry, a profession, a managerial process, or a field of study. Organization of the guides will emphasize subject access to formats such as bibliographic and numeric databases on-line, distribution databases, CD-ROM products, loose-leaf services, government publications and books, and periodical articles. Although most of the guides will serve as locators and bridges to bodies of knowledge, some may be reference books with self-contained information.

Since compiling such guides requires substantial knowledge in the organization of information or the field of study, authors are selected on the basis of their expertise as information professionals or subject specialists. Inquiries about the series and its content should be addressed to the series editor.

Wahib Nasrallah
Langsam Library
University of Cincinnati

Preface

If you approached a person on the street and asked them to describe the purpose and functions of the Federal Trade Commission (FTC), you would likely see a vacant look on their face and an answer of "I have no idea." Yet at the same time, it is highly probable that this same person is wearing clothing with detailed wear instructions, has recently purchased grocery store items with packaging explicitly stating the product's content and use, and watched commercials on television that include fine print informing him or her of exceptions and limitations regarding visual and descriptive statements made in the ad. All of this information has been made available to the consumer by the FTC and illustrate the myriad of ways in which that person's relationship to commerce and business in American society is affected by the work of the Federal Trade Commission.

The purpose of this bibliography is to assist students, researchers, legal scholars, and business persons in locating information on the FTC as reflected in scholarly journals and monographs. Since the work of the FTC is primarily challenged, debated, and affirmed in the courts, the majority of literature annotated in this book is derived from law review articles. However, journals from the fields of business and economics, political science, public administration, sociology, and history were also reviewed and included when appropriate. In this respect, this compilation may serve scholars from disciplines other than law. Political scientists will find ample studies on the political dimensions of state regulation and consumer protection; public administrators will discover research on the administration and governance of regulatory agencies; economists will encounter analyses on the economic impact of marketplace regulation; sociologists will uncover information about consumer behavior; and historians will find literature published throughout the twentieth century on the history and development of the FTC and on the broader attempts by government to regulate deceptive trade practices, protect the consumer from unfair business practices, and maintain a competitive marketplace free of monopolistic behavior.

Robert V. Labaree
Von KleinSmid Center Library
University of Southern California
June 1, 2000

Introduction

It would have been impossible to produce a truly comprehensive work representing the entire volume of literature written about the Federal Trade Commission since its inception in 1914 to early 1999. Without restrictions, this book could easily have been devoted solely to the literature of consumer protection or antitrust law enforcement. It was, therefore, crucial to impose certain restrictions on the type of material to be included in this annotated bibliography. First, only English language materials published in the United States were included. This rule was relatively easy to adhere to since the FTC has rarely been the topic of analysis in overseas journals. However, continued efforts by the FTC to regulate foreign companies doing business in the United States, coupled with the expanded globalization of business through trade and the Internet, may lead to increased attention to the work of the FTC overseas. The *Index to Foreign Legal Periodicals* and the *Public Affairs Information Service* should be consulted to obtain overseas literature on the FTC.

Second, with few exceptions, only scholarly literature was considered for inclusion. Scholarly works were defined by the type of journal, its intended readership, and the presence of references and notes. Exceptions to this rule, such as essays in popular business magazines, were made only when it could be determined that the article was the most comprehensive or detailed representation of a particular topic, had have been cited extensively in scholarly works, presented a unique of perspective, or was written by a Commissioner or other FTC official.

Finally, coverage focused only on research in which the primary point of analysis was the Federal Trade Commission. This was perhaps the most difficult rule to abide by as I researched the Commission. For example, many articles would give equal attention to examining the dual enforcement of antitrust laws by the FTC and the Antitrust Division of the Department of Justice. However, since this is one of a number of key issues shaping the legal environment in which the FTC has carried out its duties, most articles were included even if only a section was devoted to the FTC. A similar approach was used when reviewing articles examining the dual enforcement efforts of the FTC and the Federal Communications Commission as well as the FTC and the Food and Drug Administration. What follows is a more detailed explanation of the contents and scope of each chapter and section of this book.

Chapter one, "Consumer Protection," annotates books and periodical articles that examine the FTC's role in protecting the consumer from various forms of unfair business practices. There is an immense and diverse amount of literature devoted to examining the consumer protection mission of the Federal Trade Commission. The majority of this literature has been written in the past thirty-five years, paralleling the consumerism movement that began in the 1960s. Earlier literature reflects an expansion of the FTC's power in consumer protection marked by the enactment of the Wheeler-Lea Amendment to Section 5 of the FTC Act which gave the FTC power to regulate deceptive advertising.

The majority of the literature included in the first chapter can be divided into four broad categories. The first category of literature involves the FTC's application of legal doctrines, such as the doctrine of deceptive advertising and the doctrine of unsubstantiated advertising. An measurable segment of this literature is devoted to the efforts of the FTC to regulate advertising directed at children. The second category examines the Commission's efforts to educate consumers and businesses about their rights and responsibilities under the rules and regulations the FTC creates and administers. A common theme discusses the need to create a balance between regulating deceptive advertising, while at the same time, not undermining the information needs of the consumer. The third category of consumer protection literature analyzes the legal parameters in which the FTC must apply its rules and regulations. Much of this literature examines the FTC's attempt to define deception in advertising and its use of evidence to initiate action. The fourth category of literature consists of criticism directed at the FTC's attempt to protect the consumer. This criticism focuses primarily on perceptions of mismanagement and misinterpretation of the laws by the Commission. The criticism also consists of complaints by former employees of the agency regarding shifts in the FTC's mission brought about by political changes.

The following criteria has been applied in selecting the materials in the first chapter: books are chosen if their primary purpose is to analyze the FTC's role in protecting the consumer from deceptive business practices or if a significant portion of the book discusses the FTC and its relationship to consumerism. Periodical articles were selected if they focused on the FTC's role in consumer protection. Studies of action taken by the FTC against individual companies or industries are not included unless the issue, such as the regulation of children's television, was of historical importance or reflected a significant legal or policy position of the FTC. Individual actions against companies were also included if they were of a case study nature and used by the author to expand upon the larger issues of consumer protection.

Chapter two, "Antitrust Law Compliance," presents books and journal articles that examine the FTC's antitrust enforcement authority. The majority of literature in this chapter analyzes the Commission's enforcement of five specific pieces of legislation: The Sherman Antitrust Act, the Federal Trade Commission Act, the Clayton Act, the Robinson-Patman Act, and the Hart-Scott-Rodino Act. Each of these legislative initiatives cover a specific aspect of antitrust law enforcement. Much of this work addresses how effectively the FTC uses these laws to prevent monopolies and restraints on trade. A smaller portion of the literature examines the economic impact of antitrust law enforcement on the marketplace or, in some cases, on specific industries. There is also a measurable portion of mostly contemporary literature devoted to examining dual enforcement between the FTC and the Antitrust Division of the Department of Justice.

The following criteria were applied in selecting the materials for this chapter. Books were chosen if they examined antitrust law compliance from the standpoint of the FTC's impact on the marketplace or if the book or a significant portion of the book, specifically analyzed the FTC's role in antitrust law compliance. Journal articles were included if they examined the FTC's role in antitrust law enforcement or covered an important case involving the FTC and antitrust law. Also included were articles that examined the FTC's role in conjunction with the Department of Justice. Specific actions taken by the FTC against a company were not included unless the issue represented an important policy position by the agency or was of historical significance as determined by references to the issue in subsequent literature.

Chapter three, "Administrative Law and Procedure," contains references to literature that primarily examines administrative law and procedures of the FTC. For the purposes of this chapter, administrative law refers not only to the legal definition of the term, but also to research exploring the regulatory activities of the FTC within the political systems that the agency occupies. This approach was adopted because most of the legislative oversight conducted by Congress to evaluate FTC's enforcement and information gathering procedures affect the administration and organization of the agency and its ability to carry out its duties.

Chapter four, "Trade Regulation and Rulemaking Authority," examines selected books and periodical articles related to the FTC's rulemaking authority and promulgation of trade regulation rules. This literature reflects the study of the Commission's influence on business activities within specific industries, such as the cement industry, and the effects of specific rules issued by the agency to help regulate unfair and deceptive trade practices. Also included are sources that examine the constitutionality of the FTC's rulemaking authority.

Five appendices are included to supplement and enhance the content of the annotations. Appendix one outlines the history of the Federal Trade Commission derived from materials found in this book. The history is not comprehensive but intended to outline major themes and highlight specific events.

Appendix two lists the addresses and state coverage of the FTC's regional offices. Appendix three contains a glossary of terms that appear frequently in consumer protection, antitrust law, economics, and trade regulation literature. Information is also given for important pieces of legislation that fall within the enforcement jurisdiction of the FTC. When appropriate, general economic and legal words or phrases are defined within the context of specific FTC regulatory and economic responsibilities. Definitions are derived from legal dictionaries, selected FTC documents, and terminology stated in selected the law review articles within this book. Appendix four lists Internet sites related to the content of this book. The sites are listed alphabetically by title under several broad subject headings. Inclusion of sites in this list were determined from surveying current professional literature and scholarly web directories. Appendix five contains the full text of the Federal Trade Commission Act as it was drafted in 1996. The Act is included because its provisions are central to research represented in the citations of this book.

Methodology and Form of Entry

Every attempt was made to acquire and review potentially valuable bibliographic sources. Most were identified using the WorldCat database of the OCLC FirstSearch online system. Extensive reliance on the references cited by authors in law review articles were also used to locate sources for possible inclusion.

In addition to the WorldCat database, a number of online and print indexes were reviewed in their entirety. In alphabetical order, these included the print or electronic versions of *ABC Pol Sci*, *ABI/Inform*, *Alternative Press Index*, *America: History and Life*, *Arts & Humanities Citation Index*, *CARL UnCover*, *Communication Abstracts*, *Current Contents*, *ERIC*, *Expanded Academic Index ASAP*, *Historical Abstracts*, *Index of Legal Periodicals*, *Index to Foreign Legal Periodicals*, *International Political Science Abstracts*, *Journal of Economic Literature*, *The Left Index*, *LEXIS/NEXIS Legal Research Library*, *MedLine*, *Political Science Abstracts*, *Public Affairs Information Service*, *Reader's Guide to Periodical Literature*, *Sage Public Administration Abstracts*, *Sage Race Relations Abstracts*, *Sage Urban Affairs Abstracts*, *Science Citation Index*, *Social Science Citation Index*, *Social Sciences Index*, *Social Work Abstracts*, *Sociological Abstracts*, *Urban Affairs Abstracts*, and *Wilson Business Abstracts*.

Each entry contains the pertinent bibliographic information required to obtain the material. Books include the author, full title, place of publication, publisher, and year of publication. References to journals include the author, title of article, name of journal, volume number, data, and pagination. Citations follow the 13th edition of the *Chicago Manual of Style*. The annotations of books attempt to summarize the contents and highlight any special features, such as appendices. Annotations of journal articles are descriptive and state the primary purpose of the article, the research methodology employed, and the author's main conclusions.

Inclusion of all relevant doctoral dissertations was considered early in this project, but abandoned when it became apparent that many would be difficult or impossible to obtain for review. The availability of *Dissertation Abstracts International* made this decision to exclude dissertations much easier.

Acknowledgments

Although countless hours were spent alone squirreled away in the study cubicles of the law libraries at American University and the University of Southern California, an endeavor of this magnitude could not have been completed without the generous support of others. To that end, I gratefully acknowledge the assistance of Gary McCann and Joanne Zich at the Washington College of Law of American University and Brian Raphael at the University of Southern California Law Center for their efforts in helping to locate materials and access legal information online.

I also gratefully acknowledge the interlibrary loan staff of both the American University and the University of Southern California. They consistently showed infinite patience during my efforts to locate and obtain obscure journal articles or find materials that had been incorrectly cited in law reviews.

And finally, compiling this bibliography required numerous visits to the FTC Library while I lived in Washington, DC. Two things stand out from these research excursions. First, the librarians and professional staff of the FTC were extraordinarily helpful in locating materials and answering my questions. And Second, I feel compelled to mention the reuben sandwiches at the Manhattan Deli across the street from the FTC building on Pennsylvania Avenue. They provided a great excuse for taking a long lunch break between the endless hours spent in FTC Library annotating law review articles on my laptop computer.

Chapter One
Consumer Protection

1   Aaker, David A. and George S. Day., eds. *Consumerism: Search for the Consumer Interest*. 4th Edition. New York, NY: Free Press, 1982. A collection of reprinted articles from a variety of journals, the book begins with an examination of the scope of the consumer protection problem and the lack of clear goals by federal agencies, such as the FTC, to address these issues. The remaining four parts of the book discuss specific examples of deceptive behavior concerning the pre-purchase phase of the buyer-seller transaction, the purchase transaction, the post-purchase phase, and problems between segments of the buying population and the seller.

2   Acheson, Eleanor D. and Mark Tauber. "Limits of FTC Power to Issue Consumer Protection Orders." *George Washington Law Review* 40 (March 1972): 496-526. Under severe criticism, the FTC has recently attempted to fashion cease and desist orders that will effectively eliminate deceptive advertising practices. After studying the legality of recent orders under Section 5 of the FTC Act, it is concluded that orders requiring restitution and orders requiring respondents to confess violations is beyond the legislatively designated purpose of cease and desist orders. Recent legislative proposals in Congress show a reluctance on the part of Congressional members to allow the full panoply of equitable remedies be made available to enforce the prohibitions articulated in Section 5. Until Congress acts, however, the FTC must yield to legislatively established and judicially recognized controls.

3   "An Act to Prohibit Unfair and Deceptive Trade Practices." *Harvard Journal of Legislation* 7 (1969): 122-153. This article presents a model statute to prohibit unfair and deceptive trade practices. The proposal includes statutory language and explanatory comments from a modified draft of the Massachusetts "Regulation of Business and Consumer Protection Act." Each part of the model covers a specific aspect of consumer protection. The essay also notes that consumer education alone will not solve the problems of deception. However, efforts such as offering of courses in consumer budgeting and purchasing made available as a regular part of secondary school education, would help to supplement the proposed legislation.

4   "Ad Substantiation Program: You Can Fool All of the People Some of the Time and Some of the People All of the Time, but Can You Fool the FTC?." *American University Law Review* 30 (Winter 1981): 429-476. Despite the recognition that deceptive advertising is an exploitive practice that harms consumers, the judicial system has been relatively unresponsive in eradicating the problem. Consumers have few options in seeking action against deceptive advertisers because of the high cost of litigation and the highly technical nature of the evidence needed to prove deception occurred. In response, the FTC initiated the Ad Substantiation Program in July of 1971. The Program requires all advertisers to submit all tests, studies, and other evidence used by an advertiser to substantiate the safety, performance, efficacy, or comparative price claim for a product. By analyzing the Program's implementation, structure and functional deficiencies, and how the goals, requirements, and enforcement procedures have eroded the Program's effectiveness, a comprehensive framework for improving the Program is proposed.

5   "ADA, FTC Clash over Specialty Announcements, Advertising." *Journal of the American Dental Association* 125 (January 1994):88, 90.
Examines the letter presented by the FTC stating that the American Dental Association's (ADA) "Principles of Ethics and Code of Professional Conduct" violates a final order issued by the Commission prohibiting the ADA from restricting the advertising of dental care services. At issue are restrictions in the code that define when and under what circumstances a dentist may imply a specialty within a particular field of dentistry.

6   Adler, Richard. Principle Investigator. *Research on the Effects of Television Advertising on Children: A Review of the Literature and Recommendations for Future Research.* Washington, DC: National Science Foundation, 1978.
Although not meant to reach a definitive plan of action regarding the effects of advertising on children, the report does provide a framework for understanding the issues involved and to analyze the literature that has been published. The report begins by providing an overview of the issues and discusses what the research has discovered. The activities of both the FTC and the Federal Communications Commission (FCC) are examined in detail, including rules and regulations advocated by the two agencies, their interpretation of evidence, and how these activities meld with Congressional actions. This is one of the most

comprehensive sources of information on the topic of the effects of advertising to children up to the mid-1970s. Includes a bibliography of governmental, journal, and monographic literature on the issue.

7   "Administrative Law–Magnuson-Moss Warranty–Federal Trade Commission Improvement Act–The FTC Can Obtain Equitable Relief for Deceptive Trade Practices." *Texas Law Review* 53 (May 1975): 831-840.

States that the Act greatly expands the FTC's power beyond traditional cease and desist orders to actively seek remedies when deceptive practices are discovered because it allows the FTC to obtain positive relief from defrauded consumers. The commentary notes, however, that there are far more complex problems associated with the Magnuson-Moss Act because it's enforcement depends upon the actions of the courts.

8   "Advertising–Undisclosed Use of Simulations in Television Commercials–a Deceptive Practice." *Vanderbilt Law Review* 18 (1965): 2008-2013.

Discusses the reasoning behind the Supreme Court's judgement in the case *FTC v. Colgate-Palmolive Co.* to uphold the FTC's order that an undisclosed mock-up of sand attached to a plexiglass sheet used to show the moisturizing power of Rapid Shave shaving cream, is deceptive advertising. While the commentary agrees with the ruling, it is noted that further judicial review will need to take place to narrow the initial broad pronouncement.

9   Adams, David G. and Marlene Feigin Schwartz. "Consumer Protection–The Magnuson-Moss Act." *Annual Survey of American Law* (1976): 257-283

The Magnuson-Moss Act has two main components: Title I, the Warranty Act which establishes nationally uniform minimum standards of disclosure for written warranties on certain consumer goods and, Title II, the Federal Trade Commission Improvement Act which broadens the FTC's jurisdiction through increased rulemaking authority and enforcement capability. This essay concentrates on outlining the major provisions of Title I and the rules that have promulgated under it.

10   Alexander, George J. "Federal Regulation of False Advertising."
University of Kansas Law Review 17 (1969): 573-585.

Critical essay of the FTC's attempts to regulate false and misleading advertising. Specific examples are discussed to back this assertion. To improve its consumer protection mission the FTC should either provide, or force sellers to provide, consumers with basic information, implement a pro-competitive advertising policy with specific measures to protect the marketplace as well as the consumer, to reconsider its policy to judge products on a comparative basis, and to engage in testing products in markets where substantially inadequate consumer information is provided.

11   Alexander, George J. *Honesty and Competition: False Advertising
Law and Policy Under FTC Administration.* Syracuse, NY: Syracuse
University Press, 1967.

Traces the FTC's administrative activities related to its consumer protection mission. The book begins with an analysis of the conflict inherent in enhancing competition while, at the same time, avoiding consumer deception. This conflict is placed within the FTC's authority to enforce deceptive behavior as defined by legislation and court rulings and examines what limitations exist in enforcing a standard of deception. The remaining chapters analyze FTC false advertising policy regarding specific types of claims on the sale of goods or services. Topics covered include claims of product capability or function, price information, trademarks and other trade symbols, testimonies and endorsements, and sales promotions. Under each topic, cases are examined to help clarify important points. Includes twenty-three appendices containing the text to FTC guides issued to assist manufacturers and other sellers in following Commission guidelines. Each guide covers a specific industry or group of industries.

12   Allan, Paul W. and Dora R. Herring. "An Update on the Changing
Standards for Promoting CPA Services." *The Practical Accountant* 24
(February 1991): 43-49.

Examines the impact on the practitioner of the agreement between the American Institute of Certified Public Accountants and the FTC in regard to advertising, solicitation, and trade names. State regulations are also reviewed with an example of one firm's attempt at contemporary advertising.

13 Alperin, Howard J. *Consumer Law: Sales Practices and Credit Regulation.* St. Paul, MN: West Publishing Co., 1986. 2 volumes.
Takes a problem-orientated approach to defining and then analyzing the issue of consumer law. Each chapter discusses a different aspect of consumer law by providing example cases and examining what impact they have on the consumer. The FTC's role figures prominently in the chapters regarding unfairness and deception, warranties, and mass media advertising. Includes tables of statutes and rules and regulations. Updated with annual pocket inserts.

14 Anderson, David and Jonathan Winer. "Corrective Advertising:The FTC's New Formula for Effective Relief." *Texas Law Review* 50 (1972): 312-333.
Uses specific cases to outline the history of the FTC's use of corrective advertising as a remedy to supplement traditional cease and desists orders. The constitutionality of corrective advertising, and its effects on advertisers, consumers, and the volume of advertising, is also examined. It is concluded that corrective advertising is a legal and powerful method of deterring deception in advertising.

15 Anderson, Sigurd. "The Struggle for the Consumer's Dollar." *Antitrust Bulletin* 8 (May-June 1963): 517-530.
In an address at the annual meeting of the Charlotte-Piedmont Better Business Bureau, the author describes the intense competition for the consumer's dollar and how this competitive environment breeds unethical behavior among some merchants. The address then outlines the two categories of work performed by the FTC to alleviate this problem--antimonopoly regulation and antideceptive acts and practices. Examples of how these categories of regulation work for the consumer are then discussed.

16 Annen, Richard J. "Horizontal Privity Under the Magnuson-Moss Warranty Act: A Practitioner's Guide." *The Notre Dame Lawyer* 51 (April 1976): 775-785.
The essay begins with a brief outline of the Act's scope and legal history, moves on to explore three distinct classes of protected consumers as defined within the Act and placing the analysis in the context of horizontal privity, and concludes with a comparative analysis of similar versions that states may use to protect the consumer. These alternatives are contained in the Uniform Commercial Code.

17   August, William and Peggy Charren. "Finding the Public in Consumer Research: A Reply to Ward." *Merrill-Palmer Quarterly* 30 (July 1984): 261-264.

Analyzes Thomas B. Ward's examination of letters sent to the FTC concerning children's television advertising. The author advocates that public opinion research regarding consumer protection issues should include information on the degree that consumers are informed about their fundamental rights with respect to the consumer issues being studied.

18   Austern, H. Thomas. "What is "Unfairness Advertising?": A Discussion of Consumer Advertising from the Point of View of the Consumer, the Government, and Industry," *The Business Lawyer* 27 (April 1972): 883-890.

Discusses the issue of "meaning" as it relates to advertising and how the FTC has created regulations that encompass, with varying degrees of success, this concept for the benefit of the consumer.

19   Baker, Eugene J. and Daniel J. Baum. "Section 5 of the Federal Trade Commission Act: A Continuing Process of Redefinition." *Villanova Law Review* 7 (1962): 517-562.

Probes in detail the legislative history and judiciary response to the "unfair methods of competition" doctrine contained within Section 5 of the FTC Act, concluding that, despite constant review by the courts and the FTC itself, the basic tenets of the statement have remained essentially intact. This article provides a clear overview of the legislative and regulatory history of the principles behind Section 5 of the FTC Act.

20   Bailey, Patricia P. "Consumer Health Law Overview: Competition Spurs Changes for Good Ill." *Journal of State Government* 62 (May/June 1989): 99-101.

Examines the effects of deregulation through antitrust suits brought up by the Department of Justice and the FTC on the health services industry, including the expansion of competition among physicians and allied health professionals. The impact on consumers is also discussed.

21   Bailey, Patricia P. and Michael Pertschuk. "The Law of Deception: The Past as Prologue." *American University Law Review* 33 (Summer 1984): 849-897.

Examines the new deception standard from two perspectives: (1) it's apparent initial use as a device to narrow the FTC's traditional deception authority as granted by Congress and (2) as a clarification of the traditional legal standard as it now appears to be applied. A detailed introduction regarding the evolution of the new standard's development and an analysis of how that standard defines deception is presented, followed by a study of the relationship between the traditional and new standards. Further historical perspective is provided by analyzing common law of deception prior to the implementation of the Wheeler-Lea Act amending Section 5 of the FTC Act. By examining the three elements of the law of deception as defined by the FTC Act (an act or practice that has the tendency or capacity to mislead consumers, that a substantial number of consumers would be mislead, and that the act or practice must be misleading in a material respect) it is concluded that proponents of the new standard did not intend to change the traditional law governing deceptive advertising.

22   Bank, Kevin M. "How Green is My Product and Package: The Federal Trade Commission's Environmental Marketing Guidelines." *Food and Drug Law Journal* 49 (1994): 499-509.

Outlines the general principles of the FTC's "Guides for the Use of Environmental Claims in Advertising" and how they apply to Section 5 of the FTC Act. The eight specific claims (general environmental benefit claims, degradable claims, compostable claims, recyclable claims, recycled content claims, source reduction claims, refillable claims, and ozone safe and ozone friendly claims) addressed by the guidelines are then examined in detail.

23   Barksdale, Hiram C. et al. "Changes in Consumer Attitudes Toward Marketing, Consumerism, and Government Regulation: 1971-1975." *Journal of Consumer Affairs* 10 (Winter 1976): 117-139.

Examines trends in consumer attitudes towards business, consumer responsibility, government regulation and price controls. Although during the period 1971 to 1975 there was little change in the level of consumer discontent, measuring consumer attitudes from a zero base would result in exaggerated interpretations of the current conditions.

24   Barnes, David W. "The Significance of Quantitative Evidence in Federal Trade Commission Deceptive Advertising Cases." *Law and Contemporary Problems* 46 (Autumn 1983): 25-47.

Argues that a restructuring of advertising regulations must occur based on "greater clarity in the presentation, litigation, and evaluation of statistical evidence" and on a more careful enjoinment of misleading messages by the FTC. Previous guidelines are examined to determine characteristics peculiar to the factual issues concerning deceptive advertising. The distinction between "practical" and "statistical" significance is examined to provide a set of principles that would help to clarify and simplify both legal proceedings and remedies in deceptive advertising.

25   Barnes, Irston R. "False Advertising." *Ohio State Law Journal* 23 (Fall 1962): 597-664.

Detailed analysis of false advertising's impact on the marketplace. The article reviews attempts by Congress, through the FTC Act and its amendments, to remedy the problem, analyzes the FTC's specific role in policing false advertising, and concludes by commenting on the benefits to consumers that the Wheeler-Lea Amendment of 1938 have brought.

26   Barry, Thomas E. "A Framework for Ascertaining Deception in Children's Advertising." *Journal of Advertising* 9 (Winter 1980): 11-18.

Criteria are explained for judging deceptive or unfair advertising, specifically when it is directed towards children. A model is given that proposes a seven step framework for better determining how deception takes place among child consumers. The steps are: pre-examination, selection of a relevant sample, determine understanding of the concepts relevant to the message in the commercial, measure responses, determine if deception exists based upon the responses, determine deception's impact, and determine appropriate action.

27   Baum, Daniel J. "The Consumer and the Federal Trade Commission." *Journal of Urban Law* 44 (Fall 1966): 71-88.

Argues that the war on poverty has not only empowered the poor, but given context and strength to the interests of consumers. An example of this is the renewed proposal to establish a cabinet level position that oversees issues concerning consumers. However, the FTC has sometimes failed to recognize that consumer interests did not necessarily parallel those of furthering competition. Areas such as price misrepresentation, list prices, and issues regarding the cigarette industry illustrate this failure. Independent agencies such as the FTC are unable to make political decisions on behalf of consumers at the enforcement level. A study of the poor consumer would lay the foundation for developing a "Department of Consumers" that would fill this gap.

28   Baum, Daniel J. "The Federal Trade Commission and the War on Poverty." *UCLA Law Review* 14 (May 1967): 1071-1088.

Comments on the lack of awareness by the poor about the FTC's mission and power to regulate deceptive advertising and the FTC's failure to become more involved with consumer problems that it views as local and outside of its preferred jurisdiction. To overcome this, the FTC must move beyond the education guides it creates and be in direct contact with poor. It is argued that the expertise and judicial power the FTC has in fighting deceptive advertising practices should be better utilized in the War on Poverty. The creation of a comprehensive program to address issues concerning the low-income consumer would lay the foundation for this endeavor.

29   Baum, Daniel J. "Truthful Disparagement Under the Federal Trade Commission Act." *Trademark Reporter* 51 (1961): 1081-1096.

Examines the regulatory environment created by the FTC in which advertisers must function and how these regulations affect what an advertiser can say about a competitor. The issue of condition of relevance in a comparative statement regarding the merits of a product, the doctrine of significance, and the concept of puffery are specifically considered.

30   Baysinger, B. D. and C. W. Lamb. "A Consumer Welfare Standard for FTC Case Selection." *Michigan State University Business Topics* 29 (Winter 1981): 58-64.

By analyzing 1,014 cases of potentially deceptive trade practices on which the FTC has ruled upon during the period 1965 through 1975, a clear picture emerges regarding the need for research to identify criteria for the FTC to use in taking action against specific advertisements. Given the vagueness of the FTC Act's mandate to protect the consumer contained in Section 5, FTC staff must use discretion in selecting targets for investigation. The authors propose a consumer welfare standard for FTC case selection and to apply this standard to the cases the FTC has initiated during the past ten years.

31   Beales, J. Howard. "What State Regulators Can Learn from Federal Experience in Regulating Advertising." *Journal of Public Policy and Marketing* 10 (1991): 101-117.

Advertising regulators at the FTC work under three fundamental principles that guide their actions: that advertising enhances competition, that regulation cannot prevent all forms of deception or misinterpretation, and that advertising cannot provide complete information. While differences are present in the application of these principles there is a virtual consensus that adherence to these principles ensures the best protection of the consumer. However, by analyzing specific examples, it is shown that state level regulators do not adhere to this broad consensus. This creates an unpredictable environment in which advertisers must function, leading to restrictive judgements based on unwanted investigation from state officials. This would restrict the type of objective product information most helpful to consumers.

32   Beales, J. Howard et al. "The Efficient Regulation of Consumer Information." *Journal of Law and Economics* 24 (December 1981): 491-539.

There has been increasing criticism regarding regulations that purport to help the consumer. This has led to an exploration of alternative ways in which to protect the consumer. One proposal has been to simply provide the consumer with more information from which to protect themselves from unsafe products or unethical sellers. Although this goal has been widely accepted, how to accomplish it has lagged behind. Although supplying more information to the consumer seems simple, it hides the fact that there are many underlying complexities involved. These complexities are explored in an effort to help seek ways that the legal system can improve information dissemination to consumers. The analysis is summarized in the form of policy recommendations.

33   Beales, Howard et al. "Consumer Search and Public Policy." *Journal of Consumer Research* 8 (June 1981): 11-22.

Examines how consumers obtain information and from what internal and external sources. Each of these sources convey different types of information to the consumer. The implications of these factors are studied in relation to government information programs.

34   Becker, Boris W. "Injunction Powers of the Federal Trade Commission: Immediate Relief from Deceptive Advertising." *Journal of Advertising* 12 (1983): 43-45.

Traces the legislative and judicial history of the FTC's injunctive powers and discusses why this facet of the FTC's power in curtailing deceptive advertising is so important in light of recent cases.

35   Belew, Joe. "Privacy and the Fair Credit Reporting Act." *Journal of Retail Banking* 12 (Summer 1990): 60-61.

Briefly discusses the impact of an FTC commentary issued May 4, 1990 that restricts the ability of lenders to use prescreened lists for credit solicitations. The proposal states that these lists can only be sent if the lender "is prepared to offer credit to every person who appears" on the list. The list cannot be used expressly for promotional purposes. The privacy implications of prescreening and notes that the credit industry should be prepared to challenge any overburdensome provisions that may be enacted.

36   Belfiore, Constance L. "Proprietary Vocational School Abuses: Can the FTC Cure Them?" *Catholic University Law Review* 24 (Spring 1975): 603-622.

Reviews data collected to date regarding the false and misleading business practices of proprietary vocational schools and the FTC's attempt to remedy the situation through an industry-wide Trade Regulation Rule. The appropriateness of the use of this Rule is reviewed within the context of the FTC's overall power to regulate an industry and concludes by detailing each provision of the Rule as it applies to this specific case.

37   Beltramini, Richard F. "Perceived Believability of Warning Label Information Presented in Cigarette Advertising." *Journal of Advertising* 17 (1988): 26-32.

Investigates the believability among young adults of the information presented in warning labels on cigarette packaging and in advertisements initiated by the FTC in 1984. Results show that a smoker's behavior was not substantially effected by the perceived believability of the warning label information.

38   Benson, David J. and Alphonse M. Squillante. "The Role of the Holder in Due Course Doctrine in Consumer Credit Transactions." *The Hastings Law Journal* 26 (1974): 427-459.

Examines the role played by the Holder-In-Due-Course Doctrine in transactions among the seller, consumer, and financier, including recent challenges to the Doctrine and the failure of sellers, consumers, and financiers to create uniformity in the treatment of holders. Among the challenges discussed is the FTC's proposed regulation designed to end the Holder-In-Due-Course Doctrine.

39   Bernacchi, M. D. "Advertising and Its Discretionary Control by the FTC: A Need for Empirically Based Criteria." *Journal of Urban Law* 52 (November 1974): 223-266.

Discusses the importance of advertising as a modern marketing tool and the development of advertising regulations, including FTC enforcement principles and procedures, to build a screening model for prioritizing investigations of emotive, persuasive, or psychological advertisements as opposed to those based on economic, rational, and informative messages. Data gathered by behavioral science and statistical techniques are presented to show its integration into the model. The model is developed as a systematic decision making process for prioritizing the selection of alleged deceptive advertising.

40   Bernard, Kent S. "Handling the News: A Proposed Approach for the Federal Trade Commission." *Arizona Law Review* 21 (1979): 1031-1048.

Analyzes the use of the term "new" among advertisers and the potential the term has for deceiving the consumer. From an analysis of nine general uses of the term by advertisers, a general theory based upon the philosophy of language is developed to determine when the term is legally valid. It is concluded that the FTC has failed to adequately provide guidance on the term's use even though the issue falls within the parameters of FTC authority.

41   Bernstein, J. S. "Federal Trade Commission Solicits Consumer Research." *Advances in Consumer Research* 23 (1996): 313-315.

The FTC requires accurate consumer behavior information in order to make informed decisions regarding the regulation of false or misleading advertising and unfair business practices. This essay reviews several examples of current issues in which more research would to be useful to the FTC in accomplishing its regulatory mission. The issues covered include: determining which types of disclosures are most effective; exploring in what ways does the Internet affect consumer behavior; examining the effectiveness of the new Telemarketing Rules in reducing consumer injury; possibly revising the "Made in the USA" product labelling standard; and improving the utility of corrective advertising and other remedies.

42   Best, Arthur. "Controlling False Advertising : A Comparative Study of Public Regulation, Industry Self-Policing, and Private Litigation." *Georgia Law Review* 20 (Fall 1985): 1-72.

This article analyzes the relative capabilities of FTC regulatory activities, private litigation, and industry self-regulation in controlling false advertising. The essay begins by studying the frequency of violations to advertising standards and the range of regulatory responses to these violations. By examining three modes of comparative processes (selecting cases, ascertaining whether ads meet established standards, and designing remedies), the author determines that private litigation offers the most efficient mode of controlling false advertising. While some claims need to be regulated by government, the FTC and other regulatory agencies should be careful in how they rule, and thus protect, the agency as well as the advertiser from the burden of unwarranted litigation. A lack of empirical data and unnecessarily restrictive interpretations of advertising content has led to problems in applying judicial treatment to section 43a of the Lanham Act. More reliance on empirical data and input from consumers will strengthen judicial and regulatory controls on false advertising, especially given the recent move towards deregulation in government.

43   Bickart, David O. "Civil Penalties Under Section 5(m) of the Federal Trade Commission Act." *The University of Chicago Law Review* 44 (Summer 1977): 761-803.

Section 5(m) of the Federal Trade Commission Improvement Act enables the FTC to seek civil penalty actions against firms that had previously not been subject to the FTC's cease and desist orders. By tracing the legislative process that ultimately led to the civil penalty provision, the author identifies potential problems that the FTC and the courts will have to grapple with in the future.

44   Bilkey, Warren J. "Government and the Consumer Interest." *American Economic Review* 49 (May 1957): 556-577.

Discusses the role of the federal government in protecting the consumer and the institutional problems that arise because the individual agencies involved in consumer protection, consumer assistance, and information gathering activities do not coordinate their efforts. Various theories are proposed within the context of normative standards applied to the economic impact of consumer interest regulation. The essay concludes with commentary regarding the article's proposals at improving regulation.

45   Bird, II, Allen W. et al. "Corporate Image Advertising: A Discussion of the Factors that Distinguish Those Corporate Image Advertising Practices Protected Under the First Amendment from Those Subject to Control by the Federal Trade Commission." *Journal of Urban Law* 51 (1974): 405-420.

Attempts to define the boundary between the First Amendment's statement that Congress cannot create a law that abridges freedom of speech and Section 12 of the FTC Act which allows the FTC to issue cease and desist orders if false advertising is present. The essay examines these fundamental ideologies with reference to corporate image advertising.

46   Bishop, Jr., James and Henry W. Hubbard. *Let the Seller Beware.* Washington, DC: National Press, 1969.

Traces the political, social, and economic factors that led to the development of consumerism during the 1960s. Throughout the history of these developments, the role of the FTC is discussed, including action by the Commission regarding specific cases and the political activities in Congress and the Executive Branch that shaped the FTC's consumer protection policies. It is concluded that it was industry's intractable position of protecting is deceptive behavior that ultimately led to the consumer movement.

47   Bloom, Paul N. "A Decision Model for Prioritizing and Addressing Consumer Information Problems." *Journal of Public Policy and Marketing* 8 (1989): 161-180.

Analyzes the factors involved in consumer information problems and presents an approach to diagnosing and prescribing remedies to help protect consumers. A decision tree is used to determine the severity of information problems in a particular market. Health claims in advertisements for Campbell Soups, price claims in commercial airline ads, and unethical trade schools are used to illustrate this approach.

48   Bock, Betty. "Consumers and the Federal Trade Commission." *Journal of Home Economics* 41 (October 1949): 441-443.
Briefly analyzes a cross section of activities initiated by the FTC to show how these activities help consumers. These activities include prohibiting false and misleading advertising, preventing monopolistic pricing agreements, and preventing the restriction of sale channels. Specific actions by the FTC are presented under each activity.

49   Boddewyn, J. J. "Advertising Regulation: Fiddling with the FTC While the World Burns." *Business Horizons* 28 (May/June 1985): 32-40.
The author questions whether the FTC and advertisers are addressing the most critical issues regarding "disturbing trends" in the advertising field. It is argued that advertisers must boost self-regulation and not leave the monitoring of advertising regulation solely to lawyers.

50   Bodnar, Janet. "Whatever Happened to the Consumer Movement?" *Changing Times* 43 (August 1989): 45-48, 50.
Notes the irony inherent in the fact that, while the nation's consumer protection organizations have become stronger despite budget cuts to the government's consumer protection agencies under Ronald Reagan, it is more difficult for individual consumers to obtain redress. However, under the Bush Administration there is hope that the government will become more active. The appointment of Janet Steiger to chair the FTC and Anne Graham to head the Consumer Product Safety Commission are described as encouraging signs that positive change will occur in the near future. Pressure placed on the FTC and other agencies by special interest groups is outlined, along with how these agencies are responding to criticism.

51   Boies, David and Paul R. Verkuil. "Regulation of Supermarket Advertising Practices." *The Georgetown Law Journal* 60 (May 1972): 1195-1223.
Discusses the issue of misleading advertising practices among supermarkets and, specifically, the conclusions of a comprehensive study conducted by the FTC confirming that many supermarkets did not deliver on promises made concerning sale items and availability. The FTC's ruling to remedy the problem is reviewed and notes that the Trade Regulation Rule is an improvement in helping consumers rather than FTC adjudication, other agency action, or litigation on the state level.

52 Bonamici, Suzanne. "The Use and Reliability of Survey Evidence in Deceptive Advertising Cases." *Oregon Law Review* 62 (1983): 561-602.

A comment stating that the FTC should incorporate survey evidence into its methods of determining and proving the meaning of challenged advertisements. Surveys and copy tests are important elements in assessing deception because, through pretrial discovery, they could predict whether or not a advertising claim is deceptive. The establishment of guidelines for the use of copy tests would insure reliable application of their results to determine deception, much more reliably than the FTC's own expertise-based but unpredictable, determinations.

53 Borowsky, Philip. "Federal Trade Commission and the Corrective Advertising Order." *University of San Francisco Law Review* 6 (April 1972): 367-385.

States that the use of corrective advertising has brought the FTC closer to realizing its full potential in alleviating false and misleading advertising. The effects of this new order should be swift and bring real change to an industry wrought with false advertising practices. However, the rendering of twenty-five percent of advertising expenditures to be used in disclosing past deceptive claims by an offender has not been clearly explained by the Commission.

54 Bower, Paul G. "New Developments in FTC Remedies." *Antitrust Law Journal* 41 (1972): 465-475.

Text from a panel discussion in which the author discusses new areas of remedies including corrective advertising, prior proof by advertisers that a claim is valid under Section 5, and the advertising substantiation program.

55 Boyer, Barry B. "Funding Public Participation in Agency Proceedings: The Federal Trade Commission Experience." *The Georgetown Law Journal* 70 (October 1981): 51-172.

Both business and Congress have criticized the practice of funding public participation in administrative proceedings. The FTC's compensation program is used to analyze the validity of such claims. The essay is arranged into three broad areas of analysis: the first examines the criteria and procedures behind the FTC's program for awarding funding to public intervenors; the second evaluates the actual implementation of the program and its partial success; the third area of analysis attempts to assess the effects of the compensation program. It is concluded that the program's ultimate success or failure cannot be ascertained because of the vagueness of its objectives as defined by the legislative process.

56   Brandel, Roland E. and James De Long. "FTC Role in Consumer Credit." *Business Lawyer (Special Issue)* 33 (February 1978): 965-980.
Sponsored by the American Bar Association Section of Corporation, Banking and Business Law, this article is a transcript of a lecture given that presents in descriptive terms what role the FTC plays in regards to consumer credit and an evaluation of what that role should be in the future, especially concerning FTC adherence to the Holder-In-Due-Course Rule.

57   Brandt, Michael T. and Ivan L. Preston. "The Federal Trade Commission's Use of Evidence to Determine Deception." *Journal of Marketing* 41 (January 1977): 54-62.
The FTC's utilization of evidence during its existence lacks precision. However, the Commission has recently shifted its reliance on internal evidence, based upon the agency's own understanding of the presence of deception, to a more external reliance based upon consumer testimony and surveys.

58   Brennen, Bruce J. "Affirmative Disclosure in Advertising and Control of Packaging Design Under the Federal Trade Commission Act." *The Business Lawyer* 20 (November 1964): 133-144.
Discusses the FTC's current regulatory programs with regard to drug advertising and food packaging. While these issues are different, when examined within the context of their impact on American industry, several similarities are uncovered. First, both require affirmative disclosure to the consumer of certain information. Second, regulation in these areas illustrates the FTC's increased activity in regulation previously left to other agencies. Third, these topics indicate advances into new fields of regulation by the FTC. Organizations associated with the food and drug industry should be aware of these activities and be prepared for the possible consequences of expanded FTC involvement.

59   Brickey, Kathleen F. "The Magnuson-Moss Act: An Analysis of the Efficacy of Federal Warranty Regulation as a Consumer Protection Tool." *Santa Clara Law Review* 18 (Winter 1978): 73-118.
Examines the scope of consumer transactions involving warranties to assess why the government felt regulation was needed. The scope of the Act's statutory power is reviewed, including its impact on specific warranty transactions, notes

regulation of implied warranties, and concludes with an examination of the limitations of liability under the Act.

60   Bright, Thomas L. and Richard L. Coffinberger. "Commercial Paper Revolution Revisited: Will the FTC Strike Again?" *Commercial Law Journal* 85 (August/September 1980): 291-293.

Reviews the traditional Holder-In-Due-Course Doctrine and the problems associated with it and the 1976 FTC modifications that are meant to overcome these problems by extending the rule to creditors.

61   Brobeck, Stephen. *The Modern Consumer Movement: References and Resources*. Boston, MA: G. K. Hall, 1990.

An annotated bibliography of books, journal articles, reports, and other secondary sources regarding the history, development, and impact of the modern consumer movement and the individuals behind it. While many citations are references to the FTC, this is a good source for finding information on other aspects of the consumer movement.

62   Brown, William F. "The Federal Trade Commission and False Advertising, I." *Journal of Marketing* 11 (July 1947): 38-46.

The first of a two part article analyzing the Wheeler-Lea Amendment to the FTC Act, noting that while the law does not broaden the FTC's fact-finding power, the courts have generally not questioned the Commission's findings.

63   Brown, William F. "The Federal Trade Commission and False Advertising, II." *Journal of Marketing* 11 (October 1947): 193-201.

Second part of a two part article regarding the Wheeler-Lea Amendment to the FTC Act. It is concluded that while the amendment does clarify the FTC's authority over all types of deceptive advertising and the procedures to pursue the deception, the Commission has been slow in using the amendment to explore avenues to curb advertising that is less obviously false.

64   Buc, Nancy L. "The Kirkpatrick Committee Report–Consumer Protection Issues." *Antitrust Law Journal* 58 (Spring 1989): 29-32.

Introductory essay concerning consumer protection activities and responsibilities of the FTC sponsored by the American Bar Association Section of Antitrust Laws' 37th Annual Spring Meeting held April 5-7, 1989 in Washington, DC. Remarks are given in response to the Kirkpatrick Committee Report on the role of the FTC in consumer protection and antitrust enforcement.

65   Bugge, Lawrence J. "Is Consumer Protection Becoming Legal Pollution?" *Wisconsin Bar Bulletin* 49 (June 1976): 15-32.

Notes that the phenomenon "of too much legalism" has permeated not only the court system but the federal regulatory arena as well. The author cites, among other things, the FTC Door-to-Door Rule, the Magnuson-Moss Warranty Act, and other FTC rulings, as examples of the rise in federal regulation. The problems associated with this are then discussed.

66   Burck, G. "High-Pressure Consumerism at the Saleman's Door." *Fortune* 86 (July 1, 1972): 70-72,92-94.

Analyzes the art of salesmanship and the New Consumerism. However, expanding the FTC's power to regulate through Trade Regulation Rules may lead to undue restrictions on business and industry.

67   Cain, Clarissa and Max Werner. "Consumers and the Oligopoly Problem: Agenda for a Reformed FTC." *Antitrust Law and Economics* 3 (Spring 1970): 9-20.

As members of the Consumer Education and Protective Association, the authors present specific reforms of the FTC, such as annual reports to Congress on the competitive and regulated sector of the economy, public disclosure as to whether competitive consumer pricing is present, and effective antitrust enforcement.

68   Calfee, John E. "The Ghost of Cigarette Advertising Past." *Regulation* 10 (November/December 1986): 35-45.

The author presents his views concerning the renewed call to ban cigarette advertising despite evidence showing that it has little if any effect on smoking habits. Outlines the FTC's efforts to regulate cigarette advertising.

69   Calvani, Terry. "Advertising Regulation: The States vs. The FTC." *Antitrust Law Journal* 58 (1989): 253-266.

Examines the FTC's past advertising enforcement policy, uses recent cases to offer ways that it can be improved, and concludes with an analysis of efforts by state attorney generals to remedy deceptive advertising practices.

70 Calvani, Terry et al. "Attorney Advertising and Competition at the Bar." *Vanderbilt Law Review* 41 (May 1988): 761-788.

Recommends less restrictions on advertising by attorneys based on an economic analysis of the effects of attorney advertising and a measurement of empirical evidence on the price and quality of legal services. The essay concludes with a discussion of the future of attorney advertising as it relates to the FTC's consumer protection mission and that the FTC can lead the way in reducing advertising restrictions.

71 Campbell, Michael E. and Wayne Phears. "Federal Trade Commission: Developments in Advertising Regulation and Antitrust Policies." *George Washington Law Review* 41 (May 1973): 880-950.

Outlines the FTC's regulatory powers over advertising and, in particular, its recent use of Sections 5 and 6 of the FTC Act to expand that power. The FTC's advertising substantiation program, the use of corrective advertising, the broadening of cease and desist orders through restitution, and clarification of limitations placed on trademark licensing and tie-ins are all examples of this expansion of regulatory power. Each example is examined in detail. Application of these remedies on antitrust cases is also examined. While it is still too early to make definitive statements regarding the effectiveness of these programs, corrective advertising offers the greatest potential in alleviating deceptive behavior.

72 Carney, James A. "Section 5 of the Federal Trade Commission Act: Unfairness to Consumers." *Wisconsin Law Review* 1972 (1972): 1071-1096.

Notes the expansion of FTC regulation into new arenas of consumer protection beyond the traditional areas of prohibiting practices which interfere with competition and practices which are deceptive. Specifically, the note analyzes the adoption of the "unfairness doctrine" and discusses several paths the FTC can take in using this doctrine to protect consumer interests. Both historical and recent legal developments, specifically the *FTC v. Sperry & Hutchinson Co.* case, are examined to estimate the impact of the unfairness doctrine upon consumers.

73 Carpenter, David W. "Implied Civil Remedies for Consumers Under the Federal Trade Commission Act." *Boston University Law Review* 54 (1974): 758-795.

By examining the statutory structure of the FTC Act, the author explores whether the implication of a private consumer right of action would actually benefit consumers by allowing them to act independently under Section 5 in cases of deceptive marketing practices. Cases where the private right of action has been used are analyzed to illustrate in what legal environment such action could take place. The case of *Holloway v. Bristol-Myers Corp.* is specifically examined to determine if private right of action would be appropriate under the FTC Act. It is concluded that private action would be permissible in only a narrow class of cases and, even in these cases, likely not to be used due to judicial economy.

74   Castleman, James A. "Advertising, Product Safety, and a Private Right of Action Under the Federal Trade Commission Act." *Hofstra Law Review* 2 (Summer 1974): 669-691.

Efforts by the FTC to enforce the provisions of the FTC Act has been retarded by the magnitude of the problem of deceptive advertising and due to restricted enforcement powers available to the Commission. A proposed remedy would be to grant consumers private right of action to enforce the FTC Act. The author discusses the historical context of private actions under the FTC Act, including analyzing specific cases and subsequent court decisions, as well as examining what factors are involved in the implementation of a private action doctrine.

75   Cavalier, Roland Mark. "Consumer Protection and Warranties of Quality: A Proposal for a Statutory Warranty in Sales to Consumers." *Albany Law Review* 34 (1970): 339-383.

This essay focuses on the need for state or federal control in the form of a minimum statutory warranty of quality over major household items and automobiles. The author begins by discussing the current laws regarding warranty quality and then examines the problem concerning the quality of consumer goods on the market and thus the need for statutory measures to protect the consumer. Given this, the author presents a proposed solution, the "Consumer Warranty Protection Act," including the terms of the proposed statute and an explanation of its benefits. The essay concludes with a study of the constitutional problems posed by such a statute.

76   Cavanaugh, Stephen W. "Advertising: The Deception Standard." *Washburn Law Journal* 18 (Spring 1979): 600-605.

Discusses the recent *Standard Oil Co. v. FTC* decision within the context of whether substantial evidence supported the FTC's position on the case and how the lack of a well defined standard of what constitutes deceptive advertising leaves advertisers "in limbo" and perpetuates overbroad FTC discretion in taking action.

77   Celnicker, Arnold C. "The Federal Trade Commission's Competition and Consumer Advocacy Program." *Saint Louis Law Journal* 33 (Winter 1989): 379-405.
This article reviews the legal foundation and history of the FTC's Competition and Consumer Advocacy Program. This program grew out of an effort to eliminate government imposed anticompetitive restraints. It's goal is to persuade federal, state, and local government officials to protect consumer welfare by increasing competition and enhancing the marketplace's ability to better allocate resources. Although the program only costs several million dollars each year, budgetary concerns are cited by some in Congress who seek to control government intervention into people's lives. The results of a survey sent to state and local government officials who received FTC comments, shows that about forty percent of the comments were "moderately effective" and thus useful to decision-makers.

78   Chaplin, Peggy. "Federal Trade Commission Protection." *The Maryland Bar Journal* 27 (March/April 1994): 14-17.
Examines the enforcement powers of the FTC to regulate deceptive advertising and outlines three consumer protection standards of Section 5 of the FTC Act: deception, substantiation, and unfairness.

79   Charlton, Francis J. and William A. Fawcett. "The FTC and False Advertising." *Kansas Law Review* 17 (1969): 599-623.
Outlines the FTC's role in regulating deceptive advertising by providing an examination of the ineffectiveness of common law protection under the Sherman and Clayton Acts and private right of action; the procedural remedies executed under Section 5 of the FTC Act; the determination of the FTC of what statements and representations constitute false advertising; and, the liability of advertising agencies who participate in creating a deceptive ad. Specific cases are discussed throughout the article to provide legal background to the discussion.

80   "Cigarette Controls: A Sick Joke So Far." *Consumer Reports* 33 (February 1968): 97-103.
Discusses efforts by the FTC and members of Congress, such as Warren G. Magnuson, to initiate warning labels on cigarette ads. Issues examined include the industry's adoption of a self-regulatory advertising code, the FTC's response in a fifty-seven page report that this code was inadequate, and legislation currently

before Congress that would affect cigarette advertising. The article ends with an analysis of the FTC's research and findings on the tar and nicotine content of 59 representative cigarette brands.

81   Clarkson, Kenneth W. and Timothy J. Muris. "Constraining the Federal Trade Commission: The Case of Occupational Regulation." *University of Miami Law Review* 35 (1980): 77-130.

Examines the FTC's occupational licensure program to illustrate the effects of and the factors involved in limiting the powers of an administrative agency. The author argues against regulating licensed occupations on economic grounds because it restricts entry into a particular business by consumers and puts limits on certain forms of competition related to advertising and solicitation. After outlining the occupational licensure program of the FTC, the essay broadens its analysis to determine how Congressional action and judicial review may influence a particular agency program.

82   Cohen, Dorothy. "Federal Trade Commission and the Regulation of Advertising in the Consumer Interest." *Journal of Marketing* 33 (January 1969): 40-44.

Presents an analysis of the FTC's mission in assuring the consumer is presented with accurate information in order to make reasoned choices within the marketplace. The results reveal several gaps in the Commission's protection. These gaps exist because consumers do not make choices based solely in economic terms. It is recommended that the FTC's regulatory framework be adjusted according to more current knowledge about consumer behavior.

83   Cohen, S. E. "Consumer Safety Net Beginning to Unravel." *Advertising Age* 53 (March 8, 1982): 28.

Editorial expressing concern over the erosion of consumer protection powers at the FTC initiated by Reaganites and Chairman James C. Miller III. It is stated that a proposed cost/benefit statutory law is a barrier to consumer protection because it only takes into account the most grievous offenses, does not allow the FTC to address problems as they arise, and represents only one tool which the FTC should use to combat deception.

84   Cohen, S. E. "War on Poverty to Stimulate Efforts by FTC, Others to Protect Public." *Advertising Age* 36 (August 30, 1965): 263.

Discusses how regulatory agencies, such as the FTC's efforts to control television advertising, are responding to studies showing that the poor are at particular risk when confronted with deceptive business practices. The effects of the "War on Poverty" on the judicial system are also examined.

85   Cohen, Tod H. "Double Vision: The FTC, State Regulation, and Deciding What's Best for Consumers." *George Washington Law Review* 59 (June 1991): 1249-1284.

Argues that the recent ruling (*California State Board of Optometry v. FTC*) by the United States Court of Appeals for the District of Columbia significantly harms consumers. The court vacated the FTC's Ophthalmic Practice Rules (Eyeglasses II) that had been designed to lower consumer costs and improve competition by invalidating certain anticompetitive state regulations. The FTC stated that sections 5 and 18 of the FTC Act gave the FTC authority to invalidate state laws and regulations that unfairly restrict competition. The court stated otherwise, asserting that the FTC lacked such power because it had not been specifically mandated by Congress. This decision presents a "significant setback" for the FTC to protect consumers because it prevents rulemaking action over state regulated industries such as medical, dental, and veterinary practices. To support the argument that the court erred, an analysis of the FTC Act is made to determine whether Congress had addressed the issue of the FTC's authority to invalidate state laws and regulations. The reasoning behind the implementation of Eyeglasses II, its procedural history, and how the court came to its decision are then discussed.

86   Colford, Steven W. "Congress Looks to Define "Unfair"." *Advertising Age* 64 (May 31, 1993): 2, 44.

Discusses efforts by Congressional leaders to provide marketers with a clear definition of unfair under the FTC Act and how this would affect attempts by consumer groups to pressure the FTC to ban advertising for entire product categories, such as alcohol or tobacco. While advertisers are willing to discuss the issue of further defining what constitutes "unfair," it is pointed out that states will take the initiative in using the unfairness doctrine if the FTC does not.

87   Collins, Tom A. "Counter-Advertising in the Broadcast Media: Bringing the Administrative Process to Bear upon a Theoretical Imperative." *William and Mary Law Review* 15 (Summer 1974): 799-844.

Considers the issue of counter-advertising in light of the FTC's proposal submitted to the Federal Communications Commission in 1972 "advocating application through administrative rulemaking of the FCC's fairness doctrine to a wide spectrum of broadcast advertisements." The positive impact of counter-advertising is detailed, followed by an examination of the fairness doctrine as a theoretical basis for counter-advertising. Constitutional, political, and economic factors are considered. It is concluded that counter-advertising, while undoubtably changing the nature of advertising, would benefit consumers by providing more complete and accurate information.

88 "Commercial Law–Consumer Protection: The Federal Trade Commission Rule for Informal Dispute Settlement Mechanisms, Promulgated Under the Magnuson-Moss Warranty-Federal Trade Commission Improvement Act, Neglects the Commercial Incentive Necessary to Secure Adoption." *Temple Law Quarterly* 49 (Winter 1976): 459-475.

Discusses the powers delegated to the FTC under new legislation created by Congress to address the need to increase the bargaining position of the consumer in purchasing transactions. The note states, however, that the Act does not reflect practical commercial considerations and is, therefore, more likely to retard both consumer and supplier satisfaction in the area of warranties rather than advancing complaint resolution.

89 "Commercial Law–Warranties–Magnuson-Moss Act Seeks to Promote Enforceability and Comprehensibility of Written Warranties." *Rutgers Camden Law Journal* 7 (Winter 1976): 379-390.

Briefly outlines the content of the Act, its impact on existing laws, and notes potential problems in its implementation.

90 "The Consumer and Federal Regulation of Advertising." *Harvard Law Review* 53 (1940): 828-842.

Provides an analysis of the efforts of various federal agencies, including the FTC, to regulate advertising. The FTC's efforts are uneven because of it's concentration on the unfairness doctrine in combating deceptive advertising, the sometime lack of support from the courts, and the slow reaction of the Commission in regards to controlling deceptive advertising, which usually occurs well after the injury had been inflicted upon the consumer. The author concludes that the centralization of control over advertising by one independent agency offers a possible solution to effectively eliminating dishonest advertising.

91   "Consumer Legislation and the Poor." *Yale Law Journal* 76 (1967): 745-792.

Presents the "Unfair Sales Practices Act" as a model statute that may be incorporated into current city ordinances, FTC regulations, or federal laws. The statute takes into account the specific buying habits of the poor consumer and the income levels that influence their buying habits. This model is an attempt to address the unique needs of the poor consumer and set parameters in which merchants can operate.

92   "Consumer Protection Legislation, 1970: A Panel." *Antitrust Law Journal* 39 (1969/70): 385-410.

Text from a panel discussion regarding current consumer legislation, including elements of some FTC rules and regulations and the expanded authority they represent.

93   Cornfeld, Richard S. "New Approach to an Old Remedy: Corrective Advertising and the Federal Trade Commission." *Iowa Law Review* 61 (February 1976): 693-721.

Despite the fact that the FTC has failed on occasions to enforce corrective advertising when presented the opportunity, corrective advertising is a potentially useful remedy for curbing consumer deception. Cases in which corrective remedies were denied or, in the case of Warner-Lambert Co., the administrative law judges statements ordering corrective measures were written in conclusory terms, offer little guidance. While recognition must be made of the difficulties in identifying residual effects, the knowledge by advertisers that a corrective order may be imposed at the end of litigation, may induce them to abandon deceptive advertising practices voluntarily, thus ending the problem of delayed profits reaped by violators.

94   "Corrective Advertising and the FTC: No Virginia, Wonder Bread Doesn't Help Build Strong Bodies Twelve Ways." *Michigan Law Review* 70 (December 1971): 374-399.

Discusses recent cases that have brought the issue of corrective advertising to the judicial forefront and the theories behind its development. By analyzing other types of affirmative disclosure made by the FTC, the Commission's statutory authority can be ascertained. Finally, the note examines the benefits corrective advertising offers to consumers and discusses how these benefits can be further enhanced.

95   "Corrective Advertising" Orders of the Federal Trade Commission." *Harvard Law Review* 85 (December 1971): 477-506.

This note argues that an expansion of the FTC's cease and desist orders to include the implementation of corrective advertising by those firms found guilty of deceptive advertising is within the statutory authority of the FTC and that they represent a viable solution to eliminating certain forms of false advertising. It is argued, though, that these orders should be carefully applied in order to parallel particular violations and when specifically suited to correct the false claim. This may be more difficult to fulfill than the prerequisites needed to employ typical cease and desist orders.

96   "Corrective Advertising: The New Response to Consumer Deception." *Columbia Law Review* 72 (February 1972): 415-431.

This comment explores the legality and probable effectiveness of the FTC's corrective advertising remedy. The comment outlines the development of the corrective advertising within the context of previous efforts by the FTC to curb false advertising. In examining the breadth of the Commission's discretion and the court's reaction to it, corrective advertising is seen as a useful addition to the legal remedies at the disposal of the FTC despite the need for modifications depending upon the nature of the specific case.

97   "Court Upholds FTC Order Requiring Advertiser of Baldness Cure to Indicate Product is Ineffective in Most Cases." *Columbia Law Review* 60 (December 1960): 1184-1187.

Outlines the cease and desist order issued by the FTC regarding the petitioner's advertisements concerning the preventive capabilities of their baldness cure products. The comment notes that the FTC may issue a cease and desist order to require a petitioner to disclose limitations on a product's effectiveness when it is revealed that the product, while maintaining some level of effectiveness, has significant limitations that could deceive the public. The issue of the FTC's power to require affirmative disclosures by advertisers is discussed in light of *Alberty v. FTC*.

98   Craswell, Richard. "The Identification of Unfair Acts and Practices by the Federal Trade Commission." *Wisconsin Law Review* 1981 (1981): 107-153.

Controversy has recently surrounded Section 5 of the FTC Act and its prohibition of "unfair acts or practices." Critics have asserted that it is too broad and vague and Congress has responded by setting a three year moratorium on the promulgation of any FTC rules governing advertising under Section 5 authority. However, criticism has focused primarily on the abstract definitions of what constitutes unfairness and not what specific acts and practices would be unlawful under any of the proposed definitions. This article identifies the circumstances by which the FTC has ruled in regards to unfairness using four broad categories of unlawful behavior and attempts to predict the conditions under which particular practices will or will not be found to be unfair.

99   Craswell, Richard. "Interpreting Deceptive Advertising." *Boston University Law Review* 65 (July 1985): 657-732.

A common problem in determining whether an advertisement is deceptive is that most advertisements do not contain explicitly false claims, but are said to imply a false claim. This has focused the political debate on the rules created to interpret ads under anti-deception laws. This has led many to approach the debate from a purely factual standpoint and not take into consideration the need to interpret an advertisement using normative or policy judgement. The elimination of some false meaning within the advertisement could lead to giving up potentially useful information. To avoid this, the selection of what constitutes false advertising must reflect an explicit policy decision whereby the elimination of the false impression outweighs the drawbacks of doing so. This standard is based upon a narrow interpretation of deceptive advertising in which the advertiser fails to take some precaution that would have reduced the net injury caused by the ad. Arguments based on consumer rights, an economic analysis of advertiser's incentives, and administrative costs are presented.

100   Cude, Brenda. "The Federal Trade Commission's Environmental Marketing Guidelines: An Academic's Perspective." In *Proceedings...39th Annual Conference of the American Council on Consumer Interests*. Columbia, MO: A.C.C.I., 1993. pp. 332-336

The author offers her perspective as an academic regarding the historical development of the FTC's guidelines for environmental marketing and the administrative process by which testimony is given in support of these guidelines. The author outlines specific principles to illustrate how these guidelines apply to advertising, labeling, and other forms of marketing and analyzes their likely impact.

101   Currie, Allan Bruce. "A Private Right of Action Under Section Five of
the Federal Trade Commission Act." *Hastings Law Journal* 22 (May
1971): 1268-1288.
Examines the need for a private right of action under Section Five of the FTC Act
because of increased unfair and deceptive acts or practices in commerce. The
essay begins with an analysis of previous cases regarding private right of action
shows that they are no longer binding under current circumstances. Reasons are
then stated as to why right to private action are necessary. Included in this is a
discussion of state remedies. The author concludes with a brief summarization of
the advantages of private action and notes that no cases have been tried on this
issue since the passage of the Wheeler-Lea Amendments.

102   Cutler, Barry J. "FTC Has Poor Record in Actions for Consumer
Redress." *The Los Angeles Daily Journal* 96 (October 18, 1983): 4.
Discusses the so far ineffective Section 19 of the FTC Act produced from the
Magnuson-Moss Act that gives the FTC power to bring class actions in court to
obtain refunds and other relief to consumers injured by deceptive practices. The
primary reason for the section's ineffectiveness, which had been predicted when
the FTC Act was amended in 1973, is the slow administrative proceedings of the
agency. It is concluded that the FTC must work harder to expedite obtaining relief
for consumers since this accelerated approach has worked in regards to antitrust
decisions in the courts.

103   Dahringer, Lee D. and Denise R. Johnson. "The Federal Trade
Commission Redefinition of Deception and Public Policy Implications:
Let the Buyer Beware." *Journal of Consumer Affairs* 18 (Winter 1984):
326-342.
Compares the current standards employed by the FTC with those proposed by
Chairman James C. Miller III. Two cases are used to illustrate the new proposal's
impact on regulatory policy. It is concluded that the proposed guidelines would
not be as effective in eliminating false advertising as current regulations and,
while they would bring some benefit to consumers, the proposed guidelines could
reintroduce the rule of caveat emptor.

104   Damron, Jeffrey D. "The Magnanamous Moss Gloss: An Overview of
the Magnuson-Moss Warranty Act." *Kentucky Bench and Bar* 55
(Summer 1991): 18-20, 50.
Gives a short background of the Act and examines its general scope and effect.

The essay also discusses what triggers action under the Act and the remedies it provides for consumers.

105 Damrosch, Lori Fisler. "Advertising, Product Differentiation, and Monopoly Power: A Critical Look at the Proposed Solutions." *Antitrust Law and Economics Review* 9 (1977): 25-48.

Offers suggestions to better define solutions to the problem of advertising and competition and, specifically, proposals to dramatically change structural conditions in a particular industry. It is pointed out that current proposals do not fully address product differentiation in certain markets because they fail to separate the issue of buyer ignorance from nonrational persuasion.

106 Darmstadter, Ruth. "Blocking the Death Blow to Funeral Regulation." *Business and Society Review* (Winter 1983): 32-36.

Examines the need for regulations in the funeral industry and the FTC's response to consumer complaints since 1972. Industry experts argue that it is unnecessary because no clear pattern of abuse has been shown, state regulatory laws have already answered consumer complaints, and the costs to the industry are prohibitively expensive. It is concluded that there is some hope that Congress will not bend to pressure from the funeral industry lobby and pass legislation supporting regulation.

107 Davidson, John R. "FTC, Robinson-Patman, and Cooperative Promotional Activities." *Journal of Marketing* 32 (January 1968): 14-17.

Analyzes the rules that govern the consumer's obligation when a product is defective and the dealer's obligation created through the enforcement of the Magnuson-Moss Warranty Act. The article provides insights into the FTC's view regarding the rule's implementation.

108 Davis, Gary E. "The FTC Proposed Rule and the Holder in Due Course." *South Dakota Law Review* 18 (Spring 1973): 516-522.

Examines the restrictions that the proposed FTC rule would have upon the status of the Holder-In-Due-Course Doctrine and discusses the results of a hearing sponsored by the FTC that called for a more expanded rule. It is noted that this rule is a major step towards the eradication of abuses under the Doctrine.

109 Davis, Rex D. "False Advertising: The Expanding Presence of the FTC." *Baylor Law Review* 25 (1973): 650-659.

Notes the controversies that have arisen as a result of the FTC's attempts to attack the diverse subtleties of false advertising and analyzes two areas of remedial action taken by the FTC to explore the possible influence on advertising that the FTC may have in the future.

110 Davis, Ronald M. "Current Trends in Cigarette Advertising and Marketing." *New England Journal of Medicine* 316 (March 19, 1987): 725-732.

Uses statistical data gathered by the FTC to analyze current trends in U. S. cigarette advertising and marketing. The data is presented to help health officials identify and predict patterns of cigarette use and to develop health promotion programs that incorporate similar marketing strategies to counteract the influence of advertising.

111 Dean, Robert Lee. "Consumer Law–Installment Debt–FTC Rule Prohibits Sellers from Accepting Consumer Credit Note or Contract or Proceeds of "Related" Loan Without Notice of Preservation of Consumer's Claims and Defenses Prominently Placed on Credit Instrument." *Villanova Law Review* 21 (October 1976): 984-994.

Examines the effects of the FTC rule that preserves a consumer's claims and defenses in areas of credit sales transactions that had traditionally been cut off. While states had attempted to address the problem, the degree of protection provided to consumers varied widely. By reallocating the risk of seller nonperformance from the consumer to the seller and their financiers, this rule provides a strong, uniform remedy for the consumer against disreputable sellers.

112 Dell, John W. "A New Antitoxin to Advertising Artifice: Television Advertising and the Federal Trade Commission." *The Notre Dame Lawyer* 37 (1962): 524-553.

Discusses particular characteristics associated with television advertising and the new proactive approach the FTC has taken in regulating false advertising and, most notably, as it relates to controlling the marketplace and harming the consumer. This comment addresses the new problems of deception and misrepresentation brought forth by the Rapid Shave Cream demonstration of superiority and other attempts by advertisers to use mock ups to depict product superiority.

113   DeMuth, Christopher C. "The FTC Tantrum Against Children's Television." *American Spectator* 12 (April 1979): 18-21, 24.

Based upon an address given to the annual meeting of the Toy Manufacturers of America, the author criticizes the FTC's recent staff report advocating a ban on television advertising directed to children under the age of eight and to put limits on advertising of highly sugared foods to children and, alternatively, that these companies finance counter advertisements by public interest groups selected by the FTC. These rules are viewed as unrealistic given the business marketplace in which they would be applied and argues that the FTC is not basing its rules on the market itself but on the values it actually promotes.

114   Dencola, Robert C. "The Magnuson-Moss Warranty Act: Making Consumer Product Warranty a Federal Case." *Fordham Law Review* 44 (1975): 273-300.

Gives background of the legislative process and the problems of consumer product warranties that led to the creation of the Act in order to analyze how the provisions of the Act interplay with those of existing state laws regarding warranties. It is concluded that the exact scope of the Act is both "vague and ill-defined" leaving its relationship to state laws inconclusive.

115   "Developing Protection for the Consumer of Future Services." *Columbia Law Review* 72 (May 1972): 926-949.

Analyzes consumer complaints regarding fraud and misrepresentation within the future services industry (schools offering vocational and recreational skills) and how state and local laws and guidelines established by the FTC have been created to address the issue. The laws are examined for effectiveness and to suggest which components of each are most likely to prove useful in helping students seek relief.

116   "Developments–Deceptive Advertising." *Harvard Law Review* 80 (March 1967): 1005-1163.

Extensive overview and analysis of deceptive advertising. The essay begins with an examination of why legislation is needed to control deceptive advertising then moves into a history of the legal controls introduced as well as the application of First Amendment doctrine to commercial speech. The essay then shifts into an analysis of the different types of legal remedies available. This includes the substantive standards used by the FTC to determine false or misleading advertising and the procedures used by the Commission to investigate, issue restraints, and ensure compliance of orders. The role of the Food and Drug

Administration (FDA), state regulations, and private regulations are then discussed in detail. This essay is an excellent introduction into the whole concept of deceptive advertising up to date of the article.

117   Devience, Jr., Alex. "Magnuson-Moss Act: Substitution for UCC Warranty Protection?" *Commercial Law Journal* 95 (Fall 1990): 323-337.

Attempts to show, through the analysis of specific cases and statutory contents, how the Act fills a void in consumer protection left by inadequate remedies under the Uniform Commercial Code. Two areas in particular fill this void: the Act expands the right of consumers to bring action in federal court for deceptive warranty practices and it creates an additional cause of action for claims of economic loss by consumers against remote sellers and manufacturers.

118   Diener, Betty. *The Strategic Marketing Implications of Consumerism*. Cambridge, MA: Marketing Science Institute, June 1974.

Report examining various dimensions of consumerism, specifically the issue of the consumer's right to be informed, to be heard when problems arise, the right to safety, to be able to choose among products and services, and how various marketing activities, such as advertising, warranty service, and product characteristics, are affected by consumerism. Different industries are examined to identify the strategic marketing opportunities available to business people in that industry. The right to information and the right to product performance under service, warranting and redress are then analyzed including what role the FTC plays in enhancing the rights of consumers through regulation in these areas.

119   Dillon, Tom. "What is Deceptive Advertising?" *Journal of Advertising Research* 13 (October 1973): 9-12.

The author argues that the most reliable source for what is deceptive advertising is the opinions of consumers and not the theorization of academics, the definitions offered by legal scholars, or information based upon the comments of professional consumerists. Well designed consumer research could provide the basis for better allocation of FTC resources to those areas which are affecting the consumer most. It would also lead to a more thorough examination of the structure of the process by which the FTC Act is enforced.

120   DiMatteo, Larry A. "Advertisers Beware: The Seventh Circuit Gives the
       FTC Free Rein in Deciding Whether Advertising is Deceptive." *Journal
       of the Academy of Marketing* 22 (Winter 1994): 89.
Examines the outcome and impact of *Kraft Inc. v. Federal Trade Commission*
in which the Seventh Circuit Court of Appeals rules that the FTC may use its own
"subjective analysis" in determining if an advertisement contains deceptive
implied claims and need not rely on consumer surveys and questionnaires. It is
concluded that the ruling's vague findings may allow the FTC to completely
circumvent the use of extrinsic evidence and does not clarify what type of survey
methodology is appropriate evaluate whether a claim is misleading or not.

121   Dixon, Paul Rand. "Government, Consumers and Retailers:
       Togetherness or Conflict?" *New England Law Review* 4 (1969): 75-82.
Expands upon the central theme that the poor frequently pay more for goods and
services by discussing observations made by the FTC when dealing with the
merchant/consumer relationship in Washington, D.C. Remedies such as the
introduction of the Federal-State Cooperation Program by the FTC in 1965,
consumer counseling, and steps to improve installment credit to poor customers
are discussed.

122   Dole, Elizabeth H. "Cost-Benefit Analysis Versus Protecting the
       Vulnerable: The FTC's Special Interest Groups." *Antitrust Law and
       Economics Review* 9 (1977): 15-27, 29-30.
Discusses the use of cost-benefit analysis as a basis for formulating regulations at
the FTC associated with protecting the consumer while at the same time
identifying areas that are not easily accommodated by the benefit measurement.
Examples include dissemination of information to consumers and the issuance of
regulations in the field of health and safety. It is concluded that government must
recognize the special needs of certain groups and that critics of overregulation
must be aware that not all regulations can be measured purely in quantitative or
economic terms.

123   Dole Jr., Richard F. "Merchant and Consumer Protection: The Uniform
       Deceptive Trade Practices Act." *Yale Law Journal* 76 (1967): 485-506.
Argues that the Uniform Deceptive Trade Practices Act ensures protection of both
the consumer and the honest merchant from deceptive behavior because it would
insure that interstate businesses obtain an equivalent degree of protection in every

state rather than in only those states that have chosen to pass deceptive advertising laws. The Act would complement laws already passes in some states. The Uniform Act allows class action enjoinment by consumers or authorizes injured merchants to bring private actions which is not possible in most circumstances because of budgetary limits placed on enforcing agencies.

124   Donner, Barry S. "Advertising of Food and Drugs: Concealing a Truth, Hinting a Lie." *Akron Law Review* 8 (Spring 1975): 456-480.

Uses specific examples of recently published advertisements promoting foods and drugs to analyze whether they represent practices that are prohibited or should be prohibited under the FTC Act and to examine issues, such as public injury versus public interest, unfairness, and the meaning of ads. Each of the thirteen examples are studied against FTC rules and regulations to create a set of four requirements that ads must satisfy in order to avoid FTC action.

125   Doran, Gideon. *The Smoking Paradox: Public Regulation of the Cigarette Industry.* Cambridge, MA: Apt Books, 1979.

Outlines the paradox that occurred when advertising for cigarettes was banned resulting in increased consumption of cigarettes, decreased marketing costs, and an increase in industry sales margins and profits. The author shows that when cigarette advertising was removed so was the effective anti-cigarette campaign broadcast free under the Fairness Doctrine. By analyzing the governments justification for regulating advertising, including the FTC's rulings regarding cigarette advertising, the effectiveness of the campaign, who benefitted from the campaign, and political and factual issues related to the formulation of such regulations, the author demonstrates that the campaign favored the industry being regulated.

126   "Double Vision: The FTC, State Regulation, and Deciding What's Best for Consumers." *George Washington Law Review* 59 (June 1991): 1249-1284.

In *California State Board of Optometry v. FTC*, the Supreme Court, absent of a specific legislative mandate, stated that rules and regulations issued by the FTC could not invalidate state laws even if those laws have the potential to be anticompetitive and thus harmful to consumers. This essay examines the legislative intent of the FTC Act to see if Congress had considered extending the FTC's authority to include invalidating anticompetitive state laws and regulations. The author then examines in detail the provisions and underlying intent of the

Eyeglasses II regulation promulgated by the Commission. It is concluded that the court's ruling was in error and that is has the potential to significantly hinder the FTC's ability to protect the consumer in anticompetitive state-regulated industries.

127   Downs, Thomas C. "Environmentally Friendly Product Advertising: Its Future Requires a New Regulatory Authority." *The American University Law Review* 42 (Fall 1992): 155-198.

Outlines the efforts by individual states and the FTC to eliminate false environmentally friendly claims by advertisers. So far, however, the response to these claims has been uneven and inconsistent. After examining legislation introduced in Congress that divides the responsibility for regulating "green" marketing claims between the FTC and the Environmental Protection Agency, it is concluded that consumers would be best served if the jurisdiction of the EPA was coupled with legislation linking green regulation with a comprehensive environmental policy. The FTC is viewed as ineffective because it has no environmental mandate and can only outlaw deceptive advertising on a case-by-case basis of enforcement.

128   Drexler, Meg. "FTC Regulation of Land Sales." *Houston Law Review* 12 (March 1975): 708-731.

Discusses the areas of consumer fraud that occur in the interstate land development industry and attempts by Congress, through the Interstate Land Sales Full Disclosure Act, and the FTC, to curb the problem. The essay begins by discussing federal regulation of land sales prior to the ILSFDA, examines the effectiveness of sanctions brought by an FTC consent order and how it compares to existing interstate land sales laws and regulations, and concludes by analyzing the failure of the Office of Interstate Land Sales to produce adequate regulations to control the problem of fraud and misrepresentation.

129   Ducoffe, Robert Hal. "Deceptive Advertising: Unprotected and Unknown." *Paper Presented at the Annual Meeting of the Association for Education in Journalism and Mass Communication.* (69th, Norman, OK, August 3-6, 1986).

Discusses the issue of defining and regulating deception in advertising and what tools the FTC uses, such as cease and desists orders, affirmative disclosure, and corrective advertising, to protect consumers. The Armstrong and Russ model of deception should not be applied in regulating false advertising because, if deception has been detected by commissioners, then no deception has occurred.

In addition, the perceptions of the commissioners may not parallel that of consumers. Although no definition of deception currently exists, techniques for detecting deception have been developed. However, causality still remains absent from these techniques thereby rendering the policy ineffectual.

130   Dyer, Robert F. and Philip G. Kuehl. "The "Corrective Advertising" Remedy of the FTC: An Experimental Evaluation." *Journal of Marketing* 38 (January 1974): 48-54.

The central theme of this essay is to evaluate the communication effectiveness of the FTC's corrective advertising policy within the context of certain statutory limitations, including the understanding that the FTC need not bear the burden of proof and that the decisions rendered do not permanently damage the firm. The evaluation reveals that corrective advertising policies are a complex communication system. Two implications for policy makers emerge--the FTC decisions could result in penalties beyond the appropriate statutory limitations and the FTC must focus more on the need to develop appropriate consumer response measures.

131   Eckinger, Robert D. "First Amendment Restrictions on the FTC's Regulation of Advertising." *Vanderbilt Law Review* 31 (March 1978): 349-373.

In regulating advertising in the consumer's interest, the courts have generally deferred to the FTC's findings of fact and selection of remedies. However, in a recent Supreme Court decision, *Virginia State Board of Pharmacy v. Virginia Consumer Council, Inc.*, the court granted First Amendment protection to commercial speech, thus, raising questions regarding the scope of the FTC's authority to regulate advertising. Elevating commercial speech to First Amendment protection creates uncertainty concerning the extent of regulation allowed and the degree of judicial review. Given this uncertainty, it is suggested that the FTC's regulatory restrictions should receive a "deferential level of scrutiny". This proposed standard would help ensure that appropriate corrective measures created by the FTC to regulate false advertising would not be impeded by court intervention based on commercial speech rights.

132   Eddy, Jonathan A. "Effects of the Magnuson-Moss Act upon Consumer Product Warranties." *North Carolina Law Review* 55 (June 1977): 835-877.

Presents a detailed analysis of the Act, previous attempts through the Uniform

Commercial Code to regulate warranties, and common problems confronted by consumers in warranty transactions. Three aspects of the Act are analyzed to determine if the provisions of the Act address specific problems and their likelihood of contributing to a solution. The essay concludes by discussing what, if any, alternative solutions should be considered.

133   "Effective Guidance Through Cease and Desist Orders: The T.V. Commercial." *Indiana Law Review* 38 (1963): 442-455.

Discusses specific attempts by the FTC to regulate advertising on television that it deems false or misleading because it exaggerates the qualities of the product and unfairly disparages a competitor's product. The action taken by the FTC against the Colgate-Palmolive Company's "sandpaper test" commercial for Rapid Shave Cream is examined in detail to illustrate how the FTC sought to create standards by which advertisers could gauge their conduct and to examine the merits of such action.

134   Eiler, Andrew. *Consumer Protection Manual.* New York, NY: Facts on File, 1984.

This book serves four purposes: explains how to present an effective negotiating strategy and make a convincing case when presented with a problem; discusses the legal system to provide the injured consumer with adequate information about how the law can help; outlines specific laws as they relate to specific disputes; and, provides sample letters that can be adapted to settle a dispute. Among the specific laws discussed are the FTC Act, the Magnuson-Moss Warranty Act, the Preservation of Consumers' Claims and Defenses Rule, and others created or enforced by the FTC to protect the consumer. How each of these laws can be used to protect the individual consumer are discussed in detail.

135   Ellis, James T. "Sewer Service and Confessed Judgements: New Protection for Low-Income Consumers." *Harvard Civil Rights-Civil Liberties Law Review* 6 (March 1971): 414-433.

Examines the issues surrounding illicit merchant practices against low income consumers and analyzes attempts by the FTC under the unfair trade practices doctrine to remedy the problems. It is noted that FTC proposals fall short of remedying the problems of fraud associated with low income consumers because the proposals fail to obtain damages when a consumer is victimized and because existing limitations on the jurisdictional authority are inhibiting the FTC's ability to fully protect the consumer.

136   Elrod, Linda D. "Federal Trade Commission: Deceptive Advertising and the Colgate-Palmolive Company." *Washburn Law Journal* 12 (Winter 1973): 133-150.

The advent of television has created an even greater need to regulate false and misleading advertising. An important case that defines and delineates proper television advertising standards is *FTC v. Colgate-Palmolive Co.* The case involved the use of a prop to demonstrate the effectiveness of Rapid Shave Shaving Cream. At issue was whether "it is permissible to simulate a quality the product actually possesses if the test or demonstration is simulated without the viewers knowledge." The FTC stated that such props are inherently deceptive. The Supreme Court agreed, with certain exceptions, and advertisers soon began to modify, discontinue, or display the word "simulation" in order to conform to the ruling. This case stands out as one of the most definitive and explanatory decisions that helps the FTC to create advertising standards and guidelines.

137   Ely, R. S. "The Work of the Federal Trade Commission." *Wisconsin Law Review* 7 (1932): 193-212.

Provides an overview of specific developments at the FTC and highlights some of the major accomplishments of the FTC since its inception. This includes regulating, and thus preserving, the integrity of the marketplace to the benefit of the general public.

138   "Emerging Issues Under the Magnuson-Moss Warranty-Federal Trade Commission Improvement Act: Part I–Warranties." *Antitrust Law Journal* 45 (Spring 1976): 72-95.

Text from a panel discussion covering various aspects of Title I of the Act, including highlighting important components of the Act and examines its impact on the regulatory behavior of the FTC.

139   Enis, Ben M. et al. "Television Advertising and Children: Regulatory vs. Competitive Perspectives." *Journal of Advertising* 9 (1980): 23.

An examination of marketing strategy and legal analysis regarding the influence of advertising on children's consumptive behavior indicates that regulation by the FTC to ban or severely restrict advertising directed to children will not solve the problem. However, harnessing the power of advertising to market the idea of more rational consumption and value determination to children, might accomplish what regulation has failed to do.

140   Eovaldi, Thomas L and Joan E. Gestrin. "Justice for Consumers: The Mechanisms of Redress." *Northwestern University Law Review* 66 (July/August 1971): 281-323.

Discusses the role of the FTC and state consumer fraud bureaus in relation to the need for more effective mechanisms to help facilitate consumer grievances. Limitations on the FTC's role in consumer protection are discussed.

141   Erxleben, William C. "The FTC's Kaleidoscopic Unfairness Statute: Section 5." *Gonzaga Law Review* 10 (Special 1975): 333-351.

Provides an overview of the unfairness doctrine as it applies to consumers rather than competitors by first examining the statute's origin and development, then by using specific cases to analyze its application, and finally, by discussing recent developments in the unfairness principle.

142   Evans, Joel R., ed. *Consumerism in the United States: An Inter-Industry Analysis.* New York, NY: Praeger Publishers, 1980.

Explores the issue of consumerism and the response by business in ten distinct industries and the role of the FTC in regulating each industry. The study is designed as an objective, empirical investigation of the consumer movement. Its purpose is to condense the enormous amount of literature that has been written on the topic to help illustrate the overall structure and impact of the movement on consumers and the business community. Each industry is analyzed by a different author.

143   "Extrinsic Misrepresentations" in Advertising under Section 5 of the Federal Trade Commission Act." *University of Pennsylvania Law Review* 114 (1966): 725-733.

Examines how the case of *FTC v. Colgate Palmolive Co.* resolved to a large degree the issue of whether the law, as stated in Section 5, extends the concept of false statements regarding the merits and qualities of a product "to misrepresentations unrelated to the product itself." It is noted that this is a new concept taken from the law in regards to deceptive advertising, but merely the first time that it has been articulated in the courts.

144   Fayne, Steven N. and Marsha J. Smith. "Dealing with Magnuson-Moss." *Cumberland Law Review* 8 (Spring 1977): 205-228.

Studies the response by warrantors to the Act with special attention paid to the final rules set forth by the FTC regarding the terms and conditions that must be disclosed in written warranties. The rules are discussed within the context of informal FTC staff opinion interpretations and actual written warranties articulated by the business community.

145   "Federal Consumer Legislation." *The Business Lawyer* 28 (March 1973): 289-321.
Text of a panel discussion covering various aspects of current, pending, and future consumer protection legislation and proposals set forth by Congress to enhance FTC powers or create a separate consumer protection agency.

146   "Federal Trade Commission: Defending the Consumer." *Consumers' Research* 72 (October 1972): 21-24.
Interview with FTC Chairman Daniel Oliver in which he explains how the FTC functions and how it protects the consumer through the application of free market principles.

147   "Federal Trade Commission-False and Misleading Advertising." *Michigan Law Review* 31 (April 1933): 804-817.
Outlines the scope of the FTC Act, and specifically Section 5, stating the Commission's jurisdiction over false and misleading advertising. With the exception of several lower court decisions that allow puffery, the courts have been active in supporting the consumer protection elements of the Act, noting further that most cease and desist orders by the FTC never reach the courts.

148   *The Federal Trade Commission in 1975: Warranties, Consumer Redress, Rulemaking.* New York: Practicing Law Institute, 1975.
This course handbook contains a collection of essays outlining the provisions of the Magnuson-Moss Warranty-Federal Trade Commission Improvement Act, the significance of the expanded rulemaking powers of the FTC under the Act, especially when concerned with consumer credit, and examines consumer redress under Section 206 of the Magnuson-Moss Act. Includes the full text of the Act, a reprint of the FTC's "Guides Against Deceptive Advertising of Guarantees" adopted April 26, 1960, and accompanying reprints of text from the *Federal Register* on the proposed Trade Regulation Rule regarding consumer credit, provisions of the disclosure of written consumer product warranty terms and considerations, and FTC's trade regulation rulemaking authority.

149 "Federal Trade Commission Prescribes Health Warnings for Cigarette Advertising." *University of Pennsylvania Law Review* 113 (December 1964): 303-311.

Brief comment arguing that the FTC's mandate to issue the Cigarette Advertising Trade Regulation Rule based on unfair trade practices under Section 5(a) and 6 of the FTC Act extends beyond the judicial definition of the FTC's scope of action. It is argued that this provision allows only enough action to eradicate the deception and does not allow for corrective advertising, which the FTC cites as permissible under Section 15 of the Act.

150 Feldman, Laurence P. *Consumer Protection: Problems and Prospects.* 2nd Edition. St. Paul, MN: West Publishing Co., 1980.

Analyzes the basic issues that arise in the consumer and seller relationship, including the evolution of the consumer protection movement, what sources of conflict occur between the consumer and the seller, and what role the federal government plays in mediating between the two groups. The author attempts to illustrate the complexities involved in the issues raised and to use this information to bridge the gap between the viewpoints of consumers and sellers. The specific role of the FTC in protecting the consumer is discussed in detail, specifically focusing on the FTC's attempts to regulate deceptive advertising. Individual remedies such as corrective advertising, counteradvertising, and ad substantiation are examined. Includes a selected list of consumer protection legislation.

151 Feldman, Sheldon. "FTC Enforcement of the Truth in Lending Act: One Year Later." *The Business Lawyer* 26 (January 1971): 835-845.

Reviews the impact of the FTC's Truth in Lending program after one year and examines its affects on consumer education and individual enforcement activities. An assessment of the program, including problems that have arisen, are also discussed.

152 Ferguson, J. D. et al. "Consumer Ignorance as a Source of Monopoly Power: FTC Staff Report on Self-Regulation, Standardization, and Product Differentiation." *Antitrust Law and Economics Review* 5 (Winter 1971-72): 79-102.

Two part FTC staff study (continued in the Spring 1972 issue, pp. 55-74) regarding self-regulation and, in particular, the role of the product-differentiation phenomena in suppressing competition in the consumer goods industry. It is argued in an introduction by the editors of the Review that the report's recommendations concerning product disclosure standards would, if adopted, make product differentiation "practically impossible," especially with regards to television advertising.

153   Finkelhor, Francis. *Legal Phases of Advertising.* New York, NY: McGraw-Hill Book Company, Inc., 1938.

The purpose of this book to put forth the legal principles applicable to advertising by analyzing specific cases related to the contents of advertisements, the relationship between advertiser and competitor, the relationship of the advertiser to the consumer, the problems associated with the medium used to relay an advertiser's message, and the problems regarding the advertiser's relationship with those groups or individuals that help to create the advertisement. Issues covered include obscenity, endorsements, unfair competition, trade-mark law, and radio advertising. The FTC is mentioned only briefly. However, the book articulates issues of false advertising and unfair competition just prior to the enactment of the Magnuson-Moss Act of 1938 which expanded the FTC's role in policing false advertising. Includes a Table of Cases and an index.

154   Foote, Susan Bartlett and Robert H. Mnookin. "The "Kid Vid" Crusade." *Public Interest* 61 (1980): 90-105.

Examines efforts by the FTC to secure authority to regulate television advertising to children, including attempts to develop criteria to review such advertising, analyze evidence of the effects of television advertising to children, and discusses appropriate roles for the FTC.

155   Ford, Gary T. and John E. Calfee. "Recent Developments in FTC Policy on Deception." *Journal of Marketing* 50 (July 1986): 82-103.

Discusses the 1983 policy statement on the meaning of deception in advertising and its relationship to the unfairness and ad substantiation policy statements. While the 1983 statement is the focus of the article, previous FTC policy regarding deception is also discussed. The elements of deception, their meaning, and implication for future policy are analyzed. The essay concludes that the new policy offers a "modest" clarification of actionable deception.

156   Forman, Jr., William H. "The Consumer Advisory Board of New Orleans: A Federal Trade Commission Experiment." *The Urban Lawyer* 4 (Fall 1972): 757-764.

An overview of the establishment by the New Orleans Office of the FTC of a

Consumer Advisory Board to examine important consumer protection issues in the New Orleans area. The article reports on the first meeting of the Board, what issues were examined, and important topics for the future.

157 Forte, Wesley E. "Fair Packaging and Labeling Act: Its Legislative History, Content and Future." *Vanderbilt Law Review* 21 (October 1968): 761-785.

Discusses the history of the Fair Packaging and Labeling Act (FPLA), focusing on its intended function and reasons for its development. The essay then explores regulations issued by the FTC and the Food and Drug Administration (FDA) pursuant to the FPLA and problems that may arise because the FPLA does not repeal or supersede the FTC Act. This situation could create the chance for conflict between the regulatory duties of the FTC and those of the FDA under the Fair Packaging Act.

158 Forte, Wesley E. "Food and Drug Administration, Federal Trade Commission and the Deceptive Packaging of Foods." *New York University Law Review* 40 (November 1965): 860-904.

Both the FDA and the FTC maintain a working agreement in regulating the distribution of deceptively packaged foods, drugs, devices and cosmetics in interstate commerce. However, only the FDA's power has been analyzed in any depth, while the FTC's powers to prevent deceptive packaging practices has remained relatively unexplored. It is argued that any perceived imbalance between the two agencies in curbing deceptive packaging is a function of inadequate appropriations for the FDA which has retarded full utilization of its powers.

159 Fortney, Anne P. "Consumer Credit Compliance: The Federal Trade Commission as Educator and Enforcer." *The Business Lawyer* 40 (May 1985): 1125-1132.

This article outlines major examples of recent FTC activity regarding consumer credit transactions and how this has led to greater compliance with the Truth in Lending Act, the Fair Debt Collection Practices Act, the Equal Credit Opportunity Act, the Fair Credit Reporting Act, and the upcoming Credit Practices Rules of the FTC. Efforts to educate creditors of their obligations under these laws and regulations are also discussed.

160   Fortney, Anne P. "Consumer Credit and the Federal Trade Commission: Sketching the New Directions." *The Business Lawyer* 39 (1984): 1305-1314.

Provides an overview of the credit compliance programs adopted by the FTC, highlighting the most important ones adopted during the past two years so as to help promote a better understanding of the elements of these programs for practitioners. Elements discussed include enforcement activity concerning the Fair Debt Collection Practices Act, the Truth in Lending Act, the Equal Credit Opportunity Act, and the Fair Credit Reporting Act. This overview is presented to help clear up misconceptions held by industry members, consumer groups, and others that are affected by these actions.

161   Foxman, Ellen R. et al. "Disclaimer Footnotes in Ads: Discrepancies Between Purpose and Performance." *Journal of Public Policy and Marketing* 7 (1988): 127-137.

Shows that advertisers and the FTC may need to develop other means besides disclaimers for conveying supplemental information to consumers because the disclaimers do not always function as a straightforward means of providing consumers with more or better information. A survey of 246 undergraduate students is used to gather data to support this position.

162   Franke, Janice R. and Deborah A. Ballam. "New Applications of Consumer Protection Law: Judicial Activism or Legislative Directive." *Santa Clara Law Review* 32 (1992): 347-426.

Investigates the creative use of state consumer protection laws within the context of government-business relationships. This creative use of the statutes has been backed by judicial review. The article focuses on whether this judicial activism is a valid perception and whether the courts are merely carrying out legislative intent. The investigation is rooted in the historical development of consumer protection laws and the role of the FTC.

163   Franklin, Christine C. "Deceptive Advertising, FTC Fact Finding and the Seventh Amendment." *Fordham Law Review* 43 (March 1975): 606-623.

Analyzes several cases brought by the FTC with regards to cease and desist orders against firms found to be in violation of the FTC Act, paralleling this with the jury trial guarantee stipulated in the Seventh Amendment of the United States Constitution. Judicial decisions make it clear that the superiority of the FTC to determine deception to the public's ability is a basic function of the agency. Given this, the decision in *United States v. J. B. Williams Co.* that awarded the defendants a jury trial on the issue of whether certain commercials were violative of the FTC's cease and desist order will prolong the avoidance tactics of deceptive advertisers and undermine the development of new methods to deal with deception.

164 "The FTC Ad Substantiation Program." *Georgetown Law Journal* 61 (July 1973): 1427-1451.

The FTC's Ad Substantiation Program is examined with special attention focused on its improvement. Three alternative or supplemental programs are offered: increase the consumer's right to know through the implementation of more consumer education programs; broaden the FTC's power to control advertising; and, initiate a judicial or legislative consumer's right of action provision enforcing substantiation requirements. These recommendations would help to improve the program as well as address criticisms.

165 "The FTC and Television: A New Rule for Misrepresentation by Test and Demonstration." *St. John's Law Review* 36 (May 1962): 274-293.

Uses the specific Colgate-Palmolive case regarding the use of props to show the moistening qualities of Rapid Shave Cream and the subsequent ruling by the Commission that such mock-ups are unlawful, to analyze the scope of Section 5 of the FTC Act in the context of the law's passage, the level of public sophistication of which the act is aimed, traditional defenses available to advertisers, and the specific problems associated with misrepresentation in television advertising. It is concluded that the act is "a reasonable rule" which takes into account consumer motivation and behavior.

166 "The FTC's Preservation of Consumers' Claims and Defenses: Consumer Security or Consumer Fraud?" *Valparaiso University Law Review* 11 (Winter 1977): 263-313.

Analyzes the scope and effect of the recent FTC regulation that attempts to protect the consumer in the modern credit process and eliminate the loopholes present in the Holder-In-Due-Course Doctrine. While the rule represents progress on the part of the FTC, it falls short of achieving absolute consumer credit protection because the scope of the rule does not extend to the creditor. The rule's effects on the cost and availability of credit, especially among low income consumers, must be studied further.

167   Gaedeke, Ralph M. and Warren W. Etcheson. *Consumerism: Viewpoints from Business, Government, and the Public Interest.* San Francisco, CA: Canfield Press, 1972.

Collection of essays that examine the new consumer movement from three perspectives: from that of the consumer, from that of the seller, and from that of consumer advocates pushing for greater governmental involvement in consumer protection. The role that the FTC plays in protecting the consumer is referred to throughout the text.

168   Gage, Robert J. "The Discriminating Use of Information Disclosure Rules by the Federal Trade Commission." *UCLA Law Review* 26 (June 1979): 1037-1083.

FTC rules are created for two reasons: to eliminate particular patterns of unfair or anticompetitive trade practices and/or to intervene when traditional market mechanisms do not provide the consumer with sufficient product information. This article discusses various issues related to the effects of the FTC's disclosure rules, including the establishment of meaningful standards, consumer awareness of the significance of the information provided, and the medium of disclosure and what costs are incurred in disclosure regulation.

169   Gard, Stephen W. "Purpose and Promise Unfulfilled: A Different View of Private Enforcement Under the Federal Trade Commission Act." *Northwestern University Law Review* 70 (1975): 274-291.

Refutes a student comment published in this review (September-October 1974) stating that private right of action should not be implied under Section 5 of the FTC Act. The comment supports this position by noting that Congress did not specifically articulate this intention. Legislative history is used as further evidence to support this view. This critique attempts to show that several important cases were not considered, that there was a misapplication of legislative history, and that there was an "indifference to the realities of the FTC enforcement of the statute."

170   Gardner, David M. "Deception in Advertising: A Conceptual Approach," *Journal of Marketing* 39 (January 1975): 40-46.

Offers a conceptual approach to understanding the issue of deception in advertising based on the interaction between the advertisement and the consumer rather then the act of deceiving. This behavioral approach focuses on three categories of deception: a completely false statement, the need for a qualification for the ad to be completely understood by the consumer, and a claim-belief advertisement that, while not making deceptive claims per se, leaves a deceptive belief or attitude about a product. The analysis of these three categories of deception are used to present a behavioral approach to detecting and measuring deception.

171   Gardner, Judy. "Consumer Report: Attacks on Advertising Continue as Agencies Work on New Regulatory Policies." *National Journal* 4 (September 9, 1972): 1427-1436.

Provides an overview of business concerns regarding increased government scrutinization of advertising practices. The essay focuses on several agencies including the FTC. Among the activities of the Commission examined is substantiation, corrective advertising, and counter-advertising. Includes a profile of Robert Pitofsky, director of the FTC's Bureau of Consumer Protection.

172   Gardner, Judy. "Consumer Report: Strengthened FTC Ready for Action Phase as New Leaders Complete Shakedown Period." *National Journal* 5 (December 29, 1973): 1931-1939.

Examines the future of the FTC under the new Chairman, Lewis A. Engman after an "active and innovative" period led by Chairman Miles Kirkpatrick. The Commission's consumer protection activities are examined in detail to help gage what direction the FTC will take under Engman's leadership. Among the areas analyzed is rulemaking, warranties, advertising, and consumer protection. The article includes a profile of Lewis A. Engman.

173   Garrett, D. Walker. "Private Rights of Action Under the FederalTrade Commission Act." *Houston Law Review* 11 (1974): 699-708.

Discusses, using specific court cases, the judicial reasoning behind why the private rights of action remedy has not been applied to the FTC Act even though the doctrine of implication has been applied to other federal regulatory statutes.

174   Gatling, D. B. "Radio Advertising and the Federal Trade Commission." *Federal Communications Bar Journal* 9 (September 1949): 74-77.

Outlines the case load, duties, and functions of the FTC's Division of Radio and Periodical Advertising. The essay begins with a brief introduction to the roles the FTC plays in declaring false or misleading advertising unlawful.

175 Gaughan, Lawrence D. "Advertisements which Identify 'Brand X': A Trialogue on the Law and Policy." *Fordham Law Review* 35 (1967): 445-476.

The author creates a fictitious conversation among a senior partner of a Wall Street law firm, a vice president for marketing of a brewery, and an executive of the advertising agency in charge of the brewery's account. The "conversation" centers on a comparative advertisement that used the fictitious beer brand and other best selling beers to show the superiority of a competing beer. The thesis of the conversation is how the federal regulatory law affects the usage of another brands name and label in comparative advertisements which had previously been considered taboo. The conversation is used to outline the issues surrounding comparative advertising and the legal parameters that allow for another brand's name to be used in an advertisement. Specific FTC cases are referred to in order to highlight out the issues involved.

176 Gellhorn, Ernest. "Proof of Consumer Deception Before the Federal Trade Commission." *Kansas Law Review* 17 (1969): 559-572.

Despite the efforts of the FTC to regulate deceptive advertising, all indications point to an increase in such practices. A particular problem is the issue of proof of consumer deception in FTC false advertising cases. This essay advocates a more active use of scientific surveys and standards for the interpretation of possible deception. This approach would help to relieve the problems of delay and ineffectiveness that currently permeates consumer protection cases. The author details at which points these scientific surveys should be applied to insure their effective use in consumer protection cases.

177 Gellhorn, Ernest. "Trading Stamps, S & H, and the FTC's Unfairness Doctrine." *Duke Law Journal* 1983 (November 1983): 903-958.

In the case *FTC v. Sperry and Hutchinson Co.*, the Supreme Court held that the FTC's authority to prohibit unfair methods of competition as stated in Section 5 of the FTC Act extended beyond Congressional intent regarding what defines unfair business practices. In so ruling, the Court upheld the FTC's authority to decide what constitutes unfair practices. This article first argues that the economic role of trading stamps was misunderstood by the Court. A more fundamental thesis is that the legal theory used in the Sperry case is "seriously flawed" because the Court relies on the legislative history of the FTC Act which is vague and uninstructive. It is concluded from the study that "the most appropriate and objective measure for testing FTC intervention under the unfairness doctrine is whether that intervention is likely to improve consumer welfare."

178 Gerstner, Eitan and James D. Hess. "Can Bait and Switch Benefit Consumers?" *Marketing Science* 9 (Spring 1990): 114-124.

By using a model of bait and switch, it is shown that the FTC's policy of making such practice illegal should be further investigated because the findings suggest that in-store promotions and price competition is enhanced by bait and switch tactics. Empirical studies in various markets could help to further the research in this area. However, progress is probably limited because stores will not cooperate fully since the practice is still illegal.

179 Gettleman, Arthur. "Advertising and the Federal Trade Commission." *Antitrust Bulletin* 7 (March-April 1962): 259-271.

As part of the proceedings from the First Legal Symposium for Franchising sponsored by the International Franchise Association, the author provides a brief history of the FTC's jurisdiction over advertising then proceeds to use a number of cases that have come before the FTC to illustrate how the agency will become more active in monitoring advertising and other business procedures as they relate to franchising.

180 Glassman, Myron and William J. Pieper. "Processing Advertising Information: Deception, Salience, and Inferential Belief Formation." *Journal of Advertising* 9 (Winter 1980): 3-10.

Examines four FTC cases dealing with the salience of health, safety, nutritional, and environmental claims to determine the effectiveness of an advertisement judged to be deceptive by the FTC. The same ads are examined after they have been modified according to FTC guidelines. Fishbein's concepts of attribute salience and inferential belief formation are applied to the cases to determine if these concepts can provide a better framework in which to determine an advertisement's deceptiveness. The study concludes that the FTC should investigate deceptiveness based not on what is said but rather how the ad is interpreted. Text of the four advertisements examined is included.

181 Goff, David H. and Linda Dysart Goff. "Regulation of Television Advertising to Children: The Policy Dispute in Its Second Decade." *Southern Speech Communication Journal* 48 (1982): 38-50.

Traces the dispute regarding television advertising to children as heard by the FTC, states the ineffectiveness of regulating agencies, and notes a rapidly evolving regulatory atmosphere in the Reagan administration.

182   Goins, Jr., E. Eldridge. "Consumer Protection: Proposed Federal Trade Commission Rule-Preservation of Buyer's Claims and Defenses in Consumer Installment Sales." *Journal of Public Law* 21 (1972): 169-188.

States that the FTC's success in obtaining judicial or legislative support in ending consumer fraud under Section 5 of the FTC Act should be applied to areas of fraudulent practices in retail installment sales. Outlines the proposed rule's effects on the law of commercial transactions and shows the proposed effects that the rule's may have on private rights now controlled by state laws.

183   Goldston, David B. "Federal Regulation of Debt Collection Practices: The Fair Debt Collection Practices Act and Section Five of the Federal Trade Commission Act." *University of San Francisco Law Review* 13 (Spring 1979): 575-612.

Notes the increased activity of government in regulating the debt collection industry, in particular through the Fair Debt Collection Practices Act and the FTC's proposed Credit Practices Trade Regulation Rule. The coverage and possible impact of both the Act and the proposed rule are examined in detail. Issues such as third party involvement are also compared in each case.

184   Gordon, Lelland James. *Economics for Consumers.* 7th edition. New York, NY: Van Nostrand, 1977.

Textbook that provides a detailed analysis the consumer, the economy, and the marketplace and the relationship among each institution. Within this analysis is an examination of the role of government regulatory agencies and their impact on the marketplace and the consumer. The book provides a better understanding of how the marketplace operates to serve, and occasionally defraud, the consumer. The issues of advertising, labeling and packaging, and information dissemination to consumers and the attempts by the FTC to regulate these issues are all covered.

185   Grady, Susan E. and Michael B. Feinman. "Advertising and the FTC: How Much Can You "Puff" until You're Legally Out of Breath?" *Administrative Law Review* 36 (Fall 1984): 399-411.

Outlines the FTC's dual mission of promoting competition within the marketplace and protecting the consumer from deceptive trade practices and false or misleading advertising. The authors then couch this mission within the concept of puffery and its use as a defense by companies accused of unfair or deceptive advertising.

186   Graf, Edward L. "Disparaging the Product: Are the Remedies Reliable?" *Duquesne Law Review* 9 (Winter 1970-71): 163-185.

Discusses the legal definition, usage, and remedies available to a business that becomes the victim of misleading disparagement in advertising, and specifically, what role the FTC and Uniform Deceptive Trade Practices Act play in controlling the phenomenon.

187   Greenhalgh, William F. "The FTC's Holder-In-Due-Course Rule: An Ineffective Means of Achieving Optimality in the Consumer Credit Market." *UCLA Law Review* 25 (April 1978): 821-861.

Analyzes the FTC's Trade Regulation Rule Concerning Preservation of Consumer's Claims and Defenses which attempts to protect consumers from having to make payments of purchased merchandise even though the seller has refused to service, repair, or replace the product as stipulated in the sales transaction. Uneven state regulation of the Holder-In-Due-Course Doctrine prompted the FTC to enact the Trade Regulation Rule. However, careful analysis of the Rule's provisions shows that it has "substantial defects." These defects are outlined. A national statute incorporating the elimination of negotiable instruments and waiver-of-defense clauses, and creating a regulation that would encourage sellers to set a uniform transaction cost figure is proposed It is argued that this national statute would accomplish more than the current FTC rule.

188   Greer, Sue. "Commercial Speech Protection and Alcoholic Beverage Advertising." *Paper Presented at the Annual Meeting of the Association for Education in Journalism and Mass Communication.* (70th, San Antonio, TX, August 1-4, 1987).

This paper presents the legal precedents for and the implications of banning alcoholic beverage advertising and the laws governing commercial speech protection. Includes a section on the role of the FTC in regulating advertising.

189   Greig, G. B. "Some Varieties of Consumer Behavior Described of the Decisions of the Federal Trade Commission." *Journal of Business* 20 (October 1947): 191-200.

Uses misrepresentation cases that have come before the courts and the FTC "in recent years" to examine two issues relating to consumer behavior: what are the components of information provided to consumers that would justify legal protection against misrepresentation and what "habits and capacities" for understanding this information do consumers possess? The first issue is addressed by examining four categories of misrepresentation cases (origin, trade status, price, and indorsement and false testimonies). Results of the study show that evaluation and understanding by the consumer of a product's performance is frequently based on content, quality, quantity, and price. However, when this information does not readily provide the rationale for buying a product, information such as endorsements and trade status are used to make the decision for the consumer.

190   Grendell, Timothy J. "Let the Holder Beware! A Problematic Analysis of the FTC Holder-In-Due-Course Rule." *Case Western Reserve Law Review* 27 (Summer 1977): 977-1009.

Notes that, while the FTC's efforts to close loopholes in the Holder-In-Due-Course Doctrine is "laudable," the new Rule contains certain substantive and procedural problems. Among these is vagueness, inadequate guidelines, and undefined terms, that undermines the Rule's ability to completely solve fraudulent behavior in consumer credit transactions.

191   Grewal, Dhruv and Larry D. Compeau. "Comparative Price Advertising: Informative or Deceptive?" *Journal of Public Policy and Marketing* 11 (Spring 1992): 52-62.

Analyzes the public policy implications of twenty-eight studies that examined comparative price advertising to determine if such a practice is informative or deceptive. Reviewing relevant literature, FTC guidelines, and selected court cases provides the basis for recommendations regarding comparative price advertising for public policy makers. The authors conclude that the meaning stated in law and public policy parallel as much as possible that of ordinary consumer's interpretations. Includes a comprehensive list of references concerning comparative price advertising.

192   Grier, III, F. Barron. "Three Aliens Visiting the World of Products Liability." *Federal of Insurance and Corporate Counsel Quarterly* 41 (Spring 1991): 341-349.

Examines the aspects of three forms of recent consumer legislation to evaluate their impact on products liability. These are: the Consumer Product Safety Act, the Magnuson-Moss Warranty Act, and state Unfair Trade Practices Acts.

193   Grimes, Warran S. "Control of Advertising in the United States and Germany: Volkswagon Has a Better Idea." *Harvard Law Review* 84 (June 1971): 1769-1800.

Compares and contrasts the German and U.S. systems of regulating advertising by first discussing the characteristics and problems associated with the American system then describing in detail the German system. The essay concludes by comparing the two and noting that the regulation of adverting in the U.S. could be strengthened by the adoption of private enforcement and by making available both temporary and permanent relief.

194   Grodsky, Jamie A. "Certified Green: The Law and Future of Environmental Labeling." *The Yale Journal on Regulation* 10 (Winter 1993): 147-227.

Demonstrates that current statutes, FTC guidelines, and common law remedies are inadequate to properly regulate the growing response by consumers for environmentally safe products. Misleading claims by manufacturers are outlined as well as the fact that current guidelines do not offer a complete picture of the product's environmental attributes and harmful trade offs. Independent third-party environmental certification is unreliable because current legal and FTC regulatory guidelines do not insure that credible programs and standards will be developed by certifiers. Only a coordinated effort among private organizations, federal policy-makers, and a government agency (most likely the EPA) will provide a comprehensive regulatory structure for regulating deceptive environmental marketing.

195   Guida, William C. "Consumer Protection–Standing–Consumers Can Bring a Private Action Under Section 5 of the Federal Trade Commission Act if Harmed by Persistent Sales Practices that Were Previously Determined Violative of Section 5(a)(1) by the Federal Trade Commission in a Consent Order Directed Against Defendant's Franchisor." *South Carolina Law Review* 28 (March 1977): 711-725.

Examines the impact of the decision handed down in *Guernsey v. Rich Plan of the Midwest* that expands the power of Section 5 of the FTC Act to include the right of private action by consumers. Details of the case are provided along with a comparative analysis of other related cases.

196   Gunther, Max. "But First, a Word Against Our Sponsor: A Government Agency Asks Television to Provide Air Time for Those Seeking to Attack Commercials." *TV Guide* 20 (June 17, 1972): 6-8, 10-12.
First of a three part article. The first part discusses the controversy surrounding the FTC's proposal to the Federal Communications Commission that television broadcast time be set aside for "counteradvertising" for groups that feel a series of advertising is giving the consumer a one-sided view of a product or service. The FTC proposes that counteradvertising be used under the following conditions: ads that concern controversial issues, ads that rely on scientific premises that are still questioned within the scientific community, and ads that do not inform consumers about the negative aspects of a product or service. The essay also discusses reaction by the advertising industry.

197   Gunther, Max. "But First, a Word Against Our Sponsor: If the Antipitchmen Win: Will Advertisers Flee Television and Kill the Industry?" *TV Guide* 20 (July 1, 1972): 14-15, 17-18.
Third of a three part article. The concluding part of this series examines the repercussions that will be felt throughout the business community if the FTC is successful in implementing its counteradvertising proposals under the Fairness Doctrine. Limited court reviews regarding counteradvertising show that the courts are receptive to its use. Nevertheless, the FCC should proceed cautiously before deciding if it will accept the FTC's recommendations.

198   Gunther, Max. "But First, a Word Against Our Sponsor: Revolution at the FTC." *TV Guide* 20 (June 24, 1972): 26-29.
Second of a three part article. The second part examines changes in the FTC that help to explain the aggressive regulatory behavior of the agency both from the perspective of people within the Commission and members of the legal and business community. Possible relationships with Ralph Nader's consumer advocacy group is also examined.

199   Haas, Jules Martin. "*Warner-Lambert Co. v. FTC*: The Possibilities and Limitations of Corrective Advertising." *New England Law Review* 13 (Fall 1977): 348-368.
Outlines the case and summarizes the reasoning behind why the court upheld the power of the FTC to order corrective advertising. However, First Amendment considerations held in *Virginia State Board of Pharmacy v. Virginia Citizens*

Consumer Council, Inc. and the need to broadly interpret Section 5 provisions in order to legally justify the use of corrective advertising leave questions as to the FTC statutory authority to use corrective advertising to remedy deception. The decision also offers insight into the problems associated with the use of the remedy in the future.

200   Haefner, James E. "Unofficial FTC Judgements of Deception vs. Adults' and Students' Judgements of Deception." *Journal of the Academy of Marketing Science* 3 (Summer 1975): 232-243.

Attempts to provide insight into the FTC's role in determining how consumers may or may not actually perceive an advertisement by conducting a study that examines whether there is agreement between adult and student overall judgements of deception and the FTC's judgements of deception, and if the perception of deception has any effects on consumer behavior, especially with respect to intentions. While the study group of students and adults did not agree with the FTC's unofficial ratings of deceptiveness, conclusions cannot be drawn until a definitive reason for the discrepancies can be determined.

201   Hailey, Gary D. "The Federal Trade Commission, the Supreme Court, and Restrictions on Professional Advertising." *International Journal of Advertising* 8 (1989): 1-15.

Analyzes the FTC's removal of public and private restrictions on advertising and other marketing practices of licensed professionals. Advertising by pharmacists and physicians is studied.

202   Halverson, J. T. "Consumer Credit Regulation by the Federal Trade Commission." *Banking Law Journal* 90 (June 1973): 479-496.

Analyzes the problems that have arisen from the FTC's enforcement activities under the Truth-in-Lending statement regarding the issuance of policy statements designed to help consumers and the business community better understand the provisions of various aspects of consumer credit regulation and how the proposed solutions would affect the banking industry. The FTC's jurisdiction over banks, and specifically, the Holder-In-Due-Course provision are examined.

203   Hammer, Sandra N. "FTC Knights and Consumer Daze: The Regulation of Deceptive or Unfair Advertising." *Arkansas Law Review* 32 (Fall 1978): 446-469.

Discusses the economic justification for the FTC's regulation of advertising, the legal sources and nature of the FTC's authority, outlines the procedures available to regulate advertising, and defines the types of orders that the FTC may issue. Concludes that the elevation of commercial speech to constitutional protection should not substantially deter the FTC from seeking other remedies, such as discouraging puffery, in fostering informative advertising.

204   Handler, Milton. "The Control of False Advertising Under the Wheeler-Lea Act." *Law and Contemporary Problems* 6 (Winter 1939): 91-110.

Analyzes the Wheeler-Lea Act within the context of three factors: the adequacy of the Act's definition of the offense, the effectiveness of the penalties imposed, and the efficiency of the methods of administration established. The author states that the Act is an inadequate first step in ending deceptive advertising because it does not attack the problem of false advertising at its source, before it is disseminated to the public. The FTC should be given the power, which has been adopted by some Better Business Bureaus, to force false advertisers to publish retractions describing what part of their prior ads were misleading.

205   Handler, Milton. "False and Misleading Advertising." *Yale Law Journal* 39 (November 1929): 22-51.

Although there is a general recognition of the growing problem of false advertising, there has been no study articulating the variety of legal devices available to combat this issue. A basic analysis of the usefulness and shortcomings of each of these devices is presented. These devices fall under three general categories: civil actions available to either purchasers or competitors; state involvement in legal proceedings; and, sanctions of various types which indirectly discourage false advertising. It is concluded that despite the availability of these legal devices, law can do little--only a change in business psychology through the work of scholars and others to educate consumers to demand useful and truthful information would insure a solution to the problem.

206   Handler, Milton. "Jurisdiction of the Federal Trade Commission over False Advertising." *Columbia Law Review* 31 (April 1931): 527-560.

Written before the Wheeler-Lea Act of 1938, this essay points out the difficulty the courts have had in determining the jurisdiction the FTC has over false and misleading advertising given the vagueness of Section 5 of the FTC Act and the lack of legal precedent established in the courts. Specific cases such as *Raladam Co. v. FTC* are discussed to support this thesis as well as to illustrate concerns regarding how the courts have been restricting the FTC's efforts in the area of consumer protection. Mistakes made by the FTC in taking on the task of controlling false advertising are discussed while acknowledging the need for such government intervention to protect the consumer.

207   Hanen, Andrew Scott. "Texas Deceptive Trade Practices Act and Magnuson-Moss: An Explosive Combination." *Baylor Law Review* 29 (Summer 1977): 559-572.

This essay first examines how the Act has enhanced and strengthened the remedy powers of the FTC in combatting false and deceptive trade practices and, second, analyzes the potential effects of Magnuson-Moss on businesses when it is applied in conjunction with the Texas Deceptive Trade Practices Act. Measured together, the combined penalties under the state and federal statutes could be particularly severe for small firms.

208   Harkrader, Carleton A. "Fictitious Pricing and the FTC: A New Look at an Old Dodge." *St. John's Law Review* 37 (December 1962): 1-28.

Examines cases that have arisen since the promulgation by the FTC of the Guides Against Deceptive Pricing. These Guides were developed in response to retailers and, to a lesser degree, manufacturers creating "reduced prices" for goods in the minds of consumers by setting a fictitious higher price or "usual" price and then selling the goods at a "lower" price which actually reflected the true selling price for the item. The essay begins with an overview of retailing since 1920. It then addresses specific deceptive advertising acts articulated in the 1958 Guides. Recent fictitious pricing cases involving manufacturers are then examined, including issues related to manufacturer sponsored sales, catalog insert sheets, and nationwide pre-ticketing. Antitrust implications are also discussed. It is concluded that manufacturers must be aware of FTC pronouncements concerning pre-ticketing and list price suggestions or run the risk of action by the FTC.

209   Harrington, John. "Up in Smoke: The FTC's Refusal to Apply the 'Unfairness Doctrine' to Camel Cigarette Advertising." *Federal Communications Law Journal* 47 (April 1995): 593-610.

With the inability of Congress to legislate an end to the highly successful "Joe Camel" advertising campaign, the FTC considered administrative action to force R. J. Reynolds to stop using the character to sell cigarettes. This note examines whether the FTC could have succeeded in ending the ad campaign based upon the agency's authority to regulate unfair business practices. After reviewing the history of such authority and past cases involving FTC attempts to regulate commercial advertisements, these powers are then applied to the specific case of Joe Camel. A study of constitutional limitations placed on the Commission in the area of commercial advertisement regulations leads the author to conclude that the FTC would likely have been successful in ending the Joe Camel ad campaign.

210   Hartland, Jr., Thomas J. "Administrative Law–Federal Trade Commission Act–Consumer Private Right of Action Recognized Under Section 5." *Vanderbilt Law Review* 29 (May 1976): 1077-1085.
Analyzes the impact of the case of *Guernsey v. Rich Plan of The Midwest* and the legal background of the private right of action under the FTC Act, concluding that the scope of the instant court decision to limit private remedy to cases in which the FTC has already ruled still leaves the issue unresolved.

211   Hausknecht, Douglas R. et al. "Advertorials: Effective? Deceptive? or Tempest in a Teapot?" *Akron Business and Economic Review* 22 (Winter 1991): 41-52.
Advertorials are advertisements that look like articles in print sources such as magazines or newspapers or are presented on television or radio as news but are in actuality simply another form of advertising. The authors define the term and identify what advertising techniques are characteristic of this marketing approach and investigates advertorials effectiveness and describes what factors might lead to questions of deception. Specific examples are used throughout the article to highlight specific points. Problems with FTC definitions of deception are briefly examined.

212   Higgins, Richard S. and Fred S. McChesney. "Truth and Consequences: The Federal Trade Commission's Ad Substantiation Program." *International Review of Law and Economics* 6 (December 1986): 151-168.
Analyzes the allocative and distributive consequences of the FTC's shift to requiring prior substantiation for advertising claims. Concludes that this practice shifted business to larger advertising and media firms.

213   Hinich, Melvin J. and Richard Staelin. *Consumer Protection and the U. S. Food Industry*. (Pergamon Policy Studies on Business). New York: Pergamon Press, 1980.
Details the government's role in regulating the food industry, including methods

employed, areas of regulatory emphasis, such as food safety, and specific problems associated with food industry regulation. An entire chapter of the book is devoted to examining the efforts of the FTC to regulate the food industry as it applies to deceptive advertising and the promulgation of a Trade Regulation Rule establishing a set of guidelines for nutritional claims by advertisers.

214   Hodge, Jr., Samuel D. "Primer on the FTC's Rule Preserving Consumer Claims and Defenses." *Uniform Commercial Code Law Journal* 11 (Spring 1979): 354-360.

Short essay aimed at informing financial institutions of their obligations based upon arrangements with the seller under the FTC's rule preserving consumer claims and defenses. Also defines what effects the new rule will have on consumer credit transactions.

215   Holden, J. W. "Umpire of Business, But the FTC Protects the U. S. Public Against Fraud." *Review of Reviews* 95 (April 1937): 36, 67.

The author notes the importance of the FTC in protecting the consumer from fraud. The essay provides brief examples of misleading business practices that the FTC has acted upon, discusses how the FTC polices the business community, and shows how the sponsorship of conferences and the issuance of reports helps industry to police itself.

216   "Holder in Due Course: Does the Consumer Pay?" *Business Lawyer* 32 (January 1977): 591-632.

Edited transcript of a program presented at the 1976 Annual Meeting of the American Bar Association on the FTC's Trade Regulation Rule on Preservation of Consumer's Claims and Defenses. The purpose of the program is to provide some timely information in understanding the Rule and how the Rule affects consumers, sellers of goods and services, and those who finance the sale of such goods and services.

217   Holland, Tommy L. "Holder in Due Course: The FTC Rule Preserving Consumers' Claims and Defenses." *Banking Law Journal* 95 (October 1978): 789-801.

Analyzes the requirements for compliance under the FTC Trade Regulation Rule on Preservation of Consumers' Claims and Defenses and, in particular, those requirements and limitations that relate to the coverage of purchase money consumer loans.

218   Hovland, Roxanne and Gary B. Wilcox, eds. *Advertising in Society: Classic and Contemporary Readings on Advertising's Role in Society*. Lincolnwood, IL: NTC Business Books, 1989.
Collection of essays devoted to one of five aspects of advertising's role in society-- its institutional aspects, sociodemographic trends, legal and regulatory issues, economic issues, and ethical issues. Four essays within the legal and regulatory issues chapter are devoted to the FTC's efforts in regulating advertising. All four are reprints of previously published articles. The book does not include an overall index.

219   Hoy, Mariea Grubbs and Michael J. Stankey. "Structural Characteristics of Televised Advertising Disclosures: A Comparison With the FTC Clear and Conspicuous Standard." *Journal of Advertising* 22 (June 1993): 47-58.
Examines the components of the FTC's 1979 staff report of "clear and conspicuous" recommendations that are to be used to provide both supplemental information to the consumer, thus enhancing their decision-making ability when purchasing a product, and protect the advertiser from accusations of misleading or deceptive television advertising. After examining the recent disclosure practice of advertisers, it is concluded that advertisers are largely ignoring the policy and only making efforts to avoid claims of false advertising.

220   Hull, Frank Mays. "Pyramid Marketing Plans and Consumer Protection: State and Federal Regulation." *Journal of Public Law* 21 (1972): 445-477.
Analyzes three different forms of pyramid marketing schemes--referral sales, founder-member purchaser contracts, and multilevel distributorships--by defining their structure and how each deceives the consumer through the misrepresentation of lucrative profits. The role of the FTC is detailed in cases where the deception occurs within its jurisdiction.

221   Hunt, H. Keith. "Decision Points in FTC Deceptive Advertising Matters." *Journal of Advertising* 6 (Spring 1977): 28-31.
Outlines the steps involved in an FTC deceptive advertising action to inform advertisers of the proper defense strategy needed to refute a complaint and provides scholars of advertising regulation an orderly framework for teaching the subject of false advertising regulation.

222   Hunt, H. Keith. "Effects of Corrective Advertising." *Journal of Advertising Research* 13 (October 1973): 15-22.

Uses the FTC's corrective ad notice given to Chevron regarding its F-310 gasoline additive, which was found to be deceptive in its assertion that it helped reduce air pollution, to analyze both the corrective ad disclosure concept and the inoculation concept to determine their effects upon public policy decisions by the FTC.

223   Hyman, Douglas W. "The Regulation of Health Claims in Food Advertising: Have the FTC and the FDA Finally Reached a Common Ground?" *Food and Drug Law Journal* 51 (1996): 191-205.

This article reviews the FTC's response to the Nutrition Labeling and Education Act of 1990 that requires the Food and Drug Administration to issue regulations concerning food labeling, including health claims. The FDA's regulations are based upon a "significant scientific agreement" substantiation standard that the FTC was thought to reject because the Commission relied primarily on standards of deception when formulating its own regulations concerning health claims of food products. However, in a twenty-eight page enforcement policy statement, the FTC endorsed the FDAs regulatory approach. This study attempts to explore why the FTC decided to adhere to the FDA's standard rather than conform to earlier policies of deception and suggests that this is a desirable position for the Commission in future regulatory efforts.

224   Hymson, Michael T. "The Magnuson-Moss Warranty-Federal Trade Commission Improvement Act: Should the Consumer Rejoice?" *Journal of Family Law* 15 (1976-77): 77-103.

Outlines the consumer protection intentions behind the Act and its relationship to existing state laws under the Uniform Commercial Code. The article concludes that, while the Act is undoubtably a needed addition to the remedies available to deceived consumers, the impact of the Act cannot be fully measured until a later time.

225   Isaacs, Leigh R. "Psychological Advertising: A New Area of FTC Regulation." *Wisconsin Law Review* 1972 (1972): 1097-1124.

Places the prevention of "unfair and deceptive trade practices" as stated in Section 5 of the FTC Act within the context of television advertising that affect the subconscious needs and desires of consumers and comments on the recent efforts, and rationale behind, the FTC's efforts to enter into regulatory areas outside of inherent product characteristics. With the possibility of new FTC regulations, the lack of adequate constitutional protection of commercial speech is also analyzed.

226   "Illusion or Deception: The Use of 'Props' and 'Mock-Ups' in Television Advertising." *Yale Law Journal* 72 (1962): 145-161.

Provides reasons why, in the case of *FTC v. Colgate Palmolive, Inc.*, the use of mock-ups was ruled deceptive under Section 5 of the FTC Act, implying that the use of props in television commercials poses a risk to injure or create a risk of injury to the consumer. In this context, the author argues that the dictum of Section 5 was used too broadly since the consumer was not "injured" by the use of a mock-up, merely deceived in the broadest sense of the law.

227   "Implied Consumer Remedy Under FTC Trade Regulation Rule: Coup De Grace Dealt Holder in Due Course?" *University of Pennsylvania Law Review* 125 (April 1977): 876-918.

Explores the impact of the FTC Rule on the adjudication of disputes between the consumer and a financier as it related to consumer credit contracts that do not include the notice to holders "that a consumer's claims and defenses may be asserted against them." The second part of the essay examines what problems are facing consumers and the responses by state judicial and legislative systems to these consumer problems. After analyzing the overall enforcement scheme of deceptive trade practices by the FTC, the specific implications of a federal right to raise claims and defenses is examined. The essay concludes by studying the impact of the Rule on existing state law remedies.

228   Israel, Glenn. "Taming the Green Marketing Monster: National Standards for Environmental Marketing Claims." *Boston College Environmental Affairs Law Report* 20 (Winter 1993): 303-333.

The explosion of environmentally friendly product advertisements has led to misleading, trivial, and deceptive advertising practices by some manufacturers because of the lack of standardization and regulation of green claims. This comment analyzes the current and proposed approaches to curb misleading or false green claims and discusses, within the context of traditional causes of action against deceptive advertisers, the strengths and weaknesses of each approach. It is noted that the FTC's environmental marketing guidelines are a good start but fails to establish minimum standards or offer specific definitions of green terms such as "recycled" or "degradable."

229   Jacobs, William W. "Consumer Litigation and Its Relationship to the Federal Trade Commission's "Unfairness" and "Deception" Standards." *University of Toledo Law Review* 16 (Summer 1985): 903-917.

As it primarily applies to advertising, this essay briefly examines recent clarifications of FTC policy regarding the concepts of unfairness and deception. This is followed by an analysis of the Ohio Consumer Sales Practices Act and how developments in FTC rules and policies "may affect future consumer litigation in Ohio."

230   Jellinek, F. "Dies, Hearst, and the Consumer: Action of the Federal Trade Commission Against Good Housekeeping." *New Republic* 102 (January 1, 1940): 10-13.

Points out that the case brought against Good Housekeeping magazine by the FTC regarding the use of the Good Housekeeping seal system on certain products and services has not been covered significantly in the newspapers and refutes the claim by Richard Berlin of the magazine that the FTC acted under pressure from communists. The author concludes that evidence so far indicates that advertising and publishing interests have cooperated in trying to suppress the consumer movement.

231   Jenkins, John A. "How to End the Endless Delay at the FTC." *The Washington Monthly* 8 (June 1976): 42-48, 50.

This article follows up on the Wellford article that appeared in the October 1972 issue of this journal (see Harrison Wellford cite), stating that the delaying tactics used by firms in the courts is sabotaging the FTC's ability to prosecute deceptive behavior and the voluminous amount of administrative rules and regulations issued by Congress to protect due process concerns has effectively "crippled the regulatory agency." A reform proposal to end these barriers to effectiveness are outlined in the conclusion.

232   Johnson, Jr., Glendon E. "The Federal Trade Commission's Power to Protect the Consumer Sued in Inconvenient Forums." *Texas Law Review* 55 (November 1977): 1416-1426.

A note examining the distant forum abuse problems that arise in protecting the consumer against the consequences of acts performed in the state by non-residents. This abuse takes two forms: allowing the place of trial to be located sufficiently far away that it is inconvenient for the defendant to appear and, under certain state statutes, allowing plaintiffs to sue nonresidents. The FTC, through the extensive scope of the unfairness doctrine, is particularly well equipped to control distant forum abuses. This extension of powers is reinforced by the courts decision in *Spiegel, Inc. v. FTC* that stated the FTC was correct in disallowing Spiegel from suing only through the Illinois court system out-of-state consumers with delinquent accounts. This practice was ruled in violation of the unfair practice doctrine of Section 5 of the FTC Act. This issue offers a practical opportunity to expand the FTC's powers to protect the consumer.

233   Johnston, Linda Osgood. "Corrective Advertising: Panacea or Punishment?" *Duquesne Law Review* 17 (1977-1978): 169-187.

A comment exploring the legality and use of corrective advertising as an FTC remedy for deceptive advertising. Through an analysis of the Warner-Lambert Company case whereby the courts ruled that corrective advertising is permissible in seeking redress for deception, and by examining the viability of corrective disclosure as a remedy for protecting the consumer, it is concluded that the FTC has exceeded the bounds of its statutory powers and that imposition of corrective advertising orders violates the advertiser's constitutional rights.

234   Jones, Mary Gardiner. "The Consumer Interest: The Role of Public Policy." *California Management Review* 26 (Fall 1973): 17-24.

Written by a former commissioner of the FTC, the essay outlines the piece-meal efforts of business and government to deal with the issues raised by consumer groups. It is increasingly recognized that government must play an affirmative role in creating a balance between the short-term and long-term interests of business and consumers. Existing antitrust and consumer protection legislation cannot cope with all the emerging needs of consumers in the 1980s. Given this, a Department of Consumer Affairs is advocated to focus nation policy on issues related to consumer protection.

235   Jones, Mary Gardiner. "Planning the Federal Trade Commission's Consumer Protection Activities." *Journal of Consumer Affairs* 3 (Summer 1974): 8-29.

Outlines the history and reasons behind the development of the FTC's Office of Policy Planning and Evaluation, explains the advantages of applying a decision-making planning process to the consumer protection activities of the Commission, and concludes that, similar to consumer groups, limited resources must be allocated wisely and based on "clearly articulated standards and values."

236   Jones, Mary Gardiner. "To Tell the Truth, the Whole Truth...." *Food Drug Cosmetic Law Journal* 26 (April 1971): 173-185.

As an FTC Commissioner, the author examines the concept of truth as it applies to behavior within the business community and discusses public concern over the essential values that make up most advertising messages.

237   Jones, Mary Gardiner. "Wanted: A New System for Solving Consumer Grievances." *Arbitration Journal* 25 (1970): 234-247.

Reviews the inadequacies of current legal mechanisms to remedy consumer grievances and discusses the need to create informal complaint-handling mechanisms. Examples of attempts to create new mechanisms are given.

238   Jordan, Ellen R. and Paul H. Rubin. "An Economic Analysis of the Law of False Advertising." *Journal of Legal Studies* 13 (June 1979): 527-553.

Considers the economics of advertising, the legal treatment of consumer and competitor suits against misrepresentation, and offers evidence regarding the effects of changing the legal environment to better reflect economic efficiency. Within this, the role of the FTC in regulating false or misleading advertising is considered. It remains to be seen if the Commission is capable of "cleaning up the marketplace."

239   "Jurisdiction Overlap Between the Federal Trade Commission and Consumer Product Safety Commission: Toward a Rational Delineation of Regulatory Duties." *George Washington Law Review* 42 (August 1974): 1114-1140.

Analyzes the proposed complaint issued by the FTC that charged twenty-six major polyurethane and polystyrene plastics producers and marketers with representing and marketing combustible plastics as nonflammable or self-extinguishing, to determine the proper roles of the FTC and the Consumer Product Safety Commission in the regulation of consumer product safety. After studying the scope of the cease and disorder order, it is concluded that the FTC may be exceeding its power, thus creating an undesirable overlap of regulatory activities between it and the Consumer Product Safety Commission. Cooperation between the two agencies would insure the best protection for consumers.

240   Karns, Jack E. "The Federal Trade Commission's Evolving Deception Policy." *University of Richmond Law Review* 22 (Spring 1988): 399-430.

Reviews the development of the current FTC deception standard that has been revised under FTC Chairmen James C. Miller III and his efforts to abolish the traditional deception standard that evolved through the courts and from the FTC. The article also attempts to determine whether significant changes in regards to the burden of proof have arisen because of this shift. Uses the Cliffdale Associates ruling to analyze how the 1983 Policy statement represented a shift in consumer protection by the FTC and how the FTC adopted a "likely to mislead" approach after the decision.

241   Kaufman, Lois and Peter M. Sandman. "Countering Children's Sugared Commercials: Do Rebuttals Help?" *Paper Presented at the Annual Meeting of the International Communication Association.* (34th, San Francisco, CA, May 24-28, 1984).

Presents the results of a questionnaire consisting of binary choices given to approximately 1,200 children to assess the effects of advertisements and disclaimers used to counter the impact of sugared food advertisements. Children shown only advertisements of sugared food made less healthy food choices than those who viewed counter advertisements. The study was conducted to assist the FTC in policy making decisions regarding sugared food advertisements on television.

242   Kaufmann, Patrick J. et al. "Deception in Retailer High-Low Pricing: A "Rule of Reason" Approach." *Journal of Retailing* 70 (Summer 1994): 115-138.

The practice of setting prices at an initially high level for a limited period of time and then offering a discounted price for the merchandise for majority of the selling season (high-low pricing) has come under increasing scrutiny by federal, state, and local authorities. Consumers can be deceived depending on the inferences they draw from the "fair" price, "market" price, or "normal" price of the merchandise. By examining the legal, public policy, consumer behavior, and retailing perspectives of high-low retailing it is concluded that "rule of reason" rather than applying a per se approach would be more effective in protecting the consumer. A suit brought against the May D & F department store by the Colorado attorney general in 1989 helps to illustrate this conclusion.

243 Kauper, Thomas E. "Cease and Desist: The History, Effect, and Scope of Clayton Act Orders of the Federal Trade Commission." *Michigan Law Review* 66 (April 1968): 1095-1210.

This is a comprehensive study of the of orders entered by the FTC under Section 2 and 3, and to some degree section 5, of the Clayton Act. The study is divided into two parts: a consideration of the effects of enforcement and other issues and to examine the content of the orders themselves, placing these parts within the context of a fixed framework of enforcement patterns. The historical background of cease and desist orders is discussed first to provide insight into their meaning and purpose.

244 Kegan, Esther O. "Consumer Class Suits: Righting the Wrongs to Consumers." *Food Drug Cosmetic Law Journal* 26 (March 1971): 130-140.

Analyzes the principles behind and effects of the use of consumer class action suits in assisting consumers who have been injured by deceptive practices. The author discusses both state and federal laws and concludes that instilling a "philosophy of cooperative effort" among various federal agencies, manufacturers, and trade associations can best address the injustices faced by individual consumers in the marketplace.

245 Kelley, Craig A. "An Investigation of Consumer Product Warranties as Market Signals of Product Reliability." *Journal of the Academy of Marketing Science* 16 (Summer 1988): 72-78.

Uses the Market Signal Theory, which posits that consumers infer a product's reliability based upon the warranty, to conduct a pre-Magnuson-Moss and post-Magnuson-Moss analysis to determine how effective the Act is as a signal of product reliability. Concludes with an examination of the marketing and public policy implications of the findings.

246 Kent, Felix H. "The FTC Rulemaking Authority." *New York Law Journal* 206 (October 18, 1991): 3.

Examines efforts by the FTC under newly appointed Chairperson Janet Steiger to regain the power to create rules based on the unfairness doctrine. The essay outlines the development of the rulemaking controversy, both within the FTC and from Congress, and analyzes the current status of its rulemaking authority.

247   Kent, Felix H. and Elaine S. Reiss. "Advertising Directed to Children."
New York Law Journal 195 (February 28, 1986): 1.

Outlines the results and findings of the FTC's hearing regarding advertising directed to children, commenting that any regulations resulting from the hearings would have extended beyond the agency's jurisdiction. The essay continues by examining the FTC's disclosure power, the restraint of the agency to regulate all advertising of a particular class of products, and concludes with a discussion of the advertising industry's attempt at self-regulation.

248   Kertz, Consuelo Lauda and Lisa Boardman Burnette. "Telemarketing Tug-of-War: Balancing Telephone Information Technology and the First Amendment with Consumer Protection and Privacy." *Syracuse Law Review* 43 (1992): 1029-1072.

Explores the exploitation of new telephone information technology by telemarketers, specifically 900-number services, live and pre-recorded telemarketing calls which use autodialing equipment, and the business use of caller ID. The statutes and regulations that have been proposed and enacted regarding these telemarketing practices is analyzed. The discussion is couched within the issue of First Amendment rights versus the rights of consumers to be free from deception and their rights to privacy. The FTC's role in regulating telemarketing practices is covered throughout the discussion.

249   Kinnear, Thomas C. and Ann R. Root. "The FTC and Deceptive Advertising in the 1980s: Are Consumers Being Adequately Protected?" *Journal of Public Policy and Marketing* 7 (1988): 40-48.

Examines the response to the issuance in 1983 of the FTC's policy statement on the meaning of deception. Opponents have taken an economic or cost-benefit approach to assessing the statement's impact on consumer protection. While the FTC's role has not changed over the past four years, factors such as budget constraints and the President's platform must be taken into consideration. However, emphasis on how the FTC and other agencies are controlling deceptive advertising in the public interest should be analyzed.

250   Kinter, Earl W. "Federal Trade Commission Regulation of Advertising." *Michigan Law Review* 64 (May 1966): 1269-1284.

Provides an historical examination of the development of federal regulation of advertising and the subsequent expansion of the FTC's jurisdiction in regulating advertising. The essay then outlines typical patterns of deception concluding that the role of the FTC in combating false advertising is essential in ensuring that consumers are provided accurate and truthful information with respect to competing goods and services.

251   Kinter, Earl W. "Federal Trade Commission Regulation of Food, Drug and Cosmetic Advertising." *Business Lawyer* 16 (November 1960): 81-97.

Analyzing the concurrent regulatory authority of the FTC and the Food and Drug Administration in regards to the enforcement of the nations food, drug, and cosmetic laws, illustrates the pluralistic approach to regulation dictated by diverse but related goals. The FTC has advantages in regulating food, drugs, and cosmetics because concentration of regulatory power in one agency simplifies procedures, the number of flexible procedures available ensures effective and expeditious remedies, and many of the deceptive practices do not pose any dangers to the health of consumers. Nevertheless, the intersection of regulatory activities by two or more agencies is a welcome remedy for consumers when an atmosphere of cooperation has been established. This has been accomplished through the "Working Agreement Between the Federal Trade Commission and Food and Drug Administration"

252   Kinter, Earl W. *A Primer on the Law of Deceptive Practices.* 2nd Edition. New York, NY: MacMillan Publishing Company, Inc., 1978.

Analyzes the various deceptive practices used to gain an unfair advantage in the overall free market system. The initial chapters of the book examine the early abuses by deceptive marketers and advertisers and the efforts by the courts, state legislatures and the FTC to combat these practices and seek remedies. The remainder of the book consists of chapters outlining specific deceptive and/or unfair business practices, such as deceptive nondisclosure, endorsements, deceptive visuals presented on television, and mail-order sales. Each deceptive practice is analyzed within the context of the laws created to offset their effects on consumers. Throughout the book the role of the FTC is examined, thus providing a comprehensive primer on the regulatory role of the FTC in combating deceptive trade practices. Appendices contain a selected bibliography, the text of the FTC Act and other federal statutes amending or affecting the FTC Act, a selection of FTC trade regulation rules, and a list of selected FTC guides.

253   Kinter, Earl W. and Christopher Smith. "Emergence of the Federal Trade Commission as a Formidable Consumer Protection Agency." *Mercer Law Review* 26 (Spring 1975): 651-688.

Argues that the Magnuson-Moss Warranty FTC Improvement Act has significantly strengthen the FTC's ability to fight deceptive practices because, 1) the Act expands the judicial power of the FTC; 2) reaffirms the Commission's authority to make publicly known trade regulation rules defining unfair or deceptive acts or practices; and, 3) bolsters the FTC's independence by granting it authority to represent itself in court proceedings. The essay begins by tracing the FTC's role in consumer protection and the legal underpinnings that give the FTC its consumer protection authority.

254   Kinter, Earl W. and J. T. Westermeier, Jr. "Obtaining Refunds for Consumers Under Section 19 of the Federal Trade Commission Act." *Syracuse Law Review* 29 (Fall 1978): 1025-1070.

The FTC Improvement Act of 1975 added an important weapon for redressing consumer abuse by authorizing the FTC to bring civil action in court to obtain redress for individuals who have been the victim of violations under existing trade regulation rules or for violating provisions of the FTC Act. However, during the past four years only two cases have been filed under Section 19 with one case being dismissed after two years of litigation and the second has become entrapped within the statutory language regarding under what conditions refunds can be handed out to consumers. This article examines the problems of statutory interpretation of Section 19, attempts by the FTC to analyze these problems, and plans proposed by the FTC to make better use of the consumer redress provisions of the Section. The article begins with an overview of Section 19's legislative history.

255   Kinkel, Dale and Donald Roberts. "Young Minds and Marketplace Values: Issues in Children's Television Advertising." *Journal of Social Issues* 47 (1991): 57-72.

Traces the development of attempts to research young children's responses to television commercials and subsequent attempts by the FTC to regulate television advertising directed at children.

256   Kirby, Larry W. "The Federal Consumer Warranty Act and Its Effect on State Law." *Tennessee Law Review* 43 (Spring 1976): 429-463.

Analyzes the following controlling definitions present in both the Act and the

Uniform Commercial Code, "consumer product," "consumer," "supplier," "written warranty," "implied warranty," and "warrantor," to determine which statute controls and to determine differences in the scope of each piece of legislation. Special attention is paid to the definitions of "consumer product" and "written warranty." The effects of giving a written warranty are then analyzed.

257   Kirkpatrick, Miles W. "Federal Regulation of Life and Disability Insurance Advertising." *Forum* 15 (Summer 1976): 1029-1039.
Outlines the unique circumstances surrounding the regulation of the insurance industry which has been dominated almost exclusively by states and expands this thesis to discuss history of the federal and state regulatory relationship, the limitations placed on federal regulation of the insurance industry by the McCarran-Ferguson Act of 1945, and the recent activities by the FTC to regulate advertising of insurance.

258   Kirkpatrick, Miles W. "Advertising and the Federal Trade Commission." *Journal of Advertising* 1 (1972): 10-12.
Discusses the adverse effects deceptive and false advertising has on the consumer's purchasing behavior and examines how this affects the competitive nature of the U.S. economic system. Also discussed is the role of self-regulation within the business community.

259   Kirkpatrick, Miles W. "The FTC as a Consumer Protection Agency." *Antitrust Bulletin* 15 (Summer 1970): 333-345.
The author comments on the FTC's historical relationship with consumerism, focusing on the future role the FTC should play in protecting the consumer.

260   Koocher, Gerald P. "APA and FTC: New Adventures in Consumer Protection." *American Psychologist* 49 (April 1994): 322-328.
Analyzes the interaction between the American Psychological Association and the FTC by outlining unique issues connected with advertising by psychologists, tracing the historical issues behind regulating advertising by professional trade organizations, and examining actions by the FTC to curb false or misleading advertising. Emphasis is placed on the FTC's impact on the APA's Ethical Principles of Psychologists and Code of Conduct and its enforcement regarding advertising. Includes the text of those provisions of the Ethical Principles directly affected by the FTC recommendations.

261   Korber, Mark F. "Federal Trade Commission Act: A Private Cause of Action for Consumers: *Guernsey v. Rich Plan of the Midwest*, 408 F. Supp. 582 (N. D. Ind 1976)." *Connecticut Law Review* 9 (Winter 1977): 294-303.
Reviews and examines the implications of the case that first set forth legal recognition that there is private cause of action available under Section 5 of the FTC Act, thus overriding previous legal notions that only the FTC could seek judicial enforcement under the provisions of the Act.

262   Kramer, Albert H. and Robert C. Burns. "FTC Comparative Ad Cases Represent Sound Policy." *Legal Times of Washington* 4 (January 25, 1982): 16, 20-21.
Uses three recent decisions to illustrate how the FTC has maintained its policy of allowing "an unfettered flow of useful information to consumers." The essay is in response to earlier criticism that the FTC's enforcement policy regarding comparative test and survey claims would force a decline in comparative advertising and thus inhibit the flow of useful information to consumers.

263   Kunkel, Dale and Bruce Watkins. "Evolution of Children's Television Regulatory Policy." *Journal of Broadcasting and Electronic Media* 11 (Fall 1987): 367-385.
Analyzes the development and regulatory history of children's television advertising including the role and activities of the grass-root organization Action for Children's Television (ACT), the Federal Communications Commission's role in formulating guidelines, the role of the FTC and its marketplace approach to broadcast regulation, and recent legislative proposals for reform. The essay concludes with an examination of the future of children's television regulation.

264   Kutner, William R. "Consumer Product Warranties under the Magnuson-Moss Act and the Uniform Commercial Code." *Cornell Law Review* 62 (April 1977): 738-767.
Gives a detailed comparative analysis of the components of warranty protection as provided under the Act and the UCC, noting that the scope of the Act supplements rather than replaces the UCC. This, unfortunately, leads to a lack of uniformity between federal and state statutes and injects a myriad of complexities into the arena of warranty protection.

265 Kyle, Jerry V. "Deceptive Advertising Practice." *Texas Law Review* 39 (October 1961): 903-912.

Buyer confidence is being undermined by several deceptive business practices. These are deceptive packaging and labeling of products, misleading quality designations, misleading price designations, bait advertising, and questionable advertising standards. After analyzing the current FTC and state legal framework for regulating these practices, it is concluded that vigorous enforcement of these regulations and the introduction of new laws designed to further standardize container sizes, designate standard grades for various products, and regulate the size and location of the contents statement on labels coupled with coordinated efforts by state and federal lawmakers would be most helpful to consumers.

266 La Barbera, Priscilla A. *Consumers and the Federal Trade Commission: an Empirical Investigation.* East Lansing: Division of Research, Graduate School of Business Administration, Michigan State University, 1977.

This study examines three aspects of consumer involvement in federal agency rulemaking: demographic characteristics, attitudes by consumers of government regulation, and marketing, consumerism, and their participation in various activities related to consumer protection. A mail survey of 420 consumers, randomly selected from ten FTC comment files concerning at least one consumer protection rule, is examined to test hypothesis' about the effectiveness of such comments, the attitudes of the consumers, and the demographic profile of the consumers who submitted comments.

267 La Barbera, Priscilla A. and William Lazer. "Characteristics of Consumer Participants in Federal Trade Commission Rule Making." *Journal of Consumer Affairs* 14 (Winter 1980): 405-417.

Uses a systematic random sample of 420 consumer responses to proposed FTC rules concerning consumer protection from November 1, 1974 to October 31, 1975 to determine their attitudes towards marketing as compared to a public sample. The survey consisted of three sections designed to gather attitudinal, activity, and demographic data. The study supports the hypothesis that those who respond to proposed FTC regulations generally express more negative attitudes than the general public.

268   Laczniak, Russell N. and Sanford Grossbart. "An Assessment of Assumptions Underlying the Reasonableness Consumer Element in Deceptive Advertising Policy." *Journal of Public Policy and Marketing* 9 (1990): 85-99.

FTC policy on deception is examined from a behavioral perspective. At issue is the "reasonable consumer" element in determining if deception has occurred. Legal precedent is used to determine the behavior dimensions and the assumptions underlying this policy approach. An empirical test of these assumptions is used in determining that when consumers become more involved with a plausible message, their cognitive responses to the message for the advertised brand are more apt to become positive.

269   Lanfranco, Leonard W. "Advertising and Regulation During the New Deal Era, 1933-1941." *Paper Presented at the Annual Meeting of the Association for Education in Journalism*. (65th, Athens, OH, July 25-28, 1982).

Traces the efforts of various national and local consumer protection organizations to pass national consumer legislation. This consumer's movement led to the restoration and expansion of consumer protection powers of the FTC through the eventual passage of the Wheeler-Lea Act which allowed the FTC to stop false advertising as well as a separate food, drug and cosmetic act (the Copeland Bill).

270   Latimer, Hugh. "Whither the FTC on Food Advertising?" *Food Drug Cosmetic Law Journal* 46 (September 1991): 503-512.

The Reagan year marked a decline in FTC activity. However, to fill what was perceived as a regulatory gap in regards to food advertising and specifically health claims made by manufacturers, states and the Food and Drug Administration initiated regulations to compensate. This created conflicts and contradictions among the varying regulatory efforts in the areas of substantiation, permissible claims, proof required, and concern over censoring prudent information. Concludes that these conflicts may have be resolved in the courts due to the complexity of the issues.

271   Lawrence, William H. and John H. Minan. "The Effect of Abrogating the Holder-In-Due-Course Doctrine on the Commercialization of Innovative Consumer Products." *Boston University Law Review* 64 (1984): 325-374.

Points out a "fundamental paradox" that arises from the regulations embodied in the FTC's Holder-in-Due-Course Rule and its application in regards to newly developed products created by consumers. While the consumer protection features of the Rule help promote commercialization and creates an attractive marketplace for purchasers of innovative products, the Rule hinders commercialization in markets involving new products and sellers with uncertain reputations because it adversely affects the availability of credit and cost. This is particularly true based upon the optimal resource allocation principle adopted by the FTC which shifts the risk of loss from the consumer buyer to the lender. The solar energy industry is examined to illustrate the specifics of this paradox. Alternatives are then proposed that would ensure the availability of adequate financing for meaningful commercialization in new products markets.

272   Leaffer, Marshall A. and Michael H. Lipson. "Consumer Actions Against Unfair or Deceptive Acts or Practices: The Private Uses of Federal Trade Commission Jurisprudence." *George Washington Law Review* 48 (May 1980): 521-564.

This essay analyzes the federal court's treatment of private claims under the FTC Act and the role the FTC plays in protecting consumer rights and gives a description of the Unfair and Deceptive Acts and Practices (UDAP) statutes, their use by state courts, and some practical aspects of the statutes. UDAP statutes provide avenues of private remedies to compensate unfair commercial practices which is not covered under Section Five of the FTC Act. An appendix lists major features of each UDAP state statute.

273   Leary, Jr., Fairfax. "Timely Demise of Holder in Due Course Doctrine." *Uniform Commercial Code Law Journal* 5 (1972): 117-131.

Examines the provisions of a proposed Trade Regulation Rule regarding "the maintenance and retention of buyers' claims and defenses in retail consumer installment sales." The rule would override the holder in due course doctrine and the loopholes present within it. Suggested modifications to the Rule are included.

274   Lee, Stephen W. "The Magnuson-Moss Warranty Act: Consumer Information and Warranty Regulation." *Indiana Law Review* 51 (Winter 1976): 397-415.

Provides an overview of the Act's provisions for protecting the consumer in transactions involving written warranties concluding that, while the goals stated in the Act are commendable, the Act falls short of providing information for consumers, increasing the quality of products, and improving the standard of warranty performance because it does not assure public access to the information needed by consumers to make an informed decision. The author recommends a complete ban on disclaimers if such information cannot be provided.

275   Lees, Gail Ellen. "Unsafe for Little Ears? The Regulation of Broadcast Advertising to Children." *UCLA Law Review* 25 (June 1978): 1131-1186.

The author states that regulation of false and deceptive advertising is necessary, but that a blanket ruling prohibiting advertising directed to children as proposed by the FTC does more harm than good. After analyzing the issue and what impact of the proposed regulations would have on children's television programming and on protected commercial speech, it is recommended that the FTC issue a trade regulation delineating and forbidding specific false or deceptive practices rather than a broad statement and to parallel this with the application of the Federal Communication Commission's Fairness Doctrine to children's food commercials.

276   Leete, Burt A. "A Look at the Consumer Warranty Problem: The Federal Solution." *The University of Toledo Law Review* 6 (Winter 1975): 351-378.

Examines the aims and objectives of the Magnuson-Moss Warranty Act to protect the consumer in areas where the Uniform Commercial Code and other federal laws have failed or are inadequate. Discusses issues regarding warranty protection as interpreted by the Act, what effect the Act will have on the UCC, and what changes have been implemented by state legislatures which affect warranties.

277   Lemke, Jr., William F. "Souped Up Affirmative Disclosure Orders of the Federal Trade Commission." *Journal of Law Reform* 4 (Winter 1970): 180-193.

Criticizes the recent proposal by the FTC to broaden its discretion and authority to issue cease and desist orders so that individuals, partners, or corporations that are the target of the order must disclose in their subsequent advertising that a cease and desist order is standing against them because of violations made during previous advertising. This move is viewed by the author as an overreaction to recent criticism of the FTC.

278   Lester, Paul A. "How to Speak Magnuson-Moss: A Primer on the New Federal Warranty Act." *The Florida Bar Journal* 52 (April 1978): 301-310.

Uses FTC rules and policy statements issued so far to discuss what products are covered under Title I, how the Act defines "warranty", what types of warranties are permitted, what regulations have been made known publicly, what are the penalties for noncompliance, what effect does the Act have on existing federal and state laws, and, finally, what are the major changes in substantive warranty law resulting from Title I.

279   Lester, Paul A. "The Magnuson-Moss Warranty Act: The Courts Begin to Talk." *Uniform Commercial Code Law Journal* 16 (Summer 1983): 119-146.

Discusses the new federal warranty terminology introduced into the field of consumer product warranties and examines both the procedural and substantive requirements of Title I of the Act using FTC rules and policy statements as a guide since there is a lack of cases to draw upon.

280   Lewis, Michael Talmadge and Gregg Lindsey Spyridon. "Preservation of Consumer Claims and Defenses: Miller's Tale Tolled by FTC (Or Is It?)." *Mississippi Law Journal* 47 (September 1976): 768-788.

Discusses problems of consumer redress under the holder in due course doctrine and efforts by the FTC to create a rule preserving consumer claims and defenses in consumer credit transactions, even though evidence is present to show that the proposed rule may limit the supply and increase the cost to consumer credit. Concludes that the proposed rule is inadequate because of the omission of creditors from the mandate of the Rule.

281   Lewis, W. H. Ramsay. "Infomercials, Deceptive Advertising and the Federal Trade Commission." *Fordham Urban Law Journal* 19 (Spring 1992): 853-874.

Of primary concern to consumer groups, broadcasters and consumers themselves is that the public will be unable to discern a paid advertisement with its paid endorsements as an objective and real talk show. This perception is further complicated by the format of the infomercials and the current requirement that only minimal identification of the paid nature of the show is needed. Despite these and other concerns the FTC has failed to issue any guidelines or rules, taking action against only the most blatant offenders. After given a brief overview of the

FTC's power to regulate deceptive advertising and examining the new infomercial format, current FTC guidelines are applied to infomercials. It is concluded that these types of advertisements are "precariously close to violating commonly held standards for deceptive advertising." Solutions to the problem are then proposed.

282   Lindahl, Martin L. "The Federal Trade Commission Act as Amended in 1938." *Journal of Political Economy* 47 (August 1939): 497-525.

The amendments to the FTC Act of 1914 embodied in the Wheeler-Lea Act of 1938 came about for two reason: to broaden the authority of the FTC over unfair competition to include all unfair trade methods regardless of whether competitors were affected by them and to provide a more effective means for the Commission to regulate false advertising of food, drugs, devices, and cosmetics. The Wheeler-Lea amendments also strengthened enforcement procedures regarding cease-and-desist orders. These reasons, the nature of the amendments, and the probable affect they will have are analyzed in detail. While the amendments do add significant authority to the FTC, it is concluded that they fall short of clarifying and strengthening the Commission's investigatory powers.

283   Lipinski, Ronald L. "Consumer Product Warranties: The FTC Steps In." *The John Marshall Journal of Practice and Procedure* 9 (Spring 1976): 887-904.

Discusses the legal requirements and content of the Act and how it will improve consumer redress in transactions involving written warranties. The essay begins with an overview of the Act's development, then discusses its scope, applicability, and major provisions. The essay concludes with a review of how the Act will ultimately benefit the consumer by forcing the manufacturer to keep performance claims truthful and to honestly evaluate the performance claims of their products.

284   Loevinger, Lee. "Attack on Advertising and the Goals of Regulation." *Conference Board Record* 10 (January 1973): 23-28.

Discusses the two dimensions of the FTC's role in challenging deceptive, misleading or unfair advertising--policing falsehoods and requiring advertisers to disclose essential information so consumers can make informed decisions.

285   Loevinger, Lee. "The Politics of Advertising." *William and Mary Law Review* 15 (Fall 1973): 1-13.

Highly critical essay regarding the FTC's request of the Federal Communications Commission to use the FCC Unfairness Doctrine to require "regularly scheduled counter-advertising on a broad scale." Rather than being motivated by consumer protection issues, the author argues that the proposal is political in nature and offers fifteen specific reasons why it should not be implemented.

286   Lovett, William A. "Private Actions for Deceptive Trade Practices." *Administrative Law Review* 23 (May 1971): 271-290.

Comments on the problems associated with a lack of a compensatory right of action for victims of consumer fraud at both the state and federal level, noting that what little has been done at the state level is weak or underfinanced and that opportunities for federal rights of action under Section 5 of the FTC Act have not been "fully appreciated."

287   Lucas, Laurie A. and Alvin C. Harrell. "1994 Update on the Federal Fair Debt Collection Practices Act." *The Business Lawyer* 49 (May 1994): 1385-1394.

In reviewing the increasing amount of case law under the Fair Debt Collection Practices Act, the author outlines recommendations made by the FTC concerning "the formalization of criteria required in disclosure notices" and clarification regarding how often Miranda warnings must be given. A review of the case law reveals many of the concerns articulated by the FTC in its recommendations. The essay examines problems associated with the Act from the perspective of debtors, creditors, and lawyers.

288   Ludwig, Dean C. and Judith A. Ludwig. "The Regulation of Green Marketing: Learning Lessons from the Regulation of Health and Nutrition Claims." *Business and Professional Ethics Journal* 11 (Fall/Winter 1992): 73-91

States that the current debate concerning green marketing and the FTC's response of issuing preliminary guidelines should be placed with the context of prior experience in regulating health and nutrition claims. By analyzing the regulatory response to health and nutrition claims by the FTC and the Food and Drug Administration, policy makers can learn what direction the "green revolution" will be taking during the next decade and thus respond accordingly. However, it is noted that only cooperation among marketers, the scientific community, and policy makers will prevent consumer confusion and misinformation.

289   Luehr, Paul H. "Guiding the Green Revolution: The Role of the Federal Trade Commission in Regulating Environmental Advertising." *Journal of Environmental Law* 10 (1992): 311-336.

Discusses the origins of the environmental marketing movement and the reaction to it by state legislators and federal regulators, articulates the problems surrounding the lack of scientific knowledge about how to measure a product's impact on the environment and the vagueness of environmental slogans, and examines what options are available to the FTC in regulating the industry, informing consumers, and protecting the environment.

290   Lurie, Howard R. "Consumer Complaints: A Proposed Federal Trade Regulation Rule." *University of Michigan Journal of Law Reform* 5 (Spring 1972): 426-435.

Addresses the issue of consumer complaints, noting how it is frequently difficult for consumers to rely on the government to remedy a problem and that businessmen can safely ignore most consumer complaints. The author proposes a trade rule that would require any business person to respond to a consumer complaint within thirty days or be in violation of unfair trade practice under Section 5 of the FTC Act. The proposed rule would also establish a Consumer Complaints Register--a public document that would encourage prompt action by the business community. The essay concludes with the text of the proposed rule.

291   Lyons, Robert S. "Misleading Advertising and the Federal Trade Commission." *Intramural Law Review of New York University* 12 (March 1957): 221-233.

Examines the nature of misleading advertising under the FTC Act and the Wheeler-Lea Amendment of 1938. The essay uses cases to outline what factors are involved in initiating action, specific practices that the Commission condemns, and the courts reactions to those actions. The note concentrates on the FTC's power to regulate advertising prior to the Wheeler-Lea Amendment.

292   MacIntyre, Everette and Theodore P. Von Brand. "Unfair Methods of Competition as an Evolving Concept--Prelude to Consumerism." *St. John's Law Review* 44 (1970): 597-625.

Places current legislation to protect the consumer within a historical perspective by examining the FTC's contribution to consumer protection through the "unfair methods of competition" provision of the FTC Act. It is pointed out that the competitive concept doctrine within an open market reflects the views of Woodrow Wilson as well as public disenchantment with the judicial interpretation of the Sherman Act. The implications involving the FTC's consumer protection responsibilities rooted in antitrust legislation are then evaluated.

293   MacLeod, William C. "FTC Consumer Protection Activities." *Antitrust Law Journal* 57 (Spring 1988): 163-167.

Provides a current overview of the FTC's consumer protection activities. It is noted that the FTC has not expanded its promulgation of trade regulation rules but, in the areas of interstate consumer fraud, unfair debt collection, and in defining what constitutes a deceptive violation, the FTC has made significant progress.

294   MacLeod, William C. and Robert A. Rogowsky. "Consumer Protection at the FTC during the Reagan Administration." In *Regulation and the Reagan Era: Politics, Bureaucracy, and the Public Interest.* New York: Holmes and Meier, 1989.

Examines the consumer protection mission of the FTC in light of Reagan's shift away from government regulation and how this shift differed from previous administrations during the past twenty years. Specifically examined is the appointment of economist James C. Miller III as the FTC's chairman and what affect this had on the agency's approach to remedy unfair practices. Concludes that this infusion of economic thought into the consumer protection procedures of the Commission will remain for some time to come.

295   Magnuson, Warren G. and Jean Carper. *The Dark Side of the Marketplace: The Plight of the American Consumer.* Englewood Cliffs, NJ: Prentice-Hall, 1972.

Written by one of the creators of the Magnuson-Moss Warranty Act, this book analyzes the issue of deception in the marketplace, examines the individuals or groups that perpetrate it, outlines the frequently inadequate laws created to remedy deceptive practices within the marketplace, and sets forth proposals for new laws to help the consumer, and in particular, the poor. This analysis is placed within an understanding that deception is controlled by the seller. Specific examples of deception within the cigarette industry, credit and debt collection, and medical and health fields are examined in detail to back up this position.

296   "The Magnuson-Moss Amendments to The Federal Trade Commission Act: Improvements or Broken Promises?" *Iowa Law Review* 61 (1975): 222-259.

Begins by describing the provisions of the original FTC Act and its development prior to the amendments, then explains the changes that have been created as a result of the amendments. An evaluation of their effectiveness in providing consumers with a means of protection and an analysis of the FTC's ability to carry out the provisions set forth in the statute are then presented. It is noted that the FTC must demonstrate a willingness to use the new enforcement powers given to it by Congress in order to fully help the plight of the injured consumer.

297   Maher, Jr., John A. "Two Little Words and FTC Goes Local." *Dickinson Law Review* 80 (1976): 193-217.

Analyzes the possible involvement of the FTC as a regulator of local business activities now that the words "or affecting" have been added to Section 5(a) of the Act. The FTC's jurisdiction has been changed from activities concerning "in commerce" to those concerning "in or affecting commerce." The insertion of these words has affected the enforcement powers of the FTC considerably because almost all unfair or deceptive practices, although local in character, affect interstate commerce. This change in focus and its possible effects are analyzed in detail.

298   Mann, Richard A. and Metin Gurol. "An Objective Approach to Detecting and Correcting Deceptive Advertising." *Notre Dame Law Review* 54 (October 1978): 73-101.

The FTC controls deceptive advertising in two phases: detecting deceptive advertising and fashioning remedies to deter and correct the abuses. It is argued that the FTC has implemented these phases without an objective methodology. The author presents a model for such an approach using the *Warner-Lambert Co. v. FTC* case to illustrate its application. The FTC's efforts in detecting deception and the agency's use of corrective advertising are discussed first to provide background. The methodology proposed uses consumer surveys as a basis for improving FTC remedies, thus ensuring the protection of both consumers and honest business people.

299   Markey, Edward J. "Section 5 of the Federal Trade Commission Act: A Source of Protection for Competitors and Consumers." *Boston College Industrial and Commercial Law Review* 12 (April 1971): 982-996.

Uses the recent case of *Sperry & Hutchinson Co. v. FTC* to illustrate the notion that the FTC has outlived its usefulness and is incapable of performing its dual mission of antitrust enforcement and direct consumer protection. The decision is also used to show areas of untapped potential in the use of FTC powers. It is concluded that if the Sperry & Hutchinson case is affirmed, it would indicate that the FTC is fully capable of performing its duties well and is, in fact, more a victim of unresponsive courts than failure to use its power effectively.

300   Maronick, Thomas J. and Ronald W. Stiff. "Evaluating the Impact of Consumer Protection Regulations: The Federal Trade Commission Experience." *Policy Studies Review* 2 (1983): 495-505.

Shows that the sampling methods used by the FTC in evaluating the effectiveness of Bureau of Consumer Protection activities is recognized by the Commission and that this method is important in making future policy changes.

301   Marx, Gary S. "Section 43(a) of the Lanham Act: A Statutory Cause of Action for False Advertising." *Washington and Lee Law Review* 40 (Spring 1983): 383-420.

Discusses the implications of a proposed shift in FTC activity regarding action against false advertising. Chairman James C. Miller III stated that he intends "to encourage the FTC not to regulate actively in this area." The practical result of this if successfully implemented is that consumers and business people will have to rely heavily upon private remedies to counter increased deceptive advertising practices. The weight of this private remedy would subsequently fall almost exclusively on one federal statute--section 43(a) of the Lanham Act. The rest of the article outlines the history of this statute, how the Lanham Act has been applied in cases regarding comparative advertising, and concludes that the courts are just beginning to fully explore the potential to protect consumers against false advertising embodied in the Lanham.

302   Mathois, Alan and Mark Plummer. "The Regulation of Advertising by the Federal Trade Commission: Capital Market Effects." *Research in Law and Economics* 12 (1989): 77-93.

Empirical study that examines the effects of imposing a cease and desist order on a company for false advertising by drawing from 136 cases during the period of 1963 to 1985. This is done within the context of the FTC's regulation of advertising and capital market events analysis. Results show that significant costs can be incurred by a firm not directly associated with the implementation of the case. In addition, the amendments of 1975 to the FTC Act seem to have increased the FTC's ability to deter false and misleading advertising.

303 Matthews, Richard H. "A Guide to Federal Warranty Legislation: The Magnuson-Moss Act." *University of Richmond Law Review* 11 (Fall 1976): 163-176.

The purpose of this essay is to give the practicing attorney an overview of the provisions of the Act, including background surrounding its creation, disclosure provisions, what federal standards are established, and its methods of enforcement.

304 Matteoni, Norman E. "A New Antitoxin to Advertising Artifice– Television Advertising and the Federal Trade Commission." *The Notre Dame Lawyer* 37 (May 1962): 524-538.

Discusses the implications of the FTC's ruling in the Colgate-Palmolive case regarding a sand covered plexiglass prop used to show the effectiveness of Rapid Shave shaving cream. In stating that the use of such props is misleading, the FTC is further expanding its aggressive role in regulating false television advertising. Analyzes in detail the implications of ruling and the subsequent statement by the new Chairman, Paul Rand Dixon, regarding the FTC's mission to eliminate false and misleading advertising to protect the consumer and the marketplace in which they shop.

305 Matteoni, Norman E. "Rapid Shave in the First Circuit Court of Appeals: Television Advertising and the Federal Trade Commission (Part II)." *The Notre Dame Lawyer* 38 (1963): 350-354.

Comments on the results of the First Circuit Court of Appeals ruling regarding the case of *Colgate-Palmolive Co. v. FTC* in which the FTC issued a reworded Proposed Final Order under the demands of the Court of Appeals. Although the FTC has withdrawn the case, the author suggests that, if the FTC has not tired of the battle, the case is of sufficient importance to warrant an appeal to the Supreme Court. Article is a follow-up on the essay presented in the May 1962 issue of *The Notre Dame Lawyer* by the same author.

306   Mazis, Michael B. et al. "A Framework for Evaluating Consumer Information Regulation." *Journal of Marketing* 45 (1981): 11-21.

A framework for assessing alternative policy approaches to marketplace information dissemination is presented, incorporating economic, consumer behavior, and legal theory. A "Remedies Continuum" created from this framework to better assess the cost and benefits of consumer information regulation is presented.

307   McAuliffe, Robert. "The FTC and the Effectiveness of Cigarette Advertising Regulation." *Journal of Public Policy and Marketing* 7 (1988): 49-64.

Argues that the policies implemented by the federal government and the FTC to regulate cigarette advertising has not had the intended effect over the past three decades. The fact that the ban on broadcast advertising of cigarettes did not affect the consumer consumption is given as an example.

308   McCaffrey, James J. "Advertising and the Federal Trade Commission: A Reposte." *Journal of Advertising* 2 (1973): 16-19.

While the author notes that increased regulation of advertising by the FTC has led to a greater awareness of product performance by advertisers and has forced advertisers to be "more specific and accurate" about the products and services being advertised, FTC actions have also overstepped the bounds of authority. The FTC's advertising substantiation program is cited as an example.

309   McChesney, Fred S. "Consumer Ignorance and Consumer Protection Law: Empirical Evidence from the FTC Funeral Rule." *The Journal of Law and Politics* 7 (Fall 1990): 1-72.

Uses the development and provisions of the FTC's Funeral Industry Practices Rule to explore whether consumers are significantly ignorant of the laws conceived to protect them and whether mandatory disclosure laws offer useful information to consumers. It is concluded that, because the Rule was fashioned under false empirical assumptions, it has not benefitted consumers and has, in fact, burdened both consumers and producers with undue costs.

310   McGonagle, Jr., John J. "Arbitration of Consumer Disputes." *Arbitration Journal* 27 (1972): 65-84.

Details new approaches by the FTC and other consumer affairs officials and groups in handling consumer complaints since traditional litigation approaches are no longer acceptable.

311 McGrew, Thomas J. "Advertising Issues Avoided by FTC in Past Year." *Legal Times of Washington* 7 (January 7, 1985): 12, 15, 16, 17.
Discusses FTC activities during 1984 concerning advertising and concludes that the FTC was not as active as it should have been in pursuing some cases. Issues regarding a legal standard application to deceptive advertising cases and a review of the ad substantiation program failed to materialize. The article goes on to analyze specific cases that developed during the year and provides an overview of state court activities concerning advertising law.

312 McGrew, Thomas J. "FTC Should Provide Forum for Consumer Gripes." *Legal Times of Washington* 6 (February 20, 1984): 12.
Commentary stating the ineffectiveness of the current FTC Mail Order Rule. It is pointed out that consumers are unlikely to take advantage of the rule, that the Rule provides no rights, and that the dishonest seller ends up receiving no punishment because FTC staff may not act upon the merchant. An amendment to the law is proposed that would create a more service orientated consumer protection policy based on the implementation of a forum for consumers to voice their grievances.

313 Mendez, John L. "The New FTC Trade Regulation Rule on Holder in Due Course." *Houston Law Review* 13 (May 1976): 789-799.
Examines the reasons behind the implementation of the Holder-In-Due-Course Doctrine and what effects the new rule will have on consumer credit transactions. The article then analyzes these issues as they relate to the legal environment in Texas.

314 Merritt, J. Wesley. "New FTC Rule: Preservation of Claims and Defenses in Consumer Credit Transactions–Uniform Protection Comes to the Scene." *Uniform Commercial Code Law Journal* 9 (1977): 65-79.
Discusses the new FTC rule concerning consumer credit transactions under which three cutoff devices (the negotiable instrument, waiver of defenses clause, and vendor-related loan) are ruled unfair because they separate the consumer's duty to pay from the seller's duty to perform. Statutory protection within several states are examined to show the need for uniformity in the degree of preservation of consumer's claims and defenses.

315   Miller, John A. "Federal Trade Commission Activities Related to Consumer Information." *Journal of Consumer Policy* 1 (Winter 1977): 62-76.

Discusses past and present activities, policies and problems related to traditional FTC action, and responsibilities, especially in regards to the more recent information related responsibility, of the FTC. Concludes with speculation about the future role of the FTC in the area of consumer protection.

316   Miller, Rachel and Lawrence Kanter. "Litigation Under Magnuson-Moss: New Opportunities in Private Action." *Uniform Commercial Code Law Journal* 13 (Summer 1980): 10-31.

Discusses the various causes of action under the Act and examines how it has modified the nature of the private action. Various proposals to enhance the remedy powers of the Act put forth by Congress are also studied.

317   Millstein, Ira M. "The Federal Trade Commission and False Advertising." *Columbia Law Review* 64 (1964): 439-499.

Traces the development and use of regulatory powers by the FTC to control false and misleading advertising. The article focuses on the standard used by the FTC to determine the meaning behind an ad and considers how this standard may embody a limitation on freedom of speech. The author places the FTC's role in advertising in proper perspective by recognizing that the advertising "industry" is actually a diverse set of industries that does not embody one set of problems, that there is no statistical methods for assessing whether the FTC's efforts have actually led to more or less truthful advertising, and recognizing that the variety of advertising mediums also complicates the issue. It is concluded that, while the FTC is well equipped to deal with false advertising on a case-by-case basis, this approach will prove increasingly unwielding in dealing with the anticipated growth of advertising in the future.

318   Millstein, Ira M. "Kid-Vid Decision Creates Conflict between Two Functions of FTC." *The National Law Journal* 2 (February 18, 1980): 33.

Examines the recent ruling handed down in *Association of National Advertisers, Inc. v. FTC* that allows the current FTC Chairman Michael Pertschuk to participate in a rule making proceeding despite his apparent prejudgment of the issue of advertising directed to children. This ruling will only escalate the debate regarding the role of the FTC in regulating children's advertising. In addition, allowing the five FTC commissioners to participate in the rule-making procedures, pits the FTC's impartial adjudicatory role against its rule-making role.

319   Millstein, Ira M. "Federal Consumer Protection: Are Class Suits an Answer?" _The Record of the Association of the Bar of the City of New York_ 26 (November 1971): 664-670.

Text of a paper delivered at a forum sponsored by the Committee on Post-Admission Legal Education examining the arguments for and against the use of class actions to remedy fraudulent behavior directed toward consumers. Among the problems discussed are those inherent in Section 5 of the FTC Act.

320   Mintz, Morton. "The FTC in Fat City." _The Progressive_ 37 (October 1973): 8-9.

Criticizes the FTC for allowing margarine and oil makers to conduct advertising campaigns stating that polyunsaturated fats and oils reduce the chance of getting heart disease because they help to lower levels of cholesterol in the blood even though the FTC admits that the evidence for such claims is inconclusive.

321   Moewe, James A. "Consumers, Class Actions and Costs: An Economic Perspective on Deceptive Advertising." _UCLA Law Review_ 18 (1971): 592-615.

Argues that the best solution for overcoming deceptive advertising is not to strengthen existing regulatory and remedial methodologies, but to implement new consumer education programs that would compliment rather than agitate the functioning of a competitive economy.

322   Molotsky, Irvin. "The FTC: Consumer Watchdog or "Federal Trade Commission." _The Los Angeles Daily Journal_ 97 (June 14, 1984): 4.

Examines the philosophical split among the FTC's Commissioners regarding whether consumers have benefitted from the more accommodating position of the majority of Reagan appointed Commissioners rather than its previous adversarial position in regulating industry.

323   Montague, Gilbert Holland. "Unfair Methods of Competition." _Yale Law Journal_ 25 (1915): 20-41.

Early essay analyzing the issue of "unfair methods of competition" as stated in

Section 5 of the FTC Act. The article summarizes the divergence of opinion among members of Congress concerning the meaning of unfair competition and how this new legal concept promises to add an important chapter to common law in the United States.

324   Moore, Charles R. "Deceptive Trade Practices and the Federal Trade Commission." *Tennessee Law Review* 28 (1961): 493-515.

Reviews the regulatory activities of the FTC, its methods of enforcement, and its investigative powers and procedures as they relate deceptive trade practices. The essay focuses on specific cases to highlight key issues.

325   Moore, Charles R. "Regulation of Deceptive Practices by the Federal Trade Commission." *Food Drug Cosmetic Law Journal* 16 (February 1961): 102-115.

Discusses the role of the FTC in regulating deceptive practices, including the chief legal remedies available to the FTC, the economic justifications for eliminating false and misleading advertising, the relationship the FTC maintains with other agencies that regulate in the consumer's interest, and what methods are used to test products to determine the propriety of their advertising claims.

326   Moore, Ellen M. and Kelly F. Shuptrine. "Warranties: Continued Readability Problems After the 1975 Magnuson-Moss Warranty Act." *The Journal of Consumer Affairs* 27 (Summer 1993): 23-36.

Examines the readability and understandability levels of 121 warranties from ten categories of consumer durables using two statistical measures--the Flesch Count and the Fog Index. The study concludes that the Act may have actually increased problems of readability because it led to an increase in the number of limited warranties, which tend to have more difficult reading levels. Given this, the FTC should initiate cooperative efforts with companies to make warranties easier to read.

327   Moorman, Christine and Linda L. Price. "Consumer Policy Remedies and Consumer Segment Interactions." *Journal of Public Policy and Marketing* 8 (1989): 181-203.

Presents a framework for examining consumer and market problems as a function of consumer segment interaction patterns. The efficacy of regulatory remedies is shown to be affected by the type (positive, negative, or no spillovers among consumer segments) and extent of these interaction patterns. Obstacles, such as the need for large data requirements from regulatory agencies and that policy decisions are made by various regulatory agencies with varying agendas, threaten to undermine the potential contributions of this approach to remedy policy selection and implementation.

328   "More Consumer Action by the FTC." *Nation's Business* 58 (January 1971): 38-40.

Interview with the newly appointed FTC Chairman Miles Kirkpatrick. Kirkpatrick discusses his views on consumer protection and the consumer protection mission of the FTC given the current "big business" environment in America.

329   Morris, Jeffrey W. "The Magnuson-Moss Warranty-Federal Trade Commission Improvement Act: Protecting Consumers through Product Warranties." *Washington and Lee Law Review* 33 (Winter 1976): 163-179.

Discusses the provisions of the Act as it relates to expanding consumer protection enforcement remedies of the FTC and examines how the Act modifies existing Uniform Commercial Code provisions regulating written warranty transactions. Notes that the Act actually illustrates "more of a congressional policy than a master plan for consumer protection" until judicial review can help give it substance.

330   Morse, Richard L. D. "A Consumer's View of FTC Regulation of Advertising." *University of Kansas Law Review* 17 (1969): 639-650.

Despite a respectable record of positive activities to regulate deceptive advertising behavior, criticism of the Commission has increased. This essay provides an overview of the underlying factors contributing to the recent disenchantment with the FTC by consumer activists such as Ralph Nader and others.

331   Muehling, Darrel D. and Norman Kangun. "The Multi-Dimensionality of Comparative Advertising: Implications for the Federal Trade Commission." *Journal of Public Policy and Marketing* 4 (1985): 112-128.

Argues that the FTC to must change its perception that all comparative advertising is homogeneous. Comparative advertising represents a class of advertisements that encompasses a variety of dimensions, such as number of brands compared against the product being marketed. A complete understanding of these complexities must be attained before adequate policies can be formulated that ensure consumer well-being. In addition, this study raises eleven new questions regarding how to evaluate the effectiveness of different dimensions of comparative ads.

332   Mueller, Willard F. "Advertising, Monopoly, and the FTC's Breakfast Cereal Case: An Attack on Advertising." *Antitrust Law and Economics Review* 6 (1973): 59-72.

The author criticizes University of Chicago professor Yale Brozen's paid advertisement criticizing the FTC's advertising activities stating that he had written the paper under the sponsorship of New York based public relations firm. The author further states that criticism of the FTC is unfounded and based on unsound economic analysis. Brozen is also criticized for failure to disclose his relationship with ITT-Continental, a firm currently under investigation by the FTC.

333   Muris, Timothy. "The Consumer Protection Mission: Guiding Principles and Future Direction." *Antitrust Law Journal* 51 (Fall 1982): 625-632.

Written by the director of the FTC's Bureau of Consumer Protection, this article reviews James C. Miller's first year as Chairman of the FTC and outlines the organizational changes that have occurred in the areas of litigation and rulemaking as well as proposals to define unfairness and deception. This renewed commitment to traditional law enforcement was needed to restore respect to the agency.

334   Murphy, Daniel J. "The Ethics of Retail Price Advertising." *The Antitrust Bulletin* 6 (1961): 419-432.

As director of the Bureau of Deceptive Practices, Federal Trade Commission, the author discusses the ethical framework behind deceptive or false advertising, specifically as it relates to the fictitious pricing of products. Several cases are used to illustrate key points.

335   Murphy, Daniel J. "The Federal Trade Commission of the 1960s: What are Some of the Recent Changes in Procedures and How is the FTC Giving Additional Protection Against Unfair Business Practices?" *Journal of Marketing* 27 (April 1963): 1-5.

Discusses the FTC's efforts since the expansion of the Commission's administrative powers under the Wheeler-Lea Amendment of 1938, to protect both the business community and the consumer from deceptive business practices. Enforcement procedures, such as consent orders, hearings, and restraining orders, are examined. The article concludes with an outline of the agency's activities during the 1962 fiscal year.

336   Nadel, Mark V. *The Politics of Consumer Protection*. Indianapolis, IN: Bobbs-Merrill Company, Inc., 1971.

The purpose of this book is to examine from a public policy perspective the history of federal consumer protection policy and the development of the consumer protection movement in America. The author offers a critical look at the efforts by Congress and federal agencies such as the FTC to help protect the consumer and analyzes the role of the media and consumer advocates, such as Ralph Nader, in influencing public policy. The book concludes with a cost and benefits analysis of marketplace defects that affect consumers collectively in approximately the same way and reviews the findings from the previous chapters to study the consumer representation of a particular interest and how that affects the formulation of public policy.

337   Neuman, W. Lawrence. "Crisis and Growth in U.S. Antitrust Policy Activity: A Study of the Federal Trade Commission's Policy Actions, 1915-1970." *Current Perspectives in Social Theory* 10 (1990): 293-331.

This essay presents a quantitative time-series analysis of the enforcement actions of the FTC, suggesting that increased U.S. antitrust activity parallels popular protest movements that threaten dominant class legitimacy.

338   "New Chance for Consumers?" *Economist* 232 (July 26, 1969): 35-36, 39.

Discusses the recent criticism of the FTC in light of Richard Nixon's appointment of an American Bar Association commission to investigate the FTC. Traces the history of the FTC's legal mandate to protect the consumer and punish deceptive advertisers. Includes an organizational chart of the agency.

339   Newberg, Herbert B. "Federal Consumer Class Action Legislation: Making the System Work." *Harvard Journal on Legislation* 9 (January 1972): 217-259.

Examines the type of pressure that has been placed upon Congress to create more effective legislation to protect the consumer from fraud. After discussing the types of abuses, their economic effects, and administrative problems associated with them, the essay analyzes the provisions of three pieces of proposed legislation as they relate to the enforcement powers of the Department of Justice and the FTC.

340   Nicks, Stephan J. "Speak No Evil: Known Defects in the FTC's Used Car Rule." *Journal of Consumer Policy* 10 (March 1987): 69-87.

Traces the development, legal challenge to, and subsequent reissue of the FTC's Used Car Rule. Although the section of the rule that required dealers to disclose known defects to prospective purchasers had been legally upheld by the Supreme Court after having been vetoed by Congress, the FTC has decided to delete this disclosure rule for various reasons. In doing so, the FTC has insured a continuation of the status quo in the used car industry.

341   "Nontraditional Remedies for the Settlement of Consumer Disputes." *Temple Law Quarterly* 49 (Winter 1976): 385-427.

Analyzes nontraditional remedies for consumer redress due to deceptive business practices under the premise that current institutions and practices are inadequate in meeting the needs of consumers. Each area of failure with suggestions for improvement is examined, including those that fall under the jurisdiction of the FTC.

342   Ohlenforst, Cindy Morgan. "Big Brother's War on Television Advertising: How Extensive is the Regulatory Authority of the Federal Trade Commission?" *Southwestern Law Journal* 33 (June 1979): 683-701.

Discusses the FTC's efforts to ban advertising directed to children and how the proposed rules may step beyond the statutory authority of the Commission. Recent cases are examined to explore the constitutionality of the proposed rules and how they may conflict with the recent Supreme Court decisions that established a level of protection for commercial speech. While the FTC has been relatively free of judicial limits on its regulation of advertising, these court cases impose new limits on the broad discretion and power afforded the FTC in the past.

343   Olans, Judith L. and John F. Dobbyn. "Federal Regulation of False Advertising." *Boston College Industrial and Commercial Law Review* 5 (1964): 704-738.

Student commentary tracing the need, history, and status of current statutory regulation of advertising, what methods the FTC uses in detecting false advertising, the standards applied to define what constitutes false advertising, and the formal proceedings used in dealing with deceptive advertising. Given this analysis it is concluded that all regulatory power regarding false advertising must be concentrated in the FTC and greater effectiveness can be achieved by incorporating the skills of state attorneys in patrolling deceptive practices.

344   Oliver, Daniel. "Federal Trade Commission: Defending the Consumer."
Consumers Research 72 (October 1989): 21-24.
Outlines the consumer protection functions of the FTC and describes how free
market principles are used to guide its consumer protection mission. Oliver
describes changes that have occurred at the agency during his tenure as Chairman
and how these changes have helped consumers.

345   Oliver, Daniel. "How the FTC Serves the Consumer." _Consumers
Research_ 71 (August 1988): 18-20.
Summarizes the areas of enforcement under the FTC's jurisdiction, noting the
positive move by the Reagan Administration to lesson these powers, then
discusses the role of antitrust enforcement in aiding consumers through the
promotion of a free market environment.

346   Oliver, Lauren. "Regulation of Children's Advertising--A Three Party
Discussion: The FTC, the First Amendment, and the Parents." _Paper
Presented at the Annual Meeting of the Association for Education in
Journalism and Mass Communication_ (70th, San Antonio, TX, August
1-4, 1987).
Begins with an analysis of the controversy regarding advertising directed at
children under the age of twelve, presents arguments for and against regulation of
such advertising, and discusses the role of the FTC, the First Amendment, and
parents in regulating such commercials. The author argues against regulation.
Extensive footnotes are included.

347   O'Meara, Vicki A. "FTC Deceptive Advertising Regulation: A Proposal
for the Use of Consumer Behavior Research." _Northwestern University
Law Review_ 76 (February 1982): 946-979.
The FTC primarily relies upon its own interpretation as to what advertisement
constitutes deceptive advertising and how consumers will understand an ad claim.
This approach has been backed up by the courts which give great deference to
FTC findings of deception. However, research into sources of consumer
information, the influence different kinds of information has on the decision-
making process, and factors, such as brand loyalty, indicates that deception is a
complex issue to decipher. This research indicates that the FTC's assumptions

regarding the persuasive effects of advertising "may not conform to the empirical realities concerning the causes of consumer product choices." The comment begins by studying the legal foundations of deceptive advertising regulation, focuses on the potential for over-regulation, then analyzes the potential these studies have in assisting the FTC in determining if deception has occurred.

348 Orlans, Melvin H. "FTC Regulation of OTC Drug and Cosmetics Advertising." *Food Drug Cosmetic Law Journal* 36 (March 1981): 100-105.

Presents a brief policy outline of how the FTC approaches the regulation of cosmetics advertising as well as specifically examining various past and present FTC projects that directly impact the cosmetic industry with regard to comparative advertising, restitution, and rulemaking proceedings.

349 "An Overview of Consumer Legislation Enacted and Pending from the Point of View of Its Impact on the Corporation." *The Business Lawyer* 27 (November 1971): 93-110.

Text from a panel discussion examining the shortcomings of current legislation and FTC regulations on protecting the consumer, the impact of the consumer movement on pressuring Congress to be more proactive in creating remedies that protect consumers, and offers criticism of the FTC's "virtually unlimited discretion" in granting remedial relief.

350 Oxendale, Candice Lance. "The FTC and Deceptive Trade Practices: A Reasonable Standard?" *Emory Law Journal* 35 (1986): 683-727.

Analyzes the divergence of views within the FTC concerning the most effective approach to provide consumer protection against deception. Central to this debate is the issuance of a new standard that attempts to clarify the term "deception." The new policy represents an attempt to articulate a standard that could be uniformly applied to actions taken under Section 5 of the FTC Act. An examination of the history of deception enforcement is offered to show how the current debate arose and analyzes the comments of the dissenting commissioners, who wanted enforcement to be grounded on a more individualized basis, to show the struggle within the Commission and to help determine how the FTC's deception jurisdiction should be enforced.

351   Packer, Bonnie. "Federal Trade Commission Rule on the Preservation
of Consumers' Claims and Defenses: What Price Protection?" *Santa
Clara Law Review* 16 (1976): 815-857.
Critical analysis of the FTC's trade regulation rule that abolishes the Holder-In-
Due- Course Doctrine that created problems related to interlocking loans in
consumer transactions. Two methods of consumer financing, the merchant's use
of a negotiable instrument or consumer credit contract with a bank or finance
company that he or she has maintained some prearrangement with, and, the
"interlocking" lender whereby the consumer secures a "direct" loan from a lender
who is somehow connected to the merchant, are examined to discuss the manner
in which the FTC attempts to protect consumer claims and defenses. It is
concluded that the rule is too sweeping and could thus have an adverse affect on
consumer credit.

352   Palmer, R. C. "Federal Trade Commission Jurisdiction over Insurance
Advertising." *Insurance Law Journal* (February 1964): 69-76.
The McCarran-Ferguson Act provides that FTC jurisdiction over the business of
insurance "to the extent that such business is not regulated by law." This essay
discusses the present status of the FTC's jurisdiction in this area and attempts to
resolve issues not addressed so far by the courts. It is concluded that the FTC does
have jurisdiction over insurance advertising mailed from one state to residents of
another.

353   Patka, Carl F. "Of Diapers, Lawnbags, and Landfills: The Federal Trade
Commission Cracks Down on False Advertising in the Environmental
Marketplace." *Loyola Consumer Law Reporter* 5 (Winter 1993): 43-
50.
Addresses the issue of false or misleading advertising as it relates to the
environmental attributes of products and how this has led to the issuance of
voluntary environmental marketing guidelines by the FTC to assist government
and industry in measuring the basis for claims of "recyclable," "ozone safe," and
"compostable." Specific claims are examined, followed by an analysis of whether
these guidelines were issued illegally because mandated opportunity for public
input was bypassed.

354   Pauker, Molly. "The Case for FTC Regulation of Television Advertising
Directed Toward Children." *Brooklyn Law Review* 46 (1980): 513-546.
Children are disadvantaged in their attempts to make complex consumer

judgements for several reasons. First, young children (before the age of six or seven) are unable to focus beyond one facet of a situation and thus fail to see the significance of other factors around them. Second, children tend to view the world from a literal sense and are therefore unable to deal with abstract concepts. Finally, children also fail to understand the underlying persuasive or selling intent inherent in advertising. Growing public awareness of this and the subsequent concern about the physical and psychological harm advertising could inflict upon children led to the FTC initiating a trade regulation rulemaking proceeding regarding television advertising directed to children. This essay analyzes the power of the FTC to issue regulations in this area within the context of the FTC Act, examines the issue of children's advertising as an inherently deceptive trade practice, and concludes that First Amendment issues regarding commercial speech, broadcasting, and the rights of children do not create barriers to this "much needed reform."

355 Peeler, C. Lee. "Pharmaceutical Advertising: A Federal Trade Commission Perspective." *Journal of Pharmaceutical Marketing and Management* 7 (1992): 157-167.

Discusses the FTC's approach to regulating over-the-counter drug advertising claims, outlines specific pending advertising cases that involve food advertising and FTC actions regarding over-the-counter fringe products, such as baldness cures, examines the FTC's compliance program and, finally, analyzes areas of future action by the FTC as related to over-the-counter drug advertising.

356 Peeler, C. Lee and Michelle K. Rusk. "Commercial Speech and the FTC's Consumer Protection Program." *Antitrust Law Journal* 59 (Fall 1990): 985-996.

Discusses the FTC's consumer protection program within the legal parameters of the commercial speech doctrine spelled out by the United States Supreme Court. The FTC's policy on unfair advertising and the implementation of rules only when substantial consumer injury is shown, parallels the commercial speech doctrine of ensuring the free flow of commercial information. This parallel becomes clearer in light of current FTC initiatives in advertising regulation.

357 Peeler, C. Lee and Susan Cohn. "The Federal Trade Commission's Regulation of Advertising Claims for Dietary Supplements." *Food and Drug Law Journal* 50 (1995): 349-355.

The authors outline the two primary principles that govern FTC regulatory enforcement of advertising: advertising may not be false or misleading and advertisers must be able to substantiate any objective claims regarding their product's benefits for consumers. This is usually based upon scientific evidence. These principles are then used to explore in what ways the FTC has attempted to regulate health-related claims in advertisements for dietary supplements and how the newly enacted Dietary Supplement Health and Education Act of 1994 may affect the FTC's regulatory efforts in this area.

358   Peltzman, Sam. "The Effects of FTC Advertising Regulation." *Journal of Law and Economics* 24 (December 1981): 403-459.

The author views the empirical study presented as only an initial exercise in analyzing the effects of the FTC's regulation of false or misleading advertising due to a lack of sufficient data from product and advertising markets and collateral statistics from the capital market to draw upon. However, the underlying methodology used, which takes into account the actions of first time buyers, can be expanded upon to further show the effects of regulation on the product market, the advertising market, and the capital market. The article concludes with two separate comments on the study's findings.

359   Pepper, Horace G. "Action by the Federal Trade Commission against Untruthful Advertising Since 1940." *Louisiana Law Review* 6 (December 1945): 429-453.

Progress towards curbing deceptive advertising has moved forward because the courts have become more aggressive in backing FTC decisions, an introduction of new legislation, and through trial and error on the part of the Commission in attempting to enforce regulation. This comment discusses in detail these issues and subsequent developments in the principles of what constitutes unfair and misleading advertising. Application of these principles is also examined.

360   Pertschuk, Michael. "Consumer Priorities, Macro-Concentration, and the Scope of the FTC's Deconcentration Authority." *Antitrust Law and Economics Review* 9 (1977): 31-42.

Excerpts of questions and answers extracted from written responses presented to the Senate Commerce Committee by Michael Pertschuk as part of the nomination process to the chairmanship to the FTC. The questions and answers focus on Pertschuk's views regarding the FTC's legal authority to deconcentrate an industry merely because the industry exhibits a high concentration level and is imposing an inflated price on the consumer. This position of deconcentration represents a new position for the Commission.

361 Pertschuk, Michael. "Regulatory Reform Through the Looking Glass." *American Bar Association Journal* 65 (April 1979): 556-560.
Outlines the FTC's philosophy of rooting out unfair advantages in the marketplace through review sessions, examining possible overlap with other regulatory agencies, and by systematically evaluating the impact of regulation on the economy. Argues that recent re-evaluation and reform must be initiated with the public interest in mind above all else.

362 Pertschek, Michael. *Revolt Against Regulation: The Rise and Pause of the Consumer Movement.* Berkeley, CA: University of California Press, 1982.
As a former chairman of the FTC, the author provides insight into the consumer's movement during the 1960s, 1970s and the early 1980s, tracing the legislative actions of Congress to regulate business through the FTC and the political repercussions of such action. The author concludes by reflecting on what was learned over the course of regulating business in the consumer interest during his tenure at the FTC.

363 Pertschuk, Michael. "The Safety Cap Unsealed." *Bill of Rights Journal* 17 (December 1984): 13-20.
Excerpted from a report on the FTC's work from 1977-1984, the author expresses concern for what is viewed as the erosion of consumer protectionism and antitrust progress made by the FTC during the Nixon/Ford/Carter appointed administrations. Central to this erosion is the confrontational rather than cooperative nature of the current FTC leadership with Congress as well as efforts by the Reagan appointed commission to sidetrack current rule initiatives. The results of delaying or eliminating rule initiatives set up by previous commissioners is outlined.

364 "Pertschuk's FTC: Consumerist Takeover?" *Media Decisions* 12 (November 1977): 76-78.
As the new Chairman of the FTC, Michael Pertschuk states he will move the FTC forward into a more aggressive consumer protection agency, focusing not only on the regulation of deceptive trade practices, but on the issue of unfairness in advertising. Despite Pertschuk's enthusiasm for creating "the country's largest public interest law firm", many voice skepticism that even Pertschuk, a long time

consumer advocate from Congress, may not be able to change the direction of the FTC bureaucracy. However, it is noted that Pertschuk more than anyone else may be able to change the priorities within the FTC to better protect the consumer.

365   Peters, Kenneth G. "How the Magnuson-Moss Warranty Act Affects the Builder/Seller of New Housing." *Real Estate Law Journal* 5 (Spring 1977): 338-363.
Examines what is covered and not covered under the Act as it applies to the home-building industry, offering an overview of the Act's requirements, analyzing specific provisions under the law that home builders must be aware of, and summarizing dispute settlement mechanisms.

366   Petty, Ross D. "FTC Advertising Regulation: Survivor or Casualty of the Reagan Revolution." *American Business Law Journal* 30 (May 1992): 1-34.
Analyzes the policy statements and case laws during the period of mid-1978 through mid-1988 to illustrate the changes made during the Reagan administration in regards to the FTC's advertising enforcement program. Further contrast is provided by analyzing more recent changes under the Bush administration. While two important changes have benefitted consumers (the pursuit of fraud cases in federal court so that the misleading ads could be quickly stopped and the assets of the advertisers could be preserved for later redress to consumers and the regulation of advertising restraints imposed by professional societies on their members), the "Reagan FTC" failed to permanently restrict advertising regulation and, in pursuing this end, actually created the total burden of advertising regulation to increase. In addition, advertisers had to deal with private litigation and state regulation that was more burdensome than prior FTC regulation.

367   Petty, Ross D. *The Impact of Advertising Law on Business and Public Policy.* Westport, CT: Quorum Books, 1992.
Examines advertising law from a public policy perspective, using challenges against false or misleading advertising by the FTC and others to measure the impact of how various regulatory and legal methods affect the consumer and market consumption. The book begins with an overview of advertising from a behavioral science perspective and couches advertising law within First Amendment parameters. Petty then examines in detail the regulatory impact of FTC activities and the effects of the Lanham Act. Specific cases are then used to analyze the public policy aspects of advertising law. The book concludes with

proposals for improving advertising law by reducing the costs of regulatory enforcement. Antitrust laws are used in the analysis to help expand on the public policy analysis when appropriate.

368 Petty Ross D. "Regulating Product Safety: The Information Role of the U.S. Federal Trade Commission." *Journal of Consumer Policy* 18 (December 1995): 387-415.

Although the FTC is not seen as a "safety agency," this study of Commission regulation of product information labelling illustrates that, in fact, it is. After reviewing the FTC's consumer protection program under provisions of both the unfair methods of competition doctrine and the unfair or deceptive acts and practices doctrine, the paper examines three issues associated with regulating product safety information: 1) preventing pre-purchase deception of safety claims in advertising; 2) regulating the omission of safety information; and 3) regulating safety information during product use rather than in pre-purchase disclosures. The study finds that FTC regulation of product safety information is focused on the first and second categories. However, it is concluded that the FTC should become more active in regulating misleading product-use information. This would help the agency contribute not only to preventing pre-purchase deception, but enable the FTC to contribute to reducing product-related injury. A number of court cases are described throughout the study.

369 Petty, Ross D. "Supplanting Government Regulation with Competitor Lawsuits: The Case of Controlling False Advertising." *Indiana Law Review* 25 (Spring 1992): 351-395.

By examining policy arguments, the legal requirements for proving false advertising, the cases themselves, and several examples of specific types of cases, it is shown that the Lanham Act has surpassed the FTC Act as the predominant means of regulating advertising, especially in the areas of comparative claims and disposable products. However, despite past criticism, the FTC's enforcement agenda and rulemaking actions does benefit consumers. A detailed legal comparison of the acts is presented.

370 "The Pfizer Reasonable Basis Test–Fast Relief for Consumers but a Headache for Advertisers." *Duke Law Journal* 1973 (1973): 563-597.

The Pfizer opinion issued by the FTC in 1972 established that the FTC would not only seek action when fraud or falsity is present, but also proactively investigate unsubstantiated claims by advertisers. This potentially new arena of regulatory activity is in marked contrast to previous decades of inconsistent enforcement against consumer fraud. This comment examines the background and rationale of the Pfizer decision within the context of the unfairness doctrine established in Section 5 of the FTC Act and discusses the future implications of the Pfizer ruling.

371   Pitofsky, Robert. "Beyond Nader: Consumer Protection and the Regulation of Advertising." *Harvard Law Review* 90 (February 1977): 684-701.

Discusses the legal and economic justifications for governmental intrusion into the marketplace to better protect consumers from deceptive behavior by advertisers, examines the traditional principles governing advertising regulation by the FTC, and concludes with a study of more recent, non-traditional remedies, such as corrective advertising, which go beyond the methods proposed by Ralph Nader and other consumer advocates, taking into account the function of advertisers within the marketplace.

372   Pitofsky, Robert. "An FTC View of Advertising." *Conference Board Record* 10 (January 1973): 29-31.

Analyzes two fundamental dimensions of the FTC's advertising regulation program: the Commission's traditional role in policing false advertising and the agency's more recent efforts to require disclosure of essential information about a product to aid the consumer in making an informed decision about competing products. The author discusses the issue of consumer sovereignty within the marketplace, the unfairness doctrine, and briefly notes new remedial approaches to protecting the consumer.

373   Pleiss, Larry T. "Deceptive Advertising and the Federal Trade Commission: A Perspective." *Pepperdine Law Review* 6 (Spring 1979): 439-483.

Traces the historical development of the FTC's regulation of false or misleading advertising to provide a conceptual perspective on the issue of deceptive advertising. Existing and proposed remedies are then discussed followed by an analysis of the commercial speech doctrine under the First Amendment as articulated in the Virginia Pharmacy Board decision. It is concluded that the decision opens up many questions regarding the parameters in which advertisers must operate that previously had been considered judicially closed.

374   Pollak, Dale and Bruce Teichner. "The Federal Trade Commission's Deceptive Enforcement Policy." *DePaul Law Review* 35 (1985): 125-159.
Examines the development of the FTC's deception standard and the authority of the Commission to enforce the policy through adjudication and rulemaking to determine the impact of the new Deception Enforcement Policy created under the Chairmanship of James C. Miller III which includes a reformulated definition of deception. Four cases decided under the new policy are analyzed to determine the new policy's ramifications. It is concluded that this new standard "creates unparalleled confusion in the law of deception" because it varies considerable from widely accepted case law principles.

375   Pollay, Richard W. "Deceptive Advertising and Consumer Behavior: A Case for Legislative and Judicial Reform." *Kansas Law Review* 17 (1969): 625-637.
Examines the recent resurgence of consumerism and consumer protection and the expected parallel expansion of regulatory activities by the government. It is argued that careful examination of current legislation and practices should take place in order to both learn from past practice and to ensure the effectiveness of future activities. A proposal for creating deception criteria based on psychological research (actual versus hypothetical evidence) is offered.

376   Pope, Daniel. "Advertising as a Consumer Issue: An Historical View." *Journal of Social Issues* 47 (1991): 41-56.
Advertising has been of primary concern to consumers since the early Twentieth Century. This essay analyzes the development of the "truth in advertising" movement and efforts by the FTC to regulate advertising. De-regulation is also discussed as a new approach to promote consumer well-being.

377   Popper, Lewis M. "The New Federal Warranty Law: A Guide to Compliance." *The Business Lawyer* 32 (January 1977): 399-416.
Provides an overview the Magnuson-Moss Warranty Act, examines its impact on protecting the consumer, and analyzes the regulatory complexities of the Act, including its regulatory scheme and substantive requirements. Private and governmental remedies available to enforce the terms of the Act are briefly covered.

378   Powell, Jon T. "Protection of Children in Broadcast Advertising: The Regulatory Guidelines of Nine Nations." *Federal Communication Bar Journal* 26 (1973): 61-75.

Hearings before the FTC have accomplished little in defining what controls should be adopted to regulate advertising directed to children. By examining regulations of Australia, Cyprus, Finland, Great Britain, Hong Kong, Ireland, Malta, the Netherlands, and New Zealand that have been able to formulate some precise regulations, specific themes and patterns emerge that help to better understand the underlying principles involved.

379   Preston, Ivan L. "A Comment on Defining Misleading Advertising and Deception in Advertising." *Journal of Marketing* 40 (July 1976): 54-59.

Argues that the authors of two articles published in the *Journal of Marketing*, while contributing to the concept of deception, fail to take into full account what the FTC has contributed to the issue. The FTC's usage of the term "misleading" and the methodology used by the FTC in determining deception are discussed as well. Responses to the comment follow.

380   Preston, Ivan L. "Data-Free at the FTC?: How the Federal Trade Commission Decides Whether Extrinsic Evidence of Deceptiveness is Required." *American Business Law Journal* 24 (Fall 1986): 359-376.

Examines the opposing viewpoints expressed by the FTC stating that, one, "the Commission can determine the meaning of an advertisement without necessarily resorting to assessments of consumer perception or other expert testimony" and two, "there also may be instances where claims cannot be inferred from a facial examination of the advertisements and resort to extrinsic evidence is necessary." These competing viewpoints embrace the broader issue of whether FTC regulation should be expanded or contracted. The direction taken will be determined by how cases in the future will be handled.

381   Preston, Ivan L. "The Definition of Deception in Advertising and Other Commercial Speech." *Catholic University Law Review* 39 (Summer 1990): 1035-1079.

Proposes a full statement of the legal definition of deceptiveness in advertising that would eliminate or reduce the vagueness surrounding the issue that previous definitions have failed to address. Additions to the definition are also discussed that take into account the interdisciplinary nature of the issue, incorporating both legal and behavioral concepts. The essay begins by outlining the conceptual and measurement elements of how deceptiveness is currently defined.

382   Preston, Ivan L. "Description and Analysis of FTC Order Provisions Resulting from References in Advertising to Tests or Surveys." *Pepperdine Law Review* 14 (1987): 229-312.

This article examines FTC actions against advertisements that "misrepresent the existence of tests or surveys as support for selling claims." Both physical science and social science methodology is applied to the problem with a content analysis used as the method for studying the issue. FTC order provisions are separated into four types--advertisements showing tests actually being performed, advertisements that cite a test or survey, advertisements that cite tests or surveys but that do not cite explicit reference to tests or surveys that accompany the claim, advertisements that have no explicit references but that imply a reasonable basis exists to imply that the claims are truthful. Each of these categories are examined in detail. The essay then compares these findings with specifications articulated by the FTC as acceptable or unacceptable characteristics of tests or surveys. The essay concludes that the advertising community "operated at a level of its own conscious choice" that led to some advertisers making statements about tests or surveys under the mere threat of prosecution.

383   Preston, Ivan L. "Extrinsic Evidence in Federal Trade Commission Deceptiveness Cases." *Columbia Business Law Review* 1987 (1987): 633-694.

Examines and compares the types of extrinsic evidence used to resolve two issues that require evidence when the FTC is determining if deceptiveness occurred: what expressly stated or implied messages are conveyed to consumers "following exposure to a challenged sales communication" and takes on the burden of showing that messages conveyed are deceptive because they falsely depict the advertised item. The article begins by examining the nature of extrinsic evidence and its role in deception cases. This is followed by an analysis of two "highly regarded forms" of extrinsic evidence, consumer research and expert testimony. The essay concludes by discussing indirectly useful evidence and evidence rejected by the FTC as unacceptable for determining the message a sales communication conveys. Extrinsic evidence under provisions of the Lanham Act are also described.

384   Preston, Ivan L. "The Federal Trade Commission's Identification of Implications as Constituting Deceptive Advertising." *University of Cincinnati Law Review* 57 (Spring 1989): 1243-1310.

This article focuses on the implications conveyed in advertising to consumers. An example that illustrates the characteristics of this issue is the claim by the FTC that, in speaking only of the nutritional qualities of Wonder Bread, it was alleged that the advertising "implied to consumers that its product was unique through statements speaking explicitly only of nutritional qualities." At issue was not explicitly false statements within the content of the ad, but that the implied nutritional uniqueness of the product led to the deception of consumers. This and other implications are identified in various FTC cases since 1970 to show what advertisers must do to both cope with regulators and to defend against the burden of having their messages scrutinized for deceptiveness.

385   Preston, Ivan L. "The FTC's Handling of Puffery and Other Selling Claims Made 'By Implication'." *Journal of Business Research* 5 (1977): 155-181.

Analyzes the FTC's attacks on misrepresentations in advertising based on the premise of implication, as opposed to direct misrepresentation. During the period 1970 through 1976 the FTC has increasingly seen advertiser's literal statements as containing more implications to the public. This expansion in meaning from advertiser's messages can be seen specifically in the FTC's interpretation of puffery. This and other misrepresentations are used to examine the consequences of the FTC's increased attention to misrepresentation by implication. However, further action by the courts and study by researchers must occur before a full understanding of the issues becomes clearer.

386   Preston, Ivan L. *The Great American Blow-Up: Puffery in Advertising and Selling*. Madison, WI: University of Wisconsin Press, 1975.

Analyzes the issues of deception and false and misleading advertising within the context of "puffery," showing that this concept offers a chance for advertisers to make unsubstantiated claims without fear of legal challenge. The development of the concept of puffery and the arguments presented by the business community supporting its use are examined along with what effects puffery has on the marketplace and on the practices of advertisers. A comprehensive examination of the FTC's view of puffery is offered. It is concluded from the evidence presented that puffery is indeed a deceptive practice and should be severely regulated.

387   Preston, Ivan L. "Regulatory Positions Toward Advertising Puffery of the Uniform Commerce Code and the Federal Trade Commission." *Journal of Public Policy and Marketing* 16 (1997): 336-346.

Presents an overview of how puffery in advertising is regulated through provisions of the Uniform Commercial Code and deception statements by the FTC. An assessment of both interpretations leads the author to conclude that, while planned changes in the UCC to combat fraudulent puffery, it remains far behind the FTC and Lanham Act. Empirical survey evidence of consumer responses to the semantics of puffery should be incorporated into all regulatory provisions.

388   Preston, Ivan L. *The Tangled Web They Weave: Truth, Falsity, and Advertisers*. Madison, WI: University of Wisconsin, 1994.

Examines the relationship between consumer protection laws that attempts to regulate false claims made by advertisers, the actions by advertisers to circumvent these regulations, and the harm that these actions have on consumers. Advertisers are able to avoid these laws because many of the statutes are too narrowly defined, and thus, allow advertisers to either make false claims or avoid disclosing the entire truth. In describing the problems associated with the current consumer protection laws, the author offers suggestions on how to improve them based on the actions of consumers rather than "the law's erroneous assumptions about how we act." References to the policies and procedures of the FTC are made throughout the text, especially with regards to how the FTC determines falsity in advertising claims.

389   Preston, Ivan L. and Jef I. Richards. "Consumer Misrepresentation and Deceptive Advertising: A Response to Professor Craswell." *Boston University Law Review* 68 (March 1988): 431-438.

Response to an article in the July 1985 issue of the *Boston University Law Review* by Richard Craswell in which he proposed a standard of viewing deceptive advertisements "only if the advertiser failed to take some precaution that would have reduced the net injury caused by the ad." Craswell's standard is partially based on the assumption that substantial costs will often be incurred when the FTC orders or prohibits the rewriting of deceptive advertising. The authors disagree with this assumption and state that little cost would be incurred because most advertising claims that create a level of miscomprehension can be easily reduced or eliminated without undue cost burdens.

390   Preston, Ivan L. and Jef I. Richards. "Consumer Miscomprehension as a Challenge to FTC Prosecutions of Deceptive Advertising." *John Marshall Law Review* 19 (Spring 1986): 605-635.

A challenge to the FTC's established procedure concerning deceptive advertising is the issue of miscomprehension by consumers. The established interpretation holds that a violation exists if a portion of the public is deemed by the Commission to have been misled by an advertising claim, even if the deception occurs within a minority of consumers. Advertisers point out that all messages are miscomprehended on an average of thirty percent according to studies. Since advertisers are not responsible for this level of miscomprehension they should not be subjected to restraints when miscomprehension occurs among fewer than thirty percent of consumers. An analysis of advertising claims alleged to be deceptive by the FTC shows that the proper benchmark by which to measure and evaluate the level of miscomprehension is the concept of ineradicable miscomprehension, or rather, the ability to reduce or eliminate the miscomprehension through the editing of the message.

391   Preston, Ivan L. and Jef I. Richards. "A Role for Consumer Belief in FTC and Lanham Act Deceptive Advertising Cases." *American Business Law Journal* 31 (May 1993): 1-29.

Analyzes the concept of belief by consumers of advertisements, stating that a regulatory policy aimed at preventing an advertising campaign based on the ad creating only a false understanding fails to serve the primary goal "of regulating claims that could harm the consumers or competitors." The role of belief is examined within the context of reported cases involving the FTC and in formal statements issued by the FTC. It is concluded that results support the explicit incorporation of the belief element into the determination of deceptiveness.

392   Pridgen, Dee. "Advertising and Marketing on Cable Television: Whither the Public Interest?" *Catholic University Law Review* 31 (Winter 1981): 227-271.

Argues that by learning from history and planning ahead for coming technical developments, cable television can become a medium of accurate consumer information without "heavy-handed" government regulation. Part I explores the advertising and marketing environment of cable television. Part II provides an overview of federal attempts to regulate selling. Part III examines the cable industry's efforts to provide a private security force to scrutinize advertising, with an emphasis on self-regulation. And, Part IV raises the issue of the cablecasters responsibility for the commercials it disseminates, arguing that these consumer protection issues would be best addressed during the franchise negotiating process with local governments.

393   Prigden, Dee and Ivan L. Preston. "Enhancing the Flow of Information in the Marketplace from Caveat Emptor to Virginia Pharmacy and Beyond at the Federal Trade Commission." *Georgia Law Review* 14 (Summer 1980): 635-680.

Adapted from an FTC staff report, *Consumer Information Remedies*, this essay examines the historical development of commercial speech regulations, focusing on those FTC remedies that have enhanced the dissemination of information in the marketplace. Section one describes what historical factors led to FTC law protecting the consumer from misinformation. Section two examines the measures taken by the FTC's legislative authority to prompt sellers to disclose information to the public. Section three analyzes recent First Amendment developments that have aided in the flow of information in the marketplace. Section four discusses current and future FTC initiatives related to professional advertising and comparative advertising.

394   "Private Enforcement and Rulemaking Under the Federal Trade Commission Act: Expansion of FTC Responsibility." *Northwestern University Law Review* 69 (1974): 462-488.

Uses the decisions rendered in two cases, *National Petroleum Refiners Association v FTC*, which upheld the FTC's power to make substantive rules governing unfair and deceptive trade practices, and, *Holloway v. Bristol-Myers Corp.*, which refused to imply there was a private right of action from Section 5 of the FTC Act. This comment demonstrates that, while the two verdicts appear contradictory, they are consistent and could help both individuals within the business community and consumers.

395   "Proposed FTC Regulation of Consumer Financing." *Georgetown Law Journal* 60 (June 1972): 1563-1579.

Examines the background, scope, weaknesses and probable market impact of the FTC's new proposal concerning consumer installment credit. It is concluded that a number of uncertainties exist regarding the proposed rule, but that the rule represents a positive step forward in ensuring a higher degree of responsibility among installment sellers and financiers.

396   Randolph, Jr., Leroy and Douglas Whitman. "The Last Nail in the Coffin of the Holder in Due Course Doctrine." *American Business Law Journal* 14 (1977): 311-331.

Discusses the implications and possible effects of a new amendment to the FTC Trade Regulation Rule that is designed to protect the claims and defenses rights of consumers who purchase on credit and incur obligation to financial institutions. The history of the doctrine and recent court and legislative efforts to monitor the issue are outlined.

397   Rathe, Todd A. "The Gray Area of the Green Market: Is It Really Environmentally Friendly? Solutions to Confusion Caused by Environmental Advertising." *The Journal of Corporation Law* 17 (Winter 1992): 419-458.

Examines the sources of confusion in environmental advertising for consumers, discusses case-by-case adjudication under general deceptive advertising laws to eliminate this confusion and how current FTC regulations can be used to control deceptive green advertisements, and concludes by analyzing the two primary approaches to controlling deceptive green marketing--uniform guidelines and a national "green seal" program. It is concluded that neither approach alone would be sufficient, but that a combination of the two would eliminate the sources of confusion for consumers.

398   Reed, Omer Lee. "The FTC and Corrective Advertising: Act One." *American Business Law Journal* 17 (Summer 1979): 246-256.

Examines the repercussions of the recently concluded *Warner-Lambert Co. v. FTC* case for advertisers, including what role Warner-Lambert played in regard to defining corrective advertising. Also examined are the roles played by the administrative law judge, the FTC, and the Court of Appeals. Although the case offered little in terms of what the future holds, it is expected that the FTC will vigorously pursue corrective advertising as a regulatory remedy.

399   Reed, Omer Lee. "The Psychological Impact of TV Advertising and the Need for FTC Regulation." *American Business Law Journal* 13 (Fall 1975): 171-183.

Presents a model of how television commercials motivate the buying habits of consumers and to compare this understanding with the FTC's response to television advertising through provisions of the FTC Act. The author notes that little has been done by the FTC to prevent misleading psychological advertising.

400   Reed, Omer Lee and John L. Coalson, Jr. "Eighteenth Century Legal Doctrine Meets Twentieth Century Marketing Techniques: FTC Regulation of Emotionally Conditioning Advertising." *Georgia Law Review* 11 (1977): 733-782.

Dictated by economic and psychological factors and the emergence of technology that renders it possible, marketing psychologists have increasingly used computers, sophisticated personality inventory techniques, and multivariate statistical analyses to pinpoint specific emotional needs of consumers and apply that to advertising. However, because the FTC has so far concentrated its efforts in regulating advertising based upon deception, little effort has been put forth to control advertising based on the unfair portrayal of emotional satisfaction in ads. A proposed conceptual model is presented that would serve as the basis for the regulation of deceptive advertising.

401   "The Regulation of Advertising." *Columbia Law Review* 56 (November 1956): 1018-1111.

Analyzes in detail three levels of regulation of advertising--federal, including outlining the role of the FTC, state regulation, and self-regulation within the industry. Includes a statutory appendix of cases relevant to the issue of advertising regulation.

402   "Regulation of Corporate Image Advertising." *Minnesota Law Review* 59 (November 1974): 189-222.

Corporate image advertising sells "ideas" rather products. It represents the sum of impressions created by numerous public relations activities of the corporation. The purpose of such advertising is not to sell products, but to create an overall favorable impression of the company. However, unlike public relations, it is conducted through paid advertising. This note outlines the development of corporate image advertising, evaluates its protection under the First Amendment, and concludes by discussing possible FTC regulation of careless image advertisers.

403   Reich, Robert B. "Consumer Protection and the First Amendment: A Dilemma for the FTC?" *Minnesota Law Review* 61 (1977): 705-741.

Analyzes the recent Supreme Court ruling that commercial speech affords at least some free speech protection under the First Amendment within the context of the undefined statement of unfair or deceptive practices contained in the FTC Act. It is argued that the FTC should not significantly alter its mission to accommodate the ruling because, by pursuing actions that fulfill its consumer protection mission, it is fulfilling its constitutional responsibilities as well. This fact depends, however, on the court's continued understanding of the FTC's role in protecting the consumer from false or misleading advertising practices.

404   Reich, Robert B. "Preventing Deception in Commercial Speech." *New York University Law Review* 54 (1979): 775-805.

Explores the efforts of the Supreme Court and some lower courts in balancing the rights of advertisers with the rights of consumers now that the Supreme Court has recently ruled that commercial speech affords similar constitutionally protected status as non-commercial speech. By examining the premises that underlie the court's decisions and linking this into a plausible economic model, one can better understand the parameters in which the government must operate in regulating deception.

405   Remsberg, Steven A. "Divesting the FTC of Exclusive Enforcement of the Federal Trade Commission Act: *Guernsey v. Rich Plan of the Midwest.*" *University of Pittsburgh Law Review* 38 (1976): 113-133.

Examines the district court's ruling implying that there is a private right of action available to consumers rooted in the recently amended language of the FTC Act, public policy, and judicial precedent exclusive of recent Supreme Court rulings. The note also explores the potential for more effective consumer protection in the federal court system through private enforcement "supplemented by FTC intervention in the litigation process."

406   "Restitution for Consumer Fraud Under Section Five of the Federal Trade Commission Act." *Valparaiso University Law Review* 10 (Fall 1975): 69-125.

Outlines the changes that have occurred at the FTC in response to criticism regarding its role in regulating deceptive advertising practices. These changes include prohibiting the use of mock-ups or props to show the effectiveness of products, providing methods by which consumers can gain redress from deceptive advertising practices, and limiting the amount of contractual indebtedness which providers of certain consumer services can cause a consumer to incur. These and other remedies that have not received specific judicial review show an increase in authority sanctioned by the courts. The most important of these changes is the authority to order restitution. This essay argues that, while this remedy is not specifically stated in the FTC Act, its authority in this area does stem from the broad powers to define and prevent unfair acts and practices.

407   Rice, David A. "Consumer Unfairness at the FTC: Misadventure in Law and Economics." *George Washington Law Review* 52 (May-August 1984): 1-66.

Examines and critiques policy formulation under the FTC Act as it specifically relates to the rulemaking implementation of the FTC's consumer unfairness regulatory authority and points out the consequences of misuse of economic theory and analytical methods in developing legal decision criteria. While it is recognized that such FTC enforcement efforts are constitutional, ambiguous or incomprehensible restrictions are especially suspect under First Amendment doctrine.

408   Richards, Jef I. *Deceptive Advertising: Behavioral Study of a Legal Concept.* Hillsdale, NJ: Lawrence Erlbaum Associates, Inc., 1990.

The purpose of this book is to provide a critical analysis of early studies of deceptive advertising, outline the legal perspective of deception including efforts by the FTC to define deception, expand the issue of deceptiveness to include the perspective of behavioral researchers, propose a model for defining and measuring deception, and concluding by testing this method for measuring deceptiveness and comparing it to those used by the FTC.

409   Richards, Jef I. "FTC or NAAG: Who Will Win the Territorial Battle?" *Journal of Public Policy and Marketing* 10 (Spring 1991): 118-132.

Argues that there is no inherent legal conflict among the regulatory efforts of states to restrict national advertising and those of federal agencies such as the FTC. The recent challenge by the National Association of Attorney Generals (NAAG) regarding the historical preeminence of the FTC as the primary regulator of advertising in America is examined, including a discussion of the legal issues involved and a prediction of the outcome.

410   Richards, Jef I. and Ivan L. Preston. "Proving and Disproving Materiality of Deceptive Advertising Claims." *Journal of Public Policy and Marketing* 11 (Fall 1992): 45-56.

Analyzes the legal requirement of materiality to provide behavioral researchers a better understanding of how this doctrine applies to advertising claims made by the FTC. The essay notes the development of the doctrine and criticisms that have arisen over time regarding its application. The study concludes with a discussion of how materiality shifts the burden of proof from the FTC to the advertiser and the problems inherent in building a legal defense concerning materiality. Topics for future research are also presented.

411   Richards, Jef I. and Ivan L. Preston. "Quantitative Research: A Dispute Resolution Model for FTC Advertising Regulation." *Oklahoma Law Review* 40 (Winter 1987): 593-619.

Presents a model of jointly commissioned behavioral research to determine deceptive advertising practices without the accompanying costs and negative publicity that is produced by traditional FTC action. The paper points out changes in the FTC that must take place in order for the model to work. An example run is described incorporating the model's concepts, showing that, if implemented, the model would work to the FTC's benefit.

412   Richards, Jef I. and Richard D. Zakia. "Pictures: An Advertiser's Expressway Through FTC Regulation." *Georgia Law Review* 16 (Fall 1981): 77-134.

While the FTC has spent a great deal of time and effort in developing guidelines and regulating the written content of advertisements, little time has been spent in developing guidelines regarding visual content. The general regulation of advertising is examined first to provide some context followed by an analysis of the psychological methods used by advertisers, and a discussion as to why the regulation of visual advertising is needed. A model regulation is then proposed.

413   Riegert, Robert A. "An Overview of the Magnuson-Moss Warranty Act and the Successful Consumer-Plantiff's Right to Attorneys' Fees." *Commercial Law Journal* 95 (1990): 468-485.

One of the most important ways that the Act strengthens consumer protection in regards to written warranties is the provision that allows plaintiffs to recover attorneys' fees and court costs when they prevail. This essay provides a summary of the twelve sections of the Act, the prerequisites needed for recovery of court costs and attorney fees by the consumer, and outlines specific problems present in the application of the Act.

414   Ringold, Debra Jones et al. "The Informational Content of Cigarette Advertising: 1929-1986; Counting Advertising Assertions to Assess Regulatory Policy: When It Doesn't Add Up; Filters, Flavors...Flim-Flam, Too! On "Health Information" and Policy Implications in Cigarette Advertising." *Journal of Public Policy and Marketing* 8 (1989): 1-39.

A content analysis of 568 cigarette advertisements during the period 1926-1986 found that the most explicit claims are about health, the structure of the cigarette, and taste. The authors comment on the study's findings and whether the findings will lead to greater information for consumers through better advertisements.

415   Robert, Jane A. "The FTC Legend in Louisiana." *Louisiana Law Review* 48 (July 1988): 1435-1441.

Discusses the provisions of the Preservation of Consumers Claims and Defenses Rule enacted by the FTC in 1976 which requires the insertion of a notice in all consumer credit transactions. This Rule was created to offset inadequacies inherent in the Holder-In-Due-Course Doctrine. However, evidence from Louisiana case law involving Holder-In-Due-Course abuses shows that there is a continued problem related to the Rule's enforcement by the courts. The comment concludes with a plea to the judiciary to recognize and enforce the regulation.

416   Roberts, Barry S. "The Magnuson-Moss Federal Warranty Act and Failure of Its Essential Purpose, Uniform Commercial Code 2-719(2)." *The Business Lawyer* 33 (April 1978): 1845-1858.

Examines the problems associated with certain exclusions set forth in the Act, such as the exemption of goods purchased solely for commercial or industrial purposes, and discusses how these exemptions may present confusion among consumers because of reliance on the Uniform Commercial Code to fill the gap left by these exemptions.

417   Roberts, Barry S. and Richard A. Mann. "The Magnuson-Moss Federal Warranty Act and Uniform Commercial Code Section 2-719: Further Reflections and Recent Developments." *Arizona State Law Journal* 1979 (1979): 765-781.

Although the primary purpose of the Act is to facilitate consumer redress under existing laws, there are instances where the Act's provisions will prove inadequate and the consumer will have to rely upon remedies under state laws that use the Uniform Commercial Code as its statutory foundation. These alternative bases for recovery of consequential damages are examined in detail with attention paid to how the Act effects these remedies.

418   Roberts, Charley. "FTC Blamed for Rise in Deceptive Ads." *The Los Angeles Daily Journal* 102 (June 6, 1989): 7.

Short essay discussing the concerns of consumer advocate organizations, members of the advertising industry, and Congress over the issue of deceptive advertising and criticism by some that the FTC has reduced its enforcement activities despite what is viewed by many as increased abuses.

419   Rohner, Ralph J. "For Lack of a National Policy on Consumer Credit...": Preliminary Thoughts on the Need for Unified Federal Agency Rulemaking." *The Business Lawyer* 35 (November 1979): 135-148.

While Congress has attempted to regulate the consumer credit field, primarily through the Consumer Credit Protection Act of 1968, it has fallen short of fully protecting the consumer from deceptive practices. The lack of a national policy on consumer credit has created sometimes conflicting agency rulemaking among the Federal Reserve Board, the FTC, and the states. Clearly Congress, through the Subcommittee on Unified Rulemaking, must set forth a national consumer credit policy either through an existing agency or through a new entity.

420   Rohner, Ralph J. "Holder in Due Course in Consumer Transactions: Requiem, Revival, or Reformation?" *Cornell Law Review* 60 (April 1975): 503-568.

Analyzes the conceptual framework of the Holder-In-Due-Course Doctrine, noting consumer financing patterns, judicial interpretations, legislative developments, and detailing state and federal statutes. The author attempts to find common threads of reform amongst the "scattergun nature" of governmental regulatory efforts and court interpretations. Reference to the FTC's Trade Regulation Rule regarding consumer credit transactions and other guidelines set forth are noted throughout the text.

421   Rotfeld, Herbert J. and Ivan L. Preston. "The Potential Impact of Research on Advertising Law: The Case of Puffery." *Journal of Advertising Research* 21 (April 1981): 9-17.

Uses the issue of puffery in advertising to illustrate the difference in meaning that occurs when the regulators use empirical rather than nonempirical information to determine if deception exists. This can be especially true in the FTC's use of nonempirical data prior to the 1970s based on past legal decisions and in some cases, the message itself. Responding to complaints about the need to incorporate more empirical evidence, the FTC began adopting a commitment to using behavioral data and behavior scientists on the witness stand during cases. Research done on advertising in general and on puffery in particular is analyzed to show that puffery posses a capacity to deceive and therefore must be regulated. It is concluded that the FTC should base its decisions concerning puffery on empirical data and no longer on nonempirical information. Whether this data will be fully recognized in legal proceedings is somewhat dependent on the complete commitment of FTC lawyers to the use of empirical data in their arguments.

422 Roth, Mark D. "*Sadat v. American Motors Corporation*: Limiting Consumer Remedies Under Magnuson-Moss and the New Car Buyer Protection Act." *The John Marshall Law Review* 19 (Fall 1985): 163-177.

Reviews the impact of the Illinois Supreme Court's ruling that states because the Magnuson-Moss Act does not "specifically afford consumers injunctive relief," traditional equity considerations--irreparable harm and inadequate remedy at law--must be met before damages can be awarded. This decision essentially marks the downfall of consumer protection in Illinois as it relates to the purchasing of automobiles.

423 Rothchild, Donald P. "The Magnuson-Moss Warranty Act: Does It Balance Warrantor and Consumer Interests?" *The George Washington Law Review* 44 (March 1976): 335-380.

Analyzes in detail the balance of warrantor and consumer interests under the provisions of the Magnuson-Moss Warranty Act to determine its potential impact on the marketplace. The article begins by detailing the common law foundation of warranty transactions, examines legislation concerning warranties prior to the enactment of the Act, including provisions set forth in the Uniform Commercial Code, discusses the imbalance between warrantor and consumer created by this legislation, and concludes with an analysis of the specific rules under the Act and the mechanisms for enforcement.

424 Sachs, Elisabeth A. "Health Claims in the Marketplace: The Future of the FDA and the FTC's Regulatory Split." *Food and Drug Law Journal* 48 (1993): 263-283.

The FDA and the FTC have shared the responsibility for regulating health claims for food products because it was felt consumers viewed advertisements and labels differently. However, this has led to some contradictions between the enforcement guidelines of the two agencies. An analysis of the FDA's and FTC's approaches to health claim regulation, specific examples of action by the agencies, and consumer perceptions of advertising and labeling illustrates the need for a continued bifurcated system of enforcement in which the FTC enforce FDA guidelines and continue to take action against claims that are not FDA approved.

425   Safer, Ronald S. "The Magnuson-Moss Act Class Action Provisions: Consumers' Remedy or an Empty Promise?" *The Georgetown Law Journal* 70 (June 1982): 1399-1419.
States that the requirement that plaintiffs notify individually every class member whom they can identify under Rule 23 of the Federal Rules of Civil Procedure as it applies to class action suits should be voided when class actions are brought forth through the Magnuson-Moss Warranty Act because it undermines efficacy of the class action mechanism of the Act. Analysis shows that suspending the individual notice rule would not violate the due process rights of absent or unnotified class members.

426   Samini, Keyvan. "Third Party Extended Warranties and Service Contracts: Drawing the Line Between Insurance and Warranty Agreements." *Ohio State Law Journal* 54 (Spring 1993): 537-556.
Discusses the growth of third party service contracts that are intended to extend manufacturer warranties, offer financial reimbursement for needed repairs, or replace the product. Abuse by these third party contractors has led to an increased awareness by both state and federal authorities that regulation is needed. This essay discusses specific cases relevant to the issue and points out the inadequacies of the Magnuson-Moss Warranty Act, which does not provide a comprehensive regulatory structure for controlling fraud among third party contractors.

427   Sandoval, Rodolpho. "A Critical Analysis of the Cooling-Off Period for Door to Door Sales." *Chicano Law Review* 3 (1976): 110-147.
This essay critically examines the FTC's "Cooling-Off Period for Door-To-Door Sales" rule promulgated on October 18, 1972. The Rule is the result of hearings sponsored by the FTC regarding the tactics of door-to-door salespeople. Of particular interest to Hispanics, is the provisions of the Rule that address problems associated with non-English speaking consumers who are taken advantage of by vague or overly complicated contractual obligations. The analysis is placed within

an historical context and follows with definitions of deceptive practices that led to the Rule's implementation. The article concludes with an examination of the impact of the Rule, stating that, while useful, more legislation is needed to better inform and, thereby, protect Spanish speaking consumers.

428 Sauer, Raymond and Keith B. Leffler. "Did the Federal Trade Commission's Advertising Substantiation Program Promote more Credible Advertising?" *American Economic Review* 80 (1990): 191-203.

Prior to the FTC's initiation of the Advertising Substantiation Program (ASP), which put the burden of proof concerning deceptive advertising on the advertisers rather than the Commission, the FTC had done a poor job of policing such behavior. The new program established in 1970 has also promoted more credible advertising according to the authors.

429 Scanlon, P. D. "Brand Advertising and the FTC: Catching the Seed, Ignoring the Weed." *Antitrust Law and Economic Review* 7 (1974-75): 21-28.

Presents the recognition by the FTC that brand-name advertising can retard effective price competition and raise consumer prices through a concurring opinion expressed by Commissioner Mayo J. Thompson regarding the dismissal of a merger case challenging United Brand's acquisition of a number of lettuce farms in California. By dismissing the case the author argues that the FTC places greater emphasis on regulating brand-selling in a previously competitive marketplace, but is not willing to take action against inflated prices that have already been imposed in other industries.

430 Scanlon, Paul D. "We Can Enforce the Law or Help Consumers: Which Do You Want Us to Do?" *Antitrust Law and Economics Review* 7 (1974-75): 47-100.

Presents in chronological order the text of ten memos written by FTC Commissioner Mayo J. Thompson that outline suggestions for action by the agency against certain industries as well as criticism by the Commissioner regarding how cases are selected for action by the field offices. These memos offer unique insight into the policy making process of consumer protection and antitrust enforcement at the FTC.

431   Schabacker, Mark M. "Magnuson-Moss Federal Court Class Actions: Federal Right Without a Federal Forum." *Cumberland Law Review* 11 (1980): 133-161.

Commentary that examines what factors are present that undermine the class action provisions of the Act. The requirement that action can only proceed with at least one hundred "named plaintiffs" has proven to be the greatest barrier to class action because the term named plaintiffs is not defined in the Act. Several courts have dismissed actions because one hundred persons were not specifically named as plaintiffs. While analysis shows that Congress' intent to reserve the federal courts for only the most significant cases under the Magnuson-Moss Warranty Act has succeeded, it has also created no actions in the federal courts. Congress must reassess this position if consumers are to have a forum for seeking remedies under the Act.

432   Schaffer, William A. "Physician Advertising in the United States Since 1980." *International Journal of Advertising* 8 (1989): 25-33.

Traces the history of advertising by physicians and the subsequent regulations placed upon it by the states. These regulations prevented consumers from obtaining information regarding physician services. In 1980, the FTC found that these restrictions restrained trade within the industry and ordered them discontinued. Future issues regarding the content of physician advertisements are then discussed.

433   Schechter, Roger E. "The Death of the Gullible Consumer: Towards a More Sensible Definition of Deception at the FTC." *University of Illinois Law Review* 1989 (1989): 571-623.

Examines the controversy and debate surrounding the FTC's definition of deception in advertising, the goals of the deception definition to prevent physical and psychological harm to the consumer, protect competition, preserve ethical standards, and analyze competing definitions. The author concludes that existing proposals fail and sets forth a definition that is based on surveys of targeted consumers, linking the notion of deception to the probability that a challenged advertisement will induce consumer action.

434   Schechter, Roger E. "Letting the Right Hand Know What the Left Hand's Doing: The Clash of the FTC's False Advertising and Antitrust Policies." *Boston University Law Review* 64 (March 1984): 265-323.

Examines how the FTC exercises discretion in selecting cases and designing remedies concerning false advertising. Of particular concern is the issuance of cease and desist orders by the Commission to firms operating similar advertising campaigns and selling competing products. These orders frequently create a disparity of treatment by subjecting one firm to tighter controls than its competitors are subjected to. This disparity creates antitrust concerns because the market structure can be changed if consumers view the products or services of the constrained firm to be less attractive and if there is disparate freedom to advertise within the marketplace. It is concluded that in order to ensure fairness within a concentrated marketplace, a firm must be permitted to show that disparate treatment would adversely affect the market structure. In such cases, the FTC should refrain from intervention and if the Commission should proceed, the courts should rule that the FTC has abused its discretion as a matter of antitrust law.

435   Scherb, Cynthia Weber. "Trade Regulation–The FTC Policy Statement on Deception: A New Standard, or a Restatement of the Old?" *Journal of Corporation Law* 10 (Spring 1985): 805-816.

Discusses the October 1983 statement by the FTC that set forth standards on deceptive advertising. The arguments of the Commissioners who advocated the position presented in this statement, as well as the arguments against the statement by Commissioners Patricia Bailey and Michael Pertschuk, are analyzed. The majority's arguments advocating the statement are then tested against prior cases to determine whether new standards have in fact been implemented. It is concluded that the dissenters have overreacted to the possible changes that would occur when the statement is implemented, however, charges of "heavy-handed tactics" used by Chairman James C. Miller appear well founded.

436   Schmitt, Michael A. and Susan D. Kovac. "Magnuson-Moss vs. State Protective Consumer Legislation: The Validity of a Stricter State Standard of Warranty Protection." *Arkansas Law Review* 30 (Spring 1976): 21-34.

After outlining the historical development of the Act and warranty coverage under the Uniform Commercial Code, the author examines preemption problems associated with incorporating the provisions of the Act with those of state laws. It is concluded that, in order to facilitate cooperative consumer protection between state and federal authorities, the FTC should establish a procedure to review and validate stricter state laws when they exist or have been put forth by the states' attorney general.

437   Schnabel, Morton. "Conscious Parallelism and Advertising Themes: The Case for "Comparative" Advertising." *Antitrust Law and Economics Review* 7 (1974-75): 11-20.

Examines the issue of conscious parallelism--present when a firm fails to change any variable, such as price, quality of the product, or the nature of its advertising, that it can control--and how the lack of comparative advertising within a marketplace of significant product differences may be a prime indicator that implicit collusion is present.

438   Schoenfeld, Andrea F. "Consumer Report: FTC's New Boldness Tests the Limits of Its Authority." *National Journal* (January 30, 1971): 207-219.

Comprehensive examination of the FTC's revitalization under a friendly White House administration and the plans under way to seek expanded authority from Congress. This revitalization is discussed within the context of advertising, innovations in consumer protection over the last year, antitrust activities, and industry compliance with Commission regulations. Concludes that the FTC has set lofty goals that can only be realized if the FTC meets the court challenges that will most likely arise if the proposed innovations and extended authority are implemented.

439   Schroeder, Milton R. "Private Actions Under the Magnuson-Moss Warranty Act." *California Law Review* 66 (January 1978): 1-36.

Examines the new federal warranty law by outlining its content and analyzing how it compares with the law of warranty that has evolved from the Uniform Commercial Code. Special attention is paid to the ambiguities created by the language of the Act and the interplay between it and existing state laws.

440   Schwartz, Martin L. "The Marketing of Funeral Services: Past, Present, and Future." *Business Horizons* 29 (March/April 1986): 40-45.

Discusses the implications of the 1982 Funeral Rule for the funeral industry by examining the guidelines the FTC set forth and their subsequent impact on the industry. The funeral industry's response to these questionable guidelines has improved the image of the industry, however.

441   Schwartz, Teresa M. "Regulating Unfair Practices Under the FTC Act: The Need for a Legal Standard of Unfairness." *Akron Law Review* 11 (Summer 1977): 1-28.

Analyzes past and proposed use of the unfairness doctrine to illustrate the need for trade regulation rules that cover the elimination of the Holder-In-Due-Course Doctrine in consumer credit transactions, remove restraints in eyeglass and prescription drug advertising, and regulate unfair practices in, among others, the industries of hearing aids, funeral services, used motor vehicles, and debt collection. The author concludes that a more strict definition of unfairness needs to be established based predominantly on whether substantial harm has occurred in order to avoid the promulgation of unnecessarily, burdensome, or vague rules.

442   "Scope of the Jurisdiction of the Federal Trade Commission over False and Misleading Advertising." *Yale Law Journal* 40 (February 1931): 617-630.

A comment on the growing number of false advertising cases before the FTC over the past decade and how this growth has been criticized by some as outside of the FTC's stated mission to maintain open competition. The expanded jurisdiction of controlling false advertising is put into jeopardy by the decision rendered in the *Raladam Co. v. FTC* case. In this case, the Raladam Company was ordered to no longer represent its product "Marmola" as a scientific thyroid cure for obesity unless it was accompanied by a statement saying the product should only be taken under the direction of a physician. The court ruled that the terms "scientific" and "safe" were matters of opinion and did not fall within the jurisdiction of the FTC's mission of ensuring open competition. However, congressional debates during the creation of the FTC indicate that there was a strong desire among the public to maintain not only fair competition, but to enforce "higher standards of commercial practice within that competition."

443   Sebert, Jr., John A. "Obtaining Monetary Redress for Consumers Through Action by the Federal Trade Commission." *Minnesota Law Review* 57 (December 1972): 225-287.

The limited nature of remedies under the FTC Act has prevented the FTC from becoming an effective forum for seeking redress of consumer grievances. The fact that Section 5 of the Act does not have a specific provision for consumer redress has commonly been cited as the reason why this issue has not been pursued. However, precedent has already been set in the Curtis Publishing Company case in which consumers were not informed that they may accept, not only substitute subscriptions to other magazines in leu of the suspension of publishing of the *Saturday Evening Post*, but a refund of their money for the unexpired portion of their subscription. In the case, it was asserted that, in certain instances, the FTC did have the statutory authority to require a respondent to refund money or property that it had obtained from its costumers through deceptive practices. Existing statutory authority under similar circumstances is examined with recommendations offered to expand the FTC's role in this area.

444   Seligman, Daniel. "The FTC Presents: The Great Sandpaper Shaving Case." *Fortune* 70 (December 1964): 131-133, 188, 190, 192, 194.
Critical analysis of the FTC's efforts to ban the further broadcasting of the Rapid Shave "sandpaper beard" commercial in which plexiglass covered with sand is substituted for sandpaper in demonstrating Rapid Shave's effectiveness in giving a close shave. The issue is examined from a philosophical perspective examining issues of puffery and the reasoning behind creating regulations based on how a consumer perceives reality in advertising. The specific Rapid Shave case is examined in detail.

445   Serafino, James M. "Health Claims Substantiation: FTC Policy and FDA Proposals." *Food Drug Cosmetic and Medical Device Law Digest* 10 (January 1993): 42-47.
Reviews FTC guidelines regarding the substantiation of health food claims in advertising and summarizes the proposed requirements set forth by the Food and Drug Administration to set minimum levels of nutrients that, if reached, would negate health claims for a product. It is argued that a comparison of the standards set by both agencies, while sharing similar goals, may lead to disparate results in actual application.

446   Sfifas, Peter M. "Who Should Validate the Advertising of Health Care Professionals?" *International Journal of Advertising* 8 (1989): 17-23.
Although the FTC plays a major role in policing deceptive advertising in the United States, neither the FTC nor the states have the resources to actively pursue false advertisers. Professional voluntary organizations are thus in the best position to police such behavior, but are reluctant to do so because of the threat of costly antitrust litigation. This lack of protection emphasizes the need for the FTC to cooperate with these organizations to curtail deceptive advertising.

447   Shaw, Bill M. "Magnuson-Moss Warranty-Federal Trade Commission Improvement Act." *South Texas Law Journal* 17 (1976): 229-242.

Provides a systematic analysis of the provisions of the Act and its potential impact on consumers, the marketplace, and the judicial system. Specific industries within the marketplace are examined to highlight important issues.

448   Shearer, Tom E. "The National Government and False Advertising." *Iowa Law Review* 19 (1933): 28-53.

Outlines the role of the federal government in regulating false advertising. Among the agencies profiled is the FTC. Analysis of specific court cases is used to illustrate how the agency performs its primary mission to prohibit unfair methods of competition.

449   Silverglade, Bruce A. "Harmonizing Food Labeling and Advertising Regulation." *Food Drug Cosmetic Law Journal* 46 (November 1991): 861-868.

The FTC has refused to bring its food advertising policies regarding health and nutrition into line with the Food and Drug Administration, the Department of Agriculture, and Congress. This article discusses how the FTC's policy undermines the policies of other government agencies and presents steps needed to alleviate the inequity this creates in regulating food advertising.

450   Silvestri, Stephen M. "Trade Regulation: The Federal Trade Commission has the Authority to Order Corrective Advertising to Dispel the Effects of Past Deception." *Catholic University Law Review* 27 (Summer 1978): 803-817.

Outlines the implications of the *Warner-Lambert Co. v. FTC* case in expanding the FTC's remedy seeking power to include the use of corrective advertising to dispel the effect of past illegal practices. A major disadvantage of this remedy is the delay often associated with FTC action. It is also noted that the FTC must exercise care in implementing corrective advertising so as to eliminate specifically retained beliefs.

451   Simon, Morton J. *The Law for Advertising and Marketing.* New York: W.W. Norton and Company, Inc, 1956.

Provides comprehensive coverage of the history and legal relationship between the advertiser and advertising agencies and examines in detail the property law of advertising, legal problems associated with advertising, marketing and merchandising issues, and attempts by government, including the FTC, to control advertising. Cases are cited when needed. Throughout the text, the FTC is discussed in regards to its regulatory responsibilities, its relationship with the advertising industry, and its issuance of Trade Regulation Rules. Includes a table of cases.

452   Smith, Christopher. "The Magnuson-Moss Warranty Act: Turning the Tables on Caveat Emptor." *California Western Law Review* 13 (1977): 391-429.

Gives a detailed overview of the legislative history of the Act, its provisions, and examines its enforcement by the FTC. The author notes that, while it may be too early to discern whether the Act creates a more competitive market for warranty terms and product quality, the Act does establish a basic level of consumer protection that will impact all buyers, sellers, and manufacturers.

453   Smith, Christopher and Christian S. White. *FTC Trade Regulation: Advertising, Rulemaking, and New Consumer Protection.* Corporate Law and Practice Course Handbook Series Number 303. New York, NY: Practicing Law Institute, 1979.

A collection of essays that accompany an educational program given by the Practicing Law Institute in April and May of 1979. Each essay covers a different aspect of consumer protection law and practice. After two introductory essays on the FTC's role in regulating advertising, specific cases, the issue of advertising directed to children, and selected regulatory rules are analyzed. Other essays cover such topics as obtaining information from the FTC, an examination of the Magnuson-Moss Warranty Act, and the role of the FTC in private actions for consumer injury under state laws.

454   Smith, Samuel A. "Brand Advertising and "Price Performance Labeling": A Modest Proposal." *Antitrust Law and Economics Review* 7 (1974-75): 29-46.

Examines the economic efficiency of the FTC's efforts to regulate deceptive advertising. It is suggested that the FTC should concentrate its efforts not on misinformation, but rather the lack of information in the marketplace. The primary difficulty in informing the consumer is that there is a wide variety of information needs based on the product. Only by identifying which products are currently being sold with inadequate information can one begin to solve the problem.

455   Sobel Lester A., ed. *Consumer Protection.* New York, NY: Facts on File, 1976.

Records and categorizes the scattered efforts of government agencies to curb deceptive behavior towards consumers. The book is based upon developments recorded in the weekly reports issued by Facts on File during the late 1960s through the first half of the 1970s. Each chapter covers a specific topic, such as food, and further divides that into more specific subcategories. The efforts of the FTC are extensively chronicled in regards to advertising and labeling regulation. The book ends with a chapter outlining the development of the current consumers movement and a guide to deceptive advertising acts and practices.

456   Sommer, Jr., A. A. "Random Thoughts on Disclosure as "Consumer" Protection." *The Business Lawyer* 27 (November 1971): 85-91.

Expresses misgivings about the expanded use of disclosure in other areas of consumerism besides protecting investors and discusses how the current reliance upon disclosure as a philosophy of federal securities regulation is increasing viewed as inadequate within the securities field.

457   Squillante, Alphonse M. "The New Federal Warranty Disclosure Standards for Written Warranties of Consumer Products, Part I." *Commercial Law Journal* 80 (November 1975): 477-479.

Provides an overview of the Magnuson-Moss Warranty Act, including an examination of important provisions and expansion of the enforcement powers of the FTC.

458   Squillante, Alphonse M. "Remedies Provided by the Magnuson-Moss Warranty Act." *Commercial Law Journal* 92 (Winter 1987):366-383.

Discusses the remedies provided under the Act and compares the anticipated effects of the Act upon the buyer-warrantor relationship, noting that suppliers have become more sophisticated in providing warranties that don't increase the chance of liability. Enforcement by the FTC is specifically examined.

459   Stadfeld, L. Seth. "The FTC Franchise Disclosure Rule and Its Impact on Chapter 93a of the Massachusetts General Laws: A Source of Protection for Consumer Entrepreneurs." *Western New England Law Review* 2 (1980): 681-720.

Explores the impact of the FTC Trade Regulation Rule covering the issue of widespread deception and unfair business practices within the sale of business opportunities or franchises on developing law under chapter 93a of the Massachusetts General Laws. While comparative in its analysis, the essay examines in depth the contents of the Rule, what conduct violates provisions of the Rule, its potential impact on the marketplace, its effect on unfairness and deception analysis, and the applicability of the Rule to nonfranchising commercial transactions.

460   Starek, Roscoe B. and Lynda M. Rozell. "The Federal Trade Commission's Commitment to On-Line Consumer Protection." *John Marshall Journal of Computer and Information Law* 15 (Summer 1997): 679-702.

This essay begins by briefly describing the consumer protection laws that the FTC enforces and placing the enforcement of those laws within the conceptual framework of online commerce. Among the most important rules promulgated by the FTC or statutes that fall within the agency's jurisdiction having direct application to the online marketplace is the Mail or Telephone Order Merchandise Rule, the Fair Credit Billing Act, and the Electronic Fund Transfer Act. The application of these rules are then described from the perspective of protecting the consumer conducting transactions on the Internet. The next section examines law enforcement actions by the FTC involving online marketing followed by a review of non-regulatory methods of protecting the consumer in online commerce. The article concludes by analyzing in what ways the FTC is informing itself of the growing online environment and what enforcement issues are raised by this new commerce.

461   Stein, Murray. "Testimonial Advertising and the Federal Trade Commission." *George Washington Law Review* 17 (April 1949): 340-353.

Editorial that examines the legal ramifications of the *Northam Warran Corp. v. FTC* case, arguing that the FTC's regulatory power in the area of testimonial advertising had been severely restricted. In the case, the Commission issued a cease and desist order because it was not disclosed that substantial sums of money had been paid for the testimonials and endorsements of its products by individuals. The courts overturned the commission's order stating that "if the testimonials involved...represent honest beliefs of the indorsers, there is no misrepresentation." The editorial states that the courts have now handed advertisers the legal rationale to use testimonial advertising as a competitive technique.

462   Stephan, Robert T. "National Consumer Protection Enforcement."
Antitrust Law Journal 58 (1989): 247-251.

As the Attorney General for the state of Kansas, the author discusses the state attorney general's role in national consumer protection enforcement, including cooperative efforts between them and the FTC in regards to telemarketing fraud.

463   Sterk, Stewart E. "Law of Comparative Advertising: How Much Worse is Better than Great." *Columbia Law Review* 76 (1976): 80-112.

Regulating deception in cases of comparative advertising is only partially addressed by the actions of the FTC because the issue only represents a small element of the FTC's overall regulatory efforts. Private enforcement offers an alternative, but is hindered by requirements for recovery depending on whether the cause of action is defined as defamation, disparagement, or unfair competition. None of the avenues of redress can be fully effective until there is a recognition of the unique nature of comparative advertising abuses and the implementation of solutions based specifically on eliminating abusive comparative advertising.

464   Sterk, Stewart E. "Consumer Protection Via Increased Information."
Journal of Marketing 31 (April 1967): 48-52.

Analyzes the question, "Do consumers have a right to be informed, as distinct from a right not to be deceived?" and related issues regarding the full disclosure of packaging information to help curb false advertising. Government efforts to help regulate industry is outlined, including terms of sale information, standards, and consumer advisory services. Concludes that full disclosure may be not only the most economical approach to protecting the consumer, but may also alleviate the need for further restrictions.

465   Stevens, William S. "Unfair Competition: A Study of Certain Practices and Their Relation to the Trust Problems in the United States, Part One and Part Two." *Political Science Quarterly* (June 1914 and September 1914): 282-306 and 406-490.

Written from an economists' standpoint, this early two part essay attempts to define and explain the phenomenon of unfair competition. Although the article was written several months before the FTC was created, it provides an excellent historical perspective on how economists, politicians, and lawyers struggled with the issue of unfair competition in the marketplace and its adverse affects on consumers. Issues such as local price cutting, the lease, sale or purchase of items as a condition for the lease, sale or purchase of required items, preferential contracts, and simple threats, intimidation and coercion are analyzed in detail.

466   Stevenson, Thomas H. and Linda E. Swayne. "Guidelines for Comparative Advertising in Industrial Trade Publications." *Journal of Business and Industrial Marketing* 3 (Winter 1988): 37-44.

Examines the motivation behind an advertiser's marketing tactic of comparing two or more products to promote the benefits of their product. This study tracks the use of comparative advertising in industrial trade publications over a period of time to what competitive advantages are used in the ads, what is the pattern of usage among different trade journals, what long-term strategies in advertising does this tactic illustrate, and what is the nature of trade journal advertising. The impact of FTC guidelines allowing comparative advertising is examined as well.

467   Stone, Alan. "The FTC and Advertising Regulation: An Examination of Agency Failure." *Public Policy* 21 (1973): 203-234.

Presents a theory of administrative conduct based upon an analysis of the Wheeler-Lea Act to help explain the agencies performance which is viewed as severely lacking in the area of consumer protection.

468   Strasser, Kurt A. "Magnuson-Moss Warranty Act: An Overview and Comparison with UCC Coverage, Disclaimer, and Remedies in Consumer Warranties." *Mercer Law Review* 27 (Summer 1976): 1111-1145.

Begins with an overview of the provisions of the Act followed by a comparative analysis, with specific code sections, of the Uniform Commercial Code. Cases are cited only when they represent a substantial change in the application of UCC rules. Remedies set forth in the Act are also examined.

469   Stuart, Fredric., ed. *Consumer Protection from Deceptive Advertising.* (Hofstra University Yearbook of Business Series 10, Volume 3). Hempstead, NY: Hofsta University Press, 1974.

A collection of essays divided under four headings--The Role of Government as Protector, The Role of Advertisers and Consumers, Attacks on Common Deceptive Practices, and, Deceptions Aimed at Special Groups--that analyze various aspects of consumer protection and advertising. Most of the essays examine FTC advertising policies and rulemaking procedures and their effectiveness in protecting the consumer.

470   Sturdivant, Frederick D., ed. *The Ghetto Marketplace*. New York: The
Free Press, 1969.

Divided into two parts, this book focuses on "the marketplace of the urban ghetto"
by gathering materials that analyze the vulnerability of the poor to unfair or
misleading practices by merchants. The first part examines the unique
characteristics of the ghetto marketplace and the specific unfair practices that take
place. Included in this analysis is the text of the FTC Report on Installment Credit
and Retail Sales Practices of District of Columbia Retailers. The second part
contains a collection of materials discussing ways to remedy the situation,
including an essay by Mary Gardiner Jones examining the role of the FTC in
controlling deception aimed at the poor. Includes a selected bibliography.

471   Sturley, Michael F. "The Legal Impact of the Federal Trade
Commission's Holder in Due Course Notice on a Negotiable Instrument:
How Clever are the Rascals at the FTC?" *North Carolina Law Review*
68 (June 1990): 953-978.

Argues that since the FTC's notice does not override provisions of the Uniform
Commercial Code, a gap in consumer protection coverage exists because, by
requiring only a "notice" that any holder will be subject to claims, Article 3 of the
Uniform Commercial Code still "would permit a holder in due course to take a
negotiable instrument free of most claims and defenses." The author feels that the
argument as to why this gap exists by White and Summer in their commercial law
treatise is incorrect and offers other explanations, all of which underscore the need
for revisions to the rules.

472   Sullivan, E. Thomas and Brian A. Marks. "The FTC's Deceptive
Advertising Policy: A Legal and Economic Analysis." *Oregon Law
Review* 64 (1986): 593-635.

Analyzes the recent changes in FTC policy regarding deceptive advertising with
special attention paid to the legal and economic aspects of the new enforcement
policy statement. Specific factors examined include incentives, burden allocation,
transaction costs, and welfare tradeoffs resulting from the new legal standard. The
concept of Pareto optimality is applied to determine the effects the policy has on
firms, consumers, and the FTC. Case law developed prior to changes made to the
deceptive advertising policy of the Commission are examined, followed by an
analysis of specific parts of the policy. The author then discusses the justification
for government intervention and the effects of the new standard on the economy.
Concludes that, while a comparison of the costs and benefits of the case law and

the new policy is difficult without empirical evidence, the new standard does create textual ambiguities and legal uncertainties because it is unclear how much the new standard will rely on government enforcement to achieve the efficient level of deception.

473   Sweeney, Charles A. "Federal Trade Commission Control of False Advertising of Foods, Drugs, and Cosmetics." *Food Drug Cosmetics Law Journal* 12 (October 1957): 605-616.

Outlines the various legal remedies available to the FTC in controlling false advertising of foods, drugs, and cosmetics, including the Wheeler-Lea Amendment. Discusses specific instances of abuse, outlines the working agreement between the FTC and the Food and Drug Administration, and shows how the increasing volume of advertising complicates efforts to serve the public interest.

474   Sweeney, Charles A. "Packaging Responsibilities of the FTC." *Food Drug Cosmetic Law Journal* 22 (March 1967): 165-168.

The Director of the Bureau of Deceptive Practices discusses the FTC's responsibility under the Fair Packaging and Labeling Act and the regulations placed on business to help them conform to the act.

475   Tancredi, James J. "Corrective Advertising–The Federal Trade Commission's Response to Residual Deception." *Connecticut Law Review* 10 (Summer 1978): 1035-1055.

The FTC's power to issue cease and desist orders against abusive advertisers can terminate a deceptive advertising campaign, yet it cannot redress the residual misimpressions present in the minds of consumers. This opens the door to allowing the wrongdoer to continue benefitting from the deception. In *Warner-Lambert Co. v. FTC*, the use of corrective advertising was affirmed as a remedy to residual misimpressions. This note discusses the implications of the case, from which sources this power is inferred or defined, and what limitations the First Amendment places on corrective advertising.

476   Tanner, Sue A. "The FTC Holder in Due Course Rule: Neither Creditor Ruination nor Consumer Salvation." *Southwestern Law Journal* 31 (Winter 1977): 1097-1123.

Analyzes the criticism leveled at the Holder-In-Due-Course Doctrine and outlines arguments by members of the consumer credit industry against provisions of the FTC Trade Regulation Rule attempting to alleviate problems with the doctrine. The Rule is viewed as inadequate because it only partially abrogates the Holder-In-Due-Course Doctrine and affected transactions to which the doctrine does not apply. In addition, further confusion arose due to the haphazard implementation of the Rule by the FTC. However, the author notes that some of the criticism has been overstated by the industry due both to a misunderstanding of the Rule's provisions and to put pressure on Congress to suspend it.

477   Tedlow, Richard S. "From Competitor to Consumer: The Changing Focus of Federal Regulation of Advertising, 1914-1938." *Business History Review* 55 (1981): 35-58.

The FTC's attempts to punish deceptive advertising practices up until the passage of the Wheeler-Lea amendments was ineffective. With their passage, however, the FTC was granted needed support through the definition of what constituted false advertising and by imposing new penalties for violations of FTC orders.

478   Thain, Gerald J. "Advertising Regulation: The Contemporary FTC Approach." *Fordham Urban Law Journal* 1 (1973): 349-394.

As Assistant Director for National Advertising, Bureau of Consumer Protection of the FTC, the author offers his perspective on the efforts of the FTC to regulate advertising. Divided into two parts, the first section of the article discusses the Commission's traditional activities of adjudication and rule-making and the expansion of theories of violation and standards of proof under Section 5 of the FTC Act articulated through current cases before the FTC. The second section examines alternatives that are meant to supplement and enhance traditional forms of adjudication and rule-making.

479   Thain, Gerald J. "Consumer Protection: Advertising–The FTC Response." *The Business Lawyer* 27 (April 1972): 891-906.

Text of remarks presented at a program of the Food, Drug and Cosmetic Law Division of the American Bar Association in New York on July 7, 1971. The author covers five broad topics the FTC is involved in: food advertising, advertising directed to children, the "unfairness doctrine," the impact of television advertising, and examples of specific types of advertising attacked by the FTC as unlawful. The remarks conclude by examining the effects of these activities on the business community.

480   Thain, Gerald J. "Corrective Advertising: Theory and Cases." *New York Law Forum* 19 (Summer 1973): 1-34.
Reviews the history of efforts to invoke the corrective advertising remedy, discusses the legal theories used to support this as well as the philosophical basis for supporting such action, and analyzes the evidence used to invoke the remedy and how successfully this evidence has been received. Specific cases involving corrective advertising are noted throughout the essay.

481   Thain, Gerald J. "Credit Advertising and the Law: Truth in Lending and Related Matters." *Washington University Law Quarterly* 1976 (Spring 1976): 257-276.
While pressure by the FTC on industries such as cigarette manufacturers to require more information be disseminated to the consumer is often important in alleviating misrepresentations, such disclosure requirements regarding credit terms under the Truth in Lending Act do little to protect consumers who have trouble obtaining credit. The role of the FTC in regulating credit advertising is discussed in detail as well as the FTC's powers to impose sanctions for unlawful credit advertising.

482   Thain, Gerald J. "Drug Advertising and Drug Abuse: The Role of the FTC." *Food Drug Cosmetic Law Journal* 26 (1971): 487-499.
Examines the possible link between over-the-counter (OTC) drug advertising and drug abuse. The essay is couched within the framework of a study conducted by the FTC showing that, while there is no solid evidence of a causal relationship, there was the existence of a strong belief that OTC drug advertising has led to drug abuse, children's drug use, and excessive OTC drug use. The author states that the basis of this belief can be attributed to advertising techniques developed during the past twenty years. Corrective advertising and affirmative disclosure are discussed as remedies available to the FTC when deception occurs.

483   Thain, Gerald J. "Food Advertising: The FTC Past Positions Present Posture and Signposts on the Road to the Future." *Food Drug Cosmetic Law Journal* 28 (October 1973): 617-627.
Reviews FTC activities related to food advertising by focusing on two areas of advertising regulation that has recently been strengthen by recent court decisions and may have a possible effect on the food industry--the unfairness doctrine and the FTC's rulemaking authority. Both of these issues are discussed in detail with regards to the future.

484   Thain, Gerald. "Suffer the Hucksters to Come Unto the Little Children?:
Possible Restrictions of Television Advertising to Children Under
Section 5 of the Federal Trade Commission Act." *Boston University
Law Review* 56 (July 1976): 651-684.
The purpose of this article is to outline the nature of concerns voiced by parents,
educators, and others regarding advertising directed at children and discuss the
possible adverse impact these advertisements may have on children. These
concerns have led to the possible restriction of children's television advertising by
the FTC under Section 5 of the FTC Act. The unfairness doctrine of Section 5 is
analyzed through specific cases to show that the FTC is aware that the nature of
the audience is a relevant factor in determining if an advertisement if unfair to the
consumer. Arguments that restrictions would infringe upon the free speech rights
of advertisers, that such regulations would put an unfair burden upon broadcasters,
and that further research is required to justify prohibition of children's advertising
are found to be insufficiently persuasive. A "modest proposal" is offered as to
what action the FTC should take in regulating children's advertising.

485   Thain, Gerald J. *Television Advertising to Children and the Federal
Trade Commission: A Review of the History and Some Personal
Observation.* Department of Advertising, College of Communications.
Working Paper 9. Urbana, IL: University of Illinois, July 1981.
Text of remarks delivered at the University of Illinois in which the author reviews
the FTC's regulatory activities related to television advertising directed toward
children. The essay begins by tracing the issues involved and the reasons for
intervention in the form of a proposed trade regulation rule by the FTC.
Opposition to the agency's regulatory efforts centered on three issues:
infringement of free speech guaranteed by the First Amendment, the Rule would
represent an unfair burden placed on television rather than all media, and
additional research is missing to make a fully rationalized federal regulation. The
three issues are then examined in detail. Recent relevant research is then examined
followed by some personal observations and recommendations.

486   Thompson, Mayo J. "Advertising and the FTC: The Role of Information
in a Free-Enterprise Economy." *Antitrust Law and Economic Review*
6 (1973): 73-82.
Essay discussing the author's views regarding advertising's primary purpose to
provide information to potential buyers. This thesis is presented within the context
of what effects this has on the nation's economic system. The author states his

opinions based on a background in business.

487   Thompson, Mayo J. "Government Regulation of Advertising: Killing the
Consumer in Order to Save Him." *Antitrust Law and Economic Review*
8 (1976): 81-92.
Critical analysis of the "unreasonable" rules and regulations created by the FTC
to protect consumers from harmful ads.

488   Tiffany, Marcy J. K. "Consumer Protection: The Nuts and Bolts of an
FTC Investigation." *Antitrust Law Journal* 60 (1991): 139-146.
Outlines the procedures taken by the FTC when it investigates issues regarding
consumer protection. This article provides an examination as to what initiates an
investigation, how the FTC decides to react, possible reaction by the firm or
industry under investigation, legal parameters of an investigation, and aggressive
nature of some of the investigations undertaken by the FTC.

489   Tolchin, Susan J. and Martin Tolchin. *Dismantling America: The Rush
to Deregulate*. Boston, MA: Houghton Mifflin, 1983.
Provides an overview of the reasons why government regulates the marketplace
and examines the political environment during the 1970s and early 1980s that led
to the perception that the marketplace was being overregulated. Particular
attention is paid to the antiregulatory efforts of Ronald Reagan. Throughout the
text the effects of this antiregulatory movement on the FTC is examined. The
authors conclude with a criticism of this "rush to deregulate" and the shift of
consumer protection responsibilities from the federal government to the state
legislators, noting in detail the costs to consumers of social deregulation.

490   "Towards Greater Equality in Business Transactions: A Proposal to
Extend the Little FTC Acts to Small Business." *Harvard Law Review*
96 (May 1983): 1621-1640.
Examines how the provisions of Little FTC Acts adopted by states should extend
to protecting the small business community from the effects of deceptive trade
practices. This action would parallel the FTC Act that can be invoked to protect
business plaintiffs as well as consumers. The article begins by describing the
origin and purpose of the Little FTC Acts and then provides reasons why the Acts
should be extended to small business. The author uses those states that already
allow businesses to litigate under the Acts to create model legislative proposals
that others can use to extend the Little FTC Acts to protecting small companies.

491   "Trade Regulation: Use of Undisclosed Mock-Up in Television Commercial Demonstration Held to be Deceptive Practice in Violation of Federal Trade Commission Act." *Fordham Law Review* 34 (1965): 362-368.

Provides an overview of the ruling in the case of *Colgate-Palmolive v. FTC* in which a piece of plexiglass with sand attached to it was substituted for sandpaper in order to demonstrate the moisturizing ability of Rapid Shave cream, noting that the results of the ruling put into entire question the use of props in television commercials.

492   "Translating Sympathy for Deceived Consumers into Effective Programs for Protection." *University of Pennsylvania Law Review* 114 (1966): 395-450.

The results of a field research project, this comment ascertains what protection is afforded consumers from fraudulent sellers and to examine ways to improve that protection. A fictional case study is used to point out the problems of dishonest sellers, then moves into a discussion of the consumer protection activities of nongovernmental agencies such as Better Business Bureaus, private attorneys, and legal aid societies, state and local government protection, and protection afforded consumers by the federal government. The author concludes that the consumer can be best served if state, local and federal agencies or organizations unite in their efforts to eradicate fraud and if the consumer is better educated as to recognize fraudulent behavior. These conclusions are offered as the only truly long-term solutions available. The study is based on interviews of individuals in New Jersey, Pennsylvania, and New York, that work in government or organizations and who are in a position to help the consumer.

493   Trebilcock, M. J. "Private Law Remedies for Misleading Advertising." *University of Toronto Law Journal* 22 (1972): 1-32.

The author reviews criticisms brought against the FTC in regards to the private law area for meeting contemporary problems of misleading advertising. The criticisms are generally seen as justified.

494   Tyebjee, Tyzoon T. "The Role of Publicity in FTC Corrective Advertising Remedies." *Journal of Marketing and Public Policy* 1 (1982): 111-121.

This study uses empirical data to measure the extent and effect of media publicity concerning FTC corrective advertising remedies. The STP oil additive case, in which STP agreed to withdraw certain claims about its product, shows that news about an FTC action is disseminated by means other than the corrective ad itself, most notably media coverage of the regulatory action and word-of-mouth communication.

495   Tyler, Leslie and Allen R. Erickson. "The Federal Trade Commission Today: The New Improved Improvements Act." *Hastings Constitutional Law Quarterly* 3 (Summer 1973): 849-878.

Examines the language of the FTC Improvement Act within the context of constitutional limitations based on administrative procedure and, in particular, procedural due process. Cases are noted to help clarify definitions of the Act and the judicial boundaries of its powers. It is concluded that the "radical" provisions of the Act will have an immediate impact on consumers, as well as the business community in general, regardless of future judicial interpretations.

496   "Unsolicited Merchandise: State and Federal Remedies for a Consumer Problem." *Duke Law Journal* 1970 (1970): 911-1014.

State legislators, Congress and the FTC have all attempted to regulate or eliminate the practice of sending merchandise as an offer of sale without prior solicitation or an order from the consumer. This comment outlines the objections to and obligation of consumers under common law of unsolicited merchandise and analyzes remedies set forth by state agencies, the United States Post Office, and the FTC.

497   Vercammem, Kenneth A. "Advertising and the FTC: Less Regulation Can Mean More Consumer Protection." *Corporation Law Review* 8 (Winter 1985): 49-79.

The trend towards less regulation is analyzed within the context of the FTC's role in regulating advertising and the various legal weapons at its disposal that can be used to curtail deceptive advertising. The reasonable-man test in judging deceptive advertising is a sound approach, coupled with cease-and-desist orders. This allows consumers to make sound buying decisions based on a steady flow of truthful information. Advertisement substantiation and affirmative disclosure are legal approaches the FTC should discontinue since it interferes with the market, increases costs to advertisers who have passed the cost on to consumers, and puts an undue strain upon the FTC.

498   Vollmar, Elizabeth E. "Lemon Laws: Putting the Squeeze on Automobile Manufacturers." *Washington University Law Quarterly* 61 (1984): 1125-1163.

In response to the lack of comprehensive warranty coverage beyond repair and replacement of defective parts, several states have passed "lemon laws" attempting to protect consumers that have purchased an automobile with serious defects that the dealer is unable to adequately correct. By examining the current means of recovery available to owners, it is demonstrated that the Magnuson-Moss Warranty Act does little to overcome the barriers to recovery set forth in the Uniform Commercial Code and, thus, does not contribute to remedying the situation.

499   Walker, Dale Elizabeth. "Administrative Law–Federal Trade Commission– Deceptive Advertising– Disclosure and Substantiation Requirements–Over-the-Counter Internal Analgesics (*American Home Products Corp. v. FTC*, 695 F.2nd 681 (3rd Cir. 1982))." *Duquesne Law Review* 22 (Fall 1983): 273-298.

Outlines the complaint issued against the maker of Anacin and Arthritis Pain Formula, alleging that the maker made false advertising claims regarding the products' "unique pain killing" properties over all other non-prescription analgesics. The essay traces the administrative judge's ruling that the disclosure of common ingredients contained in the product and that clinical substantiation and claims of performance are questioned within the medical community, are reasonable requirements to counter the effects of advertising found to violate the FTC Act.

500   Wall, Cynthia Shoss. "Consumer Protection–Remedies of the Federal Trade Commission–Expansion to Include Limitations of Contracts." *Tulane Law Review* 47 (February 1973): 436-446.

A note outlining the FTC's mandate from Congress, and subsequent expansion of that mandate in 1938 through the Wheeler-Lea Act, to regulate deceptive business behavior. However, in recent years the FTC has begun to experiment with affirmative and restrictive rules that expand the traditional remedies of cease and desist orders in regards to contract alterations and restrictions. While this expansion may be beyond the remedies as established by Congress, it reflects the Commission's attempt to act as a public agency outside of the bureaucratic confines of legislative action.

501   Ward, Thomas B. et al. "Opinions on Television Advertising to Children: A Content Analysis of Letters to the Federal Trade Commission." *Merrill-Palmer Quarterly* 30 (July 1984): 247-259.
Presents the results of a content analysis of 888 letters written to the FTC regarding advertising directed to children.

502   Wark, Lois G. "Consumer Report: Criticism of Advertising Prompts Agency Crackdown, Industry Self-Regulation." *National Journal* 3 (August 7, 1971): 1635-1645.
Discusses criticism directed toward the advertising industry demanding reform and the various regulatory responses by Congress and the FTC and other federal agencies to the reform issue. Industry self-regulation is also examined. Actions by the FTC against specific industries, companies, and their products are studied as well as reaction by the FTC to pressure from consumer groups.

503   Washburn, Whitney F. "FTC Regulation of Endorsements in Advertising: In the Consumer's Behalf?" *Pepperdine Law Review* 8 (March 1981): 697-745.
Analyzes the requirements, guidelines, and effects that the FTC's Guides Concerning Use of Endorsements and Testimonials in Advertising may have on advertisers. First issued in 1972 with final versions released in 1980, the guides attempt to control endorsement advertising abuses through the establishment of standards by which advertisers can measure their advertisements. However, because the guides are too narrowly drafted and do not carry the weight of law, they will have little effect. New guides with more general, substantive rules should be adopted, although this seems unlikely given the federal budget reductions of the current administration.

504   Watts, Marianne R. and Judith D. Wilkenfeld. "The Role of the Federal Trade Commission in Regulating Non-Prescription Drug Advertising and Promotion." *Journal of Drug Issues* 22 (Spring 1992): 265-276.
Focuses on the manner in which the FTC regulates advertising in general and specifically over-the-counter drugs, including basic legal principles behind the actions taken, pending legal regulations that are relevant to drug advertising, and the criteria used to investigate future drug advertising issues.

505   Wattwood, Robert. "Corrective Advertising: An Advertiser's Atonement." *University of Florida Law Review* 30 (Winter 1978): 490-500.

Uses the case of *Warner-Lambert, Co. v. FTC* to illustrate the issues surrounding corrective advertising. In this case, Listerine Mouthwash advertised that it helped alleviate the symptoms of colds and sore throats. FTC action led to the issuance by Warner-Lambert Company stating that these medicinal claims were false. Although the judicial decision regarding this and other cases of corrective advertising is reasonable, the decision failed to delineate clear regulatory boundaries of the FTC's power, thus leading to problems of concerning the extent of required disclosures and the limits on the damage caused to firms found guilty of deceptive practices. Post-order surveys offer the most effective means to measure the achievement of the goals established in issuing corrective advertising.

506   Wattwood, Robert. "FTC Regulation of TV Advertising to Children-- They Deserve a Break Today." *University of Florida Law Review* 30 (Fall 1978): 946-978.

Examines studies conducted and the data they have created to address whether advertising directed to children has had a deleterious effect on their physiological and psychological well-being. The FTC's jurisdiction to regulate advertising under the unfairness doctrine and the deception doctrine are outlined followed by an analysis of the constitutional rights of adult and children and advertisers. It is concluded that, given the special protection commonly afforded to children, the FTC staff recommendations restricting advertising directed to children falls within these parameters and "is merely a recognition of such protection in the electronic age."

507   Weiner, Lee M. "The Ad Substantiation Program: You Can Fool All of the People Some of the Time and Some of the People All of the Time, but Can You Fool the FTC?" *American University Law Review* 30 (Winter 1981): 429-476.

Criticizes the effectiveness and nature of the FTC's Ad Substantiation Program on the grounds that it has not lived up to its mission of increasing the amount of useful information to consumers, that it has not been effective in deterring deceptive advertising from continuing, and, given the evolution of sophisticated electronic technology, the Program must assess these products on an ever decreasing budget. By analyzing the implementation of the Program and the factors that have retarded its effectiveness, recommendations are proposed to make it a more effective weapon in combatting deceptive advertising. Special emphasis is placed on the recent judicial decisions that have contributed to the Ad Substantiation Program's ineffectiveness.

508   Weiner, Marcel. "Federal Trade Commission–False Advertising–Corrective Advertising Remedy." *Duquesne Law Review* 16 (1977-1978): 797-812.

In reviewing the recent decision in *Warner-Lambert Co. v. FTC*, it is stated that such broad interpretation of the FTC's cease and desist powers is currently inappropriate and dangerous because no specific guidelines have been created to control when such action is appropriate. The court decision has implied that the corrective advertising order can be applied to any advertising found to be misleading. Lower courts must act on this decision within the context of protection afforded to commercial speech.

509   Wellford, Harrison. "How Ralph Nader, Tricia Nixon, the ABA, and Jamie Whitten Helped Turn the FTC Around." *The Washington Monthly* 4 (October 1972): 5-6, 8-13.

Examines the resurgence of the FTC's activities related to consumer protection. The author notes that this evolution has occurred in a few short years after the American Bar Association and Ralph Nader published reports that were highly critical of the agency's consumer protection activities. New remedies, such as ad substantiation, corrective advertising, and counter-advertising, are all examined. Recent court cases are also examined to illustrate the FTC's renewed activity. The essay concludes with an analysis of how long this resurgence may last under the growing pressure of critics who view the Commission as being too intrusive and within the current political environment that may undermine recent efforts.

510   Welsh, David F. "Environmental Marketing and Federal Preemption of State Law: Eliminating the "Gray" Behind the "Green"." *California Law Review* 81 (July 1993): 991-1027.

Criticizes current state and federal law regulating environmental or "green" marketing by pointing out how the lack of uniformity in state laws allows some deception to go unpunished and how the federal laws, including the guidelines established by the FTC, are inadequate because they rely heavily upon regulation on a case-by-case basis. The author argues that the Environmental Protection Agency should take the lead in establishing and enforcing guidelines because the FTC does not have the expertise in environmental issues. It is also argued that federal regulations should set a minimum standard that state laws must abide by. A model for ensuring nationwide uniformity is presented.

511   Welti, Belinda. "The Need for a Statutory Definition of Deceptive Advertising." *New England Law Review* 19 (1983): 127-149.

The lack of a definitive definition of deception has left interpretation to be decided on a case-by-case basis, which creates unpredictable results. To alleviate this pattern, FTC Chairman James C. Miller III has proposed a statutory definition of deceptive practices that would limit the FTC's power by requiring the Commission to adhere more strictly to the requirements that determinations of deception be supported by substantial evidence. This evidence would be based upon the "reasonable consumer" standard. By examining the potential difficulties of the proposed definition, the author concludes that alternatives to a statutory definition of deception in advertising must be sought because Chairman Miller's proposed definition would increase the FTC's evidentiary burden and the cost of prosecution of deceptive advertisements.

512   Wenthe, Roger W. "*Warner-Lambert C. v. FTC*: Corrective Advertising Gives Listerine a Taste of Its Own Medicine." *Northwestern University Law Review* 73 (December 1978): 957-979.

Discusses the impact on the FTC's authority under expanded interpretation of Section 5 of the FTC Act due to the ruling by the United States Court of Appeals for the District of Columbia affirming the FTC's power to seek remedy through corrective advertising. Although argued by Warner Lambert that these powers do not exist, the court ruled that the FTC has authority to issue remedies that "go beyond the simple cease and desist order." It is concluded that this ruling marks a "milestone" in the expanding powers of the Commission and is a starting point for determining the proper amount of remedial discretion granted to the FTC in formulating the content, duration, and conduct affected by an order.

513   Weston, Glen E. "Deceptive Advertising and the Federal Trade Commission: Decline of Caveat Emptor." *Federal Bar Journal* 24 (Fall 1964): 548-574.

Reviews and evaluates the accomplishments of the FTC during its first fifty years of existence and offers insights into some of the current problems faced by the agency. Among the accomplishments discussed is the agency's contributions to the field of consumer law, the improvement of competition, progress in the marshalling self-regulation and consumer education, bolstering inadequate state and local consumer protection laws, and saving "substantial sums" of money for the consumer by eliminating misleading advertising and regulating deceptive trade practices. Problems discussed include jurisdictional limitations, the delay between the issuance of a formal complaint and a final cease and desist order, the problem of proving falsity in advertising claims, coordination with other federal agencies, and the lack of an adequate program to review compliance with cease and desist orders once they have been issued. The essay concludes with suggestions for implementing a "cooperative regulation" program between government regulatory agencies and industry advocated by President Lyndon Johnson.

514   Westen, Tracy. "First Amendment: Barrier or Impetus to FTC Advertising Remedies?" *Brooklyn Law Review* 46 (Spring 1980): 487-512.

Two court cases, *Virginia State Board of Pharmacy v. Virginia Citizens Consumer Council, Inc.* and *First National Bank of Boston v. Bellotti*, established for the first time that commercial speech was entitled to some measure of protection under the First Amendment. The first case established the protection and the second case extended it to include free speech protection to political statements made by corporations. This poses two fundamental problems. The first involves defining how much deceptive commercial speech can be removed efficiently without imposing on the free speech rights of advertisers. This issue is currently being addressed in the courts and by the FTC. The second, more serious, issue concerns the almost necessary, one-sided nature of commercial speech. However, this one-sidedness creates a skewed marketplace of ideas and devising a system that insures equally effective speech rights for opposing speakers may prove to be very difficult.

515   "What is False Advertising? FTC Case Against Good Housekeeping." *Business Week* (December 23, 1939): 24-26.

Analyzes the *FTC v. Good Housekeeping* case at the halfway point in the trial in which the FTC charges that Good Housekeeping's issuance of seals of approval and its guaranty ads constitute unfair competition.

516   White, Martin B. "Coping with Violations of the Federal Trade Commission's Holder in Due Course Rule." *Temple Law Review* 66 (1993): 661-696.

Examines the problems associated with the absence of voluntary language in a consumer credit contract, stating that a creditor is required to include a statement specifying that a creditor who holds the contract of a buyer is subject to the buyer's claims and defenses. The essay discusses what remedies are available when this language is left out and presents several state law theories that would help to enforce the provisions of the FTC Rule in the absence of such language.

517 Wiener, Joshua Lyle. "Are Warranties Accurate Signals of Product Reliability?" *Journal of Consumer Research* 12 (September 1985): 245-250.

Gives an overview of studies conducted by the FTC and others indicating that consumers draw inferences about a product based on its warranty and examines whether consumer inferences regarding a product's reliability are accurate. It is concluded that, because a manufacturer has an economic incentive to reduce the possibility of claims against the provisions of a warranty offered to the consumer, the warranty is an effective measure of product reliability.

518 Wilkes, Robert E. and James B. Wilcox. "Recent FTC Actions: Implications for the Advertising Strategist." *Journal of Marketing* 38 (January 1974): 55-61.

By analyzing a substantial number of recent cases, this article reviews the more important policies recently employed or proposed by the FTC and to suggest a set of guidelines by which a firm may avoid FTC intervention.

519 Williams, Robert L. "Through the Looking Glass: The FTC's Advertising Substantiation Exclusionary Rule." *The American University Law Review* 27 (1977): 76-91.

Discusses the consequences of the FTC's expansion of its advertising substantiation program through an exclusionary rule that requires an advertiser at the investigative stage of an FTC inquiry "to present...its entire evidentiary defense to a potential adjudicative complaint challenging the failure to possess a prior reasonable basis for the advertising claims for which substantiation was requested." The author argues that this provision is unconstitutional and unlawful and is unworkable because it invites a voluminous amount of investigative responses.

520 Wines, Michael. "Miller's Directive to the FTC–Quit Acting Like a "Consumer Cop." *National Journal* 13 (December 5, 1981): 49-53.

Outline how the recent appointment of James C. Miller III as chairman of the FTC marks the beginning of a radical retrenchment in FTC activities. Changes proposed by Miller are offered to help curb what is viewed by the Reagan Administration as an overextended bureaucracy into individuals lives. The changes proposed include persuading Congress to revise the FTC Act to pull back some of the FTC's power of interpreting "unfair" business practices; to promote a review of the antitrust laws; initiate a task force to determine how the FTC may influence the economic and business-related activities of other federal agencies; and, review FTC programs that are viewed by Miller as interfering in the business marketplace. Concerns expressed from consumerists, Congress, and others are included.

521 Wolinsky, Sidney M. and Janet Econome. "Seduction in Wonderland: The Need for a Seller's Fiduciary Duty Toward Children." *Hastings Constitutional Law Quarterly* 4 (Spring 1977): 249-277.

Examines the problems associated with a young child's inability to discern fact from fantasy and the implications that this presents within the complex environment of commercial advertising. The government's role in protecting children from advertising exploitation is reviewed, concluding that efforts by agencies such as the FTC are inadequate in addressing the issue. In light of this, a judicial solution of applying a fiduciary doctrine is proposed.

522 Woolley, E. M. "What the Federal Trade Commission Will Do for You." *Collier's* 58 (November 18, 1916): 7-9.

Informational essay that uses case studies of manufacturer improprieties to describe how the FTC can protect the consumer. In addition, the work of the FTC is outlined in regards to its world wide research into export barriers established overseas, its efforts to protect small business from deceptive and monopolistic behavior by larger firms, and the FTC's sponsorship of hearings in various cities around the country on topics such as foreign trade and the lumber industry.

Chapter 2
Antitrust Law Compliance

523   "ACE Legal Report: The Federal Trade Commission and Televised College Football." *Educational Record* 72 (Fall 1991): 68-69.

Examines the FTC's investigation and subsequent charges leveled at the College Football Association. The investigation involved the Association and Capital Cities, which operates ABC and ESPN, charging them "with illegally conspiring to restrain competition in the marketing of college football." The response by the Association and the goal of the FTC in disallowing the contract are discussed. An administrative judge then ruled in August 1991 that the FTC investigation was invalid because the nonprofit status of the CFA members exempted them from antitrust enforcement as "corporations."

524   Albertsworth, E. F. "Interstate Commerce, Clayton Act, Constitutional Law, Jurisdiction of Federal Trade Commission." *Illinois Law Review* 22 (November 1927): 304-309.

The author agrees with a recent Supreme Court ruling that upheld an FTC cease and desist order on the grounds that interstate commerce did exist even if the contract did not expressly state so. The contract in question left it up to the purchaser whether the shipments were to come from within the state or outside of it. Eight situations involving the possible intervention by the government with regards to interstate commerce are then defined.

525   Alexander, G. J. "New Pragmatism in Robinson-Patman Interpretations?" *Syracuse Law Review* 15 (Spring 1964): 487-505.

Evaluates the pessimism articulated by some that the recent decision in *Grand Union Co. v. FTC*, in which the Second Circuit approved the FTC's position that the receipt of discriminatory allowances was in violation of Section 5 of the FTC Act allows the FTC to apply provisions of the Robinson-Patman Act based on the literal interpretation of the law, yet also applies this decision as "a joker which it could use when strict interpretation was unavailable." It is concluded that the recent cases reviewed have done little "to erase the main thrust of previous decisions" and there is virtually no chance that the entire statute will be revised to better reflect the spirit of the Sherman Act.

526   American Bar Association. *Antitrust Law Developments.* 3rd Edition.
Chicago, IL: American Bar Association, 1992.
This two volume set is a comprehensive compilation of case law and analysis of all aspects of antitrust law. Each chapter covers a different aspect of trade restraint, monopolization, mergers and acquisitions, the Robinson-Patman Act, and other subfields. Chapter five of the first volume is entirely devoted to the Federal Trade Commission's role in antitrust enforcement, however, the FTC is discussed through the text when appropriate. Several appendices contain text of important statutes and guidelines. The books include a table of cases and subject index.

527   "America's Antitrust Diaspora: Trustbusters, Inc." *The Economist* 321
(November 9, 1991): 84-89.
This brief essay analyzes attempts by the FTC and the Department of Justice to convince the world's industrialized nations and countries of Eastern Europe to model their antitrust laws after those adopted in the United States. It is noted that attempts to "export" American models of antitrust enforcement law overseas is an attempt to ensure open markets for Western penetration in the former Soviet Union and Eastern Europe for the future.

528   *The Antitrust Dilemma.* Edited by James A. Dalton and StanfordLevin.
Lexington, MA: Lexington Books, 1973.
This book contains a collection of papers written by government and academic economists that outline a number of different views concerning antitrust law enforcement. Although no essay is entirely devoted to the role of the FTC, issues such as Commission budget allocations, criticisms of FTC activities, internal policy planning, staff reports, and specific cases involving the FTC are referred to throughout. The volume includes a bibliography and subject/case index. Papers are based on a conference held at Southern Illinois University at Edwardsville, April 26-27, 1973.

529   "Antitrust Law–Investigatory Powers–Federal Trade Commission has
Right to Obtain Private Copies of Privileged Census Information."
Vanderbilt Law Review 15 (June 1962): 1009-1016.
A legal commentary that examines a recent case (*St. Regis Paper Co. v. United States*) that held that, under section 6(b) of the FTC Act, the agency had the right to obtain private copies of census information in order to complete an investigation. The petitioner had refused on grounds that the census information

was deemed privileged under the Census Act. Although this marks another example of the judiciary system upholding the Commission's investigatory requests, two policy questions arise. First, whether the census information is necessary in an investigation under Section 7 of the Clayton Act and, second, whether there is a basic conflict between the dissemination of confidential Census Bureau reports and the investigatory powers of the FTC. In addition, the decision leaves open the possibility that the effectiveness of the Census Act will be hindered because firms may not produce full and accurate reports for fear they may be used against them in future litigation.

530   Antitrust: Price Discrimination Under the Robinson-Patman Act."
George Washington Law Review 57 (May 1989): 1093-1121.

Examines in detail the decision of *Boise Cascade Corp. v. FTC* which applied provisions of the Robinson-Patman Act to buyers who receive discriminatory price discounts. The essay begins with an analysis of the specific provisions of the Act that applied to the case, discusses the history of the Boise decision, and concludes with an examination of the decision within the context of previous applications of the Act to issues related to buyer level injury cases. Particular focus is paid to the *FTC v. Morton Salt* case in which competitive injury could be inferred without direct evidence of injury if the price discrimination occurred over a long period of time. It is concluded that the Boise decision represents "dissatisfaction with the Act" stating that the Act actually causes price distortions in the marketplace.

531   Applebaum, Harvey M. "Allowances and Services Under the Robinson-Patman Act and the Revised FTC Advertising Guides." *Antitrust Law Journal* 59 (Fall 1990): 855-869.

Discusses the scope Sections 2(d) and (e) of the Robinson-Patman Act in relation to the Revised FTC Advertising Guides. The revised guides provoked a significant amount of interest and reaction from interested parties and represent an important update of guidelines regarding the provisions of the Act. The FTC Guides list examples of typical activities under the Sections. Specific cases are used to highlight requirements under the Act, such as product availability, proportionable equality among customers, and indirect customers who purchase the product for resale. Private actions and defenses are then studied. It is concluded that the new amendments to the Guides offer an improved picture of the current state of the law and the requirements under the two sections.

532 Armentano, Dominick T. *Antitrust and Monopoly: Anatomy of a Policy Failure.* 2nd ed. New York: Wiley, 1990.

Each of the nine chapters in this book present the author's views concerning the role antitrust law enforcement plays in the American marketplace and society in general. Two chapters in particular, "Price Discrimination and the Competitive Process" and "Mergers, Competition, and Antitrust Policy," use cases litigated by the FTC to provide a framework of understanding about antitrust law and the need for reform in some areas.

533 Armentano, Dominick T. "Time to Repeal Antitrust Regulation?" *Antitrust Bulletin* 35 (Summer 1990): 311-328.

The author discusses the "moderate" shift in antitrust enforcement by such institutions as the FTC since the mid-1970s in response to criticism that traditional antitrust enforcement has been misguided and actually contributes to hampering economic growth and consumer welfare. The author summarizes the antitrust efforts of the 1980s and notes four reasons given for repealing antitrust laws: 1) equilibrium theories are not relevant to current policy purposes; 2) nonlegal "barriers to entry" literature is both confusing and the efficiencies they represent are not harmful to consumer interests; 3) cases brought against businesses engaged in an intense competitive marketplace; and 4) merger enforcement and interfirm price agreements assume that antitrust regulators can evaluate the social costs and benefits as well. It is concluded that antitrust regulation should be abolished.

534 Aronson, Clifford H. and James A. Keyte. "Cutting the Suit to Fit the Cloth: Innovative Solutions to Merger Challenges by the DOJ and FTC." *Antitrust* 6 (Summer 1992): 26-30.

Discusses the advent of more innovative merger enforcement under Section 7 of the Clayton Act, including partial divestiture, licensing of important assets or technologies, and conduct degrees meant to preserve the competitive marketplace. It is noted that, with the dissemination of the Department of Justice and FTC Horizontal Merger Guidelines, parties need to be more cognizant of alleged anticompetitive effects before entering a market. Specific considerations are then covered in detail.

535 Arquit, Kevin J. "FTC Enforcement of Section 2 of the Sherman Act." *Antitrust Law Journal* 59 (Summer 1990): 547-552.

As Director of the FTC's Bureau of Competition, the author discusses the obligation of the Bureau to enforce Section 2 of the Sherman Act. Specific cases are used to highlight the benefits of anticompetitive enforcement and to examine the advantages of independent agency antitrust regulation. Issues such as predation and monopolization are reviewed to illustrate the possible future direction of the Commission in this area.

536   Arquit, Kevin J. "Perspectives on the 1992 U.S. Government Horizontal Merger Guidelines." *Antitrust Law Journal* 61 (Summer 1992): 121-139.

Comments on the Horizontal Merger Guidelines jointly issued by the Department of Justice and the FTC and highlights the changes that have been brought about by the new guidelines. Basic components of merger analysis, such as market shares and concentration, market entry, and unilateral and competitive effects, are outlined in detail.

537   Arquit, Kevin J. and Joseph Kattan. "Efficiency Considerations and Horizontal Restraints." *Antitrust Bulletin* 36 (Winter 1991): 717-732.

Draws on the FTC's experience with the health care industry as well as Supreme Court precedents to illustrate how efficiency considerations are analyzed by the FTC, specifically what defines efficiency, what is considered unacceptable efficiency claims, and "how efficiencies are weighed against a restraint's anticompetitive potential."

538   Aulette, C. L. and A. D. Schaffer. "Legality of the "Basing Point" Pricing System: Enforcement of Price Discrimination Provisions of the Clayton Act." *Georgetown Law Journal* 33 (May 1945): 439-451.

This article discusses the early use of the basing point pricing system by members of various industries, such as steel and cement, and the declaration by the FTC that, in general, this system was illegal. Other cases are used to show how the FTC defined its enforcement of the price discrimination provisions of the Clayton which had no specific reference to the basing point system. It is concluded that, while the Supreme Court has upheld the FTC's actions against firms using a basing point system, the ambiguity in the law still leaves questions unanswered.

539   Axinn, Stephen M. "Development in Mergers and Acquisitions." *Antitrust Law Journal* 58 (Summer 1989): 403-419.

Assesses the current mergers and acquisitions environment with regards to federal enforcement, including that by the FTC, developments in the courts and the state level, and proposed legislation targeted to international competition. Provides an overview of recent litigation successes and failures of the FTC in enforcing merger guidelines.

540   Azcuenaga, Mary L. "Essential Facilities and Regulation: Court or Agency Jurisdiction?" *Antitrust Law Journal* 58 (1989): 879-886.

Comments by the FTC Commissioner regarding the essential facilities doctrine and the possible role the FTC has in it. The author notes that while specific guidelines have not been issued by the FTC, several FTC cases have covered particular aspects of the doctrine. The author notes, however, that it is more efficient to enforce Section 7 of the FTC Act rather than rely on the essential facilities doctrine of regulation.

541   Bailey, Patricia P. "Antitrust, Prices, and "Wealth Transfers": A Small-Business Perspective at the FTC." *Antitrust Law and Economics Review* 15 (1983): 51-68.

Interview with FTC Commissioner Patricia P. Bailey, who discusses what she feels are the most critical issues faced by the FTC, including political pressure from the Executive Branch, and places much of the discussion about antitrust enforcement within a small business context.

542   Baker, Eugene R. and David J. Baum. "Section 5 of the Federal Trade Commission Act: A Continuing Process of Redefinition." *Villanova Law Review* 7 (Summer 1962): 517-562.

Attempts to show that the "unfair methods of competition" statement of the FTC Act can be an effective administrative tool and is flexible enough to react to "an ever-evolving commercial dexterity and the personal impact of economic power as important dimensions of trade." This fact remains despite recent criticism that the division of antitrust authority between the Department of Justice and the FTC is harmful to the mission of ensuring a competitive marketplace. An analysis of the legislative history of the FTC Act and the judicial reaction to it are detailed to show that "the operational truth behind the Congressional mandate" and to illustrate that the scope of the provision has not been narrowed during the past fifty years.

543   Baldwin, William L. *Market Power, Competition, and Antitrust Policy.* Homewood, IL: Irwin, 1987.

Each chapter in this book focuses on issues related with "the ability of firms to exercise monopolistic control over the prices of their products and to restrict entry into their markets." The book is intended as an intermediate or upper-level undergraduate text. Issues concerning the FTC include the control of advertising, the concept of shared monopolies, trade regulation rules, and trade practice conferences. Specific cases involving the FTC are referred to throughout the text.

544 Banta, Jr., Henry M. and H. Robert Field. "FTC Orders Issued Under the Price Discrimination Law: An Evaluation." *Antitrust Law and Economics Review* 3 (Winter 1969-70): 89-118.

The authors present evidence to support the argument that price discrimination has had a minimal effect on concentration in American industry, that the Robinson-Patman Price Discrimination Act has had no significant effect upon "the structure, conduct, or performance of any important American industry," that, given severe budget constraints faced by the FTC, its efforts could be better spent on other enforcement activities, and, finally, that since price discrimination is a phenomenon of monopoly power, it should be eliminated with the traditional remedies of dissolution and divestiture.

545 Barnes, David W. "Antitrust Dialogue on Social Science, Cultural Values, and Merger Law." *Antitrust Bulletin* 33 (Winter 1988): 623-653.

Text of a panel discussion that includes Jeffrey Zuckerman, Director of the Bureau of Competition at the FTC. The purpose of the discussion is to focus on the application of social science methodology in the decision-making process of policy makers. Zuckerman's comments focus on the role of the FTC in antitrust enforcement and placing this activity within the political framework of the Reagan Administration.

546 Barnes, David W. "Defining Unfairness: Empathy and Economic Analysis at the Federal Trade Commission." *Boston University Law Review* 68 (March 1989): 349-430.

This is a comprehensive essay that attempts to define unfairness in consumer contracts as it relates to FTC activities, provides an overview of the key arguments of those who criticize the Commission's handling of measuring and defining unfairness, and describes ways to improve the FTC's approach. The Credit Practices Rule is used as a basis for examining issues related to the agency's framework of understanding regarding unfairness in consumer contracts and the relationship that it has with and cost-benefit analysis and the marketplace.

547 Baum, D. J. "Antitrust Functions of the Federal Trade Commission: Area Discrimination and Product Differentiation." *Federal Bar Journal* 24 (Fall 1964): 579-608.

Analyzes the problem noted by some economists that antitrust laws attempt to change business practices, or behavior, rather than industry structure. Economists note that the two factors are related and that an industry's structure intimately affects behavior. This essay examines how existing antitrust laws and enforcement procedures by the FTC can be directed at industry structure rather than behavior. The author discusses the underlying philosophy of the antitrust laws and the FTC's relationship to that philosophy. The author concludes by using area discrimination and product differentiation as examples of how the FTC can affect market structure.

548 Bell, Robert B. and John A. Herfort. "Justice, FTC Signal Tougher Merger Enforcement Standards." *Antitrust* 4 (Summer 1990): 5-8.

Examines recent statements made by the FTC and the Department of Justice regarding the need to police anticompetitive mergers. The FTC's position concerning entry barriers are examined as well as specific litigation relevant to the issue of anticompetitive merger behavior.

549 Benson, Bruce l. et al. "Interest Groups and the Antitrust Paradox." *Cato Journal* 6 (Winter 1987): 801-817.

Places the legislative development of antitrust laws within the framework of a struggle between small and large economic entities seeking changes in the general economic environment rather than "special favors usually associated with special interest legislation." The origin and application of Judge Robert H. Bork's antitrust paradox thesis is discussed within the context of the study. The special interest forces behind the creation of the FTC is mentioned along with other antitrust statutes.

550 Bergson, Herbert A. "Regulation v. Competition." *Insurance Law Journal* 1956 (November 1956): 703-708.

Examines reaction by the insurance industry to the McCarren Act, which shifted the burden of regulating the insurance industry back to the states with several exemptions. Background is provided on the McCarren Act provisions, referred to as Public Law 15 within the insurance industry, and then analyzes both state and FTC reaction to the Act. It is concluded that the McCarren Act will help ensure a balance between regulation and competition within the insurance industry.

551   Bethell, Tom. "Breakfastgate: The FTC vs. The Cereal Companies." *Policy Review* 16 (Spring 1981): 13-32.

Discusses the market repercussions and implications for the U. S. economy if the courts side with the FTC in its case against the four major breakfast cereal manufacturers (Kellogg Company, General Mills, Inc., General Foods Corporation, and Quaker Oats Company). The agency charges that a shared monopoly exists between the four firms because they "avoid" price competition. The essay is critical of the FTC's remedy of splitting off three new companies from Kellogg and one each from General Mills and General Foods in order to break up the shared monopoly. In outlining the major point of the case and examining the FTC's reasoning in pursuing it for over nine years, it is pointed out that no direct evidence of tacit conspiracy exists. The essay also discusses the details behind the retirement and subsequent re-employment under FTC contract of Harold Hinkes, the judge that had presided over the case since the beginning.

552   Bialkin, Kenneth J. "Government Antitrust Enforcement and the Rules of Conduct." *Journal of Accountancy* 163 (May 1987): 105-109.

Measures both the direct and indirect effects of antitrust challenges brought forward by the Department of Justice and the FTC concerning rules governing the conduct of professionals. This article addresses how these regulations have affected standards of the American Institute of Certified Public Accountants (AICPA). The author notes difficulties in creating rules of conduct that keep pace with changing law.

553   "A Bibliography of Recent Antitrust Law Developments." *Antitrust Law Journal* 49 (Fall 1981): 1635-1672.

An unannotated bibliography divided into eight sections including a section devoted to antitrust enforcement by the FTC. The bibliography covers the past five years of scholarship in law reviews.

554   Bingaman, Anne K. and Janet D. Steiger. "Policy Statements of U.S. Justice department and FTC on Antitrust Enforcement in the Health-Care Industry." *Antitrust Law and Economics Review* 25 (1994): 25-27.

This article contains the text of a press release summarizing the six points contained in the Department of Justice and FTC's "Statements of Antitrust Enforcement Policy in the Health Care Area" issued September 15, 1993. The points presented articulate areas that the government will not challenge.

555 Blumenthal, William. "Market Imperfections and Overenforcement in Hart-Scott-Rodino Second Request Negotiations." *Antitrust Bulletin* 36 (Winter 1991): 745-820.
Examines the congressional intent behind the premerger notification provisions of Section 201 of the Hart-Scott-Rodino Antitrust Improvement Act of 1976 and the problems associated with its enforcement by the Department of Justice and the FTC. Section one of the article explores the legislative history of the Act. Section two examines burdens placed on merger parties associated with the gathering of information needed to comply with Second Requests. Section three analyzes the consequences of overenforcement of the Second Requests. Concludes with a summarization of findings and offers a set of proposals for changes to the requirements under the law. Analysis is based on the premiss that the requirements of the Section are burdensome and vulnerable to various market imperfections.

556 Briggs, Taylor R. et al. "Interview With James C. Miller III, Chairman, Federal Trade Commission." *ABA Antitrust Law Journal* 51 (March/April 1982): 3-21.
Text of an interview with FTC Chairman Miller in which he discusses initiatives begun under his leadership, followed by a set of questions and answers. Issues discussed include merger analysis, industrial concentration, and court cases affecting the antitrust enforcement role of the agency.

557 Briggs, John DeQ and Stephen Calkins. "Antitrust 1986-87: Power and Access (Part I)." *Antitrust Bulletin* 32 (Summer 1987): 275-333.
A two-part review of issues and developments related to antitrust law during the past year including activities of the FTC and an examination of key cases involving the agency.

558 "The Brokerage Provisions in the Robinson-Patman Act." *Illinois Law Review* 34 (November 1939): 319-331.
Critically examines the brokerage provision (Section 2 (c)) of the Robinson-Patman Act using three cases involving the FTC: *Great Atlantic & Pacific Tea Company v. FTC*, *Biddle Purchasing Company v. FTC*, and *Oliver Brothers v. FTC*. In all three cases, the FTC's actions were deemed appropriate with regards to prohibiting payments and allowances between buyers and sellers of goods.

559 Brown, Charles G. and Daniel N. Huck. "States Enforce Antitrust: Watching the Nation's Business." *Journal of State Government* 61 (May/June 1988): 115-117.
Outlines the response by state governments to enforce antitrust laws revitalized under the Hart-Scott-Rodino Antitrust Improvement Act of 1976 and the retreat by the FTC and the Department of Justice in antitrust matters due to budget cuts and a change in litigation priorities. Joint investigations between the states are discussed, illustrating that cooperative antitrust enforcement offers serious inroads into preventing antitrust violations. Information sharing with the FTC in pre-merger notices is also covered.

560 Brown, Harold. "Franchising: New Departures for Antitrust Law on Vertical Restraints." *New York Law Journal* 188 (December 9, 1982): 1, 4, 28.
Examines how the Reagan Administration and Congress have redefined the antitrust mission of the Department of Justice and the FTC with regards to vertical restraints. Both agencies have retreated from initiating action in vertical restraint cases. The FTC has done so under the guidance of James C. Miller III, the first economist appointed Chairman of the FTC. His conservative, economic based leadership is examined in detail. Specific cases are used to help predict the future direction of the FTC.

561 Bumpass, Donald. "The Social Costs of Monopoly: They May be Greater than We Thought." *Antitrust Law and Economics Review* 9 (1977): 91-101.
Argues that the results from recent studies, including those conducted by the FTC, concerning monopoly overcharges in the manufacturing industry and their impact on society are grossly underestimated.

562 Burda, David. "Mergers Thrive Despite Wailing about Adversity." *Modern Healthcare* 22 (October 12, 1992): 26-28, 30, 32.
Argues that declarations by hospitals stating that the recent efforts by the FTC and other government agencies to stifle mergers among health service providers are invalid. The author notes that, despite government controls, collaborative ventures among hospitals continues to "flourish." The reasons for these ventures are examined. The article contains quotes from numerous health care leaders that argue for or against continued antitrust enforcement. Specific FTC actions and proposed legislation before Congress are outlined.

563 Burling, Jr., Edward and William Du Bose Sheldon. "Price Competition as Affected by the Robinson-Patman Act." *Washington and Lee Law Review* 1 (Fall 1939): 31-62.

Examines the history of federal antitrust laws to illustrate the unique nature of the Robinson-Patman Act and how this uniqueness has led to criticism that the Act actually inhibits competition rather than enhancing it. Among the issues discussed is the role of the FTC in enforcing violations of price discrimination under provisions of Robinson-Patman, what factors are involved in setting prices for manufactured goods, and how these factors interact with the provisions of the Act. It is pointed out that resolution of the conflict must occur to ensure a healthy, competitive overall economy. The essay concludes with an appendix listing FTC cases brought against firms under the Robinson-Patman Act.

564 Burns, Arthur Robert. "The Anti-trust Laws and the Regulation of Price Competition." *Law and Contemporary Problems* 4 (June 1937): 301-320.

Provides a thorough analysis of the regulation of price competition by means of federal legislation. The Sherman Act, the Robinson-Patman Act, and the FTC Act are all examined in detail, comparing and contrasting how each control affects the price competition within the marketplace. The essay concludes by examining what effects the laws have had on the organization of distribution and the price policies of manufacturers, noting that the legislation presented by Congress has led to a general erosion of competition.

565 Burrus, Bernie R. and Ralph J. Savarese. "Institutional Decision-Making and the Problem of Fairness in FTC Antitrust Enforcement." *Georgetown Law Journal* 53 (Spring 1965): 656-674.

This study analyzes problems associated with decision-making processes within the FTC as it relates to fairness in antitrust enforcement by examining current FTC practice involving agency members, hearing examiners, and agency staff and the new rules of practice and procedure adopted by the FTC. Informal procedures are also examined. Based on this analysis, recommendations for institutional fairness incorporated into agency policies and procedures are then put forward.

566 Burrus, Bernie R. and Harry Teter. "Antitrust: Rulemaking v. Adjudication in the FTC." *Georgetown Law Journal* 54 (Summer 1966): 1106-1130.

Notes a shift in the FTC's antitrust enforcement activities away from certain adjudicatory enforcement procedures and more towards the use of rulemaking proceedings. This shift is most pronounced in the statements made by the FTC commissioners. However, by examining the effects and applicability of trade regulation rules and the legality of antitrust rulemaking given legislative intentions, it is concluded that the application of trade regulation to replace the adjudicatory process in antitrust enforcement is inappropriate given the number of questions left unresolved by the Commissioners.

567   Butler, Rush C. "Amending the Anti-trust Laws." *Proceedings of the Academy of Political Science* 11 (January 1926): 103-107.

Examines the rule of conduct articulated in the Sherman Act stating that any contract that unreasonably restrains trade is unlawful. The author proposes amending the Act by repealing its criminal provisions and enacting further legislation that would establish business standards and confer on an administrative agency the authority to determine whether an agreement conforms to or violates these standards. The author argues that the FTC is the logical choice to carry out this regulatory function and, thus, may actually reduce government intrusion into the business community.

568   Cabou, Christian G. et al. "An Analytic History of Delivered Price Litigation: Do Courts Properly Distinguish Rivalrous from Collusive Instances?" *Economic Inquiry* 30 (April 1992): 307-321.

Examines the development of delivered pricing as an antitrust problem. Delivered pricing refers to the price of a unit as applied "to output that is shipped by the seller to the buyer." This is in contrast to mill pricing which refers to the price of a unit of output that is acquired at the seller's place of business. Clashes with the antitrust laws occur when this delivered price system is applied to prices set relative to the location of the seller and the point of destination (the basing-point system). This system is viewed as increasing industrial concentration. This essay examines the enforcement of the Sherman Antitrust Act, the Clayton Act, and the FTC Act with regards to delivered pricing practices and the subsequent response by the judicial system to these enforcement activities. The essay concludes that the courts have been "seriously confused" about the economics of delivered pricing systems and that the vaguely worded powers granted to the FTC has created a "pernicious" pricing environment in which firms must operate.

569   Cahan, Steve E. "Accrual Choices of Oil Firms in Response to Vertical Divestiture Litigation and Legislation." *Petroleum Accounting and Financial Management* 10 (Summer 1991):168-194.

The purpose of this paper is to analyze whether oil firms had reduced their discretionary accruals in response to an FTC antitrust lawsuit against eight companies accused of monopolistic behavior and in response to Senate Bill 2387 that would have required vertical divestiture of the oil firms. Both actions were primarily a reaction to enormous profits earned by the companies during the 1974 oil crisis. Employing a political cost hypothesis, the study indicates that the oil firms indeed lowered their discretionary accruals when the FTC and Senate actions were being considered. The study also contributes to a greater understanding of the issue because the effect of specific political actions allows causal relationships to be considered, the time-series approach enhances traditional cross-sectional tests, and the paper brings a greater focus to a set of firms that "have been used anecdotally as an example of an industry vulnerable to large political costs."

570   Cain, Clarissa and Max Weiner. "Consumers and the Oligopoly Problem: Agenda for a Reformed FTC." *Antitrust Law and Economics Review* 3 (Spring 1970): 9-20.

Text of a position paper by the Consumer Federation of America that makes numerous recommendations to help solidify the FTC's economic enforcement position. Among the recommendations is the creation of a systematic study of the oligopoly in the United States, begin annual reports to Congress and the president that cover the state of the nation's competitive economy and report on the performance of various regulated industries, expand FTC's economic investigation jurisdiction, and issue a trade regulation rule that requires advertisers to submit their advertisements prior to public consumption if certain conditions exist.

571   Calamari, Robert C. "*FTC v. Superior Court Trial Lawyers Association*: Per Se Analysis and the Supreme Court's Limitation on First Amendment Protection for Antitrust Violations." *University of Toledo Law Review* 23 (Fall 1991): 199-225.

This article examines the Supreme Court decision rendered in the *FTC v. Superior Court Trial Lawyers Association* case against the backdrop of the per se standard and the rule of reason doctrine which are applied to Sherman Act cases. The note concludes that the decision puts undue limitations on the analysis of antitrust violations and blocks future attempts "to make beneficial changes to the marketplace." Views of both the majority and dissenting opinions are examined.

572   Calkins, Stephen. "Commentary: Federal Trade Commissioner Terms are Too Long." *Antitrust* 8 (Spring 1994): 46-47.
Notes that all the present commissioners at the FTC were appointed by Republicans and, therefore, there is no one currently present to speak for the Clinton Administration. The author argues that the Congress should conform FTC commissioner terms to those of the Securities and Exchange Commission which are limited to five years rather than seven.

573   Calkins, Stephen. "Supreme Court Antitrust 1991-92: The Revenge of the Amici." *Antitrust Law Journal* 61 (Winter 1993): 269-311.
Reviews three cases involving antitrust and the Supreme Court– *FTC v. Ticor Title Insurance Co.*, *Morales v.TWA*, and *Kodak C. v. Image Technical Services, Inc.* The Ticor case involved an FTC decision "condemning five large title insurance companies' use of rating bureaus in Arizona, Connecticut, Montana, New Jersey, Pennsylvania, and Wisconsin." The Supreme Court's majority, dissent, and concurrence opinions are analyzed in detail in order to highlight key issues.

574   Calvani, Terry. "Antitrust Risks for Standards Developers." *ASTM Standardization News* 15 (October 1987): 60-66.
Antitrust officials at the FTC have paid increased attention to the standards industry. This essay first describes how antitrust laws are applicable to standards activities, then analyzes issues relevant to standards developers under current antitrust laws, and finally, describes recent FTC activities in the standards industry. Relevant issues include the amount of evidence needed to justify restrictive standards, patents, and the Noerr-Pennington Doctrine. It is concluded that, while widespread violations do not occur in the standards industry, standards officials should be aware of FTC antitrust activities.

575   Calvani, Terry. "Effect of Current Developments on the Future of the Robinson-Patman Act." *Antitrust Law Journal* 48 (Fall 1980): 1692-1709.
Recent cases involving the FTC, coupled with pronouncements by the FTC and

the Department of Justice, have had a measurable impact on the enforcement of the Robinson-Patman Act. This essay examines the implications of these developments for the future. Statistics of the FTC's involvement in Robinson-Patman Act enforcement over the past fifteen years are used to track the radical decline in their enforcement are used to place the current developments within historical context.

576   Calvani, Terry. "A Proposal for Radical Change." *Antitrust Bulletin* 34 (Spring 1989): 185-207.
The essay is based on remarks by the author (an FTC Commissioner) before the American Law Institute-American Bar Association Course of Study-Antitrust Law symposium in which he discusses three problems associated with structure of the current FTC: accountability, the alleged unconstitutionality of the agency, and the perception of unfairness. The creation of a General Counsel appointed by the President and subject to conformation by the Senate is proposed to alleviate these problems. The Counsel would serve the president and thereby leave the agency to "simply hear cases that were brought before the agency."

577   Calvani, Terry and Andrew G. Berg. "Resale Price Maintenance after Monsanto: A Doctrine Still at War with Itself." *Duke Law Journal* 1984 (1984): 1163-1204.
Reviews the correlation between resale price maintenance and its effect on the marketplace by using the rulings set forth in relevant cases, considering the antitrust policy ramifications of resale price maintenance and exploring possible reasons why it could be pro-competitive, and examining the case of *Monsanto Co. v. Spray-Rite Serv. Corp.* to illustrate the critical issues present in resale price maintenance. The essay concludes with a discussion of the implications for future litigation that the Monsanto decision provides, including the Supreme Court's refusal to reaffirm the per se illegality of resale price maintenance and supporting the treatment of evidence as stated in the Colgate decision.

578   Calvani, Terry and Neil W. Averitt. "The Federal Trade Commission and Competition in the Delivery of Health Care." *Cumberland Law Review* 17 (Spring 1987): 293-312.
Outlines the role of the FTC in regulating the health care industry within the context of both antitrust and consumer protection matters. Specific issues examined include pricing policies, advertising by health care professionals, hospital staff privileges, peer review, and group boycotts. Given specific factors

associated with these issues, it is concluded that the FTC's role should remain unobtrusive and intervention should occur only when self-regulation fails to insure a competitive marketplace.

579   Campbell, Thomas J. "Antitrust Enforcement at the FTC: An Interview, Part I." *Antitrust Law and Economics Review* 14 (1982): 91-110.

Interview with the Director of the Bureau of Competition at the FTC in which he expresses his views concerning the protection of the marketplace, consumer advocacy, and collusion among firms.

580   Campbell, Thomas J. "The Antitrust Record of the First Reagan Administration." *Texas Law Review* 64 (October 1985): 353-369.

Discusses the antitrust goals of the Reagan administration which are rooted in economic efficiency from the perspective of the consumer, including how the administration attempted to influence the activities of the FTC; this is particularly true with regards to horizontal price restraints and merger guidelines.

581   Campbell, Thomas J. "The Competition Mission: Guiding Principles and Future Directions." *Antitrust Law Journal* 51 (1982): 541-551.

Discusses the FTC's efforts in antitrust law enforcement in four specific areas: general mergers, horizontal activities, vertical activities, and intervention. Each of these areas are examined within the context of economic considerations and the "competition" between economists and lawyers within the Commission.

582   Cannon, Joseph P. and Paul N. Bloom. "Are Slotting Allowances Legal Under the Antitrust Laws?" *Journal of Public Policy and Marketing* 10 (Spring 1991): 167-186.

The authors analyzes the use of slotting allowances, or the requirement that packaged goods manufacturers pay an up-front cash payment, by retail grocers before they will put a new product on the shelf and whether these allowances are legal under current antitrust laws. Concerns stated by manufacturers, grocery retailers, and policy makers are outlined. Arguments that may be presented in cases involving small manufacturers, small retailers, and the FTC are analyzed, concluding that, while private suits may ultimately be successful, the FTC is best suited to pursue a case involving slotting allowances.

583   Carstenson, P. C. and N. H. Questal. "Use of Section 5 of the Federal Trade Commission Act to Attack Larger Conglomerate Mergers." *Cornell Law Review* 63 (1978): 841-878.

Because conglomerate mergers are mergers among large firms that are engaged in unrelated industries and thus, neither vertical nor horizontal in nature, the applicability of Section 7 of the Clayton Act has been put into question. This article attempts to show the merits of using Section 5 of the FTC Act as an appropriate alternative, given the shortcomings of the Clayton Act and the legislative history and legal interpretation of Section 5. Specific cases are referred to throughout the text to support the author's argument.

584   Cies, Ralph D. "Costing Problems Posed by the Robinson-Patman Act." *Harvard Business Review* 17 (Spring 1939): 350-355.

Hearings held by the FTC have helped to focus attention on how cost accounting procedures are effected by the Robinson-Patman Act. These effects are examined in relation to the enforcement procedures of the FTC concerning provisions of Robinson-Patman. It is concluded that cost data is based on "judgement and opinion" and that there exists no mathematical way to determine true cost. The FTC has done little to clarify the problem because it has not conducted a comprehensive study of cost accounting procedures and has ignored the judgement element in creating cost data by manufacturers.

585   Clanton, David A. "Antitrust Realities and Directions." *Chicago Bar Record* 62 (March/April 1981): 230-232, 234, 236-237, 238.

Recent criticism of antitrust laws argue that the laws hinder competitive opportunities overseas and contributes to an unhealthy competitive environment at home. As a Commissioner of the FTC, the author reviews criticism of current antitrust laws and offers five specific suggestions for improving and redefining the antitrust enforcement policy of the FTC.

586   Clanton, David A. "Evolving Antitrust World Could Use FTC Guidance." *Legal Times of Washington* 5 (March 21, 1983): 12.

Examines the "new age of enlightenment" in antitrust law enforcement, which embraces revised economic reasoning, and discusses what role the FTC plays in providing guidance.

587   Clanton, David A. "The Reagan Antitrust Legacy: The Contribution of the FTC." *Federal Bar News and Journal* 35 (June 1988): 238-241.
Studies what role the Reagan Administration has had in influencing the antitrust policies of the FTC and the long-terms effects that this influence will have. Predictions are that, regardless of the future political environment, an upsurge in antitrust enforcement activities by the FTC is likely.

588   Clanton, David A. "Report from the Federal Trade Commission." *Antitrust Law Journal* 50 (1982): 145-150.
Report by the FTC chairman concerning the role of the Commission in promoting competition and providing a forum for addressing alleged antitrust violations. The institutional philosophy embraced by the agency to accomplish this task is also covered.

589   Clanton, David A. "Trade Associations and the FTC." *Antitrust Bulletin* 22 (Summer 1977): 307-315.
As a Commissioner within the FTC, the author outlines the relationship between trade associations and the FTC. Included in the discussion is the implications and impact of recent FTC actions, the FTC's interest in relative value scales that may violate antitrust laws under the concept that such pricing scales may fix or influence the establishment of fees by physicians, and what actions trade associations can take to avoid FTC orders.

590   Clark, Barbara A. "Merger Investigations at the Federal Trade Commission: An Insider's View." *Antitrust Law Journal* 56 (1987): 765-778.
As Deputy Directory of Mergers and Administration at the FTC, the author provides insight into the merger investigation activities of the agency and the trends in remedial options. It is noted by the author that these activities are undergoing constant revision and review.

591   Clark, John W. and Mary Lou Steptoe. *The Antitrust Division and the FTC Speak on Current Developments in Federal Antitrust Enforcement 1992.* New York, NY: Practicing Law Institute, 1992.
This publication is a course handbook that examines the new joint merger guidelines of the FTC and Department of Justice. Each essay examines a different aspect of the merger guidelines, including initial observations, identification of firms in the relevant marketplace, market definition, the role of market power in

antitrust merger analysis. Papers are from a program held in Washington, DC, November 12-13, 1992 and are not indexed.

592   Clarke, Donald C. "Antitrust Law–Proposed Consent Agreement Between General Motors Corporation and Toyota Motor Corporation." *Harvard International Law Journal* 25 (Spring 1984): 421-427.

States that the consent order issued by the FTC allowing a joint venture between General Motors and Toyota to proceed contains broad implications because it may mark a relaxation of antitrust standards, specifically in regards to joint ventures between competitors. This note details the specific scope of the consent order and defines terms applicable to its provisions.

593   "Clayton Act–FTC Actions and the Requirements of Section 5." *University of Colorado Law Review* 42 (August 1970): 189-195.

Uses two recently decided cases from the Supreme Court, *Minnesota Mining and Manufacturing, Co. v. New Jersey Wood Finishing Co.* and *Lippa's Inc. v. Lenox, Inc.*, to examine the early judicial opposition to treble damages awarded in antitrust cases and the subsequent development of favorable conditions for such awards after a 1965 Supreme Court decision laid the foundation for the two recent cases. Both cases evolved out of proceedings conducted by the FTC to enforce antitrust laws. It is concluded that the trend established from these rulings indicates that a plaintiff could attempt to use an FTC order issued to enforce Section 5(a) of the FTC Act as evidence sufficient enough under the judgement of law to establish a given fact (prima facie) in a subsequent private suit.

594   Coate, Malcolm B. "Horizontal Restraints in the Professions." *Antitrust Bulletin* 34 (Winter 1989): 775-796.

Reviews the economics of horizontal restraints to set the stage for an analysis of the FTC's rule of reason standard regarding horizontal agreements within professions. It is argued that the FTC's suspect conduct standard is likely "to reduce industry output" because of overenforcement. By examining certain circumstances associated with antitrust investigations in the professions, it is concluded that market power must be taken into consideration if the rule of reason standard is to be appropriately applied.

595   Coate, Malcolm et al. "Fight, Fold, or Settle: Modelling the Reaction to FTC Merger Challenges." *Economic Inquiry* 33 (October 1995): 537-551.

The third stage of any legal dispute, as identified by legal scholars, is negotiation between a plaintiff and defendant that determines if a claim is settled or not. The path to reconciliation can lead to one of three outcomes for the firm: fighting the action, conceding wrongdoing ("folding"), or settling. This study examines this process of negotiation within the procedural framework of interaction between a private party accused of violating antitrust laws in horizontal mergers and the FTC. The primary hypothesis of the study is that the nature of a case is perhaps more important from the perspective of a firm than the competitive merits of the action itself. Applying an econometric model that measures what negotiation path a firm chooses when confronted with an FTC action supports the hypothesis that the nature of the case, and not the merits of the action, drive the merger procedure. The findings provide insight into the firm's decision-making process and the influence of politics in shaping the outcome.

596   Coate, Malcolm B. and Fred S. McChesney. "Empirical Evidence on FTC Enforcement of the Merger Guidelines." *Economic Inquiry* 30 (April 1992):277-293.

The authors utilize data gathered in a previous study of seventy horizontal mergers from 1982 through 1986 to examine whether the FTC has followed the Merger Guidelines promulgated by the Department of Justice and supported by the Reagan Administration. Subsequent studies are also incorporated into the data. After discussing the provisions of the guidelines and explaining the data used for testing, the paper concludes that the Guidelines have not been applied to FTC merger challenges. Measures of concentration support this view most vividly. It is also shown that both the Chicago School and structuralist models can predict the FTC's decisions "reasonably well" but are still inferior to the probability model that incorporates political influence variables.

597   Coate, Malcolm B. et al. "Bureaucracy and Politics in FTC Merger Challenges." *Journal of Law and Economics* 33 (October 1990): 463-482.

Uses nonpublic material from the FTC to examine decisions by the agency to challenge horizontal mergers. The analysis places the responsiveness of the FTC within the context of merger guidelines, internal agreement or disagreement among its legal personnel, and pressure from politicians. This model is tested against decisions rendered between 1982 and 1986. Among the conclusions is the apparent fact that Congressional pressure to intervene in a merger case "significantly" increases the likelihood that the FTC will act and that, while the Reagan Administration's position regarding mergers is based on economic concerns, this study shows that politics still plays a part in influencing the FTC's merger activities.

598   Cohn, Fletcher G. "Some Practical Aspects of Conducting an Antitrust Hearing Before the Federal Trade Commission." *Antitrust Bulletin* 4 (September-October 1959): 665-674.

The author outlines the policies and procedures involved in conducting an antitrust hearing. Included in the discussion is an analysis of the role of the Examiner and rules set up to insure no conflict of interest between the Examiner and the subject of the case. The increasing role economic evidence is playing in formulating action is also discussed.

599   Collins, Wayne D. "Rigor and Sophistry in the New Merger Guidelines." *The American Enterprise* 4 (March 1993): 60-71.

This article examines the Department of Justice and FTC jointly issued administrative guidelines that defines for the first time how both agencies will regulate mergers and acquisitions. These joint guidelines mark an improvement over previous guidelines because they lay the economic groundwork for analyzing the competitive consequences of horizontal consolidations and view antitrust not as an exercise in law enforcement, but as a form of economic regulation. However, three issues remain unresolved. First, the guidelines do not always present the economics correctly, leaving room for misinterpretation by attorneys and government prosecutors. Second, the guidelines fail to give meaningful guidance in several areas, which opens up the possibility for "hidden guidelines." Third, both agencies have stated that the guidelines do not define their conduct in merger litigation. This last point erodes agency accountability, adds to the hidden agenda problem, and undermines the agency's public interest mission of assisting the courts in following the best possible route in merger and acquisition litigation. The article concludes with a discussion of how the Clinton Administration will view these guidelines in light of its own regulatory agenda.

600   Colver, William B. "The Federal Trade Commission and the Meat Packing Industry." *Annals of the Academy of Political and Social Science* 82 (March 1919): 170-174.

As Chairman of the FTC, the author reports the findings of the FTC concerning combinations and agreements among a group of meat-packing firms. This control of the market is based on the division of purchases of livestock in specific and fixed percentages within the group. The FTC report on the meat-packing industry recommends that Congress pass legislation that will reestablish a competitive marketplace.

601   Comanor, W. S. "Antitrust in a Political Environment." *Antitrust Bulletin* 27 (Winter 1982): 733-752.

Examines in detail the FTC suit against Exxon Corporation as well as other suits involving oil companies to illustrate what effects the intervention of political forces have on antitrust law enforcement, including shaping its direction and influencing antitrust outcomes. No attempt is made by the author to defend or criticize the effects of political intervention, but to simply "evaluate the process of antitrust policy-making."

602   "Comments by the Section of Antitrust Laws, American Bar Association on the Proposed Revisions to the Federal Trade Commission Rules Pursuant to the Federal Trade Commission Improvement Act of 1980." *Antitrust Law Journal* 49 (Winter 1981): 389-396.

This article contains comments submitted by the American Bar Association's Antitrust Section regarding revisions to the FTC's rules of practice implementing certain sections of the FTC Improvement Act of 1980. The ABA urges the FTC "to consider a broader range of possible improvements" concerning its rulemaking procedures. The text of the specific recommendations are included.

603   Cooper, Ann. "FTC Suits Spur Congress to Protect Cities from Paying Antitrust Damages." *National Journal* 16 (August 4, 1981): 573-577.

The author studies FTC antitrust enforcement intervention in local government functions. Two suits filed against the taxicab industry in Minneapolis and New Orleans illustrate the Commission's willingness to enter into antitrust enforcement activities to compensate for inaction by local governments. However, local officials view FTC action as simply "a new form of federal meddling" and another example of an agency that has overstepped its bounds of useful authority. Interviews with city officials from Minneapolis and New Orleans are conducted to illustrate this point.

604   Copeland, Melvin T. "The Problems of Administering the Robinson-Patman Act." *Harvard Business Review* 15 (Winter 1937): 156-173.
This essay examines key issues associated with the administration and enforcement of the Robinson-Patman Act, most notably by the FTC. The procedures that need to be instituted to ensure the Act is effective and what conditions must be met within the business environment that relate to the Act's provisions are discussed in detail. Specific forms of discrimination, such as various types of discounts and advertising allowances, are then outlined. The author concludes that the FTC has been handed an important opportunity and must proceed in a responsible fashion in order to take advantage of the doctrine of price policy that has recently developed in the United States.

605   Cottin, Jonathan. "Economic Report: Increased Corporation Antitrust Suits Prompt Industry Fears of New Federal Policy." *National Journal* 5 (September 15, 1973): 1367-1373.
This essay is an analysis of the impact caused by the increased number of antitrust suits against big business by the FTC. Concern among business leaders has peaked since the FTC issued a complaint against eight of the largest oil companies that could lead to divestiture of some of their holdings. Observers note several reasons for the FTC's increased enforcement activity, including a general shift away from "nickel and dime prosecutions" to more substantial antitrust activity, a response to political pressures to address high inflation and its impact on consumers, and a more liberal interpretation by the FTC of antitrust laws beyond original Congressional intent.

606   Cousins, N. "Food for the Trust-Busters: Unpublished Report of FTC Says that a Few Large Corporations Dominate Main Food Industries." *Current History* 48 (February 1938): 26-30.
Discusses allegations reported by the FTC to the Franklin Roosevelt Administration that a few large organizations have monopolized the diary, livestock, and wheat industries. The report also examines the effects these food monopolies have had on the American family farm. Efforts by the FTC to obtain information for the eight volume report (officially known as the "Agricultural Income Inquiry") are outlined, along with reaction in Congress to the allegations contained in it.

607   Crampton, Paul S. "The DOJ/FTC 1992 Horizontal Merger Guidelines: A Canadian Perspective." *Antitrust Bulletin* 38 (Fall 1993): 665-713.
Provides a comparative analysis of the joint Department of Justice and FTC Horizontal Merger Guidelines and the Canadian Merger Enforcement Guidelines. The author notes the similarities between the two guidelines, outlines the development of each, and notes that both are a model for similar guidelines throughout the world. Market definition, concentration, competitive effects, entry, efficiencies, and failure and exiting assets are all compared in detail.

608   Curnin, Paul C. "United States Antitrust Law and Industrial Policy: International Joint Ventures and Global Competition after GM-Toyota." *Fordham International Law Journal* 9 (Spring 1986): 257-294.
The essay begins by describing the evolution of the application of U.S. antitrust laws to international joint ventures, argues that the recently settled complaint issued by the FTC challenging a joint venture between General Motors and Toyota represents an industrial policy, and concludes that antitrust law enforcement through an industrial policy is preferable to protectionist legislation. It is noted that any industry suffering from the effects of anticompetitive behavior should weigh their options under the GM-Toyota precedent.

609   Davidson, J. R. "FTC, Robinson-Patman, and Cooperative Promotional Activities." *Journal of Marketing* 32 (January 1968): 14-17.
The article begins by outlining the FTC's changing emphasis on antitrust enforcement and then uses sections 2(d) and (e) of the Robinson-Patman amendments to the Clayton Act to examine how the FTC is seeking voluntary compliance with the amendment's provisions through informal methods such as education, guidance, and advice. Reaction by industries and the business community are also discussed, noting the development by many of trade regulation rules that were created in cooperation with the FTC.

610   "Debate: The Federal Trade Commission Under Attack: Should the Commission's Role be Changed?" *ABA Antitrust Law Journal* 49 (August 1980): 1481-1497.
Text of a panel discussion that attempts to address what role the FTC has in antitrust law enforcement and protection of consumers from unfair business practices in light of recent legislation from Congress affecting the FTC. This legislation eventually took the form of the FTC Improvement Act. The panelists discuss criticisms laid out in the 1969 American Bar Association report and

examines whether those criticism are still valid today. Issues such as dual enforcement and future Congressional involvement are covered in detail.

611   Decker, R. K. "New Directions for the Federal Trade Commission: Introductory Remarks." *ABA Antitrust Law Journal* 42 (1972-72): 55-77.

Text of a panel discussion which begins by examining the impact of the *FTC v. Sperry and Hutchinson Co.* case and how the case reinforces Section 5 of the FTC Act as an independent tool in antitrust enforcement. The discussion then considers how the Sperry case will affect FTC rulemaking in the future and concludes with a discussion of corrective advertising.

612   De Jong, H. W. "Antitrust and International 'Competitiveness': The European Experience Parts I, II, III, IV." *Antitrust Law and Economics Review* 18 and 19 (1986 and 1987): Part I: 91-110; Part II: 85-110; Part III: 79-98.; Part IV: 49-64.

This is a four part interview with Dr. H. W. de Jong, a professor of economics at the University of Amsterdam. The interview provides insights into the antitrust approach of the Common Market. The most notably difference between antitrust policy between the United States and Europe is the use of economists in Europe as active members of the policy making process. In the United States economists are primarily serve as "technically expert witness in the employ of lawyers." Dr. de Jong uses the FTC as an example to back up this point and is referred to throughout the interview.

613   Delorme, Charles D., Jr. et al. "Special-Interest-Group Perspectives Before and After the Clayton and Federal Trade Commission Acts." *Applied Economics* 28 (July 1996): 773-777.

Using data of relative prices and relative industry output from 1904 to 1925 representing the eleven year period prior to and following passage of the Clayton and Federal Trade Commission Acts and comparing the results to performance data from 1890 to 1901, the eleven year period prior to and following passage of the Sherman Act, the authors support previous research showing that antitrust legislation is just as vulnerable to special interest group agendas as other forms of public interest legislation. The findings refute the central thesis of public interest theory stating that antitrust laws protect and serve the public good through market regulation and control of business behavior.

614   Demkovich, Linda E. "There's No Quick Solution Likely to the Ready-to-Eat Cereal Case." *National Journal* 9 (July 9, 1977): 1071-1075.

Reviews the FTC's case against the four largest cereal manufacturers alleging they conspired to keep competitors out of the marketplace and cooperated in maintaining high profit margins through artificially high prices, brand proliferation, heavy advertising, and special arrangements with grocery stores for premium shelf space. Remedies proposed by the FTC, legal questions, and possible outcomes are examined in detail.

615   Denger, M. L. "Unfairness Standard and FTC Rulemaking: The Controversy over the Scope of the Commission's Authority." *Antitrust Law Journal* 49 (Summer 1980): 53-108.

Provides an overview of the changes in attitudes among many scholars, critics, and government officials concerning the scope of the FTC's rulemaking authority through the Magnuson-Moss-FTC Improvement Act and it's liberal use of the unfairness standard. It is concluded that, while the promulgation of policy statements by the FTC defining its goals is an important step in addressing the concerns of critics, the agency must endeavor to continue provide further clarification as developments warrant.

616   Dilks, Russell C. "A Stepchild Gains Small Favor: The FTC and the Meeting Competition Defense Under the Robinson-Patman Act." *Business Lawyer* 21 (January 1966): 481-497.

Examines the development of the "meeting competition defense," in which prices are lowered to meet a competitors prices and its relationship to selective price discrimination violations under the Robinson-Patman Act. The analysis is placed within the context of recent FTC positions taken that attempt to put limitations on the meeting competition defense. An analysis of how these provisions relate to specific court cases is also examined. It is concluded that these tests used by the FTC offer little hope to companies thinking of using this defense in any price discrimination litigation.

617   Dingell, J. D. et al. "Dingell Report on FTC's Enforcement of the Robinson-Patman Act: "Findings" and Recommendations." *Antitrust Law and Economics Review* 3 (Summer 1970): 53-82.

The authors outline the findings and recommendations of the White House Task Force Report on Antitrust Policy as viewed by the Special Subcommittee on Small

Business and the Robinson-Patman Act. The essay specifically discusses the need for major revisions to the Robinson-Patman Act. The Act is viewed as ineffective and drawing too much of the FTC's antitrust enforcement attention away from more appropriate issues related to anticompetitive behavior, most notably oligopolies. The report also recommends the need to develop further empirical data to insure proper application of Robinson-Patman in the future.

618   "The Distinction Between the Scope of Section 2(a) and Section 2(d) and 2(e) of the Robinson-Patman Act." *Michigan Law Review* 83 (May 1985): 1584-1602.

Discusses the price discrimination distinctions between Section 2(a) and 2(d) and (e) of the Robinson-Patman Act, noting that problems may arise if a seller's discriminatory behavior falls within the scope of both sections. The comment argues that the courts should determine if Section 2(a) applies and if so, apply it to the exclusion of the other two sections. The comment concludes by presenting an analytical framework for distinguishing between indirect price discrimination from service and facility discrimination.

619   Dixon, Paul Rand. "Federal Trade Commission in 1961." *Antitrust Law Symposium* 1962 (1962): 16-28.

Reviews the activities of the FTC during 1961. Issues covered include agency reorganization, revision of its Rules of Practice, and developments in the case law.

620   Dixon, Paul Rand. "Federal Trade Commission in 1962." *Antitrust Law Symposium* 1963 (1963): 28-39.

Reviews the activities of the FTC during 1962. Issues covered include the increased number of cease and desist orders issued by the FTC and how this fits into the new reorganization efforts and developments in the case law.

621   Dixon, Paul Rand. "Federal Trade Commission in 1963." *Antitrust Law Symposium* 1964 (1964): 18-26.

Reviews the activities of the FTC during 1963. Issues covered include highlighting specific merger-related cases as well as general developments in the case law.

622   Dixon, Paul Rand. "FTC in 1966: Some Hopes and Resolutions." *Antitrust Law Symposium* 1966 (1966): 19-33.

Discusses future activities of the FTC for 1966. Issues covered include the tightening budget and its affect of agency performance, emphasis on protecting the consumer, and reviewing select cases affecting FTC actions in the antitrust arena.

623   Dixon, Paul Rand. "Some Impediments to Policy Making." *Antitrust Law Symposium* 1969 (1969): 21-28.

Under the theme "Antitrust in a Changing Society," the Chairman of the FTC addresses the issue of barriers to formulating effective long-range plans related to antitrust policy making. Three impediments are discussed: the budgetary process, the Judges Act of 1925, and Supreme Court decisions.

624   Dixon, Paul Rand. "Trademarks, the Federal Trade Commission, and the Lanham Act." *Trademark Reporter* 68 (July-August 1978): 463-470.

Based upon an address given at the United States Trademark Association's annual conference, this essay examines the relationships among trademarks, provisions of the Lanham Act, and efforts by the FTC to enforce those provisions based on maintaining competition within the marketplace. Six actions under which the Commission may take action are outlined. It is noted that, while the FTC does not commit a large amount of resources to regulating trademarks, the agency is always alert to trademarks that may have become "generic."

625   Dolan, R. J. "How an Association is Investigated and What is the Government Looking For: A Federal Trade Commission Perspective." *Antitrust Bulletin* 22 (Summer 1977): 273-286.

As Assistant Director at the FTC's Bureau of Competition, the author describes the Bureau's investigations of several national associations for evidence of horizontal restraint of trade activities and based on the FTC' concern over the growing economic power these associations wielded. The author continues by outlining what factors are taken into consideration in an investigation.

626   Dole, Elizabeth H. "Cost-Benefit Analysis Versus Protecting the Vulnerable: The FTC's Special Interest Groups." *Antitrust Law and Economics Review* 9 (1977): 15-27, 29-30.

Discusses the use of cost-benefit analysis as a basis for formulating regulations at the FTC associated with protecting the consumer while at the same time identifying areas that are not easily accommodated by the benefit measurement. Examples include dissemination of information to consumers and the issuance of regulations in the field of health and safety. It is concluded that government must recognize the special needs of certain groups and that critics of overregulation must be aware that not all regulations can be measured purely in quantitative or economic terms.

627   Dougherty, Jr., A. F. and K. M. Davidson. "Limitation Without Regulation: The FTC's Bureau of Competition Approach to Conglomerate Mergers." *Utah Law Review* 1980 (1980): 95-154.

This study analyzes the Bureau of Competition's legislative proposal that would limit firm growth among the largest companies in America through acquisitions and mergers. The proposal would allow even large firm mergers if it paralleled that action with divestiture of currently held business operations that were comparable in size. A framework of understanding is first created by describing the growth in mergers in the United States during the late 1970s. The author notes that the proposal does not eliminate mergers, just those that are used to increase a firm's size in the marketplace. The article ends with a proposed Section 7(b) to the Clayton Act followed by a subsection by subsection analysis of the Section.

628   Douglas, George W. "Antitrust Policies in the Eighties at the Federal Trade Commission." 35 *Federal Bar News and Journal* 35 (June 1988): 232-237.

Reviews a number of specific court cases in order to analyze two traditional antitrust enforcement initiatives of the FTC--nonprice vertical restraints and price discrimination under the Robinson-Patman Act. The analysis is placed within the context of policies and goals of the Reagan administration and the efforts of the FTC Chairman James C. Miller III. The essay begins with a brief overview of the development of merger policy and enforcement.

629   Dwyer, Paula. "The Reagan Revolution in Antitrust Won't Fade Away." *Business Week (Industrial/Technology Edition)* (April 18, 1988): 29.

Examines the prospects for tougher antitrust enforcement under the Bush Administration after a period of "laissez-faire" enforcement under President Reagan. It is noted, however, that the "Reagan Revolution" has had a lasting effect on antitrust policy. Foreign competition from countries such as Japan and the view that mergers should only be blocked if the consumer is harmed substantially are examples of this new view, even among Democrats. The role of the FTC within this new merger environment is briefly covered.

630   Easterbrook, Frank H. "The Limits of Antitrust." *Texas Law Review* 63 (August 1984): 1-40.

Argues that the current methods employed to enforce antitrust laws and remedy anticompetitive behavior, such as the rule of reason and the per se rule, are inadequate and an "imperfect" tool for regulating competition. An alternative approach based on a series of "filters" designed to screen out beneficial conduct but pass unwanted behavior is proposed. This approach would also allow for screening to be done on a category of case basis rather than on a case-by-case basis. Five "filters" are described: market power, relation between profit and reduced competition, adoption of identical practices, effect on output and survival of the firm, and identity of the plaintiff.

631   Eckbo, B. Epsen and Peggy Wier. "Antimerger Policy Under the Hart-Scott-Rodino Act: A Reexamination of the Market Power Hypothesis." *Journal of Law and Economics* 27 (April 1985): 119-149.

Examines a number of cases filed after 1978 by the FTC and the Department of Justice under Section 7 of the Clayton Act to determine if the Hart-Scott-Rodino Antitrust Improvements Act has enhanced the agency's ability to select anti-competitive mergers, and specifically horizontal mergers, for prosecution. The study is based on the assumption that legal constraints are present based on a study by Eckbo and Stillman that used stock price data to determine if merger challenges by the government between 1963 and 1978 did in fact represent anticompetitive behavior on the part of the firms involved. In the current study, it is concluded that there is no evidence that the Hart-Scott-Rodino Act's provision that imposes automatic delays on proposed mergers has enhanced the FTC's or Department of Justice's ability to more accurately target anticompetitive mergers for prosecution.

632   "Effect of the Robinson-Patman Act on the Work of the FTC: The Control of Price Discrimination." *Harvard Law Review* 54 (February 1941): 670-679.

Although passed only four years previously, the effects of the Robinson-Patman Act on the activities of the FTC can be measured with some accuracy. Prior to Robinson-Patman, the FTC's efforts to regulate price discrimination had been largely ineffective. However, problems related to the Act's construction, has made it difficult for the FTC to fashion a useful program to assist the business community. This essay examines specific problems with the Act and attempts by the FTC to work around them. It is concluded that, while administrating Robinson-Patman has consumed an important volume of FTC activity, the effect of this increased workload on business is "uncertain."

633   Eisner, Marc Allen. *Antitrust and the Triumph of Economics: Institutions, Expertise, and Policy Change.* Chapel Hill, NC: University of North Carolina Press, 1991.

The fundamental premise of Eisner's book is that the Reagan Revolution was not a revolution at all, but the consequence of melding economic expertise to law within the organizational frameworks of government. Reagan accomplished this by adopting Chicago school economic theories to negate long established goals of antitrust enforcement. A review of documentation and the antitrust enforcement processes at the Federal Trade Commission and the Antitrust Division at the Department of Justice are used to support this thesis. A significant portion of this work examines the political and economic forces that shaped the FTC and its antitrust enforcement activities during the Reagan Administration.

634   Ellis, William L. and John D. Eldridge. "May the Federal Trade Commission be Enjoined from Holding Its Hearing in Public on an Unfair Competition Complaint." *George Washington Law Review* 2 (January 1934): 196-202.

Discusses the details underlying a petition denied in the case of *E. Griffith Hughes, Inc. v. FTC* in which Hughes asked that the charges not be made public before the case was tried so as not to harm the company's image. It was argued that, since the FTC's power was delegated and its proceedings are not judicial, it cannot punish a firm by publicizing its charges. The court ruled that the FTC does possess the authority to make the charges public if the Commission deems such action is in the best interests of the public.

635   Elman, Philip. "Antitrust Enforcement: Retrospect and Prospect." *American Bar Association Journal* 53 (July 1967): 609-612.

Complicating antitrust law enforcement has been a number of contradictions and complexities that hinder a clear path for businesses to follow in order to avoid litigation. While antitrust laws clearly state certain guidelines and articulate easily applied rules, such as those related to price fixing and supplier boycotts, other areas of enforcement related to conglomerate mergers, oligopoly power, undue concentration, vertical integration, and dual distribution are "gray areas" that have yet to be resolved. It is noted that these issues are further complicated by the fact that the antitrust roles of the Department of Justice and the FTC have yet to be clearly differentiated.

636   Elman, Philip. "Rulemaking Procedures in the FTC's Enforcement of the Merger Law." *Harvard Law Review* 78 (December 1964): 385-392.
Outlines the implications regarding the issuance by the FTC of a Trade Regulation Rule regarding vertical mergers in the cement industry. Of particular significance is the fact that this TRR represents an important departure from the traditional approach to enforcing antitrust laws based on judicial and quasi-judicial proceedings. The disadvantages of litigation on a case-by-case basis is also examined.

637   Ely, R. S. "Work of the Federal Trade Commission." *Wisconsin Law Review* 7 (June 1932): 195-212.
Essay by an FTC staff member outlining the Commission's history, duties and procedures employed with regard to its antitrust enforcement efforts and examines the agency's present activities. The author concludes with an appraisal of the FTC's work in response to President Herbert Hoover's statements concerning the need for evaluating the existing antitrust laws.

638   Elzinger, Kenneth G. "The Antimerger Law: Pyrrhic Victories?" *Journal of Law and Economics* 12 (1969): 42-78.
An examination of legal and economic literature as well as reaction in the business community to antitrust laws tends to point to a feeling of overexpansion of Section 7 of the Clayton Act as enforced by the FTC and Department of Justice. Given this expansion in antitrust law enforcement, this essay explores the issue of effective relief under the law and what happens after a merger has been found in violation of antitrust laws or the respondents have decided to submit to the consent order without further litigation. It is shown that without effective relief as a component of antimerger statutes competition will not be restored to the marketplace and the law will not prevent future mergers that could be harmful to competition. Specific Celler-Kefauver cases (listed as an appendix in the article) brought by the Department of Justice and the FTC under the legal standards of effective relief enforcement are analyzed to define what constitutes successful, sufficient, deficient or unsuccessful relief.

639   Engman, L. A. "Report from the Federal Trade Commission." *Antitrust Law Journal* 44 (Spring 1975): 161-168.

Report by the Chairman of the FTC in which he discusses the elimination of the "Part II Procedure" that allowed firms to negotiate a settlement thirty days after notice of an investigation by the FTC. The procedure proved to be a form of delay rather than speeding up the judicial process. Another change is the elimination of the "All-State Doctrine" that required staff to have completed their investigatory work before issuing a complaint. The author concludes by describing changes in the FTC's discovery rules.

640   Erikson, W. Bruce. "Unfair Trade Practices Under Section 5 of the Federal Trade Commission Act: A Statistical Evaluation." *Antitrust Bulletin* 22 (1977): 643-671.

Uses statistical data to analyze the relationship between unfair trade practices and the competitive process, consumer welfare, levels of concentration, and the economic importance of the industries involved anticompetitive business practices. The article concludes by discussing the public policy implications of the study's results.

641   Evans, Charles D. "Anti-Price Discrimination Act of 1936." *Virginia Law Review* 23 (December 1936): 140-177.

This essay traces the birth and development of the Robinson-Patman Anti-Price Discrimination Act of 1936 in three separate sections. The first section examines the findings of the FTC after it was directed by the Senate in 1928 to investigate the marketing and distribution system of the chain store industry. The final report found that chain stores held a distinct market advantage as a result of special discounts and allowances. The second section examines the creation of the Robinson and Patman bills in response to the FTC's findings. The final section traces the "tortuous course" that these bills navigated through Congress before becoming law. The essay concludes by analyzing specific provisions of the Act and concludes that the Act, if amended, can become an important part of overall antitrust legislation. If it remains in its present form, however, it will seriously handicap business activities.

642   Faith, Roger L. et al. "Antitrust Pork Barrel." *Journal of Law and Economics* 25 (1982): 329-342.

Follows up on the study done by Richard Posner concluding that the FTC is vulnerable to the special interests of businesses and organizations located in districts of powerful members of Congress. This, Posner stated, leads to investigations that are "seldom in the public interest." This study presents empirical evidence to examine whether FTC activities favor firms that operate in the jurisdiction of members of Congress that belong to committees that oversee FTC functions and appropriations. The data is analyzed in two periods, 1961-1969 and 1970-1979, to distinguish between the period observed by Posner and the period after his study. Results of the study indicate there is a private interest relationship between Congress and the FTC. This relationship grew stronger during reform period of the 1970s.

643   "Federal Trade Commission–FTC has Power to Issue Subpoenas in proceedings to Enforce Section 2 of the Clayton Act." *Harvard Law Review* 70 (June 1956): 1476-1479.

Outlines the granting of power to the FTC to issue subpoenas in cases involving Section 2 of the Clayton Act as amended by the Robinson-Patman Act. This power was derived from provisions set forth in Section 9 of the FTC Act. The essay concludes that this decision was a proper one because the power to issue a subpoena requiring the submission of documentation is the only way to ensure effective enforcement of Section 2 of the Clayton Act. Congressional intention and previous cases are used to outline the reasoning behind the federal district court's decision.

644   "Federal Trade Commission Guides Against Deceptive Pricing, 2 Trade Reg. Rep.-7897 (FTC Jan. 8, 1964)." *New York University Law Review* 39 (November 1964): 884-889.

On January 8, 1964, the FTC adopted the revised Guides Against Deceptive Pricing which supplants the 1958 Guides Against Deceptive pricing that proved cumbersome to manufacturers because the old guides required that firms to coordinate retail prices with their list prices. The new Guides are less restrictive and articulate what is permissible conduct rather than affirmatively setting forth violative acts. The essay focuses on Guide III, which describes procedures regarding the advertising of list prices.

645   "Federal Trade Commission Proceedings and Section 5 of the Clayton Act: Application and Implications." *Michigan Law Review* 64 (April 1964): 1156-1164.

Analyzes the case *Minnesota Mining and Mfg. Co. v. New Jersey Wood Finishing Co.*, in which the Supreme Court held that proceedings instituted by the

FTC can be used as prima facie evidence in private suits and fall within the purview of Section 5(b) of the Clayton Act. This is the case with the use of Department of Justice proceedings in private suits. The reasoning behind the Court's ruling is examined as well as the implications this ruling has for future private suits in antitrust matters.

646   Ferguson, J. D. et al. "Consumer Ignorance as a Source of Monopoly Power: FTC Staff Report on Self-Regulation, Standardization, and Product Differentiation." *Antitrust Law and Economics Review* 5 (Winter 1971-72): 79-102 and (Spring 1972): 55-74.
Two part article that contains the text of FTC's staff study on self-regulation along with commentary focusing on the issue of product differentiation and its role in suppressing competition in certain consumer goods industries.

647   Fisher, Alan A. and Robert H. Lande. "Efficiency Considerations in Merger Enforcement." *California Law Review* 71 (December 1983): 1582-1696.
Detailed analysis of the effects of efficiency consideration when applied to enforcement policy under the Clayton Act, the Celler-Kefauver Amendment to the Clayton Act and the Federal Trade Commission Act. The essay begins with an analysis of Congressional and judicial relationship with the issue of market power versus efficiencies. The next section empirical and theoretical evidence is examined as well as case studies to determine the extent of resolution between the two merger perspectives. This evidence is then used to show that a balance between market power and efficiencies is "too complex and too uncertain to use on a case-by-case basis." The incorporation of efficiencies into merger analysis are then examined. The study concludes by evaluating the 1982 Merger Guidelines of the FTC and the Department of Justice. An Afterward follows the article that examines the issue of efficiencies from the perspective of Congressional interest and notes that Congress is much more interested in the use of mergers by firms to strengthen market power, raise prices, and thus harm consumers than they are with the issue of efficiencies.

648   Fisher, W. A. "Supplemental Jurisdiction of the Federal Trade Commission Under Sections 7 and 11 of the Clayton Act." *George Washington Law Review* 3 (November 1934): 81-86.
Examines the supplemental jurisdiction granted the FTC to order the divestiture of assets resulting from the violation of Section 7 of the Clayton Act. Court cases

are used to show that the inadequacies of this supplemental jurisdiction because it has been rarely employed by the FTC and also may be used by Attorney General. It is argued that the federal regulation of business practices should fall under the jurisdiction of one agency granted a range of powers dealing with all aspects of business activity.

649   Fisher, III, William H. "Sections 2(d) and (e) of the Robinson-Patman Act: Babel Revisited." *Vanderbilt Law Review* 11 (March 1958): 466-482.

Analyzes the development of the Robinson-Patman Act, the relationships the Act's provisions have with each other, and addresses problems associated with its construction and enforcement by the FTC.

650   Foer, Albert A. "The New Antitrust Guidelines: Full Speed Ahead for Business Combinations." *Business and Society Review* 44 (Winter 1983): 23-28

Discusses the Department of Justice's Merger Guidelines and their relationship to statements issued by the FTC. As a former executive in the FTC, the author criticizes the FTC's Statement Concerning Horizontal Mergers as "mundane, rambling, [and] nebulous," but states that it may, in fact, have greater influence in the long run than the Department of Justice's guidelines. This is due to the possibility that the FTC will create more stringent merger guidelines through its case-by-case development of merger guidelines rather than the Justice Department's guidelines that are based on more hypothetical provisions.

651   Fraas, Gertrude A. "Structural Shared Monopoly Under FTC 5: The Implication of the Exxon Complaint." *Case Western Reserve Law Review* 26 (1976): 613-652.

Uses the complaint issued by the FTC against eight oil firms accusing them of practicing a shared monopoly to show the advantages of using a structural analysis of the economic power within a market in enforcing antitrust laws. The note begins with an analysis of the complaint and the reasons why the FTC issued it. An examination of organizational economics and the concept of the marketplace follows to create a framework of understanding regarding the application of the proposed structural analysis. The concept of market structure is presented to study the relationship between market power and Section 5 of the FTC Act. It is concluded that the Exxon case offers an opportunity to adopt a more meaningful structural analysis approach by the courts

652   Franklin, Barbara Hackman. "Antitrust Accord: FTC, EC Agree to Share Enforcement Information." *New York Law Journal* 207 (January 2, 1992): 5.

Outlines the provisions of the pact signed between the United States and the European Community that would ensure the notification of each other in cases where antitrust enforcement may affect the other party. It is hoped that this agreement will help prevent clashes over the application of U.S. antitrust laws when applied to overseas jurisdictions. However, several antitrust lawyers stated that the agreement was "largely symbolic."

653   Freer, Robert E. "Let's Stop Kicking the Antitrust Laws Around." *Vital Speeches of the Day* 15 (January 15, 1949): 210-213.

Speech given by the Chairman of the FTC in which he outlines the scope of FTC authority in enforcing antitrust laws, examines the agency's accomplishments, specifically the Cement Institute case involving price fixing and suppression of competition, and discusses the budgetary constraints placed on the FTC that hinder its enforcement authority.

654   "FTC 5 and Robinson-Patman: Unfair Method of Legislation or Fair Method of Administration." *Villanova Law Review* 11 (Fall 1965): 113-124.

Comments on the following issue: "Whether Section 5 of the Federal Trade Commission Act can be employed by the Commission when a discriminatory practice does not come within the purview of the Robinson-Patman Act because of a technical omission which denies jurisdiction to the regulatory body under that statute." The issue is placed within the context of repeated criticisms of the Robinson-Patman Act and its legislative history.

655   "The FTC and the Sherman Act." *Chicago-Kent Law Review* 25 (June 1947): 225-232.

Argues that, based on other trade regulation statutes and their accompanying legislative background, the FTC has overstepped the bounds of its enforcement authority when applying actions under the Sherman Act. Although mentioned in the original complaint leading to the *Aetna Portland Cement Company v. FTC* case, there has so far been no review of this issue by a court of law and, therefore, the FTC should not assume legislative or judicial acceptance of this inclusion of enforcement authority.

656   "FTC Staff Report: Competition Policy in the New High-Tech, Global Marketplace." *Antitrust Law Journal* 64 (Spring 1996): 791-798.

Text of the executive summary and principal conclusions of the FTC's staff report concerning the need for the agency to adjust the FTC's competition enforcement mission so as not to impede attempts by U.S. businesses to compete in the global economy and to recognize the complex innovation involved in product development.

657   Gallagher, Michael F. "The Robinson-Patman Act." *John Marshall Law Quarterly* 2 (March 1937): 464-477.

Early legal review of the provisions of the Robinson-Patman Act, its legislative background, and the judicial attitude towards it. Among the issues discussed are the difficulties faced by the FTC in enforcing the Act.

658   Gallo, Joseph C. et al. "Guess Who Came to Dinner: An Empirical Study of Federal Antitrust Enforcement for the Period 1963-1984." *Review of Industrial Organization* 2 (1985): 106-130.

This study of antitrust enforcement during the period 1963 through 1984 continues the methodology, format and operational definitions of a study conducted by Richard Posner in the October 1970 issue of the *Journal of Law and Economics*. The statistical elements used include the number of antitrust cases initiated, how many cases the Department of Justice and the FTC won and lost, and the nature of the violations, fines, and imprisonment of the cases. The study makes special note of trends present during the Reagan administration.

659   Gantz, John. "History Suggests FTC Antitrust Case vs. Microsoft Will Flop." *InfoWorld* 13 (March 25, 1991): 42.

The author discusses the FTC's suit against Microsoft from the perspective of suits brought against IBM claiming it had a monopoly on peripheral components sold for its own computer systems, a claim similar to that brought against Microsoft. Based on suits filed against IBM, it is concluded that legal action against Microsoft will be very difficult for the FTC to win.

660   Gardner, Judy. "Consumer Report: FTC Seeks Wider Impact in Antitrust Work, Puts New Emphasis on Planning." *National Journal* 4 (July 15, 1972): 1151-1159.

Outlines the Commission's more aggressive antitrust activities to help protect the consumer from unfair business practices. It is noted that this expansion of FTC activity to target large-scale offenders reflects a general effort to revitalize the FTC. However, reaction from business leaders has been harsh. Specific actions by the FTC under the leadership of Chairman Miles Kirkpatrick are discussed, followed by an analysis of where this action will lead. A brief outline of how the FTC and the Department of Justice share antitrust enforcement responsibilities is included.

661   Gellhorn, Ernest. "Distinguished Alumni Lecture: Regulatory Reform and the Federal Trade Commission's Antitrust Jurisdiction." *Tennessee Law Review* 49 (Spring 1982): 471-510.

The article begins by articulating the distinction between the antitrust enforcement duties of the FTC and the Department of Justice's Antitrust Division; an arrangement, it is noted, based more on historical precedent than logic. FTC antitrust responsibility is then examined with respect to redundant statutory assignments, the agency's consumer protection mission, and the FTC's vulnerability to pressures from special interest groups. Six objections to unifying antitrust responsibilities are then examined in detail: political independence, flexible enforcement authority, rulemaking and adjudication powers, special expertise, small business protection, and competition in enforcement. It is concluded that problems associated with dual enforcement cannot be solved with new personnel, greater authority, or a larger budget and, therefore, consolidation must be seriously considered.

662   Gellhorn, Ernest. "The New Gibberish at the FTC." *Regulation* 2 (May/June 1978): 37-42.

Examines the FTC's new competition policy announced by Chairman Michael Pertschuk in which he states that antitrust enforcement should reflect human values rather than pure economic efficiency. The author analyzes the six main principles contained in the policy and then details two arguments as to why the policy should not be implemented. First, it is unlikely that the policy will increase competition or eliminate barriers to competition and, second, the policy represents an overbroad application of the antitrust laws. The author declares that the laws were meant to be flexible in their interpretation but were not meant to become a tool of open-ended authority for the Chairman. It is concluded that a more modest approach to antitrust enforcement be adopted.

663   Gellhorn, Ernest. "Two's a Crowd: The FTC's Redundant Antitrust Powers." *Regulation* 5 (November/December 1981): 32-42.

The author argues that the FTC's antitrust responsibilities should be eliminated based upon a reviews the antitrust enforcement record of the FTC. An analysis of major cases from 1975 to 1981 and the FTC's vulnerability to special interest groups and political pressures are used to support this position. The author systematically refutes the arguments that the FTC's responsibilities should be maintained.

664   Gellhorn, Ernest et al. "Has Antitrust Outgrown Dual Enforcement? A Proposal for Rationalization." *Antitrust Bulletin* 35 (Fall 1990): 695-743.

Criticizes the recent shifts in antitrust enforcement philosophy embraced by the FTC after the Reagan Administration, arguing that little has changed in terms of how antitrust enforcement is carried out by the agency with respect to the efforts of the Department of Justice. The author examines the "very aggressive" antitrust efforts of both agencies from 1965 to 1980 and outlines their relative strengths. The author concludes from this analysis that the Department of Justice is much better suited to antitrust enforcement and that all antitrust enforcement responsibilities should be shifted to DOJ and Section 5 of the FTC Act should be repealed to prevent future ambiguity.

665   Ginsburg, Douglas H. "The Appropriate Role of the Antitrust Enforcement Agencies." *Cardoza Law Review* 9 (March 1988): 1277-1293.

This essay explores the antitrust enforcement roles of the FTC and the Department of Justice by describing shared statutory responsibilities, such as civil action based on provisions of the Clayton and Sherman Acts, and other similarities. While there is a general consensus that both agencies share the enforcement goal of preserving competition, debate still remains concerning the allocation of agency resources devoted to competition advocacy.

666   Gladieux, Jennifer E. "Towards a Single Standard for Antitrust: The Federal Trade Commission's Evolving Rule of Reason." *George Mason University Law Review* 5 (Spring 1997): 471-523.

This study uses three recent FTC proceedings (Massachusetts Board of Registration in Optometry, California Dental Association, International Association of Conference Interpreters) to examine the issue of "whether or not pure microeconomic analysis or an integration of microeconomics and other policy concerns" can contribute to the formulation of a workable antitrust standard. The article begins by outlining FTC antitrust procedures. This is followed by a more specific analysis of the three recent cases. The next section studies how the FTC's application of an antitrust standard has evolved over time from the Massachusetts Board decision to the California Dental decision. When considering the FTC's application of a general antitrust standard to the Conference Interpreters case, it is revealed that the FTC "retains much of its formalistic distinction between the per se rule and the rule of reason" in cases that do not involve multi-firm non-merger antitrust cases.

667   Glassman, Michael L. "Changing Presumptions in Antitrust: There's More Competition Than We Thought." *Antitrust Law and Economics Review* 16 (Summer 1984): 57-90.

Contains the text of an interview of the author, former Director of the FTC's Division of Economic Evidence, discussing his work at the FTC from 1972 through 1976, including specific cases he testified or gave deposition for. During the interview, Glassman also gives his views of the FTC's work regarding horizontal mergers, price restraints and international issues related to antitrust.

668   Glazer, David L. "Clayton Act Scrutiny of Nonprofit Hospital Mergers: The Wrong Rx for Ailing Institutions." *Washington Law Review* 66 (October 1991): 1041-1060.

Discusses the differing decisions between two federal circuit courts regarding the application of the Clayton Act to nonprofit hospital mergers. After reviewing the issue of hospital mergers and antitrust law, the essay reviews statutory interpretations, the legislative history, and possible public policy considerations, concluding that provisions of Section 7 of the Clayton Act should not be applied to nonprofit hospital mergers.

669   Godfrey, T. Bruce. "*FTC v. Ticor Title Insurance Company*: More Confusion than Guidance." *Business Lawyer* 48 (February 1993): 779-787.

Analyzes the issues surrounding the Ticor case and the history of state action defense in antitrust actions. The opinions of the majority are examined in light if current antitrust laws, but the note concludes that little in the way of guidance has been set forth for future antitrust regulation.

670 Gotts, Ilene Knable. "Health Care Joint Ventures and the Antitrust Laws: A Guardedly Optimistic Prognosis." *The Journal of Contemporary Health Law and Policy* 10 (Spring 1994): 169-193.
This article discusses the antitrust implications of current health care consolidation and joint ventures and the creation of alternative delivery systems. While these changes are generally pro-competitive, antitrust enforcement agencies must be alert to joint ventures and other forms of collaborative health care systems that may be created simply to eliminate competition and restrain trade within the marketplace. Both the FTC and the Department of Justice are discussed within the context of the pro-competitive and anti-competitive effects of joint ventures.

671 Gotts, Ilene Knable. "Regulators Focusing on Antitrust Issues: Intellectual Property Transfers are Receiving Increased Scrutiny." *The National Law Journal* 16 (January 24, 1994): S12-S14.
The first year of the Clinton Administration has marked increased activity by the FTC and the Department of Justice with regards to possible antitrust violations by major corporations in the software and microprocessor fields. Most of the antitrust probes have centered on a concern by regulators that these companies could misuse the market power available to them under U.S. intellectual property laws to undermine competition or otherwise illegally expand their market position. Several examples of this activity, including investigations by the FTC, and subsequently by the Department of Justice, of possible antitrust violations by MicroSoft Corporation, are examined. This is followed by a brief discussion of the impact that these investigations have had on the industry.

672 Grady, Kevin E. "A Framework for Antitrust Analysis of Health Care Joint Ventures." *Antitrust Law Journal* 61 (Spring 1993): 765-827.
Defines the parameters of joint ventures between health care businesses by using two Supreme Court cases to determine if joint ventures among competitors are "legitimate." This analysis to coupled with statements by the FTC and other enforcement agencies to determine the efficiencies of joint ventures. Specific policy statements by the FTC regarding the health care industry are also examined to help measure their influence on planning within the health care industry.

673 Greaney, Thomas L. "A Critique: The Department of Justice, FTC Health Care Policy Statements." *Antitrust* 8 (Spring 1994): 20-25.
Begins by examining the reaction by the healthcare industry to the release of the

FTC's and Department of Justices' Joint Policy Statements Concerning Antitrust Enforcement Policy in the Health Care Area, then analyzes six provisions of the Statement: hospital mergers, the purchase of high-tech equipment, the collective provision of information by physician and purchasers, information exchanges among hospitals, joint purchasing arrangements, and physician control of health care networks. Concludes that while there are some important clarifications of interpretive principles, the Statement is best viewed as a "political communique" designed to help enhance the Clinton Administration's health care package.

674   Green, Jay. "FTC May Challenge Not-For-Profit Mergers." *Modern Healthcare* 17 (November 6, 1987): 46-48, 50, 55.

The author explores the potential impact resulting from proposed FTC challenges to nonprofit consolidations. Of particular interest is the impact of an FTC challenge on not-for-profit hospital mergers in small markets. The reasons behind increased merger activity in the nonprofit hospital industry in general and the landscape of the post-merger hospital environment are analyzed in detail and concludes with predictions of what will occur in the upcoming court battles.

675   Grimmond, Jeannie. "*E.I. Du Pont Nemours v. FTC*: Facilitating Practices Under FTC Act Section 5." *Iowa Law Review* 70 (May 1985): 1045-1060.

This article examines in detail the state of antitrust laws regarding oligopolistic behavior as it applies to the Du Pont case in which the Second Circuit court struck down the FTC's cease and desist order based on the agency's statement that "noncollusive conduct violated Section 5." The court refused to uphold the contention that oligopolistic interdependence created the potential for anticompetitive behavior. A brief overview of the Harvard and Chicago schools of economic theory are presented followed by a statement of support for the noncollusive facilitating practices approach based on the historical and legislative intent of the FTC Act, previous pricing decisions by the FTC showing "a willingness to impose liability without proof of agreement if noncompetitive effect can be shown," and the low cost of the cease and desist remedy sought. It is concluded that the decision places undue limits on the FTC's ability to use economic evidence in its antitrust enforcement mission.

676   Hagan, Willis W. "State of the Collective Liver of the Federal Trade Commissioners." *Marquette Law Review* 47 (Winter 1963-64): 342-358.

Due to the lack of moral guidance from Congress when it created the FTC, the Commission must rely upon business morality when determining if a practice is fair or unfair. However, there also exists little ethical philosophy within the business environment, forcing many to feel that the FTC overregulates. To prevent a "static, hamstrung business community," leaders must adopt a moral business approach to their practices beyond the law.

677   Hagarty, Sheila M. "The Legality of Backhaul Allowances Under the Robinson-Patman Act: An Analysis." *Dickinson Law Review* 84 (Summer 1980): 625-643.

Analyzes the legality of the use of backhaul allowances (price concessions given to individuals who transport their own goods) in light of an FTC advisory opinion that ruled such price allowances are in violation of provisions of the Robinson-Patman Act. Cost justifications and public policy considerations are reviewed to show the infeasibility of alternatives. It is concluded that the FTC should rescind its advisory opinion because it does not take into account public policy issues and its own position regarding price discrimination in uniform delivered price systems.

678   Haines, Charles Grove. "Efforts to Define Unfair Competition: The Legal Concept of Unfair Competition." *Yale Law Journal* 29 (November 1919): 1-28.

This essay published shortly after the FTC was created examines the problems associated with legally defining "unfair competition" and attempts by federal agencies, such as the FTC, and the judiciary, to provide guidance to insure a competitive marketplace. The FTC Act and the Clayton Act are both reviewed in detail. This is followed by an examination of common law and its relationship to unfair methods of competition. State law is also examined. The essay concludes by analyzing the advantages of regulating unfair competition through an administrative agency (the FTC) and compares U.S. regulatory policy with other countries.

679   Halverson, James T. "Arbitration and Antitrust Remedies." *Arbitration Journal* 30 (1975): 25-33.

Examines the FTC's policy of encouraging arbitration of dealership termination disputes. This policy was implemented because it offers an important antitrust remedy. The FTC's consent order against the Phillips Petroleum Company is used to highlight how and why the policy works. In the Phillips case, the company was charged by the FTC of using the threat of canceling the lease of its lessee-dealers to force them to purchase certain Phillip's products to the exclusion of other manufacturers. The essay concludes with an analysis of how to fashion a consent order to best fit current as well as future circumstances.

680   Halverson, James T. "FTC Antitrust Enforcement Policies with Respect to Business Practices in an Inflation and Shortage Economy." *Antitrust Law Symposium* 1975 (Summer 1977): 89-109.
This study analyzes what factors might be considered by the FTC when pursuing antitrust enforcement actions with respect to price fixing and as a result of competition problems associated with shortage conditions. The discussion is placed within the context of the double-digit inflation and high unemployment of the economy during the mid-1970s.

681   Hamilton, Milo E. and Lee Lovinger. "The Second Attack on Price Discrimination: The Robinson-Patman Act." *Washington University Law Quarterly* 22 (February 1937): 153-186.
One of the more comprehensive early studies about the impact and problems associated with the Robinson-Patman Act. The birth and development of the Act, initiated primarily because of a report promulgated by the FTC with regards to anticompetitive behavior within the chain store industry, is outlined in detail. This is followed by an examination of the Act's purpose with respect to other antitrust laws, problems that arise because of how the Act is written, including an analysis of provisions stated that guide FTC proceedings, and concludes that, although the Robinson-Patman Act is "poorly drafted and carelessly enacted," it does not mark any sweeping changes in antitrust law associated with price discrimination.

682   Handler, Milton. "Reforming the Antitrust Laws." *Columbia Law Review* 82 (November 1982): 1287-1364.
Uses specific cases to construct a model of reform regarding antitrust law in areas such as vertical restraint, mergers, state action and unfair labor practices. A section of the article is devoted to reforming the FTC arguing that the agency's aggressive antitrust enforcement conduct frequently goes beyond the parameters of the laws as interpreted by the Supreme Court. Nevertheless, the Sperry & Hutchinson decision shows that the Supreme Court has sanctioned this expansive behavior.

683   Handler, Milton. "Reforming the Antitrust Laws (Part One)." *New York Law Journal* 187 (April 5, 1982): 1, 28.

Beginning of a seven part article that examines the need for reforming the nation's antitrust laws. Part One examines some of the general issues involved as the nation approaches the centennial of the Sherman Act. Parts two through seven cover the following issues: part two (April 6, 1982, pp. 1, 26) covers vertical restraints and the need for judicial clarification of such items as exclusive dealing arrangements, territorial and customer restrictions, and resale price maintenance; part three (April 7, 1982, pp. 6, 7) covers merger law and policy; part four (April 8, 1982, pp. 4-5) covers dual enforcement and the FTC's antitrust enforcement mission; part five (April 9, 1982, pp. 26) focuses on state antitrust enforcement regulation; part six (April 12, 1982, pp. 3-4) covers the treatment of labor unions under antitrust laws; and, part seven (April 13, 1982, pp. 5-6) examines the issue of monopolization and provisions of Section 2 of the Sherman Act.

684   Handler, Milton. "Unfair Competition and the Federal Trade Commission." *George Washington Law Review* 8 (January-February 1940): 399-426.

This work outlines the improving relations between the FTC and the courts when interpreting FTC authority to regulate unfair competition. This is accomplished by examining court rulings associated with the FTC's twenty-seven methods of competition listed in the FTC's 1938 annual report describing what is deemed unfair by the Commission. It is concluded that, although the courts had limited the scope of the FTC's powers in some respects, the areas in which the FTC has been granted judicial latitude have been marked by "constructive action." A call for further legislation is made to further clarify enforcement ambiguities.

685   Hanson, Hugh C. "Robinson-Patman Law: A Review and Analysis." *Fordham Law Review* 51 (May 1983): 1113-1218.

Although the Act has been the focus of much criticism since its creation fifty years ago, it has remained primarily because it is difficult to prove the Act is directly harmful to consumers, there are a limited number of scholars interested in the complexity of the law and, thus, few available to press for sweeping change, and finally, concern for the competitor's well-being has frequently undermined the few times that criticism has actually been presented. Throughout this, the FTC has been generally supportive of the Act. This essay reviews in detail the Robinson-Patman Act and its enforcement by the FTC, followed by an exploration of various possibilities for meaningful revision. It is concluded that the Act is the result of the economic upheaval of the Great Depression and primarily protects business and industry from competition.

686   Harvey, Richard Selden. *A Manual of the Federal Trade Commission, Presenting the Origin, Development, and Construction of the Antitrust Laws, With Decisions upon the Constitutional and Unfair Trade Questions Involved, Together With the Rules of Practice, Forms, Texts of Statutes, Debates in Congress and Complete Memoranda of Anti-Trust Cases Instituted by the United States.* Washington, DC: J. Byrne and Company, 1916.

This book provides perhaps the earliest and most comprehensive analysis of the FTC's development, authority, and functions. Each chapter covers a specific area of antitrust enforcement that must be administered by the FTC and the problems associated with that area. Includes the full text of the FTC Act and other statutes as well as an annotated list of antitrust cases in the United States up to the year 1915. Includes a subject index.

687   Hawley, Ellis W. "Herbert Hoover and the Sherman Act, 1921-1933: An Early Phase of a Continuing Issue." *Iowa Law Review* 74 (July 1989): 1067-1103.

This work analyzes Herbert Hoover's involvement in antitrust debates and policy decisions from 1921 to 1933. His approach to antitrust law is discussed. This is followed by an exploration of two contrasting periods of involvement by Hoover. At several points in the text, reference to the FTC's role in antitrust law enforcement and cooperation with Hoover is made.

688   Hay, G. A. "The FTC and Pricing: Of Predation and Signaling." *Antitrust Law Journal* 52 (August 1983): 409-417.

Summarizes and offers commentary regarding two recent cases. The first involves accusations of predatory pricing by the FTC against Bordon, Inc. The second case involves an FTC opinion against four manufacturers of gasoline additives that they participated in "facilitating practices," a shared monopoly. These cases are analyzed to show that, while facilitating practices have "considerable appeal" to economists and antitrust theorists, it offers little significance to litigators or corporate planners.

689   Hayman, Russell. "The Goods or Really Exemption to Premerger Notification Under the Hart-Scott-Rodino Antitrust Improvements Act." *University of San Francisco Law Review* 17 (Spring 1983): 477-505. Comprehensive examination of the goods or realty exemption in the Hart-Scott-Rodino Act, showing that interpretations of the exemption have been inconsistent with the goals of the Act and antitrust law enforcement. An interpretation based on the acquired assets of both the buyer and seller is offered. Several hypothetical cases of acquiring assets, including some posed by the FTC, are presented to illustrate its use. Current enforcement of the Act by the FTC is detailed, noting that the Commission has failed to define the exemption provision even though it is primarily responsible for enforcing the Act. Unofficial statements from FTC staff are used to help define the agency's position.

690   Hobbs, Caswell O. "Antitrust in the Next Decade: A Role for the Federal Trade Commission." *Antitrust Bulletin* 31 (Summer 1986): 451-480. Discusses the origins of the FTC and its antitrust mission and analyzes three factors associated with its future role in antitrust enforcement. These are: 1) the original objective articulated by Congress has not, in general, been realized; 2) the boundaries of antitrust enforcement have been narrowed, thereby limiting the FTC's enforcement purview; and 3) the federal courts have significantly eroded the FTC's antitrust jurisdiction. Each of these factors are examined in detail. A prediction for the FTC's role in the next is then presented concluding that any curtailing of the FTC's antitrust role will most likely be marginal.

691   Hobbs, Caswell O. "Swings of the Pendulum: The FTC's First Seventy-Five Years." *Antitrust Law Journal* 58 (Spring 1989): 9-15. The author outlines of the legislative history and enforcement responsibility of the FTC to develop an understanding of the Kirkpatrick Committee Report on the Role of the Federal Trade Commission and its impact on agency antitrust activities.

692   Holliday, W. T. "The Anti-Trust Laws and the Federal Trade Commission Act." *Ohio Law Bulletin and Reporter* 19 (March 6, 1922): 685-710. The author systematically explains how the enforcement jurisdiction of the FTC fits within the framework of the Sherman Antitrust Act, the Clayton Act, and the FTC Act. Specific cases are used throughout the article to emphasize particular points. Among the issues discussed is the power of the FTC to examine corporate documents, price discrimination, unfair methods of competition, selling below cost, and price fixing under patent agreements.

693   Holliday, W. T. "The Federal Trade Commission: Jurisdiction and Powers of Body as Set Forth in Act Creating It, Orders Issued, and Decisions of Courts on Various Provisions of Clayton and Trade Commission Acts." *American Bar Association Journal* 8 (May 1922): 293-299.

Provides a complete overview of the legislative development and creation of the FTC Act, procedures adopted by the agency to regulate unfair competition, and the FTC's overall jurisdiction with regards to visitorial power (authority to examine corporate records and other documents relevant to an investigation), price discrimination, tying contracts, selling below cost, resale price maintenance, price fixing under patent licenses, commercial bribery, lending equipment to a customer, and conspiracy under the Sherman Antitrust Act. Specific cases are examined throughout the essay.

694   Horn, Jr., H. Chester. "Confronting the Brave New World of Antitrust Federalism." *Antitrust Bulletin* 36 (Winter 1991): 821-833.

Discusses how two recently decided Supreme Court cases, *California v. American Stores* and *California v. ARC America Corp.*, have shifted the "balance of power" in antitrust enforcement related to mergers away from the federal government, most notably the FTC, and to the states. The mission of state antitrust enforcement related to mergers, vertical and horizontal restraints, and monopolization offenses are then examined.

695   Howry, Edward F. "Utilization by the FTC of Section 5 of the Federal Trade Commission Act as an Antitrust Law." *Antitrust Bulletin* 5 (1960): 161-185.

The author reviews the current state of antitrust enforcement and attempts to discern what trends are in the future based on an examination of the legislative history of Section 5 of the FTC Act and the judicial interpretation of the Section. The application and interpretation of Section 5 by the FTC is studied in detail. The author concludes that usage of Section 5 to "round out" the Clayton Act is not a valid procedure because there is no clear line between where the Clayton Act's authority ends and the FTC's begins.

696   Hucker, Charles W. "Kennedy Seeks Limitations on Conglomerate Mergers." *Congressional Quarterly Weekly Report* 37 (March 17, 1979): 481-485.

Notes the possible resurgence of conglomerate mergers and reviews both FTC and Department of Justice proposals to regulate these mergers as well as relevant legislation presented by Senator Edward Kennedy (D-Massachusetts). The author discusses the reasons behind the current merger movement and the arguments for and against further regulation. Although passage of Kennedy's legislation is remote, the issue has come to the forefront again with hearings possibly in the near future regarding the general subject of mergers.

697   Iglehart, John K. "Adding a Dose of Competition to the Health Care Industry." *National Journal* 10 (October 7, 1978): 1602-1606.

Health care in America consists of a $163 billion dollar a year industry. Both the FTC and the Department of Justice have begun "to apply rigorous new tests to the health care industry" to ensure fair competition. The origin of this activity, initiated primarily because of a series of Supreme Court decisions, are examined in detail, followed by analysis of three areas of concern: physician advertising, physician fees, and whether domination of Blue Shield boards by physicians stifles competition. The essay concludes that the FTC's activities indicate a long-term commitment to examining the industry, but politics may enter into what direction the FTC takes in following through with its actions. Includes a detailed chronology of antitrust enforcement activity by the FTC and the department of Justice.

698   "Interview with Dennis A. Yao, Former FTC Commissioner." *Antitrust* 9 (Fall 1994): 12-16.

Interview in which former FTC Commissioner Yao reflects on the work of the FTC, its role in enforcing antitrust laws, and how Yao's business, rather than legal, background has affected his view of the FTC's mission.

699   "Interview with Stephen Calkins, General Counsel, Federal Trade Commission." *Antitrust* 10 (Fall 1995): 28-31.

Contains the text of an interview of Stephen Calkins, "a leading analyst of antitrust law and procedure" and General Counsel for the FTC. Among the issues discussed are: 1) efforts by the FTC to clarify procedures associated with preliminary injunctions; 2) the agency's relationship with the Department of Justice; 3) review of recent court cases that have affected the FTC's antitrust work, especially as it relates to the role of the General Counsel, and 4) consideration of whether or not the FTC should be more active in filing amicus briefs and participating in private cases.

700 "Interview with William S. Baer, Director, Bureau of Competition, Federal Trade Commission." *Antitrust* 10 (Summer 1996): 15-19.
This article is the text of an interview of William J. Baer, Director of the FTC's Bureau of Competition in which he discusses issues related to duel enforcement, merger policies and procedures, efficiencies, mergers within the health care industry, and the Bureau of Competition's relationship with the Bureaus of Consumer Protection and Economics.

701 "Investigatory Powers of the Federal Trade Commission." *Northwestern University Law Review* 53 (March/April 1958): 109-116.
Examines the investigatory powers of the FTC as they relate to gathering and compiling information relevant to an investigation and, for the purpose of examination, the right to copy any documentary evidence of any firm under investigated. The author states that the access and copy powers granted the FTC under certain Supreme Court rulings should be limited to complaint and pre-complaint investigations and general industry investigations when the violators are unknown. However, the author concludes that the obtaining of information for legislative or rule-making purposes is unconstitutional. A subpoena should be used in these cases.

702 Irvine, Ralstone R. "Uncertainties of Section 7 of the Clayton Act." *Cornell Law Quarterly* 14 (December 1928): 28-39.
Analyzes whether "the Clayton Act forbids one corporation from acquiring and holding the assets of a competing corporation when those assets are acquired as a result of an illegal acquisition of stock or are paid for in the stock of the acquiring corporation." The application of Section 7 of the Clayton Act has been placed in doubt due to a recent series of cases entitled *Federal Trade Commission v. Western Meat Company.* To help assess the relationship between Section 7 and the acquisition of assets and to determine if additional legislation is needed to clarify interpretation of the Clayton Act, the history and purpose of the Clayton Act is studied.

703   Jacobs, William W. "Competition in Health Care Markets: Avoiding the Antitrust Pitfalls." *University of Toledo Law Review* 17 (Summer 1986): 839-849.
Aimed at health care professionals, this article attempts to explain the legal and policy developments in antitrust law in order to avoid liability. Couched within this is an analysis of the role of the FTC in ensuring competition within the health care industry. The relationship between the FTC and industry self-regulation is examined in light of the case brought against the American Medical Association. Issues relating to advertising by physicians, commercial practices, boycotts, and mergers are then examined. It is recommended that health care professionals seek information from the FTC whenever a question of legality arises.

704   Jacobson, Raymond A. and Scott S. Megregian. "New Government Merger Rules May Stimulate Growth and Acquisition." *Business Forum* 18 (Winter/Spring 1993): 21-24.
Analyzes the possible effects of the 1992 Horizontal Merger Guidelines issued jointly by the FTC and the Department of Justice. Comparison with previous guidelines is noted with emphasis placed on new provisions regarding price discrimination and geographic markets and the new competitive effects test that helps define under what circumstances a merger or acquisition in a concentrated market should be opposed. The guideline's effects on consumer products, retail stores, defense contractors, health care, mining and natural resource, and durable goods industries are then examined.

705   Jaekels, Christopher J. "International Joint Ventures and Antitrust Policy: FTC Puts GM and Toyota in the Driver's Seat." *Wisconsin International Law Journal* 4 (1985): 64-85.
This study analyzes the FTC's provisional consent order allowing Toyota and General Motors to proceed with a joint venture to build subcompact automobiles at a factory in Fremont, California. The consent order was revised to restrict the joint venture's output, duration, and the information that could be exchanged between the two parties. This essay examines the antitrust law and policy implications of the order, the reasoning behind the FTC's acceptance of the venture, and compares procompetitive and anticompetitive effects of the venture to determine its significance in regards to future joint ventures. It is concluded that the FTC went beyond the boundaries of established antitrust law and "threatened to harm United States objectives concerning foreign industrial investment" as well as the balance of trade, forms of employment, and energy conservation.

706   James, Jr., Charles A. "Non-Merger Case Generation at the Federal Trade Commission." *Antitrust Law Journal* 54 (Winter 1985): 189-194.
The author examines which procedures are followed by the FTC when pursuing a nonmerger investigation. Specific cases are discussed to clarify what procedures are utilized. The author states that the FTC is currently active in five areas of case generation: health care professions, a parallel program of non-health care professions, horizontal restraints in the area of trade associations, non-price predation, and the exploration of antitrust exemptions in light of recent Supreme Court decisions.

707   Johnson, Ronald N. and Allen M. Parkman. "The Role of Ideas in Antitrust Policy Toward Vertical Mergers: Evidence from the FTC Cement-Ready Mixed Concrete Cases." *Antitrust Bulletin* 32 (Winter 1987): 841-883.
Reviews issues related to the enforcement of restrictions on vertical mergers by examining in detail the FTC's efforts to dissolve vertical mergers between cement and concrete firms during the 1960s and 1970s. The FTC's Economic Report was highly critical of mergers because they were seen as preventing entrance by outside firms. However, hindsight and an analysis of the cases rather than the report itself, reveal higher prices were not likely to result from the mergers. The FTC apparently concurs because it has since rescinded its "Enforcement Policy with Respect to Vertical Mergers in the Cement Industry." This episode in FTC vertical merger restriction enforcement is viewed as the impetus for new merger guidelines and a more relaxed interpretation by the judiciary.

708   Jones, Mary Gardiner. "The Golden Age of the Federal Trade Commission: Innovation and Creativity in the 60s and 70s (Part I and II)." *Antitrust Law and Economics Review* 16 (1984): 103-110 and 29-56.
Text of an interview with the former FTC Commissioner, in which she discusses her involvement with the policies of the FTC during the "Golden Age" in the 1960s and 1970s and the shift of antitrust and consumer protection goals under the James C. Miller III era.

709   Kanwit, S. W. "Federal Trade Commission and Insurance Mergers." *Insurance Law Journal* 1980 (Fall 1980): 73-78.
This article analyzes the FTC's insurance industry merger policy. It is argued that, although the McCarran-Ferguson Act provides that the antitrust laws and the FTC

Act are applicable to "the business of insurance" only, FTC premerger reporting requirements pursuant to the Hart-Scott-Rodino Act have allowed the Commission "considerable leverage to coerce settlements and impose consent orders in certain large insurance mergers."

710 Kanwit, S. W. "FTC Enforcement Efforts Involving Trade and Professional Associations." *ABA Antitrust Law Journal* 46 (Summer 1977): 640-652.

As the FTC's Regional Office Director in Chicago, the author offers his perspective on the issue of antitrust law and trade associations. Problems arise because, by their nature, they are a collection of competitors and, thus, must satisfy the combination requirements of Section 1 of the Sherman Act. This situation can be enhanced because the activities of these competitors fall within areas related to prices, distribution channels, and when competition becomes too severe the members of the association may ask the association to intervene and clashing with antitrust laws. These issues are discussed within the context of FTC action under Section 5 of the FTC Act and the Magnuson-Moss Federal Trade Commission Improvement Act of 1975.

711 Katten, Joseph. "Economic Theory as a Substitute for Evidence in Antitrust: The Difficulty of Erecting Rules of Law on Theory After Kodak." *Antitrust Law and Economics* 23 (1991): 13-34.

Text of an address given by the Assistant Director for Policy and Evaluation, Bureau of Competition at the FTC in which he discusses the implications of the Supreme Court's decision in the *Image Technical Service v. Eastman Kodak Co.* case. It is argued that the case marks the possibility of a shift in antitrust ruling back to using mere "evidence" rather than continued use of economic theory. Recent FTC cases about distribution are examined to shed light on the government's perspective antitrust rule of law.

712 Katten, Joseph. "The Role of Efficiency Considerations in the Federal Trade Commission's Antitrust Analysis." *Antitrust Law Journal* 64 (Spring 1996): 613-632.

The author examines the question of efficiencies in the area of antitrust enforcement by noting how the FTC has attempted to circumvent the difficult issue of disproving claims of efficiency. Recent efficiency claims in horizontal restraint cases have reshaped this debate and forced the FTC to consider market structures. However, as a result of this process, the FTC has taken the proper position by adopting a more disciplined approach to measuring the effects of efficiencies when applying economic analysis to antitrust enforcement.

713 Katzmann, Robert A. *Regulatory Bureaucracy: The Federal Trade Commission and Antitrust Policy.* Cambridge, MA: MIT Press, 1980. The purpose of this work is to examine in detail the "organizational and professional norms of lawyers and economists" who work in the antitrust section of the FTC to gain a framework for understanding how their actions affect policy considerations. The primary argument presented is that legal processes may not represent the most efficient or desirable means to solve economic problems. The role each component of the FTC's antitrust section, such as the commissioners, is examined in detail. The book includes a chart of the FTC's antitrust case selection process and an index.

714 Kauper, Thomas E. "Cease and Desist: The History, Effect, and Scope of Clayton Act Orders of the Federal Trade Commission." *Michigan Law Review* 66 (April 1968): 1095-1210.

Comprehensive study of the content of cease and desist orders entered by the FTC under Sections 2 and 3 of the Clayton Act. The essay is divided into two parts: a detailed analysis of enforcement and other "indirect effects" of FTC orders and an examination of the content of the orders themselves to determine, among other things, the general scope of the orders. Results of the study indicate that the FTC should not enter a cease and desist order "whenever a technical or isolated violation is found," but rather after continued violations. In addition, findings indicate that statutory changes should be initiated in the area of enforcement procedures to help broaden the efficiency of the orders.

715 Kauper, Thomas E. "The Justice Department and the Antitrust Laws: Law Enforcer or Regulatory?" *Antitrust Bulletin* 35 (Spring 1990): 83-122.

Although this article focuses on the role of the Department of Justice's Antitrust Division in antitrust enforcement, the author does spend time delving into the dual responsibilities of the Antitrust Division and the FTC. It is concluded that shifting all antitrust enforcement from one to the other agency is predicated on whether enforcement can be best achieved through judicial or administrative action.

716   Kauper, Thomas E. et al. "Interview with James C. Miller III, Chairman, Federal Trade Commission." *Antitrust Law Journal* 52 (March 1983): 3-22.

Text of an interview in which the FTC Chairman first examines how government uses the statutes, regulations and policies of the FTC "to restrain business rivalry and restrict consumer choice." The interview is followed by a question and answer period in which Miller analyzes several issues related to antitrust enforcement.

717   Keating, Kenneth B. "Myth, Reality, and the Future of Antitrust." *Antitrust Law Journal* 24 (April 1964): 59-66.

Examines three areas of antitrust law enforcement: the Robinson-Patman Act, the role of antitrust in foreign commerce, and the relationship between antitrust law and administrative regulation in the setting of transportation rates. Emphasis is placed on the Robinson-Patman Act enforcement patterns of the FTC.

718   Kindred, Kay P. "When First Amendment Values and Competition Policy Collide: Resolving the Dilemma of Mixed-Motive Boycotts." *Arizona Law Review* 34 (Winter 1992): 709-742.

The author argues that the Supreme Court erred in its decision that a group of private defense lawyers violated per se Section 1 of the Sherman Antitrust Act and Section 5 of the FTC Act in the case of *FTC v. Superior Court Trial Lawyers Association*. The Supreme Court failed to take into account the "expressive dimension" of the case. By applying the rule of reason, it is concluded that the economic and political interests (mixed motive) of the boycott was protected under the First Amendment. A model for balancing First Amendment interests with competition policy in boycott cases is then presented.

719   Kinter, Earl W. *An Antitrust Primer: A Guide to Antitrust and Trade Regulation Laws for Businessmen*. New York: MacMillan, 1973. 2nd Edition.

As a well respected authority on antitrust law, the author presents a systematic overview of antitrust law enforcement in the United States. Among the topics covered are price fixing, mergers and acquisitions, monopolies, and state antitrust enforcement. The book includes specific chapters devoted to the FTC Act and FTC policies and procedures.

720   Kinter, Earl W. "Federal Trade Commission in 1960--Apologia Pro Vita Nostra." *Antitrust Law Symposium* 1961 (1961): 21-44.

As Chairman of the FTC, the author sketches three goals that will shape the agency's antitrust philosophy in the coming years: meaningful compliance, the need for activism, and a "proper regard for due process." Each of these goals are examined in detail followed by an analysis of the Commission's activities with regards to Robinson-Patman Act and various provisions of the FTC Act. Possible solutions to problems related to Robinson-Patman are then discussed. The essay concludes with a review of agency antimerger activities during the past year.

721   Kinter, Earl W. "Fifty Years of Antitrust Enforcement." *Federal Bar Journal* 24 (Fall 1964): 510-512.

Short essay outlining the antitrust accomplishments of the FTC during the first fifty years of its existence and examines current efforts to improve antitrust enforcement procedures with regards to the Robinson-Patman Act and through various agency programs.

722   Kinter, Earl W. "Resurgens: The Federal Trade Commission in 1959." *Antitrust Law Symposium* 1960 (1960): 30-48.

Reviews the antitrust activities of the FTC during the past year and outlines what actions the agency plans to take in the near future. Specific sections of the FTC Act, Robinson-Patman, and Section 7 of the Clayton Act are examined in this context. The essay concludes by studying the court's resistance to the Commission's subpoena power and the administrative process employed by the agency.

723   Kinter, Earl W. "Recent Changes in Federal Trade Commission Discovery Practice." *Antitrust Law Journal* 37 (1968): 238-247.

Three areas of discovery practice in antitrust law enforcement are examined: changes to Commission rules involving the taking of depositions, the use of subpoenas requiring the production of documents or access to files, and the availability of investigative files of the FTC to a respondent.

724   Kinter, Earl W. "Scope of the Federal Trade Commission's Orders in Price Discrimination Cases." *Business Lawyer* 14 (July 1959): 1053-1063.

As General Counsel of the FTC, the author discusses how the FTC develops orders that best fit the public's interest, protects the rights of the respondents as well as competitors, and takes into account economic realities. The underlying principles in creating an order are reviewed, followed by an examination of specific actions against firms to specifically analyze how orders develop with regard to price discrimination cases.

725   Kinter, Earl W. and Jerry R. Selinger. "Section 7 of the Clayton Act: A survey of Enforcement Options and Opportunities." *Emory Law Journal* 29 (Summer 1980): 681-753.

Surveys the law of mergers and monopolistic business activity as it relates to Section 7 of the Clayton Act. Included in the analysis is an overview of its development and a section devoted to examining the pre-complaint investigatory tools of the FTC. Three factors may initiate involvement by the agency: a general investigation of an industry, private party complaints, and pre-merger notification requirements. The investigatory authority of the FTC is also outlined.

726   Kitch, Edmund W. "Viewpoint: Taxi Reform–The FTC Can Hack It." *Regulation* 8 (May/June 1984): 13-15.

Examines the issue of artificial entry limits placed on the taxicab market in most cities and the results of a study conducted by staff at the FTC that ultimately led to the issuance of complaints against the cities of Minneapolis and New Orleans challenging their regulation of the taxicab industry as anticompetitive and thus harmful to the consumer. This issue is used to highlight three emerging trends in antitrust law: 1) enforcers adjusting their mission to include examining the impact of government regulation on competition; 2) expansion of the Sherman Act through rulings by the Supreme Court; and, 3) reducing the scope antitrust immunity based on "state action" by the Court.

727   Kleit, Andrew N. "Efficiencies Without Economists: The Early Years of Resale Price Maintenance." *Southern Economic Journal* 59 (April 1993): 597-619.

This essay examines what factors are associated with how businesses perceive potential benefits from resale price maintenance and, specifically, "which efficiency rationales were advanced by firms" during the period 1915 through 1917. Using previously unresearched material, the rationales are placed within the context of current economic theory. Section two provides an overview and critique of several economic theories that have been used to explain resale price maintenance. Section three analyzes federal resale price maintenance case law prior to 1918. Section four examines efficiency arguments made during 1915-1917 and the diverse number of business and government leaders that showed support for resale price maintenance. Involvement by the FTC is noted throughout the article.

728   Koch, Jr., Charles H. and Beth Martin. "FTC Rulemaking Through Negotiation." *North Carolina Law Review* 61 (January 1983): 275-311. Examines the rulemaking tools available to the FTC in assuring continued competition in the marketplace and "to encourage confidence in the marketplace" through its consumer protection activities. It is noted that the consumer protection activities are as much a policing function of the market as its antitrust duties. Rulemaking through general public participation and negotiation are studied in detail followed by an analysis the balance that the agency must maintain between creating regulations and satisfying the concerns of those affected by the regulations. It is concluded from the analysis that the FTC has failed in its rulemaking activities because it has failed to take into account business interests in its decision-making processes.

729   Kovacic, William E. "Federal Antitrust Enforcement in the Reagan Administration: Two Cheers for the Disappearance of the Large Firm Defendant in Nonmerger Cases." *Research in Law and Economics Annual* 12 (1989): 173-206.
This work explores antitrust activity directed at Fortune 500 companies by the Department of Justice and the FTC during the periods of 1973-1980 and 1980-1988. The research highlights the sharp decline in antitrust enforcement activity during the Reagan Administration. Although critics viewed this as sign of abandonment of regulating the harmful behavior of large firms, the author cites factors, such as "the state of antitrust learning" and limitations in antitrust enforcement capabilities of the Department of Justice and the FTC, as reasons for the decline. Two solutions are presented to improve antitrust enforcement: the need to recruit and retain qualified staff that are not immediately lured away by better opportunities in private practice and the need to create a long-term view of antitrust enforcement and the use of their allocated resources.

730   Kovacic, William E. "The Federal Trade Commission and Congressional Oversight of Antitrust Enforcement." *Tulsa Law Journal* 17 (Summer 1982): 587-671.
Gives a comprehensive analysis of the Congressional response to FTC antitrust

enforcement activities initiated by the *1969 Report of the American Bar Association Commission to Study the Federal Trade Commission*. The findings of the Report, including proposals that the Commission devote its antitrust resources to areas of economically significant problems and that its failure to perform efficiently was primarily due to a lack of clear goals and priorities, were influential in Congressional attempts to restructure the Commission's antitrust enforcement role. An historical analysis of external influences on the agency's work is provided to help explain the antitrust efforts of the FTC during the 1970s. A detailed description of how Congress endorsed the ABA Report's findings are also examined. The findings indicate that the FTC's antitrust enforcement program of the 1970s was responsive to Congressional policy preferences.

731   Kovacic, William E. "The Identification and Proof of Horizontal Agreements Under the Antitrust Laws." *Antitrust Bulletin* 38 (Spring 1993): 5-81.

Examines the structure of antitrust legal standards meant to identify and prove the existence of horizontal agreements. Contained within this is a section devoted to analyzing of the FTC's enforcement doctrine of tacit collusion as stated under Section 5 of the FTC Act. Legal standards under the Sherman Act are also examined. Specific cases are used throughout the text to clarify certain issues. The essay concludes by suggesting better ways to devise a definition of concerted action and to create suitable methodology for proving the existence of horizontal collusion.

732   Kovacic, William E. "Public Choice and Public Interest: Federal Trade Commission Antitrust Enforcement During the Reagan Administration." *Antitrust Bulletin* 33 (Fall 1988): 467-504.

This essay uses the end of the Reagan Administration antitrust era to examine the use of the rule of reason as applied to nonprice vertical restraints as established in the case of *Continental T.V., Inc. v. GTE Sylvania Inc.* Involvement, or the lack thereof, by the FTC in creating guidelines concerning vertical restraints is mentioned.

733   Kovaleff, Theodore P., ed. *The Antitrust Impulse: An Economic, Historical, and Legal Analysis.* New York, NY: M. E. Sharpe, 1994.

This is a two volume set of essays that examine various aspects of antitrust law. The essays are arranged under three broad perspectives: historical, philosophical, and economic. Each volume has a separate subject index that leads to numerous references to the FTC and its enforcement actions and rules. Because this is a recent book, issues related to the Reagan Administration and the European Community are discussed in some detail.

734   Kramer, Thomas. "Recent Case: Antitrust Law–Restraint of Trade–Unfair Competition–Trade Regulation–In an Action Brought by the Federal Trade Commission Under Section 13(b) of the FTC Act Seeking a Preliminary Injunction Against a Proposed Merger, a Court, After Weighing the Public and Private Equities Involved, May Deny the Requested Injunction and Issue a Hold Order, Even If the Commission Demonstrates a Likelihood of Success on the Merits." *University of Cincinnati Law Review* 51 (1982): 136-148.

This legal note outlines the issues behind the Weyerhaeser Co. case in which a preliminary injunction against a possible merger with Menasha Corporation that the FTC "had reason to believe" would violate existing antitrust laws, was not granted by United States District Court for the District of Columbia, even though the court concluded that evidence did exist that the merits of the case would likely lead to successful litigation by the FTC. The court allowed the merger to take place under a hold separate order which permitted a consumerization of the merger but under the requirement that the firms would operate as separate businesses pending further legal proceedings. t is concluded that this ruling has the potential to "seriously undermine" the enforcement of antitrust laws by the FTC and others.

735   Kravitz, Katherine Betz. "Nonprofit Hospital Mergers and Federal Antitrust Law: The Quest for Compatibility." *Delaware Journal of Corporate Law* 15 (Spring 1990): 539-572.

Although focusing on the efforts of the Department of Justice to regulate mergers between nonprofit hospitals, attention is paid to the role of the FTC in its efforts to control nonprofit hospital mergers. The author concludes that the mergers do offer relief for consumers in the way of lower prices and increased quality and that these facts should override the antitrust enforcement efforts of the Justice Department and the FTC.

736   Kreider, John S. "A Brief History of the Growth of Antitrust Legislation in the United States." *Southern California Law Review* 7 (January 1934): 144-182.

Outlines the growth of various antitrust laws in response to the large consolidations that have taken place in the first quarter of this century and analyzes what aspects of the public interest are embodied in the laws, the intent of Congress, judicial interpretation of the law, as well as what rules were present to guide the court's decisions. The Sherman, Clayton, and FTC Acts are all examined. With regards to the FTC, it is noted that the agency adds little statutory authority to preventing unlawful consolidations. However, the FTC Act does create a commission that has initiated both formal practices (cease and desist orders) and informal practices (the stipulation procedure and trade practice conferences) that were previously unknown in antitrust enforcement procedures.

737   Kruse, Layne E. "Deconcentration and Section 5 of the Federal Trade Commission Act." *George Washington Law Review* 46 (January 1978): 200-232.

This article studies the possible implications and effects of the FTC attempt to break up the four largest manufacturers of breakfast cereals in what the FTC contends is a shared monopoly that violates Section 5 of the FTC Act. After briefly analyzing the economic theories behind the shared monopoly concept, an examination of legislative history of the Act and specific cases are used to show that the FTC's use of Section 5 to suppress a shared monopoly is outside the legislative intent established by Congress. The author argues that the dismantling of shared monopolies should only be exercised when it injures competitors or consumers.

738   Kuhlman, J. M. "Changing Role of the Antitrust Agencies." *Antitrust Bulletin* 9 (1964): 725-.

Examines how the Celler-Kefauver amendment to Section 7 of the Clayton Act may have changed the role of the Department of Justice and the FTC with regards to antitrust law enforcement. Recent cases indicate a shift away from behavioral analysis and greater consideration given to the structure of the private sector. Issues related to determining relevant information, the nature and extent of the evidence, and remedial measures are examined in detail.

739   Langenfeld, James L. "How Can Guidelines Reduce the Uncertainties of Antitrust Enforcement?" *Antitrust Bulletin* 32 (Fall 1987): 643-659.

Discusses the problems associated with the issuance of various antitrust enforcement guidelines by the FTC, the Department of Justice, and the National Association of Attorney Generals as they relate to Thomas Jorde's appeal for more information in regards to how the courts and enforcement agencies interpret antitrust laws (*Antitrust Bulletin*, Fall 1987, pp. 579-608). These guidelines have frequently led to inconsistent enforcement standards. However, further study should take place before "more sophisticated, less predictable, case-by-case enforcement" is abandoned for simpler and more predictable rules are implemented.

740   Langenfeld, James L. and Louis Silva. "Federal Trade Commission Horizontal Restraint Cases: An Economic Perspective." *Antitrust Law Journal* 61 (Spring 1993): 653-697.

Analyzes eighty-one FTC horizontal restraint cases brought against trade and professional associations during the period of 1980 through 1992 within the context of three economic theories of anticompetitive effect: traditional collusion, raising rival's costs, and raising their own costs. It is concluded that, in general, such cases are procompetitive. An alphabetical list of cases and a table of selected data on respondents and case resolutions are given.

741   Larson, Paul. "Federal Trade Commission, Clayton 7 and Bigness in the Dairy Industry." *Oregon Law Review* 45 (February 1966): 85-113.

Uses the FTC's antitrust enforcement activity against the four largest companies in the dairy industry as a case study to examine the FTC's "attitude toward 'bigness' and to evaluate the effectiveness of section 7 of the Clayton Act as a device for curbing growth by acquisition." The cases against Foremost Dairies Inc. and Beatrice Foods Company are the focus of this article. The Foremost decision was important because it concentrated on potential rather than actual competition "between the acquired and acquiring companies as an indicator of the probable competitive effect of a merger." Four issues are raised by this litigation: is the marketplace more stable as a result of FTC action? were any new concepts concerning the application of Section 7 developed by the FTC as a result of this litigation? did the actions taken by the Commission effectively eliminate the anti-competitive behavior found within the dairy industry? and, is the marketplace more open for small businesses as a result of the FTC's actions? It is concluded that, while the FTC feels that its actions improved the dairy market, it is too early to make a definitive judgement on the issue.

742   LaRue, Paul H. "Current Significant Issues Under the Robinson-Patman Act." *Business Lawyer* 44 (August 1989): 1293-1305.

This work discusses the Act's relationship with current antitrust enforcement ideology based on Chicago School economics that view the provisions of

Robinson-Patman as protectionist legislation. The author notes that the lack of enforcement by the FTC indicates the Chicago School's influence on FTC policy. Four issues regarding the Act are specifically analyzed: what constitutes predatory pricing?, to what degree is the "inference of injury" decision by the Supreme Court in *FTC v. Morton Salt Co.* rebuttable?, what is the current status of functional discounts?, and what satisfies the plaintiff-buyer burden of proof concerning damages?

743   Latwin, Joseph L. "Dealing with Government Antitrust Investigations." *Brooklyn Law Review* 46 (Winter 1980): 235-247.

The author focuses on the scope of authority in enforcing antitrust laws of the Attorney General of the State of New York, the Antitrust Division of the Department of Justice and the FTC. The section devoted to the FTC discusses not only investigative authority, but what procedures are available to insure compliance with FTC orders.

744   Lavik, A. Roy. "The 1990 Revisions to the FTC Guides for Advertising Allowances and Other Merchandising Payments and Services." *Antitrust Law Journal* 59 (Fall 1990): 871-887.

Examines the FTC advisory interpretations issued to help clarify provisions of the Robinson-Patman Act. The interpretations cover advertising allowances or furnishing services in both resale transactions and original sales transactions. The legal development of these guidelines are discussed in light of earlier FTC interpretations. The rest of the article analyzes specific sections of the revised guidelines.

745   Lederman, Douglas. "Antitrust Challenge to Football Group Dismissed by Judge." *Chronicle of Higher Education* 37 (August 14, 1991): A1, A26.

Discusses the reasoning behind an administrative law judge's decision to dismiss a complaint issued by the FTC against the College Football Association in regards to its television contract with Capital Cities/ABC. It was ruled that the sale of television rights was "part of the educational process and not a part of big business." The judge ruled that the FTC has no jurisdiction in matters related to nonprofit entities.

746   Lerner, Arthur N. "Federal Trade Commission Antitrust Activities in the Health Care Services Field." *Antitrust Bulletin* 29 (Summer 1984): 205-224.

The author, as Assistant Director for Health Care, Bureau of Competition at the FTC, begins by outlining the FTC's antitrust enforcement involvement in the health care field during the past decade then examines specific enforcement activities related to advertising, innovation, access to hospitals, control over joint ventures, cost containment, relative value scales, and hospital mergers. The essay then explores the agency's role in issuing advisory opinions and details future enforcement efforts such as restrictions placed on physicians by state boards, health care financing, and obstruction of cost containment measures offered by private insurers, prepayment plans and government purchasers of health services.

747   Levi, Edward H. "The Robinson-Patman Act: Is It in the Public Interest?" *Antitrust Law Journal* 1 (1952-53): 60-75.

As part of a symposium on the Robinson-Patman Act, the author articulates reasons why the Act has presented such difficult legal problems. The author contends that the root of the problem lies in the fact that the Act is a price-fixing statute that has been misinterpreted as a antimonopoly or pro-competition law. The author expands on six specific defects within the Robinson-Patman Act, including undefined terms and misleading phrases. The author then examines the conflict between Robinson-Patman and the Sherman Act, in which Robinson-Patman promotes uniformity in prices and control over prices that the Sherman and FTC Acts consider illegal. Robinson-Patman grew out of a sense that the Sherman Act was inadequate in preventing monopolies. This perception, the author notes, is not so true today.

748   Lewis-Beck, Michael S. "Maintaining Economic Competition: The Causes and Consequences of Antitrust." *Journal of Politics* 41 (1979): 169-191.

The purpose of this essay is to focus on the causes and consequences of antitrust enforcement patterns by the FTC and the Department of Justice. The author evaluates leading theories on the political and economic determinants of antitrust enforcement and follows this with an analysis of whether current antitrust enforcement helps or hinders economic competition. After applying regression models to the problem, it is concluded that both agencies fail in having any significant effect on anticompetitive mergers. The primary reason for this is the lack of resources available to combat anticompetitive behavior in a trillion-dollar economy. Further, the political climate in Congress would undermine any chance of obtaining the enormous resources needed by either agency in order to be effective.

749   Lewyn, Mark. "Going After Microsoft." *National Review* 46 (January 24, 1994): 30, 32, 34, 36, 38.
Traces the FTC's efforts to investigate Microsoft that began with an agreement between Microsoft and IBM regarding application of operating systems in high and low end markets. The article provides insight into the FTC's interpretation of attempts by Bill Gates, Chief Executive of Microsoft, to merge with other software firms to strengthen its already strong position within the software marketplace.

750   Liebeler, Wesley J. "Antitrust Law and the New Federal Trade Commission." *Southwestern University Law Review* 12 (1980/81): 166-229.
Examines antitrust complaints, decisions, and settlements from January 1, 1970 through December 31, 1980 made by the FTC with the purpose of evaluating the cost effectiveness of the Commission's antitrust activities. The cases are analyzed against a standard of maximizing consumer welfare and divided among industry-wide cases, vertical contract and mergers, and horizontal contract and mergers. The results from the study indicate that the FTC's antitrust efforts are not cost-effective and divorced from the principles of market analysis. The last fourteen pages of the article contain the text of panelist responses to Liebeler's study.

751   Liedquist, R. E. "Recent Developments in Regional Enforcement of the Antitrust Laws." *Antitrust Law Symposium* 1975 (1975): 8-48.
Written by the Deputy Director of the FTC's Bureau of Competition, this essay discusses the role of the agency's regional offices in antitrust enforcement. It begins by outlining the development of recent antitrust activity within the regional offices including distributional restraints, horizontal price fixing and collusion, price discrimination, and other areas of horizontal and vertical restraints. The discussion concludes by examining future antitrust actions by the regional offices based on FTC directives.

752   Lobrano, John Drake. "Antitrust Law: Disallowance of Contribution; Rejection of Automatic Damages; and the Diminishing Role of the FTC in Antitrust Enforcement." *Annual Survey of American Law* 1982

(1982): 49-77.
Analyzes three areas of restriction related to recent antitrust enforcement. Among the three areas covered is recent circuit court decisions that have restricted interpretation of Section 5 of the FTC Act in regards to antitrust matters. Two cases, *Official Airlines Guide, Inc. v. FTC* and *FTC v. Weyerhaeuser Co.*, are studied to illustrate this restrictive behavior by the courts. It is concluded that the court's decision marks a trend away from the previously expansive power of the agency. It is noted that this trends is likely to continue.

753   Lock, Reinier H. et al. "United States-Canada Energy Trade and Evolving Antitrust Standards in Domestic Energy Regulation." *University of Pennsylvania Journal of International Law* 11 (Spring 1989): 381-413.
Examines domestic antitrust regulation of the energy market in relation to U.S.-Canadian energy trade. Although the FTC has had limited intervention in this area it does warrant some discussion in this essay, particularly when related to sponsoring competition, regulating non-price predation, and reacting to mergers. The regulatory mandates of the FTC and the Department of Justice are also covered.

754   Loftis III, James R. and Jeanne M. Forch. "Avoiding Potential FTC Challenges: A Practical Guide to Premerger Exchanges of Information." *Antitrust* 4 (Summer 1990): 10-12.
Discusses the concern expressed by the FTC regarding unlawful information exchanged between merging firms. FTC concern focuses on the nature of the information exchanged, the reasons why it was provided, the confidentiality by which the information was treated, and whether the information is exchanged or is simply information given by the company to be bought to the company doing the buying.

755   Loughlin, J. T. "Investigation and Trial of Robinson-Patman Act Cases Before the Federal Trade Commission." *Antitrust Bulletin* 4 (November 1959): 741-784; 5 (February 1960): 45-75.
This two part article examines in detail the increased attention given to Robinson-Patman Act provisions by the FTC during the 1950s. This activity falls under two general categories: general, industry-wide investigations and special investigations that cover a particular provision of the Act. The cases are then used to illustrate the investigational methods and powers of the FTC and to show the scope of these

investigations under Sections 2(c), (d), (e), and (f) of the Robinson-Patman Act. The second part of the article examines the legal procedures involved, FTC rules of practice, and appeal process. Results of the study show that a major defect in the administration of the Act is the method of selection of cases which is outdated and based on methods employed in 1915 when the FTC began its legal investigations. An additional problem is that too many complaints have resulted in consent orders. It is concluded that the underlying problem is that the Robinson-Patman Act as it amends Section 2 of the Clayton Act is treated with differing criteria depending on the form of the discriminatory practice. This leads to uneven interpretation by the FTC and the courts.

756   Luchansky, Bill and Jurg Gerber. "Constructing State Autonomy: The Federal Trade Commission and the Celler-Kefauver Act." *Sociological Perspectives* 36 (1993): 217-240.

Builds on previous research that examines "the nature of state in capitalist societies" by studying how a government agency evolves from a position of weakness to one of strength. The passage of the Celler-Kefauver Act and how it marked the expansion of FTC authority is used to analyze this issue. Efforts by the FTC to take advantage of a less hostile political structure and to affect legislation through the gathering of resources and conducting detailed economic studies are outlined. Three theories of the state, corporate liberalism, relative autonomy, and the state-centered theory, are used to show how government actors supported, and eventually passed, the law as well as how business reacted to the Act.

757   MacDonald, George P. "US Antitrust Law as It Relates to US Joint Research and Development Ventures." *International Journal of Technology Management* 3 (1988): 123-134.

The author examines U.S. antitrust law and compares it to European Economic Community antitrust law with regards to joint research ventures. Included in the discussion is a study of provisions of the FTC Act and opinions expressed by the FTC and the Department of Justice regarding joint ventures.

758   MacIntyre, Everette. "Federal Trade Commission's Antitrust Functions: Some Practical Problems in Enforcement." *UCLA Law Review* 14 (May 1967): 997-1027.

As a Commissioner at the FTC, the author examines the role of the Commission in enforcing the antitrust doctrine and proposes the need to re-evaluate current antitrust practices in a rapidly changing economy. Central to this re-evaluation is the task of measuring how much intervention is needed to insure a competitive marketplace while, at the same time, eliminating the need for additional regulation. Among the issues discussed is the relationship between economic reality and aggregate concentration, horizontal and vertical acquisitions, and the need to assess the Commission's role with regards to price discrimination.

759   Mahaney, Mary Claire and Adrian E. Tschoegl. "The Determinants of the FTC Antitrust Activity." *Administrative Law Review* 35 (Winter 1983): 1-32.

Reports the findings of a study to examine the what political and economic factors are present that determine the antitrust enforcement activities of the FTC. The study begins by discussing relevant theories and the role of ideology in relation to regulation. To help foster a framework for understanding, the internal workings of the FTC and its relationship to the legislative and executive branches of government are detailed. The methodology of the study and its results are then outlined. It is concluded from the data that there is a "strong relationship" between the frequency of complaints issued by the Commission and variables related to politics, economics and "life-cycle" of FTC over time. It is recommended that a similar study be conducted on the Department of Justice to provide a better overall understanding of regulation.

760   Manck, Richard B. "Petroleum Conspiracy: A Costly Myth." *Public Policy* 22 (Winter 1974): 1-13.

The author evaluates a report issued by the FTC that supported earlier statements by Congress that the petroleum industry was deliberately trying "to destroy the independent refiners and marketers," to expand their own markets, and attempt to block environmental legislation. The FTC report states that eight major petroleum companies, in particular, were engaging in conduct harmful to the independent refiner and marketer. This "squeezing" by the major companies was due to two major advantages: oil import quotas and oil depletion quotas. Each argument is analyzed and evidence is presented to indicate that these advantages stated in the FTC's report are, in fact, fallacious.

761   "Marketing Under the Robinson-Patman Act." *Illinois Law Review* 31 (March 1937): 907-942.

Outlines how the Robinson-Patman Act changes provisions within Section 2 of the Clayton Act and strengthens the ability of the FTC to enforce price discrimination cases. However, the Act is silent with regards to whether discriminatory contracts concluded before the effective date of the Act will be affected. This is an important issue because it calls into question whether some firms will be able to avoid prosecution under Robinson-Patman and whether firms "can urge present invalidity as a defense." Previous laws, such as the Clayton Act, have not been limited due to the absence of an express provision that contracts existing when the statutes went into effect are exempt from prosecution. This fact would indicate that Robinson-Patman will be interpreted in the same way.

762   "Marketing: Where Marketing Cases Stand Now and What's to Come, With a New Antitrust Policy Developing." *Business Week* (August 1, 1953): 62, 64, 66.

Discusses new and pending antitrust cases brought by the FTC and the Department of Justice to clarify governmental attitudes regarding the regulation of the marketplace under the Eisenhower Administration. The influence of newly appointed FTC Chairman Edward Howrey, who advocates the use of evidence over "preconceived ideologies" and the possible influence of law professor S. Chesterfield Oppenheim, who was appointed to co-chair a national committee set up by Attorney General Herbert Brownell to study antitrust law and marketing legislation, is also discussed.

763   Markovits, Richard S. "The Limits to Simplifying Antitrust: A Reply to Professor Easterbrook." *Texas Law Review* 63 (August 1984): 41-87.

Criticizes some of the assumptions articulated by Frank H. Easterbrook as they relate to tests of legality contained in antitrust laws and the structure of antitrust litigation, related conclusions regarding the rule of reason, and his arguments that "it is more just and efficient to reject a valid antitrust claim than to accept an invalid one." The essay concludes by analyzing Easterbrook's proposal for a set of "filters" to determine whether antitrust suits should be dismissed or maintained. The author concludes that while there is a need in certain circumstances to simplify antitrust analysis, there are limits which must be recognized.

764   Matteoni, Norman E. "An Antitrust Argument: Whether a Federal Trade Commission Order is Within the Ambit of the Clayton Act's Section 5." *Notre Dame Law Review* 40 (February 1965): 158-170.

This study researches recent challenges to the reasoning that a cease and desist order issued by the FTC cannot constitute prima facie evidence of an antitrust violation and/or "toll the statute of limitations for the private suitor" in subsequent treble damage suits. This position was established in the 1923 case, *Proper v.*

John Bene and Sons. The FTC's antitrust power as established by the provisions of the Clayton Act are placed within a legislative and factual context as well as compared with the antitrust powers of the Department of Justice. While there are arguments supporting both sides of the issue, it is pointed out that a cease and desist order from the FTC does not represent conclusive evidence of a violation in subsequent litigation and, if an order were to be considered prima facie evidence, then it must be considered so under Section 11 of the Clayton Act, for other agencies, such as the Federal Communications Commission, that have specialized antitrust jurisdiction.

765   Mattern, Stephen. "Free Speech, Free Markets, and the Per Se Rule of Antitrust: *FTC v. Superior Court Trial Lawyers Association.*" *Southwestern University Law Review* 21 (1992): 1443-1463.

Discusses the Trial Lawyers case and the use of the per se rule by the Supreme Court to argue that boycotts applied to the commercial arena are in violation of Section 1 of the Sherman Act. The note begins by providing background on the Sherman Act and the Noerr-Pennington Doctrine which allows an exception to the antitrust law if the situation involves an attempt to influence governmental decisions. This issue is then placed within the context of political boycotts. A detailed analysis of the events and outcome of the Trial Lawyers case reveals the FTC's reasoning in filing a complaint. The case also is illustrative of the conflict between First Amendment rights regarding free expression, the right to petition government, and the freedom to assemble and antitrust laws that protect groups and individuals from being the targets of unfair economic pressure, attempts to control prices, or exclude competition.

766   Matthew, Dayna B. "Doing What Comes Naturally: Antitrust Law and Hospital Mergers." *Houston Law Review* 31 (Fall 1994): 813-872.

Examines what effects antitrust statutes and enforcement by the Department of Justice and the FTC have had on the hospital industry. An empirical analysis of the industry provides important insight into the "classic competition versus regulation debate." It is argued that the natural monopoly characteristics of the hospital services industry must be taken into account when attempting to hold down costs through legislative or judicial means. Enforcement of antitrust laws by the government has been "applied indiscriminately" to control consolidations that were anticompetitive. It is concluded that pure competition within the hospital industry will lead to lower health care prices is incorrect due to the unique nature of the industry.

767   McCarthy, J. Thomas. "Trademarks, Antitrust and the Federal Trade Commission." *John Marshall Law Review* 13 (Fall 1979): 151-162.
Presents arguments both for and against the FTC's policy regarding its generic name cancellation program. The article begins by discussing the role of the FTC related to trademarks. Specific points related to the FTC's activities in trademark ownership are then outlined. It is concluded that recent criticism of the FTC's program is mostly unfounded, with the exception that genericness should be left to private litigation rather than through a government agency litigation.

768   McChesney, Fred S. "Antitrust and Regulation: Chicago's Contradictory Views." *Cato Journal* 10 (Winter 1991): 775-798.
The complex "intellectual agenda" of antitrust law enforcement in the 1990s is due to two elements of the Chicago school approach: the mistaken assumption by Chicago School advocates that it has won "the antitrust war" and that much of the economic analysis that forms the basis of Chicago School antitrust enforcement philosophy is inconsistent with its own positive notions of economics. The essay begins with an historical outline of the Chicago School approach followed by how antitrust is defined by Chicago. Antitrust enforcement actions by the FTC and Department of Justice are used to help clarify the effects of Chicago School economics.

769   McChesney, Fred S. and William F. Shugart, eds. *The Causes and Consequences of Antitrust: The Public-Choice Perspective.* Chicago, IL: University of Chicago Press, 1995.
This collection of reprinted and original essays attempts to move beyond the traditional debate in antitrust law enforcement from what antitrust should do to what has it done and why. The arguments among legal and economic scholars concerning the merits of the "Chicago School" or "Harvard School" approaches to antitrust analysis have overshadowed more fundamental issues relating to its overall purpose in regulating a free economy. Most essays devote at least some analysis to the role of the FTC. The essays are divided into five sections that examine a different aspect of antitrust enforcement and public choice. The work includes a selected bibliography, addresses of contributors, and a subject index.

770   McCullough, Joseph T. "The Continuing Search for Greater Certainty: Suggestions for Improving U.S. and EEC Antitrust Clearance Procedures." *Northwestern Journal of International Law and Business* 6 (Fall 1984): 803-895.

This essay studies three areas of uncertainty related to antitrust law enforcement within the United States and the European Community. The first is, due to a heavy dependence on judicial interpretation, there is often a considerable delay in reviewing "fringe issues and gray areas" in the law; Second, even when dealing with relatively clear provisions of the law, suits can still be brought to seek further judicial clarification. Finally, uncertainty is also present when the issue of legality depends on the individual circumstances of the case. In examining U.S. reaction to uncertainties in antitrust law enforcement, the author gives a detailed analysis of the FTC's Advisory Opinion Program which attempts to inform businesses of the legality of a proposed or on-going course of action.

771   McDavid, Janet L. "Antitrust Issues in Health Care Reform." *DePaul Law Review* 43 (Summer 1994): 1045-1080.

The author argues that, among the major initiatives of the Clinton Administration, is reforming America's health care system. To insure that the health care industry remains a competitive marketplace, antitrust enforcement must represent a major component of any reform movement. The roles of both the FTC and the Department of Justice are discussed as part of an examination of possible reform plans, their relationship to antitrust laws, and proposed exemptions for health care providers.

772   McDermott, Kathleen E. "Clearing HSR Reportable Mergers Through the FTC: A Quick Look at the "Quick Look"." *Antitrust* 5 (Spring 1991): 32-35.

This article examines the problems associated with clearing reportable mergers under provisions of the Hart-Scott-Rodino Amendment and specifically second requests (requests for additional information) by the FTC. The criticisms focus on the fact these requests can be overbroad, covering material that is irrelevant to the merger process. To help the FTC obtain information on a merger without placing an undue burden on the firms involved a "quick look" policy was developed by the agency which attempts are made to provide information relevant to a specific aspect of the merger if that specific information will alleviate concerns about the transaction. The essay offers a critique of this policy and concludes that it does offer the potential to solve some of the concerns firms may have with second requests.

773   McDermott, Kathleen E. "FTC Explores the Limits of Nonmerger Enforcement." *Antitrust* 5 (Summer 1991): 34-37.

Observes that recent developments at the FTC would indicate a return to 1970s style antitrust enforcement that employed innovation tactics and intervened in areas that the FTC had previously ignored. This issue is particularly true in the field on nonmerger antitrust enforcement where a special task force was created to focus on nonmerger enforcement without the statutory constraints of merger work. Opinions from FTC personnel and others are included to shed light on the prospects for success in FTC nonmerger enforcement.

774   McKinney, Luther C. "Shared Monopolies and the FTC's Cereal Case." *Antitrust Law Journal* 47 (1978): 1127-1134.

The author shares his personal insights into the concept of shared monopolies and examines in detail the recent action taken by the FTC against the top six ready-to-eat breakfast cereal manufacturers. The author examines the economic and legal theories underlying shared monopolies and notes that there is an erosion in public confidence concerning what effects challenging shared monopolies would have on the economy.

775   McLaughlin, James A. "The Courts and the Robinson-Patman Act: Possibilities of Strict Construction." *Law and Contemporary Problems* 4 (June 1937): 410-419.

Evaluates the treatment of legislation by the courts that attempts to regulate trade. Analyzing specific cases provides insight into the development of the FTC and Clayton Acts, and more recently, the Robinson-Patman Act. Criticism of individual sections of the Robinson-Patman Act is discussed in detail. With regard to FTC enforcement of the Act, it is concluded that the agency has proceeded to take action under the Act "without any signs of intelligent discrimination" and that the suits are "badly chosen," "badly prepared," and "badly presented." The author notes that the fact that many FTC orders are reversed, helps to supports this view.

776   McLaughlin, James A. "Legal Control of Competitive Methods." *Iowa Law Review* 21 (January 1936): 274-304.

Essay that examines the political impetus for the development of legislation to combat unfair competition. Specific cases are used to illustrate what business behavior led to the creation of the Sherman, Clayton, and FTC Acts. The essay concludes by defining what competitive practices are subject to legal control.

777   Melone, Albert P. "The American Bar Association, Antitrust Legislation, and Interest Group Coalitions." *Policy Studies Journal* 11 (1983): 684-698.

This study examines the American Bar Associations lobbying activities with regards to the antitrust field. The article begins by outlining the ABA's general opposition to "innovative" change to the antitrust laws and reasons for such opposition. This pattern continues into the 1970s. By examining testimonial behavior with respect to Congressional hearings, it is shown that the ABA is more likely to side with opponents representing economically conservative business-oriented interests groups and generally argued against views expressed by consumer groups, such as the Consumer's Union, and the government (FTC). It is concluded that the ABA agrees with groups that it interacts with most frequently and this parallels finding from a previous study conducted ten years ago.

778   Mensch, Elizabeth and Alan Freeman. "Frontiers of Legal Thought I: Efficiency and Image Advertising as an Antitrust Issue." *Duke Law Journal* 1990 (April 1990): 321-373.

This article is divided into three parts: Part I traces the relationship between advertising and antitrust law during the past twenty-five years noting that during the last decade advertising has become "a preferred and even privileged" part of contemporary antitrust doctrine. Specific cases are used to illustrate this point. Part II examines why this break occurred, noting the fundamental change in FTC philosophy under Reagan appointee James C. Miller III and within the context of an active debate among economists regarding the economic meaning behind product differentiation achieved through the effects of advertising. Part III places the institution of advertising within a social and historical context. This is done to show the difficulty in defining advertising solely based on whether it is anti or pro competitive in nature. FTC involvement in both advertising and antitrust enforcement are analyzed throughout the text.

779   Miller, III, James C. "No More 'Star Trek Antitrust' at the FTC: The Taming of a Wayward Regulator." *Antitrust Law and Economics Review* 15 (1983): 69-89.

Text of an interview with FTC Chairman James C. Miller III. In it, Miller expresses concern that the FTC is going beyond the expressed intention of the law with regards to antitrust enforcement and the frequently adversarial relationship that has developed between the agency and private industry. Issues concerning predation, industry concentration and mergers are discussed in detail.

780   Minotti, A. M. "The Federal Trade Commission Takes Another Look at Dual Distribution Under the Robinson-Patman Act." *Texas Bar Journal* 44 (May 1981): 473-474, 476-482.

Uses the FTC complaint against Boise Cascade Corporation, in which the Commission states Boise participated in discriminatory price discounts with suppliers of its office products supplies, to note a rift among the Commissioners between the regulatory schemes of the Robinson-Patman and Sherman Acts as they relate to duel distribution. The FTC cited Section 2(f) of the Robinson-Patman Act as the legal foundation for action against Boise. Other cases are used to show this rift concerning what Act should be used to remedy preferential discounts between retail and wholesale distributors.

781   "Moog-Niehoff Decision–The FTC and Enforcement for Enforcement's Sake." *Northwestern University Law Review* 53 (September-October 1958): 510-520.

The cases of *Moog Indus, Inc. v. FTC* and *FTC v. C. E. Niehoff* helped to resolve the issue of court power to postpone the effect of FTC cease and desist orders under provisions of the Robinson-Patman Act. However, as this article examines, the cases did not remedy the issue of FTC cease and desist orders against a particular firm practicing price discrimination without regard for competing firms in the same industry remaining relatively unaffected by the order. The scope of the FTC power to modify cease and desist orders and the role of competitive necessity under the Robinson-Patman Act are analyzed to help define possible solutions.

782   Montague, Gilbert H. "Antitrust Laws and Federal Trade Commission, 1914-1927." *Columbia Law Review* 27 (June 1927): 650-678.

Provides a detailed overview of the birth and development of the FTC and the political climate that shaped its agenda and antitrust enforcement jurisdiction. Specific cases are used to measure the progress the agency has made in following its enforcement mission and the possible restrictions placed on the FTC when the courts and public opinion view the agency as departing from legal tradition.

783   Montague, Gilbert H. "The Commission's Jurisdiction Over Practices in Restraint of Trade: A Large-Scale Method of Mass Enforcement of the Antitrust Laws." *George Washington Law Review* 8 (January-February

1940): 365-398.

Outlines the historical development of the "unfair methods of competition" provision of the FTC Act and how the provision has developed into a powerful antitrust enforcement tool. Judicial interpretations of the provision and its application to specific issues such as unrestrained price cutting and promotion of open competition are examined in detail. The relationship between the FTC and the Attorney General is also discussed.

784 Morganfeld, I. R. "Antitrust and the Oligopoly Problem: Intellectual Pygmies at the Enforcement Agencies?" *Antitrust Law and Economics Review* 9 (1977): 15-30.

Critical examination of the flaws inherent in calling on the Department of Justice and the FTC to investigate the problem of oligopolies. Among the problems noted by the author is that such a task would cost considerable time and money, there are political influences present at both agencies that could undermine the effectiveness of such an endeavor, and there is a lack of economic expertise to evaluate the issue. This latter issue is examined in a sarcastic tone by the author.

785 Mosher, Lawrence. "Conglomerate Mergers–A Threat or a Blessing?" *National Journal* 11 (March 24, 1979): 480-484.

The essay discusses reaction within Congress to the recent increase in large conglomerate mergers and the subsequent economic concentration that this has led to. Reaction by both the Department of Justice and the FTC are examined. It is noted that there is little, if any, evidence from available data to indicate that these mergers are actually harmful to the economy and that any anti-merger bills presented in Congress are unlikely to pass without strong presidential support.

786 Mosher, Lawrence. "With the Cooperation of Its Friends, Sunkist is Pulling the FTC's Teeth." *National Journal* 12 (January 12, 1980): 49-51.

Examines a bill submitted by Congressman Mark Andrews (New York-R), that will prevent the FTC from continuing its antitrust proceedings against Sunkist Growers Inc. The bill will also abort any antitrust investigations of the nation's 7,500 agricultural cooperatives. Also detailed is the case against Sunkist and reaction by decision-makers within the FTC to Congress' "interference."

787   Mueller, Charles E. "Antitrust and Economics: The Gulf between Science and Policy in the U.S." *Antitrust Law and Economics Review* 22 (1990): 1-18.

Discusses the lack of policy input by "the scientific economic community" in the field of antitrust law. Two examples are presented to show the repercussions of this lack of scientific input. The first is the need to include economists in helping Eastern European countries transform from Communist states to a market economy. The involvement of FTC Chairwoman Janet Steiger and others from the FTC and Department of Justice in advising delegates from Czechoslovakia, Hungary, and Poland is examined, noting that many of their opinions regarding global antitrust are not supported by economists. The second example used is a critique of domestic antitrust policy as defined by FTC activities that also suffer from a lack of input by "scientific economists."

788   Mueller, Charles E. "FTC and the Monopoly Problem: Trustbusting a "Revolutionary" Concept in America?" *Antitrust Law and Economics Review* 7 (1975): 9-24.

As a attorney-advisor for the FTC during the past fifteen years, the author presents testimony to the Senate hearings on the adequacy of the state of competition in the nation's food industry. This is the text of his statement to Congress in which the agency's efforts with regards to regulating the food industry is discussed. Issues presented in the hearing includes the inadequacies of cease and desist orders, the growing numbers of monopolies in the economy, price fixing problems, and concludes by stating the economic need for a new antitrust law.

789   Mueller, Charles E. "How Antitrust Fell as Economics Rose: "Mutiny" at Justice and the FTC." *Antitrust Law and Economics Review* 22 (1990): 1-17.

There has been increased antitrust enforcement activity of the FTC under Janet Stieger. According to the author, this post-Reagan ideology is "middle of the road" and likely not to evolve into the aggressive trustbusting policies that marked the 1970s. A parallel shift in ideology is also taking place at the Department of Justice. The author examines possible barriers to this shift including conflicts between economic interests and antitrust interests. Points articulated by Marc Allan Eisner in his book *Antitrust and the Triumph of Economics* are also examined in detail to help explain these conflicts and shift from active enforcement during the 1970s to laissez-faire enforcement during the Reagan era.

790   Mueller, Charles E. "See No Monopolies, Hear No Critics: The Sad Case of the Federal Trade Commission." *Antitrust Law and Economics Review* 12 (1980): 56-72.

Highly critical essay outlining attempts by the author and others of the *Review* to file an amicus curiae brief concerning the pending case of *FTC v. E.I. DuPont de Nemours and Co.*, which was subsequently denied by a majority vote (4-1) of the FTC Commissioners. The author then delves into the reasons why the FTC is unwilling to hear its public interest critics, suggesting that, as appointees under the FTC Act, acceptance of outside counsel can be construed as an admission that they lack the public interest wisdom inferred upon them through the Congressional appointment process.

791   Mueller, Charles E. "Step 1 in Reforming U.S. Antitrust: Abolish the Economics Units at Justice and the FTC." *Wage-Price Law and Economics Review* 17 (1992): 1-20.

In a series of communications with the Clinton Administration, the author presents eleven antitrust reforms that should be instituted in 1993. The foundation of these reforms is the elimination of the economic units of the FTC and the Department of Justice and the economic theories that developed through them that "were used to kill two-thirds" of the antitrust cases brought forth during the past twelve years. Airline consolidation is used as an example of why economic theory developed during the past decade has undermined antitrust law enforcement.

792   Mueller, Charles E. "Trustbusting and the Future of Capitalism: Small Could Be Beautiful." *Antitrust Law and Economics Review* 8 (1976): 47-80 and 15-56.

Two part article containing the text of an interview with the associate editor of the *Review* and former attorney for the FTC. In the interview the author discusses a wide variety of topics, including trustbusting and political pressures, monopolies in a capitalistic society, institutional constraints on FTC antitrust enforcement, and aspects of FTC administrative procedure. The second part of the article continued in the next issue examines the role of economic analysis in FTC proceedings and its influence on the Commissioners. The article provides unique insight into the administrative procedures of the agency. The author states that the FTC is an economic agency that should be directed by economists or attorneys familiar with economic principles.

793   Mueller, Willard F. "A New Attack on Antitrust: The Chicago Case."
Antitrust Law and Economics Review 18 (1986): 29-66.
This work examines the current attack on antitrust from the political right within
the context of the Chicago School of Economics enforcement ideology. The
effects of this movement on both the Department of Justice and the FTC are
examined. Also considered is what impact this ideology will have on future
antitrust policy.

794   Mueller, Willard F. et al. *The Sunkist Case: A Study in Legal-
Economic Analysis.* Lexington, MA: Lexington Books, 1987.
This book examines in detail the case against Sunkist Growers, Inc. issued by the
FTC charging that the firm attempted to monopolize the California-Arizona citrus
industry. Access to key internal documents and personal interviews with personnel
of Sunkist provide a rich source of information normally not available in cases of
this size. The authors use this case to examine in broader terms "the marketing and
pricing policies that lie at the core of market conduct" as well as "the nature and
role of cooperative enterprise in determining market performance." Includes the
text of the FTC complaint, the Sunkist Growers, Inc., amended articles of
incorporation and bylaws, and the agreement between the FTC and Sunkist.
Includes a list of references and an index.

795   Mullenix, James W. "The Premerger Notification Program at the Federal
Trade Commission." *Antitrust Law Journal* 57 (Spring 1988): 125-131.
Traces the development of the FTC's premerger notification program since it
began in 1978 and what impact it has had in merger enforcement by the
Commission. Three issues are then analyzed in detail: inadvertent failure to file
a premerger notification, exemption of purchases made exclusively for the
purpose of investment, and the use of transactions or devises to avoid filing under
the program. It is noted that the premerger notification program is an important
component of the FTC's merger enforcement activities.

796   Muris, Timothy J. "Antitrust Enforcement at the FTC: The Atomistic
Problem." *Antitrust Law and Economics Review* 15 (1983): Part I: 91-
110; Part II: 11-18.
Two part interview with the current Director of the FTC's Bureau of Competition
in which he discusses the role of the FTC in antitrust regulation. Issues covered
include specific roles regarding mergers and monopolies, specific remedies the
FTC uses to control, and antitrust enforcement problems confronted by the FTC.

797   Muris, Timothy J. "Kirkpatrick Committee Report: Antitrust Issues." *Antitrust Law Journal* 58 (Spring 1989): 25-28.

As part of a discussion regarding the Kirkpatrick Committee Report on the Role of the FTC, the author discusses the key principles in the Report related to mergers and non-merger cases. The Commission's involvement with the health care industry is used to an example of future what future action the FTC should take in antitrust law enforcement.

798   Neale, A. D. *The Antitrust Laws of the U.S.A.* Cambridge: Cambridge University Press, 1970. 2nd Edition.

Meant as a comprehensive, one-volume reference to the antitrust laws of the United States, this book provides a good foundation for understanding the complexities of antitrust enforcement. Included in its analysis are numerous cites and examinations of the FTC's role in antitrust enforcement. The book is divided into sixteen section, with each covering a different area of antitrust law. Among the issues covered are remedies, monopolistic practices, mergers and acquisitions, resale price maintenance, and various agreements among competitors.

799   Nelson, Philip B. "Reading Their Lips: Changes in Antitrust Policy Under the Bush Administration." *Antitrust Bulletin* 36 (Fall 1991): 681-697.

Explores possible changes in antitrust law enforcement based on statements by appointees of the Bush Administration and a survey of twenty-four antitrust attorneys. The antitrust bar's perception of the success or failure of the policies stated by the attorneys and appointees are also examined. It is concluded that these statements indicate an adoption of a more active antitrust policy by the Department of Justice and FTC in the near future.

800   "The New Federal Trade Commission and the Enforcement of the Antitrust Laws." *Yale Law Journal* 65 (November 1965): 34-85.

Comprehensive analysis of the FTC's "new" direction in antitrust law enforcement since the agency gained a Republican majority as the result of the appointment of Chairman Edward F. Howrey in March of 1953. Among the issues discussed relating to the "new" FTC are formal enforcement procedures, the use of voluntary enforcement of antitrust laws, enforcement of Section 3 of the Clayton Act, exclusive dealing contracts, tying arrangements, enforcement of Robinson-Patman, territorial price discrimination, and administrative expertise as presumed by the Supreme Court in the Standard Stations case. It is concluded that while the

FTC actions are misguided with regards to territorial price discrimination, judicial review remains to correct such actions. The current actions of the FTC represent an important improvement in antitrust enforcement by the agency.

801   Nguyen, Xuan Nguyen and Frederick W. Derrick. "Hospital Markets and Competition: Implications for Antitrust Policy." *Health Care Management Review* 19 (Winter 1994): 34-43.

This study considers issues related to the application of federal antitrust laws by the FTC and the Department of Justice to hospital mergers. Central to this issue is whether competition among hospitals contributes to lower health care costs. The joint merger guidelines of the FTC and the DOJ are analyzed and framed within the context of defining the product market and delimiting the geographic marketplace of hospital services. A literature review is then conducted showing that, because hospitals compete on a nonprice basis, competition leads to higher prices, lower occupancy rates, and reduced efficiency. It is concluded that the 1992 merger guidelines offer an improvement over previous guidelines, but it remains to be seen if the enforcement of the guidelines will improve conditions in light of the Clinton Administration's desire to create highly concentrated provider networks.

802   Noakes, Wayne C. and William S. Hendon. "Large Firms and Small Firms: Enforcement of the Clayton Act." *Antitrust Bulletin* 11 (1966): 949-962.

Examines patterns of enforcement by the FTC with regards to the Clayton Act and, specifically, whether the Clayton Act is enforced against large firms more than smaller ones. The study also attempts to determine what sections of the Act are used or not used in enforcement proceedings. Data from 335 cases decided between January 1958 and June 1962 are analyzed. Results from the study indicate that large firms were not specifically targeted. FTC enforcement motivation was primarily based on whether the agency could win the case (which it did 95% of the time) and not on economic efficiency. Data also revealed that most cases were enforced under Section 2 of the Clayton Act with Sections 3, 7, and 8 largely unenforced. It is concluded that large firms in highly concentrated industries are investigated less frequently and thus have an advantage over small firms in less concentrated industries.

803   Oliver, Daniel. "Current FTC Merger Policy and Enforcement of the Antitrust Laws as They Relate to Mergers." *Antitrust Law Journal* 56 (1987): 755-764.
Outlines the antitrust laws enforced by the FTC that related to mergers and reviews the policies behind these enforcement activities. Also covered are the agency's procedures and highlights features of the constitute action by the FTC in challenging a possible merger. Two charts are included that summarize the merger enforcement of the FTC during the past nine years.

804   Oliver, Daniel. "Federal and State Antitrust Enforcement: Constitutional Principles and Policy Considerations." *Cardozo Law Review* 9 (March 1988): 1245-1275.
Examines state antitrust enforcement activities in relation to antitrust policies and guidelines established by the FTC by reviewing the FTC's enforcement activities, discussing how states can complement these efforts, and detailing the need for national conformity. The case of *California ex rel. Van de Kamp v. Texaco, Inc.* is studied in detail to provide a concrete example of state action involving mergers and acquisitions.

805   Oliver, Daniel. "Revolution in Antitrust: Competition Deserves More than Lip Service." *The Credit World* 76 (March/April 1988): 18-20, 22-23, 26.
The integration of economic analysis into the enforcement of antitrust laws and the ways in which this phenomenon evolved from academics to the courts and eventually adopted by federal agencies is the focus of this work. Examples of anti-competition actions by the FTC are presented that have had a measurable effect on consumer welfare. The essay concludes with the text of a question and answer session after remarks made at the Center for the Study of American Business, Washington University, St. Louis.

806   Oliver, Daniel. "The Role of the Federal Trade Commission in Formulating and Implementing Competition Policy." *Federal Bar News and Journal* 34 (June 1987): 200-205.
As Chairman of the FTC, the author details the three key principles that guide his leadership of the Commission: that competition is the best way to ensure "optimal allocation of society's resources and maximizes consumer welfare; that restraints on competition erode consumer welfare; and that government is the primary

source of restraint on consumer welfare. The author then focuses on five components of the agency's competition program that reflect these principles: mergers and acquisitions, distributional arrangements, horizontal restraints, and competition policy. The role of state antitrust enforcement is also detailed.

807   Oppenheim, S. Chesterfield. "Administration of the Brokerage Provision of the Robinson-Patman Act." *George Washington Law Review* 8 (January-February 1940): 511-544.

The brokerage provision of the Robinson-Patman Act is the only provision that has been tested by judicial review. The interpretation of the brokerage provision, its legislative history, the rationale for brokerage services, and various aspects of the FTC's enforcement of the Section 2(c) of the Act are examined to show what principles underlay its creation and enforcement.

808   Oppenheim, S. Chesterfield. "Federal Antitrust Legislation: Guideposts to a Revised National Antitrust Policy." *Michigan Law Review* 50 (1952): 1139-1244.

Explores whether the three major antitrust laws, the Clayton Act, the Sherman Act, and the FTC Act and accompanying lesser laws constitutes a sound public policy in antitrust enforcement. Issues highlighted include whether the legislative intent behind these laws represents a sound approach; whether or not the laws have been properly executed; does sufficient cohesion exist among the varying laws; and what is the type and quality of protection to competition embodied in these laws. Although these issues have been around for awhile, changes to the antitrust laws have been "piecemeal" with no comprehensive revision attempted by Congress. The author then details eleven recommended steps to revising the national antitrust policy.

809   Oppenheim, S. Chesterfield. "Guides to Harmonizing Section 5 of the Federal Trade Commission Act with the Sherman and Clayton Acts." *Michigan Law Review* 59 (April 1961): 821-854.

Examines the FTC's authority in enforcing the Clayton Act, the Sherman Act, and Section 5 of the FTC Act in order to evaluate the FTC's use of Section 5 without taking into account the complexities of the other statutes. The author attempts to create a model for harmonizing antitrust enforcement through the three laws and to discuss the extent of Congressional intervention needed to ensure effective competition under a national antitrust policy. Specific cases are used to provide an understanding of the provisions of each statute.

810   Ordover, Janusz A. and Jonathan B. Baker. "Entry Analysis Under the 1992 Horizontal Merger Guidelines." *Antitrust Law Journal* 61 (Summer 1992): 139-146.

Examines the issue of entry as defined in the Department of Justice's 1984 Merger Guidelines and the FTC merger guidelines of 1992. The new Guidelines place the analysis of entry between two types: uncommitted and committed. Uncommitted firms enter for short term periods to reap quick profits. Committed firms enter for an extended period of time and are primarily concerned with long-term profit potential. It is concluded that the economic framework of the new guidelines provide a consistently logical "explanation of the way the prospect of entry may deter or counteract possible harmful competitive effects of mergers" and helps to organize facts to facilitate this evaluation.

811   Palmer, Alan K. "Regulation, Professional Responsibility, and Market Forces in the Health Care Field." *Journal of Medical Education* 54 (April 1979): 275-283.

This essay begins with a discussion of the FTC's role in antitrust enforcement, focusing on efforts to regulate unfair methods of competition within the health care industry. FTC activities have increased in this field due to the fact that health care is a necessity for consumers, a significant portion of the consumer's dollar is spent on health care, and health care costs have risen considerably during the past decade. These issues and the FTC's competition program are studied in detail.

812   Paul, Robert D. "The FTC's Increased Reliance on Section 13(b) in Court Litigation." *Antitrust Law Journal* 57 (Spring 1988): 141-148.

The purpose of this essay is to examine the use of Section 13(b) of the FTC Act in merger regulation and consumer protection enforcement. The case of *FTC v. Weyerhaeuser Co.* is used to illustrate usage of the preliminary injunction proviso. Two more recent preliminary injunction suits cases are also outlined.

813   Pearson, Richard N. "Section 5 of the Federal Trade Commission Act as Antitrust: A Comment." *Boston University Law Review* 47 (Winter 1967): 1-19.

Commentary discussing the court system's broad interpretation of Section 5 of the FTC Act as an antitrust enforcement tool, noting that this broad usage is "becoming the uncaged giant of the antitrust laws." Central to problems associated with Section 5 usage is when the law is applied independent of the Sherman and

Clayton Acts. This issue is further complicated by the fact that Section of the FTC Act addresses two separate modes of conduct: deceptive or dishonest practices and restraint of trade. It is concluded that an open-ended interpretation of Section 5 does more harm than good with regards to competition in a marketplace. The decision of *Brown Shoe Co. v. United States* is used to illustrate this point. The Commission should rely on the rule of reason rather than the per se rule in its application of Section 5 to antitrust enforcement.

814   Peoples, Jr., James. "Merger Activity and Wage Levels in U.S. Manufacturing." *Journal of Labor Research* 10 (Spring 1989): 183-196.

The purpose of this study is to determine what type of mergers provide workers with higher-than-average or lower-than-average wages. Two primary sets of data were used: information about an individual employee's personal characteristics, wages, regional place of work, and the industry in which the individual worked full-time was gathered from the March 1981 Current Population Survey and information obtained from the 1979 FTC Large Mergers and Acquisitions Series that gave the value of acquisition assets for large acquisitions. Results suggest that industries composed of firms created through horizontal, vertical, and product extension mergers "received significantly higher wages than other workers."

815   Peritz, Rudolph J. "The Predicament of Antitrust Jurisprudence: Economics and the Monopolization of Price Discrimination Argument." *Duke Law Journal* 1984 (December 1984): 1205-1295.

The central assertion of those who support the "Law and Economics Approach" to antitrust analysis is that there is a fundamental conflict in antitrust enforcement if there is a failure to take into account "both rational economic analysis and political 'populist' concerns." This article analyzes this claim and the strategies behind it from the perspective of contemporary philosophy and social theory. The issue of price discrimination under the Robinson-Patman Act is used because antitrust scholars agree that the statutory interpretation and doctrinal development of the Act is incoherent and because the provisions of the Act have only marginal importance. Contained within this analysis is a section devoted to the FTC's interpretation and enforcement of Robinson-Patman.

816   Perry, A. R. "Jurisdiction of the Federal Trade Commission– Multiple Basing Point System–Unfair Method of Competition–Price Discrimination." *Southern California Law Review* 22 (February 1949):

164-175.
Defines the elements of a multiple basing point system, examines how a basing point arrangement creates an unhealthy business environment for competitors that are excluded from the system, and analyzes how the Supreme Court in the case, *Federal Trade Commission v. Cement Institute*, upheld the FTC's challenge that the basing point system constitutes a restrain on trade under provisions of the Sherman Act. The essay concludes by briefly examining the economic characteristics and impact of the system and its abolition.

817   Pertschuk, Michael. "Consumer Priorities, Macro-Concentration, and the Scope of the FTC's Deconcentration Authority." *Antitrust Law and Economics Review* 9 (1977): 31-42.
Text of excerpted questions and answers to the nominee for Chairman of the FTC. The dialogue is part of the Pertschuk's confirmation hearing before the Senate Commerce Committee. Among the issues covered is the seemingly new position that the FTC will activity investigate industries with high concentration and setting priorities in allocating resources for antitrust and consumer protection activities.

818   Pertschuk, Michael. "Inflation Paradox: Business Regulation of Business." *Antitrust Law and Economics Review* 10 (1978): 53-59.
Text of an address given in Chicago in which the FTC Chairman discusses business supported regulations with regards to price fixing and suppressing innovation and efforts to regulate unfair industry conduct.

819   Pertschuk, Michael. "The Reagan Antitrusters and Fundamental Values: Fairness and Free-Market Economics at the FTC." *Antitrust Law and Economics Review* 15 (1983): 37-49.
Interview with outgoing chairman Michael Pertschuk in which he expresses his disdain for certain programs initiated by the FTC under Republican political pressure and states that their is a fundamental "lack of faith in the antitrust laws." The interview also includes insight into Pertschuk's future intentions after his chairmanship ends.

820   Pertschuk, Michael. "Report from the Federal Trade Commission." *Antitrust Law Journal* 47 (April 1978): 765-773.
Discusses the role of the Commission as an advocate for competition, focusing on the current trend in government towards deregulation. The FTC has eliminated

over one hundred obsolete trade regulation rules to help streamline efficiency and to ensure a competitive marketplace. Also examined is the need for further reform.

821   Pertschuk, Michael. "Report from the Federal Trade Commission." *Antitrust Law Journal* 48 (April 1979): 629-636.

Examines the FTC's efforts to seek alternative enforcement strategies beyond the case-by-case approach and to systematically review priorities within the agency's enforcement procedures. Three broad categories of enforcement are then previewed: taking action to eliminate the harmful effects of excessive market power, investigating areas of the economy and industries that are of vital importance to the consumer, and continuing to pursue traditional areas of enforcement related to mergers, vertical restraints, and compliance.

822   Pertschuk, Michael et al. "FTC and "No-Fault" Monopolies: It's Against the Single-Firm Variety!" *Antitrust Law and Economics Review* 10 (1978): 21-36.

Text of statements issued by the FTC to the National Commission for the Review of Antitrust Laws and Procedures and Commissioner Paul Rand Dixon. The statements are preceded by commentary discussing main points and notes the alarming rise in rhetoric concerning anti-monopolistic regulation by the government and specifically the FTC. The essay is critical of the FTC's attempts to regulate shared monopolies and oligopolies.

823   Pfunder, M. R. "Premerger Notification After One Year: An FTC Staff Perspective." *Antitrust Law Journal* 48 (August 1979): 1487-1501.

Explores from the perspective of FTC enforcement, the premerger notification program required under the Hart-Scott-Rodino Act. The essay begins by outlining the basic scheme of the program and the criteria that must be met before the program is initiated. An overview of the first year of the program's enforcement is then provided, including what transactions are investigated, an exemption from the program of transaction whose total assets where less than fifteen million dollars, the monitoring of merger activity by the FTC, the issuance of and compliance with second requests and reasons for noncompliance. It is concluded that the program is a success and has not placed any undue burden upon the business community.

824   Phillips, Charles F. "Robinson-Patman Anti-Price Discrimination Law and the Chain Store." *Harvard Business Review* 15 (October 1936): 62-75.

The author studies the development of the Robinson-Patman Act and its relationship to the growth of chain stores in the United States, an issue first investigated by the FTC in its Final Report on the Chain Store Investigation. Also important in the Act's development was the hearings conducted by the Patman Committee concerning the American Retail Federation. The article begins by examining price discrimination among large chain stores and is followed by a study of the price discrimination section of the Clayton Act. Concludes by comparing the original Section 2 of the Act and the amended Section to determine the merits of the revised Section under Robinson-Patman.

825   Pierson, Dianne E. "Antitrust Analysis in Uncertain Times: *FTC v. Superior Trial Lawyers Association.*" *Creighton Law Review* 24 (December 1990): 125-153.

Examines the judicial interpretation of the Superior Court Trial Lawyers Association case, which held that a group boycott by the Association placed undue constraints of trade under Section 5 of the FTC Act and Section 1 of the Sherman Antitrust Act. The decision is unique because the Supreme Court based its ruling not on the rule of reason but rather the pre se doctrine. This represents a departure from recent rulings. The rule of reason and pe se doctrines are studied in detail. This is followed by a study of the court's current antitrust analysis as compared to previous rulings.

826   Pitofsky, Robert. "Antitrust in the Next 100 Years." *California Law Review* 75 (May 1987): 817-833.

In focusing on cartels, mergers and predation to outline the current "minimalist" approach to antitrust enforcement, the author attempts to predict what the next century of antitrust law will look like. Renewed interest in the enforcement of the provisions of the Robinson-Patman Act by the FTC is mentioned as one of the catalysts to a more aggressive antitrust movement in future.

827   Poer, Albert A. "The New Antitrust Guidelines: Full Speed Ahead for Business Combinations." *Business and Society Review* (Winter 1983): 23-28.

Provides an analysis of the separate development of antitrust guidelines promulgated by the FTC and the Department of Justice. While much of the legal literature has focused upon the "elegant" presentation of the Justice Department, little has been said about the Commission's "Statement Concerning Horizontal Mergers." It is noted that this should not be viewed as an indication that the FTC guidelines are inadequate, but that, in the long run, they may be more influential in determining what constitutes an unacceptable corporate merger because they take into account practical considerations.

828   Pogue, R. W. "Effects on Other Merger Transactions: Does the Government Abuse Its Newly Granted Power?" *Antitrust Law Journal* 48 (August 1979): 1471-1486.

Critically examines the FTC enforcement of the Hart-Scott-Rodino Act and the problems associated with the statute requirement for advance merger notification. The author analyzes the FTC's enforcement within the context of legislative intent, noting that Congress wanted to create a balance between notification of very large mergers while, at the same time, avoid placing undue burdens on the business community. Each of these intentions are studied in detail to determine why they have not been followed.

829   Pollard, Michael R. "The Essential Role of Antitrust in a Competitive Market for Health Services." *Milbank Memorial Fund Quarterly/Health and Society* 59 (Spring 1981): 256-268.

The author reviews the role of antitrust law in insuring a competitive marketplace within the health care services industry. The essay begins by defining what is competition in the health care industry. The author notes that it is an industry conditioned to believe that normal forces cannot exist in the marketplace. The evolution of antitrust in public service industries is examined, noting that antitrust analysis of health care can proceed down two paths--the rule of reason and per se violations. This is followed by a study of how to assure competitive conditions in the health care marketplace. The essay concludes by considering self-regulation as a viable alternative to antitrust regulation.

830   Pollock, Earl E. "Pre-Complaint Investigations by the Federal Trade Commission." *Antitrust Bulletin* 9 (January-February 1964): 1-26.

FTC investigations consist of one of the following: general investigations of conditions and practices in a specific industry or segment of the economy or pre-complaint investigations that are conducted to determine if a particular company violated any antitrust laws or FTC regulations. This essay analyzes how the "New Look" FTC and reorganization of its investigative staff has impacted pre-complaint investigation procedures in the areas of expediting trial hearings, consent orders, and voluntary compliance.

831   Porter, Richard H. "The Federal Trade Commission v. the Oil Industry: An Autopsy on the Commission's Shared Monopoly Case Against the Nation's Eight Largest Oil Companies." *Antitrust Bulletin* 27 (Winter 1982): 753-820.

Examines chronologically the history and legal development of the FTC's complaint against eight oil companies claiming that they engaged in a shared monopoly. In light of its recent demise after eight years of litigation, the author points out the lessons learned from the case and the difficulties the FTC had in pursuing it. It is concluded that hindsight indicates that the effort was not worth the cost because the FTC failed to conduct an adequate pre-trial investigation of the matter and the Commission was hindered by its own administrative rules governing adjudicative proceedings.

832   Posner, Richard A. "A Statistical Study of Antitrust Enforcement." *Journal of Law and Economics* 13 (1970); 365-419.

Outlines antitrust enforcement by the FTC, the Department of Justice, state agencies and private plaintiffs to show that: 1) the collection and analysis of statistical data can be useful to in effective antitrust enforcement; 2) there are a number of important implications related to comprehensive data collection for antitrust law enforcement; and 3) weakness in the application of existing statistics do exist. The author uses these points to illustrate ways in which to improve antitrust enforcement. The author concludes with suggestions for improving the gathering and dissemination of data by the FTC and Justice Department and notes the importance of statistics in creating reliable antitrust policy planning for the future.

833   "Powers of the Federal Trade Commission in Prohibiting Unfair Methods of Competition." *Yale Law Journal* 43 (June 1934): 1338-1340.

Analyzes the impact of the Supreme Court's decision in *Federal Trade Commission v. R. F. Keppel and Brothers*, in which the Supreme Court overturned a lower court decision stating that the FTC's powers under Section 5 of the FTC Act "extended only to those practices which had previously been condemned as unfair under the Act, or which were unfair at common law, or which tended toward the restraint of trade or the creation of monopoly." The lower court ruled that since R. F. Kepple and Brothers had employed a method of unfair competition not previously used, and thus deemed illegal, the FTC had overstepped its bounds of authority. The Supreme Court overturned this ruling, and in so doing, greatly increased the effectiveness of the FTC's authority to suppress questionable competitive behavior.

834   Praeger, Bruce J. and Paul T. Denis. "Regulatory, Legislative, and Administrative Changes Relating to Hart-Scott-Rodino Premerger Notification." *Antitrust Law Journal* 56 (Fall 1987): 817-838.

Discusses the potential impact of final rules promulgated by the FTC that amend Hart-Scott-Rodino Premerger Notification Rules. The purpose of these rules is to codify prior interpretation by staff of the FTC's Premerger Notification Office, make technical changes to the Notification and Report Form and, most importantly, to close a loophole that allowed newly formed partnerships to make an acquisition regardless of size without being subject to the notification provisions of the Act. The author then discusses bills pending in Congress related to the Act. The essay concludes with an analysis of the procedures adopted by the FTC in acting on compliance investigations and discusses how businesses can to avoid them.

835   Preston, Warren P. and John M. Conner. "An Economic Evaluation of Federal Antitrust Activity in the Manufacturing Industries, 1980-1985." *Antitrust Bulletin* 37 (Winter 1992): 969-996.

This study analyzes whether there is behavioral evidence during the first half of the Reagan Administration of a "change in the economic standards of antitrust enforcement" as indicated in the allocation of antitrust activity in the manufacturing sector. Among the objectives of the study is to measure the level of professional activity devoted to antitrust enforcement by the FTC and the Department of Justice and to test if there is any change in these agencies related to the process of resource allocation. The results parallel previous works, indicating that there is a strong relationship between antitrust activity and industry size. The study also reveals that present findings show a more effective use of economic determinants in determining resource allocation.

836   "Prima Facie Effect of Federal Trade Commission Orders in Clayton Act Treble Damage Actions." *Duke Law Journal* 1970 (April 1970): 351-373.

Discusses the trend towards the shared responsibility in antitrust law enforcement between private litigants and government agencies such as the FTC, specifically focusing on the admissibility of FTC orders as prima facie evidence in private treble damage suits. Prima facie evidence refers to evidence that is sufficient to establish a given fact without the need for additional evidence. In other words, evidence that stands on its own merits. Specific cases are used to illustrate the development of this trend as well as problems associated with it due to outside pressures placed on the FTC to pursue anticompetitive behavior.

837   Proxmire, William. "Oligopoly Investigation Part I and II." *Antitrust Law and Economics Review* 3 (Fall 1969): 7-24 and (Winter 1969): 9-26.

Text of communications between the FTC and Senator William Proxmire and Congressman Benjamin S. Rosenthal regarding the allocation of FTC resources by specific industry and a request by Proxmire to conduct an investigation of oligopolies in the United States. The second part is the text of the FTC's reply to the request.

838   "Public Interest as a Jurisdictional Requirement Under Section 5 of the Federal Trade Commission Act." *Harvard Law Review* 43 (December 1929): 285-289.

A brief note questioning a court's decision against enforcing an FTC order based on the grounds that the order is not in the public's interest. The note points out that Section 5 of the FTC Act only sets a standard of which anticompetitive practices are unlawful, giving the agency "the power to proscribe the prohibitive practices," and outlining the procedures of the FTC. It is concluded that the Court was incorrect in suppressing the order by the FTC based upon the concept of "public interest."

839   Queen, Thomas W. "Recent Developments in Federal Antitrust Legislation." *Antitrust Law Journal* 54 (July 1985): 383-404.

Among the developments discussed by the author is the possibility of new legislation intended to further define FTC authorization in the area of antitrust enforcement jurisdiction. Stumbling blocks to previous attempts at FTC reauthorization is covered. The introduction of a bill regarding state enforcement of the FTC Act is also outlined.

840   Rahl, James A. "Conspiracy and the Antitrust Laws." *Illinois Law Review* 44 (1950): 743-768.

The author states that conspiracy is synonymous with the concept of combination when describing illegal mergers and acquisitions under the antitrust laws. This essay studies two Sherman Act cases, *United States v. New York Great Atlantic & Pacific Tea Co.* and *United States v. Armour & Co.*, to determine the future direction of antitrust policy in the United States and the possible impact of the law's expanding scope. A number of references are made to the role of the FTC Act and the Clayton Act.

841   Rahl, James A. "Does Section 5 of the FTC Act Extend the Clayton Act?" *Antitrust Bulletin* 5 (1960): 533-549.

Discusses the implications of the FTC's assertion that it has both the power and duty to "supplement and bolster" Section 2 of the amended Clayton Act under provisions articulated in Section 5 of the FTC Act. This position was stated in the recent Grand Union Company case. Criticism of the Grand Union decision, as well as historical support for it, are discussed in detail followed by an analysis of the application of the "spirit" test in current Robinson-Patman cases.

842   Raig, Reva Mae. "Administrative Law: Federal Trade Commission: Unfair Competition: Misrepresentation of Business Status." *Cornell Law Quarterly* 24 (April 1939): 413-416.

A brief comment concerning the Circuit Court of Appeals for the Second Circuit's decision to uphold an FTC finding that a vendor of jewelry cannot refer to itself as a "Wholesale Jeweler" with regards to its sales because, in this case, the firm was not a true wholesaler and thus in clear violation Section 5 of the FTC Act. By establishing the fact that a sale is not wholesale if it is actually a sale to the ultimate customer, the FTC has provided business with a clear standard to guide future practice.

843   Rauschert, J. P. "The FTC and the Sherman Act." *Chicago-Kent Law Review* 25 (June 1947): 225-232.

A comment arguing that the FTC's cause of action under the Sherman Act in the case of *Aetna Portland Cement Company v. FTC* is beyond the agency's legal jurisdiction. Both the specific language of the FTC Act and the legislative intent surrounding its passage show that the FTC has overstepped its authority. However, until it is addressed by the courts there remains a measure of ambiguity.

844   "Recent Trends in Interpretation of the Federal Trade Commission Act."
Michigan Law Review 32 (June 1934): 1142-1154.

Commentary examining recent cases involving the FTC, noting the fact that courts appear more likely to interpret the scope of agency antitrust activities more liberally than in the past. An overview of recent interpretations of cases is used to illustrate this point and to show how it has hampered the FTC efforts in fighting anticompetitive behavior in the business community.

845   Reisner, Alan K. "Applicability of NEPA to Antitrust Law Enforcement Proceedings." *Connecticut Law Review* 10 (Fall 1977): 177-191.

Details the content of the recent Mobile Oil case in which the District Court for the Southern District of New York held that the FTC must adhere to laws set forth in the National Environmental Policy Act. The court ruled that the FTC's antitrust complaint against Mobile Oil was premature because the FTC did not prepare an environmental impact statement prior to seeking action. The comment concludes that the court interpretation of the environmental impact statement requirement is too broad and could hinder future FTC action against the oil companies if it must become a part of FTC proceedings.

846   "Report on the Committee on Antitrust." *Energy Law Journal* 15 (1994): 157-174.

Summarizes specific cases related to energy that are brought under federal antitrust laws. Included among the cases is the impact of the state immunity doctrine that was established in *FTC v. Ticor Title Insurance Co.*

847   Rhodes, Thomas W. et al. "Antitrust Enforcement in the Southeastern United States in the 1970s." *Georgia State Bar Journal* 18 (November 1981): 74-76, 78, 80.

This article examines trends in antitrust enforcement in the Southeastern region of the United States based on statistics gathered or provided by the Atlanta offices of the FTC and the Department of Justice. Enforcement by the Justice Department, the FTC, and private parties are studied in detail. Date from the FTC revealed that most investigations involved mergers. The food industries received the most attention. Finally, statistics show that little more than half the cases were settled by consent decrees.

848   Riegel, Quentin. "FTC in the 1980s: An Analysis of the FTC Improvements Act of 1980." *Antitrust Bulletin* 26 (Fall 1981): 49-486. Describes the legislative history of the FTC Improvements Act of 1980 as it specifically relates to Congressional attempts to revise its rulemaking authority and curb its aggressive actions regarding children's advertising, regulation over the funeral industry, product standards and certification programs, the insurance industry, and the use of trademarks that have become "generic" in the minds of consumers. Also discussed are attempts by members of the House of Representatives to grant Congress veto powers over any future FTC rules. The essay concludes with an analysis of miscellaneous provisions and addresses what lies ahead for the FTC.

849   Rill, James F. et al. "U.S. Department of Justice and Federal Trade Commission Horizontal Merger Guidelines of 1992 (Parts I and II)." *Antitrust Law and Economics* 23 (1991): 52-74 and 69-90. Two part article that outlines in detail the following antitrust enforcement components of the 1992 Merger Guidelines released by the Department of Justice and the FTC: its purpose, with commentary regarding its underlying policy assumptions and a general overview; market definition, measurement, and concentration; examination of potential adverse competitive effects of mergers; entry analysis; efficiencies; and, company or division failure and exiting assets. The preface to each part of the article implies that the Merger Guidelines are the result of a political agenda and that, instead of preventing horizontal mergers that enhance or create market power, the record and public statements by officials from both agencies show that, in practice, the guidelines actually promote market power.

850   "The Robinson-Patman Act in Action." *Yale Law Journal* 46 (January 1937): 447-482. A comment outlining the provisions of the Robinson-Patman Act and measuring the Act's impact on various business practices related to "the marketing organization of the main consumers' goods industries." The commentary uses the drug industry as a case study to illustrate major issues. The business practices covered are wholesaler's discounts, quantity discounts, freight allowances, terms of sale, advertising allowances, the use of "push money," or allowances given to wholesalers and retailers as a means of encouraging special selling efforts of the wholesaler's or retailer's products, the use of store "demonstrators" offered to favored customers, free deals, private brands, as well as the use of various marketing practices not specifically covered by Robinson-Patman. The enforcement efforts of the FTC are outlined when appropriate. It is concluded that the Act is neither capable of preventing monopolistic behavior nor consistent with established antitrust enforcement laws.

851   "The Robinson-Patman Act: Some Prospective Problems of Construction and Constitutionality." *Harvard Law Review* 50 (November 1936): 106-125.
Early analysis of the possible effects of price discrimination under provisions of the Robinson-Patman Act by the FTC. Among the issues examined is Congressional intent, quality differences, differences in methods of sale and quantity, functional classification, brokerage allowances, advertising allowances, changes in market conditions, interpretation of cutting prices by a defendant to meet competition, the right to refuse to sell, criminal provisions, interstate transactions, and issues related to the Act's enforcement and relationship to existing long-term contracts entered before the Act was passed by Congress. Problems associated with each issue are examined systematically.

852   "Robinson-Patman Bill." *Georgetown Law Journal* 24 (May 1936): 951-961.
This article examines the provisions of the Robinson and Patman bills before Congress in light of recent FTC action against the chain store industry. The need for regulating the chain store industry is analyzed, including the enormous growth and size of the retail stores and the possible impact they may have on smaller firms. Particular attention is paid to the price discrimination aspects of the bill, describing how the bill attempts to forbid quantity discounts and other forms of price discrimination not covered by Section 2 of the Clayton Act. The note concludes that, given ambiguities related to what authority Congress has in regulating intrastate transactions, there are important constitutional questions associated with the bill.

853   Rockefeller, Edwin S. *Antitrust Counseling for the 1980s.* Washington, DC: The Bureau of National Affairs, Inc., 1983
The purpose of this book is to provide an overview of federal antitrust law and to analyze recent shifts in the antimonopoly environment. Among the issues examined are relationships with competitors, distribution of goods and services, price discrimination, mergers, and enforcement and compliance. The role of the FTC Act and the Commission is mentioned throughout the text. The work

includes the text of FTC Advisory Opinions, a table of cases, and a subject index.

854   Rockefeller, Edwin S. "The Federal Trade Commission's Potential for Making Purposeful Antitrust Policy." *Federal Bar Journal* 24 (Fall 1964): 541-547.

Argues that the performance of antitrust enforcement duties by the FTC and the Department of Justice has been "erratic, fitful, and too short on purposeful objectives." This is partially due to an overemphasis on method, process, and procedure and not enough emphasis within enforcement agencies to ask systematically why an action should be taken to guide the U. S. economy, according to the author. However, it is stated that, given the flexible nature of the legislation governing the actions of the FTC, the FTC holds the most promise for breaking out of this enforcement framework and creating a more rational regulatory policy.

855   Rockefeller, Edwin S. and Robert L. Wald. "Antitrust Enforcement by the Federal Trade Commission and the Department of Justice: A Primer for Small Business." *Dickinson Law Review* 66 (Spring 1962): 251-267.

Outlines provisions of the principle antitrust statutes administered by the Department of Justice, those administered by the FTC, statutes administered by both agencies, and those governing private antitrust litigation. The essay specifically discusses how these laws affect the activities of small business and what provisions of each set of laws is most critical in defining competitive environment of small business.

856   Roll, D. L. "Dual Enforcement of the Antitrust Laws by the Department of Justice and the FTC: The Liaison Procedure." *Business Lawyer* 31 (July 1976): 2075-2085.

Reviews the dual antitrust enforcement arrangements between the FTC and the Department of Justice. The article focuses on the formal 1948 liaison agreement between the two agencies, how this agreement has been supplemented by subsequent correspondence and "informal understandings," and uses this to illustrate present problems in dual enforcement. Arguments against dual enforcement are also detailed. The author concludes that since Congress is unlikely to shift antitrust enforcement duties to only one agency, present liaison procedures, while not perfect, are likely to continue.

857   Rosch, J. Thomas. "Future FTC Enforcement of Section 2." *Antitrust Law Journal* 59 (Summer 1990): 543-546.

Brief essay outlining the author's reasons why the FTC should be the "sole guardian" of Section 2 of the FTC Act with regards to antitrust law enforcement rather than sharing duties with the Department of Justice. The specialized mission of the FTC could provide important input into the development of merger law and can act as an amicus in private litigation.

858   Rosch, J Thomas and Hajime Tada. "The Antitrust Risks of Management Services Organizations, Medical Foundations, and Integrated Delivery Systems." *Topics in Health Care Financing* 20 (Spring 1994): 37-45.

By examining the antitrust implications of creating a fully integrated health service delivery system, it is shown that such an arrangement actually poses less risk in violating antitrust laws than a less integrated system. Antitrust issues related to FTC and Department of Justice review of integrated systems are discussed along with the impact of guidelines promulgated by both agencies. The essay ends by outlining specific points that must be considered by health care providers to minimize the risk of antitrust violations.

859   Rose, M. E. "Federal Trade Commission Enforcement of Section 3 of the Clayton Act." *George Washington Law Review* 8 (January-February 1940): 639-670.

Analyzes the FTC's enforcement of Section 3 of the Clayton At which prohibits "exclusive dealing arrangements" and "tying contracts" in which a seller sells merchandise under the condition that the purchaser only work with that specific dealer and refrain from buying goods from competitors. To enhance his or her position in the transaction a seller may enforce a tying contract involving the leasing of equipment on the condition that it can be used only with supplies of the lessor. Both tying clause arrangements and exclusive dealer arrangements are examined using specific cases as a basis for understanding the provision. Analysis reveals that the FTC has not effectively enforced the provision in the few times it has been invoked.

860   Rosen, Gerald R. "FTC's Tough Trustbuster." *Duns Review* 105 (February 1975): 51-52, 86.

Examines the shift in the FTC's mission from a primarily consumer protection orientated agency to an antitrust one due to the appointment by President Gerald

Ford of Lewis Engman as it's chairman. This essay outlines the reasons behind this shift, examines some of the cases that the FTC is pursuing, defines what remedies are available to the FTC in eliminating monopolistic behavior, and discusses future action by the agency, all while under the leadership of Chairman Engman.

861 Rosner, Bernat. "Buyer Liability Under the Robinson-Patman Act." *Antitrust Law Journal* 59 (Fall 1990): 889-900.

Examines judicial and FTC interpretation of buyer liability law as defined in Section 2(f) of the Robinson-Patman Act. There are three fundamental elements of this section: a buyer must possess a "certain kind of knowledge in order to bring it within Section 2(f); incentive to purchase or receipt must be present in the transaction; and, the item or service induced or received must be a price that is prohibited by Section 2 of the Clayton Act. The A & P case involving the bidding war between Borden and Bowman for A & P's private label milk business is used to address the problems associated with these elements.

862 Ross, Thomas W. "Winners and Losers Under the Robinson-Patman Act." *Journal of Law and Economics* 27 (October 1984): 243-271.

Noting the lack of empirical studies done on the effects of the Act, a capital market analysis of chain store stocks and data related to food brokers' commissions during the mid to late 1930s is reported. The effects of FTC enforcement after the Act's passage are then examined to determine what damage is incurred by firms selected for investigation and how extensive this damage is based on whether the cases ended in consent decrees, dismissals, or cease and desist orders. The results show that the Act had harmful effects on grocery store chains but otherwise had little effect on other chains and grocery manufacturers. There is also evidence that food brokers benefitted. This research is recommended as a first step in understanding the effects of the Act.

863 Rowe, Federick M. "Evolution of the Robinson-Patman Act: A Twenty Year Perspective." *Columbia Law Review* 57 (December 1957): 1059-1088.

Chronicles the "conflict, compromise, and confusion" that has surrounded the Robinson-Patman Act over the past twenty years. It is noted that at the foundation of these problems is the Act's undue restrictions on pricing freedom that runs counter to the Sherman Act and general antitrust policy that promotes free and competitive pricing. The development of the Act and its legislative history is covered in detail followed by an analysis of enforcement patterns by the FTC. The essay concludes with an overview of current Congressional activity that is attempting to strengthen the Act.

864   Rowe, Frederick M. "The Federal Trade Commission's Administration of the Anti-Price Discrimination Law." *Columbia Law Review* 64 (March 1964): 415-438.
Appraisals of the FTC's enforcement policy regarding false or deceptive advertising, policing deceptive trade practices, and traditional antitrust issues such as mergers have been more a question of efficiency rather than direction. The one exception to this has been the FTC's enforcement activity of price discrimination under the Robinson-Patman Act. This article details the problems associated with the Act, including its inability to either restrain aggressive price discrimination or protect small firms. Four areas of FTC interpretations of the Act are analyzed: failure to create realistic criteria "for appraising the competitive character and impact of price variations"; erosion of the seller's right to meet lower competitor prices; needless extension of the scope of the Act's Brokerage Clause in Section 2(c); and, magnification of deficiencies by promoting industry-wide trade restraints. It is concluded that FTC enforcement of the Act has restrained more competition than it has promoted.

865   Rowe, Frederick M. *Price Discrimination Under the Robinson-Patman Act*. Boston, MA: Little, Brown, 1962.
Perhaps the most complex and misunderstood area of antitrust law enforcement concerns the Robinson-Patman Act of 1936. This book attempts to provide a concise and clear explanation of the Act's birth, development, and subsequent application within the marketplace. Central to the author's examination is the FTC's interpretation of the Act and how that has shaped the direction of price discrimination law during the fifty years after Robinson-Patman's enactment. Includes an appendix that traces the legislative history of the Act, including texts of bills and Congressional committee reports, a table of cases, and an index.

866   Saret, Larry. "Unfairness without Deception: Recent Positions of the Federal Trade Commission." *Loyola University Law Journal* 5 (Summer 1974): 537-561.
The *FTC v. Sperry and Hutchinson Co.* case has resulted in considerable attention to the use of the unfairness doctrine. However, the FTC has rarely applied its principles, showing that, while the FTC wants to increase its regulatory

authority, it wants to do so within the legislative parameters of Section 5. This article examines the historical development of the unfairness doctrine, its legal applications, and how it can be utilized by the FTC as a tool for enforcement within the greater context of the "public interest."

867   Sawyer, A. E. "The Commission's Administration of Paragraph 2(a) of the Robinson-Patman Act: An Appraisal." *George Washington Law Review* 8 (January-February 1940): 469-510.

Analyzes the development of standards in determining price discrimination related to injury to competition, "cost justification of quantity differentials," and setting prices to meet competition. The essay reviews research based on complaints issued by industry, cases involving Robinson-Patman Act provisions, and accompanying commentary to build a framework for understanding the Act's application. It is concluded that, based on the study's findings, the FTC should be commended for moving methodically and thoroughly in cases involving the Act. The article concludes with a fold-out summary of FTC proceedings under the Robinson-Patman Act.

868   Scanlon, Paul D. "Confirmation Hearings on the New FTC Chairman: Some Questions from the Review." *Antitrust Law and Economics Review* 6 (Winter 1972-73): 15-43.

Begins with an analysis of the Senate Commerce Committee's hearing on the nomination of Lewis A. Engman as the new FTC Chairman, outlining the views of this journal's editors regarding what direction the FTC should take concerning oligopolies, the integration of economic analysis into FTC enforcement procedures, and shared monopolies. This is followed by the text of thirteen questions and the subsequent answers by Engman submitted by the editors to the Senate confirmation hearing.

869   Scanlon, Paul D. "Policy Planning at the FTC: A Commissioner Who Really Believes In It?" *Antitrust Law and Economics Review* 6 (1973): 35-58.

This is an editorial expressing hope that the new FTC Commissioner Mayo J. Thompson is a signal away from agency "secrecy" and marks the beginning of substantial agency policy planning for the future. To illustrate this new movement as it relates to antitrust law enforcement, the text of policy planning memos written by Thompson are included. Of particular interest is Thompson's proposal to create a procedure whereby economists review FTC cases.

870   Scher, Irving. "Recent Federal Trade Commission Developments." *Antitrust Law Journal* 46 (Summer 1977): 950-964.

As Chairman of the FTC's Committee Section of Antitrust Law, the author examines recent developments in FTC efforts to expand the scope of its unfairness doctrine beyond coverage of antitrust laws, efforts to preempt state controls, and discusses the recent *Warner Lambert Co v. FTC* case that involved the FTC's authority under FTC Act Section 5 provisions to order corrective advertising.

871   Scher, Irving. "Single-Firm Conduct: The Government's and Antitrust Section's Views." *Antitrust Law Journal* 59 (Summer 1990): 527-534.

Discusses the difficulties faced by government enforcement agencies, including the FTC, when challenging monopolization conduct by single-firms. The author notes the need for a careful balance between deterring monopolistic conduct while not stifling competition. Specific reference is made to the FTC's experience in challenging monopolistic practices.

872   Schildkraut, Marc G. et al. "FTC Policy on Predation: No Problem if There is at Least One Surviving Competitor." *Antitrust Law and Economics Review* 23 (1991): 17-32.

Critical essay commenting on the apparent dichotomy between FTC and Department of Justice support for predatory pricing (selective price cutting in a narrow geographic area or involving small levels of products for brief periods of time), while condemning the behavior of discounters whose routine price-cutting is passed on to the consumer on a daily basis. Reaction in the form of letters exchanged between the authors and the *Review* are used to back up this claim. The text of the letters are included.

873   Schwartz, Louis B. "The New Merger Guidelines: Guide to Governmental Discretion and Private Counseling or Propaganda for Revision of the Antitrust Laws?" *California Law Review* 71 (March 1983): 575-603.

Examines the purpose, provisions and effects of the new Merger Guidelines promulgated by the Department of Justice. The author states that the Guidelines primary function will be to support "whatever decision the Department wants to make in particular cases" and that they are being created to promote Chicago School economics within the enforcement purview of the FTC and DOJ without Congressional action. Differences between the Justice Department and the FTC regarding merger criteria, such as market definition, are also discussed.

874   Schwartz, Maurius. "The Perverse Effects of the Robinson-Patman Act." *Antitrust Bulletin* 31 (Fall 1986): 733-757.
Discusses the more subtle and unintended effects of Robinson-Patman on competition and distribution efficiency. Its effects on competition includes preventing selective discounts to large buyers which insulates sellers from undue pressure, the exchange of competitively sensitive information between firms under provisions of the Act, overprotecting competitors when unsystematic price discrimination exists, and the vagueness of the Act concerning various pricing moves (notably with regards to practices that erode aggressive pricing). Distribution efficiency is affected because the Act discourages buyer initiative, hampers promotional activities, promotes the adoption of substitute business practices, and contains intrinsic ambiguity supported by complex case law. It is concluded that the Act serves as an example of what occurs when a clear goal (ending price discrimination) is applied to the complexities of business activity. This should be taken into consideration when formulating future legislation.

875   Seesel, John H. "Non-Merger Investigations and Enforcement Procedures at the Federal Trade Commission." *Antitrust Law Journal* 54 (Winter 1985): 181-188.
Outlines current FTC activity and reviews cases in the area of nonmerger antitrust enforcement as it relates to monopolization, horizontal restraints, vertical restraints, and price discrimination. Case development initiated by public or internal investigations is examined, followed by a description of both initial-phase investigation procedures and full-phase investigation procedures. Factors related to how an investigation moves from the initial to full stage is analyzed.

876   Seib, C. B. "Congress Ready to Sharpen Antimerger Tools." *Nations Business* (May 1956): 42-43, 53-54, 58, 60.
This essay explores the merger wave that have swept through the American business climate during the Eisenhower Administration and outlines possible steps to be taken by Congress in response to this expansion. Among the steps discussed is allocating more funds to the FTC and the Department of Justice and passing legislation that will strengthen existing antitrust laws and the agency's authority. Further expansion of antitrust authority is also examined if the merger wave continues. This article is followed by an interview with FTC Chairman John W. Gwynne.

877   Seldman, A. G. and A. R. Connelly. "Commission's Power to Conduct Field Investigations." *Antitrust Law Journal* 14 (1959): 12-17.

As part of a panel discussion, this essay examines the Commission's authority to seek information to protect the nation's economy from deceptive trade practices, monopolies, and predation. Specific sanctions under the FTC Act are outlined as well as the motivation behind actions by attorneys within the Bureau of Investigation. Specific cases are used to illustrate the boundaries of FTC investigatory authority.

878   Seligson, Harold P. "The Extent of the Jurisdiction of the Federal Trade Commission over Unfair Methods of Competition." *American Bar Association Journal* 9 (November 1923): 698-701.

The author attempts to measure the scope of FTC enforcement jurisdiction regarding unfair methods of competition as stated in Section 5 of the FTC Act based on the decisions of specific court cases and internal procedure within the FTC. Factors that should be taken into account by the courts when determining whether the Commission's jurisdiction should be restricted or extended are analyzed in detail.

879   Sharp, Benjamin S. "FTC Antitrust Remedies: In the Classic Tradition." *Antitrust Law Journal* 50 (1982): 83-94.

Gives background concerning the FTC's legal authority of enforcement in order to discuss four activities of the agency: divestiture and injunctions, patent licensing, fencing in remedial provisions, and consumer redress. The author notes that the agency focuses most of its activities on more traditional antitrust remedies rather than "innovative remedies."

880   Shenefield, John H. "Open Letter to the New President of the United States." *Cardozo Law Review* 9 (March 1988): 1295-1304.

Briefing paper submitted to the President of the United States requesting that the new administration shift away from the deregulation and "do no harm" approach to antitrust enforcement of the recent past and arguing the need for an aggressive enforcement policy. This argument is based on the fact that, while deregulation may have introduced competition in industries previously cartelized, it may have also increased harmful business behavior directed at the consumer. The author recommends increasing the FTC's budget and appointing the next Assistant Attorney General from the professional ranks of antitrust law.

881 Shughart II, William F. "Don't Revise the Clayton Act, Scrap It!" *Cato Journal* 6 (Winter 1987): 925-932.

Outlines revisions to the language of the Clayton Act as proposed by the Reagan Administration. These changes encompassed changing the litmus test used to determine if a merger violates antitrust laws, requiring antitrust agencies to base their actions of Department of Justice guidelines, Exempting import-injured industries from the antimerger law for a period of five years, placing restrictions of treble damages, and relaxing prohibitions against interlocking directorates. This new direction, however, is based on "outmoded economic thinking" and would hinder efficient allocation of productive resources within the economy. Two areas are examined to illustrate these concerns: Department of Justice merger guidelines and premerger notification requirements in the Hart-Scott-Rodino Act. The role of the FTC is mentioned throughout the text.

882 Shughart II, William F. and Robert D. Tollison. "The Positive Economics of Antitrust Policy: A Survey Article." *International Review of Law and Economics* 5 (June 1985): 39-57.

Uses a select amount of positive literature regarding antitrust law enforcement policy to suggest that "the antitrust bureaucracy operates much like regulatory bureaucracy in general." The literature falls under three broad categories: case output, the costs and benefits of antitrust enforcement, and organizational behavior of the FTC and the Antitrust Division of the Department of Justice. A positive approach to analyzing the literature helps to understand the motivations behind the individuals who enforce the law and to show that standard critiques based on identifying good or bad cases or good or bad laws is an ineffective approach to analyzing antitrust enforcement law.

883 Silcox, Clark R. "Unfair Methods of Competition in Antitrust Cases Under Section 5 of the FTC Act." *Antitrust Bulletin* 29 (Fall 1984): 423-474.

Analyzes FTC Act cases decided under Section 5 to reveal that there is little experience by the Commission in dealing with the issue of incipient trade restraints, the status of a marketplace before an actual injury to competition has occurred. Recent efforts by the FTC, though, have been undertaken to expand Section 5 proscription of unfair methods of competition and to bolster or supplement provisions of the Sherman or Clayton Acts. An examination of the cases shows that the FTC was unsuccessful in its expansionary competition policy because it fails to take into account "new factual scenarios and forms of conduct" that reflect how the antitrust laws should be enforced.

884   Singer, James W. "Big is Back in Favor–But Only If It Promotes Economic Efficiency." *National Journal* 13 (April 4, 1981): 573-577. This article analyzes the Reagan's Administration's shift towards a more narrow interpretation of antitrust law enforcement. This shift reflects the perception that current antitrust laws are restricting America's ability to compete abroad and that there is a "new awareness of efficient business practices." It also marks the beginning of traditional approaches to antitrust law enforcement by the FTC and the Department of Justice. The recent history behind this shift is studied in detail through interviews with decision-makers in the FTC and Department of Justice.

885   Singer, James W. "Regulatory Report: FTC Stresses Antitrust Effort as Weapon in Battle against Inflation." *National Journal* 6 (October 19, 1974): 1567-1581. Marked by the beginning of Lewis A. Engman's term as Chairman of the FTC, the Commission has begun an aggressive effort to use antitrust enforcement as a tool in controlling inflation, preserving competition, and protecting consumer rights. Investigations, for example, in the areas of energy, food, vocational schools, franchising, and debtor's rights are outlined. The essay also provides viewpoints from the agency's commissioners about the FTC's mission in promoting competition and protecting the consumer. Congressional debate in both the House and Senate concerning the FTC's authority and support from the Ford Administration for the agency's new aggressiveness are discussed as well.

886   "60 Minutes with the Honorable Janet Steiger, Chairman, Federal Trade Commission." *Antitrust Law Journal* 59 (Spring 1990): 3-23. Contains the remarks of Chairman Janet Steiger presented to the ABA Antitrust Section's Annual Spring Meeting in which she examines issues related to agency funding, the FTC's relationship with states and other groups, new nonmerger initiatives, and merger enforcement. The remarks are followed by the text of an interview that follows up on issues brought forth in the speech and various other issues not specifically covered previously.

887   "60 Minutes with the Honorable Janet Steiger, Chairman, Federal Trade Commission." *Antitrust Law Journal* 61 (Summer 1992): 187-210. Introduction by Stieger and interview of her by a group of panelists in which she provides an overview of the antitrust activities of the FTC and highlighting the

Antitrust Law

new joint Merger Guidelines recently issued. This is cited as an example of the "maturity" of the agency's antitrust enforcement. Specific changes brought about by the guidelines are examined. The interview contains reaction to the guidelines by Steiger as they relate to specific cases and criticisms leveled against the agency.

888   Slade, Roger. "Federal Obstruction of State Antitrust Enforcement: The Second Circuit Finds No Place for State Participation in the Fast World of Mergers." *Brooklyn Law Review* 52 (1986): 591-608.

The passage of the Hart-Scott-Rodino Antitrust Improvements Act has significantly increased state involvement in antitrust enforcement by allowing state law enforcement officials to sue violators on behalf of the citizens of the state. The FTC has cooperated by allowing access to premerger information by state officials. However, the case of *Lieberman v. FTC* was brought forth because the FTC had recently declined to share some information. The author concludes that the ruling against the state attorney generals in Lieberman will cripple state antitrust law enforcement, noting that the Second Circuit's failed to take into account that Congress forbid public access to information but not states.

889   Sloan, J. B. "Antitrust: Shared Information Between the FTC and the Department of Justice." *Brigham Young University Law Review* 1979 (1979): 883-910.

Examines issues, such as due process and self-incrimination, related to the gathering of information in the pursuit of an antitrust enforcement case by one agency (FTC) and the use of that information by another agency (Department of Justice) in a later criminal proceeding. This article discusses possible defenses available to corporations that are forced to disclose information as part of an antitrust investigation and that may be prosecuted on simultaneous or subsequent criminal or civil proceedings. The antitrust enforcement of each agency is examined to create a framework of understanding concerning these issues. Remedies associated with administrative, civil, and criminal law are then analyzed. It is concluded that the sharing of information boils down to a matter of ethics.

890   Slomsky, Antia J. "Washington Turns Up Antitrust Heat on Doctors." *Medical Economics* 68 (August 5, 1991): 42-48.

The Reagan Administration marked a period of declining federal antitrust enforcement and deregulation. However, this period has ended and among the first targets for antitrust investigation are physicians. The rising costs of health care have prompted the FTC, the Department of Justice, and state agencies to more aggressively pursue charges of price fixing and trade restraint within the health care field. Specific activities by the FTC are outlined separately.

891   Soloman, Richard A. "Why Uncle Sam Can't Lose a Case Under Section 7 of the Clayton Act." *American Bar Association Journal* 53 (February 1967): 137-142.

Discusses the expansion of the concept of "submarket" through recent actions by the FTC and its subsequent reaffirmation by the courts in cases brought under Section 7 of the Clayton Act. The author states that this expansion of the definition of a relevant market as it relates to the competitive effects of a challenged merger is misguided because the FTC and the courts have not taken into account the business context of the paperwork (evidence) amassed by a company during its operation. Also discussed is the theme in Section 7 cases that diversification and expansion is best achieved through internal growth rather through mergers. The author concludes that this view of a relevant market is not reflective of the realities of business commerce.

892   Sproul, Jr., Robert G. "United States Antitrust Laws and Foreign Joint Ventures." *American Bar Association Journal* 54 (September 1968): 889-895.

Examines the increasing interest in foreign joint ventures by the Department of Justice and the FTC despite the state of uncertainty that exist in regards to how U.S. antitrust laws apply to these ventures. Court rulings have not been helpful in clarifying how these laws apply either. The author discusses recent trends in joint ventures and offers advice to practicing attorneys regarding what might constitute violations of the rule of reason doctrine and the per se rule while enhancing the contracting party's freedom to do business.

893   Starek III, Roscoe B. "Health Care and Antitrust Enforcement at the FTC." *Antitrust Law and Economics Review* 25 (1994): 19-32.

The author explores the role of the FTC in enforcing antitrust laws in the field of health care and, specifically, the impact of statements issued by the FTC and the Department of Justice clarifying antitrust enforcement policies related to hospital mergers, high-technology joint ventures, joint purchasing arrangements, information sharing, and physicians joint ventures. A description of each issue covered and its potential impact on the health care field is examined.

894   Starek III, Roscoe B. "Health Care and Antitrust Enforcement at the FTC." *Wage-Price Law and Economics Review* 18 (1994): 19-32.

During the first three quarters of this century, antitrust laws generally had not been applied to the health care field. However, a variety of new cases have arisen that focus on issues of interstate commerce and "learned professions" which have led to FTC regulation of health care services. This paper reviews policy statements governing FTC regulatory actions in the areas of hospital mergers, high-technology joint ventures, joint purchasing agreements, information sharing, and physicians joint ventures. In each case, the type of resistance exhibited by the industry is discussed.

895   "State Action Exemption and Antitrust Enforcement Under the Federal Trade Commission Act." *Harvard Law Review* 89 (February 1976): 715-751.

Although the case of *Parker v. Brown* established that the Sherman Act was not intended by Congress to apply "to state agents acting in furtherance of state policies or to private parties acting under the direction of state law," the precise scope of the exemption as it relates to Section 5 of the FTC Act has never been resolved in court. This note argues that the state exemption established in Parker should not apply to Section 5. This position is based on existing case law and rationales behind the Sherman Act. Nevertheless, the FTC should seek a balance between the interests articulated in state laws and those promulgated by the FTC.

896   Stedman, John C. "Twenty-Four Years of the Robinson-Patman Act." *University of Wisconsin Law Review* 1960 (March 1960): 197-226.

Analyzes the birth and development of the Robinson-Patman Act and reviews the controversies surrounding its enforcement by the FTC during the past twenty-four years. Also examined is the legislative intent behind the creation of the Act. The author then evaluates the Act's provisions and its administration and concludes that further legislation is needed to modify its language to improve its performance as it relates to price discrimination, the protection of small businesses, and exclusive arrangements between suppliers and buyers.

897   Steinberg, Harry. "Oligopolistic Interdependence: The FTC Adopts a "No Agreement" Standard to Attack Parallel Non-Collusive Practices." *Brooklyn Law Review* 50 (Winter 1984): 255-300.

Discusses the implications inherent in the FTC's decision that four manufacturers of antiknock gasoline additives practiced unfair methods of competition in an oligopolistic industry under Section 5 provisions even though they arrived at pricing decisions independent of one another. In other words, there was no collusive behavior among the manufacturers. This note argues that proof of agreement was inadequately factored into the FTC's decision. The note analyzes the concept of "agreement" in antitrust enforcement law, analyzes the legislative intent behind the Sherman and Clayton Acts, and concludes that the Ethyl Corporation decision represents an attempt to redefine the concept of trade regulation and not to prevent anticompetitive behavior. An editors note follows stating that the Second Circuit court vacated the FTC's order.

898   Steiner, Robert L. "RPM, Distribution Restraints, and the Growth of Discounting: The Importance of Vertical Competition." *Antitrust Law and Economics Review* 15 (Spring 1983): 73-96.

As a visiting professor in the FTC's Bureau of Economics, the author gives his views regarding the Baxter-Bork-Posner thesis that all vertical restraints should be treated the same, but notes that the restraints are presumptively illegal because "they tend to retard the growth of more efficient forms of retailing." Steiner also discusses the impact of the Baxter-Bork-Posner thesis on contemporary economic thinking as it relates to antitrust law theory.

899   Steptoe, Mary Lou and David Balto. "Finding the Right Prescription: The FTC's Use of Innovative Merger Remedies." *Antitrust* 10 (Fall 1995): 16-20.

The purpose of this article is to examine FTC antitrust efforts regarding the divestiture of sufficient facilities in cases in which there is "competitive overlap involving multiple production facilities and distribution outlets." The authors argue that divestiture of production assets is not necessarily the most efficient merger remedy and offers four alternative arenas for seeking mergers remedies. These are: 1) mergers impacting research and development; 2) the reputation of the company; 3) distribution assets; and 4) an input in the production process. The article concludes with a list of practical advice in negotiating concept orders in cases where innovative remedies may be needed.

900   Stevens, W. H. S. "Resale Price Maintenance as Unfair Competition." *Columbia Law Review* 19 (June 1919): 265-285.

Several issues have arisen regarding resale price maintenance after the findings and order by the FTC against the Cudahy Packing Company. First, resale price maintenance complaints have already been issued by the FTC as a violation of

Section 5 of the FTC Act. Given the widespread use of this practice, further activity by the FTC in this area is likely unless legislation is passed. Second, the Cudahy case offers the first insight into the theories of the Commission with regards to resale price maintenance practices. Third, these theories are of particular interest with regards to orders issued that may be carried to the Circuit Court of Appeals. This offers a further opportunity to examine Commission theories on resale price maintenance. And fourth, findings promulgated by the FTC appear to show that the agency is basing its actions more on the unfair effect of resale price maintenance on jobbers, manufacturers, and consumers rather than considerations of restraint and monopoly power.

901 Strenio, Jr., Andrew J. "The FTC's Administrative Dilemma." *Environmental Law* 20 (Fall 1990): 35-47.

As a Commissioner of the FTC, the author discusses the implications of criticisms leveled against the FTC in the Kirkpatrick Report, focusing on three variables mentioned in the Report regarding antitrust enforcement: resources of the Commission, leadership and guidance to its staff, to the public, and to the consumer through the Consumer and Competition Advocacy Program, and case selection criteria. The essay concludes with an analysis of the FTC's antitrust agenda for the 1990s.

902 Stryker, David M. "The Federal Trade Commission, Injunctive Relief, and Allegedly Anticompetitive Mergers: Preliminary Relief Under the Federal Trade Commission Act." *Indiana Law Journal* 58 (Spring 1982/83): 293-317.

Examines preliminary relief under Section 13(b) of the FTC Act and what standards should be adopted by the courts in evaluating which FTC requests should be granted. Judicial analysis should be based on the specific facts of a case and the courts should determine whether preliminary relief is in the consumer's best interest. The author proposes that, in light of the fact that full-stop orders are generally not practical, interim relief should be adopted along with the traditional divestiture remedy should be used. By not taking into account considerations of equity, the FTC and the courts have interpreted Section 13(b) provisions too narrowly.

903 "Subpoena Power of FTC in Clayton Act Proceedings Upheld." *Columbia Law Review* 57 (June 1957): 890-893.

Discusses the implications of the *Menzies v. Federal Trade Commission* case in which the FTC's power, under Section 9 of the FTC Act, to issue subpoenas was affirmed. It is noted that this ruling conforms to previous rulings permitting broad use of administrative subpoenas to enhance the enforcement of provisions of the Clayton Act in the public interest.

904   Taylor, Jr., Stuart. "What To Do with the Microsoft Monster." *The American Lawyer* 15 (November 1993): 72-83.

The author examines the growth of the Microsoft Corporation into a world leader in the software industry under the guidance of Bill Gates. The development of it's operating system has led several competitors to accuse Microsoft of anti-competitive behavior. This essay outlines the three-year battle waged by Microsoft against the FTC and recently taken up by the Department of Justice's Antitrust Division. Specific charges made by competitors are analyzed, followed by an examination of how the government responded to these charges. It is concluded that Microsoft "probably" did commit acts of monopolistic predation, but to sue the corporation may lead to a long, unproductive period of litigation similar to what happened in the case of *U.S. v IBM* that lasted from 1969 until 1982 and could ultimately harm one of the few industries where the United States is a global leader.

905   Terborgh, George W. "Judicial Construction of the Meaning of Unfair Methods of Competition." *Journal of Business* 2 (January 1929): 50-64.

In creating legislation, Congress is frequently confronted with two alternatives: create a broad, general statute which gives the judicial system latitude in interpreting and applying the act, or on the other hand, create legislation that is detailed and defines specific courses of action in enforcement by the courts. The disadvantage of the first approach is that it may promote confusion and conflicting judicial interpretations. The disadvantage with the second approach is that it may be too inflexible and rigid to be an effective piece of legislation. Section 5 of the FTC Act was created under the first principle. This essay examines the consequences of this decision by Congress and notes that confusion still remains. Four phases of judicial interpretation are then analyzed to illustrate this point.

906   Thompson, Mayo J. "FTC Strikes Again: Rooting Out "Low" Prices in the Bread Industry." *Antitrust Law and Economics Review* 7 (1975): 85-96.

Text of FTC Commissioner Mayo J. Thompson dissent in the complaint filed by the Commission against ITT Continental Baking Company which was charged with predatory pricing to drive out competition in certain cities in violation of the Robinson-Patman Act and the FTC Act. In the statement, Thompson states that the case represents a poor use of FTC resources because it does fall within public interest criteria of Section 5(b) of the FTC Act.

907   Thompson, Mayo J. "Mergers, Monopolization, and Marketing: The Problem of Priorities at the FTC." *Antitrust Law and Economics Review* 7 (1974): 27-36.

As an FTC Commissioner, the author offers his views on the FTC's activities and interpretation of mergers and economic efficiency and whether "efficiency" represents a constraint of merger law enforcement as well as the issue of monopolies and what factors are involved in consumer injury due to monopolistic activities. The author concludes by offering a set of personal guidelines that define for marketers the agency's view of mergers and monopolization, noting that a balance must be struck between consumer and business interests.

908   Thompson, Mayo J. "Monopoly, Competition, and Free Enterprise: Toward an Economic Point of No Return." *George Washington Law Review* 42 (August 1974): 901-920.

Discusses the scope of the FTC's antitrust enforcement, including its legislative mandate and the size of its influence on the nation's economy, and examines the agency's resource allocation given these antitrust law compliance responsibilities. The author then analyzes FTC case selection to determine if the Commission could proceed in a more efficient manner. Case selection analysis is conducted with regards to mergers and monopolization and advertising and consumer law, followed by an examination of the concept of free enterprise in American society.

909   Tincher, W. R. "Practical Aspects of Conducting Antitrust Proceedings: Post Hearing." *Antitrust Bulletin* 4 (September-October 1959): 683-691.

As the Assistant Director of the FTC's Antimonopoly Bureau of Litigation, the author offers insights into the post-hearing phase of an antitrust proceeding before a Commission hearing examiner in which the validity of a decision should be issued based on legal precedents and principles. Much of the information presented is based on the FTC's Rules of Practice for Adjudicative Proceedings.

910   Todd, Ronald G. "Real Estate Transactions Become Targets for Antitrust Scrutiny." *Real Estate Review* 18 (Fall 1988): 72-77.
Analyzes the impact of provisions of the Hart-Scott-Rodino Antitrust Improvements Act on the real estate field. Although there are indications that real estate would be exempt under the Act, the vagueness of the law does not preclude this. Interpretation of the "realty provision" by the FTC is discussed, including areas of exemption and the failure of the Act to clarify issues related to property transfers and treatment of property rights. The essay concludes by offering practical suggestions for real estate practitioners about provisions of the Act and premerger notification rules.

911   Tollison, Robert D. "Economic Analysis at the FTC: An Interview." *Antitrust Law and Economics Review* 14 (1982): 45-90.
Text of an interview with the Director of the FTC's Bureau of Economics in which Tollison discusses his views on predation, rulemaking, and specific programs initiated by the Bureau of Economics to combat unfair practices and collusion. The interview concludes with Tollison's views on Chairman James C. Miller III and what his leadership means for the future.

912   "Trade Rules and Trade Conference–The FTC and Business Attack Deceptive Practices, Unfair Competition, and Antitrust Violation." *Yale Law Journal* 62 (May 1953): 912-953.
Examines the recent attempt by the FTC to streamline its "antiquated" antitrust enforcement procedures and enhance the impact of its enforcement by developing methods that promote industry-wide cooperation and informal enforcement. The essay begins by outlining the FTC's enforcement procedures. This is followed by a detailed analysis of the trade practice conference program, its aftermath with regards to future actions against deception business practices and unfair competition, and its impact on competitive behavior. The essay then examines in detail the use of trade rules by the FTC and their impact on competition. It is concluded that the trade conference offers important step forward in industry self-regulation and cooperation. Trade rules must be written carefully however, so as not to create "custom-made" rules that may help specific firms. Both programs are helpful in offsetting an understaffed FTC.

913   "Treatment of Delivery Services Under Section 2(e) of the Robinson-Patman Act." *George Washington Law Review* 51 (August 1983): 727-745.

Discusses discriminatory practices associated with the delivery of goods in relation to provisions of Robinson-Patman and describes the impact of these practices on both the consumer and the buyer's ability to resell goods. This impact can take the form of inhibiting marketing strategies, inventory maintenance, or scheduling and pricing. Interpretations by the FTC and the Justice Department are used to help clarify the Act's impact on delivery services. It is concluded after this analysis that both offer little guidance.

914   "Unfair Competition at Common Law and Under the Federal Trade Commission." *Columbia Law Review* 20 (March 1920): 328-333.

This essay reviews the scope of FTC jurisdiction in light of the fact that there is a lack of guidance provided by common law. Particular examples of unfair practices prohibited by the Commission are outlined.

915   "Use of Section 5 of the Federal Trade Commission Act in Robinson-Patman Enforcement: A Desirable End through Questionable Means." *Duke Law Journal* 1963 (Winter 1963): 145-153.

Examines the approval through a recent court ruling of the FTC's authority to issue cease and desist orders under Section 5 of the FTC Act against firms participating in price discrimination. Prior to the ruling it was unclear whether the FTC had the authority to issue cease and desist orders under provisions of the Robinson-Patman Act. It is concluded that the two statutes cannot be used interchangeably in some situations and that the court's ruling may not curb anticompetitive behavior because Supreme Court rulings and commentary from legal and economic scholars indicate that enforcement of Robinson-Patman may have an adverse effect on competition.

916   Vaill, E. E. "Federal Trade Commission: Should It Continue as Both Prosecutor and Judge in Antitrust Proceedings?" *Southwestern University Law Review* 10 (1978): 763-794.

The author advocates a "long overdue and meaningful" transformation of the FTC from both a prosecutional and judicial agency to one that is solely a prosecutional agency with judicial responsibilities shifted to the federal courts. This thesis is supported by examples of criticism leveled at the agency's adjudication functions since the FTC's early history. The author then outlines recommendations of President Carter's National Commission for the Review of Antitrust Laws and Procedures and presents practical suggestions for reforming the FTC's antitrust, rulemaking, and consumer protection adjudicative functions

917   Wallace, Jr., James H. "Recent Developments in Federal Antitrust Legislation." *Antitrust Law Journal* 52 (Summer 1983): 479-512.

Examines various developments in antitrust law enforcement during the past couple of years, including an extended discussion of FTC reauthorization legislation pending in both houses of Congress. Among the issues covered is the subject of state-regulated professionals, unfair acts and practices, agricultural cooperatives, rulemaking, legislative review of FTC trade regulation rules, and the potential closing of regional offices. The article concludes with an appendix charting the status of antitrust legislation in 98th Congress.

918   Wallace, Robert A. and Paul H. Douglas." Antitrust Policies and the New Attack on the Federal Trade Commission." *University of Chicago Law Review* 19 (Summer 1952): 684-723.

Evaluates arguments that are intended to support discontinuing the FTC as an antitrust enforcement agency and offers reasons why such arguments are invalid. These new attacks on the FTC are made by groups and individuals who feel that the Commission has overstepped the bounds of sensible antitrust enforcement and, in so doing, actually hindered business growth. The essay focuses on arguments made by William Simon in a 1952 issue of the *University of Chicago Law Review* (p. 297) that the FTC has failed to be informative, created confusion with respect to antitrust law enforcement, and has pursued "unorthodox ideologies." Simon recommends transferring the antitrust functions of the FTC to the Department of Justice and economic analysis functions to the Department of Commerce. Simon also stated that the FTC's "finding of facts be subject to review based on the weight of evidence."

919   Ward, Alan S. "The Federal Trade Commission and Unfair Methods of Competition in Foreign Commerce." *Antitrust Law Journal* 40 (1971): 806-809.

This essay briefly discusses the FTC's antitrust responsibilities with regards to foreign companies and commerce, and specifically, how that jurisdiction encompasses provisions of the Webb-Pomerene Act. Future roles are also examined in light of specific cases.

920   Weinberger, Caspar W. "Federal Trade Commission of the 1970's." *Antitrust Law Journal* 39 (1969-70): 411-426.

The Chairman of the FTC discusses the future of the FTC in the next decade.

Antitrust Law

Topics covered include possible restructuring of the agency, reaction to recent criticism of the FTC by the American Bar Association, influence of the consumer protection movement, and the devotion of Commission resources towards problems arising from the Robinson-Patman Act.

921   Weinberger, Caspar W. "Federal Trade Commission: Progress and a New Profile." *Case Western Reserve Law Review* 22 (November 1970): 5-10.

Text of an address delivered before the Fourth Annual Antitrust Institute of the Ohio State Bar Association in Akron, Ohio, May 14, 1970, in which the former FTC chairman outlines the steps to be adopted by the Commission to ensure a proper and efficient use of agency authority under Section 5 of the FTC Act given the prospects for additional power granted to the FTC by Congress. This renewed commitment to preventing unfairness in the marketplace is juxtaposed against criticism leveled at the FTC during the 1960s.

922   Weingast, Barry R. and Mark J. Moran. "Bureaucratic Discretion of Congressional Control? Regulatory Policymaking by the Federal Trade Commission." *Journal of Political Economy* 91 (October 1983): 765-800.

Uses recent changes in the FTC's antitrust enforcement policy and the relationship of these changes to Congressional action to develop a basis for a model of agency decision-making based on proposition that agency actions are controlled by the legislature. The study reviews attacks against FTC policy by Congress and the agency's response to such attacks. While it cannot be concluded that a lack of Congressional monitoring means that there is no legislative control, the study does show that "the FTC is remarkably sensitive to changes in subcommittee composition" and reveals that these subcommittees have a greater influence on the FTC's decision-making process that Congress as a whole.

923   Willcox, Thomas C. "Beyond the Pale of the Sherman and Clayton Acts: The Federal Trade Commission's "Invitation to Collude" Doctrine as a Deterrent to Violations of the Antitrust Laws." *Antitrust Bulletin* 39 (Fall 1994): 623-651.

Examines four recently issued consent decrees that allege invitations by companies to their competitors to engage in price fixing (invitations to collude doctrine). The first three decrees were issued even though the companies refused to accept the invitation. The fourth decree does fall within the scope of the

267

doctrine. The essay begins by analyzing the historical and legal background of Section 5 of the FTC Act as it relates to price fixing to help determine what factors led to the issuance of the consent decrees. Various arguments to support or eliminate the invitation to collude doctrine are then presented. It is concluded that the doctrine should continue to be enforced because of it serves as an important deterrent to price-fixing.

924   Wilson, Robert A. "Barriers to Trustbusting: "Efficiency" Myths and Timid Trustbusters." *Antitrust Law and Economics Review* 9 (1977): 19-39.

Reviews recent literature commenting on problems associated with antitrust law enforcement and then proceeds to discuss various factors that impede the enforcement of antitrust legislation. Among the factors addressed are political influences hindering both the FTC and the Department of Justice, the need to be comprehensive in discovering monopolized industries, and pricing structures within an industry.

925   Wilson, Robert D. "Federal Trade Commission Orders and the Clayton Act Section 5: A Reexamination." *Antitrust Bulletin* 12 (Spring 1967): 27-47.

Examines the recent Supreme Court ruling in *New Jersey Wood Finishing Co. v. Minnesota Mining and Manufacturing Co.* in which the courts reaffirmed the Congressional intention that national antitrust enforcement be based upon "a two-pronged regulatory scheme." However, the court also reaffirmed previous opinions that the FTC Act is not "an antitrust law within the purview of Sections 5(a) and 5(b) of the Clayton Act."

926   Withrow, Jr., James R. "Investigations by the Federal Trade Commission--As Seen by the Potential Respondent." *Antitrust Law Journal* 29 (1965): 81-106.

This article provides insight into antitrust proceedings as perceived by a firm being investigated. Among the problems confronted by private practitioners is the method by which a client is first notified that an investigation is to be conducted and the large amount of information that is needed to understand what powers are available to the FTC. The most important powers are the authority to force a firm to file annual or special reports and to answer specific inquiries in writing, the power to subpoena witnesses and the production of documentary evidence, and power to obtain copies of any documentary evidence held by the firm being investigated. The paper concludes with an appendix that discusses these three powers and the text of a question and answer session concerning the author's study.

927 Wood, B. Dan and James E. Anderson. "The Politics of U.S. Antitrust Regulation." *American Journal of Political Science* 37 (February 1993): 1-39.

An economic or bureaucratic theory of antitrust regulation fails because they do not take into account the overall institutional framework within which the regulation is applied. The authors adopt an "overhead democracy" theory to formulate a political explanation of antitrust regulation. This theory states that under the American constitutional system, "elected officials should be able to mold the preferences of nonelected bureaucrats and hold them accountable for their actions." Data from the Department of Justice's Antitrust Division is used to measure the relative importance of politics, bureaucracy, and economics in the government's use of antitrust laws to maintain competition and suppress monopolistic behavior. The essay begins by analyzing FTC enforcement activities and cites studies that show bureaucratic influence on FTC antimerger activities.

928 Woods, R. Kyle. "Functional Discounts and Integrated Distribution Under the Robinson-Patman Act." *Emory Law Journal* 37 (Summer 1988): 799-833.

Examines the validity under provisions of the Act of granting functional discounts to buyers who participate in both wholesale and retail functions ("integrated buyers"). The analysis is placed within the context of the recent decision by the FTC in the Boise Cascade Corp. case. The essay begins by reviewing the history of the Act in relation to functional discounts and then discusses FTC decisions regarding the discounts. It is concluded that the agency missed an opportunity to promulgate new rules that would be "more consistent with current distribution systems."

929 Yao, Dennis A. and Susan S. DeSanti. "Antitrust Analysis of Defense Industry Mergers." *Contract Law Journal* 23 (Spring 1994): 379-395.

This essay examines the role of the FTC in antitrust analysis of defense industry mergers within the context of current downsizing in the industry due to the reduction of the defense procurement budget. Three cases in which the FTC obtained preliminary injunctions are analyzed to determine on a case-by-case basis what factors led to the decision by the FTC that the mergers posed a threat to open competition within the defense industry. The article concludes by analyzing what role the Department of Defense plays in antitrust analysis.

930   Zimmerman, E. M. "The Federal Trade Commission and Mergers." *Columbia Law Review* 64 (March 1964): 500-523.
Studies the 1950 amendment to Section 7 of the Clayton Act and discusses the implications this has on future FTC enforcement regarding mergers. Specific court cases are used to help define how the revised Act is fashioned by the agency's work and how ambiguities are resolved. Three potential issues are analyzed in light of the revision: the opportunity to develop substantive doctrine, the question of relief under the Act, enhancement of the Commission's ability to investigate, and enhancement of its guidance function. These potential issues are compared to actual Commission policies and procedures to illustrate its effectiveness in enforcing merger law.

931   Zuckerman, Jeffrey I. "The FTC's Approach to Merger Analysis: Is Anyone Out There Paying Attention?" *Antitrust Law Journal* 57 (Spring 1988): 115-124.
Examines the difference in merger enforcement between the Department of Justice and its guidelines and the FTC, which has its own set of guidelines. Four specific differences are stated. First, additional supply in the market due to a new entry is only considered after a year by the FTC rather than immediately considered in defining the market. Second, an acquisition cannot have anticompetitive effects if there is an absence of barriers to entry. Third, the FTC has adopted a "two-tier approach" to defining entry barriers. And fourth, the FTC has not articulated a specific time period to measure impediments to entry.

Chapter Three
Administrative Law and Procedure

932   "Administrative Law–FTC Denied Substantive Rulemaking Power."
            University of Kansas Law Review 21 (Winter 1973): 198-211.
Until the federal court decision *National Petroleum Refiners Association v.
FTC*, the Federal Trade Commission's authority to issue Trade Regulation Rules
under guidelines established by the Administrative Procedure Act (APA) had
never been judicially challenged. The author argues that the court's decision to
diminish the agency's rulemaking authority in this case is based on false pretenses.
By analyzing the language and legislative history of the FTC Act, its relationship
to APA, and similar judicial interpretations of rules and regulation guidelines in
other "administrative enabling statutes," it can be shown that rulemaking is a
viable alternative to adjudication.

933   "Administrative Law–Judicial Review–The Issuance of a Complaint by
            an Administrative Agency is Not "Final" Agency Action and Pre-
            enforcement Review is Therefore Not Available Under the
            Administrative Procedure Act–*Federal Trade Commission v. Standard
            Oil Co.* (101 S. Ct. 488)." *George Washington Law Review* 50
            (January 1982): 349-369.
Examines the availability of pre-enforcement review of agency action within the
context of the reversal by the United States Supreme Court of a lower courts
decision that a suit brought by Standard Oil Company of California to terminate
FTC administrative complaint proceedings against the company, even though the
administrative hearing had been dismissed, must continue under the grounds that
the issuance of a complaint constitutes final agency action reviewable under the
Administrative Procedure Act. This comment examines the test established to
determine what constitutes final agency action and discusses the doctrines of
"ripeness," "finality," and "exhaustion." It is concluded that the finality test
established in the Standard Oil decision provides the courts with the needed
flexibility to make "common sense decisions."

934   "Administrative   Law–Magnuson-Moss   Warranty-Federal   Trade
            Commission Improvement Act–The FTC Can Obtain Equitable Relief
            for Deceptive Trade Practices." *Texas Law Review* 53 (May 1975): 831-
            840.

John Heater had guaranteed to the merchants participating in his program, entitled "Honor All Credit Cards," that he would extend credit to all holders of selected credit cards and "that the customer would be billed and the payments remitted to the merchant regardless of whether the amounts owed had been paid by the customer." However, Heater rarely made the remittance payments and the FTC found his program to be an unfair trade practice under Section 5. The FTC ordered Heater to reimburse the deceived customers. The Ninth Circuit Court ruled that this order was beyond the FTC's power because the order was penal, compensatory, and retroactive. Passage of the Magnuson-Moss Warranty-Federal Trade Commission Improvement Act now provides the FTC the power to commence a civil action. The creation of this power is the basis of the legal comment.

935   "Administrative Law–Powers of Agencies– An Order of the Federal Trade Commission Must Have the Concurrence of a Majority of the Full Commission." *Harvard Law Review* 80 (May 1967): 1589-1593.

Reviews the case of *Flotill Prods., Inc. v. FTC* in which it was ruled that the issuance of a cease and desist order by the FTC must have the concurrence of the majority of the full commission before proceeding with an order. It is argued that congressional intent is too vague, therefore, the courts must uphold the agency's majority of quorum rule even if the courts are concerned that a minority of the Commission may issue orders "without the benefits of deliberation" by absent members of the Commission.

936   Anderson, Sigurd. "Federal Trade Commission–What Is It and What Does It Do?" *South Dakota Law Review* 4 (Spring 1959): 117-148.

This essay outlines the development of the FTC in a positive light and its role in regulating business, the powers it possesses under congressional intent, and its organization. The author defines the various statutes under FTC jurisdiction and remedies available under provisions of the FTC Act.

937   Auerbach, Carl A. "Federal Trade Commission: Internal Organization and Procedure." *Minnesota Law Review* 48 (January 1964): 383-522.

This article is a comprehensive examination of the organization and procedural activities of the FTC. It is divided into seven parts covering the following issues within the context of internal organization and procedure: principle FTC bureaus, organization for planning, delegation of authority, consent settlement procedures, efforts to secure industry-wide compliance, the process of formal adjudication, and the form and scope of orders. Based upon this analysis, the author systematically summarizes recommendations to improve the efficiency of the agency. This article represents the best and most detailed insight into the internal operations of the FTC from the agency's inception to the point of publication of this paper.

938   Baker, Jonathan B. "Continuous Regulatory Reform at the Federal Trade Commission." *Administrative Law Review* 49 (Fall 1997): 859-874.

During the past twenty years, a movement has been under way by Congress and the President to incorporate cost benefit analysis into administrative agency decision-making processes. The FTC has emerged as one of the most proactive regulatory agencies in this area by systematically reviewing old rules and procedures and terminating them is they are deemed unnecessary. This article highlights internal approaches to regulatory reform that are guided primarily by the FTC's Bureau of Economics. By continually employing a cost benefit analysis to decision-making, "continuous" regulatory reform becomes an integral part of the day-to-day work of the Commission.

939   Baum, Daniel J. "Program of Enforcement: Comment and Correspondence between Congressman Rouch and the Federal Trade Commission." *Administrative Law Review* 16 (Fall 1963): 42-49.

Examines the recent establishment by the Department of Justice Antitrust Division's program review section, which is modeled after the Program Review Officer of the FTC. The experience with this review model by the FTC is the focus of this essay and contains the correspondence between the FTC and Congressman J. Edward Rouch (D-Indiana). As a member of the Government Operations Committee and the Intergovernmental Relations Subcommittee, Rouch was instrumental in pointing out concerns with the enforcement efforts of the FTC that eventually led to the establishment of the Program Review Officer.

940   Baum, Daniel J. "Reorganization, Delay and the Federal Trade Commission." *Administrative Law Review* 15 (Winter-Spring 1963): 92-110.

Explores the continued delay in formal litigation at the FTC despite efforts from private and presidential sources to speed up the process of adjudication. Commission reorganization, revised rules of procedure, and the delegation of some agency functions have also failed to increase efficiency. This comment argues that delay will continue so long as the Commission is "unselective" in the cases it pursues in fulfilling its statutory mission. It is concluded that primary reliance on a case-by-case approach will perpetuate the delays. However, the issuance and adoption of industry-wide trade regulation rules offers hope that the situation will not continue indefinitely.

941 Baum, Daniel Jay. "Federal Trade Commission Orders under the Robinson-Patman Act." *Administrative Law Review* 16 (Fall 1963): 80-98.

This is an essay that examines factors associated with the need to issue a cease and desist order when a company refuses to comply with FTC edict, analyzes the scope of these orders, and their limits and their effectiveness. Also discussed are four areas in which a respondent may attempt to constrict the effectiveness of an order and how the FTC has responded to such actions. Throughout the article references to judicial input are noted.

942 Beer, Henry Ward. "Federal Trade Commission and Its Due Process of Law." *Notre Dame Lawyer* 7 (January 1932): 170-184.

A reprint that originally appeared in *The New York Law Journal* discussing the impact of the ruling by the Supreme Court in *FTC v. Raladam Co.* that the FTC had overstepped its administrative power. Similar cases are used to show the reasoning behind the Court's decision to limit agency authority.

943 Bennett, Joel P. "Post-Compliant Discovery in Administrative Proceedings: The FTC as a Case Study." *Duke Law Journal* 1975 (March 1975): 329-346.

The purpose of this article is to: 1) review the history and background of discovery in civil and administrative proceedings; 2) compare discovery under both the Federal Rules of Civil Procedure and the FTC's Rules of Pactice;3) analyze post-complaint discovery under FTC rules and judicial interpretation of those rules;and 4) evaluate the efficiency of the Commission's rules with respect to complex cases such as the pending case against the eight major oil companies. It is concluded that FTC rules are cumbersome because each requested deposition and subpoena is likely to be the object of litigation, thus leading to unnecessary delay. Adoption of the Federal Rules of Civil Procedure would help address these problems.

944   Boyer, Barry B. ""Funding Public Participation in Agency Proceedings: The Federal Trade Commission Experience." *Georgetown Law Journal* 70 (October 1981): 51-172.

Analyzes the implementation and impact on administrative proceedings of the FTC's compensation provision over a four year period within the context of the Commission's authority to fund public participation in administrative proceedings. Recent political and economic factors have led to a criticism that this funding represents expensive and "one-sided subsidies for proponents of additional regulation." The author examines the validity of this criticism and concludes that aggressive regulatory behavior by the agency during the late 1970s led to hostility among members of Congress and others, thereby, undermining the possible benefits that direct funding of public participation may have afforded.

945   Boyer, Barry B. "Too May Lawyers, Not Enough Practical People: The Policy-Making Discretion of the Federal Trade Commission." *Law and Policy Quarterly* 5 (1983): 9-33.

On April 30, 1980, the FTC was shut down by Congress because it had failed to pass legislation allocating the agency funds for the upcoming fiscal year. Although funds were made available the next day, the incident reflects the growing dissatisfaction Congress had for the FTC's regulatory agenda. Procedural controls promulgated in the Magnuson-Moss Act failed "to produce politically acceptable results." This essay examines why this strategy failed and how later attempts articulated through the FTC Improvements Act of 1980 reflected an altered strategy by Congress to control agency decision-making procedures.

946   Budnitz, Mark E. "The FTC's Consumer Protection Program During the Miller Years: Lessons for Administrative Agency Structure and Operation." *The Catholic University Law Review* 46 (Winter 1997): 371-451.

It is generally understood that during the 1970s, Chairman Michael Pertschuk created an aggressive consumer protection program that hindered commerce and labelled the FTC as the "national nanny." During the 1980s, Chairman James C. Miller III governed the agency to the other extreme by reining in consumer protection activity to the point of being accused of acquiescing to the special interest demands of business. This article attempts to step beyond these generalizations by examining the consumer protection program of the FTC during the Miller years, the cases brought by the Commission, and Miller's management philosophy and style. Using elements of time and process as they relate to how the agency decided to proceed in enforcement matters, this study sheds light on the "competitive forces" outside of the agency, such as Congress and the institutional context of the agency, that define the boundaries that the chairman must effectively function within. Various theories are put forth that attempt to explain why the chairman promoted certain positions or engaged in particular activities during his tenure, noting the usefulness or inadequacies of each in explaining behavior. The article concludes by exploring the policy implications of Miller's chairmanship and the implications for further study of other administrative agencies.

947   Cary, George S. and Marian R. Bruno. "Merger Remedies." *Administrative Law Review* 49 (Fall 1997): 875-887.

The author outlines efforts by the FTC's Bureau of Competition to evaluate the effectiveness, both procedurally and substantively, of merger remedies and the use of divestitures to address competition concerns. Recently, seven new approaches to reviewing mergers have emerged: shorter divestiture periods; identification of acceptable buyers in advance; broader asset packages to be divested; support of a "crown jewel provision" that "expands the assets to be divested should the respondent fail to divest the original package in the time allotted"; inclusion of hold separate agreements, whereby a facility or business to be divested is operated independently of the respondent's business until the FTC finds a suitable buyer; and using initial public offerings. The essay concludes by considering civil penalties in cases where a firm has failed to divest in a timely manner.

948   Condon, Ann E. "*Federal Trade Commission v. Compagnie De Saint-Gobain-Pont-A-Mousson* International Service of Administrative Process." *George Washington Journal of International Law and Economics* 16 (1981): 119-141.

Analyzes the service of administrative documents abroad, such as investigatory subpoenas sent by registered mail, that was adopted by the FTC, and how the decision by the United States Court of Appeals for the District of Columbia to strike down the FTC's authority to issue such documents will make it much more difficult for the agency to investigate foreign companies operating in the United States. It is concluded that the FTC and other regulatory agencies should be allowed, through congressional action, to reach foreign corporations that have real or potential effects within the U.S. marketplace, although agencies should confer with the State Department before taking action.

949   Connor, Martin F. "The Defense of Abandonment in Proceedings Before the Federal Trade Commission." *Georgetown Law Journal* 49 (Summer 1961): 722-736.

This article criticizes of the FTC's slow investigative and adjudicatory processes with regards to cease and desist orders issued against firms found to be in violation of FTC rules or regulations. It is noted that, not only do companies have only a one in eight chance of avoiding a cease and desist order once a complaint is issued, but there is a likelihood that the practice under question has been discontinued long before the determination of legality has been made. To avoid this situation and to accelerate the adjudicatory process, the author proposes the following rules of reason concerning the defense of abandonment: should a practice be halted before an investigation begins, it should be considered a move of good faith on the part of the respondent; the respondent should receive the most favorable judgement by the FTC upon discontinuance; and, no inference should be derived from a respondents discontinuance of a practice.

950   Connor, Martin F. "FTC Procedure Revisions: A Critique." *Villanova Law Review* 7 (Spring 1963): 359-388.

Discusses the various opinions about the efficiency of the FTC and then specifically analyzes the potential impact of the agency's amended and revised rules governing its adjudicatory proceedings in light of its record of antitrust law enforcement procedures. Upon noting the subtle differences between the Commission and a court, it is concluded that the new rules reflect a step forward in producing a more efficient adjudicative process, but that more needs to be done.

951   Cooper, Scott. "Technology and Competition Come to Telecommunications: Reexamining Exemptions to the Federal Trade Commission Act." *Administrative Law Review* 49 (Fall 1997): 963-988.

This article addresses two issues: the underlying reasons why a dual regulatory structure exists in the United States, particularly as the issue relates to the FTC and Federal Communications Commission, and the need to shift away from industry-specific regulation and move towards a competitive open marketplace model of consumer protection in relation to the emergence of new technologies. Three area of consumer protection in a digital environment have arisen that must be confronted by regulatory agencies: advertising in electronic commerce, resale of telephone services, and electronic funds transfer.

952   Copeland, Melvin T. "The Problem of Administering the Robinson-Patman Act." *Harvard Business Review* 15 (Winter 1937): 156-173.
Reviews provisions of the Robinson-Patman Act, then examines the problems with dual enforcement between the FTC and the Department of Justice. Forms of discrimination, such as outright price variations, trade and quantity, term, and cash discounts, and advertising allowances, are examined with dual enforcement in mind. Administration of the Act parallels problems of public administration associated with business regulation in general.

953   Craswell, R. "Identification of Unfair Acts and Practices by the Federal Trade Commission." *Wisconsin Law Review* 1981 (1981): 107-153.
This paper attempts to predict within what conditions specific practices will be determined as unfair under provisions of Section 5 of the FTC Act by cataloging the most common commercial practices that have already been determined as unfair through litigation. This study is considered by the author to be important because little attention has been paid to the issue. Most studies have focused on defining unfairness in the abstract with little regard to what specific acts and practices would be rendered unlawful under the proposed definitions. The author notes that considerations guiding the Commission's actions have varied widely depending on the circumstances under which the FTC has ruled. It is concluded that future decisions regarding what constitutes unfairness must be based on past decisions rather than treating them on a case-by-case basis.

954   Davis, Ewin L. "Influence of Federal Trade Commission's General Investigations." *Federal Bar Association Journal* 3 (April 1938): 145-148, 180.
This essay briefly discusses the effects of general investigations by the FTC on various legislative acts, such as the Grain Futures Act of 1921 and the Securities Act of 1933, and concludes by exploring pending federal and state legislation.

955   Davis, Ewin L. "Influence of the Federal Trade Commission's Investigations on Federal Regulation of Interstate Electric and Gas Utilities." *George Washington Law Review* 14 (December 1945): 21-29.
The author examines actions taken by the FTC against deceptive practices within the utility industries and how these actions influenced the passage of the Federal Power Act of 1935 and expansion of regulatory authority to the Federal Power Commission. The findings of the FTC's investigation of the utility industries and

the provisions of the Federal Power Act are outlined.

956   Denger, Michael L. "The Unfairness Standard and FTC Rulemaking: The Controversy over the Scope of the Commission's Authority." *Antitrust Law Journal* 49 (Summer 1980): 53-108.

This study briefly reviews several developments during the past ten years that have led to an expansion of FTC authority and that are currently being challenged by Congress and special interest groups. This review helps to place current criticism into proper context and to highlight unresolved issues arising from the controversy over the scope of the Commission's authority. Among the issues discussed is the undefined breadth of the FTC's unfairness standard and undefined limits under provisions of Magnuson-Moss rulemaking authority. Concerning whether the unfairness standard should be modified, the author examines several issues: the lack of a meaningful delineation between unfair methods of competition and unfair acts or practices; the apparent intentional decision by the FTC to leave the unfairness standard vague; the failure to development consistently applied criteria for determining unfairness; the fact that the use of value-orientated rather than factually-orientated criteria does not lead to a meaningful standard for determining unfairness; and the failure of courts to establish meaningful guidelines. The essay concludes by stating what restrictions should be placed on the FTC's power to impose preventive requirements in trade regulation rules.

957   Dixon, Paul Rand. "Administrative Delay Revisited." *Antitrust Law Journal* 37 (1968): 281-288.

As the incoming Chairman of the FTC, the author reviews early criticism of the FTC that focused on procedural fairness. While the Administrative Procedure Act has done much to alleviate this concern, a new issue expressed by President John F. Kennedy was the regulatory delay experienced at many federal agencies. This delay is primarily due to the adoption of cumbersome administrative procedures in response to earlier criticism. Efforts by the FTC to meet these criticisms are then examined.

958   Dixon, Paul Rand. "Disqualification" of Agency Members: The New Challenge to the Administrative Process." *Antitrust Law Symposium* (1965): 13-30.

Discusses "the present rash of bias cases" involving the FTC and other independent agencies. Three types of cases are defined: hearing cases that generally do not cover a new principle of law, cases related to the "separation of functions," and "speech" cases in which speeches were viewed as prejudging actions against several oil companies suspected of price fixing. It is concluded that these cases arise because of the perceived need for a neutral judge or administrator, a concept not only considered impossible to attain, but undesirable as well.

959   Dixon, Paul Rand. "The Federal Trade Commission: Its Fact-Finding Responsibilities and Powers." *Marquette Law Review* 46 (Summer 1962): 17-28.

Studies the development of the FTC, the underlying reasons behind its creation in 1914, and examines the processes available to the agency in conducting an investigation. Three distinct compulsory processes exist: subpoena power regarding both witnesses and documents, right of visitation or access to documentary evidence or firms, and the power to require corporations to submit annual and/or special reports. It is concluded that these powers, refined through judicial review, will provide a precise set of enforcement tools that will speed proceedings and sharpen the FTC's focus.

960   Dixon, Paul Rand. "Practice and Procedure before the Federal Trade Commission." *New York Law Forum* 9 (March 1963): 31-63.

The author addresses the issue of judicial unfairness inherent in administrative delay and examines how this is reflected in FTC practice and procedure. As Chairman, Dixon discusses the underlying difficulties in antitrust enforcement that create delays and bring criticism stating that the agency's enforcement of rules is unfairly administered.

961   Dixon, Paul Rand. "Program Planning at the Federal Trade Commission." *Administrative Law Review* 19 (July 1967): 408-415.

Text of an address given at American University before the Washington (DC) Conference on Business-Government Relations in which the FTC chairman articulates the agency's program planning efforts. These efforts encompass agency goals and priorities, planning for the efficient allocation of scarce resources, and maintaining flexibility of organization in order to respond to new challenges; each of these issues are summarized in detail.

962   Dixon, William D. "Federal Trade Commission Advisory Opinions." *Administrative Law Review* 18 (Fall 1965): 65-79.

Outlines the history and development of advisory opinions, delineates the contents of these opinions from others, and examines specific issues associated with advisory opinions produced by the FTC at the request of the requesting party, including the substance of the opinions and the possible impact of more advisory opinions issued by the FTC in the future.

963   Eisner, Marc Allen. "Bureaucratic Professionalization and the Limits of the Political Control Thesis: The Case of the Federal Trade Commission." *Governance: An International Journal of Policy and Administration* 6 (April 1993): 127-153.

Uses a case study of the FTC to explore how political control by Congress impacts policy changes within the organizational framework of an agency. Literature in this area so far has failed to take into account the relationship between the organizational structure of an agency and policy changes imposed by Congress. This study indicate that the growing role of economists in setting antitrust enforcement priorities has had more impact on driving agency policy than Congressional oversight or presidential appointments.

964   Elman, Philip. "Administrative Reform in the Federal Trade Commission." *Georgetown Law Journal* 59 (March 1971): 777-860.

Drawing from his experience as an FTC Commissioner, the author outlines the principle failures of the FTC during the 1960s. Among these is the failure to clearly define the agency's role in regulatory enforcement, the use or misuse of broad sets of criteria to determine how to apply the law in administrative proceedings that taxes the FTC's resources, the lack of decisions based on the public's need, the absence of planning in selecting cases for litigation, and issues related to the agency's unique nonjudicial functions and authority. Analysis of these issues is followed by an examination of the FTC's relationship with Congress. The essay concludes with suggestions for internal reorganization and personnel changes.

965   Elman, Philip. "Agency Decision-Making: Adjudication by the Federal Trade Commission." *Food Drug Cosmetic Law Journal* 19 (October 1964): 508-512.

Attempts to answer the question of whether the FTC can effectively "discharge the function of adjudication fairly and impartially" given the variety and complexity of administrative tasks it must perform. Administrative duties of Commission members and the personal standards that guide them are reviewed.

966   Elman, Philip. "Federal Trade Commission and the Administrative Process." *Antitrust Bulletin* 8 (July-August 1963): 607-616.

As a commissioner at the FTC, the author offers his personal insights into administrative processes within the FTC and current problems associated with them. Among the issues addressed are the problems of delay in adjudicative proceedings, the benefits associated with industry-wide trade regulation rules, and the need to revise the process by which complaints are issued, and to improve the formulation of cease and desist orders created remedy specific violations found.

967   Ely, R. S. "Work of the Federal Trade Commission." *Wisconsin Law Review* 7 (June 1932): 195-212.

Examines the history of he FTC, its powers and duties, the procedures employed to carry out its mission, and highlights specific developments in its work. Concludes by discussing the significance of the Commission's work concerning the regulation of unfair business practices.

968   Engman, Lewis A. "Report from the Federal Trade Commission." *Antitrust Law Journal* 44 (Spring 1975): 161-168.

Report outlining procedures promulgated in the *Federal Register* that will affect the course of future agency investigations. Among these is the abolition of the "Part II" procedures, the creation of new discovery rules for cases in adjudication, and the elimination of the "All-State Doctrine," which essentially stated that all staff investigations must be completed before the agency could take action. Concludes by examining three elements of the Magnuson-Moss Act: rulemaking, civil penalties for knowing violations, and consumer redress, noting that the new legislation is welcomed by the FTC.

969   "Evidence, Federal Trade Commission Hearings: Proponent Must Show Good Cause for Evidence to he Received in Camera." *Minnesota Law Review* 46 (March 1962): 778-785.

In order to ensure that sensitive information concerning a company is not revealed, specific documents can be placed "in camera" and thus be excluded from the public record. The FTC recognizes two classes of materials that can be placed in camera: trade secrets and business records. The exclusion of trade secrets from the public record is usually granted. However, it is noted that harm created by the disclosure of business records, such as profit margins, price lists, and customer lists, is generally difficult to measure and frequently represent little, if any, harm to the individual company or market. It is concluded that the standard of serious injury to the company should be applied to all in camera requests.

970 Evins, J. L. "The Federal Trade Commission." *Tennessee Law Review* 16 (April 1941): 772-779.
A brief essay outlining the history and development of the FTC, including its statutory responsibilities and enforcement procedures. The FTC's work as it specifically relates to the Robinson-Patman Act and the Wheeler-Lea Act are also examined.

971 "Federal Trade Commission and Reform of the Administrative Process." *Columbia Law Review* 62 (April 1962): 671-707.
The article analyzes in detail the "administrative malaise" within the FTC related to policy-making, procedure, and personnel. Problems associated with the agency's administrative process are complicated by sporadic new rules, court rulings, and an unpredictable executive branch. Among the platforms articulated at the 1960 Democratic Party convention was Reorganization Plan No. 4 of 1961 for the FTC. This, coupled with Kennedy appointees to the Commission, offers a chance to improve agency relations with Congress and the Presidency and provide guidance in creating new regulatory procedures. Both of these issues are studied in detail. The essay includes an organizational chart and an appendix outlining the agency's budget and regulatory activities.

972 Fox, Eleanor M. "Chairman Miller, the Federal Trade Commission, Economics, and Rashomon." *Law and Contemporary Problems* 50 (Autumn 1987): 33-55.
The first part of this article discusses, in general, the role of the chairman in setting agency priorities and affecting policy, and then examines in detail the appointment by President Ronald Reagan of James C. Miller III as FTC Chairman in 1981. Miller's appointment is unique in that he was the first economist, rather than attorney, to hold the position. The article then details the political environment at the time of Miller's appointment, outlining his general approach to antitrust enforcement and consumer protection. Part three analyzes three cases that were decided by a divided Commission. Miller's role in applying economics to the outcome are analyzed. The article concludes by noting that Miller's

chairmanship raised the level of economics-related dialogue within the agency and his positions in the three cases analyzed showed that "political philosophy drives economic analysis." Miller's continuation of Michael Pertschuk's policy of maintaining open discussions about FTC policy indicated a willingness to keep the FTC's economic policies and presumptions transparent.

973   "Freedom of Information Act and the Federal Trade Commission: A Study in Malfeasance." *Harvard Civil Rights-Civil Liberties Law Review* 4 (Spring 1969): 345-377.

As part of an investigation of the FTC by six legal students and scholars under the guidance of Ralph Nader, it became apparent that the information disclosure policies and procedures of the Commission needed to be reviewed. This comment uses the author's experience as a member of the investigative project to examine the legislative history and intention of the Freedom of Information Act (FOIA) and its implementation by the FTC. It is argued that the FTC frequently attempts to circumvent FOIA requests through regulations, exemptions, and operational obstacles to dissemination. The comment concludes with recommendations for reform within the FTC to eliminate barriers to information dissemination.

974   Freer, Robert E. "The Federal Trade Commission–A Study in Survival." *Business Lawyer* 26 (July 1971): 1505-1526.

Outlines key components of the American Bar Association's report on the FTC that stated changes to the agency must take place if it is to remain a viable government institution. In reaction to this, the FTC has become much more aggressive and gained positive accolades from President Richard Nixon concerning its consumer protection activities. The author notes that this transformation is due in large part to effective management initiated under the new Chairman, Caspar W. Weinberger. Specific cases brought by the FTC are used throughout the text to support this position. Includes two organization charts to illustrate the agency's new administrative organization.

975   Freer, Robert E. "The Federal Trade Commission Practice and Procedure." *Federal Bar Association Journal* 6 (July 1945): 387-398.

Overview of the policies and procedures of the FTC as they relate to enforcement of the FTC Act and the Clayton Act, as amended by Robinson-Patman. The essay begins with a general review of FTC jurisdiction and investigational procedure, followed by a more detailed analysis of formal enforcement procedures.

976   Freer, Robert E. "Federal Trade Commission Procedure." *American Bar Association Journal* 26 (April 1940): 342-343, 370.

Brief essay by the Chairman of the FTC reviewing the specific provisions of laws under FTC jurisdiction and outlines how the FTC proceeds in pursuing a case and evaluating the findings.

977   French, John D. "Federal Trade Commission and the Public Interest." *Minnesota Law Review* 49 (January 1965): 539-552.

Analyzes the public interest clause within the FTC Act, its importance in relation to the burdensome FTC procedures frequently imposed on private litigants, and how it places a limitation on agency authority. Whether or not the Commission has complied with this clause is then examined within the framework of judicial review of specific cases. It is concluded that a per se application to all cases is "dangerous" and the rule of reason must be employed given the broad scope and indefinite terminology of antitrust laws.

978   "FTC 5 and Robinson-Patman: Unfair Method of Legislation or Unfair Method of Administration." *Villanova Law Review* 11 (Fall 1965): 113-124.

Examines criticism raised concerning enforcement by the FTC of the Robinson-Patman Act and places this criticism within the context of legislative intent and administrative enforcement. The issue of whether or not the FTC can use Section 5 of the FTC Act "when a discriminatory practice does not come within the purview of the Robinson-Patman Act because of a technical omission which denies jurisdiction to the regulatory body under the statute" is studied in detail. Specific cases are used to show how judicial review has affected the administration of Section 5.

979   Gaskill, Nelson B. "Public Interest versus Private Interest in the Federal Trade Commission Act." *Academy of Political Science Proceedings* 11 (January 1926): 121-131.

As a former Commissioner, the author argues that the FTC has the potential to do a lot of good in the future. Critics argue that the agency's administration has not adhered to the original intent of the Federal Trade Commission Act to assist business in prospering. The FTC has also been ineffective because there is a lack of common understanding between the FTC and the courts concerning guiding principles. By examining selected court decisions and placing the argument within the conceptual framework of the public interest, a "partial solution" is offered.

980   Gellhorn, Ernest. "The Treatment of Confidential Information by the Federal Trade Commission: Pretrial Practices." *University of Chicago Law Review* 36 (Fall 1968): 113-184.

This article builds on previous studies of FTC treatment of confidential business information by analyzing practices prior to the hearing stage and examines what should be the FTC's confidentiality policies at the pre-trial and investigative stage. By gathering data from FTC decisions at the pretrial stage, the author attempts to create a set of standards that will assist in determining whether sensitive information should be disclosed in cases where it appears current policy is inadequate. The work concludes by offering standards to determine if the data warrants confidential treatment during the investigative process and how this information can be protected.

981   Gellhorn, Ernest. "The Treatment of Confidential Information by the Federal Trade Commission: The Hearing." *University of Pennsylvania Law Review* 116 (January 1968): 401-434.

Examines the following questions related to FTC practice involving confidential business information: what constitutes confidential information? who shall decide what is confidential in an investigation? and how should this data be handled? Related to these issues are concerns about why the material is deemed sensitive, for what purpose is disclosure or discovery sought, and in what way is the information harmful to the respondent. This essay focuses on the treatment of confidential information during the trial stage of FTC proceedings and concludes by stating that the Commission should re-evaluate its confidentiality procedures given the lack of judicial scrutiny and oversight during the hearing.

982   Gercke, Joseph J. "Post Order Compliance–Procedures and Reports." *Antitrust Law Journal* 37 (1968): 269-274.

The author comments on the methodologies used with regard to post-order compliance procedures and, more specifically, how they affect final orders in the restraint of trade field. The essay outlines what procedures are involved in issuing a final order and parallels them with provisions stated in the Commission's Rules of Practice. It is noted that the role of the Compliance counsel is to listen and react to the respondent so that the FTC is better informed of the issues involved.

983   Graves, Kristin and Bruce Hall. "Crisis at the FTC." *Human Ecology Forum* 18 (Summer 1980): 28-31.

Analyzes the repercussions of increased authority granted to the FTC through the Magnuson-Moss Amendment, and specifically, trade regulation rules which extend regulatory power to entire industries. Opposition expressed to Congress by various business groups that may be subject to proposed trade regulation rules has led to only two rules being implemented while most have been halted. After describing a number of proposed legislative remedies, the authors argue that the FTC is a critical element to government regulation of business because reform efforts are vulnerable to special interest groups.

984   Haase, Eric. "Proposals for Reform of Federal Trade Commission Procedure." *The Trademark Reporter* 40 (March 1950): 197-210.

This article reviews five proposals made since 1940 to examine procedures within the FTC. These proposals are: 1) the Report of Attorney-General's Committee on Administrative Procedure that promulgated three recommendations, all concerning, to some degree, the dissemination of information; 2) the Reece Bill sponsored by B. Carroll Reece (R., Tennessee) that attempted to address issues raised in the Attorney-General report; 3) the Administrative Procedure Act sponsored by the American Bar Association that attempted to standardize practices among administrative agencies; 4) the O'Hara Bill sponsored by Rep. Joseph P. O'Hara and its subsequent reintroduction the following session; and 5) the Hoover Commission Report.

985   Hagan, Willis W. "Ethics, Marketing and the Federal Trade Commission." *American Business Law Journal* 5 (Fall 1967): 171-184.

Examines the issue of fairness, both as it applies to provisions of the FTC Act and as it relates to ethical decisions as it applies to fairness to competitors and the consuming public. Ambiguity exists because the FTC Act does not define what business practices should be considered unfair. Through both judicial review and the Commission's work, examples of unfair practices are defined that would most likely initiate agency action. The ethical decision-making framework of the FTC is placed within both a legal and marketing dimension.

986   Handler, Milton. "Constitutionality of Investigations by the Federal Trade Commission." *Columbia Law Review* 28 (June 1928): Part One 708-733; Part Two (November 1928): 905-937.

This is a comprehensive analysis of the constitutionallty of the exercise of investigative powers by the FTC. The essay begins by analyzing the legislative history of the agency, followed by a study of whether such investigations reflect unreasonable search and seizure, whether requests for information regarding production and intrastate sales are equivalent to regulating intrastate commerce and thus outside the jurisdiction of the federal government, and whether "such inquiries result in a deprivation of property without due process of law." A number of cases are used throughout the article to highlight specific points.

987   Hankin, Gregory. "Conclusiveness of Federal Trade Commission's Findings as to Facts." *Michigan Law Review* 23 (1925): 233-271.

Examines the issue of whether the finding of fact, if supported by testimony by the FTC, is actually considered conclusive by the courts when sent to the Circuit Court of Appeals. The FTC Act and the Clayton Act both state that the Commission's findings as to facts shall be conclusive if they are supported by testimony. The findings of other administrative bodies are used to study this issue. Using the results of specific cases it is concluded that there is evidence to support the provision that testimony remain conclusive in tying contracts, but may not be as definitive when examining other cases.

988   Henderson, Gerard Carl. *Federal Trade Commission: A Study in Administrative Law and Procedure.* New Haven, CT: Yale University Press, 1924.

This book contains chapters that cover the following topics: the agency's political and legislative history, procedures of the FTC, finding of facts, deceptive and dishonest practices, and practices which restrain trade. Each of these topics are examined in detail within the context of administrative law and practice. The book concludes that, despite criticisms concerning the details of FTC administration and proceedings and procedures, the "fundamental policy embodied in the FTC Act is sound." Includes an appendix to the text of the FTC Act and the Clayton Act, an index of cases cited, and a subject index.

989   Henke, Michael J. "Federal Trade Commission Hearings: Rights of a Non-Party to Protect Its Witnesses and Documents." *American University Law Review* 21 (September 1971): 130-155.

There are several important risks associated with the testimony of non-party witnesses in restraint of trade hearings: sensitive business information can be revealed by such witnesses, the witnesses are usually representing the best interests of competitors, and the non-party witness may be required by the FTC to submit documents containing important business records. This article explores the devises available to non-party witnesses to protect themselves from revealing sensitive information during the course of a hearing. It is concluded that the FTC should adopt procedures and rules outlined by the author to insure protection against revealing sensitive business or trade information.

990   Herring, E. Pendleton. "Politics, Personalities and the Federal Trade Commission." _American Political Science Review_ 28 (December 1934): 1016-1029 [Part One]; 29 (February 1935): 21-35 [Part Two].

Focuses on the FTC's relationship with the business community, Congress, and the President to reveal what economic and political influences these institutions have had on the administrative experience of the FTC. Complicating the relationships among these institutions is the underlying influence of special interest and economic groups. The two part essay sets the stage for future FTC action by examining the legislative intent behind the agency's creation and analyzing the "cautious" administrative procedures of FTC enforcement provisions. The essay concludes by detailing the political agendas of those most closely associated with the FTC's mission and activities.

991   Hoffman, J. E. "Participating Effectively in TRR Proceedings at the FTC." _Food Drug Cosmetic Law Journal_ 32 (May 1977): 200-215.

While provisions of the Magnuson-Moss Warranty and Federal Trade Commission Improvement Act have greatly strengthened the FTC's authority to issue sanctions against those found in violation of its rules, the amendment also enhances the ability of respondents to participate in FTC proceedings. This essay offers suggestions on how the food and drug industries can participate effectively in these proceedings. This article provides a clear chronology of the FTC's procedures in a Trade Regulation Rule proceeding.

992   Hoge, J. F. "Federal Trade Commission: A Revaluation of Its Responsibilities." _Michigan State Bar Journal_ 29 (December 1950): 13-18, 34.

The author, an experienced lawyer dealing with FTC litigation matters, outlines the increased power of the FTC since it was first formed in 1914 under President Woodrow Wilson. The extension of adjudication powers has evolved from a regulation of business to a process "of policing and punishment." This thesis is supported by an examination of litigation proceedings, Commission procedure, and appeals from the FTC.

993   Houck, Stanley B. "Jurisdiction and Procedure of the Federal Trade Commission." *Illinois Law Review* 15 (March 1921): 518-526.

This article provides a step-by-step review of the procedures underlying FTC activities. At the time of this writing, only one Supreme Court case had been decided concerning the work of the FTC, therefore, it is concluded that much of the ambiguity inherent in the language of the FTC Act has yet to be effectively interpreted. The article concludes that the primary source of attacks on the FTC are the result of clients being accused of misdeeds rather than a reflection of flawed procedures in carrying out the agency's mission.

994   Howry, Edward F. "Federal Trade Commission: A Revaluation of Its Responsibilities." *American Bar Association Journal* 40 (February 1954): 113-117.

The text of a speech given by the Chairman of the FTC in which he addresses how the FTC should proceed administratively in its efforts to ensure a vigorous economy free of unfair business practices. Among the issues covered is a re-examination of congressional purpose in creating the FTC, the need to explore better approaches to measuring standards of proof, including the revitalization of the Bureau of Industrial Economics, the establishment of more guidelines in Robinson-Patman cases, and a recommendation to create a Bureau of Consultation to act as an advisor and consultant to small business.

995   Johnson, Shirley Z. "Treatment of Confidential Documents by the Federal Trade Commission." *Antitrust Law Journal* 46 (Winter 1978): 1017-1061.

Explores the relationship between the treatment of confidential documents received from respondents by the FTC, most notably in light of proposed amendments to FTC rules, and provisions of two statutes that govern the disclosure of confidential documents: the Freedom of Information Act and the Trade Secrets Act. A number of court cases are used to illustrate the need for a Commission rule that explicitly prohibits the disclosure of trade secrets and confidential documents.

996   "Judicial Review of Administrative "Reason to Believe". *William and Mary Law Review* 23 (Fall 1981): 139-164.

Analyzes the application of finality criteria and the underlying principles of judicial review of agency actions by the Supreme Court in the case of *FTC v.*

Standard Oil of California. It is concluded that the Supreme Court misapplied the finality doctrine because it "focused on Standard Oil's allegations as if Standard had attacked the substantive basis for the FTC's finding" rather than the fundamental issue of "whether the FTC made a determination that it had reason to believe that Standard violated the law." In so doing, the court has insulated the FTC from prosecutional discretion in cases involving finality and opened the door for politically motivated adjudicative proceedings.

997   Kennedy, Edward M. "Professor Elman and the Changing Federal Trade Commission: A Comment." *Georgetown Law Journal* 59 (March 1971): 861-863.

Commentary on the criticism levelled at the FTC by the President's Advisory Council on Executive Organization (the Ash Council) recommending that the FTC be abolished and subsequent criticism by former FTC Commissioner Philip Elman that became the basis for critical reports from Ralph Nader and the American Bar Association. The focus of this criticism has been that the agency is unresponsive to the needs of the American public and too bureaucratic. Elman's work has led to a blueprint for structural change and incremental reform that provides a solid foundation for building a more responsive agency.

998   Kinter, Earl W. "Current Ordeal of the Administrative Process: In Reply to Mr. Hector." *Yale Law Journal* 69 (May 1960): 965-977.

Response to Louis J. Hectors resignation from the Civil Aeronautics Board submitted to President Eisenhower and his subsequent speech before the Section of Administrative Law of the American Bar Association. Within these documents Hector criticizes governmental regulation and the administrative process. As Chairman of the FTC, the author outlines the need for "careful questioning of unstated assumptions" and the need to conduct detailed study and analysis before the reforms articulated by Hector and others who represent the "new criticism" calling for administrative reform to be carried out.

999   Kinter, Earl W. "Recent Changes in Federal Trade Commission Discovery Practice." *Antitrust Law Journal* 37 (1968): 238-247.

Describes specific rule changes relating to prehearing discovery in adjudicative proceedings, the reasons behind the changes, and their possible impact in future actions. The changes are meant to provide a balance between precomplaint investigative powers of the FTC and the provision of thorough postcomplaint discovery to a respondent and involve depositions, subpoenas, the availability of

Commission files, as well as the protection of confidential business information.

1000   Kinter, Earl W. "The Revitalized Federal Trade Commission: A Two-Year Evaluation." *New York University Law Review* 30 (June 1955): 1143-1193.

The author refutes claims among some members of Congress that the "new" FTC is "using the Robinson-Patman Act to protect big business," that the rule of reason is being misapplied, and that the Commission has ignored the intent of Congress to control unfair practices by asking firms to merely "meet competition." By examining administrative and procedural developments, defining the work of agency in antitrust litigation, and outlining specific court decisions, an argument is made that the past two years have actually been quite productive and that the agency has taken measurable strides in combatting unfair business practices.

1001   Kolak, Raymond P. "Standard Setting in Agency Adjudications Under the Federal Trade Commission Improvement Act." *George Washington Law Review* 46 (January 1978): 233-250.

Section 205 of the Magnuson-Moss Warranty/Federal Trade Commission Improvement Act effectively switches the establishment of legal standards from administrative rulemaking to agency adjudication. This essay examines the impact of that change and discusses in what ways the courts may support or resist new enforcement procedures beyond reliance on cease and desist orders prior to 1975. The essay concludes that the Improvement Act may fail to adequately serve advance notice of possible violations. Therefore, the FTC should inform possible defendants of the standards which the agency believes apply to the case and to publish these standards in the *Federal Register* to ensure greater dissemination of information.

1002   Kolasky, William J., Jr. and James W. Lowe. "The Merger Review Process at the Federal Trade Commission: Administrative Efficiency and the Rule of Law." *Administrative Law Review* 49 (Fall 1997): 889-914.

There has been a steady decline during the past decade regarding the impact court cases have had in shaping "the content and direction" of general antitrust legislation and merger review procedures specifically. This essay examines the impact of the Hart-Scott-Rodino Premerger Notification Act, the underlying reasons why this act has had such broad impact, and the ways in which issues such as merger reviews are now conducted in an informal manner that avoids older models of antitrust enforcement at the FTC and the Department of Justice.

1003   Kovacic, William E. "Product Differentiation: Administrative Adjudication and the Use of New Economic Approaches in Antitrust Analysis." *George Mason Law Review* 5 (Spring 1997): 313-320.

Several new approaches to analyzing and examining antitrust-relevant economic behavior have recently developed. However, these innovations in antitrust analysis "may fit awkwardly into existing frameworks of doctrine and policy." It is argued in this essay that the administrative adjudication processes of the FTC offer the best forum for testing and implementing new methodologies for studying the impact of mergers on competitiveness and other issues. Unfortunately, congressional intent to establish an antitrust enforcement agency superior to the federal courts and empowered with personnel who were experts in the fields of antitrust analysis and competition policy have not been realized despite the opportunity to use "extraordinary" investigative powers. The use of new analytical techniques gives the FTC an opportunity to overcome past deficiencies, but only if the Commission conducts internal audits of its activities on a regular basis to improve policy and relies on external audits from outside agencies, such as the General Accounting Office, to review specific cases and offer suggestions for improving enforcement processes.

1004   Kovacic, William E. "The Quality of Appointments and the Capability of the Federal Trade Commission." *Administrative Law Review* 49 (Fall 1997): 915-961.

The author argues that, while the appointment of Robert Pitofsky as FTC Chairman in April of 1995 has brought considerable expertise and leadership to the Commission, all too often Commissioners are appointed to the FTC possessing a limited understanding of the consumer protection and antitrust policymaking responsibilities of the agency. The article begins by reviewing how Congress envisioned the FTC as a regulatory agency and compares this to the author's conceptualization of what constitutes an effective Commissioner. This criteria is then used to measure the quality of individual appointments. The essay concludes by describing how inadequate appointments have undermined the FTC's mission. Four approaches to improving appointments in the future are presented: reduce the number of commissioners, make the vetting process more rigorous, incorporate the recommendations of advisory bodies, and shift the focus of performance reviews to commissioners after thy have left the agency. Includes three appendices listing chairmen of the FTC, commissioners and their term in office, and the pre-appointment professional backgrounds of commissioners.

1005   LaRue, Paul H. "FTC Expertise: A Legend Examined." *Antitrust Bulletin* 16 (Spring 1971): 1-31.

Administrative expertise refers to "the specialized knowledge imputed to regulatory agencies which appellate courts are supposed to respect upon review of agency action." In the case of the FTC, however, it is argued that this assumption of expertise is invalid and that the courts should be more active in reviewing FTC judgements. A detailed examination of the FTC's perceived expertise by the courts is used to support this thesis.

1006   Lewis, John. "Discovery Techniques and the Protection of Confidential Data in FTC Proceedings." *Administrative Law Review* 21 (June 1969): 457-470.

This essay begins with a review of pretrial discovery techniques and then proceeds to examine in detail how the FTC ensures the protection of confidential documents sought through the discovery process. Five specific methods of discovery under the Commission's Rules of Practice for Adjudicative Proceedings are examined: admission as to facts and documents, orders requiring access, depositions, subpoenas, and prehearing conferences.

1007   Liebling, Jeffrey H. "Judicial Usurpation of the F.T.C.'s Authority: A Return to the Rule of Reason." *The John Marshall Law Review* 30 (Fall 1996): 283-319.

This study examines the relationship between the original intent of Congress to grant broad authority to the FTC by purposely leaving certain provisions of the FTC Act ambiguous or undefined and the efforts of the federal courts to limit the agency's power. After providing historical background information, the author analyzes judicial interpretation of FTC powers, uses recent court cases to outline trends in narrowing authority, and concludes by discussing the impact of this trend on agency enforcement activities. A brief proposal of changes to Section 5 of the FTC Act meant to reinvigorate FTC regulatory powers is also described.

1008   Long, Thad G. "The Administrative Process: Agonizing Reappraisal in the FTC." *George Washington Law Review* 33 (March 1965): 671-691.

Reviews recent developments at the FTC concerning the agency's "new attitude" with regards to cease and desist orders. Under initiatives formulated under the guidance of Commissioner Philip Elman, the FTC has begun to draft cease and desist orders that address more specifically the elements of abuse and, in so doing, has better defined its powers beyond those granted to the courts. Combined with the fact that in several instances the FTC dismissed the case because it would not advance long-range enforcement policies, this new approach reflects a commitment by the FTC to achieve compliance on an industry-wide, rather than company-by-company, basis.

1009 Lu, Haoran. "Presidential Influence on Independent Commissions: A Case of FTC Staffing Levels." *Presidential Studies Quarterly* 28 (Winter 1998): 51-67.

The author examines requested, appropriated, and actual staffing levels at the FTC from fiscal year 1923 through fiscal year 1990 to determine the effectiveness of the Nixon-Ford, Carter, and Reagan administration's influence on independent commissions as it is expressed through the process of controlling staffing within the agency. The study finds that presidents do use staffing levels as a tool for shaping agency behavior and that this influence is manifested in different forms related to the size, duration, or direction (positive or negative) of the action. However, it is concluded that presidents face real limits in using staffing levels to control agency policy.

1010 MacIntyre, A. Everette and Joachim J. Volhard. "Federal Trade Commission." *Boston College Industrial and Commercial Law Review* 11 (May 1970): 723-783.

This is a comprehensive article analyzing the functions of the FTC, including its legislative history and relationship to the three branches of government, and its rules of practice. This is followed by a detailed examination of the successes and failures of the agency and the impact external forces have had on its work. The article concludes by exploring recent developments in antitrust enforcement activities through the use of court cases to highlight specific issues and to project into the future what challenges and opportunities face the FTC.

1011 MacIntyre, A Everette and Joachim J. Volhard. "Federal Trade Commission and Incipient Unfairness." *George Washington Law Review* 41 (March 1973): 407-445.

Places claims by critics that, since its inception, the FTC is ineffective, inefficient, and unfair with regards to carrying out legislative intent and the desire "to arrest trade restraints in their incipiency." A source of the problems experienced by the FTC that has subsequently fed the fires of criticism is the mixed results of court decisions dealing with the issue of incipiency. On some occasions the courts appear to understand the Commission's intent, while on other occasions, the courts have focused more on the function of judicial review. The inconsistent history of the theory of incipiency has resulted in only a few cases being disposed of in favor of the FTC during the period 1914-1934. It is concluded that only after a continuation of decisions by the FTC and the courts and the resulting process of inclusion and exclusion, will a meaningful and workable definition of incipiency be formulated.

1012   Malone, Thomas H. "Meaning of the Term "Public Interest" in the Federal Trade Commission." *Virginia Law Review* 17 (May 1931): 676-689.

The concept of "in the public interest" can invoke a number of interpretations. This essay examines the term as it applies to Section 5 of the FTC Act and frames it within the following question: "When may a proceeding concerning unfair business practices be deemed to the interest of the public?" By examining the text of commentary by judges in court cases specifically associated with Section 5, a "true test" of what defines "in the public interest" can be ascertained.

1013   Maronick, Thomas J. "Copy Test in FTC Deception Cases: Guidelines for Researchers." *Journal of Advertising Research* 31 (December 1991): 9-17.

Advertisers face numerous difficulties in predicting how the FTC will determine if an ad is unfair or deceptive. This is complicated by the fact that only recently has the FTC incorporated empirical evidence into its evaluation procedures. Nine standards derived from previous cases in which non-expert evidence was used are described that should be applied to the development of copy-test extrinsic data by a firm under FTC investigation.

1014   Mayer, F. C. "Settlement Procedures at the Federal Trade Commission." *Antitrust Law Journal* 37 (1968): 261-268.

This article examines problems and issues associated with FTC settlement procedures. Among the most important is the need for selective enforcement due to a lack of resources. Although every complaint is considered to meet its obligation, the Commission must choose what cases warrant an investigation. Describing how priorities are set and what alternatives are available to supplement investigations, such as business education and general community and voluntary compliance, encompasses this essay.

1015   Mayer, Robert N. and Debra L. Scammon. "Intervenor Funding at the FTC: Biopsy or Autopsy?" *Policy Studies Review* 2 (February 1983): 506-515.
Intervenor funding refers to the practice of "reimbursing groups and individuals for expenses incurred in participating in regulatory agency proceedings." The FTC was the first agency to begin intervenor funding and maintained the largest such program until 1980 when Chairman James C. Miller III halted the program for philosophical reasons. After examining arguments both supporting and criticizing the use of intervenor funding practices, the authors present the results of a survey sent to funded and non-funded applicants to help assess its effectiveness in promoting consumer representation. It is concluded that effectiveness of the program suffered due to time constraints and the lack of a comparable model. Although other alternatives exist to promote consumer representation, no other program with a mission of nurturing grass roots consumer participation has been proposed.

1016   McFarland, Carl. *Judicial Control of the Federal Trade Commission and the Interstate Commerce Commission, 1920-1930: A Comparative Study in the Relations of Courts to Administrative Commissions.* (Harvard Studies in Administrative Law, v. 5). Cambridge, MA: Harvard University Press, 1933.
There are two dominant theories regarding the relationship between the courts and administrative agencies. The older theory views both institutions as functioning within a single system of law, but with the courts wielding dominant authority. Developed during the past fifty years, the other theory views the relationship as a dual system of administrative justice in which there is a division of function between the two institutions so that some administrative decisions are final while others are subject to judicial review. This book examines this more recent theory within the constructs of judicial control of the Interstate Commerce Commission and the Federal Trade Commission. Through an analysis of judicial-administrative "doctrines, principles, and policies under which the commissions have been treated," it is revealed that each agency differs greatly in terms of its relationship to the courts and the nature of judicial control despite the fact they both developed under similar circumstances.

1017   Mechem, John Leland. "Change in Policy in the Federal Trade Commission." *American Bar Association Journal* 11 (October 1925): 637-641.

Among the many criticisms levelled against the FTC was the issue of publicity of changes in cases against a company. While the FTC was prompt when informing the public of actions taken against a company for possible violation of the law, the agency generally failed to provide any follow up information if the case was dismissed. In addition, if notification was publicized, it would be accompanied only with brief statements of "without prejudice" or "now fully advised of the premises." This resulted in firms bearing the stigma of wrong-doing even if the case had run its course and had not resulted in action against the respondent. Unfortunately, neither the Wadsworth-Williams Bill (H. R. 11793), submitted to Congress on January 20, 1925, nor revisions of rules within the agency address the issue of ensuring that an accompanying statement of reason for dismissal is provided.

1018   Mezines, Basil J. and Lewis F. Parker. "Discovery before the Federal Trade Commission." *Administrative Law Review* 18 (Winter-Spring 1966): 55-74.

The authors examines changes in rules regarding pre-trial discovery procedures adopted by the Commission after 1961 in response to criticism that the presentation of evidence in "piece-meal fashion by allowing intervals between hearings" was not consistent with Federal Rules of Civil Procedure. Specific cases are used to analyze procedural problems concerned with the release of confidential information in the FTC proceedings. It is concluded that the FTC's new rules will help alleviate concerns that administrative proceedings are not as fair as judicial ones and that the withholding of some evidence will still ensure confidentiality related to sensitive business information.

1019   Montague, Gilbert H. "The New Policy and Procedure of the Federal Trade Commission." *Academy of Political Science Proceedings* 11 (January 1926): 132-135.

A brief essay outlining the new procedures implemented by the FTC that will throw out all cases currently on the agency's docket involving private conflicts that can be resolved in the courts. The author concurs that these cases are inappropriate for agency review. In so doing, the Commission is then free to move more effectively towards fair regulation of American industry.

1020   Moran, Mark J. and Barry R. Weingast. "Congress as the Source of Regulatory Decisions: The Case of the Federal Trade Commission." *American Economic Review* 72 (May 1982): 109-113.

Uses the FTC to illustrate the close ties between Congress and regulatory agencies and to show that this relationship is governed by subtle and non-obvious linkages. The study reveals close parallels between not only Congressional intent and agency action, but between the actions of the agency and the policies of the Senatorial oversight subcommittee. Statistical analysis reveals a "remarkable" FTC sensitivity to congressional preference.

1021   Murphy, Patrick E. "Strategic Planning at the FTC." _Journal of Public Policy and Marketing_ 3 (1984): 56-66.

This paper outlines the creation of an Office of Management Planning within the Bureau of Consumer Protection of the FTC, focusing on the issue of strategic planning within the agency. The essay begins by reviewing the historical use of strategic planning and examines the specific activities of the new consumer protection planning office. The paper concludes by examining five problems that arose in implementing the Office of Management Planning and the formulation of a long-term strategic plan. These problems illustrate the fact that strategic planning at the federal government level is only appropriate when applied to certain programs and agencies.

1022   Nelson, David A. "Administrative Law–Judicial Control–Appellate Review of Federal Trade Commission Proceedings." _Michigan Law Review_ 57 (June 1959): 1190-1214.

Commentary analyzing the extent of control exhibited by the judiciary over the FTC. The purpose of this examination is to offer insight into the possible outcome of judicial review regarding an appeal beyond the full Commission. Supreme Court cases involving the FTC since 1914 and cases presented to the court of appeals since 1947 are used. The study concludes with several recommends based upon those of the Hoover Commission Task Force on Legal Services and Procedures, including the recommendation that a "Trade Section" of the Administrative Court be created to take over adjudicative functions of the FTC.

1023   Nelson, T. H. "Politicization of FTC Rulemaking." _Connecticut Law Review_ 8 (Spring 1976): 413-448.

Three issues are addressed: 1) a brief history of the FTC to reveal the "immense power" concentrated in the agency and to show that it extends well beyond Congressional intent; 2) the need for further checks on FTC power and argues that the new Administrative Procedure Act, while declared to be cumbersome by its critics, is in fact providing some protection against administrative action that ignores public interest; and 3) a review of rulemaking procedures required by the Magnuson-Moss Act is used to illustrate the politicization of the rulemaking process and the effectiveness of recent enactments to expand the scope of judicial review of FTC actions.

1024 Nystrom, P. C. "Input-Output Processes of the Federal Trade Commission." *Administrative Science Quarterly* 20 (March 1975): 104-113.

A case study of the FTC to demonstrate a new model for examining organizational response patterns to change in the environment. Quantitative research methodologies were applied to the workflow of complaints, financial resources allocated by Congress, and cases brought before the federal courts to create this conceptual model for understanding input and output processes.

1025 Parnes, Lydia B. and Carol J. Jennings. "Through the Looking Glass: A Perspective on Regulatory Reform at the Federal Trade Commission." *Administrative Law Review* 49 (Fall 1997): 989-1006.

The author examines challenges faced by the FTC in carrying out its mission in the 1990s and, in so doing, builds a framework for evaluating recent efforts of the FTC to in reform its regulations and rulemaking and enforcement procedures. It is concluded that the adoption of creative solutions to new consumer protection problems has positioned the FTC well for the next century.

1026 Pollock, Earl E. "Pre-Complaint Investigations by the Federal Trade Commission." *Antitrust Bulletin* 9 (January-February 1964): 1-26.

This essay outlines the underlying purpose and intent of two types of FTC investigations: general investigations that result in "the filing of a report of organizing and analyzing the information gathered," and pre-complaint investigations that conclude with a decision as to whether to proceed with litigation or to dismiss charges. The original intent of the investigative functions of the FTC was to pursue general investigations. However, recent actions by the FTC indicate that the agency is now devoting more of its resources to pre-complaint investigations that could lead to litigation. By briefly discussing the selection of matters to be investigated, the reorganization of the investigative staff, the impact of recent procedural changes on pre-complaint investigations, and increased use of investigational hearings, it is concluded that the FTC is practicing procedural "brinkmanship" that could undermine its image of fairness.

1027   Posner, Richard A. "The Federal Trade Commission." *University of Chicago Law Review* 37 (Fall 1969): 47-89.
This work examines the history of criticism levelled at the FTC, specifically focusing on the major landmark studies (Gerald Henderson's report of 1924, the Hoover Commission's 1949 Report, the 1960 Landis Report, the Auerbach Report of 1964, Ralph Nader's attack in 1969, and the 1969 Report of the American Bar Association). The author argues that this criticism is based upon "two dubious and largely unexamined assumptions": 1) that the administrative process utilized in combatting restraints of trade and consumer fraud is a sound policy and that it is only the execution of this policy that has created inefficiency, and 2) that the ineffectiveness of the agency is a product of "historical accident rather than of the inherent conditions of government regulation." Failure to consider these points has created a unnecessarily narrow framework for understanding the problems within the FTC. The article concludes by stating that, as an alternative to the FTC, greater reliance should be placed on market processes and on a system of judicial rights and remedies.

1028   *Public Choice and Regulation: A View from Inside the Federal Trade Commission.* Robert J. Mackay, James C. Miller III, and Bruce Yandle, editors. Stanford, CA: Hoover Institution Press, 1987.
This collection of essays examines the role of external forces, such as Congressional action, and internal forces, such as organizational structure and incentives, that influence the FTC's antitrust and consumer protection polices and procedures. A positive economic approach is adopted to show the politics underlying regulation. Specific issues addressed by the contributors are arranged in three parts: the relationship between the FTC and Congress, empirical studies of program activities, and the internal management and budgeting within the agency.

1029   "Public Interest as Jurisdictional Requirement Under Section 5 of the Federal Trade Commission Act." *Harvard Law Review* 43 (December 1929): 285-289.
The article examines a decision by the Supreme Court refusing to enforce an order by the FTC, not because it lacked merit, but on the grounds that "the filing of the complaint before the Commission was not in the public interest." The problem, as argued in this comment, is rooted in the interpretation of Section 5, the placement of the public interest clause in paragraph three, and the issue of whether this preliminary determination by the FTC is within the court's jurisdiction.

1030   Reilly, John R. "The Role of the Federal Trade Commission." *Food Drug Cosmetic Law Journal* 22 (June 1976): 338-343.

This study discusses what role the FTC will play in interpreting and enforcing the Fair Packaging and Labeling Act of 1966 and in what ways the Commission is preparing to enforce mandatory labeling of all consumer goods, excluding food, drugs, and cosmetics. By outlining the enforcement staff's duties and noting extensive revisions to the FTC's Rules of Practice, three procedures come to light: proposing regulations, holding adjudicative hearings on matters pertaining to the provisions of the Fair Packaging and Labeling Act, and disseminating final regulations under judicial review.

1031   Roundtree, George S. "Advisory Procedures of the Federal Trade Commission." *Journal of the Bar Association of the District of Columbia* 31 (May 1964): 164-169.

Outlines the mission and purpose of the Division of Advisory Opinions, one of three Divisions within the Bureau of Industry Guidance. The Division was established by Chairman Paul Rand Dixon to give business the opportunity to receive authoritative opinion from the agency concerning proposed course of action. Prior to the establishment of the Advisory Opinion Division, business had to rely upon the "personal views" of staff for information which was not binding. The issuance of official opinion also helps business avoid litigation.

1032   Rowe, Frederick. M. "The Federal Trade Commission's Administration of the Anti-Price Discrimination Law." *Columbia Law Review* 64 (March 1964): 415-438.

The Robinson-Patman Act is a piece of legislation that is surrounded by confusion because it was the product of a political compromise between the conventional antitrust mission of preserving fair competition under provisions of the Clayton Act, while at the same time, adhering to the National Retailer's Association's "live and let live" philosophy of enforcement. By examining numerous anti-price discrimination cases, this study attempts to show that the FTC has victimized small business through its enforcement policies. It is concluded that only Congressional action intended to re-evaluate Robinson-Patman will relieve the Commission's administration of the burden of rationalizing the Act under adversarial litigation conditions and help to deflect criticism levelled at the agency for its enforcement policies.

1033   Scanlon, Paul D. "Policy Planning at the FTC: A Commissioner Who Really Believes in It?" *Antitrust Law and Economics Review* 6 (1973): 35-58.

This essay discusses the appointment of Mayo J. Thompson to be an FTC Commissioner. The author offers a highly positive assessment of Thompson, especially with regards to his record of policy planning and sharing information about agency intentions. An analysis of Thompson's policy planning memorandums, the full-text of which are included with this essay, are used to support the thesis that he will bring a much needed focus to the agency.

1034   Schechter, Roger E. "A Retrospective on the Reagan FTC: Musings on the Role of an Administrative Agency." *Administrative Law Review* 42 (Fall 1990): 489-517.

The purpose of this article is to review the overall enforcement performance of the FTC during the decade of the 1980s, most notably under the Reagan Administration. The agency has again received criticism that its enforcement of both antitrust and consumer protection rules has diminished to unacceptable levels. By outlining changes that have taken place under the direction of James C. Miller III and other Reagan appointees, a set of guiding principles are offered that will help energize the agency's enforcement agenda in the 1990s under the direction of Janet Steiger, President Bush's appointee to be FTC Chairman.

1035   Scherer, Frederic M. "Sunlight and Sunset at the Federal Trade Commission." *Administrative Law Review* 42 (Fall 1990): 461-487.

Among the early mandates given to the FTC was to gather and disseminate information concerning the functions of American industry. This mandate has been eroded in the 1980s under the direction of the Reagan Administration appointees. Industry studies produced in other government agencies only partially fill the gap and academic institutions cannot always be relied upon because they obtain much of their data from government sources. By exploring the underlying rationale for establishing a "sunshine" mandate and the subsequent actions by commissioners in the 1980s, it is revealed that FTC data collection is crucial to a coherent antitrust enforcement strategy.

1036   Schuknecht, Barbara Himes. "Administrative Adjudication–A New Legal Standard for Its Use–*Ford Motor C. v. FTC*, 673 F.2d 1008 (9th Cir. 1981), cert. denied, 103 S. Ct. 358 (1982)." *Washington Law*

Review 58 (July 1983): 633-648.

Although the courts have generally refused to specify in what situations an agency must use rulemaking or adjudication procedures, the recent case of *Ford Motor C. v. FTC* may indicate a shift away from this position. In the Ford Motor Company case, the Ninth Circuit Court of Appeals dismissed the case because the FTC had "abused its discretion by relying on adjudication." The comment notes that this is an "inadvisable" ruling because it creates an overly broad legal standard governing when rulemaking must be applied and, thus, may undermine an agency's flexibility in determining how to proceed. This flexibility is essential in maintaining an effective administrative process.

1037   Seidman, Albert G. "The Commission's Power to Conduct Field Investigations." *Antitrust Law Journal* 14 (1959): 12-17.

This essay examines specific provisions of the FTC Act and available remedies that relate to the agency's quasi-judicial power to conduct field investigations of corporations that may have violated the law. These investigations are intended to promote the voluntary acquisition of company documents in order to evaluate whether monopolistic or unfair business activities have been practiced. The author concludes by urging private attorneys to cooperate fully with FTC investigations.

1038   Seidman, Albert G. "What's New–What's on Top at the Federal Trade Commission?" *Food Drug Cosmetic Law Journal* 17 (March 1962): 181-187.

The article reviews the major changes in procedure under the direction of Chairman Paul Rand Dixon. Among the changes described in the revised Rules of Practice is the dissemination of a proposed complaint to the respondent and public announcements of proceedings and the holding of hearings in one venue. The agency has also re-organized staff structure to facilitate administrative involvement in agency activities. The article concludes by describing recent trends in FTC proceedings involving food, drugs, and cosmetics and with regards to rigged television commercials.

1039   Shaw, A. W. "How the Federal Trade Commission will Handle Cases." *System: The Magazine of Business* 28 (August 1915): 221-223.

In this editorial essay, the author outlines the rules of practice of the FTC as they relate to handling complaints, specifically noting that the procedures will help to streamline the process and make it easier for businesses to obtain information quickly. The essay goes on to express hope that the FTC will meet its goals by acting on statements made by its vice-chairman to assist small businesses and "help the average businessman."

1040   Simon, David M. "Extraterritorial Service of Administrative Subpoenas: *Federal Trade Commission v. Compagnie De Saint-Gobain-Pont-A-Mousson.*" *Law and Policy in International Business* 13 (1981): 847-870.

Outlines the Gobain decision and its impact. In this case, the Court of Appeals for the District of Columbia held that the FTC was not authorized by Section 9 of the FTC Act to serve subpoenas by registered mail to foreign nationals outside of the United States because the action was "contrary to generally recognized principles of international law." Although the ruling was specifically related to registered mail, it can be implied that the only way to issue an extraterritorial subpoena is through international judicial assistance. It is concluded that the decision unnecessarily restricts the FTC's authority to investigate foreign firms operating in the United States and places an "insurmountable" burden on the FTC's ability to investigate foreign firms under the agency's statutory mandate.

1041   Simon, William. "Case Against the Federal Trade Commission." *University of Chicago Law Review* 19 (Winter 1952): 297-338.

The author argues that dual enforcement of antitrust between the Attorney General's office and the Federal Trade Commission is not in the public's interest because they have conflicting views of economic philosophy and objectives regarding the enforcement of antitrust statutes. The FTC has failed primarily due to its staff, its uneven interpretation of Congressional intent, and its adherence to "unorthodox ideologies." Through a detailed analysis of inconsistent actions associated with antitrust and functional pricing cases, the author attempts to show that the Commission has inflicted injury on the economy. The article concludes with three recommendations: 1) remove all antitrust responsibilities from the FTC and transfer them to the Department of Justice, 2) transfer industry studies from the FTC's Bureau of Industry Economics to the Department of Commerce, and 3) "weight of evidence" should be used to review all Commission orders.

1042   "Small Business before the Federal Trade Commission." *Yale Law Journal* 75 (January 1966): 487-503.

Outlines criticism of antitrust enforcement procedures and policies directed at the FTC as they specifically relate to their affect on small business. Data gathered from 179 firms responding to a survey (out of approximately 500 queried) was analyzed from three perspectives–selection of cases, investigation of cases, and pre-hearing settlement of the cases–to determine the factual basis for criticism claiming that FTC antitrust actions unduly harm small business. The study concludes that small firms are more likely to be subjected to formalized proceedings. A number of reasons for this are proposed, including the expediency in prosecuting violators, the desire to avoid litigation because small firms have less resources, and the fact that small firms are more likely harmed by negative exposure of their corporate image in public hearings. Each of these issues must be addressed to protect small business from the disproportionate impact of FTC actions.

1043   Smith, J. Clay. "Practicing Communications Law– The Tangents: The Federal Communications Commission and the Federal Trade Commission." *Administrative Law Review* 32 (Summer 1980): 457-476.
Examines the overlapping regulatory responsibilities of the Federal Communications Commission and the FTC as it relates to granting and reviewing broadcast licenses by the FCC and the regulation of false or misleading advertising by the FTC. Although the FCC does not possess the authority to regulate advertising, there is legal precedence showing that the FCC has threatened to withdraw broadcast licenses when companies have practiced false advertising. This has led to industry self-regulation. With the establishment of liaison procedures between the FCC and the FTC in 1972, an agreement was reached placing primary enforcement responsibilities with the FTC. However, gaps remain that may require congressional intervention to resolve.

1044   Stevens, W. H. S. "The Advantage of Preventing Unfair Competition through an Administrative Body." *Annals of the American Academy of Political and Social Science* 82 (March 1919): 231-246.
By analyzing the procedures associated with regulation of unfair competition through court decisions, private right of action, and the Department of Justice, the author argues that regulation through an administrative body (the FTC) is the most appropriate and effective means of controlling monopolistic behavior. The author goes on to review the administrative structure of the FTC, its enforcement methods, and the nature of FTC orders under judicial review, noting that judicial review will have a major impact on shaping the construction and interpretation of the Act.

1045   Stevens, W. H. S. "Changes in the Federal Trade Commission's Legal Procedure." *Academy of Political Science Proceedings* 11 (January 1926): 136-142.

Avoiding a discussion about their validity, the author examines legal issues surrounding two new procedural changes adopted by the FTC. The first states that "all cases shall be settled by stipulation unless the public interest demands otherwise." The second procedural change stipulates that a respondent will be given an opportunity before the Board of Review to show cause as to why the complaint should be withdrawn. Paralleling these are rules regarding the publicity of complaints. Each set of changes and rules are examined in detail to reveal key questions about their impact in the future.

1046   Stewart, Jr., Charles E and C. Daniel Ward. "FTC Discovery: Depositions, the Freedom of Information Act and Confidential Documents." *Antitrust Law Journal* 37 (1968): 248-260.

Examines three issues relating to the passage by Congress of the Freedom of Information Act and the revision by the FTC of its rules of procedure. The first issue concerns changes in the taking and use of depositions for purposes of discovery. The second issue examines the potential impact of the Freedom of Information Act on the discovery of information contained in the FTC's files. The final issue involves the protection of confidential informers in light of the Freedom of Information Act.

1047   Stolle, Dennis P. "The FTC's Reliance on Extrinsic Evidence in Cases of Deceptive Advertising: A Proposal for Interpretive Rulemaking, *Kraft, Inc. v. FTC*, 970 F.2d 311 (7th Cir. 1992), cert. denied, 113 S. Ct. 1254 (1993)." *Nebraska Law Review* 74 (1995): 352-373.

Many members of the legal community were "shocked" by the FTC's actions with regards to the Kraft, Inc. court decision because it appeared that the Commission failed to consider relevant extrinsic evidence and relied solely on its own reasoned analysis when determining if deceptive advertising had occurred. The article begins by exploring the background and history of the FTC's decision in the Kraft case. The next part provides further background on the standard of deception applied by the FTC. This is followed by an analysis of why the decision is firmly grounded in good policy but fails as a legal ruling. It is concluded that the issuance of policy statements and the development of precedent has failed. Such actions should be replaced with administrative rulemaking procedures that clarify the use of extrinsic evidence.

1048 Stone, Alan. *Economic Regulation and the Public Interest: The Federal Trade Commission in Theory and Practice.* Ithaca, NY: Cornell University Press, 1977.

This work outlines the history of the FTC and examines the work of the agency in regulating monopolies, protecting the consumer, and analyzing economic trends in the domestic marketplace. Motivated by concerns expressed at various levels that the FTC is ineffective in meeting its goals, the author places these activities within the context of regulatory conduct and social action. The final chapter discusses alternative models of controlling business based upon a set of "core values" that have stood the test of time and that "serve human well-being," including safety and health, truthful information, permissible profits by companies, and intended, unintended or incidental externalities that result from corporate activity.

1049 Strenio, Jr., Andrew J. "The FTC's Administrative Dilemma." *Environmental Law* 20 (1990): 35-47.

This is the text of an address given at the Conference on Antitrust Law Under the New Administration in which the author uses the American Bar Association's Report on the FTC as the basis for examining how the agency's antitrust enforcement activities are impacted by the resources available to the Commission, leadership and guidance among FTC staff, and the criteria used in selecting cases. The essay concludes with commentary about the future agenda of the FTC and what impact the American Bar Association Report may have in shaping that agenda.

1050 Swanson, Carl L. "Revolution at the Federal Trade Commission." *American Bar Association Journal* 57 (February 1971): 132-134.

This essay briefly outlines the "quiet revolution" that took place at the FTC on February 25, 1970 when, under the direction of Chairman Caspar W. Weinberger, the agency announced sweeping changes to appoint new consumer protection staff, create law enforcement coordinating committees, and establish consumer advisory councils, among other initiatives. This consumer-focused revitalization of the FTC is described as a decentralization of operations.

1051 Title, Peter S. "Administrative Law–Federal Trade Commission–Authority to FTC to Issue Substantive Rules is Upheld." *Tulsa Law Review* 48 (April 1974): 697-703.

Examines a federal district court decision to uphold the authority of the FTC to issue Trade Regulation Rules arising from a case brought against the agency by thirty-four oil companies and two refinery companies stating that the FTC had overstepped its bounds of jurisdiction by requiring gas pumps to show the octane level of the gasoline they dispense. Trade Regulation Rules carry more enforcement weight than Trade Practice Rules because they "are definitive statements of illegal activity." It is concluded that this expansion of power is within congressional intent.

1052   Towle, Griffith. "Representing a Franchisor in an FTC Investigation." *Franchise Law Journal* 16 (Summer 1996): 11-14.

First of a two part piece, this essay examines the underlying processes associated with an FTC investigation of a franchisor. Among the issues discussed are what factors that may lead to an investigation, the difference between initial and full phase investigations, access to information, compulsory procedures, civil investigative demands, and consent order agreements.

1053   Towle, Griffith. "Representing a Franchisor in Litigation with the FTC." *Franchise Law Journal* 17 (Summer 1997): 9-13.

Second of a two-part piece that outlines the law governing FTC enforcement actions directed at franchisors, the various ways in which the FTC may attempt to prove a case, and how counsel can formulate an effective defense to refute evidence presented by the Commission.

1054   "United States--Attorney General--Administrative Law--Attorneys Authorized to Represent the United States in Court--Extent of Authority of Counsel for the Federal Trade Commission." *Minnesota Law Review* 32 (May 1948): 606-623.

This note asks the question: to what extent is the FTC authorized to conduct litigation through its own attorneys? The author points out that, while Congress can authorize agencies to use lawyers unconnected from the Department of Justice, these authorizations are frequently ill-defined, as in the case of the FTC. A review of the enforcement of cease and desist orders, injunctions against false advertising, and orders to secure corporate information show that proposed legislation to transfer "all personnel employed in positions of attorney or in any other positions requiring the services of" attorneys to the Department of Justice does not address the problem. A uniform enforcement act for orders promulgated by administrative agencies is offered as a solution.

1055   Vernon, D. H. "Labyrinthine Ways: The Handling of Food, Drug, Device and Cosmetic Cases by the Federal Trade Commission since 1938." *Food Drug Cosmetic Law Journal* 8 (June 1953): 367-393.

This article comprehensively analyzes the formal proceedings employed by the FTC since the passage in 1938 of the Wheeler-Lea Amendment, specifically as it affects the marketing and advertising of food and drugs. The author uses specific cases to question FTC procedures concerning findings of fact, choice of remedy, affirmative disclosures, and role in protecting the consumer. It is concluded that informal procedures and close adherence to congressional intent will address most contemporary problems.

1056   Wald, Robert L. "FTC Settlement Procedures." *Litigation* 5 (Spring 1979): 8-11, 47-48.

This essay briefly considers whether the FTC's current settlement procedures conform to provisions of the Administrative Procedure Act and provides practical advice concerning corporate rights during pre-complaint investigations and during adjudication.

1057   Watkins, Myron W. "An Appraisal of the Work of the Federal Trade Commission." *Columbia Law Review* 32 (February 1932): 272-289.

This article seeks to establish whether the FTC has accomplished its goals and what its prospects are for the future. After reviewing the work of the FTC since its inception in 1914, the author outlines a plan that adheres to sound economic necessities and constitutional requirements. The Bureau of Corporations would be granted the responsibility of reviewing "corporate charters" upon approval by the FTC. The Bureau of Trade Associations would be authorized to issue industry-wide licenses to organizations. The Bureau of Commercial Practices would be given the work of the legal division of the FTC. And finally, made up of economists with employment that is free from political appointments, the Bureau of Industrial Coordination would be granted an advisory role.

1058   Weinberger, Caspar W. "Arbitration and the Federal Trade Commission." *Arbitration Journal* 25 (1970): 65-72.

In this address at the annual meeting of the American Arbitration Association, the author discusses the social and economic reform taking place at the FTC with the intent of expanding the remedies available to the agency in combatting unfair business practices. Among the considerations mentioned here is the possible reliance on arbitration as a means of withholding prosecution proceedings. Also outlined is the need for the Commission to better inform minority groups of their rights as consumers.

1059   Weinberger, Caspar W. "Federal Trade Commission: Progress and a New Profile." *Case Western Reserve Law Review* 22 (November 1970): 5-10.

The essay examines steps taken by the FTC to ensure proper enforcement of Section 5 provisions of the FTC Act and to outline new initiatives by the agency that will hopefully lead to expanded authority to act in deceptive practices matters and to ensure fairness in the marketplace, including the power to seek preliminary injunctions and the ability to assess civil penalties, and award damages to consumers injured through the actions of a corporation.

1060   Weingast, Barry R. and Mark J. Moran. "Bureaucratic Discretion or Congressional Control? Regulatory Policymaking by the Federal Trade Commission." *Journal of Political Economy* 91 (October 1983): 765-800.

The purpose of this study is to examine how regulatory behavior of government agencies is shaped by a legislature and, in so doing, create a model of decision-making that is based upon the premise that regulatory agencies are controlled by the legislature. Recent changes at the FTC initiated by Congress is used to test assumptions about the model. Using empirical evidence gathered from changes in legislative support for an active or inactive FTC on Congressional oversight committees, strong evidence is provided supporting the position that the legislature wields substantial control over the regulatory behavior of the FTC, most notably through the actions of committees and subcommittees.

1061   Weingast, Barry R. and Mark J. Moran. "The Myth of Runaway Bureaucracy: The Case of the FTC." *Regulation* 6 (May/June 1982): 33-38.

Many recent proposals to reform regulatory agencies are based upon the theory that they are independent from congressional control. Supporters of this theory point out the small number of oversight hearings and the perfunctory consideration Congress gives to appointments of agency officers as evidence to support agency independence. The proposals are, therefore, intended to bridge the gap between independence and control. However, the authors argue that this is not the case and that, in fact, agencies parallel the desires of Congress very closely. The activities of a "runaway" FTC during the 1970s is used as a case study to support this hypothesis and to reveal that control is frequently obtained through a "subtle bureaucratic incentive system."

1062 West, William Floyd. "Judicial Rulemaking Procedures in the FTC: A Case Study of Their Causes and Effects." *Public Policy* 29 (Spring 1981): 197-217.

This article focuses on the rulemaking procedures outlined in the Magnuson-Moss Act of 1974 that require the FTC to hold oral hearings in which any proposed rules are subject to analysis and cross-examination and that requires rules to be based exclusively on the evidence presented in hearing transcripts and all written submissions. Although it is inconclusive as to whether these provisions will improve or diminish the FTC's rulemaking authority, the movement in Congress away from informal rulemaking to a more judicialized procedure does reflect a explicit response to industry and special interest concerns over those of consumer advocates. The greatest impact of judicialized procedures has been delays in responding quickly to an ever-changing business environment.

1063 West, William Floyd. "Politics of Administrative Rulemaking." *Public Administration Review* 42 (September/October 1982): 420-426.

This study analyzes the politics of FTC rulemaking procedures as it relates to consumer protection, revealing that the political determinants of FTC policy have a negative effect on the ability of the agency to implement Trade Regulation Rules as a means of exerting control over industry. This approach is preferred over a case-by-case adjudication method.

1064 Wilkie, William L. "Affirmative Disclosure at the FTC: Communication Decisions." *Journal of Public Policy and Marketing* 6 (1987): 33-42.

Builds on the author's previous research into the area of affirmative disclosure orders issued by the FTC. The study is divided into two sections. The first section looks at four factors that affect communication decisions: timing, the number of instances the consumer will confront the disclosure, the presentation level of the disclosure ("intensity"), and "distinctiveness," referring to the extent to which the disclosure is viewed by the consumer in relation to competing stimuli. The second section examines these factors as well as other variables, such as placement of the disclosure on the product, that shape the effectiveness of the communication to the consumer.

1065   Wilkie, William L. "Affirmative Disclosure at the FTC: Objectives for the Remedy and Outcomes of Past Orders." *Journal of Public Policy and Marketing* 4 (1985): 91-111.

Provides an extensive analysis of the nature of disclosure orders issued by the FTC during a seven year period beginning in the late 1970s, and examines them within the conceptual framework of a consumer protection enforcement remedy. Using the example of new cigarette warning labels to study broad policy objectives underlying their use and impact on the consumer, a measurement of the outcome of the orders based upon empirical evidence can be ascertained. It is concluded that the FTC does not consider empirical evidence to the degree needed to determine the substantive impacts of its disclosure orders. The types of impacts and sources of information that the FTC could utilize are also described.

1066   Wilkie, William L. "Affirmative Disclosure at the FTC: Theoretical Framework and Typology of Case Selection." *Journal of Public Policy and Marketing* 2 (1983): 3-15.

The author describes a theoretical framework intended to provide insights into the specific dimensions of affirmative disclosures as a form of remedy. The framework fulfills both the operational function of classifying specific types of affirmative disclosures and evaluating the effectiveness of different types of disclosures under a variety of circumstances. This paper focuses on one of five categories of the framework, "the Nature of the Problem," to illustrate which cases selected by the FTC needed an affirmative disclosure remedy.

1067   Wilkie, William L. "Affirmative Disclosure: Perspectives on FTC Orders." *Journal of Public Policy and Marketing* 1 (1982): 95-110.

An "evaluative framework" is developed in this study to help classify the effectiveness of FTC disclosures, orders, and cases. The framework consists of five parts: the nature of the problem, objectives for the remedy, strategy for the disclosure, tactical disclosure decisions, and outcomes of the orders. By applying each of these parts to over 200 disclosures during a seven-year period, four policy recommendations are offered: 1) distinguish between rule making and case orders for information disclosure, 2) maintain and extend the effectiveness of disclosures to the consumer level, 3) adopt a policy statement outlining goals that distinguish between rule making and disclosure orders, and 4) obtain systematic feedback concerning the impact of the FTC's orders. The essay concludes with four additional recommendations regarding the management of disclosures.

1068   Williams, Mark A. "Standards of Disqualification for Federal Trade Commissioners in Hybrid Proceedings: *Association of National Advertisers v. FTC.*" *Washington and Lee Law Review* 37 (Fall 1980): 1359-1370.

This essay examines clarification of due process requirements associated with the disqualification of an FTC commissioner from rulemaking or hybrid rulemaking proceedings by the District of Columbia Circuit Court. By examining the standard of disqualification first promulgated in the *Cinderella Career and Finishing School v. FTC* case and later reversed in the case of *Association of National Advertisers v. FTC*, a standard that focuses on the proper role of administrators rather than agency procedures is proposed as a compromise to ensure unbiased proceedings.

1069   Williams, Samuel L. "Investigations by the Federal Trade Commission." *Antitrust Law Journal* 29 (1965): 71-80.

Explores in detail the procedures adopted by the FTC when investigating a company that may have violated FTC rules. Particular attention is paid to the actions of individual lawyers in the field offices, policies used to ensure confidentiality, and the formal and informal procedures used to obtain information. The FTC usually does not have to use its formal powers of investigation, such as issuing administrative subpoenas, to obtain information, but rather, relies on "the persuasiveness and ingenuity of its field attorneys and the honesty and integrity of the business community" to acquire factual information about a case. When corporations or industries do not cooperate it is usually done so under the assumption that facts can be concealed from the FTC attorneys indefinitely or it is used as a delaying tactic.

1070   Williamson, Peter W. "Federal Trade Commission–Adjudicatory Proceedings–Receipt of Evidence in Camera." *Michigan Law Review* 60 (March 1962): 647-650.

Explores the ruling in an adjudicatory hearing pursuant to a complaint filed by the FTC that held that confidential evidence gathered for the investigation cannot be placed "in camera" (not made a part of the public record) unless the evidence contains highly secret business information that could clearly harm the interests of the respondent. This essay examines this issue within the context of today's highly competitive marketplace and notes that the FTC "apparently can compel public disclosure only when it is in direct control of the procedures under which such material is received as evidence." Respondents may also resort to private litigation and settlement to ensure protection of confidential information, such as, manufacturing processes and consumer lists.

1071   Wilson, Robert D. "Judicial Review of Federal Trade Commission Action: An Analysis of Factors Influencing the Courts." *Antitrust Bulletin* 13 (Winter 1968): 1271-1305.

This study considers the factors associated with judicial review of FTC actions, using both tangible and intangible evidence, to show that the reviewing courts do not apply uniform standards when considering the use of cease and desist orders. Courts are more likely to respond to the statute involved, "the unamity of the Commission in issuing the order," and the attitude of the court concerning antitrust laws and the role of the FTC in enforcing those laws.

1072   Yandle, Bruce. "Federal Trade Commission Output and Costs: Cycling through the Zone of Political Wrath." *Social Science Quarterly* 67 (September 1986): 517-533.

This work examines the institutional history of the FTC as it relates to its discharge of duties (output) within the legislative arena. By outlining the controversies the agency has experienced with Congress and the parallel changes in budget and costs associated with FTC activities over time, it is revealed that agencies such as the FTC function within a political "safe zone" of operation and that stepping beyond that zone may incur the wrath of Congress.

1073   Yao, Dennis A. and Christa Van Anh Vecchi. "Information and Decisionmaking at the Federal Trade Commission." *Journal of Public Policy and Marketing* 11 (Fall 1992): 1-11.

This paper analyzes the extrinsic evidence associated with the interpretation of false advertising under rules promulgated by the FTC and provisions of the Lanham Trade-Mark Act. By applying a Bayesian statistical decision making model to determine how much extrinsic evidence is utilized in determining the validity of a claim that an advertisement is false, it is revealed, in a quantitative manner, how prior interpretations about an advertisement's meaning is modified by new information about the product. This leads to the conclusion that "the statistical reliability of survey evidence may often be as important to the Commission's (and by implication Lanham Act courts') decision making as the reported estimate of the percentage of consumers who perceive a given message."

Chapter Four
Trade Regulation and Rulemaking Authority

1074   Acarregui, Richard A. "Trade Regulation–Deceptive Trade Practices–The Federal Trade Commission Act and Recent Oregon Legislation." *Oregon Law Review* 45 (February 1966): 132-139.

In its efforts to regulate unfair trade practices, the FTC is hindered by a number of factors, including the possibility of lengthy hearings and judicial review, the wording of Section 5 of the FTC which restricts FTC authority to interstate commerce, and the large volume of cases the agency must litigate. This article describes each factor and reviews provisions of the Oregon Consumer Protection Act intended to compensate for limitations in FTC authority.

1075   Albertsworth, E. F. "Interstate Commerce, Clayton Act, Constitutional Law, Jurisdiction of Federal Trade Commission." *Illinois Law Review* 22 (November 1927): 304-309.

Examines a recent decision by the Supreme Court (*Federal Trade Commission v. Pacific States P. T. Association*), in which the FTC's right to issue a cease and desist order to prevent a uniform price fixed by members of an association engaged in interstate commerce was upheld because the action of the interstate association fell within the parameters of the Clayton Act. The comment outlines eight specific scenarios that could lead to further government regulation of interstate commerce. It is concluded that, although the Supreme Court ruled correctly in granting FTC authority over interstate commerce, the eight types of legal relationships described in this commentary should serve as a warning that old principles of legal doctrine must not be applied uniformly as new scenarios arise.

1076   Albertsworth, E. F. "Trade Regulation–What is the Matter of Public Interest to Justify Issuance of Complaint by the Federal Trade Commission–Judicial Review of Administrative Action." *Illinois Law Review* 24 (March 1930): 815-819.

There are two fallacies associated with FTC trade regulation authority over interstate commerce. First, is the ability of the FTC to interfere in the internal affairs of private enterprise and the second is that the FTC has authority to scrutinize unfair competition practices of "practically any private business." The Commission cannot investigate a business for unfair interstate trade practices under the pretenses established by unrelated orders. In addition, the FTC must show that an investigation is in the public interest. This essay outlines three issues concerning what constitutes authority within the realm of "public interest" that are the result of the Supreme Court's ruling in *Federal Trade Commission v. Klesner*. Each factor helps to further define the administrative boundaries within which the FTC can operate when regulating unfair business practices across state lines.

1077   Angel, Arthur R. "How a FTC Staff Attorney Makes a Record in a FTC Rulemaking Proceeding." *Antitrust Bulletin* 22 (Summer 1977): 327-339.

Examines three basic "elements of proof" relevant to rulemaking and decision-making proceedings under provisions of the Magnuson-Moss Act: 1) proof that a violation of a proposed rule has taken place; 2) proof that the trade regulation rule is a fair and effective remedy; and 3) proof that there will be minimal burden placed on the company. Each factor is described in detail as it relates to the formulation of policy and procedure within the FTC and concludes by noting how participation in rulemaking proceedings by trade associations can greatly affect the validity and quality of an inquiry.

1078   Austern, H. Thomas. "Five Thousand Dollars a Day: An Inquiry into the Civil Penalty Consequences of Violation of a Federal Trade Commission Cease and Desist Order." *Kentucky Law Journal* 51 (Spring 1963): 481-525.

Presented to the Antitrust Section of the American Bar Association, this paper outlines the perceived cycle from strict limitations on FTC regulatory authority to more liberal application of power. Currently agency cease and desist orders can carry a large monetary civil penalty and violation of Section 5 of the FTC Act or the Robinson-Patman Act also could bring financial penalty. This potential of significant monetary penalties is examined in detail, with special attention paid to the scope, application, extent, and reasonableness placed on respondents by these monetary burdens. Also considered are the policies in place that dictate the writing of the orders and the penalties imposed on violators. It is concluded that broad compliance with FTC rules can only be accomplished if the agency avoids issuing "obscurely phrased and broadly applicable cease and desist orders."

1079   Badal, Robert G. "Restrictive State Laws and the Federal Trade Commission." *Administrative Law Review* 29 (Spring 1977): 239-264.

During the past several decades, states have become increasingly active in regulating unfair business practices, usually created through the business license requirement. However, in some cases, these state laws harm industries and the free market economy. This article examines the relationship between state authority and the FTC's power to regulate unfair business practices, arguing that, when the FTC views a state regulation or law as a serious anti-competitive effect, the FTC has the authority to issue rules that supersede conflicting state regulations. This statement is made on the basis of the FTC's legal mandate, its rulemaking authority, and the provisions of a proposed trade regulation rule regarding the advertisement of eyeglasses and corrective lenses. This trade rule is a useful case study because it directly conflicts with existing state regulations. The conclusion outlines the scope of agency authority to limit state actions and notes that the Supreme Court's promulgation of the "state action" doctrine established in the *Parker v. Brown* case does not pose an obstacle to FTC authority.

1080   Barnett, E. Howard. "Green with Envy: The FTC, the EPA, the States, and the Regulation of Environmental Marketing." *Environmental Lawyer* 1 (February 1995): 491-512.

Both the FTC and the Environmental Protection Agency regulate the marketing products based on environmental attributes, such as "green packaging" or "recyclable." This essay examines the approaches to green marketing regulation by both agencies and state programs. The author describes the shortcomings associated with the FTC regulations, but acknowledges that they have been mostly successful. It is concluded that uneven regulations among the FTC and EPA and various state agencies discourages companies from becoming environmentally conscious.

1081   Baughman, Wilber Norman. "The Federal Trade Commission and the Rule of Evidence." *Journal of the District of Columbia Bar Association* 5 (September 1938): 397-406.

This article analyzes the issue of whether regulatory agencies, in this case the FTC, should be governed by the same rules of evidence as those that are present in the courts. The issue is rendered even more ambiguous by the fact that neither the FTC Act nor the FTC Rules of Practice deal with what evidence the agency receives or how and in what way the rules of evidence can be invoked. By reviewing pertinent court rulings, the author concludes that the FTC has been conservative in its pursuit of evidence even though it is not bound by the same rules that govern rules of evidence in the courts.

1082   Bazen, Horace Buchanan. "Bill to Remove the Fact-Finding Power of the Federal Trade Commission." *Georgetown Law Journal* 37 (November 1948): 59-65.

The underlying intention of H.R. 3871 is to remove the quasi-judicial authority of the FTC in unfair trade practice cases by amending provisions contained in Section 5 of the FTC Act. The amendment would force the FTC to file a complaint with the appropriate district court rather than adjudicate the matter through an agency hearing. This note argues against the bill by noting that the complexities of current business practices justifies the need for the expertise and fact-finding authority of the FTC. Also, since FTC procedures do not violate due process of law, time should be given to determine if sections 5 and 11 of the Administrative Act can ensure adequate safeguards in quasi-judicial proceedings.

1083   Bell, Ann M. "Trade Regulation–Use of Registered Mail by Federal Trade Commission to Subpoena Foreign Citizens Abroad Violates International Law." *Vanderbilt Journal of Transnational Law* 14 (Summer 1981): 663-676.

This article examines the legal history and underlying reasoning behind the decision to vacate the *FTC v. Compagnie de Saint-Gobain-Pont-a-Mousson* case in which the Commission issued a subpoena by registered mail to a company in Paris that was found to have violated the FTC Act. The court ruled that the agency's statutory power to investigate foreign company activities affecting the price of competitive products in the United States did not implicitly permit the FTC to use registered mail for service of an investigatory subpoena because such action violates international law.

1084   Bennett, Joel P. "Post-Complaint Discovery in Administrative Proceedings: The FTC as a Case Study." *Duke Law Journal* 1975 (1975): 329-346.

The purpose of this study is to analyze the complex dynamics of pre-trial discovery in administrative adjudicatory proceedings to develop relevant evidence in an investigation. The author outlines the history of discovery in civil and administrative proceedings under the Federal Rules of Civil Procedure and the FTC's Rules of Practice. In comparing the two procedures, and with special attention to the case law involving the Commission, the author concludes that the

FTC should adopt the discovery provisions of the Federal Rules of Civil Procedure because current Rules of Practice have led to litigation that result in preliminary delays and inefficiency.

1085   Benston, George J. "The Costs of Complying with a Government Data Collection Program: The FTC's Line of Business Report." *Journal of Accounting and Public Policy* 3 (Summer 1984): 123-137.

This article focuses on the perceived burden placed on companies required to gather and report detailed data as required by the FTC's Line of Business Program. The General Accounting Office's survey of nine firms in 1974 and detailed estimates of the cost of complying with the program by five companies resisting the compliance in U.S. District Court, show that there is a significant difference between company estimates of burden and those stated by the FTC. The author suggests two factors that help explain this difference: varying expectations and incentives between the demands of the FTC and the firms required to disseminate that data and different procedures for estimating costs. It is concluded that the FTC's cost estimates are invalid. Suggested improvements to the Line of Business Program should include an independent agency, such as the GAO, being responsible for estimating costs and improve the quality of data collected by conducting a statistically random sample of respondents.

1086   Berger, Raoul. "Removal of Judicial Functions from Federal Trade Commission to a Trade Court: A Reply to Mr. Kinter." *Michigan Law Review* 59 (December 1960): 199-229.

The author responds in detail to FTC Chairman Earl W. Kinter's criticism of the American Bar Association's proposal to create an administrative Trade Court by commenting on several key points noted by Kinter regarding how a Trade Court could harm rulemaking authority and quasi-judicial control. The author argues that the Trade Court offers a viable alternative to an agency that has lost the public's confidence to issue unbiased judgements.

1087   Berlow, Alan. "Federal Trade Commission: Business Wants Congress to Limit Powers of Agency." *Congressional Quarterly Weekly Report* 37 (August 11, 1979): 1647-1651.

This essay discusses complaints by business interests that see the FTC as overly aggressive in carrying out its authority to issue rules designed to provide consumers with more information about products or services in the funeral home and used car industries. The author outlines Congressional reaction to these complaints and the various bills intended to limit the FTC's authority to investigate, focusing on the FTC's attempt to regulate television advertising directed at children. Also, outlined are attempts by Congress to pass a legislative veto bill that would grant Congress the power to veto any proposed FTC regulations. The essay concludes that, while the House of Representatives will likely pass a legislative veto bill attached to FTC authorization in the coming year, it is not likely to pass in the Senate.

1088   Berman, J. "New Policy of Federal Trade Commission and Recent Decisions on Trade Regulation." _Commercial Law Journal_ 59 (September 1954): 240-244.

Examines recent reforms in the areas of trade regulation and antitrust policy in light of the new Republican administration, with special emphasis on new initiatives developed at the FTC under Chairman Howry. These initiatives are: to establish a Bureau of Consultation, revise application of the "per se" violation test, create an advisory committee to help administer provisions of the Robinson-Patman Act, avoid conflict with the Antitrust Division of the Department of Justice and the work of the Food and Drug Administration, and solicit the advise of outside management engineers to recommend the elimination of excess paper work. The essay also reviews recent reforms of the Robinson-Patman Act and legislative developments in antitrust policy.

1089   Black, David L. "New Federal Trade Commission Franchise Disclosure Rule: Application to Distributorship Arrangements." _Business Lawyer_ 35 (January 1980): 409-433.

This article reviews the "Disclosure Requirements and Prohibitions Concerning Franchising and Business Opportunity Ventures" trade regulation rule that requires offerors of certain franchising and business opportunity ventures to disclose information about their business activities. The impact of this rule on distributorship arrangements is analyzed, followed by a discussion of exemptions under the trade rule that affect distributorship. An appendix is included that summarizes the twenty categories of disclosure information that must be provided to the FTC.

1090   Bloom, Lawrence H. "Applicability of NEPA's Environmental Impact Statement Requirement of Federal Trade Commission Adjudications." _Albany Law Review_ 42 (Spring 1978): 506-521.

Analyzes the conflict between provisions of the FTC Act and the National

Environmental Policy Act of 1969 (NEPA). Under NEPA, an environmental impact statement must be filed when a government agency or legislative action is viewed as potentially affecting the environment. However, FTC adjudicatory and rulemaking proceedings are exempt from this process. This raises two questions: to what extent is the FTC exempt from NEPA rules? and second, if an exemption does not exist, at what point in the proceedings is the FTC required to file an environmental impact statement? Relying on a number of court cases, the author addresses these concerns in detail and concludes that effective compliance with NEPA rules can only take place if a draft impact statement is issued early in the rulemaking proceedings.

1091   Brandel, Roland E. and John A. Sodergren. "FTC and Banking: Power without Limit." *ABA Banking Journal* 74 (June 1982): 203-204, 207, 209, 211.

The authors argue that the broad authority granted to the five FTC Commissioners to prohibit conduct deemed to be unfair or deceptive represents a threat to the banking industry because compliance with FTC rules will place an undue burden on the resources of financial service companies. The article reviews a number of issues associated with the FTC's "unfairness jurisdiction." The central problem, as stated by the authors, is that "when Congress delegated practically unlimited power to the FTC, it abdicated its legislative function of democratically determined public policy." Among the issues discussed to support this assertion are problems defining unfairness, inadequate safeguards against FTC abuse of power, inherent drawbacks of legislative veto power, judicial review, the lack of expertise, and the potential effect of FTC rules on the Uniform Commercial Code and state laws. It is argued that the banking industry must lobby Congress to repeal Section 18 of the Magnuson-Moss Act.

1092   Braucher, Jean. "Defining Unfairness: Empathy and Economic Analysis at the Federal Trade Commission." *Boston University Law Review* 68 (March 1989): 349-430.

The author attempts to answer the question "What is unfair?" as it applies to consumer contracts and, specifically, FTC attempts to formulate rules governing its jurisdiction to regulate unfair business practices within the business framework of consumer contracts. The author defends the Commission's authority in this area and uses the FTC's Credit Practices Rule as a example of a flawed, but significant attempt by the agency to define its role in regulating consumer contracts deemed to be unfair under provisions of FTC Act. Currently this definition of unfairness focuses on the issue of gross inefficiency. This path to effective regulation should be followed and the urge to police consumer contracts should be avoided since taxes and transfer payments offer the most effective means of achieving redistribution.

1093   Brennan, Bruce J. "Affirmative Disclosure in Advertising and Control of Packaging Design Under the Federal Trade Commission Act." *Business Lawyer* 20 (November 1964): 133-144.

This essay discusses the current regulatory activities of the FTC in the area of food and drug advertising. Two issues in particular are examined in detail: 1) efforts to require affirmative disclosures of drug side effects and contraindications and, in the case of food products, more rigid rules concerning the true volume of product in a container; and 2) in what ways these programs illustrate an expansion of regulatory activity by the Commission into areas previously left to other agencies.

1094   Brin, Jr., Royal H. "Jurisdiction of the Federal Trade Commission in the Field of Insurance." *Texas Law Review* 37 (December 1958): 198-206.

Brief essay that uses selective judicial decisions to explore the FTC's regulatory jurisdiction in the insurance industry. This jurisdiction is contrasted with current state litigation against insurance companies, arguing that FTC enforcement is likely to occur only as it applies to interstate mail-order insurance business and to supervise enforcement by the states if it is shown that a state statute is inadequate or "enacted only for the purpose of depriving the federal government of jurisdiction."

1095   Brown, Mary L. and Lynn R. Price. "Federal Trade Commission Franchise Disclosure Rule." *John Marshall Law Review* 13 (Spring 1980): 637-677.

The purpose of this commentary is to examine the FTC's "Disclosure Requirements and Prohibitions Concerning Franchising and Business Opportunity Ventures" trade regulation rule issued in 1971. By examining in detail the definition of a franchiser, the FTC's rulemaking authority, and the rule's impact on business, it is argued that the rule is an ineffective tool for preventing fraud in franchising and should be simplified or eliminated.

1096   Calvani, Terry. "An FTC Commissioner's View of Regulating Lawyers." *American Bar Association Journal* 70 (August 1984): 70-72.

Opinion piece by the author outlining under what conditions the FTC may pursue enforcement of antitrust and consumer protection regulations as they apply to lawyers. The debate has generally focused on an "all-or-nothing" interpretation of FTC intentions. Enforcement should either be aggressively pursued or lawyers and other professional should be exempt from regulation. The author argues that the FTC should retain its right to enforce antitrust and consumer protection laws regardless of the profession involved.

1097   Carlson, M. B. "Fierce Fight over Deregulation at the Federal Trade Commission." *California Lawyer* 3 (January 1983): 40-43, 60-61.
Overview of efforts by external constituencies and Chairman James C. Miller III to reform the enforcement activities of the FTC in light of criticism that the agency is out of control, has squandered resources pursuing inconsistent policies, and overextended its regulatory authority. After a brief history of the "modern FTC" beginning in 1970, the author describes various programs to regulate children's television advertising, deceptive practices in the used car, funeral home and mobile home industries and how the changing climate in Congress, coupled with uneven results, has led to calls to terminate the era of regulatory activism.

1098   Casey, Sharon C. "Franchisors and the FTC: State Regulation and Federal Preemption." *Harvard Journal of Law and Public Policy* 3 (1980): 155-190.
Recent efforts by the FTC to regulate franchises raises compelling issues concerning the power of the quasi-legislative agency to preempt state law, conflicting requirements under different state laws, and in what ways the relationship between FTC and state regulatory efforts affect the businesses being regulated. The essay begins by reviewing the development of the disclosure rule governing franchise behavior. Part two examines provisions of the rule in comparison to existing state regulations. The third section analyzes the FTC's quasi-legislative rulemaking authority and to what extent this power can preempt state rules. It is argued in the conclusion that the FTC should have adopted the states uniform disclosure document rather than promulgate new rules. The FTC's preemption power has not been clearly defined, an issue that Congress must address given this study's findings.

1099   Clanton, David A. "Trade Associations and the FTC." *Antitrust Bulletin* 22 (Summer 1977): 307-315.
Text of a paper given at the 13th Annual Symposium of the Antitrust Law Committee of the Bar Association of the District of Columbia, in which the author

discusses specific efforts by the FTC to regulate trade associations, most notably in the area of health services. Three statutory powers, the promulgation of trade regulation rules, pursuit of civil penalties under provisions of the Magnuson-Moss Act, and use of injunctive relief under Section 13(b) of the FTC Act, are highlighted due to their possible impact on trade associations.

1100   Clark, Richard C. "Unfair Trade Practices–Packers and Stockyards Act–Federal Trade Commission Lacks Jurisdiction over Grocery Chain Owning Meat Packing Plant." *Notre Dame Lawyer* 33 (December 1957): 121-123.
Brief legal note outlining the court's decision in the *Food Fair Stores v. FTC* case, in which the Commission had issued a complaint against a retail supermarket organization that had acquired a meat packing plant, claiming that because the stores also sold fresh and canned meats, the organization had used a "co-operative advertising" scheme involving receipt of discriminatory advertising allowances to gain an advantage over competitors. The court ruled that, under provisions of the Packers and Stockyards Act of 1921, the FTC did not have jurisdiction in the meat packing industry because the Act vested exclusive control and regulation of the industry to the Secretary of Agriculture.

1101   Clarkson, Kenneth W. and Timothy J. Muris. "Constraining the Federal Trade Commission: The Case of Occupational Regulation." *University of Miami Law Review* 35 (November 1980): 77-130.
This article examines external constraints placed on an administrative body by focusing on the occupational licensure program of the FTC and possible rules that may be promulgated as a result of this program. The essay begins by arguing from an economic perspective that occupational regulation is unnecessary and harms the consumer by constricting the marketplace. The next section outlines the development of the occupational licensure program of the FTC. The following sections analyze the likelihood that the program will produce significant rules that preempt state regulations in light of three factors: 1) internal agency issues associated with the allocation of resources in support of the program, consistent although ineffective opposition by some people within the agency, and the relationship of the program as originally conceived, to new activities; 2) Congressional support or opposition to a particular program; and 3) the constraint of judicial review of agency actions to enforce trade regulation rules. Findings from this study indicate that FTC preemption of state intent is likely to take the form of additional regulation rather than deregulation and that Congress is

generally unable to require or prevent specific enforcement activities. Judicial review offers a somewhat more likely control over FTC regulatory rules but, absent of a cost-benefit analysis, the courts offer little additional constraints.

1102 "Critique of the Administrative Conference Report on Federal Trade Commission Rulemaking, Panel Discussion." *American Bar Association Antitrust Law Journal* 48 (1979): 1755-1794.

Panel discussion in which participants examine the underlying causes of Congressional unrest over recent FTC rulemaking activities under the expanded authority granted by the Magnuson-Moss Act. The concern of Congress is most clearly manifested in the most recent appropriations bill singling out the agency as the "leading candidate for a legislative veto provision."

1103 Cushman, Robert E. "The Constitutional Status of the Independent Regulatory Commissions." *Cornell Law Quarterly* 24 (December 1938): 13-53; (February 1938): 163-197.

This purpose of this two part article is to review comprehensively the legal character and political place of independent regulatory commissions, including the FTC. The first part examines commission behavior within the conceptual framework of the constitutional separation of powers and how that doctrine defines agency organization, functions and relations with other governmental bodies. The second part examines the legal and constitutional relationships independent commissions maintain with Congress, the Executive Office, and the judicial system, In so doing, this study attempts to reveal the complex constitutional problems associated with underlying public purpose of independent agencies and how the three branches of government have addressed these problems with varying degrees of success.

1104 Daniels, William G. "Judicial Review of the Fact Findings of the Federal Trade Commission." *Washington Law Review and State Bar Journal* 14 (January 1939): 37-51.

As stated in Section 5 of the FTC Act and Section 11 of the Clayton Act, Congress had taken the process of gathering evidence out of the hands of the courts and placed it within the administrative function of the FTC with regards to pursuing claims of unfair competition and monopolistic behavior. The role of the courts were to determine if the actions of the Commission are based upon substantial evidence. However, the courts appear hesitant to fully accept FTC findings of evidence by administrative means, substituting their own findings for those of the

FTC. A series of doctrines to help guide their actions has been developed, but this comment argues, by considering a number of recent cases, the courts continue to maintain considerable latitude when weighing the validity of Commission findings of fact.

1105 Dell'Ario, A. Charles. "FTC Attempts to Abolish Vicarious Liability Defenses for Deceptive Sales Practices: Strict Liability for Manufacturers?" *Hastings Law Journal* 25 (April 1974): 1142-1164.
This note examines "three general types of sale-distribution arrangements" and how various respondents succeed in avoiding vicarious liability for deceptive practices despite the broad powers granted to the FTC. When confronted with a cease and desist order regarding deceptive sales practices, a manufacturer may attempt to avoid the action by reorganizing its sales group into a "nominally separate business entity." Based upon current case law, this note examines two untested theories based on latent power to control deceptive practices and the doctrine of strict products liability to regulate the separateness of business entities. It is concluded, however, that only through Congressional action, rather than relying on the courts, can a meaningful remedy for vicarious liability be formulated.

1106 Dietrich, Ronald. "The FTC and Regulation Affecting Banks." *Banking Law Journal* 89 (June 1972): 514-523.
Although the FTC does not directly regulate the banking industry, it nevertheless has jurisdiction over specific functions of the industry, most notably as a result of provisions promulgated in the Truth-In-Lending Act. This essay explores the FTC's Truth-In-Lending enforcement program and the possible ways in which the issuance of policy statements may affect the banking industry and its relationship to bank regulatory agencies. Also discussed are the implications for the financial community of two proposed trade regulation rules concerning holder-in-due-course activities and billing practices.

1107 Doherty, Brian. "Masters of Manipulation." *Reason* 29 (March 1998): 54-55.
The FTC claims that a chiropractor who writes, publishes and sells brochures describing the work of chiropractors contains misleading information based on the fact that the standard of "competent and reliable scientific evidence" has not been used to support specific claims made in the brochures. Using this case as an example, the author argues that the FTC is "a dragon with big teeth" that will use

the excuse that the brochure is commercial speech to circumvent First Amendment rights of free speech.

1108   Drexler, Meg. "FTC Regulation of Interstate Land Sales." *Houston Law Review* 12 (March 1975): 708-731.

This essay explores the implications inherent in the FTC's recent entry into real estate sales transactions by examining the Commission's actions against GAC Corporation, a leading land sales and development company, and by reviewing the regulation of land sales by the Office of Interstate Land Sales created under provisions of the Interstate Land Sales Full Disclosure Act of 1974. The author argues that the consent order issued against GAC Corporation by the FTC highlights inadequacies in the Land Sales Full Disclosure Act to protect the consumer. The FTC's consent order also illustrates the fact that the consumer protection authority of the Commission can be an effective means for regulating land sales.

1109   Dyer, Thomas M. and James B. Ellis. "The FTC's Claim of Substantive Rule-Making Power: A Study in Opposition." *George Washington Law Review* 41 (December 1972): 330-347.

During the first half of its history, the FTC limited its enforcement methods to adjudicatory processes. Rules were issued occasionally but they took the form of advisory opinions. However, in 1962, the FTC issued a Rule of Practice that formed the basis for issuing substantive rules intended to have the force of law. Authority to create trade regulation rules was provided under provisions of Section 5 and 6(g) of the FTC Act. The FTC claims that the substantive rules are necessary for the effective and efficient execution of its regulatory responsibilities. This has led to considerable debate as to the legality of these claims by the Commission. This article examines the content of Sections 5 and 6(g), including their history and development, and concludes that, in fact, they do not provide the legal basis for creating trade regulation rules.

1110   Ellison, Newell W. "Court Review of Federal Trade Commission Orders." *Food Drug Cosmetic Law Quarterly* 1 (June 1946): 239-252.

The provisions of the Reece Bill (H. R. 2390) are intended to expand the scope of judicial review of findings of fact and orders of the FTC by amending Section 5 of the FTC Act. The author outlines several reasons why the Reece Bill is needed in order to address inadequacies in the current system of judicial review of FTC activities.

Trade Regulation

1111   Elman, Philip. "The New Constitutional Right to Advertise." *American Bar Association Journal* 64 (February 1978): 206-210.

The author examines the impact of recent Supreme Court rulings that commercial speech is protected by the First Amendment on affirmative disclosures, ad substantiation, and corrective statements. Although the rulings clearly place the burden of showing that deception exists on the FTC in statements commercial speech regulated by an Commission order, the ruling also reaffirms the fact that advertisers must adhere to the truth in advertising doctrine to avoid possible FTC regulation.

1112   Erickson, W. Bruce. "Unfair Trade Practices Under Section 5 of the Federal Trade Commission Act: A Statistical Evaluation." *Antitrust Bulletin* 22 (Fall 1977): 643-671.

Using empirical evidence, this study describes unfair trade practices as defined under provisions of the FTC Act as they relates to four issues: the competitive process, consumer welfare, levels of concentration within the industries that are subject to allegations of unfair trade practices, and the economic importance of industries. A total of 9,119 alleged unfair trade practices during the period 1945 to 1967 were classified according to twenty-nine trade practice categories (for example, "product misrepresentation") derived from sixty-three classes of trade practices used by the FTC. By employing a Spearman rank-order correlation coefficient among the four issues and related to the twenty-nine trade practice categories, it is revealed that the four highest ranked categories of trade practices closely parallels the FTC's enforcement activities, supporting the contention that the agency closely follows its Congressional mandate.

1113   "Federal Trade Commission Act, Amendments Under the Wheeler-Lea Act." *New York University Law Quarterly Review* 16 (November 1938): 121-125.

A note reviewing the expected positive impact that the Wheeler-Lea Act should have in addressing FTC Act deficiencies that have become apparent during its first twenty-four years of existence; this is especially true as it relates to the literal construction of the unfair methods of competition doctrine which had severely hindered the FTC's actions because the agency was burdened with showing that the action injured the consumer.

1114   "Federal Trade Commission–Recent Trends in Interpretation of Federal Trade Commission Act." *Michigan Law Review* 32 (June 1934): 1142-1154.

Brief commentary that attempts to explain the underlying reasons why "the judiciary has clearly been unfriendly" to the FTC, noting that this is likely due to the court's unwillingness to grant broad powers to new federal agencies, especially one that acts as "both judge and jury" in cases falling within Section 5 provisions, and because investigations under Section 6 are in conflict with the Fourth and Fifth Amendments of the United States Constitution. The commentary concludes that the relationship between the courts and the FTC are easing somewhat over time and that this will lead to a more effective enforcement agency.

1115   "Federal Trade Commission Act–Amendments Under the Wheeler-Lea Act." *New York University Law Quarterly Review* 16 (November 1938): 121-125.

This commentary briefly outlines the ways in which the Wheeler-Lea Amendment to the FTC Act will result in a "marked improvement" concerning the Commission's powers of enforcement.

1116   "The Federal Trade Commission Act of 1938." *Columbia Law Review* 39 (February 1939): 259-273.

This article examines in detail four changes to the FTC Act due to passage of the Wheeler-Lea Act: 1) shifts the emphasis from having to prove injury to a competitor to showing injury to the consumer; 2) makes false advertising a criminal act as it discovered to defraud or mislead the consumer or if the advertisement is injurious; 3) grants the FTC temporary injunction powers in cases if the FTC has reason to believe an advertisement may be false or misleading; and 4) requires that a respondent must file for review in the Court of Appeals a cease and desist order within sixty days or the order becomes final. The article concludes that problems with the Wheeler-Lea Amendment do exist but that it is an important step forward in preventing false advertising.

1117   Fietkiewicz, John M. "Section 14 of the Lanham Act: FTC Authority to Challenge Generic Trademarks." *Fordham Law Review* 48 (March 1980): 437-470.

Under Section 14 of the Lanham Act, the FTC has the authority to petition for cancellation of a trademark on the grounds that it has become a common descriptive name. This article examines the *FTC v. Formica Corp.* case, the first instance in which the FTC uses the generic word doctrine to petition for removal of a trademark. In the case, the agency alleges that the term "formica" had become a generic word in the marketplace. The article explores the negative reactions among business leaders that has prompted the introduction of legislation in Congress intended to limit FTC authority under provisions of the Lanham Act. The author concludes that it is premature to assume that neither consumers nor competitors will benefit from the FTC's actions, therefore, Congress should refrain from passing legislation until the impact of the case can be assessed.

1118   Filene, Lincoln. "Voluntary Control of Unfair Business Practices." *Harvard Business Review* 17 (Summer 1939): 434-441.

This article analyzes the development of voluntary action by business groups through trade associations to ensure "self-education and self-regulation" among companies within a particular industry. The author outlines efforts by various business groups to achieve voluntary regulation of unfair practices in producer-distributor transactions and the relationship these efforts have with government regulators, most notably the FTC. A set of six steps are proposed that delineate the process for creating an effective voluntary self-regulation and that would satisfy government regulators.

1119   Fisher, Richard M. "FTC v. Funeral Industry: Round One." *Lincoln Law Review* 11 (1980): 193-203.

This article begins by examining the funeral home industry, how a typical funeral home is managed, and the development of licensing boards and other forms of state regulation of the industry. The remainder of the article analyzes the underlying reasons why the FTC formulated a set of proposed Funeral Industry trade regulation rules, their relationship to existing state regulations, and how, through its statutory jurisdiction to regulate industry, the FTC rules may provide a single means for regulating the industry which has been governed by widely varying state regulations.

1120   Fisher, William A. "Supplemental Jurisdiction of the Federal Trade Commission Under Section 7 and 11 of the Clayton Act." *George Washington Law Review* 3 (November 1934): 81-86.

Examines the Supreme Court case *Arrow-Hart and Hegeman Electric Co. v. FTC* to illustrate how problems remain with regards to the FTC's authority to order divestiture of assets under Section 7 of the Clayton Act when it is determined that the acquisition of stock of one company by another leads to the lessening of competition. The central argument is that the FTC is an administrative body with restricted powers to order property or other assets to be divested. It is argued that this narrow interpretation of FTC authority has rendered the FTC ineffective in regulating anticompetitive stock acquisitions.

1121   Fraizer, C. C. "Federal Trade Commission Jurisdiction?" *Insurance Counsel Journal* 22 (October 1955): 467-471.

Citing a number of cases, this study explores the efforts of the FTC to regulate the insurance industry. The FTC took action against seventeen companies based on the findings of a study it conducted of the industry alleging that the insurance companies used misleading advertising in promotional and solicitation materials. The author describes attempts by the companies to fight FTC jurisdiction over the industry and the relationship between FTC regulatory efforts and those of the states.

1122   Freer, Robert E. "Practice Before the Federal Trade Commission." *George Washington Law Review* 7 (January 1939): 283-303.

In an address to the Cincinnati Bar Association, the author outlines the enforcement activities of the FTC, the scope of its jurisdiction as described by the Sherman and Clayton Acts, and how recent amendments to the FTC Act, such as Wheeler-Lea, have broadened its powers. The essay concludes by exploring agency investigatory practices, judicial review and enforcement of cease and desist orders, the role of trade practice conferences, and the nature of general investigations.

1123   "FTC Has Power to Issue Subpoenas in Proceedings to Enforce Section 2 of the Clayton Act (*FTC v. Menzies* 145 F Supp 1964)." *Harvard Law Review* 70 (June 1956): 1476-1479.

Reviews the *FTC v. Menzies* case, which held that, while Section 11 of the Clayton Act does not specifically confer subpoena power on any enforcement agencies, it is clear that the FTC can assume this power through Section 9 of the FTC Act. This argument is viewed as an important judicial decision because the availability of subpoena power in proceedings is essential in ensuring comprehensive enforcement.

1124   "FTC Substantive Rulemaking: An Evaluation of Past Practice and Proposed Legislation." *New York University Law Review* 48 (April

1973): 135-170.

Reviews the development of substantive rulemaking by the FTC in 1962 and the subsequent debate in legal and political circles concerning the validity of trade regulation rules as a means for regulating industry and protecting the consumer. Prior to substantive rulemaking, the FTC relied on voluntary compliance, case-by-case adjudication procedures, or interpretive "guides" intended to inform business of the rules under the FTC Act. Each of these were either ineffective in regulating industry-wide violations or were expensive and time consuming. This note examines the debates surrounding the creation of trade regulation rules as an alternative to previous enforcement procedures and discusses how proposed legislation to amend the FTC Act may affect the agency's substantive rulemaking authority.

1125   Gage, Robert J. "Discriminating Use of Information Disclosure Rules by the Federal Trade Commission." *UCLA Law Review* 26 (June 1979): 1037-1083.

Information disclosure rules are those regulations that require producers of consumer products to disseminate material information about products and services that, if otherwise unknown to the consumer, would affect their purchasing behavior. This article examines the function of information in the marketplace, the failure of private market to adequately inform consumers about products and services, and the effect of insufficient information on the marketplace. The next section discusses options available to policy makers to formulate effective information disclosure rules and the appropriate roles of both federal agencies and industry. The article concludes by examining in detail efforts by the FTC to improve consumer information primarily through the issuance of trade regulation rules.

1126   Gard, Stephen W. "Purpose and Promise Unfulfilled: A Different View of Private Enforcement Under the Federal Trade Commission." *Northwestern University Law Review* 70 (May-June 1975): 274-291.

The author responds to an essay that appeared in this law review the previous year that endorsed the *Holloway v. Bristol-Myers Corp.* decision that states that a consumer is not entitled to redress pursuant to the FTC Act if that person has suffered economically due to an unfair or deceptive trade practice. The author argues that a misapplication of legislative history, the omission of several key court cases, and "an indifference to the realities of the FTC's enforcement of the statute" has misrepresented the issue of private enforcement under the FTC Act.

It is concluded, after re-examining court cases and legislative intent, that "it would be entirely appropriate" to imply a private right to action under provisions of the FTC Act.

1127   Garner, Donald W. and Darrell W. Dunham. "FTC Rule 433 and the Uniform Commercial Code: An Analysis of Current Lender Status." *Missouri Law Review* 43 (Spring 1978): 199-234.

This study analyzes the Guidelines on Trade Regulation Rule Concerning Preservation of Consumers' Claims and Defenses that attempted to circumvent a variety of mostly ineffective state regulations concerning hold-in-due-course transactions. However, the rule is not entirely effective. This is due to the fact that the rule does not regulate actions by the lender because the Commission is forbidden to regulate banks, which falls within the regulatory purview of the Federal Reserve Board. The implications for consumers that lenders are not regulated under provisions of the rule is the focus of this essay. It is concluded that this "half step" in regulating holder-in-due-course transactions leads to good faith compliance by lenders. True regulation can only be achieved if the FTC and Federal Reserve Board work together to formulate a comprehensive rule.

1128   Geismar, John. "Commercial Speech and the FTC: A Point of Departure from the Traditional First Amendment Analysis Regarding Prior Restraint." *New England Law Review* 16 (1980-1981): 793-829.

Studies in what ways FTC use of prior restraint may or may not be consistent with the expansion of First Amendment protection to include commercial speech. The article begins by reviewing the relationship between provisions of the FTC Act and commercial speech. This is followed by an analysis of the concept of prior restraint in light of First Amendment protection granted to commercial speech and the extent to which this protection applies. It is concluded that prior restraint would not inflict a heavy burden on either business or the consumer. Although the Supreme Court did not consider prior restraint when granting First Amendment protection to commercial speech, upholding FTC authority to require affirmative disclosures would seem to indicate that no problem exists. Nevertheless, the possibility, however unlikely, that the FTC could censor an advertiser must be resolved.

1129   Goldberg, Victor P. "Enforcing Resale Price Maintenance: The FTC Investigation of Lenox." *American Business Law Journal* 18 (Summer 1980): 225-258.

Using public and nonpublic files from the Federal Trade Commission, the author investigates the FTC's complaint against Lenox Inc. charging that Lenox utilized a restricted distribution system that incorporated resale price maintenance. The essay begins by outlining the reasons why a company would adopt a policy of resale price maintenance to restrict distribution of its products. The next section is devoted to describing the history of the FTC investigation of Lenox and the hearings conducted to examine the rationale of Lenox's policy. The third section describes the FTC decision to issue a cease and desist order within the context of dealer services and the nature of the Lenox retailing system. The author concludes that, while the FTC proceeded correctly in investigating Lenox, especially as it relates to conforming to previous case law, the fact that Lenox had created its policy to also conform to previous case law prevented the FTC from extending its investigation to the entire distribution system. The article ends with an appendix containing the text of the order modifying the original cease and desist order.

1130   Goldberg, Victor P. "Resale Price Maintenance and the FTC: The Magnavox Investigation." *William and Mary Law Review* 23 (Spring 1982): 439-500.

This essay examines the issue of resale price maintenance as it relates to the 1971 FTC investigation of Magnavox. By sifting through the contents of documents produced at the Commission as a result of the investigation, the author discovers "enough relevant material to provide a fairly good picture of the nature of Magnavox's marketing system." This fact illustrates how these files can be utilized by scholars to examine the validity of investigations by the FTC and to explore the nature of a corporation's marketing strategies. After outlining the history of the Magnavox investigation, the essay describes the marketing strategy of Magnavox and its competitors and details the internal structure of Magnavox's marketing strategy and relationship with distributors and sellers. The essay concludes with an analysis of the ways in which Magnavox enforced resale price maintenance through "aggressive" vertical restrictions. The text of the FTC consent order is included with the article.

1131   Greenhalgh, William F. "FTC's Holder-in-Due-Course Rule: An Ineffective Means of Achieving Optimality in the Consumer Credit Market." *UCLA Law Review* 25 (April 1978): 821-861.

This essay examines in detail the holder-in-due-course doctrine and efforts by state courts and legislatures to restrict the application of the doctrine that required consumers to pay for goods and services on an installment plan even if the seller unjustly refuses to repair or replace the product as stated in the sales transaction. However, the degree of protection for the consumer is not consistent because state laws are not uniform. The FTC's Trade Regulation Rule Concerning Preservation of Consumer's Claims and Defenses is an attempt to ensure uniform protection for consumers regardless of the jurisdiction where the sales transaction occurred. The purpose of this Rule is to allow consumers to break their contracts with lenders if the seller violates provisions of the sales transaction. The author explores the effectiveness of the Rule within the context of economic optimality (exists when all costs for an item are reflected in its price) and concludes that the Rule should be replaced by "national legislation" which would ban the use of negotiable instruments and waiver-of-defense clauses and would base "the regulation of vendor-related loans on factors designed to maximize lenders' incentives to set a uniform transaction cost figure for screening seller reliability" and negotiate adverse economic consequences associated with nonpayment by the buyer.

1132   Guttman, David Saul. "FTC's Newly Recognized Power to Issue Substantive Intra-Agency Rules or Why the Sleeping Beauty of Section 6(g) was Awakened by Court Order." *Loyola University Law Journal* 5 (Winter 1974): 107-139.

This paper reviews the ways in which the FTC has been hindered in its regulatory efforts because the Commission, unlike other regulatory agencies such as the Federal Communications Commission, did not have binding substantive rulemaking authority at its disposal and examines FTC efforts to formulate substantive rulemaking through the issuance of trade regulation rules that would not conflict with its statutory mandate. A number of court cases are used to illustrate attempts by the FTC to issue industry-wide regulations, but it is concluded that the FTC's substantive rulemaking authority is beyond the intention of those who viewed the agency as seeking remedies only by adjudication.

1133   Halverson, James T. "Consumer Credit Regulation by the Federal Trade Commission." *Banking Law Journal* 90 (June 1973): 479-496.

Examines FTC involvement in consumer credit regulation under provisions of the Truth-In-Lending Act, with special attention paid to assignee and hold-in-due-course liability, the timing of credit disclosures, and the sale of credit insurance, and, provisions of the Fair Credit Reporting Act, focusing on FTC interpretation of the practice of publishing credit guides by credit bureaus and the practice of prescreening the creditworthiness of consumers. Also examined are FTC trade regulation rules and how they reflect FTC jurisdiction over the banking industry.

1134   Halverson, James T. "Federal Trade Commission's Injunctive Powers Under the Alaskan Pipeline Amendments: An Analysis." *Northwestern University Law Review* 69 (January-February 1975): 872-885.

The Trans-Alaska Pipeline Authorization Act of 1973 amends Section 13 of the FTC Act and empowers the Commission to seek an injunctive relief if the agency has "reason to believe" that a possible violation of the provisions of the FTC Act may exist and that it is in the interest of the public to launch an investigation. Prior to the amendment, the FTC's powers were severely diminished because the agency could not take action before a merger or violation nor could the Commission preserve the status quo until administrative hearings were completed. In the case of false or misleading advertising, the advertisement would be withdrawn by the time the investigation was completed, thereby rendering the cease and desist order a moot point. The author argues that the preliminary injunctive powers granted to the FTC under the Pipeline Amendment have eliminated this "loophole." The essay concludes by predicting the ways in which the FTC may utilize its new injunction authority in future investigations.

1135   Hankin, Gregory. "Judicial Review of the Federal Trade Commission's Orders." *Illinois Law Quarterly* 6 (June 1924): 264-295.

There are a number of reasons why a case involving the FTC may be ruled in favor of the defendant. This study focuses on cases "decided on the question of whether the orders issued are within the meaning of the provisions" of the FTC or Clayton Acts. The paper begins by describing cases concerning misleading advertising, acts against competitors, and acts against consumers in which cease and desist orders have been affirmed. An exploration of cases in which the courts found the defendant to be in violation of Clayton Act provisions follows. The second part of the article examines cases in which the order has been annulled. The author concludes by describing the underlying reasons why the courts ruled against the FTC.

1136   Hankin, Gregory. "Validity and Constitutionality of the Federal Trade Commission Act." *Illinois Law Review* 19 (May 1924): 17-43.

Published ten years after the FTC Act was created, this study examines criticism aimed at the FTC, stating that its statutory authority is invalid and unconstitutional because of the "indefiniteness" of the language of the Act. The author notes that this argument illustrates a central conflict in the formulation of law: the need for specific language to prevent ambiguity versus the need in complex social systems for broad-based language encompassing general rules of conduct. The author uses a number of court cases to examine this issue and places them within the conceptual framework of the delegation of legislative power.

1137 Heekin, Thomas D. "Insurance–Regulation Under the McCarran-Ferguson Act–FTC Jurisdiction Not Oust by a State Statute Purporting to Control Deceptive Advertising Mailed to Other States." *Michigan Law Review* 59 (March 1961): 794-798.

Examines the implications surrounding the *Travelers Health Association v. FTC* case in which a cease and desist order was voided by the courts because the state of Nebraska had a law in place to regulate the insurance industry and how the emergence of mail-order insurance businesses has intensified the debate concerning the Congressional intent in using the phrase "regulated by state law" in the McCarren-Ferguson Act.

1138 Heller, Lawrence J. "Practice before the Federal Trade Commission." *Commercial Law League Journal* 35 (May 1930): 225-229.

Brief essay reviewing the statutory authority of the FTC and its activities to enforcement antitrust laws against firms practicing unfair methods of competition. Recent enforcement actions by the FTC are described, noting the general judicial support for such actions, and concludes that the FTC "serves as a healthy arm of the law" that is needed to control illegal business activities.

1139 Hobbs, C. O. "Legal Issues in FTC Trade Regulation Rules." *Food Drug Cosmetic Law Journal* 32 (September 1977): 414-422.

The author expresses reservations about the viability of the Magnuson-Moss Act to enhance the FTC's enforcement authority in a meaningful way, most notably as this issue relates to the whether FTC rulemaking is a legislative or adjudicative function. In addressing this topic the author examines the legal rights of respondents involved in trade regulation rule proceedings, the role of FTC staff in the rulemaking process, the remedial powers granted the FTC under Magnuson-Moss, and the scope of judicial review itself in determining the validity of FTC powers under Magnuson-Moss.

1140 Hogan, Sara Greenwood. "FTC Rulemaking: The Standard for Disqualification of a Biased Commissioner." *St. Mary's Law Journal* 12 (1981): 734-753.

In the case, *Association of National Advertisers v. FTC*, the United States Court of Appeals for the District of Columbia ruled that a rigorous standard for disqualifying biased commissioners must be established during a rulemaking procedure in order to protect the interests of the respondent. This comment discusses previous standards of disqualification within the conceptual framework of adjudicatory and rulemaking procedures, most notably with regards to the *Cinderella Career and Finishing School, Inc. v. FTC* case in which it was ruled that FTC Chairman Paul Rand Dixon should have been disqualified from the hearing because he made a public speech that indicated he had prejudged the facts of the case and the *Vermont Yankee Nuclear Power Corp. v. Natural Resources Defense Council* case in which the Supreme Court ruled that the Court of Appeals stepped beyond its judicial authority when it required agencies to follow rulemaking procedures that were not stated in the Administrative Procedure Act. The essay concludes that the FTC Improvements Act of 1980 may reduce the opportunity for commissioner bias but that care must be taken to ensure that the consumer protection authority of the agency is not diminished.

1141   Howry, Edward F. "Federal Trade Commission: A Revaluation of Its Responsibilities." *American Bar Association Journal* 40 (February 1954): 113-117.

Contains the text of a speech before the University of Michigan's Institute on Federal Antitrust Law in which the FTC Chairman outlines the underlying intent of Congress in creating the FTC and the need to explore standards of proof for measuring possible injury inflicted on competition in the marketplace, to develop "guiding yardsticks" to help businesses better understand distribution costs and other issues associated with the Robinson-Patman Act, to formulate a Bureau of Consultation to assist businesses in understanding antitrust laws, and to promulgate definitive pleadings in cases involving complex economic and legal issues.

1142   Howry, Edward F. "Some Thoughts on Commission Fact Finding and Judicial Review." *Antitrust Law Journal* 14 (1959): 32-38.

Examines critical reviews by the courts of appeals of the FTC's fact finding administration functions. The author uses several cases in which the courts found that the FTC had misinterpreted the law, leading to a finding of fact on the wrong issues. Two deficiencies in FTC procedures for reviewing a hearing examiner's findings exist. First, the FTC's decisions should constitute an "authentic public record' and, as such, should be published with an index and classified according to "the areas of discretion within which the hearing examiner may rule." And second, there is an absence of a uniform standard for evaluating the findings of the hearing examiner.

1143   Hyman, Paul M. "Participating in a TRR." *Food Drug Cosmetic Law Journal* 32 (August 1977): 369-379.

The purpose of this essay is to outline trade regulation rule procedures and practices, including the role of the presiding officer, the process for promulgating the rule, participation in a hearing, problems associated with group representation in a hearing, participation in an informal pre-hearing conference, and possible conclusions of the FTC. It is pointed out that, as more respondents are involved in trade regulation rule proceedings, the process will be refined and improved.

1144   "Insurance--Federal Trade Commission--Regulation by State Where Unfair Trade Practice Originates Does not Oust FTC Jurisdiction Under McCarran Act." *Vanderbilt Law Review* 14 (March 1961): 656-662.

The McCarran-Ferguson Act places severe limitations on the FTC's authority to regulate the insurance industry. This essay briefly explores the implications of the *Federal Trade Commission v. Travelers Health Association* decision to void an FTC cease and desist order directed at an insurance company in the state of Nebraska that was found to have engaged in false and deceptive interstate advertising. The court ruled that the McCarran-Ferguson Act prevented the FTC from issuing its own regulations because the state of Nebraska already had a state law regulating insurance companies. However, it is concluded that effective control of deceptive interstate practices in the insurance industry has been hindered by this decision because the states do not employ uniform regulations.

1145   "Investigatory Powers of the Federal Trade Commission." *Northwestern University Law Review* 53 (March-April 1958): 109-116.

Examines the "access and copy" authority of the FTC which, under Section 9 of the FTC Act, enables the Commission to have access as well as permission to copy documents during an investigation as part of its efforts to gather evidence. Using the recent *FTC v. American Tobacco Co.* case, this paper argues that copy and access powers should be available to the Commission only in complaint and pre-complaint investigations. When the FTC exercises this power to serve legislative or rule making purposes, it should be considered an unauthorized and unconstitutional action. It is argued that the FTC should be granted leniency in using subpoena power to obtain information. A number of court cases are described to support the conclusions of the author.

1146   Jeffrey, Thomas G. "The Federal Trade Commission's Power with References to Stock Acquisitions." *St. Louis Law Review* 16 (December 1930): 55-63.

The author uses several key court cases, but most notably *International Shoe Company v. Federal Trade Commission*, as the basis for exploring the FTC's authority to regulate the acquisition of stock in a merger transaction. The author points out that this case was not consistent with previous cases concerning the acquisition of assets and its relationship to the existence of competition. The Supreme Court ruled against the FTC in the International Shoe case, however, and as the author points out, the Court not only ruled against the findings of the FTC as to whether competition existed, but launched its own fact-finding investigation of the case ruling that competition was not diminished to the point of injuring the public. It is concluded that, in this respect, the Supreme Court assumed the position of the FTC as the investigatory body, thereby further confusing interpretations of the Clayton Act.

1147   Jones, Mary Gardner. "The Importance of Credit in Our Competitive Economy and the Role of the Federal Trade Commission." *New England Law Review* 4 (Spring 1969): 111-119.

As a Commissioner of the FTC, the author reviews the Truth-In-Lending Act and the ways in which the FTC anticipates enforcing its provisions. Included in the discussion is the formulation of an effective enforcement program once the Act goes into effect, how state credit disclosure laws inform the FTC's enforcement protocol, and the expected contribution of business in helping to enforce the Act.

1148   "Jurisdictional Fetter on the FTC." *Yale Law Journal* 76 (July 1967): 1688-1700.

This note argues that the FTC should be granted greater leniency in regulating local firms in direct competition with interstate concerns. The case of *FTC v. Bunte Bros.*, in which the court held that it was never the intention of Congress to grant FTC jurisdiction over local firms which may affect but are not associated with interstate commerce, is used to explore this issue. It is concluded that a complete reversal of the Bunte case is unlikely because it would give the FTC jurisdiction over all business activities. Nevertheless, Section 5 of the FTC Act should be interpreted to mean that the Commission has jurisdiction over local firms that use unfair practices to gain an advantage over interstate firms that happen to be in direct competition with the offending local company.

1149 "Jurisdictional Overlap between the Federal Trade Commission and the Consumer Product Safety Commission: Toward a Rational Delineation of Regulatory Duties." *George Washington Law Review* 42 (August 1974): 1114-1140.

In a consent order accepted by producers and marketers of polyurethane and polystyrene plastics, the FTC found that the manufacturers knowingly deceived consumers by selling and advertising combustible products labelled as nonflammable. The FTC required the firms not only to cease the misrepresentation and notification of past users of the product, but to establish a five million dollar research program "to minimize the hazards associated with the use of plastics products." This remedy overlaps the jurisdiction of the newly created Consumer Product Safety Commission (CPSC). This note examines this overlap within the framework of the statutory authority of the CPSC and attempts to outline the proper roles for each agency. It is concluded that the FTC overstepped its cease and desist powers to regulate industry. An "intermediate liaison committee" charged with ensuring formal coordination between the two agencies is recommended to resolve the issue of regulatory overlap.

1150 Kantorczyk, Todd D. "How to Stop the Fast Break: An Evaluation of the 'Three-Peat' Trademark and the FTC's Role in Trademark Law Enforcement." *UCLA Entertainment Law Review* 2 (Winter 1995): 195-228.

The term "three-peat" has become a widely used phrase in sports jargon to describe a team that has the opportunity to win a third consecutive championship. Using a public perception test, it is determined that the term "three-peat" has become a generic name for any event occurring three times consecutively. Designating a term as generic and outside the purview of trademark laws is primarily determined in private litigation. This comment argues that actions by the FTC would offer the most effective and efficient means of determining if a term is generic because the agency has no stake in future profits and can thereby act as an unbiased mediator. This is not the case in private actions to remove trademark restrictions.

1151 Kaplan, Eugene. "Federal Trade Commission and Equitable Remedies." *American University Law Review* 25 (Fall 1975): 173-199.

The courts found in *Heater v. FTC* that the FTC did not have the authority to order restitution as a remedy to correct an unfair practice. Using congressional remarks made during Senate and House of Representative debates during the formulation of the FTC Act and court decisions during the past twenty years, the author argues that the FTC possesses the power to issue and enforce equitable remedies, including seeking restitution, divestiture, and rescission. Only two exceptions are apparent: 1) the FTC cannot enforce its own order but rather, apply to the appropriate district court for civil penalty actions against firms found to be in violation of a cease and desist order, and 2) an order must be issued based solely on serving the public interest. It is argued that equitable remedies must be available to the FTC because prohibition of the unfair practice may not entirely serve the public's interest.

1152   Keating, William J. "FTC Authority to Order Compulsory Trademark Licensing: Is "Realemon" Really Real Lemon?" *Dickinson Law Review* 85 (Winter 1981): 191-199.

The author argues that the FTC does not possess the de facto authority to promulgate the remedies of compulsory trademark licensing because its use is based on "misconceptions" regarding the development of trademark rights and this remedy undermines the application of trademarks rights as a means of protecting the consumer from product confusion. Based on the case law, the author argues that it remains unclear why the FTC would pursue cancellation of a trademark. In response to the FTC's actions against the Formica Corporation, Congress threatened to withhold funding for any efforts by the Commission to render the company's name generic, but the FTC retains its ability to petition for cancellation of a trademark.

1153   Keller, Joseph E. "The Enlarged Jurisdiction of the Federal Trade Commission (Wheeler-Lea Act)." *Journal of the District of Columbia Bar Association* 5 (July 1938): 306-323.

The author explains the impact of the expanded enforcement powers of the FTC under provisions of the Wheeler-Lea Act from the perspective of three issues central to the Act: 1) broaden powers of the Commission to include "unfair or deceptive acts or practices"; 2) strengthen cease and desist orders by ensuring that they become final if a respondent does not act within sixty days; and 3) render more effective enforcement authority over false advertising of food, drug, device and cosmetic products and services.

1154   Kelley, William T. and James W. Cassedy. "The Federal Trade Commission Act as Amended by the Wheeler-Lea Act." *Food Drug Cosmetic Law Quarterly* 2 (September 1947): 315-334.

The purpose of this study is to explore the relationship between the provisions of the Wheeler-Lea Act that prohibits false advertising of foods, drugs, medical devices, and cosmetics and the Federal Food, Drug, and Cosmetic Act of 1938. Special attention is paid to the enforcement procedures outlined in each statute, interpreting congressional intent, and evaluating current case law. In order to avoid an overlap in administrative efforts, the FTC Commissioners issued a statement clarifying the conditions under which the FTC would seek to minimize or eliminate duplication of enforcement efforts that is created by the two statutes.

1155   Kesterbaum, Lionel. "Rulemaking Beyond APA: Criteria for Trial-Type Procedures and the FTC Improvement Act." *George Washington Law Review* 44 (August 1976): 679-709.

Although there has been a movement in Congress of late to create legislation that relies on "the function and judgement" of administrative agencies to a greater extent than in the past, there is also a diminished confidence in administrative agencies to formulate broad policies. This has undermined actions to formulate a more meaningful procedural framework of rulemaking. This article uses the FTC Improvement Act and the Commission's actions to enforce its provisions as an opportunity to examine reliance on "trial-type" hearings and the criteria needed to ensure its successful application in rulemaking procedures. It is concluded that abandonment of the "single-minded adherence to Administrative Procedure Act notice-and-comment procedures" and move towards a hearing with the possibility of cross-examination in a trial-type setting is only appropriate if the nature of the evidence is considered.

1156   Kinter, Earl W. et al. "Effect of the Federal Trade Commission Improvements Act of 1980 on the FTC's Rulemaking and Enforcement Authority." *Washington University Law Quarterly* 58 (1980): 847-859.

The authors examine and describe FTC Improvement Act provisions associated with the confidentiality of business records, use of civil investigative demands rather than subpoenas in pre-complaint consumer protection investigations, granting both houses of Congress the authority to veto implementation of a trade regulation rule, and restricts investigations of the insurance industry. It is concluded that, while certain restrictions have been placed on the FTC by the Act, its fundamental enforcement authority remains intact.

1157   Kirkpatrick, Miles W. "FTC Rulemaking in Historical Perspective." *Antitrust Law Journal* 48 (August 1979): 1561-1569.

This essay outlines the impact of the Magnuson-Moss Act on the FTC's efforts to protect consumers. The author notes that passage of the Act was an expression of confidence in the agency by Congress. However, less than four years after the Act was passed, FTC appropriations are "under siege" due to perceptions in Congress that the agency's rulemaking activities have "run amuck." This essay attempts to explain, in a historical context, why the dramatic shift in opinion regarding the FTC's enforcement activities has taken place and suggests ways in which the Commission can be brought closer in line with the sentiments in Congress.

1158   Kittelle, Sumner S. and Fred E. Campbell. "Power of the Federal Trade Commission to Require Informative Labeling of Textiles." *Boston University Law Review* 20 (January 1940): 23-36.

The creation of affirmative trade regulation rules as the result of a trade practice conference represents a new approach to consumer protection. This article examines in detail the rule promulgated by the FTC that requires an affirmative statement indicating fiber content on all textile products and discusses the authority of the FTC to make such rules since such power is not explicitly stated in the FTC Act. The author argues that the issue is complicated by the fact that: 1) the only tool available to enforcing the rule are cease-and-desist orders, and 2) questions exist concerning whether failure to disclose the content of fabrics violates the FTC Act. It is concluded that the only solution to misleading labelling of textile products is through Congressional action and not FTC rules.

1159   Knapp, Susan J. "Commercial Speech, the Federal Trade Commission and the First Amendment." *Memphis State University Law Review* 9 (Fall 1978): 1-56.

This study begins by detailing the history and development of constitutional protection granted to commercial speech. The next part examines the impact that recent extensions of those protection have had on commercial speech deemed misleading or false under provisions of the FTC Act. The third part places this expanded constitutional protection within the administrative and enforcement framework of the FTC's efforts to seek truthfulness in advertising. In addition to the importance of defining false or misleading advertising, the author evaluates the standard of intelligence used in determining if an ad is false or misleading as well as judicial review of FTC actions, with special attention paid to the relationship between corrective advertising requirements and the protection of commercial speech. Case law is utilized to argue that corrective advertising may violate constitutional protection of commercial speech.

1160 Koch, Jr, Charles H. and Beth Martin. "FTC Rulemaking through Negotiation." *North Carolina Law Review* 61 (January 1983): 275-311. This essay focuses on the mandate of the FTC to ensure a free and open marketplace and reviews agency enforcement activities in light of criticisms, primarily within the business community, that the FTC is more of an impediment to a competitive marketplace than a facilitator. A reason for some of this criticism is the fact that the FTC moves from one generation of regulatory devices to the next without considering past experiences, leading to uneven guidance of business practices. To alleviate this problem, the authors argue that a systematic procedure should be created to determine "when [each rulemaking process] can be used most efficiently." Businesses should, therefore, be involved with the implementation of an informal process of negotiation among the FTC, commercial interests, and consumer protection groups to create a "broad regulatory device" that serves as the foundation for applying traditional remedies.

1161 Kolak, Raymond P. "Standard Setting in Agency Adjudications Under the Federal Trade Commission Improvement Act." *George Washington Law Review* 46 (January 1978): 233-250. This note explores initial civil actions by the FTC to recover penalties for unfair and deceptive trade practices under Section 205 of the Magnuson-Moss-FTC Improvement Act. Section 205 permits the agency to rely on legal standards developed as a result of administrative cease and desist proceedings in subsequent actions against persons not involved with the administrative proceedings. The article focuses on this standard setting function, the impact of Section 205 on formulating standards, judicial review of agency actions based on standard setting, and potential problems with the application of standards. It is concluded that issues of enforcement delay and deterrence should be alleviated to some degree by Section 205. However, the effectiveness of adjudicative standards is based on the filing of a civil penalties suit by the FTC and the cease and desist order used to show that an unfair practice has occurred.

1162 Kuzow, Michael F. "FTC and the Generic Doctrine: A New Rx for Pharmaceutical Trademarks." *Tulsa Law Journal* 15 (1979): 327-347. Examines the legal and business ramifications of the order by an administrative law judge of the FTC to cancel the trademark of "REALEMON" and Formica on

347

the grounds that both trademarks had become generic in the minds of consumers. Given these actions by the FTC, the author outlines why these decisions have broad implications for the pharmaceutical industry and how the enforcement of substitution laws (laws which list brand name drugs and their therapeutically equivalent substitutes) offers a more desirable remedy to high priced pharmaceutical products without compromising trademarks.

1163 Laczniak, Gene R. and Anne Curley. "Public Participation in Rulemaking by the Federal Trade Commission: A Survey of Some Recent Experiences." *Journal of Consumer Affairs* 15 (Summer 1981): 32-45.

The authors use a telephone survey of forty-six funding recipients involved with the FTC's public participation program to evaluate its effectiveness. The program involves the distribution of monies to organizations or the public that facilitates their involvement in federal rulemaking under provisions of the FTC Improvement Act. Although the findings indicate that participants were "very positive" about their involvement in the program, criticisms levelled at the program are used to formulate the following recommendations by the authors: place the funding outside of the agency to alleviate perceptions of biased disbursements of funding, improve the dissemination of information about the program, and develop an evaluation mechanism to review past participation in the program for those requesting renewals of their grants.

1164 Lasky, Michael C. and Stuart Lee Friedel. "Word from Washington: New FTC Developments." *Public Relations Quarterly* 38 (Winter 1993-94): 29-31.

The authors discuss four issues under FTC enforcement authority that is of particular interest to public relations executives in helping to avoid possible violations of the law. These issues are: telemarketing activities, the Mail Order Rule, regulation of food claims, and the regulation of diet and fitness claims in advertisements.

1165 Lemke, William F. "The Federal Trade Commission's Use of Investigational Subpoenas." *Loyola University Law Journal* 1 (Winter 1970): 15-32.

Most information required by the FTC during an investigation is submitted voluntarily by the respondent. However, when a company refuses, the FTC has three options available to it: 1) authorization under Section 6(b) of the FTC Act to acquire special reports concerning the firm's business activities; 2) right of access to documentary evidence under provisions of Section 9; and 3) the power to issue a subpoena, also authorized under Section 9. This essay discusses the use of subpoenas in non-adjudicative, investigational proceedings when no complaint has been issued and the fact that subpoenas, unlike special reports, are not limited to corporations under investigation, but can be used to secure testimony and company records from firms not directly involved in litigation and of individuals who are in business as sole proprietors. The applicability of the Administrative Procedure Act and case law is used to conclude that subpoenas are an "effective and flexible tool" for obtaining documentary evidence.

1166 Lemke, William F. "Souped Up Affirmative Disclosure Orders of the Federal Trade Commission." *University of Michigan Journal of Law Reform* 4 (Winter 1970): 180-183.

The author argues that the FTC has overstepped its authority when it proposed that some cease and desist orders include a statement requiring respondents to acknowledge in all subsequent advertising that a cease and desist order is standing against them as a result of an FTC finding of false or misleading statements in previous advertisements. A critique of affirmative disclosure requirements is offered based on a review of the history and nature of cease and desist orders and the content of orders issued against Standard Oil of California and the Coca-Cola Corporation.

1167 Lewis, Wayne K. "Regulation of Attorney Debt Collectors: The Role of the FTC and the Bar." *The Hastings Law Journal* 35 (March 1984): 669-706.

Given the passage of the Fair Debt Collection Practices Act (FDCPA) and its authority to prohibit a broad range of debt collection practices, an increasing number of attorneys have become more involved in debt collection. This essay examines attorney debt collection activities and whether or not, as well as to what extent, they are governed by the FTC's authority to regulate of debt collection practices. The author concludes that, while the FTC likely does possess the power to regulate attorney debt collection practices, neither it nor the states are unable to ensure that consumers are protected against unfair practices. The authors recommend that the most practical and effective means of protecting the consumer is for bar associations to aggressively adopt standards of conduct and affirmative obligations in their code of ethics and to rigorously enforce these codes.

1168   Liebling, Jeffrey H. "Judicial Usurpation of the F.T.C.'s Authority: A Return to the Rule of Reason." *John Marshall Law Review* 30 (Fall 1996): 283-319.

The purpose of this study is to analyze the conflicting relationship that has recently arisen between Congressional intent to grant broad powers to the FTC and current attempts by the courts to curtail FTC actions. Among the underlying reasons for establishing the FTC, the author argues, is to establish an administrative organization endowed with economic and business expertise that facilitates determining what constitutes unfair methods of competition. However, as recent judicial decisions show, the courts are beginning to make factual determinations regarding unfair competition. An exploration of the legislative history of the FTC and subsequent interpretations of FTC authority by the courts is used to examine the problem. The author concludes that Congress should consider reiterating its original intent and specifically limiting the judiciary in areas governed by the FTC Act.

1169   Likoff, Bruce L. "The Federal Trade Commission's Remedial Power: Commission Efforts." *Annual Survey of American Law* 1973/74 (Summer 1974): 701-716.

Highlights criticisms of ineffectiveness leveled at the FTC's traditional use of cease and desist orders based on delays in obtaining them and the lack of remedial alternatives. The essay examines the validity and effectiveness of recent FTC efforts to overcome these problems as well as other statutory developments associated with the FTC's remedial powers.

1170   Lindahl, Martin L. "Federal Trade Commission Act as Amended in 1938." *Journal of Political Economy* 47 (August 1939): 497-525.

Examines the reasons for passage of the Wheeler-Lea Act and the possible impact it may have in shaping the enforcement activities of the FTC. Among the issues discussed is the extension of FTC jurisdiction over unfair and deceptive acts and practices, the meaning of new language in Section 5, the regulation of false advertising and its significance, and the strengthening of enforcement procedures through FTC orders. Although Wheeler-Lea does not address central concerns about the FTC's overall record of achievement, it reflects a renewed attention to trade regulation.

1171   Linder, B. J. and Allan H. Savage. "The Line of Business Program: The FTC's New Tool." *California Management Review* 21 (Summer 1979): 57-63.

The article examines the development of the FTC's Line of Business Program and explores why, after only three years, it has evolved into a source of legal controversy between the Commission and business. It is concluded that problems associated with defining and classifying the number and types of segments of a particular company and the financial burden of complying with gathering data, places the entire program in jeopardy.

1172   Lipinsky de Orlov, Lino S. Jr. "*Katherine Gibbs School v. FTC* (612 F 2d 658): Restricting the Federal Trade Commission's Trade Regulation Rulemaking Authority Under the Magnuson-Moss Act." *New York University Law Review* 56 (April 1981): 183-205.

The Katherine Gibbs School decision is important because it struck down several elements of the trade regulation rule affecting the school, and thus, represents the first case to challenge the validity of a trade regulation rule subsequent to changes to the Commission's rulemaking authority under provisions of the Magnuson-Moss Act. This study notes that, since the FTC has decided not to challenge this decision, the case represents "the outer boundaries" of regulatory authority of trade regulation rules and other remedies directed at a single industry. However, this ruling is subject to criticism on two levels. First, the court incorrectly interpreted Magnuson-Moss when it required the FTC to specifically define those unfair and deceptive acts that led to the promulgation of the trade regulation rule. Second, the court failed to accord the Commission sufficient rulemaking authority to invalidate the refund and job placement disclosure provisions of the trade regulation rule. It is concluded that the court should have used the substantial evidence standard to evaluate the FTC's factual determinations. Since it did not, future courts should not follow this decision.

1173   Maher, John A. "Rule of Law and FTC: Thesis and Antithesis? Some Proposals." *Dickinson Law Review* 86 (Spring 1982): 403-446.

Analyzes the issue of unfairness in light of the *FTC v. Sperry and Hutchinson Co.* decision and attempts by the FTC Commissioners to renounce as a non-exclusive substantive rule of "S & H standards" established by the courts to future actions of antitrust enforcement by the agency. The author argues that this interpretation of the Sperry case by Commission personnel and articulated in a letter sent to the Senate Committee on Commerce borders not only on FTC arrogance, but is a political action intended to influence Congress. The essay concludes with a proposal to amend the FTC Act that reaffirms Commission jurisdiction over all antitrust enforcement matters, but restricts the application of the unfairness doctrine to situations where merchants coerce or materially mislead the consumer and to patterns of conduct "having effects normally associated with coercion and constructive fraud."

1174   Mansfield, Cathy Lessor. "The Federal Trade Commission Holder Rule and Its Applicability to Student Loans: Reallocating the Risk of Propriety School Failure." *Wake Forest Law Review* 26 (1991): 635-667.

In many cases when students are seeking loans under the Higher Education Act of 1965 to help pay for their education, the college or university chooses one or two lenders that it conducts business with and processes the loans for student rather than having the student go directly to the lender, such as a bank, for funding. However, this process can be abused by institutions whose sales representatives convince economically deprived individuals to apply. Often, the author argues, these individuals are asked to sign loan documents without knowing their rights as consumers should they default on the loan and the seller (in this case the school) does not fulfill its obligations to provide an education. Ultimately, if an individual does default on a loan, the federal government must cover uncollectible student loan obligations. The author argues that abuses by schools falls within the FTC's jurisdiction because student loans are purchase money loans possessing a finance charge within the meaning of the FTC's Rule on Preservation of Consumer's Claims and Defenses and the "FTC Holder Rule."

1175   Marble, Roland D. "Federal Regulation of Life Insurance by the Federal Trade Commission." *Federation of Insurance Counsel Quarterly* 30 (Summer 1980): 319-334.

The purpose of this essay is to examine FTC efforts to regulate the life insurance industry. The investigation, begun in December of 1976, focuses on four issues: 1) does the life insurance industry provide adequate cost information to life insurance purchasers; 2) what type of information is most likely to be useful for consumers; 3) what would be the impact on insurance companies and consumers if cost information was disseminated; and 4) what actions should the FTC take to ensure that any problems are remedied in a timely manner. The author argues that the investigation is misguided and FTC actions are based on "unsound assumptions" and "an incorrect premise" regarding the nature of the life insurance industry and the charges levelled against the industry pose a serious public relations crisis. The essay concludes by outlining various congressional actions that are in response to attempts by the FTC to create industry-wide rules and regulations and intended to limit the Commissions regulatory authority.

1176 Marinelli, Arthur J., Jr. "Federal Trade Commission's Authority to Determine Unfair Practices and Engage in Substantive Rulemaking." *Ohio Northern University Law Review* 2 (1974): 289-298.

This article examines the ways in which recent criticism directly at the FTC's consumer protection efforts has motivated the agency to broaden its definition of "unfair methods of competition beyond the letter or spirit of antitrust statutes" and the authority of the FTC in substantive rulemaking proceedings.

1177 McChesney, Fred S. "Regulating without Evidence: The FTC's "Cooling Off" Rule." *Journal of Contemporary Studies* 7 (Winter 1984): 57-70.

Underlying the larger debate about trade regulation rules has been a discussion concerning the level of evidence needed to justify FTC regulation of the marketplace. This study notes that Commission appointees under President Ronald Reagan have insisted that the burden of proof be placed on proponents of a new rule and not the respondents. To support the position that quantitative evidence must form the basis to promulgate a rule before the government intervenes, the author examines systematic evidence gathered ten years after the "Cooling-Off Rule" was created that regulates direct, door-to-door selling. The rule was a response to consumer "horror stories" rather than factual evidence. However, evidentiary data from the recent study show that the rule is unwarranted, harms the consumer, and overstates problems that have already been addressed in the industry.

1178 Miller, Randall G. "*National Petroleum Refiners Association v. Federal Trade Commission* (340 F Supp 1343): Authority of FTC to Promulgate Trade Regulation Rules." *South Dakota Law Review* 18 (Winter 1973): 243-250.

In the National Petroleum Refiners Association case, the U.S. District Court of the District of Columbia ruled that the FTC did not possess the authority to issue trade regulation rules that had the effect of substantive law because the FTC Act only grants the Commission rulemaking power concerning the internal rules of organization, practice, and procedure. This note examines the underlying reasoning of the court's decision, criticism of the ruling, and its implications for future enforcement actions. It is concluded that enforcement must be pursued solely on a case-by-case basis and must rely on cease and desist orders until Congress deems otherwise through new legislation.

1179   Millon, David. "International Trade: FTC Service of Subpoena Abroad–FTC Improvements Act of 1980, Pub. L. No. 96-252, 13, 94 Stat. 374, 380 (1980)." *Harvard International Law Journal* 22 (Spring 1981): 458-464.

Section 13 of the FTC Improvements Act of 1980 gives the FTC permission to issue investigatory subpoena abroad under provisions of the Federal Rules of Civil Procedures to gather evidence from overseas firms. This comment examines the implications of this amendment for servicing a subpoena, including the fact that a subpoena "carries with it a direct threat of sanctions for noncompliance." The remainder of the essay explores how international law limits the power of the amendment and how growing resistance to U.S. judicial and administrative proceedings has led to laws in a number of nations prohibiting its citizens from producing documents required by the subpoena. It is concluded that sensitivity to foreign sovereignty is the only way to ensure cooperation.

1180   "Moog-Niehoff Decision–The FTC and Enforcement for Enforcement's Sake." *Northwestern University Law Review* 53 (September-October 1958): 510-520.

Although the Supreme Court, in its decision regarding the *Moog Indus. Inc. v. FTC* and *FTC v. C. E. Niehoff & Co.* cases, resolved the conflicting ruling of the Seventh and Eighth Circuit courts as to the power of the courts to postpone cease and desist orders issued by the FTC under the Robinson-Patman Act, the Supreme Court failed to resolve situations in which the FTC makes its cease and desist order immediately effective for one set of companies but allows competitors to continue discriminatory practices. Ironically, this can result in restrained companies under the original cease and desist order to go out of business, thereby undermining competition. This note examines the procedural and substantive impact of this decision on antitrust policy. Three solutions to this problem are offered: multi-party proceedings, increased use of trade practice conferences, and delay of an order's effectiveness.

1181   Moore, Charles R. "Regulation of Deceptive Practices by the Federal Trade Commission." *Food Drug Cosmetic Law Journal* 16 (February 1961): 102-115.

As Assistant Director on Deceptive Practices, Bureau of Investigation of the FTC, the author reviews in historical context the basic purpose of laws administered by the agency, remedies available to the Commission in preventing unfair methods of competition and deception of consumers, and recent forms of deceptive behavior. Also outlined is the FTC's relationship to other agencies and the development of methods for testing products to determine the validity of advertising claims.

1182 Morrison, James J. "Judicial Review of Facts Found by the Federal Trade Commission." *Tulane Law Review* 4 (June 1930): 638-646.

This legal comment examines the judicial review of the FTC as it specifically relates to the extent of power delegated to the agency by Congress. Three early court cases are reviewed that have placed limits on the authority of the FTC. It is concluded that these decisions illustrate a tendency by the courts "to supersede the findings of fact and inferences to be drawn therefrom by the Commission." The author argues that these actions by the courts directly contradict the intent and purpose of the FTC and Clayton Acts with regards to the finding of facts supported by testimony to be conclusive.

1183 Mueller, Charles E. "Access to Corporate Papers Under the FTC Act." *University of Kansas Law Review* 11 (October 1962): 77-105.

Three investigative powers are granted to the FTC under Section 9 of the FTC Act: 1) authority to require reports from companies; 2) power to issue subpoenas; and 3) power to send agency attorney-investigators to corporations under investigation with the intent of gathering documents in support of an investigation. Although the process of accessing corporate papers during an investigation has been "in daily use" since the agency's inception, it has rarely been challenged in court. The purpose of this article is to examine the history of this authority and to review those cases in which access power has been challenged in court.

1184 Muris, Timothy J. "Regulatory Policymaking at the Federal Trade Commission: The Extent of Congressional Control." *Journal of Political Economy* 94 (August 1986): 884-889.

The author refutes a study conducted by Weingast and Moran that uses the FTC as a model for showing that Congress exerts substantial control over the decisions of federal agency decisions. While acknowledging that Congress can shape the boundaries within which the FTC can exert its authority, Congress has little power to affect specific projects. It is also argued that Weingast and Moran used incomplete information to support their conclusion and they failed to consider the liberal ideological and career goal dimensions of the agency's staff despite a movement towards conservatism in Congress during the late 1970s.

1185 Muris, Timothy J. "Rules Without Reason: The Case of the FTC." *Regulation* 6 (September/October 1982): 20-26.
The author criticizes the FTC's record of achievement since the Magnuson-Moss Act was passed in using trade regulation rules to regulate unfair practices and protect the consumer from deception by focusing on two interrelated issues. First, the agency has failed to obtain reliable evidence in deciding whether to regulate. Issues related to the use of internal expertise, anecdotal evidence, expert testimony, or systematic projectable evidence is examined to support this statement. Second, FTC rulemaking is not governed by "a clear substantive theory" to explain how the rule will alleviate deception rather than relying on market forces. In addition, explicit statements concerning the way in which a challenged practice violates provisions of the FTC Act are absent from the proceeding.

1186 Offen, Neil H. "How FTC Proposed Rules Affect Trade Associations and Their Members." *Antitrust Bulletin* 22 (Summer 1977): 317-354.
Reviews proposed laws before Congress to grant specific lawmaking power to the FTC after its authority was challenged in the *National Petroleum Refiners Association v. FTC* case. Among the issues addressed are current procedures in the FTC Procedures and Rules of Practice that apply to Magnuson-Moss rulemaking, responses by trade association lawyers to rulemaking procedures, remedial provisions stemming from consumer protection initiatives, and self regulation efforts within an industry.

1187 O'Hara, Joseph P. "The Federal Trade Commission's Power over Trademarks." *Trademark Reporter* 38 (June 1948): 613-621.
In a paper read before the 17th Annual Meeting of the United States Trade-Mark Association, the author outlines the conditions under which the FTC may investigate possible violations of trademark laws, discusses the likely procedures that the agency will force a company under investigation to follow, and concludes by describing the O'Hara bill introduced by the author into Congress that is intended to remedy opportunities of abuse during investigations by the FTC.

1188   Orlans, Melvin H. "Phase I of the FTC's Food Advertising Rule: Its Scope and Impact." *Food Drug Cosmetic Law Journal* 36 (May 1981): 220-228.

This essay discusses Phase I of the FTC's food advertising rulemaking proceedings, which encompasses natural, organic, and health food claims, energy and weight control claims, and fat, fatty acid, and cholesterol claims in food advertising. The essay begins by outlining the scope of the rule then shifts into analyzing substantive provisions of the Rule, including energy claims, weight control claims, "natural food" claims, content claims, and health claims. Because some provisions have not been completed, the essay is not meant to be a definitive interpretation of the Rule.

1189   Oxendale, Candace Lance. "The FTC and Deceptive Trade Practices: A Reasonable Standard?" *Emory Law Journal* 35 (Summer 1986): 683-727.

The term "deception" in Section 5 of the FTC Act has never been statutorily defined and Congress declined to do so when formulating the Act in 1914. In late 1983, the FTC issued a controversial policy statement that attempted to define what constitutes deception. The controversy is primarily the result of conflict within the Commission, which only passed by a three to two margin among the commissioners, and is grounded in "a fundamental philosophical difference" of opinion concerning how best to protect the consumer. By examining the development of the statement, relevant cases involving what constitutes a deceptive act, and its possible ramifications for the future, it is concluded that the policy statement does offer a measure of standards for deception violations.

1190   Paynter, Donald G. "Federal Trade Commission–Trade Rule on Games of Chance in the Food Retailing and Gasoline Industries–16 C.F.R. 419.1 (1969)." *Ohio State Law Journal* 31 (Summer 1970): 610-617.

The purpose of this trade regulation rule is to prevent the use of deceptive or unfair practices by the food retailing and gasoline retail industries in their promotions of games of chance under provisions of Section 5 of the FTC Act. This commentary places the promulgation of this rule in historical context by examining the *FTC v. R.F. Keppel and Bros., Inc.* case in which it was determined that inducements to purchase candy with the opportunity to redeem the price of the candy or receive other prizes amounted to a lottery. When gasoline and food retailers began games of chance as a non-price competitive device in 1964, dealers began complaining that the games were susceptible to cheating and the FTC widened its investigation based on additional statements that the games were unfair and deception trade practices. The commentary concludes that the rule will lead to one of three outcomes: the rule will create the illusion of honesty but the games will continue to adversely affect the consumer, the regulation may prove to eliminate unfair practices, or the rule will be viewed "to be so obnoxious" that retailers will simply end the games. The third statement is considered most likely to occur with no benefit to the consumer.

1191   Pelgro, Michael J. "Authority of the Federal Trade Commission to Order Corrective Advertising." *Boston College Law Review* 19 (July 1978): 899-938.

This article looks at the FTC's authority to issue orders of corrective advertising to remedy cases in which the advertisement found to be false has a sustained impact on the consumer beyond the point at which the respondent complies with the cease and desist order. Using the case of *Warner-Lambert v. FTC*, the historical basis for FTC authority in issuing orders of corrective advertising is reviewed. The next section considers whether corrective advertising falls within the legal parameters of affirmative disclosure of "unfavorable product characteristics." The third section supports the contention that corrective advertising is an appropriate extension of affirmative disclosure power. The final section uses the *Warner-Lambert* decision to present guidelines concerning under what circumstances corrective advertising may be used in the future.

1192   "Permissible Scope of Cease and Desist Orders: Legislation and Adjudication by the FTC." *University of Chicago Law Review* 29 (1962): 706-727.

Traces the development of the legal parameters defining the permissible scope of FTC cease and desist orders and analyzes problems related to the breadth of the orders "from the standpoint of legislative and judicial function which they perform." This analysis is performed to help in understanding the nature and effect of the orders and what factors should be considered to determine their proper scope. Orders issued by the National Labor Relations Board in cases of unfair labor practices are used for comparative purposes.

1193   Perry, Alan R. "Jurisdiction of the Federal Trade Commission–Multiple Basing Point System–Unfair Method of Competition–Price Discrimination." *Southern California Law Review* 22 (February 1949): 164-175.

Examines in detail the *FTC v. Cement Institute* decision in which the Supreme Court overturned a Court of Appeals ruling by stating that a "multiple-basing point system" is inherently a practice of unfair competition and price discrimination. Central to this ruling was that, in order to maximize the benefits of participating in the point system, internal regulation by a group of companies in the form of boycotts, dismissal of uncooperative employees, organized opposition to building new manufacturing plants by companies outside of the basing point consortium, and distribution of phantom freight charges among participants, all contributed to unfair competition within the cement industry. The article outlines possible economic effects of the basing point system and its abolition.

1194   Powell, Dennis R. "Scope of Current Questionnaire Investigations by the Federal Trade Commission." *Notre Dame Lawyer* 37 (March 1962): 379-389.

The author examines the recent practice of the FTC to disseminate questionnaires to corporate officers and legal counsels with the intent of gathering information about possible industry-wide violations of the Robinson-Patman Act and to obtain information concerning possible mergers and acquisitions. The authority to seek industry-wide information through questionnaires under Section 6 of the FTC Act is examined in detail along with an analysis of possible legal issues that may arise as a result of this method of investigation. Using extensive quotes from cases that involved gathering information from questionnaires, the author concludes that the results of the method are promising, most notably with regards to addressing the problem of personnel shortages at the FTC.

1195   "Power of the Federal Trade Commission to Order a Corporation to Divest Itself of Physical Property and Assets Obtained through Unlawful Intercorporate Shareholdings." *University of Pennsylvania Law Review* 75 (March 1927): 463-468.

Comment that analyzes three recent cases involving the FTC (*FTC v. Western Meat Co.*, *FTC v. Thatcher Mfg. Co.*, and *FTC v. Swift and Co.*) in light of provisions in the Clayton Act granting authority for the Commission to order companies to desist from intercorporate shareholding and require the companies involved to retransfer property gained from the acquisition of the shares. However, the Supreme Court ruled in favor of the FTC in only one case, leading the author of this note to conclude that the courts are not basing their decisions on Congressional intent, but rather on current economic principles.

1196 "Power of the Federal Trade Commission to Order Divestiture of Physical Property." *Columbia Law Review* 26 (May 1926): 594-600.

The Congressional intent underlying Section 7 of the Clayton Act is to ensure that certain effects brought forth by a company's acquisition of a competitor's stock, such as restraint of trade, development of monopolies, and lessening competition, are regulated by the FTC. This comment examines the issue of FTC authority to divest property under Section 7 of the Clayton Act and Section 5 of the FTC Act, noting that special consideration must be given to the fact that the FTC is an administrative agency. It is concluded that, while it is doubtful the FTC has authority of divestiture under Section 7 of the Clayton Act, the FTC does have the power to order a company to divest stock acquired from a competitor if the result is lessening of competition under Section 5 of the FTC Act.

1197 Preston, Ivan L. "Extrinsic Evidence in Federal Trade Commission Deceptiveness Cases." *Columbia Business Law Review* 1987 (1987): 633-694.

This study examines the types of extrinsic evidence used by the FTC when determining if an advertising message disseminated to consumers falsely depicts a product. Using previous research on the subject, the author notes that the Commission has no written guidelines concerning the application of extrinsic evidence, creating ambiguity among respondents regarding how best to gather evidence. This study builds on this fact by examining the nature of extrinsic evidence and its treatment by the FTC in decisions and opinions spanning the past twenty years. This is followed by a study of the two major forms of extrinsic evidence described in sections two and three: consumer research in the form of surveys or open-ended and forced choice questions, and the use of expert testimony. Section four and five examine indirectly useful evidence and evidence which is rejected because it is irrelevant or is grounded in poor methodology. Section six briefly compares and contrasts the handling of extrinsic evidence between Lanham Act and FTC cases. The author concludes by reviewing acceptable and unacceptable uses of extrinsic evidence with the purpose of creating guidelines for the future.

1198 "Private Enforcement and Rulemaking Under the Federal Trade Commission Act: Expansion of FTC Responsibility." *Northwestern University Law Review* 69 (July-August 1974): 462-488.

This article examines two recent cases: *National Petroleum Refiners Association v. FTC*, in which it was ruled that the FTC had the power to make substantive rules regulating unfair or deceptive business practices, and *Holloway v. Bristol-Myers Corp.*, in which the court "refused to imply a private right of action from Section 5 of the FTC Act." The rulings appear contradictory because, on the one hand, the FTC is granted broad authority to regulate industries, while at the same time, denying consumer lawsuits against a company under provisions of the FTC Act. However, by exploring issues associated with private remedies for consumers under the FTC Act, the legislative history of the FTC Act, and the legal basis of the FTC's rulemaking authority, it is concluded that the contradictory nature of the rulings "reflects that balanced nature of the FTC Act."

1199 "Proposed Legislation Amending the Federal Trade Commission Act." *Georgetown Law Journal* 25 (May 1937): 976-985.

Proposed legislation to amend the FTC Act encompasses three issues: 1) make unfair or deceptive acts and practices in commerce unlawful, authorize the Commission to seek enforcement in the Circuit Court of Appeals of orders that have been disobeyed by respondents, and make all cease and desist orders final after sixty days unless the respondent seeks court review prior to end of sixty days; 2) expand the meaning of corporation to include trusts and to expand the meaning of documentary evidence to include all corporate financial records; and 3) that a person must claim privilege against self-incrimination prior to testifying or providing evidence. This article reviews these three issues in detail and concludes that the amendments will benefit consumers.

1200 "Proposed FTC Regulation of Consumer Financing." *Georgetown Law Journal* 60 (June 1972): 1563-1579.

Legal comment that examines the development, scope, weaknesses, and validity of the proposed trade regulation rule, "Preservation of Buyer's Claims and Defenses in Consumer Installment Sales." The author argues that, although the proposed rule does not apply to interlocking sales and contains "too much legal jargon" to be understood by most consumers with regard to the preservation of defenses, it is concluded that the proposed rule helps alleviate inconsistent regulation in the states and courts and provides a higher degree of responsibility among both merchants and financiers.

1201 Quinn, James P. "The Responsibilities of the FTC Under Public Law 15." *Insurance Law Journal* 1956 (December 1956): 778-800.

The author is critical of FTC attempts to regulate the insurance industry through trade regulation conference compliance procedures despite the provisions of

Public Law 15, which declares the insurance industry to be governed primarily by the regulations of individual states and Section 2 of the FTC Act which excludes Commission authority in the insurance industry because the insurance industry does not constitute interstate commerce.

1202   Rabkin, Jeremy. "Rulemaking, Bias, and the Dues of Due Process at the FTC." *Regulation* 3 (January/February 1979): 43-47.

The author examines the decision in *National Advertisers v. FTC*, in which the court was ruled that the FTC Chairman should have declined to participate in the agency's procedures to formulate proposed regulations against television advertising directed at children, to discuss "the futility of our efforts to reconcile broad regulatory authority with popular government" by means of judicial review.

1203   Ragan, William J. "Constitutional Law–Federal Trade Commission Asserts Jurisdiction over Insurance Advertising in Interstate Commerce." *Notre Dame Lawyer* 32 (March 1957): 319-324.

Discusses the arguments both for and against the complaint issued by the FTC alleging that an insurance company practiced false and misleading advertising in brochures sent across state lines. This activity represented interstate commerce, thereby falling within the jurisdiction of the FTC. Complicating matters, the complaint was issued under newly promulgated provisions of the McCarran-Ferguson Act and it preempted state laws. Although several Supreme Court decisions have been issued concerning Congressional intent, it remains unclear whether the FTC, through an extension of Congressional intent, should issue uniform regulation of interstate commerce even if state laws are preempted, or if FTC regulations should be issued only in conjunction with state regulation that is more closely tied to the insurance industry. It is concluded that the FTC must resist regulating interstate aspects of insurance transactions because it undermines Congressional intent and likely undermines, rather than compliments, state regulations.

1204   "Recent Trends in Interpretation of the Federal Trade Commission Act." *Michigan Law Review* 32 (June 1934): 1142-1154.

The courts have traditionally been reluctant to grant broad powers to administrative agencies. With regards to the FTC, this position has been supported by perceptions that the agency is inefficient due to poorly written legislation and its own personnel. However, this note argues that recent decisions by the courts indicate that the judiciary is viewing enforcement behavior of the FTC as more efficient. In addition, with the exception of investigatory powers under Section 6, defects in the FTC Act are "not particularly important." Given this, the Commission should be granted a broader scope of authority by the judiciary as intended by Congress.

1205 "A Revised Federal Trade Commission Act–The Wheeler-Lea Amendment." *University of Pennsylvania Law Review* 86 (May 1938): 757-765.

The Wheeler-Lea Act represents the first major revision of the FTC's authority since its inception and has shifted the agency's regulatory enforcement from the curtailment of monopolistic practices to one charged with arbitration of disputes between business and the protection of consumers from the effects of unfair business practices. This article examines how the amendments change the jurisdictional powers of the agency, remove procedural deficiencies, and regulate false and misleading advertising. Special attention is paid to legislative intent and possible effects on future regulatory endeavors.

1206 Rodell, F. "Regulation of Securities by the Federal Trade Commission." *Yale Law Journal* 43 (December 1933): 272-280.

This essay explores the FTC's authority to regulate, through the issuance of cease and desist orders, the sale of improperly registered securities within the legal framework of the Federal Securities Act. The author studies the dynamics of enforcement of security sales and the barriers that hinder the FTC's ability to enforce the Federal Securities Act. It is concluded that the courts, Congress, and the FTC must work together to ensure that the central purpose of the Federal Securities Act (to protect consumers from losing money in unscrupulous financed business enterprises) is realized to the fullest degree possible.

1207 Ronald, James H. "The Jurisdiction of the Federal Trade Commission over Paid Testimonial Advertising." *George Washington Law Review* 1 (January 1933): 249-258.

The purpose of this note is to examine the judicial review of a cease and desist order issued by the FTC against the Northam Warren Corporation in which it was determined that well-known women from "the social and theatrical world" were paid to give testimonials about the quality of "Cutex" brand manicure preparations in advertisements. The FTC argued that withholding the fact that the company paid for testimonials was the equivalent of false representation. The courts ruled against the FTC because such action did not lead to a monopoly or restraint of trade nor did paid testimonials mislead the public since their statements were admittedly truthful. Based on an analysis of Section 5 of the FTC Act, the author argues that the courts were correct in their ruling and that the FTC had overstepped its jurisdictional boundaries.

1208   Rosengarten, Ronald Marshall. "Scope of Federal Trade Commission Rulemaking: *Katherine Gibbs School v. FTC.*" (612 F 2d 658)." *New England Law Review* 16 (1980-81): 917-977.

The Katherine Gibbs School case was the first to challenge the FTC's authority to promulgate substantive trade regulation rules under provisions of the Magnuson-Moss Warranty-FTC Improvement Act and, as such, was the first opportunity for the courts to interpret the Commission's rulemaking authority under the Act. After reviewing FTC rulemaking authority prior to Magnuson-Moss and the provisions of the Act, an examination is made of the court's opinion that the FTC's trade regulation rule on vocational schools was inadequate in some areas, including issues raised by petitioners but not considered by the court. The author concludes that, because the Second Circuit court did not clearly articulate why certain provisions of the rule were substantially flawed, it will be difficult for the Commission to measure how newer rules will survive judicial scrutiny.

1209   Rushefsky, Norman and Herbert I. Cantor. "FTC Section 5 Powers and the Pfizer-Cyanamid Imbroglio: Where Do We Go from Here, or You Ain't Seen Nothing Yet." *Journal of the Patent Office Society* 51 (July 1969): 414-445.

This article describes the case of *Charles Pfizer and Co. v FTC*. The case involved the development of the antibiotic drug tetracycline through similar processes employed by both the Charles Pfizer Company and American Cyanamid Corporation. At issue was a claim of interference between the companies during their attempt to patent the product. During the proceeding, the FTC charged in a complaint against Pfizer that it "made false, misleading, and incorrect statements" and that both Pfizer and Cyanamid withheld information during the patent application process. Under the authority of Section 5 of the FTC Act the Commission issued a cease and desist order directing both companies to license the tetracycline product "to any domestic applicant." The order was vacated by the Sixth Circuit Court on the grounds that Chairman Paul Rand Dixon should have excused himself from the proceeding and that the patent examiner should have been allowed to testify. However, this case was the first in which the FTC used compulsory licensing of patents as a remedy for Section 5 violations. The article analyzes in detail the implication of this new regulatory approach for the future.

1210   Schwartz, Teresa M. "Regulating Unfair Practices Under the FTC Act: The Need for a Legal Standard of Unfairness." *Akron Law Review* 11 (Summer 1977): 1-28.

The vaguely worded 1975 amendments to the FTC Act has allowed the Commission to broadly interpret the statutory term "unfair...acts and practices." One of the manifestations of this broad interpretation of regulatory authority is the issuance of trade regulation rules rather relying solely on cases-by-case enforcement. The author examines the provisions of these rules to illustrate the point that, while the vaguely worded statute does provide the agency with the flexibility to explore innovative ways to protect the consumer from unlawful acts and practices, it also leaves the Commission vulnerable to judicial reversals and more restrictive legislation in the future. The author concludes that a single standard of the theory of unfairness should be formulated by the Commission based primarily on substantial harm determined from an economic and social analysis of the marketplace.

1211   Seidman, Albert G. "The Commission's Power to Conduct Field Investigations." *Antitrust Law Journal* 14 (1959): 12-17.

This article begins by outlining the "arsenal of weapons" available to the FTC in its exercise of quasi-judicial functions intended to regulate unfair or deceptive practices and prevent monopolies. This is followed by an examination of the Commission's power to require corporations to furnish information upon FTC request during an investigation, including the legal basis for obtaining corporate documents, the authority to conduct investigational hearings and issue subpoenas, and the authority to visit corporations with the intent of gathering information.

1212   Seligson, Harold P. "Trade Regulation: The Extent of the Jurisdiction of the Federal Trade Commission Over Unfair Methods of Competition." *American Bar Association Journal* 9 (1923): 698-701.

Brief article examining the legislative intent of the FTC Act and the agency's enforcement authority over unfair business practices. By reviewing specific court cases and the historical analysis of other scholars, the author argues that the FTC's jurisdiction extends beyond the regulation of unfair competition for the purpose of preventing monopolies or undue restraint of trade, but includes practices that are injurious to competitors and consumers.

1213   Seyffer, Richard R. "Due Process in FTC Rulemaking." *Arizona State Law Journal* 1979 (1979): 543-562.

During the preliminary proceedings of the FTC's attempt to pass an administrative rule intended to control the content of television advertising directed at children, federal district judge Gerhard Gesell ruled that Chairman Michael Pertschuk was biased towards the case based on public statements Pertschuk had made alleging that television advertisers "manipulate children's attitudes." This comment argues that this decision challenges current Supreme Court doctrine and explores whether constitutional due process can provide the basis for dismissal of an FTC commissioner during a rulemaking proceeding under provisions of the Magnuson-Moss Federal Trade Commission Improvement Act.

1214   Shanklin, William L. and Herbert G. King. "Evaluating the FTC Cooling Off Rule." *Journal of Consumer Affairs* 11 (Winter 1977): 101-106.

Analyzes the application of the FTC's Cooling-Off Rule to a door-to-door sales company to show that the rule does not lead to customer cancellations in direct sales transactions. The rule's purpose is to curb abuses in door-to-door sales transactions by requiring that consumers are informed of their right to cancel and that the seller must provide a written receipt or contract concerning any sale over twenty-five dollars. Each of these rights are examined in detail. The article concludes that the rule is a model regulation that enables a purchaser to be better informed of their rights as a consumer.

1215   Shipley, David E. "Generic Trademarks, the FTC, and the Lanham Act: Covering the Market with Formica." *William and Mary Law Review* 20 (Fall 1978): 1-32.

Although there exists several avenues for declaring a trademark to be generic, this article focuses on the FTC's authority under Section 14 of the Lanham Act to petition for cancellation of a trademark on the grounds that the term has become a common descriptive word. The case of *FTC v. Formica Corp.* is examined in detail to show that the FTC's policy "is highly inappropriate and...could have damaging effects on consumers and industry." By analyzing the causes, evidence, and burden of proof associated with determining if a trademark has become generic, the author argues that the FTC should limit its actions under provisions of Section 5 of the FTC Act to only those cases in which it can be demonstrated that consumer deception or harm to the marketplace if the trademark remains registered will occur. Market forces should provide an adequate measure concerning the genericness of a trademark.

1216   Silvestri, Stephen M. "Trade Regulation: The Federal Trade Commission Has the Authority to Order Corrective Advertising to Dispel the Effects of Past Deception. *Warner-Lambert Co. v. FTC*, F.2d 749 (D.C. Cir. 1977), cert. denied, 435 U.S. 950 (1978)." *Catholic University Law Review* 27 (Summer 1978): 803-817.

Examines the implications underlying the expansion of power granted the FTC in the Warner-Lambert case that grants the agency the authority to compel a company to disseminate corrective advertising so that misimpressions caused by past advertisements can be dispelled. Although a corrective advertising order helps alleviate the problem of excessive delay associated with other remedies, the author concludes that the FTC must limit the scope of corrective advertising to only instances of eliminating false impressions among consumers.

1217   Skrapits, Frank M. "Jurisdiction of the Federal Trade Commission over the Accident and Health Insurance Industry." *Georgetown Law Journal* 45 (Fall 1956): 85-99.

This study examines the history of court decisions concerning government regulation of the insurance industry and the precedent set in the 1944 case of *United States v. South-Eastern Underwriters Association*. The study's findings indicate that, while states are regulating insurance companies within the expressed provisions of the McCarran-Ferguson Act and several companies investigated by the FTC have accepted jurisdiction in the form of taking consent orders, this does not necessarily mean that admission of jurisdiction in a consent order represents FTC authority to regulate insurance companies nor does it imply the state regulation is effective. It is concluded that despite these issues, states are prohibited from regulating interstate commerce such as mail order insurance schemes, therefore, uniform regulation of the insurance industry must rest with the FTC.

1218   Stolle, Dennis P. "The FTC's Reliance on Extrinsic Evidence in Cases of Deceptive Advertising: A Proposal for Interpretive Rulemaking. *Kraft, Inc. v. FTC*, 970 F. 2nd 311 (7th Cir. 1992), cert. denied, 113 S. Ct. 1254." *University of Nebraska Law Review* 74 (1995): 352-373.

The Kraft case reaffirmed the FTC's authority to regulate commercial speech based on the agency's own expertise rather than extrinsic evidence. This note studies the court's decision to uphold the Commission's authority to determine when commercial speech is deceptive based on procedural history, but also examines the court's determination that the agency must reduce uncertainty regarding its intentions in the future by adopting a consistent position on extrinsic evidence. The author outlines a theoretical proposal for an interpretive rule that restrains agency discretion and defines under what circumstances the FTC relies on extrinsic evidence. The outcome of such a rule would be increased fairness, a higher standard of substantive quality, and greater efficiency.

1219   Stradley, Leighton P. "Constitutionality of Compulsory Statistical Reports to the Federal Trade Commission: How Far can Federal Trade Commission Control Compel Private Companies to Submit Reports to the Commission." *University of Pennsylvania Law Review* 76 (November 1927): 19-28.

This article attempts to answer the following question: How can the FTC, as an administrative agency, force a company to produce reports and disseminate statistics that fall within the parameters of private correspondence and trade secrets? Using previous scholarship and case law, the author reiterates court decisions that define FTC power to gather corporate information under Section 6 of the FTC Act as applying only to interstate commerce and to plenary authority where Congress exercises visitation powers over corporations. However, it is also pointed out that the FTC must adhere strictly to Section 6 guidelines, an issue emphasized by the courts on several occasions that are described in the article.

1220   "Substantive Rulemaking and the FTC." *Fordham Law Review* 42(October 1973): 178-196.

Examines the legal debate concerning the FTC's decision in 1964 to amend its General Procedures and Rules of Practice to permit the promulgation of trade regulation rules. The essay begins by outlining the basis of the agency's claim that it possesses the authority to issue substantive rules, focusing in particular on Section 6(g) of the FTC Act. Section three explores the legal controversy of rulemaking versus adjudication leading up to the *National Petroleum Refiners Association v. FTC* ruling. Section four places the debate within historical context by exploring the legislative history of the FTC Act. This is followed by a description of cases that have, over time, expanded the FTC's rulemaking authority. It is concluded that substantive rulemaking has the potential to benefit the public so long as the FTC does not overreach its authority in the area.

1221   "Substantive Rule-Making in the Federal Trade Commission: The Validity of Trade Regulation Rules." *Iowa Law Review* 59 (February 1974): 629-639.

The *National Petroleum Refiners Association v. FTC* case is important because, for the first time, the courts affirmed the position that the FTC possesses the authority to make rules and regulations with the force and effect of law in order to carry out the agency's statutory purpose to regulate against unfair acts and practices in commerce. A legal debate has raged since the implementation of trade regulation rules by the FTC. This article focuses on the issue of whether substantive rulemaking is legislative in nature or merely interpretive of the law. The FTC states that trade regulation rules are substantive rather than either legislative or interpretive. However, the author argues that the FTC has overstepped its authority because the trade regulation rules preclude the respondents from litigating the facts associated with the rule, thereby undermining the respondents rights to an adjudicative hearing. Furthermore, the author notes that the National Petroleum ruling was reached based on policy considerations and "judicial decisions of questionable applicability," leading to a broad interpretation of powers that require Congressional clarification.

1222   Tifford, John M. "Federal Trade Commission Trade Regulation Rule on Franchises and Business Opportunity Ventures." *Business Lawyer* 36 (April 1981): 1051-1059.

Describes the purpose and intent of the FTC's trade regulation rule governing the presale disclosure requirements and business opportunity ventures of franchises. Among the issues discussed are the underlying reasons why the FTC felt compelled to issue the rule, the definition of a franchise, the types of disclosures required, what constitutes unfair acts and practices under Section 5 of the FTC Act as applied to franchises and the enforcement options available to the agency, and the relationship of the rule with state disclosure laws.

1223   Tollefson, A. M. "Judicial Review of the Decisions of the Federal Trade Commission." *Wisconsin Law Review* 4 (October 1927): 257-302.

After describing the origin and purpose of the FTC and its procedures for enforcement of the Sherman Antitrust Act and the Clayton Act, the author examines judicial review of the FTC in four areas: 1) the constitutionality of the statutes establishing the FTC and their construction with regards to defining the scope of its powers; 2) questions involving the jurisdiction of the FTC with regards to enforcement in the public's interest, that an order does not become invalid after an unfair practice has been discontinued, and concerning the right to divest property and stock in cases of unlawful acquisition during merger proceedings; 3) general court decisions involving questions of law associated with combination sales, price maintenance, and the sufficiency of the complaint; 4) the finding of fact by the FTC with regards to testimony, the nature of admissible evidence, and the weight and credibility of the evidence. The essay concludes by comparing the finality of findings of the FTC and the Interstate Commerce Commission.

1224   Turley, J. Wayne. "Federal Trade Commission Improvement Act Section 5(m)(1)(B): Minimum Alterations to Preserve Constitutionality." *Arizona State Law Journal* 1981 (1981): 1029-1048.
The author states that the ambiguous language contained in Section 5(m)(1)(B) of the Federal Trade Commission Improvement Act gives the agency enforcement powers that are unconstitutional. Although the FTC has so far been lenient in applying this Section during the Commission's enforcement activities, its provisions concerning final cease and desist orders and due process, especially as it relates to adequate representation, reasonable notice, and appropriate judicial review, are lacking proper procedures to ensure that the law does not lead to unconstitutional actions by the agency. The author concludes by suggesting five measures that could correct flaws in the Section: 1) allow non-parties the opportunity to review pre-enforcement actions so that they may challenge the scope of FTC orders; 2) for those cases not subject to judicial review, provide a broad interpretation of trial de nova leading to relitigation; 3) make notices issued to potential non-parties as explicit as possible regarding the scope of the investigation; 4) "liberally grant petitions to intervene" and be open to input from those affected by a trade regulation rule; and 5) allow non-parties to appeal orders that have been issued against the initial respondents.

1225   Tyler, Leslie and Allen R. Erickson "Federal Trade Commission Today: The New Improved Improvements Act." *Hastings Constitutional Law Quarterly* 3 (Summer 1976): 849-878.
The authors examines the legislative history of the FTC and its development as a regulatory agency affecting both businesses and the consumer. Most recently, Congress passed the Magnuson-Moss-Federal Trade Commission Improvement Act that "radically" reshapes the regulatory landscape governed by the Commission. This note examines key provisions of this legislation and its relationship to constitutional limitations on administrative procedure. It is

concluded that, although the issue of due process has been adequate addressed in the Magnuson-Moss Act, constitutional issues regarding civil penalties and consumer redress remain untested. Only after interpretations by the courts will the impact of the latter two issues be resolved.

1226 Verkuil, Paul R. "Preemption of State Law by the Federal Trade Commission." *Duke Law Journal* 1976 (May 1976): 225-247.

The purpose of this study is to investigate the possible impact FTC authority to issue trade regulation rules may have on preempting state laws. At the center of the policy debate is the issue of whether a balance can be struck between the need to reform an eclectic amalgamation of state laws that "have distorted the competitive marketplace since the 1930s" and the overall desired notions of state sovereignty and independence. The author uses the prescription drug price advertising trade regulation rule to build a framework for understanding the debate because it was the first rule to directly address the question of preemption and because it is likely to serve as a vehicle for judicial review. After analyzing in detail congressional intent underlying the power of the FTC to preempt state law, the author concludes that the issue can best be addressed using the judicial analysis expressed in the *Parker v. Brown* case (the "Parker doctrine"), despite the 1975 amendments to the FTC Act that permit the Commission to declare a preemption of state rules when they are in conflict with federal regulations.

1227 Walker, Mary M. "Mail-Order Insurance: The FTC Rides Again." *Maryland Law Review* 24 (Fall 1964): 417-431.

The proliferation of mail-order insurance companies prompted the FTC in 1964 to issue the Mail Order Insurance Guides detailing special rules describing types of conduct that may lead to violations of existing antitrust laws. The FTC promulgated the laws because state-by-state regulations were viewed by the agency as ineffective and inconsistent. This article reviews the FTC guidelines in detail and compares its provisions to similar guidelines contained in the Maryland state regulations. The purpose is to examine possible jurisdictional problems associated with the co-existence of the two laws and the impact on effective regulation of the mail order insurance industry. The analysis suggests that Maryland has limited power over both licensed and unlicensed insurers. In addition, foreign insurers who do not own property in the state and in cases when Maryland must rely on processes in another state, may also undermine effective enforcement. Given these facts, it is concluded that in such instances, FTC guidelines can be effective in regulating mail order insurance companies.

1228   Ward, Peter C. "Restitution for Consumers Under the Federal Trade Commission Act: Good Intentions or Congressional Intentions?" *The American University Law Review* 41 (Summer 1992): 1139-1197.
Argues that the courts have frequently disregarded legislative intent in order to secure redress for consumers who have been injured by deceptive business practices. By allowing the FTC to circumvent statutory procedures so that consumers can be compensated for their injury, the courts have undermined the constitutional system that mandates a separation of powers among the branches of government. To support this thesis, the author examines the FTC's authority to issue cease and desist orders, their legislative history, and how specific cases have led to an expansion in their authoritative power. It is concluded that a proper balance can be met between FTC restitution authority and legislative intent, however, this balance must be sought through Congressional action and through the courts.

1229   Waters, Timothy J. "How Legal Counsel for a Trade Association Participates in an FTC Rulemaking Proceeding and Protects His Members." *Antitrust Bulletin* 22 (Summer 1977): 341-354.
The author analyzes the role of legal counsel for a trade or professional association engaged in an FTC rulemaking proceeding. Two basic principles are outlined: rulemaking is an integral part of the FTC's enforcement activities and effective participation in a rulemaking procedure by members of an association are best served if the interest of the members are actively represented. The mechanisms of rulemaking proceedings are outlined, including initial notice of a proposed rule, pre-hearing conferences, and the submission of written comments,

1230   Weiss, Stephen E. "Creating the GM-Toyota Joint Venture: A Case in Complex Negotiation." *Columbia Journal of World Business* 22 (Summer 1987): 22-37.
The purpose of this study is to examine the dynamics of an international business venture and to outline the strategic implications for businesses contemplating international collaboration. Particular attention is paid to the actors involved in the General Motors-Toyota case and the role of the FTC during the negotiation process. The Commission monitored the process to ensure that no antitrust violations occurred and issued a consent order that made sure "the companies follow through with the agreement as planned." The author then briefly notes how the FTC shaped the overall negotiation process.

1231 West, William F. "Judicial Rulemaking Procedures in the FTC: A Case of Their Causes and Effects." *Public Policy* 29 (Spring 1981): 197-218.
A critical provision of the Magnuson-Moss Act of 1974 was the restriction placed on FTC proceedings that required the agency to hold oral hearings that would facilitate cross examination and rebuttal of proposed rules and the requirement that final decisions are to be based exclusively on the evidence gathered during a proceeding. This study analyzes the reasons why Congress imposed such restrictions on the FTC, concluding that judicialized procedures have led to a more rigorous exploration of factual decision-making processes. However, the restrictions have also led to delays. The implications of these delays are that man-hours are likely to be focused on one proceeding longer, thereby, constricting the number of issues that can be considered at any one time and undermining the flexibility and timeliness afforded an agency procedure over Congressional legislation.

1232 West, William F. "The Policies of Administrative Rulemaking." *Public Administration Review* 42 (September/October 1982): 420-426.
This study examines the FTC's use of trade regulation rules as a preferred administrative tool of enforcement over case-be-case adjudication methods to illustrate the political implications of adopting rulemaking as the dominant means of protecting the consumer. After reviewing the FTC's early application of rulemaking and the subsequent resistance of regulated industries, the author explores how the struggle between advocates of trade regulations rules and anti-regulatory groups in industry and Congress led to greater awareness of various constituencies that ultimately shape the political environment that the FTC occupies. It is concluded that the Commission's experience is illustrative of a key irony in administrative regulation: that "vague statutory policy" may enhance the opportunity to use rulemaking but, at the same time, bureaucratic politics may render the approach less feasible.

1233 Whipple, Douglas P. "Analysis of the FTC Line of Business and Corporate Patterns Reports Litigation." *Cleveland State Law Review* 28 (1979): 83-114.
In order to create a comprehensive database of statistical information intended to inform the processes of policy planning, economic analysis, and antitrust enforcement procedures at the FTC, the agency created two corporate report programs, "The Line of Business Report Program" and "The Corporate Patterns Report Program," that were issued to primarily large conglomerates requesting

information. Although the corporations resisted due to the cost imposed on companies to produce the data and the unclear intent of how the data would be used by the FTC, the Supreme Court forced the corporations to comply by refusing to intervene in the dispute. This article reviews the dispute and offers alternatives to current procedures related to creating a fair balance between preventing agency "fishing expeditions" and the need for the FTC to gather information about an increasingly complex marketplace.

1234 White, P. A. "FTC: Wrong Agency for the Job of Adjudication." *American Bar Association Journal* 61 (October 1975): 1242-1245.

As a former chief counsel for the FTC in its case against eight petroleum manufacturing firms charged with joint monopolization, the author outlines the FTC's evolving enforcement activities given its entrance into more complex matters of litigation and recent procedural reforms within the organization. The author argues that the FTC and Congress have properly moved away from traditional administrative concepts, but further efforts must be made to ensure a federal judiciary in which all Commission cases are decided in federal court.

1235 Williams, R. L. "Authority of Federal Agencies to Impose Discovery Sanctions: The FTC–A Case in Point." *Georgetown Law Journal* 65 (February 1977): 739-771.

This article provides a comprehensive analysis of recent attempts by the Federal Trade Commission to exercise the power to decree substantively similar discovery sanctions that parallel the court's authority to impose penalties on respondents who fail to comply with orders to produce documents or other evidence. The FTC adopted rule 3.38 in its Rules of Practice and Procedure in 1972. Similar to rule 37(b)(2) of the Federal Rule of Civil Procedure, the FTC rule is intended to describe under what conditions sanctions would be imposed on a respondent if they were to withhold evidence. The author concludes that the FTC discovery sanctions are improper because they deny, either in whole or in part, a respondent's right to a judicial hearing concerning the authority and legality of FTC charges before sanctions are imposed, the rule circumvents the ability of the respondent to produce substantial evidence refuting FTC charges, and, while it is true that all discovery sanctions may be subject to judicial review, the appellate process is time consuming and expensive.

Appendix One
History of the FTC

Ours is a government of laws, which must be administered by men.
To say that the Federal Trade Commission cannot be depended upon
helpfully to administer these regulatory statutes is to say that our
government is a failure. Men have been found who understand the
spirit of the Federal Trade Commission Law and who administer it
in harmony with its spirit. Therefore men can and will be found in the
future who will administer the law with the same sympathetic
understanding.

> Rush C. Butler
> Former Chairman, Committee on
> Federal Trade Commission for
> U.S. Chamber of Commerce,
> 1926

The Federal Trade Commission (FTC) was created under provisions of
the Federal Trade Commission Act of 1914. Along with the Clayton Antitrust Act
passed by Congress that same year, this Progressive Era legislation represented a
broad mandate by political leaders to bring order to the increasingly diversified,
dynamic, and complex business landscape of early twentieth century America.
The FTC was conceived as an independent federal agency with quasi-judicial
authority to prohibit "unfair methods of practice" and to uphold its regulatory
mission only in "the interest of the public." These fundamental tenets of purpose
were intended to promote the competitive process by eliminating monopolistic
behavior and restraints of trade. The grand assumption of political leaders at the
time was that, freed from the harmful effects of collusion within industry and the
deceptive methods and misrepresentation of businesses intent on placing profit
before ethics, the American economy would be empowered to grow in a manner
that would enhance America's position in the new global economy, while at the
same time, respecting the private rights of consumers in the marketplace.

Since its inception, however, the FTC has been at the heart of constant,
and often heated debate within public policy and legal circles concerning the
overall effectiveness of the Commission in carrying out its primary
responsibilities. The criticism has ranged from claims that the FTC is simply
ineffective or invisible in the government's battle against unfair methods of
competition to accusations that the FTC actions have been damaging to open

competition and actually harmed consumers in the process. Advocates for a strong FTC have countered that the agency is capable, but is frequently hindered by conflicting political agendas in Congress and poorly formulated interpretations of regulatory laws in the federal courts.

Before tracing the conflicted history of the Federal Trade Commission, it is instructive to step back for a moment and examine several decades prior to the passage of the FTC Act. Understanding the history of regulatory reform leading up to this point in time accomplishes two things: it places the story of the FTC in proper historical context and it lays the groundwork for understanding the political, economic, and social forces that have acted upon the Commission throughout its history.

Prelude to the Federal Trade Commission, 1880-1914

The FTC evolved from demands by the consuming public and small business to reign in the anticompetitive practices of large Progressive era monopolies. It was during this period that the foundations of our nation's corporate capitalist economy, the modern regulatory state, and internationalist foreign policy were developed. Rapid industrialization led to significant concentrations of corporate power, primarily in those industries essential to fueling America's economic engine, such as transportation (railroads) and manufacturing (steel). This transformation of corporate assets and market relationships did not take place within a political and social vacuum, but occurred in an environment where tangible wealth was growing at a phenomenal rate and political leaders were committed to reconfiguring America's values and institutions to facilitate expansion of the new corporate-capitalist order. This new economic order was also considered the vehicle for promoting the nation's interests abroad. Domestically, industrial concentration, created at least in part by a wave of corporate mergers from 1897 to 1902, was leading many legislators to believe that firms were either competing unfairly amongst themselves or were monopolies that restrained trade and harmed consumers.

The nation's railroad interests were singled out as a particularly egregious violator of fair business practices. During a time of rapid westward expansion prior to 1870, the railroad industry operated almost entirely free from government restraints. However, discriminatory pricing, exorbitant shipping rates, and exclusive dealings led to public demands by farmers and small business leaders to reform the industry. In response, Congress passed the Interstate Commerce Act in 1887, thereby establishing the nation's first regulatory agency.

History

The Interstate Commerce Commission (ICC) was created to regulate railroad commerce among the states and to prescribe reasonable and non-discriminatory shipping rates. The agency was also intended to regulate discriminatory preferences among railroad customers that often gave discounted rates to preferred customers.

Shortly after Congress addressed the discriminatory pricing and monopolistic abuses of the railroad industry, legislators passed the Sherman Antitrust Act in 1890. This Act was created to regulate monopolistic behavior throughout American industry and was passed in response to the public's principle objection to the fact that large corporate trusts were able to raise prices without consideration of market conditions. By the 1910s however, both the Sherman Act and the Instate Commerce Commission proved inadequate in regulating the monopolies. There are several reasons underlying this fact. First and foremost, the courts had failed to fully comprehend the damage inflicted on the public by large industrial conglomerates. Although the Instate Commerce Commission mandated "just and reasonable rates" for shipping, Congress had failed to define the concepts of just and reasonable. This positioned the agency poorly in relation to the courts interpretations of its purpose and authority. The regulatory authority imbedded in the provisions of the Sherman Act was also hindered by undefined concepts of unfair practices–what exactly was to be considered "unfair" and under what conditions and at which level should regulations be invoked in response to a particular business practice?

Presidential leadership under Theodore Roosevelt and Woodrow Wilson continued to identify market concentration with harm to an open capitalist economy, but the courts, lacking any precedent, continuously ruled in the favor of business, thereby undermining the intention of the Progressive Era legislation. This conflict between legislative and executive intent versus judicial review came to a head in the "rule of reason" doctrine handed down by the Supreme Court in 1911. In the decisions against both the American Tobacco Company and Standard Oil Company–each firm clearly dominant within its respective market–the Court ruled that the companies had violated provisions of the Sherman Act by placing an "undue restraint" on interstate commerce in an attempt to monopolize the marketplace and ordered them to broken up into several separate companies. Although the Supreme Court had supported the underlying principles of antitrust law in making its decision, the Court's choice to invoke the terms "reasonable" and "undue" left open the possibility for further judicial interpretation beyond the boundaries of legislative intent. In this sense, the courts were holding that restriction of competition did not necessarily imply that there was an attempt to

377

illegally restrain trade or form a monopoly. This interpretive legacy would provide the conceptual reasoning for creating the FTC as well as the challenges that it would face throughout its history.

As a result of the Supreme Court's application of common law, both the Sherman Act and the ICC (although considered an administrative success at the time) were increasingly viewed by the legislative and executive branches of government as ineffective. During the 1912 presidential election, all three major political parties–Progressive, Republican, and Democratic–added planks to their campaign platforms stating an intention to reformulate antitrust regulation in light of recent court decisions. With the Republican party split, Woodrow Wilson easily won the 1912 election and immediately advocated for the creation of an Interstate Trade Commission.

Wilson envisioned this new regulatory agency to have two roles in regulating business. First, the agency would act as a clearinghouse of information that would inform business leaders of regulatory initiatives and educate the consumer. Second, the new agency would regulate industry "where the processes of the courts or the natural forces of correction outside of the courts are inadequate to adjust the remedy to the wrong in a way that will meet all the equities and circumstances of the case." In this way Wilson laid the foundation for the creation of an independent regulatory agency with quasi-judicial authority to enforce existing antitrust laws.

The Federal Trade Commission and Its Duties, 1914-1936

When the FTC Act was passed in 1914, Congress had granted the new agency two overarching powers to regulate trade and enforce the nation's antitrust laws. One power was the authority to issue restraining orders against unfair methods of competition. The other regulatory power identified by the Act was to investigate economic conditions within industry for the purpose of determining, among other things, combinations in restraint of trade and unfair practices and business conditions that could adversely restrict an open, capitalist economy. As a function of this regulatory responsibility, the Commission was expected to disseminate investigatory findings to the Attorney General, Congress, the President, and, in some cases, the public. The main provisions of the FTC Act created a board of five commissioners to be appointed by the President and approved by the Senate. It was held that no more than three commissioners could be affiliated with the same political party. Commissioners serve seven-year terms with an annual salary of $10,000. A Commission chairman would be determined from its own membership and that individual was expected to serve for one year in that position. Commissioners were forbidden to engage in any other business activities while in office and the President had the authority to dismiss a Commissioner if that individual were found to be neglect in his or her duty. The final Act included a total of eleven sections, some of which are highlighted below.

The earliest work of the FTC was to follow through on the remaining responsibilities of the Bureau of Corporations. Section Three of the FTC Act provided that all pending investigations and proceedings were to be continued by the FTC. Employees formally in the Bureau were to automatically become employees of the FTC. In addition, Section Three stipulated that all record, papers, and property of the Bureau, as well as all unexpended funds, were to become property of the new Commission.

Section 5 declared unfair methods of competition to be unlawful and empowered the FTC to prevent individuals, partnerships, or corporations (except banks and common carriers) from using unfair methods of competition in commerce. The section specified the processes by which the Commission is to proceed to prevent any practices found to be unfair and how appeals may be made to the U. S. Court of Appeals. Section 5 provided for the exclusive jurisdiction of the Circuit Court of Appeals to enforce, set aside or modify any orders issued by the Commission, although it was understood that final judgements and decrees were subject to review by the Supreme Court. However, findings of fact by the FTC, if supported by evidence, were to be considered conclusive. Finally, this section articulates the methods by which complaints, orders, and other quasi-judicial actions of the Commission may be served on offenders.

Section 6, as written in 1914, conferred upon the Commission the authority to gather and compile information concerning investigations of corporations engaged in commerce as it relates to their organization, business activities, conduct, and practices as well as their relationship to other corporations, associations, and individuals. This section also required, among other things, that corporations engaged in commerce file annual or special reports with the commission and furnish any information upon request of the agency, make recommendations upon request to the Attorney General for adjusting the business of any corporation found to be in violation of the antitrust laws, and to promulgate portions of information derived from its investigations and disseminate its reports and decisions in manner best adapted for public consumption.

Section 8 granted the President the authority to require any federal department or other agency to furnish the Commission with any records or documents relating to any corporate activities pertinent to FTC actions.

Section 9 gave the Commission the authority to issue subpoenas to require the attendance and testimony of witnesses and the production of documentary evidence relating to an investigation and to apply to any court actions that would enforce compliance with the Commission's order. Refusal would be interpreted as being in contempt of court.

Section 10 provided penalties for refusal to attend or testify in a hearing, for false documentation or statements of fact, destruction or removal of documents, and refusal of access to documents during an investigation by the FTC. This section also defined penalties for any Commission employees who knowingly disclose information obtained by the agency, without authority to do so by the Commission.

Paralleling the passage of the FTC Act in 1914 was the omnibus Clayton Antitrust Act, which authorized the FTC to issue restraining orders to prevent corporations from exercising business practices deemed in violation of sections 2, 3, 7, and 8 of the Clayton Act. Section 11 of the FTC Act provided procedures by which the Commission could issue cease and desist orders and, in mergers cases, orders of divestiture. The sections of the Clayton Act enforced by the FTC covered a variety of business practices.

Section 2 of the Clayton Act related to price discrimination. It forbade any price discrimination practices intended to damage or destroy the business of a competitor. A specific intent to "injure" had to be shown in order to render a price discrimination illegal under the Clayton Act.

Section 3 related to exclusive or "tying" agreements that made it a criminal offense to lease or sell goods or to fix a price, discount or rebate, on the condition that the leasee or purchaser not use or otherwise deal with the goods of a competitor. This section also related to agreements in which a manufacturer would require its wholesale and retail distributors not to handle the product's of the manufacturer's competitors.

Section 7 prohibited stock purchases found to be made, not solely on the grounds of investment, but rather, acquired in whole or in part of another corporation engaged in similar businesses with the deliberate intention of lessening competition or facilitating the formation of subsidiary corporations.

Section 8 contained a paragraph making it unlawful for any person to be a director in any two or more corporations engaged in interstate commerce or foreign trade that are deemed to be competitors. The House version of the original Clayton bill contain a provision that stated such violations only apply to corporations with assets and undivided profits of over $1,000,000. However, the final Senate version eliminated this monetary stipulation.

History

During the first decade of its existence, the FTC conducted work against unfair business practices based primarily on the content of the Clayton and FTC Acts, although each case against a violator presented in Court provided new clarifications to the underlying meaning of unfairness . Two modifications to the provisions of the FTC Act occurred during this period, though. The first was the Export Trade Act, better known as the Webb-Pomerene Act, that became law on April 10, 1918. This act exempted all associations engaged solely in export trade from the provisions of the Sherman Antitrust Act, and granted the FTC authority to inquire into the activities of such associations and compel them to produce reports the Commission might require. If the Commission were to determine that laws were violated, a recommendation for prosecution could be forwarded to the Attorney General. To facilitate the FTC's authority in this area, powers were expanded to include unfair practices and methods used in export trade against competition engaged in export trade, even though the illegal acts are committed outside of the territorial jurisdiction of the United States.

In 1921, the Packers' and Stockyards' Act became law. It granted broad powers to the Secretary of Agriculture over the business practices and operations of meat packers, stockyards, and livestock commission houses. Section 408 of this Act removed all FTC jurisdiction in these areas as far as that jurisdiction was conferred by the content of the Packers' and Stockyards' Act.

During U.S. involvement in World War I, the FTC was called upon to perform two additional functions related to its mission. The first was to issue confidential reports to the government regarding costs of production. A total of 284 reports were filed during the conflict. The second call to action was initiated by Woodrow Wilson's executive order of October 12, 1917 that delegated certain powers to the Federal Trade Commission related to the use of licenses, trademarks, print labels, and copyright during the War and to order that an invention remain secret and that the issuance of a patent be suspended until the end of the War. Under these provisions the FTC issued 2,940 orders to keep patents or inventions secret.

By the late 1920s, the Commission had organized itself under three broad divisions. The Administrative division was responsible for carrying on the general business of the FTC and was under the Secretary of the Commission. The Secretary was responsible for disseminating information from the FTC to other agencies in the federal government. The Legal Division was subdivided into the trial branch and the investigatory branch. This division was primarily responsible for enforcing Section 5 of the FTC Act and Sections 2, 3, 7, and 8 of the Clayton Act. The Economic Division consists of economists in charge of supporting the general work of the Commission on matters pertaining to econometric modeling and economic policy issues and to investigate price discrimination, tying contracts, intercorporate stockholdings, and interlocking directorates under the Clayton Act.

Under this organizational structure, the Commission pursued a number of investigations related to possible violations of the nation's antitrust laws. To some, each case was seen as more precisely defining the scope and authority of the FTC. To critics, though, the aggressive antitrust enforcement of the agency after World War I and into the 1930s was an indication of an agency quickly losing sight of its public purpose and legislative intent. Two court cases illustrate this period of regulatory ambition and contradiction

A hearing before the FTC determined that the Western Meat Company was in violation of Section Seven of the Clayton Act because of its acquisition of stock and properties held by the Nevada Packing Company. The FTC ordered Western to divest itself of these stocks and properties. The company refused and appealed to the Circuit Court of Appeals in San Francisco. The Court ruled that sufficient evidence existed to justify the actions of the FTC. Western Meat requested a rehearing which was granted and in that second ruling the Court modified its original ruling by holding that the authority of the FTC was restricted to only requiring a divestiture of stock but did not extend to the Nevada Packing Company plant and property. In response to this limitation placed on its regulatory power, the FTC petitioned the Supreme Court which upheld the original findings of the FTC and reversing the Circuit Court's ruling.

In the case of *American Tobacco Company v. FTC* in 1924, the Commission had ordered the company to provide access to all of its records and documents as part of the agency's trade practices investigation. The Supreme Court, in an unanimous decision, rejected the Commission's request on the grounds that right of access to documents and corporate records are limited to only those materials which are shown to likely contain evidence pertinent to the investigation. The Supreme Court held that, even in investigations of possible illegality, regulatory agencies must show probable cause that the law has been violated before the courts will enforce a subpoena. In this way, the decision avoided specific reference to the concept of unreasonable search and seizures under the Fourth Amendment and to whether Section 5 of the FTC Act, therefore, violated the Fourth Amendment.

These are but two of many cases that the FTC pursued during the two decades after World War I that both expanded and restricted the judicial boundaries of the agency's regulatory powers. This period also marked the beginning of heated debates about the effectiveness and social legitimacy of the Commission itself. The agency had experienced a relatively quiet period shortly after its birth in which the hopes and aspirations of a new regulatory era muted most criticism of the FTC. Business interests had been critical of the FTC since its establishment in 1914, but since they were viewed as the enemy by policy-makers, their complaints were largely dismissed. However, it did not take long before some in Congress where calling for the abolishment of the FTC as a failed experiment in controlling business. On some occasions the agency was forced to adopt new policies for controlling business. For example, the Commission decided that proceedings of alleged violations of unfair trade practices would not be entertained if the controversy was private and did not suppress competition in a manner affecting the public. However, many of these shifts in policy resulted only in accusations that the agency was too lenient towards business. Ironically, the agency was viewed as overly aggressive during its earliest history.

The criticism took a number of forms. Much of this criticism took the form of statements about the unwieldiness of what was now perceived to be a bloated bureaucratic agency incapable of fine-tuning the hidden complexities of American business to the benefit of all. Others were critical of the FTC's perceived failure to embrace proper legislative intent when pursuing regulatory investigations of industry. To some, the agency's aggressive stance in testing the boundaries of its authority in the courts was wasteful and ill-advised. Still others viewed the agency, not as independent, but often prone to manipulation from the political agendas of special interest groups within Congress resulting in investigations being halted and undermining the overall mission of the Commission. These critics often identified the link between agency actions and the annual appropriations from Congress as a serious threat to regulatory autonomy.

As a result of mounting criticism of the FTC, many in Congress called for revisions to the FTC Act and the passage of additional regulatory laws intended to strengthen the government's ability to control monopolistic behavior and unfair business practices. What resulted was a set of sweeping changes to the regulatory landscape of America in the years just before World War II.

New Directions for the Federal Trade Commission, 1936-1960

With mounting criticism directed at the FTC, policy-makers and President Franklin D. Roosevelt were faced with essentially two choices–abolish the FTC and begin anew or strengthen and preserve the FTC through legislative action. Although several threats to close the Commission surfaced during the first forty years of its existence, liberal supporters in Congress argued that the agency should be granted additional powers under the assumption that, as a result, the agency's value would then become apparent. The first order of business for President Roosevelt was to overhaul the membership of the Commission's leadership.

The laissez-faire Commission under the Republic administrations of Warren G. Harding, Calvin Coolidge, and Herbert Hoover led President Roosevelt to target the FTC as an agency in need of review. He began by filling two open Commissioner positions with liberal appointees sympathetic to the President's desire to maintain a strong regulatory agency. Three Commissioners remained, having been appointed by previous administrations. President Roosevelt, in seeking a majority of Commissioners who would align themselves with his policies, sought the resignation of William E. Humphrey, an old guard conservative. Humphrey refuted the President's continued requests to leave office, knowing the fact that there was no evidence of inefficiency, neglect of duty or malfeasance during his time in office, which were defined in the FTC Act as the only justifications for Executive removal of an FTC Commissioner.

Ignoring this provision of the law, Roosevelt took advantage of his overwhelming public approval rating and simply declared that there was a vacancy within the FTC and appointed the liberal Republican, George C. Mathews of Wisconsin to replace Humphrey. The Supreme Court subsequently found the dismissal of Humphrey to have violated the law and required that Humphrey's widow receive monetary compensation equivalent to the salary Humphrey would have received had he been in office for the remainder of his term. What followed from 1934 through 1941was a remarkable period of stability within the FTC.

During the Roosevelt presidency, a number of important legislation was passed that had significant impact on the mission and functions of the FTC. For example, the National Recovery Act (NRA) set forth industry-wide codes of fair competition. Although a provision of the National Recovery Act stated that in no way should these standards be construed to interfere with the work of the FTC, the relationship between National Recovery Act codes and the FTC's mandate to set forth standards of fair competition within industry was ambiguous. However, Section 3b of the NRA did require the FTC to treat violations of industry codes in the same manner as violations of other rules of fair competition and Section 6c of the National Recovery Act required the FTC to investigate any possible code violations at the request of the President. In short, the NRA removed the FTC's power of ultimate decision from those cases involving NRA code violations. This situation continued for only a short period of time while the National Recovery Act remained a viable piece of legislation before judicial review severely handicapped its power.

The Federal Security Act of 1933 had a much greater impact on the work of the FTC but, like the NRA, it remained law only briefly. The Federal Security Act was intended to protect the public from unscrupulous sales of securities by requiring full disclosure about any security sold in instate or foreign commerce or through the mail. The provisions of the Federal Security Act required that the FTC to administer the law by ensuring that complete and accurate information was made available to the purchaser. The Commission was not permitted to evaluate the validity of the security as an investment. The FTC lacked experience in the area of securities claims and was hindered by a limited budget. In June 6, 1934, though, these challenges were rendered moot by the passage of new legislation establishing the Securities and Exchange Commission.

The National Recovery Act and the Federal Securities Act were short-lived pieces of legislation. However, during the period in which they remained viable laws, both had a tremendous impact on the work of the FTC and its allocation of resources. The Robinson-Patman Act of 1936 that amended Section 2 of the Clayton Act and the Wheeler-Lea Amendment to the FTC Act both had a considerably greater and significantly longer impact on the FTC, however. Both were responsible for establishing new paths of regulatory responsibility for the agency and, as such, setting off a new firestorm of criticism directed at the work of the agency.

On June 19, 1936, the Robinson-Patman Act was passed by Congress. The purpose of this amending legislation was to revise and strengthen the regulatory authority of Section 2 of the Clayton Act. When passed in 1914, Section 2 was intended to make it unlawful to discriminate between purchasers in the price charged for goods in interstate commence. According to the 1936 Annual Report of the FTC, the Clayton Act set forth four requirements under which such a transaction would violate the law: the effect of the price charged between purchasers would lesson competition; the difference in price is not due to variance of quality or quantity; the discrimination is not "in good faith to meet competition"; and, the discrimination is not the result of "bona fide" transactions and does not restrain trade. Provisions of the Clayton Act granted the Commission the authority to enforce this set of requirements. However, critics viewed these requirements as overly broad and open to judicial interpretation to be effective and, as a result, the FTC did not actively pursue cases based on Section 2 of the Clayton Act.

The Robinson-Patman Act was passed to substantially revise and strengthen Section 2 by removing the legal ambiguities that had hindered enforcement initiatives by the FTC since its inception in 1914. First, Robinson-Patman reduced the amount of proof needed to show the anticompetitive effects of price discrimination by adding a clause against discrimination that might "injure, destroy, or prevent competition." Second, the amendment made brokerage fees illegal. Third, the legislation made the acceptance or inducement of a discriminatory price an unlawful action. Finally, Robinson-Patman granted the FTC with more authority to pursue successfully cases of illegal price discrimination.

At first glance, the Robinson-Patman Act appeared to substantially clarify and strengthen Section 2 of the Clayton Act and indirectly supplement provisions of the Sherman Antitrust Act. Legal and public policy scholars have argued that this was simply not the case. The Robinson-Patman Act was firmly grounded in a desire by small business retailers to control the rapid growth of large retail chain stores that could undersell their smaller competitors. Robinson-Patman has been criticized since its inception as a law, intended not to promote competition, but as a means for maintaining the status quo within the retail marketplace economy by protecting small business from the methods large chain stores allegedly used to gain a competitive advantage over smaller rivals.

Although the FTC aggressively pursued investigations under Robinson-Patman, the work of the investigations proved to be more costly than other actions of the agency because a judgment as to possible price discrimination required detailed cost accounting analysis. Often this task was hindered because firms under investigation did not support adequate cost accounting systems. These situations most often required the FTC to conduct a time study of each operation involved in the sale and distribution of the product associated with the alleged price discrimination.

In general, criticism of the Robinson-Patman Act has centered on two fatal flaws. First, the Act has been ineffective in controlling the growth of large retail chain stores and the subsequent disappearance of small retail operations. Ironically, the law that small business had helped formulate and promote through Congress also hindered the competitive position of small business by undermining their ability to establish cooperatives and other programs that helped small firms compete against the inherent advantages of the large chain stores. The second fatal flaw of Robinson-Patman concerned the inability of the courts to interpret Robinson-Patman within the regulatory framework of other antitrust laws. This was due in part to the fact that Robinson-Patman proved ineffective in identifying those forms of price discrimination that are a manifestation of anticompetive practices from those forms that are simply the result of marketplace efficiency. In short, Robinson-Patman did not condemn discriminatory prices, only low prices because the Act failed to require proof that economic harm had been committed.

Caught within this quagmire of legislative ambiguity and the failure of the courts to come up with clear linkages between the enforcement provisions of Robinson-Patman and other antitrust legislation sat the Federal Trade Commission. In this environment, the FTC became embroiled in new criticism about its legislative intent and public purpose.

The final important piece of legislation affecting the work of the FTC during the Roosevelt Administration and beyond was passage of the Wheeler-Lea Amendments to the FTC Act in 1938. These amendments were passed due to continued criticism that the original FTC Act was inadequate in addressing the increasingly complex issues of the day and marked a dramatic shift in the regulatory mission of the agency for two reasons in particular. First, the Wheeler-Lea Act provided for a civil penalty action in any district court for violation of a final cease and desist order. Finality was determined either through the affirmation of the court of appeals or at the end of sixty days if no appeal was pursued by the respondent. Civil penalties for each offense were brought by the Attorney General at the request of the FTC. Prior to the passage of Wheeler-Lea, cease and desist orders issued under provisions of the 1914 FTC Act were enforceable only by appellate courts in contempt proceedings after the order was adopted as the court's decree. This process proved slow and arduous for all involved. Wheeler-Lea was thus, in part, an attempt to streamline regulatory proceedings, creating a more responsive and efficient Commission.

Second, Wheeler-Lea dramatically expanded the authority of the FTC to include regulating false advertising of foods, drugs, cosmetics, and curative or corrective devices. To understand this shift in proper context, one must step back to 1919 and the case of *Sears, Roebuck & Co. v. FTC.* This case marked the first time that the FTC had taken action against a firm based primarily on the tenets of consumer protectionism. The FTC sought action against Sears because the company had advertised that their prices for tea and sugar were lower than their competitors due to their larger buying power. The FTC found this claim to be false. The courts upheld the FTC's findings, not for reasons concerning possible harm to the consumer, but because the claim was found to likely injure smaller competitors in the marketplace. This decision reaffirmed the FTC's regulatory authority under Section 5 provisions but denied agency action based on possible injury to the consumer.

In 1931, the landmark case of *FTC v. Raladam* was decided by the Supreme Court. In this case, the court held that the Commission could not prohibit false advertising if there is no evidence that the action injures a competitor. The ruling effectively halted any further actions by the FTC to pursue regulatory enforcement on the basis that the unfair business practice of false advertising was inherently harmful to the consumer. Despite this setback, the decision by the Supreme Court galvanized support in Congress to redefine and expand the powers of the FTC to include consumer protection and this eventually led to passage of the Wheeler-Lea amendments to the FTC Act. With Wheeler-Lea removing the obligation of the FTC to demonstrate injury to competition, the Commission was free to regulate against deceptive advertising. The challenge for the FTC then shifted to the issue of defining deception within the conceptual framework of advertising and consumer behavior and in response to judicial review of agency regulatory tactics in this area.

The concept of deception is found when the advertisement perceived by the buyer either differs from reality or affects buying behavior to the detriment of the consumer. In some cases, action is taken simply because the advertisement contains a blatantly false statement about the product. The more difficult issue for regulators is determining an advertisement that is not obviously false, but the perceptual process of the buyer generates an impression that the statement is deceptive. Judicial review of FTC actions against false advertising helped to define the boundaries between the legitimate promotion of a product and deceptive behavior intended to gain an unfair advantage over a competitor buying disseminating false information about a product or service.

One important issue was determining to what degree must the deception occur to trigger regulatory action by the FTC based on the consumer's level of cognition. In the 1944 case of *Charles of the Ritz Dist. Corp. v. FTC*, for example, the Commission found that the trademark "Rejuvenence" was associated with a makeup cream in a manner which promised the skin restored to a youthful complexion. The District Court agreed that such language may imply that this product actually does ensure a youthful look and, therefore, upheld the FTC's position that it can "insist on the most literal truthfulness in [an] advertisement." The court noted that the law was not intended to merely protect the expert consumer, but "the vast multitude which includes the ignorant, the unthinking and the credulous."

A second important issue concerned clarifying the general impression of an advertisement. In the case of *P. Lorillard Co. v. FTC*, the cigarette company Lorillard had emphasized in its advertising an article that appeared in

Reader's Digest that listed the tar and nicotine content of cigarettes providing evidence that all cigarettes were harmful. The Lorillard brand was shown on the list to have the lowest levels of each ingredient even though the margin was exceptionally small. The courts upheld the FTC action because it was determined that, although the fact that Lorillard did have the lowest level of tar and nicotine, the overall impression of the advertisement created a false impression that the levels tar and nicotine were in some way less harmful to consumers than other brands.

A third clarification involved the FTC's right to require the use of complete disclosure in correcting a misconception. For example, the FTC required baldness cures to reveal the fact that the condition is hereditary and unlikely to respond to medical treatments. In another case, the FTC required Geritol to state in its advertisements that the "tired feelings" it was purported to alleviate could possibly be due to factors the product could not address. In these cases, the courts established that deception could also occur if incomplete information was disseminated.

The famous case of *Colgate-Palmolive v. FTC* established the judicial position that the FTC could only act if an advertisement contained a material untruth. To demonstrate the moisturizing qualities of its Rapid Shave shaving cream product, a television commercial showed the product applied to simulated sandpaper (sand on a sheet of plexiglass). The FTC ruled the demonstration as deceptive because, as the agency noted, sandpaper can only be "shaved" if it is presoaked in a liquid to loosen the sand particles. In addition, the FTC ruled that the mock-up used to simulate the sandpaper was also deceptive. In the latter position, the courts rejected the Commission's position, since the use of the mock-up was not intended to affect purchase decisions. The FTC then revised its position to note that mock-ups could be determined as deceptive only if they were intended to illustrate visually a quality material to selling the product and influencing consumer behavior.

A final clarification from the courts in the years soon after the passage of the Wheeler-Lea Amendment concerned the concept of puffery. Puffery is exaggeration that takes the form of either a subjective statement of opinion that is likely not true in the literal sense but would be otherwise impossible to prove or puffery is an exaggeration that is an outright spoof of reality. The fact that certain forms of puffery were permissible was affirmed in the 1946 case of *Carlay v. FTC*. Carlay manufactured and sold vitamin-enhanced candy that was promoted as part of weight reduction plan. It was stated that eating one or two pieces of the candy before a meal would be an "easy," "simple," and , "safe" way to reduce an individuals desire to eat fattening or starchy foods. The issue of whether eating a piece of Carlay candy before a meal would help reduce one's appetite was not in dispute. However, the FTC stated that claims theat the plan was "easy" were deceptive. The court ruled against the agency's position by stating that, "what was said was clearly justifiable, under the circumstances, under those cases recognizing that such words as 'easy,' 'perfect,' 'amazing,' 'prime,' 'wonderful,' 'excellent,' are regarded in law as mere puffing or dealer's talk upon which no charge of misrepresentation can be based."

Underlying these regulatory actions against false advertising by the FTC was a growing consumer movement that began during the 1890s in response to food additives and pure food legislation, matured during the 1930s when dangerous and useless medicines became the focus of Congressional action leading to the creation of the Food and Drug Administration, and then waned during World War II and the 1950s. The 1960s marked a new era of consumer activism and new consumer protection legislation. As one of the most visible agencies responsible for protecting the consumer, the Federal Trade Commission was swept up in the consumer movement of the 1960s and, as a result, became a target of heated debates about the social legitimacy of the agency and it's ultimate effectiveness as a regulatory agency.

The Federal Trade Commission and Consumerism, 1961-1979

As with any federal agency, the Federal Trade Commission does not function independent from the social and economic systems in which it occupies. During the period in which the agency was testing the boundaries of regulatory consumerism, a public outcry was developing in response to evidence that industry was placing profit before consumer safety. The development of consumerism has its roots in the postwar increase in an educated and economically self-sufficient middle class that became increasingly more politically conscious.

The mobilization of a consumer movement can be attributed to three factors that helped to create an organized movement for change in business practices. First, public officials participated in a comprehensive propaganda campaign touting the virtues of the "American way of life." This way of life focused considerable attention on the acquisition of material goods superior to those found anywhere else. Second, the business community greatly expanded the amount of money it spent on advertisements promoting the quality of their products. Third, these advertising campaigns placed a substantial emphasis on alleged improvements to the products. However, in many cases the improvements actually meant an increase in complexity and this ultimately led to more functional parts that were vulnerable to breakdowns and in need of frequent repair.

As a result of these factors and coupled with the promotion of the "new American way of life," the new middle class of America experienced a great rise in expectations about the quality, performance, durability, and reliability of goods and services. However, with the increased complexity of products, Americans were becoming less patient with the need to repair these goods. In addition, the increased complexity meant that it was often no longer possible for the average consumer to fix his or her own appliances, but had to rely upon the expertise of others. These services were often expensive and contributed to consumer dissatisfaction over product imperfections. The new, highly-educated and upwardly mobile middle class began to organize and to demand new legislation and more effective enforcement of existing regulatory laws.

From this movement, several high profile consumer advocates arose to target the most egregious violators. The public interest lawyer Ralph Nader took on the automobile industry with the publication of his 1964 report, *Unsafe At Any Speed*, which provided clear evidence that faulty engineering, construction, and design had been responsible for the high rate of death among people in automobile accidents. Product liability lawyer Edward Swartz was a leading advocate calling for safer toys for children. The surgeon general's staff was principally responsible for restricting the promotion of cigarettes. Quite often the work of these individuals were supported by well-financed organizations such as National Consumer's League that pressured Congress to eliminate unsafe business practices. In response, legislators passed three laws concerning fair packaging, truth-in-lending, and warranties that directly impacted the regulatory mission of the FTC.

Although it had been long recognized that the shape of a package and the labeling on it affected consumer buying habits, only two orders between 1956 and 1964 involving deceptive packaging were entered by the FTC. Five related orders were brought against book publishers for selling books without notifying the consumer that the works were abridgements. However, by the mid-1960s abuses involving packaging of products led to legislative action. This action was based on two concepts affecting consumer behavior. The first involved the theory that the size and appearance of the package implicitly make certain claims about the products qualities just as words do. For example, consumers assume that a can or box is completely full. Deception occurs, however, when the product on the shelf is only partially full. This deception allows the company to either place less product in a competitor's similar-sized container and thereby maintaining an unfair advantage over that competitor, or the company can reduce the quantity of the product while maintaining the same price, thereby enhancing its profit bargain for that item.

The second form of deception involves packaging design and graphics. This is also shown to affect consumer purchasing behavior. Products packaged in a certain form, such as the Welch Grape Juice Company placing jellies and jam preserves in drinking glasses, has become an important competitive tool. However, these variations, absent of standardization, were confusing to consumers. In addition, terms such as "large economy size" or "family size" were used to imply savings even when this was not the case based on per unit purchases.

In response to these forms of deception, the Fair Packaging and Labeling Act was passed by Congress in 1966. Authority under the Act was divided among three agencies–the Food and Drug Administration, the FTC, and the Department of Commerce. The FTC was responsible for preparing regulations governing the terms manufacturers could use, such as "giant" or "economy size," to describe the package, but was prevented from establishing any rules concerning the size, shape, weight, or dimensions of the package. The FTC was also responsible for issuing regulations governing the use of these promotional phrases relating to price. The Fair Packaging and Labeling Act also required the FTC to promulgate rules regarding the use of common or usual names of commodities on packaging. And finally, the Act allowed the FTC to make rules regarding the relationship between the size of the package and the amount of product within, provided that specific qualities such as settling during shipment are taken into account.

A second law passed in response to the early consumer movement was the Truth-In-Lending Act. Originally introduced to Congress in 1960 as the Consumer Credit Protection Act, the purpose of this legislation was to require full disclosure of all annual terms and conditions associated with a financial transaction. Although the Act met early resistance from lending organizations, the legislation eventually passed under the assumption that full disclosure did not substantially affect consumer purchasing habits. Although the Act was heralded as a major consumer protection law at the time of its passage, it has had a minimal impact on the consumer. Nevertheless, the FTC has entered numerous orders under the Truth-In-Lending Act. The Commission's jurisdiction is divided between it and several other agencies, most notably the Federal Reserve Board. The FTC does not cover banks, or other financial institutions, but focuses on retail establishments. In the years immediately after the Act's passage in 1968, orders were entered by the FTC against mostly small retailers claiming that they either failed to disclose certain information explicitly required by the Act or that ambiguous terminology was used that could lead to confusion.

The third consumer advocacy law directly affecting the work of the FTC was the Magnuson-Moss–Federal Trade Commission Improvement Act. This Act became law on January 4, 1975, but it did not mark the beginning of FTC regulation against deceptive warranties and product guarantees. For example, the FTC had attempted to regulate unrestricted language of warranties in the automobile industry since the 1930s. During the 1960s, the agency was particularly aggressive in pursuing actions against watch makers who claimed an unlimited warranty when, in fact, certain limitations were placed on the transactions. The challenge of the new law was to infuse some standardization in the area of warranties but to do so in a way that did not stifle competition.

Congress intended the Magnuson-Moss Act to accomplish three things: 1) ensure that consumers have available to them complete information about warranty terms and conditions and are thereby empowered to know what to expect if something goes wrong; 2) ensure that consumers could compare warranty coverage before buying so that consumers would have the opportunity to choose a product with the best combination of price, features, and warranty coverage to meet their specific needs; and, 3) promote competition on the basis of warranty coverage by encouraging sales promotion on the basis of warranty coverage and among companies to meet consumer preferences through various levels of warranty coverage. The Act did not pertain to whether a company should use a warranty or not and only applied to written warranties, but the new law did outline thirteen specific pieces of information that must be present in a warranty that is offered to a consumer. These specifications included such things as requiring companies to clearly identify the party or parties to whom the warranty is extended and to include a statement instructing the consumer of the time at which the warrantor will perform any obligations under the warranty.

Finally, the Magnuson-Moss Act required companies to issue either full warranties or limited warranties. Full warranties were characterized as those in which there is no limit in the duration of implied warranties, service is provided to anyone who owns the product during the warranty period, the warranty service is provided free of charge, including such costs as returning the product or removing and reinstalling the product, the consumer is offered a choice to either a replacement or a full refund if the product cannot be repaired in a reasonable period of time, and the buyer is not required to perform any duty as a precondition for receiving service under the terms of the warranty. Any variations to these provisions would imply a limited warranty for consumers.

Each of these three laws–the Fair Packaging and Labeling Act, the Truth-In-Lending Act, and the Magnuson-Moss–Federal Trade Commission Act–grew out of a desire among consumer protection advocates to prevent unfair business practices that directly affected consumer behavior, while at the same time, permitting some competition to remain. These laws did not necessarily lead the FTC into new regulatory territory. However, they helped to clarify the FTC's role as a key federal agency committed to helping protect the consumer from deceptive business practices. The highly organized and unified consumer movement of the mid to late 1960s was critical in defining the FTC's jurisdiction in regulating packaging, financial transactions, and warranties. It did not take long, however, for these same mer advocacy groups, headed by high profile individuals, to focus their social agendas on the FTC itself.

The most high profile attacks on the FTC arising from the consumer movement were contained in reports issued separately by Ralph Nader and his group of young consumer protection advocates ("Nader's Raiders") and the American Bar Association, each were published only months apart in 1969. Both reports were highly critical of the FTC's overall administrative and regulatory performance. The Nader report placed much of the blame for the Commission's perceived inefficiency on a lack of qualified personnel and poorly formulated decision-making. The Nader report argued that the FTC spent a disproportionate amount of time and effort focused on peripheral regulatory matters that would result in little gains for the consumer, while at the same time, ignoring consumer fraud perpetuated by large firms advertising in the mass media. Paralleling the social justice movement of the 1960s, the Nader report also criticized the FTC for ignoring the poor and minority groups who were particularly vulnerable to deceptive practices. The report issued by the American Bar Association criticized the FTC on similar grounds, arguing that the agency was focused on trivial regulatory pursuits rather than committing itself to tackling consumer fraud that caused the most harm to those least able to protect themselves.

The FTC responded to these criticisms by claiming that the charges in the Nader and ABA reports were greatly exaggerated and that, in fact, the agency has been extraordinarily bold in its enforcement activities. Officials within the FTC argued that much of the consumer fraud was perpetuated by racketeers and other criminals that, due to the nature of their activities, were immune to regulatory remedies such as cease and desist orders or voluntary compliance. The problem thus was not an issue of FTC personnel or the agency's organization structure, but rather was a symptom of statutory deficiencies governing the regulatory remedies available to the Commission.

The Magnuson-Moss–Federal Trade Commission Act of 1975 was instrumental in promoting warranty reform. The Act was also instrumental in expanding the Commission's jurisdiction in matters of antitrust enforcement. The Act opened up court representation so that the FTC no longer had to rely on the attorney general to be agency's representative. The law gave the FTC authority to prescribe rules defining what acts or practices were unfair or deceptive. For the first time, Magnuson-Moss gave the Commission power to take violators of its trade regulation rules directly to court to obtain civil penalties. Furthermore, the Act allowed the FTC to request the courts to order the refunding of money, the paying of damages, or the rewriting of specific contract clauses if firms were unfair to consumers. In short, Magnuson-Moss gave the FTC expressed authority to formulate substantive rules that had industry-wide impact. FTC regulators no longer were required to show that an act was deceptive, only that the act violated the conditions of a specific trade regulation rule. With this new enforcement authority, it did not take long before the FTC had entered a new era of aggressive antitrust regulation after 1970, promoted in large part by the same consumer interest groups that had criticized the agency in the late 1960s.

Although there were setbacks, judicial review of FTC actions appeared to parallel legislative actions that enabled the FTC's ability to seek innovative regulatory remedies. For example, in the 1976 case of *Spiegel, Inc. v. FTC* the Seventh Circuit court ruled that the Commission had the power to prohibit a practice specifically permitted by a state statute pursuant to its unfairness authority under Section 5 of the FTC Act. The case of *Warner-Lambert Co. v. FTC* also expanded the agency's authority when the District of Columbia Circuit court ruling allowed the FTC to demand in a cease and desist order that affirmative action be taken to correct deceptive advertising. These two cases highlight a period in which the FTC's work was greatly expanded to encompass the philosophical goals of social responsibility.

In 1977, Michael Pertschuk was appointed chairman of the FTC after serving fourteen years as chief counsel to the Senate Commerce Committee chaired by Senator Warren G. Magnuson. The Committee under Magnuson represented, in many respects, the legislative focal point of reform efforts intended to greatly strengthen the power of the FTC. With this in mind, Pertschuk set out to expand antitrust regulations based, not on abstract principles of economic efficiency, but rather on humanistic concerns within the context of the nation's democratic and social values. With this progression to the chairmanship of the Commission, coupled with liberal judicial review of FTC actions, Pertschuk felt empowered to guide the FTC into a new era of expansionist regulatory policy.

In early 1978, Pertschuk tested the boundaries of socially responsible regulation when he initiated an investigation of the entire industry of television advertising aimed at children. The action was focused in two areas: a ban on television advertising of presweetened breakfast cereals, and a broader ban on all advertising directed at children, which was advocated by the Boston consumerism group, Action for Children's Television. The FTC faced a number of vexing issues related to regulating children's advertising, such as what is children's programming? Whose values should dictate the content of the programs? What distinctions should be made among different age groups? Despite these questions, the agency went forward with its investigation under pressure from consumer advocates. Within months, however, a consortium of companies and trade associations had formed a unified front to block the FTC from regulating children's television advertising. Along with similar resistance from associations and companies to trade regulation rules directed at the funeral industry and line-of-business reporting, the legislative mandate that had created a favorable political environment in Congress for an aggressive Commission was beginning to wane.

By the end of 1979, a serious backlash was forming within all three branches of government to regain control over the expansive rulemaking represented by the FTC's actions against big business interests such as children's television advertisers and the funeral industry. The consumerism agenda began to witness major defeats in the courts as well, specifically with regards to the case of *Illinois Brick Co. v. FTC* that limited antitrust recoveries to direct purchasers and middlemen. In Congress, a clear message was sent to consumerists when legislators refused to establish a new federal consumer protection agency. Executive oversight was also about to make a dramatic turn away from expansionist antitrust regulation when Ronald Reagan, soon after he was elected President, appointed James C. Miller III as the new chair of the FTC.

The Federal Trade Commission in the New Republican Era, 1980-1992

The transitional period between the reign of Michael Pertschuk's expansionist philosophy based on the tenets of consumer protectionism and the beginning of James C. Miller's tenure as chairman of the FTC was a time when Congress attempted to significantly reduce the agency's rulemaking authority. On a much broader scale, the political climate in Washington was changing significantly. The central issue underlying the question of how wealth should be distributed in the United States was no longer centered on issues of social justice and protectionism, but was now focused on viewing regulation as a means for promoting economic efficiency in the marketplace. At the center of this controversy was the authorization of funding for the FTC tied to legislation intended to place restrictions on FTC enforcement activities and to forge a better relationship between the Commission and the business world.

Passed May 28, 1980, the Federal Trade Commission Improvements Act contained several provisions intended to place restrictions on FTC enforcement activities. For example, Section 3 forbid the agency from releasing any trade secret or any commercial or financial information gathered during the course of an investigation. This section was in response to the FTC releasing data obtained under a subpoena from the Tobacco Institute and several cigarette companies stating that possible reductions in cigarette sales would likely occur should a ban on smoking in public buildings be instituted.

Also attached to the amendment was a legislative veto proposal that would give Congress veto power over any rules promulgated by the FTC. This was a particularly controversial issue. The legislative veto was enacted into law as Section 21 of the FTC Improvement Act of 1980 and meant that, for the first time in American history, Congress had the power to veto any actions of an independent regulatory agency without the president's approval. During the debate and because appropriations for the agency were tied up in the legislation, the FTC shut down for a day on May 1, 1980, the first agency ever closed due to a lapse in appropriations from Congress. The controversy surrounding the possible constitutionality of the legislative veto provision was not resolved until President Jimmy Carter intervened, accepting the provision as a necessary condition for ensuring the future viability of the FTC. Within three years the Supreme Court ruled that the legislative veto was unconstitutional.

By the time Ronald Reagan took office, changes within the agency had already begun. Agency funding had been cut by five percent for fiscal year 1981 and was to be cut by an additional eleven percent for fiscal year 1982. This forced the FTC to cut back considerably on its enforcement activities. With the resignation of Michael Pertschuk as chairman, David A. Clanton took over on an interim basis until President Reagan appointed a permanent successor. Republican James C. Miller III of Georgia was eventually chosen as the new leader of the FTC, replacing Paul Rand Dixon who had retired, and although there was some resistance to his appointment, his nomination passed the Senate by a vote of ninety-two to two.

Miller was a conservative regulator who fundamentally changed the Commission's emphasis from social to economic regulation. Miller believed that the prior work of the FTC was misguided because it was based on perceptions of the consumer as ignorant and uninformed and that business was composed of villainous conglomerates intent on destroying America's free market economy. Miller refocused advertising substantiation requirements on only the most egregious violators and, although not formally challenged by the courts, Miller announced that the requirements would only be issued against individual companies rather than on an industry-wide basis. In addition, Miller called for the FTC to revert back to more traditional regulatory activities by going after only advertisements of products proven to be dangerous to the consumer rather than simply deceptive. Finally, Miller promoted regulatory policies that were intended to facilitate the flow of information to the consumer. The idea was that, if most consumers in the marketplace possess adequate information, then there would be no need for the government to regulate business. In short, Miller intended to create an FTC that would facilitate economic activity in the aggregate rather than place what he saw as arbitrary restrictions on business activities. Central to this philosophy was a desire to significantly reduce rulemaking proceedings and rely more heavily on adjudication.

The rise of economic conservatism did not mean that the FTC was abdicating its responsibility to pursue cases against violators of the antitrust laws, although these actions were met with decidedly mixed results. For example, Miller promoted a strong campaign against antitrust exemptions for professional groups. At the center of this action was the American Medical Association, which claimed that the FTC had overstepped its authority in attempting to regulate a nonprofit professional organization. Upholding the lower court's decision, the Supreme Court, in *American Medical Association v. FTC*, decided in favor of the FTC to regulate the professional pricing and advertising practices of professional organizations. Under considerable lobbying efforts by the AMA, Congress considered reversing the ruling thereby prohibiting the FTC from preempting state regulations in this area. However, given the rising costs of health care and general demands by the public to reform the health care industry, Congress refused to acquiesce to the AMA demands and those of other professional organizations by passing a compromise bill giving the FTC the authority to regulate only the business practices of nonprofit professional groups and preventing the FTC to interfere in the work of state licensing boards that governed issues of medical competence.

Miller's term as chairman of the FTC had lasted only fifty months when, in 1985, he left the FTC to become head of the Office of Management and Budget after David Stockman resigned. Nevertheless, the impact Miller had on reshaping the FTC was significant. In general, his commitment to requiring economic justification for developing any antitrust or consumer protection initiatives succeeded in establishing a non-adversarial relationship between the agency and the business community. Miller's objective of reducing the Commission's rulemaking activity was also successful, although it should be noted that his elimination of certain on-going proceedings were begun during Republican administrations and not during Pertschuk's tenure in office. Finally, Miller was instrumental in advocating for a statutory clarification of the unfairness doctrine, which remained overly broad and vague. Although he ultimately failed to convince Congress to pass legislation incorporating his proposal to codify the FTC's recommended definition of unfairness, Miller succeeded in convincing Congress to defeat measures that would have narrowed the Commission's jurisdiction with regard to regulating professional groups and commercial advertising. After James C. Miller III resigned as chairman, the FTC was chaired by Terry Calvani and Daniel Oliver for the remainder of the 1980s until Janet Steiger took over in August of 1989. During the time between 1986 and 1995, several important initiatives occupied the work of FTC officials.

The broadest initiative concerned reforming the administration of trade regulation rules. Recognizing that rules that were appropriate at the time they were developed may now be obsolete due to the introduction of new laws or changes in technologies and marketing techniques, the FTC adopted a plan in 1992 to review all trade rules at least once every ten years. In addition, the FTC also began reviewing the appropriateness of Industrial Guides and other interpretive policies related to business practice guidelines. The early 1990s also marked the beginning of new rulemaking proceedings involving workshop conferences intended to bring together representatives from all groups possibly affected by a proposed trade regulation rule. The purpose of these conferences was not to build a consensus for action, but to promote meaningful dialogue among the various stakeholders that identifies key issues that need to be addressed.

The FTC during this period also issued revised joint Horizontal Merger Guidelines with the Department of Justice's Antitrust Division. The primary purpose of these guidelines was to prevent mergers determined to have an anticompetitive effect on the marketplace, while at the same time, encouraging firms to merge if the combination could enhance competition. The merger guidelines were intended to articulate the conditions under which certain types of mergers that would be challenged by these antitrust enforcement agencies and to lend a sense of predictability to the enforcement actions of each agency. The 1992 guidelines replaced both the 1984 Merger Guidelines released by the Department of Justice and the 1982 Statement Concerning Horizontal Merger Guidelines issued by the FTC. These guidelines represented a new direction for the FTC under Janet Steiger who called for a reorientation of enforcement priorities, particularly in the area of mergers. On a broader scale, the emphasis of revised rulemaking procedures and merger guidelines represented a gradual shift away from regulation to the enforcement of existing laws.

In the Spring of 1995, Robert Pitofsky assumed leadership of the FTC. By this time, two major issues had matured to the point that they dramatically affected the work of the Commission—emerging information technologies and their affect on commerce, and the growing global marketplace. In response, the Commission commenced hearing to examine the continued viability of current consumer protection and antitrust laws in light of these two issues. The hearings involved a broad range of constituents affected by the work of the FTC, including experts in law, economics, marketing, consumer behavior, and consumer education. From this discussion, a number of themes were identified that helped lay the groundwork for future enforcement and regulatory priorities of the agency.

Under Pitofsky, the FTC also attempted to foster private sector self-regulation. The purpose of these workshops was to facilitate solutions to problems within specific markets without having to resort to costly and time-consuming rulemaking procedures. Related to these activities, the FTC continued to encourage a wide array of self-regulatory actions within industry.

Finally, the FTC under Pitofsky has been characterized as an agency that actively seeks partnerships with others to create more meaningful and lasting enforcement initiatives. For example, inspection results of dairy products such as milk and of juice beverages revealed significant short-filling of containers. To address the problem, the FTC worked closely with federal agencies, such as the Department of Agriculture and the Food and Drug Administration, and the weights and measurement authorities in over twenty states, to determine the facts and development appropriate remedies. Partnerships had also been sought to help publicize consumer rights under certain trade regulation rules. This approach has succeeded in facilitating the dissemination of consumer fraud information through non-traditional channels like including information on billing statements or public billboards.

These programs and initiatives succeeded on another level as well—they ensured a relatively quiet period for the agency. Although the FTC was active in asserting its authority to review mergers, some of which were particularly well-publicized in mid-1990s, there was relatively little criticism of the FTC's social and economic legitimacy during this period. This period of relative stability was likely the result of significant regulatory reform efforts that have reduced the number of rules and guides by about one-third, increased attention to harmonization with current antitrust laws, and facilitated the pursuit of non-regulatory solutions to problems.

The Federal Trade Commission Today and In the Future

At the beginning of a new century, the Federal Trade Commission has, for the most part, continued down this path, although the agency has become increasingly intertwined in the ambiguities of Internet-based commerce and its implications for promoting new forms of fraud and deception. Of particular concern is the issue of privacy. The FTC recently promulgated recommendations to Congress that would help protect consumer privacy online. Paralleling earlier efforts to find non-regulatory means of addressing consumer protection issues, the FTC has begun to sponsor workshops with the Department of Commerce focusing on how alternative dispute resolution programs may contribute to fostering consumer confidence without unnecessarily burdening business, and to explore the use of alternative dispute resolution as one means of providing transparent and effective redress for consumers engaged in online transactions.

It appears that emerging technologies will continue to grow in economic importance relative to the distribution of wealth in America and across the globe. As old forms of deception and unfairness are transposed onto the new digital environment, a review of the current initiatives and activities of the FTC listed on its web site appears to show that the Commission is taking a proactive position in regulating deception on the Internet. The 2000 presidential election could also determine to a large degree if Robert Pitofsky and other personnel continue to lead the FTC in the near future.

Today, the regulatory functions of the Federal Trade Commission are organized within three bureaus, each subdivided further into divisions. The Bureau of Competition enforces the antitrust laws within the administrative jurisdiction of the Commission. The Bureau of Consumer Protection is responsible for investigating instances of alleged unfair and deceptive business practices and to foster compliance with FTC rules and regulations in this area. This Bureau is also responsible for educating the public and the business community about the laws the agency enforces. The Bureau of Economics advises FTC personnel on the economic issues by preparing economic surveys of markets and analysis of economic conditions. Areas of analysis cover any aspect of FTC authority. A complete description of the FTC, including an organizational chart, can be found in the current edition of the *Federal Regulatory Directory*.

Appendix Two
Regional Offices

East Central Regional Office
Federal Trade Commission
1111 Superior Avenue, Suite 200
Cleveland, OH 44114-2507
The East Central Region serves the residents of the following states: Delaware, Maryland, Michigan, Ohio, Pennsylvania, Virginia and West Virginia as well as the District of Columbia.

Midwest Regional Office
Federal Trade Commission
55 East Monroe Street, Suite 1860
Chicago, IL 60603-5701
The Midwest Regional Office serves the residents of the following states: Illinois, Indiana, Iowa, Kansas, Kentucky, Nebraska, North Dakota, Minnesota, Missouri, South Dakota, and Wisconsin.

Northeast Regional Office
Federal Trade Commission
1 Bowling Green
New York, NY 10004
The Northeast Region serves the residents of the following states: Connecticut, Maine, Massachusetts, New Hampshire, New Jersey, New York, Rhode Island, and Vermont.

Northwest Regional Office
Federal Trade Commission
2896 Federal Building
915 Second Avenue
Seattle, WA 98174.
The Northwest Regional Office serves the residents of the following states: Alaska, Idaho, Montana, Oregon, Washington and Wyoming.

Southeast Regional Office
Federal Trade Commission
Suite 5M35
60 Forsyth Street, SW
Atlanta, GA 30303-2322
The Southeast Region serves the residents of the following states: Alabama, Florida, Georgia, Mississippi, North Carolina, South Carolina, and Tennessee.

Southwest Regional Office
Federal Trade Commission
1999 Bryan Street, Suite 2150
Dallas, TX 75201-6808
The Southwest Regional Office serves the residents of the following states: Arkansas, Louisiana, New Mexico, Oklahoma, and Texas.

Western Regional Office
Federal Trade Commission
901 Market Street, Suite 570
San Francisco, CA 94103

Western Regional Office
Federal Trade Commission
10877 Wilshire Blvd., Suite 700
Los Angeles, California 90024
The Western Region has two offices serving the residents of the following states: Arizona, Northern California, Southern California, Colorado, Hawaii, Nevada and Utah.

Appendix Three
Glossary of Terms

Acquisition.....a merger. It includes all forms of mergers and acquisitions, including statutory mergers and acquisition of stocks or assets, whether for cash or securities or both.

Ad Substantiation Program.....prior to the dissemination of an advertisement, requires that an advertiser be able to submit to the FTC all tests, studies, or other information that purport to substantiate any representation made concerning the product's safety, performance, efficiency, or comparative price.

Adjudicative Proceedings.....administrative procedure. Instituted to resolve a complaint that alleges that a company is engaging in anti-competitive or unfair or deceptive acts or practices. Adjudicative proceeding begins after the commission has conducted an investigation and issued a formal complaint alleging some form of illegal behavior. Respondent has 30 days to answer complaint and either stops illegal practice and makes restitution, or if seeks to dispute charge, an administrative law judge is named and a hearing is scheduled.

Advisory Opinion.....issued by the FTC in response to a request from a company, organization, or other entity requesting clarification or interpretation of a rule or regulation in order to predict how the FTC might act upon the firm's proposed action. This is frequently used by merging firms to seek a nonbinding opinion from the agency in regards to possible antitrust violations.

Affirmative Disclosure Order.....an order that requires advertisements to include a statement that the product may not be totally effective for everyone who uses it.

Amicus Briefs.....a written document submitted to the court by a third party in support of a party's position on a legal question. The amicus brief provides information to the court and urges a judgement compatible with the interests of the party submitting it. The amicus participant ("friend of the court") is typically representing a special interest group.

Antideceptive Practice.....a vast range of FTC activity concerning "unfair" or deceptive acts or practices in commerce (most are cases of false 0r misleading advertising); all cases arising under Section 12 and most cases arising under Section 5 of the FTC Act are antideceptive practice cases.

Antimerger Case.....a case brought under the provisions of Section 7 of the Clayton Act as amended in 1950 by the Celler-Kefauver Act and Section 5 of the FTC Act, which forbids corporate mergers or stock acquisitions where the effect may be to lesson substantially competition or tend to create a monopoly in any line of commerce.

Application for Complaint.....a letter from the public which alleges commercial wrongdoing on the part of a business firm or individual.

Assurance of Discontinuance.....an informal means of obtaining compliance with the law without launching an investigation or using mandatory compliance procedures.

Attorney Examiner.....field office attorney who investigate cases (also known as "attorney investigators").

Attorney in Charge.....the manager of a Federal Trade Commission field office.

Bait and Switch.....a deceptive practice by a seller that uses a low-priced item to lure consumers into the store (the bait), then induces the consumer to purchase higher-priced models by failing to sufficiently stock the lower-priced item or by disparaging the less expensive item (the switch).

Cartel.....cartels occur when firms in a market seek to maximize their profits by agreeing to raise prices and restrict output.

Case-by-case.....an approach to the regulation of deceptive behavior or merger activity in which enforcement is issued through the process of litigating individual cases.

Caveat Emptor.....Latin for "let the buyer beware," this refers to the doctrine that the purchaser assumes all the risk in regards to a product's quality and purported performance. It is not designed to protect the seller, but rather, summarizes the maxim that the consumer should investigate, judge and test the product before purchase. Consumer protection rules and regulations issued by the FTC have minimized the impact of this doctrine.

Cease and Desist Order.....formal order issued by the FTC that legally prohibits a business entity from continuing a deceptive practice or misleading advertisement. It is the administrative agency equivalent of an court injunction.

Celler-Kefauver Amendment.....enacted in 1950, it expands restrictions articulated in the Clayton Act of 1914 with regards to merger activity.

Chicago School of Antitrust Regulation.....revisionist view of antitrust regulation that developed in the early 1960s. It de-emphasizes antitrust law as an economic form of regulation and advocates antitrust enforcement from a public policy and consumer welfare framework of understanding. Those who defend traditional antitrust policies are frequently identified with Harvard School antitrust regulation.

Class Action.....a lawsuit that involves a group of individuals that possess a similar interest in regards to the subject matter of the lawsuit. Class action suits are usually allowed when it is impractical to name every individual involved in the suit.

Clayton Act.....enacted in 1914, Section 7, amended in 1950 by the Celler-Kefauver Act, prohibits mergers or acquisitions of stock or assets where the effect may be substantially to lesson competition or to tend to create a monopoly in any line of commerce in any section of the country. Other provisions include a prohibition on price discrimination (which, as amended, is referred to as the Robinson-Patman Act), and various procedural provisions (including a provision for private actions for violation of antitrust laws).

Closing.....when a completed investigation is deemed to have shown no violation of the law, or shown a minor violation not feasible for prosecution, it is recommended that the whole case be "closed" (also known as "dropped").

Collusion.....occurs when two or more business enterprises reach an agreement to deceive or otherwise mislead consumers or harm competition.

Comment Period.....period of time specified in an initial notice of proposed rulemaking in which the public may submit written data, views, or arguments on any topic related to fact, law, or policy.

Commercial Speech.....speech that constitutes advertising or other forms of expressive behavior that promotes a product or service for profit or other business purposes.

Common Law.....refers to a collective body of law that derives its authority, not from legislative enactment, but through usages and customs prior to the American Revolution and is derived in general from judicial decisions.

Comparative Pricing......allows consumers to rate the prices charged by a seller for goods or services that have been compared to other sources. In advertising, the price comparison may be made with the advertiser's own previous prices or other prices, or the same or comparable goods.

Complaint.....a formal public statement of charges against a respondent which the Bureau of Litigation believes it can prove. A complaint is drafted by the Bureau of Litigation but must be approved by the Commission itself.

Concentration Ratio.....the aggregate market share of the number of firms with respect to which the concentration ratio is computed.

Conglomerate.....refers to an acquisition which is neither vertical nor horizontal. Includes product extension and market extension mergers.

Consent Order.....administrative procedure/negotiations. Orders issued by the commission in which a company neither admits nor denies violating the law, but agrees to discontinue certain practices and to take some type of affirmative action to rectify past actions. Proposed consent order is published in the *Federal Register* and is open for public comment for 60 days. Comments then are considered by the commission in deciding whether to issue the order in final form.

Consumerism.....refers to a movement characterized by a greater awareness by consumers as to their presence in the marketplace and a recognition by advocacy groups or organizations for the need to protect the consumer from deceptive business practices and misleading or unfair selling methods.

Cooling Off Rule......remedy mandating a three-day "cooling-off" period on most door-to-door sales contracts. During this period buyers may rescind their contracts merely by notifying the seller. Applies to door-to-door transactions in which the seller or his representative personally solicits the sale of a product or service and the buyer's agreement or offer to purchase is made at a place other than the place of business of the seller.

Corporate Image Advertising.....the practice by a firm to advertise an image rather than product and in this way promote an overall favorable impression of the company in the minds of consumers.

Corrective Advertising.....a consumer protection remedy supported by the FTC at one time that attempted to use the persuasive power of advertising to offset the effects on the consumer of a previously misleading or false claim. It would have required firms to issue advertisements that would "correct" the misleading claims and thereby reduce the deceptive harm imposed on consumers.

Counteradvertising......a form of remedy intended to educate consumers about a product. Possible conditions that could justify mandating the use of counteradvertising are advertisements that concern controversial issues, advertisements that rely on scientific premises that are still questioned within the scientific community, and advertisements that do not inform consumers about the negative aspects of a product or service.

Debtor.....person who owes a payment or financial obligation to another.

Deception.....in advertising, the act of misleading or misrepresenting the characteristics a product or service. When applied to sales practices, it has been defined by the FTC to mean a deceptive act that is likely to deceive a consumer acting reasonably under the circumstances of the sales transaction.

Deconcentration.....the act of breaking up a highly concentrated group of firms that control a inordinate amount of the market in a particular industry and thus hinder competition within that market.

Divestiture.....in antitrust law, refers to a court order to sell certain assets, such as a subsidiary or division, in order to comply with merger and acquisition guidelines.

Division of Compliance.....the unit in the General Counsel's Office responsible for gaining and maintaining compliance with all outstanding cease and desist orders.

Economic Reports.....produced by the Bureau of Economics, these studies provide a detailed economic analysis of various markets and industries, focusing on the economic effects of regulation and on issues that are of importance to antitrust and consumer protection law enforcement.

Enjoinment.....similar to an injunction or restraining order, it directs a person or firm to abstain or desist from a particular act or to require a certain action to be performed.

Exclusive Dealings.....an arrangement in which a buyer agrees to purchase products or services for a period of time from only one supplier and is not allowed to purchase competing products or services from another supplier.

Exhaustion Doctrine......considered an expression of executive and administrative autonomy that prevents premature interference with agency processes, thereby allowing the agency to function effectively by correcting its own errors and utilizing its expertise. The policies underlying the exhaustion doctrine are: (1) keeping the administrative process free from premature interruptions; (2) letting the administrative agency acquire the factual background necessary for decision making; (3) allowing the agency to use its skills and its expertise; (4) facilitating prompt resolution of the issue; (5) preserving administrative and executive autonomy; (6) promoting administrative efficiency and judicial economy; and (7) improving agency effectiveness and morale.

Extraterritorial.....beyond the physical or juridical boundaries of a specific state or country.

Extrinsic Evidence.....message conveyed by an advertisement that consists of any evidence of deception apart from the communication itself. There are two major categories of extrinsic evidence: consumer research involving a survey data or observation of consumers and expert testimony.

Fair Packaging and Labeling Act.....section five of this 1982 Act gives the FTC the authority to issue rules concerning the packaging and labeling of any commodity not covered by the Federal Food, Drug, and Cosmetic Act of 1982.

Fairness Doctrine......derived from a provision of the Federal Communications Act, it is the means by which the FCC assures that the public can hear representative views on controversial issues. In a regulatory context, the concept provides that opposing parties should be given fair or equal opportunity to articulate their viewpoints.

Finality Doctrine......an order or decree which holds that a district court may not, for purposes of appeal, render a judgement final which is provisional or interim. Finality means that the judgement must dispose of at least a single substantive claim.

Fishing Expedition.....refers to investigations that seek information without a definite purpose in hopes of eliciting some significant findings.

Formal Case.....a case in which a complaint has been issued by the FTC.

Green Marketing.....the use of environmental terms such as "recyclable" and "degradable" by advertisers to promote the characteristics of a product or service as being environmentally safe.

Guides Program.....one of the Bureau of Consultation's means of obtaining voluntary compliance with FTC laws by spelling out in layman's language fairly explicit guidelines regarding the legality or illegality of specific practices.

Hart-Scott-Rodino Antitrust Improvement Act.....grants broad regulatory powers by requiring a waiting period to obtain antitrust clearance from either the Department of Justice or the FTC before a merger can take place.

Hearing Examiner.....an official who hears litigated cases as does a judge in a civil court of original jurisdiction; he then writes initial decision which is submitted to the FTC for final action; the examiner also approves consent settlements before they are submitted to the FTC.

Heller Report.....management survey of the FTC conducted by Robert Heller and Associates of Cleveland in 1953-54 and became effective July 1, 1954. The FTC was reorganized primarily based on recommendations from the Report.

High-Low Pricing......the practice of setting prices at an initially high level for a limited period of time and then discounting the merchandise for the bulk of the selling season. Inherent deception occurs when the higher price is referenced in advertising and store signage as the "regular," "former," or "original" price.

Holder-in-Due-Course.....an individual who accepts a bill of exchange (promissory note, bank check or other negotiable instrument for the payment of money) at face value and in good faith absent of any notice that the instrument is overdue, subject to any claim against it or other action.

Horizontal Merger.....a merger among competing firms that are on the same level of the distribution chain. Horizontal price fixing refers to an agreement among firms on the same level of the distribution chain to avoid competition by charging the same price.

Implied Warranty.....under state law in connection with sale by supplier of a consumer product, this term refers to the reasonable duration of quality of a product or service after purchase, although it makes no inchoate promise that may become enforceable after the delivery of goods or services.

In Camera.....evidence gathered during an investigation that is not made a part of the public record.

Infomercial.....a commercial, usually thirty minutes in length, that demonstrates the use of a product or describes a service and usually takes the form of an entertainment show.

Informal Case or Matter.....any case which is in a stage preliminary to the issuance of a complaint.

Intellectual Property......refers to any product or idea that results from creative process, research, or design and that can be protected under federal law, including copyrightable works, ideas, discoveries, and inventions.

Intervenor Funding.....refers to the practice of reimbursing groups and individuals for expenses incurred during participation in regulatory agency proceedings.

Joint Venture.....an association of persons or companies that are engaged in an activity for profit in which generally all members of the venture contribute assets and share in the risk.

Lanham Trade-Mark Act.....establishes a comprehensive system of federal registration of trademarks and other marks of identification. The Act gives the FTC the power to petition the Commissioner of Patents for the cancellation of a mark under certain circumstances.

Legal Advisor.....a senior attorney who provides legal advice and assistance to other lawyers in the agency.

Legislative Intent.....refers to the reasoning behind why a law was created by Congress or other legislative body.

Little FTC Act.....in a general sense, this refers to any consumer protection or deceptive trade practice legislation adopted in one form or another by a state. In a more narrow interpretation, it is a piece of legislation adopted by a state that is specifically modeled after the FTC Act.

Magnuson-Moss Warranty Act.....passed in 1975, this law represents the most comprehensive legal regulation of consumer product warranties. The Act requires manufacturers and retailers who market products covered by written warranties to make full disclosure of the warranty terms, including scope or warranty protection and how long the warranty lasts and how the warranties are enforced and methods of redress for unsatisfied customers. In addition, the Act requires that the warranty's provisions be written in simple and readily understandable language.

Market.....a collection of buyers and sellers whose transactions determine the price of a commodity or service. The buyers or sellers, or both, may and do trade in various parts of the market, which may be accessible areas within which traders or commodities or services move, or accessible products whose prices exert a decisive influence upon the price of the commodity or service in question.

413

Market Extension.....refers to a conglomerate merger involving two firms which produce goods which are identical or substitutable but are sold in different geographical markets.

McCarran-Ferguson Act.....legislation enacted by Congress in 1945 declaring that states can continue to regulate the insurance industry, while at the same time, protecting the business activities of insurance companies from federal regulation because it does not constitute interstate commerce.

Mock up.....the use of props in television advertising to show particular attributes or characteristics of a product.

Monopoly.....refers to the market structure of a particular industry in which only one firm is present. It also refers to a firm's power to dominate or control a market segment. This power is generally manifested in the firm's ability to control prices or exclude competitors.

Multiple Price Basing System......In its simplest from, this refers to a producer that manufacturers a product at points A and B, and sells it to all buyers at a price computed by adding to a mill price the freight tariff from point A, for example; this is so even though the goods may be shipped to a buyer from the mill at point B. Point A is considered the "basing point" and, from the standpoint of freight delivery, three facts become clear from the use of this system: 1) if the producer supplies the buyer from the mill at B and pays less actual freight on the shipment than the tariff from point A to the buyer, the producer has acquired the differential commonly referred to as "phantom freight"; 2) if the producer has to pay more actual freight on the shipment than the tariff from A to the buyer, the producer will be said to have "absorbed freight" and 3) from these observations a third follows stating that the "mill net" cost–the total price received for the goods minus the actual freight tariff paid by the producer–will vary as between buyers located at different points because the total price received by the producer upon deliveries from point B correlate to factors other than the actual costs of production or delivery.

Newness......refers to the use of the term "new" as it is applied by advertisers to describe the quality or state of a current product that is substantially dissimilar from an earlier product. The concept is primary applied to the ways in which it can be applied deceptively in advertising.

Noerr-Pennington Doctrine.....provides immunity from antitrust challenge for efforts to influence legislative, executive, administrative, and adjudicatory conduct by government as it relates to First Amendment rights of free speech and the right to petition for redress of grievances. The doctrine does not override competition policy in cases where the offending party engaged in flagrant, corrupting activity such as bribery or intentional misrepresentation or has initiated governmental process to harass its victims rather than to achieve the redress or resolution that the invoked process legitimately could offer.

Oligopoly.....a market structure in which there is a small number of large suppliers within a particular industry.

Oral Argument.....the oral portion of an appeal proceeding before the FTC; both FTC and respondent's counsel offer their views on a decision made by the hearing examiner.

Per Se Doctrine.....the concept that certain antitrust activities, such as price fixing, are inherently anti-competitive and injurious to the consumer and, therefore, action taken against such activity need not be supported with evidence that injury to the consumer or the marketplace actually occurred.

Predation.....action taken that is meant to drive out all competitors in a market regardless of fairness or whether such action would benefit the consumer. When applied to pricing, it refers to the setting of prices well below appropriate measure of cost with the intent of eliminating competitors and subsequently raising prices to recoup the losses incurred from the predatory move. Predatory pricing is also said to have the effect of disciplining competitors who otherwise refuse to cooperate in keeping prices at monopoly levels or is intended to depress the market value of rivals' assets enabling the predator to purchase these assets at below-market prices.

Prehearing Conference.....hearing before an administrative law judge to consider issues related to FTC procedures in a case. Hearings can be called to help clarify or simplify issues, to expedite the presentation of evidence, and/or other matters that will assist in the efficient and orderly disposition of proceedings.

Premerger Notification.....requirement that a corporation intending to acquire another firm notify the FTC or other regulatory agency that such action is about to take place. It is intended to prevent mergers that could be anti-competitive or monopolistic from proceeding. This requirement is embodied in the Hart-Scott-Rodino Antitrust Improvement Act of 1976.

Pretrial Discovery......refers to statutory or procedure devices, such as a written request to produce documents, used by parties prior to a trial to gather evidence.

Price Discrimination.....the practice of charging different prices to consumers when the cost of the product or service remains the same for the seller. Illegal price discrimination occurs when it is determined that the price difference cannot be justified on the basis of either specific cost savings or established in good faith to meet the lower price of a competitor.

Price Fixing.....an agreement among competitors for the purpose of raising, depressing, or freezing prices of a product or group of products or a service or group of services.

Private Action.....refers to the right of an individual to seek direct redress through a lawsuit

Product Extension.....refers to a conglomerate merger involving two firms which produce goods which are not identical or substitutable but may be related in methods of production or distribution.

Promulgate.....to make officially known to the public.

Prop.....*see* Mock-Up.

Puffery.....the practice of advertisers to exaggerate or place extravagant praise upon a product or services' qualities just short of deception. Puffery is allowed because the claim is so outrageous that a "normal" consumer would know immediately that the claim is an exaggeration.

Remedy.....any number of actions taken by a regulatory agency to reverse the harmful effects that have occurred because of deceptive trade practices or misleading or false advertising. Corrective advertising is an example of a remedy.

Resale Price Maintenance.....an agreement between a supplier and its distributors on resale prices.

Respondent.....alleged violator of an FTC-administered statute; a defendant.

Restraint of Trade.....a barrier that restricts interaction between firms conducting business trade practices. A conspiracy in restraint of trade exists when two or more firms or individuals agree to some unlawful practice relating to the free flow of commerce.

Right of Visitation.....power granted to the FTC during an investigation to examine any documents of a corporation deemed vital to the case.

Ripeness Doctrine......dictates that courts should avoid premature entanglements in agency decisions until it has been determined that the case has matured to a point of requiring judicial action. Ripeness reflects a judgment that the disadvantages of a premature review may prove too abstract or unnecessary, therefore outweighing the additional costs of post-implementation litigation.

Robinson-Patman Case.....restraint of trade cases in alleged violations of Sections 2(a), (c), (d), (e), and (f) of the Clayton Act as amended by the Robinson-Patman Act of 1936, which forbids commercial discrimination in price, service, or facilities where the effect may be to lessen competition.

Rule of Reason.....test applied to antitrust litigation in which all factors must be considered regarding the alleged violation. The plaintiff must show that actual harm to competition occurred and not simply that the practices were "unfair." The rule of reason does not apply to per se antitrust violations.

Section 6 Case.....an investigation conducted by correspondence under the authority of Section 6 of the FTC Act, which gives the FTC broad powers of inquiry; the law requires that recipients of FTC questionnaires answer all questions under oath.

Self-Regulation.....a concept that promotes regulation from within an industry usually through a set of guidelines, rules, or standards. Self-regulation is sometimes supported within an industry as a preferable alternative to government imposed regulation.

Shared Monopoly.....a small group of firms in a particular industry that act uniformly in regards to setting prices or other harmful business practices and is meant to exclude entry by other firms or otherwise suppress competition.

Sherman Antitrust Act.....the first major antitrust law, enacted in 1890. Section 1 prohibits contracts, combinations, and conspiracies in restraint of trade. Section 2 prohibits monopolization or attempts to monopolize.

Slotting Allowances......fees paid by a manufacturer to a retailer for the retailer's shelf space.

Special Legal Assistants.....the legal research and opinion writing staff who help the FTC decide procedural appeals and make final case dispositions.

Stipulation.....a publicized voluntary agreement (lacking the force of law such as a consent settlement has) to cease and desist from minor violations of FTC laws.

Substitution Laws.....laws which list brand name drugs and their therapeutically equivalent substitutes.

Tacit Collusion.....refers to firms conspiring to fix prices without overtly communicating with each other. This can accomplished by various means, including public announcements, changes in pricing policy, changes in output levels, or other neutral means. This type of anticompetitive cooperation is referred to as "facilitating practices."

Telemarketing......refers to the use of the telephone as a medium to sell, promote, or solicit goods and services.

Tentative Assignment.....a procedure whereby a trial attorney is assigned to a case still pending in the Bureau of Investigation in order that he may familiarize him or herself with the case as it develops and help guide the course of its investigation.

Trade Practice Conference.....a voluntary compliance procedure administered by the Bureau of Consultation in which the FTC meets with industry leaders to develop the content of a proposed set of trade practice rules.

Trade Regulation Rule.....rules that set standards and define which industry practices the commission holds to be unfair and deceptive. Commission was authorized to issue Trade Regulation Rules (TRR) by the Magnuson-Moss Warranty-FTC Improvement Act of 1974. TRRs have the force of law and can apply to an entire industry or be limited to industries in a specific geographic area. Published in the *Federal Register* and public hearings are conducted by a presiding officer. Final decision is made by the commission.

Trade Secrets......the systematic accumulation of information regarding business competitors and their products.

Trial Attorneys.....attorneys in the Bureau of Litigation who plead cases before hearing examiners and the FTC, and who negotiate consent settlement.

Truth-in-Lending Act.....requires that consumers seeking credit term information such as finance charge and the amount of periodic payments be fully disclosed during the consumer loan transaction. The Act is intended to promote the informed use of credit by consumers. The information is released in the form of a disclosure statement. (15 U.S.C.A. Section 1601 et seq.)

Tying Arrangements.....a marketing method in which a seller will sell one product or service (the "tying" product or service) only under the condition that the buyer also purchase an additional product or service (the "tied" product or service). Also known as a tying contract.

Unfair Methods of Competition.....an undefined phrase contained within the FTC Act that generally refers to activities that suppress competition within the marketplace. The "unfairness doctrine" refers to the manner by which the FTC operates in enforcing the unfair methods of competition portion of the FTC Act and the principles that guide its enforcement actions.

Uniform Deceptive Trade Practices Act.....passed in 1964, this act attempts to bring consistency into the state laws of unfair competition and deceptive trade practices. Two specific areas of deceptive trade practices or unfair competition are addressed by the Act: trademarks and false or misleading advertising. Among the most important provisions is the elimination of the need for proof of competition between parties as a prerequisite to relief.

Uniformity.....in the literature of this book, the term generally refers to cooperation among regulatory entities to create one rule or standard that does not differ over time or is applicable under all circumstances. Uniformity is sought when it is felt that it would lead to more efficient regulation.

Vertical Merger.....a merger among firms that function on different levels of the manufacture and distribution chain. Although the firms may not be in direct competition with one another, the merger could enhance the newly merged business enterprise ability to compete in the marketplace.

Voluntary Compliance.....the program of securing general voluntary law observance through various informal means; administered by the Bureau of Consultation.

Webb-Pomerene Act.....provides an exemption from the antitrust laws with regards to partnerships that are created for the sole purpose of engaging in export trade as long as trade within the United States or trade of a domestic competitor is not restrained. The Act imposes a registration requirement upon every export association that must be filed with the FTC within thirty days.

Wheeler-Lea Amendment.....greatly expands the FTC's authority by amending Section 5 of the FTC Act to allow the protection of the consumer without having to prove any simultaneous threat to competitors and by adding Section 12 to the FTC Act. This section specifically empowers the FTC to prevent false or misleading advertising.

Written Warranty.....under the Magnuson-Moss Warranty Act, this is defined as any written affirmation of fact or written promise made in connection with the sale of a consumer product by a supplier to a buyer which relates to the nature of the material or workmanship and affirms or promises that such material or workmanship is defect free or will meet a specified level of performance over a specified period of time.

Appendix Four
Internet Resources

Law Directories and Search Engines

ABA Administrative Procedure Database
    http://www.law.fsu.edu/library/admin

The Antitrust Case Browser
    http://www.stolaf.edu/people/becker/antitrust/antitrust.html

Competition Online
    http://www.clubi.ie/competition/compframesite/WorldsBiggestAnt
iTrustSitesList.html

Find Law
    http://findlaw.com

U.S. Government Sites

Consumer.Gov
    http://www.consumer.gov/index.htm

Consumer Product Safety Commission
    http://www.cpsc.gov

Department of Justice
    http://www.usdoj.gov

Environmental Protection Agency
    http://www.epa.gov

Federal Communications Commission
    http://www.fcc.gov

Federal Consumer Information Center
    http://www.pueblo.gsa.gov

Federal Trade Commission
   http://www.ftc.gov

Food and Drug Administration
   http://www.fda.gov

Professional Associations

American Bar Association
   http://www.abanet.org/antitrust/

Special Interest Groups

American Antitrust Institute
   http://www.antitrustinstitute.org

Antitrust Policy
   http://www.antitrust.org/index.htm

Better Business Bureau
   http://www.bbb.org

Consumer.Net
   http://www.consumer.net

Consumer World
   http://www.consumerworld.org

National Conference of Administrative Law Judges
   http://www.abanet.org/jd/ncalj/home.html

National Fraud Information Center
   http://www.fraud.org

Regulation.Org
   http://www.regulation.org

Appendix Five
The Federal Trade Commission Act

AN ACT To create a Federal Trade Commission, to define its powers and duties, and for other purposes.

Be it enacted by the Senate and House of Representatives of the United States of America in Congress assembled, That a commission is created and established, to be known as the Federal Trade Commission (hereinafter referred to as the Commission), which shall be composed of five Commissioners, who shall be appointed by the President, by and with the advice and consent of the Senate. Not more than three of the Commissioners shall be members of the same political party. The first Commissioners appointed shall continue in office for terms of three, four, five, six, and seven years, respectively, from September 26, 1914, the term of each to be designated by the President, but their successors shall be appointed for terms of seven years, except that any person chosen to fill a vacancy shall be appointed only for the unexpired term of the Commissioner whom he shall succeed: *Provided, however,* That upon the expiration of his term of office a Commissioner shall continue to serve until his successor shall have been appointed and shall have qualified. The President shall choose a chairman from the Commission's membership. No Commissioner shall engage in any other business, vocation, or employment. Any Commissioner may be removed by the President for inefficiency, neglect of duty, or malfeasance in office. A vacancy in the Commission shall not impair the right of the remaining Commissioners to exercise all the powers of the Commission.

The Commission shall have an official seal, which shall be judicially notice

42. Employees; expenses

Each commissioner shall receive a salary, payable in the same manner as the salaries of the judges of the courts of the United States. The commission shall appoint a secretary, who shall receive a salary, and it shall have authority to employ and fix the compensation of such attorneys, special experts, examiners, clerks, and other employees as it may from time to time find necessary for the proper performance of its duties and as may be from time to time appropriated for by Congress.

With the exception of the secretary, a clerk to each Commissioner, the attorneys, and such special experts and examiners as the Commission may from time to time find necessary for the conduct of its work, all employees of the Commission shall be a part of the classified civil service, and shall enter the service under such rules and regulations as may be prescribed by the Commission and by the Director of the Office of Personnel Management.

All of the expenses of the Commission, including all necessary expenses for transportation incurred by the Commissioners or by their employees under their orders, in making any investigation, or upon official business in any other places than in the city of Washington, shall be allowed and paid on the presentation of itemized vouchers therefor approved by the Commission.

Until otherwise provided by law, the Commission may rent suitable offices for its use.

The General Accounting Office shall receive and examine all accounts of expenditures of the Commission.

43. Office and place of meeting

The principal office of the Commission shall be in the city of Washington, but it may meet and exercise all its powers at any other place. The Commission may, by one or more of its members, or by such examiners as it may designate, prosecute any inquiry necessary to its duties in any part of the United States.

44. Definitions

The words defined in this section shall have the following meaning when found in this subchapter, to wit:

"Commerce" means commerce among the several States or with foreign nations, or in any Territory of the United States or in the District of Columbia, or between any such Territory and another, or between any such Territory and any State or foreign nation, or between the District of Columbia and any State or Territory or foreign nation.
"Corporation" shall be deemed to include any company, trust, so-called Massachusetts trust, or association, incorporated or unincorporated, which is

organized to carry on business for its own profit or that of its members, and has shares of capital or capital stock or certificates of interest, and any company, trust, so-called Massachusetts trust, or association, incorporated or unincorporated, without shares of capital or capital stock or certificates of interest, except partnerships, which is organized to carry on business for its own profit or that of its members.

"Documentary evidence" includes all documents, papers, correspondence, books of account, and financial and corporate records.

"Acts to regulate commerce" means subtitle IV of title 49 and the Communications Act of 1934 (47 U.S.C. 151 et seq.) and all Acts amendatory thereof and supplementary thereto.

"Antitrust Acts" means the Act entitled "An Act to protect trade and commerce against unlawful restraints and monopolies," approved July 2, 1890; also sections 73 to 77, inclusive, of an Act entitled "An Act to reduce taxation, to provide revenue for the Government, and for other purposes," approved August 27, 1894; also the Act entitled "An Act to amend sections 73 and 76 of the Act of August 27, 1894, entitled "An Act to reduce taxation, to provide revenue for the Government, and for other purposes," approved February 12, 1913; and also the Act entitled "An Act to supplement existing laws against unlawful restraints and monopolies, and for other purposes," approved October 15, 1914.

"Banks" means the types of banks and other financial institutions referred to in section 57a(f)(2) of this title.

45. Unfair methods of competition unlawful; prevention by Commission

(a) Declaration of unlawfulness; power to prohibit unfair practices; inapplicability to foreign trade

●(1) Unfair methods of competition in or affecting commerce, and unfair or deceptive acts or practices in or affecting commerce, are hereby declared unlawful.

●(2) The Commission is hereby empowered and directed to prevent persons, partnerships, or corporations, except banks, savings and loan institutions described in section 57a(f)(3) of this title, Federal credit unions described in section 57a(f)(4) of this title, common carriers subject to the Acts to regulate commerce, air carriers and foreign air carriers subject to part A of subtitle VII of title 49, and persons, partnerships, or corporations insofar as they are subject to the Packers and Stockyards Act, 1921, as amended (7 U.S.C. 181 et seq.), except as provided in section 406(b) of said Act (7 U.S.C. 227(b)), from using unfair methods of competition in or affecting commerce and unfair or deceptive acts or practices in or affecting commerce.

●(3) This subsection shall not apply to unfair methods of competition involving commerce with foreign nations (other than import commerce) unless -

    (A) such methods of competition have a direct, substantial, and reasonably foreseeable effect -

        (i) on commerce which is not commerce with foreign nations, or on import commerce with foreign nations; or

        (ii) on export commerce with foreign nations, of a person engaged in such commerce in the United States; and

(B) such effect gives rise to a claim under the provisions of this subsection, other than this paragraph. If this subsection applies to such methods of competition only because of the operation of subparagraph (A)(ii), this subsection shall apply to such conduct only for injury to export business in the United States.

(b) Proceeding by Commission; modifying and setting aside orders

Whenever the Commission shall have reason to believe that any such person, partnership, or corporation has been or is using any unfair method of competition or unfair or deceptive act or practice in or affecting commerce, and if it shall appear to the Commission that a proceeding by it in respect thereof would be to the interest of the public, it shall issue and serve upon such person, partnership, or corporation a complaint stating its charges in that respect and containing a notice of a hearing upon a day and at a place therein fixed at least thirty days after the service of said complaint. The person, partnership, or corporation so complained of shall have the right to appear at the place and time so fixed and show cause why an order should not be entered by the Commission requiring such person, partnership, or corporation to cease and desist from the violation of the law so charged in said complaint. Any person, partnership, or corporation may make application, and upon good cause shown may be allowed by the Commission to intervene and appear in said proceeding by counsel or in person. The testimony in any such proceeding shall be reduced to writing and filed in the office of the Commission. If upon such hearing the Commission shall be of the opinion that the method of competition or the act or practice in question is prohibited by this subchapter, it shall make a report in writing in which it shall state its findings as to the facts and shall issue and cause to be served on such person, partnership, or corporation an order requiring such person, partnership, or corporation to cease and desist from using such method of competition or such act or practice. Until the expiration of the time allowed for filing a petition for review, if no such petition has been duly filed within such time, or, if a petition for review has been filed within such time then until the record in the proceeding has been filed in a court of appeals of the United States, as hereinafter provided, the Commission may at any time, upon such notice and in such manner as it shall deem proper, modify or set aside, in whole or in part, any report or any order made or issued by it under this section. After the expiration of the time allowed for filing a petition for review, if no such petition has been duly filed within such time, the Commission may at any time, after notice and opportunity for hearing, reopen and alter, modify, or set aside, in whole or in part any report or order made or issued by it under this section, whenever in the opinion of the Commission conditions of fact or of law have so changed as to require such action or if the public interest shall so require, except that (1) the said person, partnership, or corporation may, within sixty days after service upon him or it of said report or order entered after such a reopening, obtain a review thereof in the appropriate court of appeals of the United States, in the manner provided in subsection (c) of this section; and (2) in the case of an order, the Commission shall reopen any such order to consider whether such order (including any affirmative relief provision contained in such order) should be altered, modified, or set aside, in whole or in part, if the person, partnership, or corporation involved files a request with the Commission which makes a satisfactory showing that changed conditions of law or fact require such order to be altered, modified, or set aside, in whole or in part. The Commission shall determine whether to alter, modify, or set aside any order of the Commission in response to a request made by a person, partnership, or corporation under paragraph (FOOTNOTE 1) (2) not later than 120 days after the date of the filing of such request. (FOOTNOTE 1) So in original. Probably should be "clause."

(c) Review of order; rehearing

Any person, partnership, or corporation required by an order of the Commission to cease and desist from using any method of competition or act or practice may obtain a review of such order in the court of appeals of the United States, within any circuit where the method of competition or the act or practice in question was used or where such person, partnership, or corporation resides or carries on business, by filing in the court, within sixty days from the date of the service of such order, a written petition praying that the order of the Commission be set aside. A copy of such petition shall be forthwith transmitted by the clerk of the court to the Commission, and thereupon the Commission shall file in the court the record in the proceeding, as provided in section 2112 of title 28. Upon such filing of the petition the court shall have jurisdiction of the proceeding and of the question determined therein concurrently with the Commission until the filing of the record and shall have power to make and enter a decree affirming, modifying, or setting aside the order of the Commission, and enforcing the same to the extent that such order is affirmed and to issue such writs as are ancillary to its jurisdiction or are necessary in its judgement to prevent injury to the public or to competitors pendente lite. The findings of the Commission as to the facts, if supported by evidence, shall be conclusive. To the extent that the order of the Commission is affirmed, the court shall thereupon issue its own order commanding obedience to the terms of such order of the Commission. If either party shall apply to the court for leave to adduce additional evidence, and shall show to the satisfaction of the court that such additional evidence is material and that there were reasonable grounds for the failure to adduce such evidence in the proceeding before the Commission, the court may order such additional evidence to be taken before the Commission and to be adduced upon the hearing in such manner and upon such terms and conditions as to the court may seem proper. The Commission may modify its findings as to the facts, or make new findings, by reason of the additional evidence so taken, and it shall file such modified or new findings, which, if supported by evidence, shall be conclusive, and its recommendation, if any, for the modification or setting aside of its original order, with the return of such additional evidence. The judgment and decree of the court shall be final, except that the same shall be subject to review by the Supreme Court upon certiorari, as provided in section 1254 of title 28.

(d) Jurisdiction of court

Upon the filing of the record with it the jurisdiction of the court of appeals of the United States to affirm, enforce, modify, or set aside orders of the Commission shall be exclusive.

(e) Exemption from liability

No order of the Commission or judgement of court to enforce the same shall in anywise relieve or absolve any person, partnership, or corporation from any liability under the Antitrust Acts.

(f) Service of complaints, orders and other processes; return

Complaints, orders, and other processes of the Commission under this section may be served by anyone duly authorized by the Commission, either (a) by delivering a copy thereof to the person to be served, or to a member of the partnership to be served, or the president, secretary, or other executive officer or a director of the corporation to be served; or (b) by leaving a copy thereof at the residence or the principal office or place of business of such person, partnership, or corporation; or (c) by mailing a copy thereof by registered mail or by certified mail addressed to such person, partnership, or corporation at his or its residence or principal office or place of business. The verified return by the person so serving said complaint, order, or other process setting forth the manner of said service shall be proof of the same, and the return post office receipt for said complaint, order, or other process mailed by registered mail or by certified mail as aforesaid shall be proof of the service of the same.

(g) Finality of order

An order of the Commission to cease and desist shall become final-
●(1) Upon the expiration of the time allowed for filing a petition for review, if no such petition has been duly filed within such time; but the Commission may thereafter modify or set aside its order to the extent provided in the last sentence of subsection (b).
●(2) Except as to any order provision subject to paragraph (4), upon the sixtieth day after such order is served, if a petition for review has been duly filed; except that any such order may be stayed, in whole or in part

429

and subject to such conditions as may be appropriate, by-
>(A) the Commission;
>
>(B) an appropriate court of appeals of the United States, if
>>(i) a petition for review of such order is pending in such court, and
>>
>>(ii) an application for such a stay was previously submitted to the Commission and the Commission, within the 30-day period beginning on the date the application was received by the Commission, either denied the application or did not grant or deny the application; or
>
>(C) the Supreme Court, if an applicable petition for certiorari is pending.

●(3) For purposes of subsection (m)(1)(B) of this section and of section 57b(a)(2) of this title, if a petition for review of the order of the Commission has been filed-
>(A) upon the expiration of the time allowed for filing a petition for certiorari, if the order of the Commission has been affirmed or the petition for review has been dismissed by the court of appeals and no petition for certiorari has been duly filed;
>
>(B) upon the denial of a petition for certiorari, if the order of the Commission has been affirmed or the petition for review has been dismissed by the court of appeals; or
>
>(C) upon the expiration of 30 days from the date of issuance of a mandate of the Supreme Court directing that the order of the Commission be affirmed or the petition for review be dismissed.

●(4) In the case of an order provision requiring a person, partnership, or corporation to divest itself of stock, other share capital, or assets, if a petition for review of such order of the Commission has been filed-
>(A) upon the expiration of the time allowed for filing a petition for certiorari, if the order of the Commission has been affirmed or the petition for review has been dismissed by the court of appeals and no petition for certiorari has been duly filed;
>
>(B) upon the denial of a petition for certiorari, if the order of the Commission has been affirmed or the petition for review has been dismissed by the court of appeals; or
>
>(C) upon the expiration of 30 days from the date of issuance of

a mandate of the Supreme Court directing that the order of the Commission be affirmed or the petition for review be dismissed.

(h) Modification or setting aside of order by Supreme Court

If the Supreme Court directs that the order of the Commission be modified or set aside, the order of the Commission rendered in accordance with the mandate of the Supreme Court shall become final upon the expiration of thirty days from the time it was rendered, unless within such thirty days either party has instituted proceedings to have such order corrected to accord with the mandate, in which event the order of the Commission shall become final when so corrected.

(i) Modification or setting aside of order by Court of Appeals

If the order of the Commission is modified or set aside by the court of appeals, and if (1) the time allowed for filing a petition for certiorari has expired and no such petition has been duly filed, or (2) the petition for certiorari has been denied, or (3) the decision of the court has been affirmed by the Supreme Court, then the order of the Commission rendered in accordance with the mandate of the court of appeals shall become final on the expiration of thirty days from the time such order of the Commission was rendered, unless within such thirty days either party has instituted proceedings to have such order corrected so that it will accord with the mandate, in which event the order of the Commission shall become final when so corrected.

(j) Rehearing upon order or remand

If the Supreme Court orders a rehearing; or if the case is remanded by the court of appeals to the Commission for a rehearing, and if (1) the time allowed for filing a petition for certiorari has expired, and no such petition has been duly filed, or (2) the petition for certiorari has been denied, or (3) the decision of the court has been affirmed by the Supreme Court, then the order of the Commission rendered upon such rehearing shall become final in the same manner as though no prior order of the Commission had been rendered.

(k) "Mandate" defined

431

As used in this section the term "mandate," in case a mandate has been recalled prior to the expiration of thirty days from the date of issuance thereof, means the final mandate.

(l) Penalty for violation of order; injunctions and other appropriate equitable relief

Any person, partnership, or corporation who violates an order of the Commission after it has become final, and while such order is in effect, shall forfeit and pay to the United States a civil penalty of not more than $10,000 for each violation, which shall accrue to the United States and may be recovered in a civil action brought by the Attorney General of the United States. Each separate violation of such an order shall be a separate offense, except that in a case of a violation through continuing failure to obey or neglect to obey a final order of the Commission, each day of continuance of such failure or neglect shall be deemed a separate offense. In such actions, the United States district courts are empowered to grant mandatory injunctions and such other and further equitable relief as they deem appropriate in the enforcement of such final orders of the Commission.

(m) Civil actions for recovery of penalties for knowing violations of rules and cease and desist orders respecting unfair or deceptive acts or practices; jurisdiction; maximum amount of penalties; continuing violations; de novo determinations; compromise or settlement procedure

●(1)

(A) The Commission may commence a civil action to recover a civil penalty in a district court of the United States against any person, partnership, or corporation which violates any rule under this chapter respecting unfair or deceptive acts or practices (other than an interpretive rule or a rule violation of which the Commission has provided is not an unfair or deceptive act or practice in violation of subsection (a)(1) of this section) with actual knowledge or knowledge fairly implied on the basis of objective circumstances that such act is unfair or deceptive and is prohibited by such rule. In such action, such person, partnership, or corporation shall be liable for a civil penalty of not more than $10,000 for each violation. (B) If the Commission determines in a proceeding under subsection (b) of this section that any act or practice is unfair or deceptive, and issues a final cease and desist order, other than a consent order, with respect to such act or practice, then the Commission may commence a civil action to obtain a civil penalty in a district court of the United States against any person, partnership, or corporation which engages in such act or practice-

> (1) after such cease and desist order becomes final (whether or not such person, partnership, or corporation was subject to such cease and desist order), and
>
> (2) with actual knowledge that such act or practice is unfair or deceptive and is unlawful under subsection (a)(1) of this section. In such action, such person, partnership, or corporation shall be liable for a civil penalty of not more than $10,000 for each violation.

(C) In the case of a violation through continuing failure to comply with a rule or with subsection (a)(1) of this section, each day of continuance of such failure shall be treated as a separate violation, for purposes of subparagraphs (A) and (B). In determining the amount of such a civil penalty, the court shall take into account the degree of culpability, any history of prior such conduct, ability to pay, effect on ability to continue to do business, and such other matters as justice may require.

●(2) If the cease and desist order establishing that the act or practice is unfair or deceptive was not issued against the defendant in a civil penalty action under paragraph (1)(B) the issues of fact in such action against such defendant shall be tried de novo. Upon request of any party to such an action against such defendant, the court shall also review the determination of law made by the Commission in the proceeding under subsection (b) of this section that the act or practice which was the subject of such proceeding constituted an unfair or deceptive act or practice in violation of subsection (a) of this section.

●(3) The Commission may compromise or settle any action for a civil penalty if such compromise or settlement is accompanied by a public statement of its reasons and is approved by the court.

(n) Standard of proof; public policy consideration

The Commission shall have no authority under this section or section 57a of this title to declare unlawful an act or practice on the grounds that such act or practice is unfair unless the act or practice causes or is likely to cause substantial injury to consumers which is not reasonably avoidable by consumers themselves and not outweighed by countervailing benefits to consumers or to competition. In determining whether an act or practice is unfair, the Commission may consider established public policies as evidence to be considered with all other evidence. Such public policy considerations may not serve as a primary basis for such determination.

46. Additional powers of Commission

The Commission shall also have power-

(a) Investigation of persons, partnerships, or corporations

To gather and compile information concerning, and to investigate from time to time the organization, business, conduct, practices, and management of any person, partnership, or corporation engaged in or whose business affects commerce, excepting banks, savings and loan institutions described in section 57a(f)(3) of this title, Federal credit unions described in section 57a(f)(4) of this title, and common carriers subject to the Act to regulate commerce, and its relation to other persons, partnerships, and corporations.

(b) Reports of persons, partnerships, and corporations

To require, by general or special orders, persons, partnerships, and corporations, engaged in or whose business affects commerce, excepting banks, savings and loan institutions described in section 57a(f)(3) of this title, Federal credit unions described in section 57a(f)(4) of this title, and common carriers subject to the Act to regulate commerce, or any class of them, or any of them, respectively, to file with the Commission in such form as the Commission may prescribe annual or special, or both annual and special, reports or answers in writing to specific questions, furnishing to the Commission such information as it may require as to the organization, business, conduct, practices, management, and relation to other corporations, partnerships, and individuals of the respective persons, partnerships, and corporations filing such reports or answers in writing. Such reports and answers shall be made under oath, or otherwise, as the Commission may prescribe, and shall be filed with the Commission within such reasonable period as the Commission may prescribe, unless additional time be granted in any case by the Commission.

(c) Investigation of compliance with antitrust decrees

Whenever a final decree has been entered against any defendant corporation in any suit brought by the United States to prevent and restrain any violation of the antitrust Acts, to make investigation, upon its own initiative, of the manner in which the decree has been or is being carried out, and upon the application of the Attorney General it shall be its duty to make such investigation. It shall transmit to the Attorney General a report embodying its findings and recommendations as a result of any such investigation, and the report shall be made public in the discretion of the Commission.

(d) Investigations of violations of antitrust statutes

Upon the direction of the President or either House of Congress to investigate and report the facts relating to any alleged violations of the antitrust Acts by any corporation.

(e) Readjustment of business of corporations violating antitrust statutes

Upon the application of the Attorney General to investigate and make recommendations for the readjustment of the business of any corporation alleged to be violating the antitrust Acts in order that the corporation may thereafter maintain its organization, management, and conduct of business in accordance with law.

(f) Publication of information; reports

To make public from time to time such portions of the information obtained by it hereunder as are in the public interest; and to make annual and special reports to the Congress and to submit therewith recommendations for additional legislation; and to provide for the publication of its reports and decisions in such form and manner as may be best adapted for public information and use: *Provided,* That the

Commission shall not have any authority to make public any trade secret or any commercial or financial information which is obtained from any person and which is privileged or confidential, except that the Commission may disclose such information to officers and employees of appropriate Federal law enforcement agencies or to any officer or employee of any State law enforcement agency upon the prior certification of an officer of any such Federal or State law enforcement agency that such information will be maintained in confidence and will be used only for official law enforcement purposes.

(g) Classification of corporations; regulations

From time to time classify corporations and (except as provided in section 57a(a)(2) of this title) to make rules and regulations for the purpose of carrying out the provisions of this subchapter.

(h) Investigations of foreign trade conditions; reports

To investigate, from time to time, trade conditions in and with foreign countries where associations, combinations, or practices of manufacturers, merchants, or traders, or other conditions, may affect the foreign trade of the United States, and to report to Congress thereon, with such recommendations as it deems advisable.

(i) Investigations of foreign antitrust law violations

With respect to the International Antitrust Enforcement Assistance Act of 1994 (15 U.S.C. 6201 et seq.), to conduct investigations of possible violations of foreign antitrust laws (as defined in section 12 of such Act (15 U.S.C. 6211)).

Provided, That the exception of "banks, savings and loan institutions described in section 57a(f)(3) of this title, Federal credit unions described in section 57a(f)(4) of this title, and common carriers subject to the Act to regulate commerce" from the Commission's powers defined in clauses (a) and (b) of this section, shall not be construed to limit the Commission's authority to gather and compile information, to investigate, or to require reports or answers from, any person, partnership, or corporation to the extent that such action is necessary to the investigation of any person, partnership, or corporation, group of persons, partnerships, or corporations, or industry which is not engaged or is engaged only incidentally in banking, in business as a savings and loan institution, in business as a Federal credit union, or in business as a common carrier subject to the Act to regulate commerce.

The Commission shall establish a plan designed to substantially reduce burdens imposed upon small businesses as a result of requirements established by the Commission under clause (b) relating to the filing of quarterly financial reports. Such plan shall (1) be established after consultation with small businesses and persons who use the information contained in such quarterly financial reports; (2) provide for a reduction of the number of small businesses required to file such quarterly financial reports; and (3) make revisions in the forms used for such quarterly financial reports for the purpose of reducing the complexity of such forms. The Commission, not later than December 31, 1980, shall submit such plan to the Committee on Commerce, Science, and Transportation of the Senate and to the Committee on Energy and Commerce of the House of Representatives. Such plan shall take effect not later than October 31, 1981.

No officer or employee of the Commission or any Commissioner may publish or disclose information to the public, or to any Federal agency, whereby any line-of-business data furnished by a particular establishment or individual can be identified. No one other than designated sworn officers and employees of the Commission may examine the line-of-business reports from individual firms, and information provided in the line-of-business program administered by the Commission shall be used only for statistical purposes. Information for carrying out specific law enforcement responsibilities of the Commission shall be obtained under practices and procedures in effect on May 28, 1980, or as changed by law.

Nothing in this section (other than the provisions of clause (c) and clause (d)) shall apply to the business of insurance, except that the Commission shall have authority to conduct studies and prepare reports relating to the business of insurance. The Commission may exercise such authority only upon receiving a request which is agreed to by a majority of the members of the Committee on Commerce, Science, and Transportation of the Senate or the Committee on Energy and Commerce of the House of Representatives. The authority to conduct any such study shall expire at the end of the Congress during which the request for such study was made.

46a. Concurrent resolution essential to authorize

After June 16, 1933, no new investigations shall be initiated by the Commission as the result of a legislative resolution, except the same be a concurrent resolution of the two Houses of Congress.

47. Reference of suits under antitrust statutes to Commission

In any suit in equity brought by or under the direction of the Attorney General as provided in the antitrust Acts, the court may, upon the conclusion of the testimony therein, if it shall be then of opinion that the complainant is entitled to relief, refer said suit to the Commission, as a master in chancery, to ascertain and report an appropriate form of decree therein. The Commission shall proceed upon such notice to the parties and under such rules of procedure as the court may prescribe, and upon the coming in of such report such exceptions may be filed and such proceedings had in relation thereto as upon the report of a master in other equity causes, but the court may adopt or reject such report, in whole or in part, and enter such decree as the nature of the case may in its judgment require.

48. Information and assistance from departments

The several departments and bureaus of the Government when directed by the President shall furnish the Commission, upon its request, all records, papers, and information in their possession relating to any corporation subject to any of the provisions of this subchapter, and shall detail from time to time such officials and employees to the Commission as he may direct.

49. Documentary evidence; depositions; witnesses

For the purposes of this subchapter the Commission, or its duly authorized agent or agents, shall at all reasonable times have access to, for the purpose of examination, and the right to copy any documentary evidence of any person, partnership, or corporation being investigated or proceeded against; and the Commission shall have power to require by subpoena the attendance and testimony of witnesses and the production of all such documentary evidence relating to any matter under investigation. Any member of the Commission may sign subpoenas, and members and examiners of the Commission may administer oaths and affirmations, examine witnesses, and receive evidence.

Such attendance of witnesses, and the production of such documentary evidence, may be required from any place in the United States, at any designated place of hearing. And in case of disobedience to a subpoena the Commission may invoke the aid of any court of the United States in requiring the attendance and testimony of witnesses and the production of documentary evidence.

Any of the district courts of the United States within the jurisdiction of which such inquiry is carried on may, in case of contumacy or refusal to obey a subpoena issued to any person, partnership, or corporation issue an order requiring such person, partnership, or corporation to appear before the Commission, or to produce documentary evidence if so ordered, or to give evidence touching the matter in question; and any failure to obey such order of the court may be punished by such court as a contempt thereof.

Upon the application of the Attorney General of the United States, at the request of the Commission, the district courts of the United States shall have jurisdiction to issue writs of mandamus commanding any person, partnership, or corporation to comply with the provisions of this subchapter or any order of the Commission made in pursuance thereof.

The Commission may order testimony to be taken by deposition in any proceeding or investigation pending under this subchapter at any stage of such proceeding or investigation. Such depositions may be taken before any person designated by the commission and having power to administer oaths. Such testimony shall be reduced to writing by the person taking the deposition, or under his direction, and shall then be subscribed by the deponent. Any person may be compelled to appear and depose and to produce documentary evidence in the same manner as witnesses may be compelled to appear and testify and produce documentary evidence before the Commission as hereinbefore provided.

Witnesses summoned before the Commission shall be paid the same fees and mileage that are paid witnesses in the courts of the United States and witnesses whose depositions are taken and the persons taking the same shall severally be entitled to the same fees as are paid for like services in the courts of the United States.

50. Offenses and penalties

Any person who shall neglect or refuse to attend and testify, or to answer any lawful inquiry or to produce any documentary evidence, if in his power to do so, in obedience to an order of a district court of the United States directing compliance with the subpoena or lawful requirement of the Commission, shall be guilty of an offense and upon conviction thereof by a court of competent jurisdiction shall be punished by a fine of not less than $1,000 nor more than $5,000, or by imprisonment for not more than one year, or by both such fine and imprisonment.

Any person who shall willfully make, or cause to be made, any false entry or statement of fact in any report required to be made under this subchapter, or who shall willfully make, or cause to be made, any false entry in any account, record, or memorandum kept by any person, partnership, or corporation subject to this subchapter, or who shall willfully neglect or fail to make, or to cause to be made, full, true, and correct entries in such accounts, records, or memoranda of all facts and transactions appertaining to the business of such person, partnership, or corporation, or who shall willfully remove out of the jurisdiction of the United States, or willfully mutilate, alter, or by any other means falsify any documentary evidence of such person, partnership, or corporation, or who shall willfully refuse to submit to the Commission or to any of its authorized agents, for the purpose of inspection and taking copies, any documentary evidence of such person, partnership, or corporation in his possession or within his control, shall be deemed guilty of an offense against the United States, and shall be subject, upon conviction in any court of the United States of competent jurisdiction, to a fine of not less than $1,000 nor more than $5,000, or to imprisonment for a term of not more than three years, or to both such fine and imprisonment.

If any persons, partnership, or corporation required by this subchapter to file any annual or special report shall fail so to do within the time fixed by the Commission for filing the same, and such failure shall continue for thirty days after notice of such default, the corporation shall forfeit to the United States the sum of $100 for each and every day of the continuance of such failure, which forfeiture shall be payable into the Treasury of the United States, and shall be recoverable in a civil suit in the name of the United States brought in the case of a corporation or partnership in the district where the corporation or partnership has its principal office or in any district in which it shall do business, and in the case of any person in the district where such person resides or has his principal place of business. It shall be the duty of the various United States attorneys, under the direction of the Attorney General of the United States, to prosecute for the recovery of the forfeitures. The costs and expenses of such prosecution shall be paid out of the appropriation for the expenses of the courts of the United States.

Any officer or employee of the Commission who shall make public any information obtained by the Commission without its authority, unless directed by a court, shall be deemed guilty of a misdemeanor, and, upon conviction thereof, shall be punished by a fine not exceeding $5,000, or by imprisonment not exceeding one year, or by fine and imprisonment, in the discretion of the court.

51. Effect on other statutory provisions

Nothing contained in this subchapter shall be construed to prevent or interfere with the enforcement of the provisions of the antitrust Acts or the Acts to regulate commerce, nor shall anything contained in this subchapter be construed to alter, modify, or repeal the said antitrust Acts or the Acts to regulate commerce or any part or parts thereof.

52. Dissemination of false advertisements

(a) Unlawfulness

It shall be unlawful for any person, partnership, or corporation to disseminate, or cause to be disseminated, any false advertisement-
●(1) By United States mails, or in or having an effect upon commerce, by any means, for the purpose of inducing, or which is likely to induce, directly or indirectly the purchase of food, drugs, devices, services, or cosmetics; or
●(2) By any means, for the purpose of inducing, or which is likely to induce, directly or indirectly, the purchase in or having an effect upon commerce, of food, drugs, devices, services, or cosmetics. (b) Unfair or deceptive act or practice The dissemination or the causing to be disseminated of any false advertisement within the provisions of subsection (a) of this section shall be an unfair or deceptive act or practice in or affecting commerce within the meaning of section 45 of this title.

53. False advertisements; injunctions and restraining orders

(a) Power of Commission; jurisdiction of courts

Whenever the Commission has reason to believe-

●(1) that any person, partnership, or corporation is engaged in, or is about to engage in, the dissemination or the causing of the dissemination of any advertisement in violation of section 52 of this title, and

●(2) that the enjoining thereof pending the issuance of a complaint by the Commission under section 45 of this title, and until such complaint is dismissed by the Commission or set aside by the court on review, or the order of the Commission to cease and desist made thereon has become final within the meaning of section 45 of this title, would be to the interest of the public,

the Commission by any of its attorneys designated by it for such purpose may bring suit in a district court of the United States or in the United States court of any Territory, to enjoin the dissemination or the causing of the dissemination of such advertisement. Upon proper showing a temporary injunction or restraining order shall be granted without bond. Any suit may be brought where such person, partnership, or corporation resides or transacts business, or wherever venue is proper under section 1391 of title 28. In addition, the court may, if the court determines that the interests of justice require that any other person, partnership, or corporation should be a party in such suit, cause such other person, partnership, or corporation to be added as a party without regard to whether venue is otherwise proper in the district in which the suit is brought. In any suit under this section, process may be served on any person, partnership, or corporation wherever it may be found.

(b) Temporary restraining orders; preliminary injunctions

Whenever the Commission has reason to believe-

●(1) that any person, partnership, or corporation is violating, or is about to violate, any provision of law enforced by the Federal Trade Commission, and

●(2) that the enjoining thereof pending the issuance of a complaint by the Commission and until such complaint is dismissed by the Commission or set aside by the court on review, or until the order of the

Commission made thereon has become final, would be in the interest of the public-

the Commission by any of its attorneys designated by it for such purpose may bring suit in a district court of the United States to enjoin any such act or practice. Upon a proper showing that, weighing the equities and considering the Commission's likelihood of ultimate success, such action would be in the public interest, and after notice to the defendant, a temporary restraining order or a preliminary injunction may be granted without bond: *Provided, however,* That if a complaint is not filed within such period (not exceeding 20 days) as may be specified by the court after issuance of the temporary restraining order or preliminary injunction, the order or injunction shall be dissolved by the court and be of no further force and effect: *Provided further,* That in proper cases the Commission may seek, and after proper proof, the court may issue, a permanent injunction. Any suit may be brought where such person, partnership, or corporation resides or transacts business, or wherever venue is proper under section 1391 of title 28. In addition, the court may, if the court determines that the interests of justice require that any other person, partnership, or corporation should be a party in such suit, cause such other person, partnership, or corporation to be added as a party without regard to whether venue is otherwise proper in the district in which the suit is brought. In any suit under this section, process may be served on any person, partnership, or corporation wherever it may be found.

(c) Service of process; proof of service

Any process of the Commission under this section may be served by any person duly authorized by the Commission-

> ●(1) by delivering a copy of such process to the person to be served, to a member of the partnership to be served, or to the president, secretary, or other executive officer or a director of the corporation to be served;
> ●(2) by leaving a copy of such process at the residence or the principal office or place of business of such person, partnership, or corporation; or
> ●(3) by mailing a copy of such process by registered mail or certified mail addressed to such person, partnership, or corporation at his, or her, or its residence, principal office, or principal place or business.

The verified return by the person serving such process setting forth the manner of such service shall be proof of the same.

(d) Exception of periodical publications

Whenever it appears to the satisfaction of the court in the case of a newspaper, magazine, periodical, or other publication, published at regular intervals-

●(1) that restraining the dissemination of a false advertisement in any particular issue of such publication would delay the delivery of such issue after the regular time therefor, and

●(2) that such delay would be due to the method by which the manufacture and distribution of such publication is customarily conducted by the publisher in accordance with sound business practice, and not to any method or device adopted for the evasion of this section or to prevent or delay the issuance of an injunction or restraining order with respect to such false advertisement or any other advertisement,

the court shall exclude such issue from the operation of the restraining order or injunction.

54. False advertisements; penalties

(a) Imposition of penalties

Any person, partnership, or corporation who violates any provision of section 52(a) of this title shall, if the use of the commodity advertised may be injurious to health because of results from such use under the conditions prescribed in the advertisement thereof, or under such conditions as are customary or usual, or if such violation is with intent to defraud or mislead, be guilty of a misdemeanor, and upon conviction shall be punished by a fine of not more than $5,000 or by imprisonment for not more than six months, or by both such fine and imprisonment; except that if the conviction is for a violation committed after a first conviction of such person, partnership, or corporation, for any violation of such section, punishment shall be by a fine of not more than $10,000 or by imprisonment for not more than one year, or by both such fine and imprisonment: Provided, That for the purposes of this section meats and meat food products duly inspected, marked, and labeled in accordance with rules and regulations issued under the Meat Inspection Act (21 U.S.C. 601 et seq.) shall be conclusively presumed not injurious to health at the time the same leave official "establishments."

(b) Exception of advertising medium or agency

No publisher, radio-broadcast licensee, or agency or medium for the dissemination of advertising, except the manufacturer, packer, distributor, or seller of the commodity to which the false advertisement relates, shall be liable under this section by reason of the dissemination by him of any false advertisement, unless he has refused, on the request of the Commission, to furnish the Commission the name and post-office address of the manufacturer, packer, distributor, seller, or advertising agency, residing in the United States, who caused him to disseminate such advertisement. No advertising agency shall be liable under this section by reason of the causing by it of the dissemination of any false advertisement, unless it has refused, on the request of the Commission, to furnish the Commission the name and post-office address of the manufacturer, packer, distributor, or seller, residing in the United States, who caused it to cause the dissemination of such advertisement.

55. Additional definitions

For the purposes of sections 52 to 54 of this title-

(a) False advertisement

● (1) The term "false advertisement" means an advertisement, other than labeling, which is misleading in a material respect; and in determining whether any advertisement is misleading, there shall be taken into account (among other things) not only representations made or suggested by statement, word, design, device, sound, or any combination thereof, but also the extent to which the advertisement fails to reveal facts material in the light of such representations or material with respect to consequences which may result from the use of the commodity to which the advertisement relates under the conditions prescribed in said advertisement, or under such conditions as are customary or usual. No advertisement of a drug shall be deemed to be false if it is disseminated only to members of the medical profession, contains no false representation of a material fact, and includes, or is accompanied in each instance by truthful disclosure of, the formula showing quantitatively each ingredient of such drug.

●(2) In the case of oleomargarine or margarine an advertisement shall be deemed misleading in a material respect if in such advertisement representations are made or suggested by statement, word, grade designation, design, device, symbol, sound, or any combination thereof, that such oleomargarine or margarine is a dairy product, except that nothing contained herein shall prevent a truthful, accurate, and full statement in any such advertisement of all the ingredients contained in such oleomargarine or margarine.

(b) Food

The term "food" means (1) articles used for food or drink for man or other animals, (2) chewing gum, and (3) articles used for components of any such article.

(c) Drug

The term "drug" means (1) articles recognized in the official United States Pharmacopoeia, official Homeopathic Pharmacopoeia of the United States, or official National Formulary, or any supplement to any of them; and (2) articles intended for use in the diagnosis, cure, mitigation, treatment, or prevention of disease in man or other animals; and (3) articles (other than food) intended to affect the structure or any function of the body of man or other animals; and (4) articles intended for use as a component of any article specified in clause (1), (2), or (3); but does not include devices or their components, parts, or accessories.

(d) Device

The term "device" (except when used in subsection (a) of this section) means an instrument, apparatus, implement, machine, contrivance, implant, in vitro reagent, or other similar or related article, including any component, part, or accessory, which is-

●(1) recognized in the official National Formulary, or the United States Pharmacopeia, or any supplement to them,

●(2) intended for use in the diagnosis of disease or other conditions, or

in the cure, mitigation, treatment, or prevention of disease, in man or other animals, or

●(3) intended to affect the structure or any function of the body of man or other animals, and which does not achieve any of its principal intended purposes through chemical action within or on the body of man or other animals and which is not dependent upon being metabolized for the achievement of any of its principal intended purposes.

(e) Cosmetic

The term "cosmetic" means (1) articles to be rubbed, poured, sprinkled, or sprayed on, introduced into, or otherwise applied to the human body or any part thereof intended for cleansing, beautifying, promoting attractiveness, or altering the appearance, and (2) articles intended for use as a component of any such article; except that such term shall not include soap.

(f) Oleomargarine or margarine

For the purposes of this section and section 347 of title 21, the term "oleomargarine" or "margarine" includes-

●(1) all substances, mixtures, and compounds known as oleomargarine or margarine;

●(2) all substances, mixtures, and compounds which have a consistence similar to that of butter and which contain any edible oils or fats other than milk fat if made in imitation or semblance of butter.

56. Commencement, defense, intervention and supervision of litigation and appeal by Commission or Attorney General

(a) Procedure for exercise of authority to litigate or appeal

●(1) Except as otherwise provided in paragraph (2) or (3), if-

(A) before commencing, defending, or intervening in, any civil action involving this subchapter (including an action to collect a civil penalty) which the Commission, or the Attorney General on behalf of the Commission, is authorized to commence, defend, or intervene in, the Commission gives written notification and undertakes to consult with the Attorney General with respect to such action; and

(B) the Attorney General fails within 45 days after receipt of such notification to commence, defend, or intervene in, such action; the Commission may commence, defend, or intervene in, and supervise the litigation or, such action and any appeal of such action in its own name by any of its attorneys designated by it for such purpose.

●(2) Except as otherwise provided in paragraph (3), in any civil action-

(A) under section 53 of this title (relating to injunctive relief);

(B) under section 57b of this title (relating to consumer redress);

(C) to obtain judicial review of a rule prescribed by the Commission, or a cease and desist order issued under section 45 of this title; or

(D) under the second paragraph of section 49 of this title (relating to enforcement of a subpoena) and under the fourth paragraph of such section (relating to compliance with section 46 of this title);

the Commission shall have exclusive authority to commence or defend, and supervise the litigation of, such action and any appeal of such action in its own name by any of its attorneys designated by it for such purpose, unless the Commission authorizes the Attorney General to do so. The Commission shall inform the Attorney General of the exercise of such authority and such exercise shall not preclude the Attorney General from intervening on behalf of the United States in such action and any appeal of such action as may be otherwise provided by law.

●(3)

(A) If the Commission makes a written request to the Attorney General, within the 10-day period which begins on the date of the entry of the judgment in any civil action in which the Commission represented itself pursuant to paragraph (1) or (2), to represent itself through any of its attorneys designated by it for such purpose before the Supreme Court in such action, it may do so, if

(i) the Attorney General concurs with such request; or

(ii) the Attorney General, within the 60-day period

which begins on the date of the entry of such judgment-

(a) refuses to appeal or file a petition for writ of certiorari with respect to such civil action, in which case he shall give written notification to the Commission of the reasons for such refusal within such 60-day period; or

(b) the Attorney General fails to take any action with respect to the Commission's request.

(B) In any case where the Attorney General represents the Commission before the Supreme Court in any civil action in which the Commission represented itself pursuant to paragraph (1) or (2), the Attorney General may not agree to any settlement, compromise, or dismissal of such action, or confess error in the Supreme Court with respect to such action, unless the Commission concurs.

(C) For purposes of this paragraph (with respect to representation before the Supreme Court), the term "Attorney General" includes the Solicitor General.

●(4) If, prior to the expiration of the 45-day period specified in paragraph (1) of this section or a 60-day period specified in paragraph (3), any right of the Commission to commence, defend, or intervene in, any such action or appeal may be extinguished due to any procedural requirement of any court with respect to the time in which any pleadings, notice of appeal, or other acts pertaining to such action or appeal may be taken, the Attorney General shall have one-half of the time required to comply with any such procedural requirement of the court (including any extension of such time granted by the court) for the purpose of commencing, defending, or intervening in the civil action pursuant to paragraph (1) or for the purpose of refusing to appeal or file a petition for writ of certiorari and the written notification or failing to take any action pursuant to paragraph 3(A)(ii).

●(5) The provisions of this subsection shall apply notwithstanding chapter 31 of title 28, or any other provision of law.

(b) Certification by Commission to Attorney General for criminal proceedings

Whenever the Commission has reason to believe that any person, partnership, or corporation is liable for a criminal penalty under this subchapter, the Commission shall certify the facts to the Attorney General, whose duty it shall be to cause appropriate criminal proceedings to be brought.

57. Separability clause

If any provision of this subchapter, or the application thereof to any person, partnership, or corporation, or circumstance, is held invalid, the remainder of this subchapter, and the application of such provisions to any other person, partnership, corporation, or circumstance, shall not be affected thereby.

57a. Unfair or deceptive acts or practices rulemaking proceedings

(a) Authority of Commission to prescribe rules and general statements of policy

●(1) Except as provided in subsection (h) of this section, the Commission may prescribe-
(A) interpretive rules and general statements of policy with respect to unfair or deceptive acts or practices in or affecting commerce (within the meaning of section 45(a)(1) of this title), and
(B) rules which define with specificity acts or practices which are unfair or deceptive acts or practices in or affecting commerce (within the meaning of section 45(a)(1) of this title), except that the Commission shall not develop or promulgate any trade rule or regulation with regard to the regulation of the development and utilization of the standards and certification activities pursuant to this section. Rules under this subparagraph may include requirements prescribed for the purpose of preventing such acts or practices.
●(2) The Commission shall have no authority under this subchapter, other than its authority under this section, to prescribe any rule with respect to unfair or deceptive acts or practices in or affecting commerce

(within the meaning of section 45(a)(1) of this title). The preceding sentence shall not affect any authority of the Commission to prescribe rules (including interpretive rules), and general statements of policy, with respect to unfair methods of competition in or affecting commerce.

(b) Procedures applicable

●(1) When prescribing a rule under subsection (a)(1)(B) of this section, the Commission shall proceed in accordance with section 553 of title 5 (without regard to any reference in such section to sections 556 and 557 of such title), and shall also (A) publish a notice of proposed rulemaking stating with particularity the text of the rule, including any alternatives, which the Commission proposes to promulgate, and the reason for the proposed rule; (B) allow interested persons to submit written data, views, and arguments, and make all such submissions publicly available; (C) provide an opportunity for an informal hearing in accordance with subsection (c) of this section; and (D) promulgate, if appropriate, a final rule based on the matter in the rulemaking record (as defined in subsection (e)(1)(B) of this section), together with a statement of basis and purpose.

●(2)

(A) Prior to the publication of any notice of proposed rulemaking pursuant to paragraph (1)(A), the Commission shall publish an advance notice of proposed rulemaking in the Federal Register. Such advance notice shall-
(i) contain a brief description of the area of inquiry under consideration, the objectives which the Commission seeks to achieve, and possible regulatory alternatives under consideration by the Commission; and
(ii) invite the response of interested parties with respect to such proposed rulemaking, including any suggestions or alternative methods for achieving such objectives.
(B) The Commission shall submit such advance notice of proposed rulemaking to the Committee on Commerce, Science, and Transportation of the Senate and to the Committee on Energy and Commerce of the House of

Representatives. The Commission may use such additional mechanisms as the Commission considers useful to obtain suggestions regarding the content of the area of inquiry before the publication of a general notice of proposed rulemaking under paragraph (1)(A).

(C) The Commission shall, 30 days before the publication of a notice of proposed rulemaking pursuant to paragraph (1)(A), submit such notice to the Committee on Commerce, Science, and Transportation of the Senate and to the Committee on Energy and Commerce of the House of Representatives.

●(3) The Commission shall issue a notice of proposed rulemaking pursuant to paragraph (1)(A) only where it has reason to believe that the unfair or deceptive acts or practices which are the subject of the proposed rulemaking are prevalent. The Commission shall make a determination that unfair or deceptive acts or practices are prevalent under this paragraph only if-

(A) it has issued cease and desist orders regarding such acts or practices, or

(B) any other information available to the Commission indicates a widespread pattern of unfair or deceptive acts or practices.

(c) Informal hearing procedure

The Commission shall conduct any informal hearings required by subsection (b)(1)(C) of this section in accordance with the following procedure:

●(1)

(A) The Commission shall provide for the conduct of proceedings under this subsection by hearing officers who shall perform their functions in accordance with the requirements of this subsection.

(B) The officer who presides over the rulemaking proceedings shall be responsible to a chief presiding officer who shall not be responsible to any other officer or employee of the Commission. The officer who presides over the rulemaking proceeding shall make a recommended decision based upon the findings and conclusions of such officer as to all relevant and material evidence, except that such recommended decision may be made by another officer if the officer who presided over the proceeding is no longer available to the Commission. (C) Except as required for the disposition of ex parte matters as authorized by law, no presiding officer shall consult any person or party with respect to any fact in issue unless such officer gives notice and opportunity for all parties to participate.

●(2) Subject to paragraph (3) of this subsection, an interested person is entitled-

(A) to present his position orally or by documentary submission (or both), and

(B) if the Commission determines that there are disputed issues of material fact it is necessary to resolve, to present such rebuttal submissions and to conduct (or have conducted under paragraph (3)(B)) such cross examination of persons as the Commission determines (i) to be appropriate, and (ii) to be required for a full and true disclosure with respect to such issues.

●(3) The Commission may prescribe such rules and make such rulings concerning proceedings in such hearings as may tend to avoid unnecessary costs or delay. Such rules or rulings may include (A) imposition of reasonable time limits on each interested person's oral presentations, and (B) requirements that any cross-examination to which a person may be entitled under paragraph (2) be conducted by the Commission on behalf of that person in such manner as the Commission determines (i) to be appropriate, and (ii) to be required for a full and true disclosure with respect to disputed issues of material fact.

●(4)

(A) Except as provided in subparagraph (B), if a group of persons each of whom under paragraphs (2) and (3) would be entitled to conduct (or have conducted) cross-examination and who are determined by the Commission to have the same or similar interests in the proceeding cannot agree upon a single representative of such interests for purposes of cross-examination, the Commission may make rules and rulings (i) limiting the representation of such interest, for such purposes, and (ii) governing the manner in which such cross-examination shall be limited.

(B) When any person who is a member of a group with respect to which the Commission has made a determination under subparagraph (A) is unable to agree upon group representation with the other members of the group, then such person shall not be denied under the authority of subparagraph (A) the opportunity to conduct (or have conducted) cross-examination as to issues affecting his particular interests if (i) he satisfies the Commission that he has made a reasonable and good faith effort to reach agreement upon group representation with the other members of the group and (ii) the Commission determines that there are substantial and relevant issues which are not adequately presented by the group representative.

(5) A verbatim transcript shall be taken of any oral presentation, and cross-examination, in an informal hearing to which this subsection applies. Such transcript shall be available to the public.

(d) Statement of basis and purpose accompanying rule; "Commission" defined; judicial review of amendment or repeal of rule; violation of rule

●(1) The Commission's statement of basis and purpose to accompany a rule promulgated under subsection (a)(1)(B) of this section shall include (A) a statement as to the prevalence of the acts or practices treated by the rule; (B) a statement as to the manner and context in which such acts or practices are unfair or deceptive; and (C) a statement as to the economic effect of the rule, taking into account the effect on small business and consumers.

●(2)

(A) The term "Commission" as used in this subsection and subsections (b) and (c) of this section includes any person authorized to act in behalf of the Commission in any part of the rulemaking proceeding.

(B) A substantive amendment to, or repeal of, a rule promulgated under subsection (a)(1)(B) of this section shall be prescribed, and subject to judicial review, in the same manner as a rule prescribed under such subsection. An exemption under subsection (g) of this section shall not be treated as an amendment or repeal of a rule.

●(3) When any rule under subsection (a)(1)(B) of this section takes effect a subsequent violation thereof shall constitute an unfair or deceptive act or practice in violation of section 45(a)(1) of this title, unless the Commission otherwise expressly provides in such rule.

(e) Judicial review; petition; jurisdiction and venue; rulemaking record; additional submissions and presentations; scope of review and relief; review by Supreme Court; additional remedies

●(1)

(A) Not later than 60 days after a rule is promulgated under subsection (a)(1)(B) of this section by the Commission, any interested person (including a consumer or consumer organization) may file a petition, in the United States Court of Appeals for the District of Columbia circuit or for the circuit in which such person resides or has his principal place of business, for judicial review of such rule. Copies of the petition shall be forthwith transmitted by the clerk of the court to the Commission or other officer designated by it for that purpose. The provisions of section 2112 of title 28 shall apply to the filing of the rulemaking record of proceedings on which the Commission based its rule and to the transfer of proceedings in the courts of appeals.

(B) For purposes of this section, the term "rulemaking record" means the rule, its statement of basis and purpose, the transcript required by subsection (c)(5) of this section, any written submissions, and any other information which the Commission considers relevant to such rule.

●(2) If the petitioner or the Commission applies to the court for leave to make additional oral submissions or written presentations and shows to the satisfaction of the court that such submissions and presentations would be material and that there were reasonable grounds for the submissions and failure to make such submissions and presentations in the proceeding before the Commission, the court may order the Commission to provide additional opportunity to make such submissions and presentations. The Commission may modify or set aside its rule or make a new rule by reason of the additional submissions and presentations and shall file such modified or new rule, and the rule's statement of basis of purpose, with the return of such submissions and presentations. The court shall thereafter review such new or modified rule.

●(3) Upon the filing of the petition under paragraph (1) of this subsection, the court shall have jurisdiction to review the rule in accordance with chapter 7 of title 5 and to grant appropriate relief, including interim relief, as provided in such chapter. The court shall hold unlawful and set aside the rule on any ground specified in subparagraphs (A), (B), (C), or (D) of section 706(2) of title 5 (taking due account of the rule of prejudicial error), or if

> (A) the court finds that the Commission's action is not supported by substantial evidence in the rulemaking record (as defined in paragraph (1)(B) of this subsection) taken as a whole, or
>
> (B) the court finds that-
>
>> (i) a Commission determination under subsection (c) of this section that the petitioner is not entitled to conduct cross examination or make rebuttal submissions, or
>>
>> (ii) a Commission rule or ruling under subsection (c) of this section limiting the petitioner's cross examination or rebuttal submissions, has precluded disclosure of disputed material facts which was necessary for fair determination by the Commission of the rulemaking proceeding taken as a whole. The term "evidence," as used in this paragraph, means any matter in the rulemaking record.

●(4) The judgment of the court affirming or setting aside, in whole or in part, any such rule shall be final, subject to review by the Supreme Court of the United States upon certiorari or certification, as provided in section 1254 of title 28.

●(5)

> (A) Remedies under the preceding paragraphs of this subsection are in addition to and not in lieu of any other remedies provided by law.
>
> (B) The United States Courts of Appeal shall have exclusive jurisdiction of any action to obtain judicial review (other than

in an enforcement proceeding) of a rule prescribed under subsection (a)(1)(B) of this section, if any district court of the United States would have had jurisdiction of such action but for this subparagraph. Any such action shall be brought in the United States Court of Appeals for the District of Columbia circuit, or for any circuit which includes a judicial district in which the action could have been brought but for this subparagraph.

(C) A determination, rule, or ruling of the Commission described in paragraph (3)(B)(i) or (ii) may be reviewed only in a proceeding under this subsection and only in accordance with paragraph (3)(B). Section 706(2)(E) of title 5 shall not apply to any rule promulgated under subsection (a)(1)(B) of this section. The contents and adequacy of any statement required by subsection (b)(1)(D) of this section shall not be subject to judicial review in any respect.

(f) Unfair or deceptive acts or practices by banks, savings and loan institutions, or Federal credit unions; promulgation of regulations by Board of Governors of Federal Reserve System, Federal Home Loan Bank Board, and National Credit Union Administration Board; agency enforcement and compliance proceedings; violations; power of other Federal agencies unaffected; reporting requirements

●(1) In order to prevent unfair or deceptive acts or practices in or affecting commerce (including acts or practices which are unfair or deceptive to consumers) by banks or savings and loan institutions described in paragraph (3), each agency specified in paragraph (2) or (3) of this subsection shall establish a separate division of consumer affairs which shall receive and take appropriate action upon complaints with respect to such acts or practices by banks or savings and loan institutions described in paragraph (3) subject to its jurisdiction. The Board of Governors of the Federal Reserve System (with respect to banks) and the Federal Home Loan Bank Board (with respect to savings and loan institutions described in paragraph (3)) and the National Credit Union Administration Board (with respect to Federal credit unions described in paragraph (4)) shall prescribe regulations to carry out the purposes of this section, including regulations defining with specificity such unfair or deceptive acts or practices, and containing requirements prescribed for the purpose of preventing such acts or practices. Whenever the Commission prescribes a rule under subsection (a)(1)(B) of this section, then within 60 days after such rule takes effect each such Board shall promulgate substantially similar regulations prohibiting acts or practices of banks or savings and loan institutions described in paragraph (3), or Federal credit unions described in paragraph (4), as the case may be, which are substantially similar to those prohibited by rules of the Commission and which impose substantially similar requirements, unless (A) any such Board finds that such acts or practices of banks or savings and loan institutions described in paragraph (3), or Federal credit unions described in paragraph (4), as the case may be, are not unfair or deceptive, or (B) the Board of Governors of the Federal Reserve System finds that implementation of similar regulations with respect to banks, savings and loan institutions or Federal credit unions would seriously conflict with essential monetary and payments systems policies of such Board, and publishes any such finding, and the reasons therefore, in the Federal Register.

● (2) Enforcement. - Compliance with regulations prescribed under this subsection shall be enforced under section 1818 of title 12, in the case of

> (A) national banks, banks operating under the code of law for the District of Columbia, and Federal branches and Federal agencies of foreign banks, by the division of consumer affairs established by the Office of the Comptroller of the Currency;
> (B) member banks of the Federal Reserve System (other than national banks and banks operating under the code of law for the District of Columbia), branches and agencies of foreign banks (other than Federal branches, Federal agencies, and insured State branches of foreign banks), commercial lending companies owned or controlled by foreign banks, and organizations operating under section 25 or 25(a) (FOOTNOTE 1) of the Federal Reserve Act (12 U.S.C. 601 et seq., 611 et seq.), by the division of consumer affairs established by the Board of Governors of the Federal Reserve System; and (FOOTNOTE 1) See References in Text note below.
> (C) banks insured by the Federal Deposit Insurance

Corporation (other (FOOTNOTE 2) banks referred to in subparagraph (A) or (B)) and insured State branches of foreign banks, by the division of consumer affairs established by the Board of Directors of the Federal Deposit Insurance Corporation. (FOOTNOTE 2) So in original. Probably should be "(other than."

●(3) Compliance with regulations prescribed under this subsection shall be enforced under section 1818 of title 12 with respect to savings associations as defined in section 1813 of title 12.

●(4) Compliance with regulations prescribed under this subsection shall be enforced with respect to Federal credit unions under sections 1766 and 1786 of title 12.

●(5) For the purpose of the exercise by any agency referred to in paragraph (2) of its powers under any Act referred to in that paragraph, a violation of any regulation prescribed under this subsection shall be deemed to be a violation of a requirement imposed under that Act. In addition to its powers under any provision of law specifically referred to in paragraph (2), each of the agencies referred to in that paragraph may exercise, for the purpose of enforcing compliance with any regulation prescribed under this subsection, any other authority conferred on it by law.

●(6) The authority of the Board of Governors of the Federal Reserve System to issue regulations under this subsection does not impair the authority of any other agency designated in this subsection to make rules respecting its own procedures in enforcing compliance with regulations prescribed under this subsection.

●(7) Each agency exercising authority under this subsection shall transmit to the Congress each year a detailed report on its activities under this paragraph during the preceding calendar year. The terms used in this paragraph that are not defined in this subchapter or otherwise defined in section 1813(s) of title 12 shall have the meaning given to them in section 3101 of title 12.

(g) Exemptions and stays from application of rules; procedures

●(1) Any person to whom a rule under subsection (a)(1)(B) of this section applies may petition the Commission for an exemption from such rule.

●(2) If, on its own motion or on the basis of a petition under paragraph (1), the Commission finds that the application of a rule prescribed under subsection (a)(1)(B) of this section to any person or class or (FOOTNOTE 3) persons is not necessary to prevent the unfair or deceptive act or practice to which the rule relates, the Commission may exempt such person or class from all or part of such rule. Section 553 of title 5 shall apply to action under this paragraph. (FOOTNOTE 3) So in original. Probably should be "of."

●(3) Neither the pendency of a proceeding under this subsection respecting an exemption from a rule, nor the pendency of judicial proceedings to review the Commission's action or failure to act under this subsection, shall stay the applicability of such rule under subsection (a)(1)(B) of this section.

(h) Restriction on rulemaking authority of Commission respecting children's advertising proceedings pending on May 28, 1980

The Commission shall not have any authority to promulgate any rule in the children's advertising proceeding pending on May 28, 1980, or in any substantially similar proceeding on the basis of a determination by the Commission that such advertising constitutes an unfair act or practice in or affecting commerce.

(i) Meetings with outside parties

●(1) For purposes of this subsection, the term "outside party" means any person other than (A) a Commissioner; (B) an officer or employee of the Commission; or (C) any person who has entered into a contract or any other agreement or arrangement with the Commission to provide any goods or services (including consulting services) to the Commission.

●(2) Not later than 60 days after May 28, 1980, the Commission shall publish a proposed rule, and not later than 180 days after May 28, 1980, the Commission shall promulgate a final rule, which shall authorize the Commission or any Commissioner to meet with any outside party concerning any rulemaking proceeding of the Commission. Such rule shall provide that-

(A) notice of any such meeting shall be included in any weekly calendar prepared by the Commission; and

(B) a verbatim record or a summary of any such meeting, or of any communication relating to any such meeting, shall be kept, made available to the public, and included in the rulemaking record.

(j) Communications by investigative personnel with staff of Commission concerning matters outside rulemaking record prohibited

Not later than 60 days after May 28, 1980, the Commission shall publish a proposed rule, and not later than 180 days after May 28, 1980, the Commission shall promulgate a final rule, which shall prohibit any officer, employee, or agent of the Commission with any investigative responsibility or other responsibility relating to any rulemaking proceeding within any operating bureau of the Commission, from communicating or causing to be communicated to any Commissioner or to the personal staff of any Commissioner any fact which is relevant to the merits of such proceeding and which is not on the rulemaking record of such proceeding, unless such communication is made available to the public and is included in the rulemaking record. The provisions of this subsection shall not apply to any communication to the extent such communication is required for the disposition of ex parte matters as authorized by law.

57a-1. Omitted

57b. Civil actions for violations of rules and cease and desist orders respecting unfair or deceptive acts or practices

(a) Suits by Commission against persons, partnerships, or corporations; jurisdiction; relief for dishonest or fraudulent acts

●(1) If any person, partnership, or corporation violates any rule under this subchapter respecting unfair or deceptive acts or practices (other than an interpretive rule, or a rule violation of which the Commission has provided is not an unfair or deceptive act or practice in violation of section 45(a) of this title), then the Commission may commence a civil action against such person, partnership, or corporation for relief under subsection (b) of this section in a United States district court or in any court of competent jurisdiction of a State.

●(2) If any person, partnership, or corporation engages in any unfair or deceptive act or practice (within the meaning of section 45(a)(1) of this title) with respect to which the Commission has issued a final cease and desist order which is applicable to such person, partnership, or corporation, then the Commission may commence a civil action against such person, partnership, or corporation in a United States district court or in any court of competent jurisdiction of a State. If the Commission satisfies the court that the act or practice to which the cease and desist order relates is one which a reasonable man would have known under the circumstances was dishonest or fraudulent, the court may grant relief under subsection (b) of this section.

(b) Nature of relief available

The court in an action under subsection (a) of this section shall have jurisdiction to grant such relief as the court finds necessary to redress injury to consumers or other persons, partnerships, and corporations resulting from the rule violation or the unfair or deceptive act or practice, as the case may be. Such relief may include, but shall not be limited to, rescission or reformation of contracts, the refund of money or return of property, the payment of damages, and public notification respecting the rule violation or the unfair or deceptive act or practice, as the case may be; except that nothing in this subsection is intended to authorize the imposition of any exemplary or punitive damages.

(c) Conclusiveness of findings of Commission in cease and desist proceedings; notice of judicial proceedings to injured persons, etc.

●(1) if (A) a cease and desist order issued under section 45(b) of this title has become final under section 45(g) of this title with respect to any person's, partnership's, or corporation's rule violation or unfair or deceptive act or practice, and (B) an action under this section is brought with respect to such person's, partnership's, or corporation's rule violation or act or practice, then the findings of the Commission as to the material facts in the proceeding under section 45(b) of this title with respect to such person's, partnership's, or corporation's rule violation or act or practice, shall be conclusive unless (i) the terms of such cease and desist order expressly provide that the Commission's findings shall not be conclusive, or (ii) the order became final by reason of section 45(g)(1) of this title, in which case such finding shall be conclusive if supported by evidence.

●(2) The court shall cause notice of an action under this section to be given in a manner which is reasonably calculated, under all of the circumstances, to apprise the persons, partnerships, and corporations allegedly injured by the defendant's rule violation or act or practice of the pendency of such action. Such notice may, in the discretion of the court, be given by publication.

(d) Time for bringing of actions

No action may be brought by the Commission under this section more than 3 years after the rule violation to which an action under subsection (a)(1) of this section relates, or the unfair or deceptive act or practice to which an action under subsection (a)(2) of this section relates; except that if a cease and desist order with respect to any person's, partnership's, or corporation's rule violation or unfair or deceptive act or practice has become final and such order was issued in a proceeding under section 45(b) of this title which was commenced not later than 3 years after the rule violation or act or practice occurred, a civil action may be commenced under this section against such person, partnership, or corporation at any time before the expiration of one year after such order becomes final.

(e) Availability of additional Federal or State remedies; other authority of Commission unaffected

Remedies provided in this section are in addition to, and not in lieu of, any other remedy or right of action provided by State or Federal law. Nothing in this section shall be construed to affect any authority of the Commission under any other provision of law.

57b-1. Civil investigative demands

(a) Definitions

For purposes of this section:
●(1) The terms "civil investigative demand" and "demand" mean any demand issued by the commission under subsection (c)(1) of this section.
●(2) The term "Commission investigation" means any inquiry conducted by a Commission investigator for the purpose of ascertaining

whether any person is or has been engaged in any unfair or deceptive acts or practices in or affecting commerce (within the meaning of section 45(a)(1) of this title) or in any antitrust violations.

●(3) The term "Commission investigator" means any attorney or investigator employed by the Commission who is charged with the duty of enforcing or carrying into effect any provisions relating to unfair or deceptive acts or practices in or affecting commerce (within the meaning of section 45(a)(1) of this title) or any provisions relating to antitrust violations.

●(4) The term "custodian" means the custodian or any deputy custodian designated under section 57b-2(b)(2)(A) of this title.

●(5) The term "documentary material" includes the original or any copy of any book, record, report, memorandum, paper, communication, tabulation, chart, or other document.

●(6) The term "person" means any natural person, partnership, corporation, association, or other legal entity, including any person acting under color or authority of State law.

●(7) The term "violation" means any act or omission constituting an unfair or deceptive act or practice in or affecting commerce (within the meaning of section 45(a)(1) of this title) or any antitrust violation.

●(8) The term "antitrust violation" means-

> (A) any unfair method of competition (within the meaning of section 45(a)(1) of this title);
> (B) any violation of the Clayton Act (15 U.S.C. 12 et seq.) or of any other Federal statute that prohibits, or makes available to the Commission a civil remedy with respect to, any restraint upon or monopolization of interstate or foreign trade or commerce;
> (C) with respect to the International Antitrust Enforcement Assistance Act of 1994 (15 U.S.C. 6201 et seq.), any violation of any of the foreign antitrust laws (as defined in section 12 of such Act (15 U.S.C. 6211)) with respect to which a request is made under section 3 of such Act (15 U.S.C. 6202); or
> (D) any activity in preparation for a merger, acquisition, joint venture, or similar transaction, which if consummated, may result in any such unfair method of competition or in any such violation.

(b) Actions conducted by Commission respecting unfair or deceptive acts or practices in or affecting commerce

For the purpose of investigations performed pursuant to this section with respect to unfair or deceptive acts or practices in or affecting commerce (within the meaning of section 45(a)(1) of this title); all actions of the Commission taken under section 46 and section 49 of this title shall be conducted pursuant to subsection (c) of this section.

(c) Issuance of demand; contents; service; verified return; sworn certificate; answers; taking of oral testimony

●(1) Whenever the Commission has reason to believe that any person may be in possession, custody, or control of any documentary material or tangible things, or may have any information, relevant to unfair or deceptive acts or practices in or affecting commerce (within the meaning of section 45(a)(1) of this title), or to antitrust violations, the Commission may, before the institution of any proceedings under this subchapter, issue in writing, and cause to be served upon such person, a civil investigative demand requiring such person to produce such documentary material for inspection and copying or reproduction, to submit such tangible things, to file written reports or answers to questions, to give oral testimony concerning documentary material or other information, or to furnish any combination of such material, answers, or testimony.

●(2) Each civil investigative demand shall state the nature of the conduct constituting the alleged violation which is under investigation and the provision of law applicable to such violation.

●(3) Each civil investigative demand for the production of documentary material shall-

(A) describe each class of documentary material to be produced under the demand with such definiteness and certainty as to permit such material to be fairly identified;

(B) prescribe a return date or dates which will provide a reasonable period of time within which the material so demanded may be assembled and made available for inspection and copying or reproduction; and

(C) identify the custodian to whom such material shall be made available.

●(4) Each civil investigative demand for the submission of tangible things shall-

(A) describe each class of tangible things to be submitted under the demand with such definiteness and certainty as to permit such things to be fairly identified;

(B) prescribe a return date or dates which will provide a reasonable period of time within which the things so demanded may be assembled and submitted; and

(C) identify the custodian to whom such things shall be submitted.

●(5) Each civil investigative demand for written reports or answers to questions shall-

(A) propound with definiteness and certainty the reports to be produced or the questions to be answered;

(B) prescribe a date or dates at which time written reports or answers to questions shall be submitted; and

(C) identify the custodian to whom such reports or answers shall be submitted.

●(6) Each civil investigative demand for the giving of oral testimony shall-

(A) prescribe a date, time, and place at which oral testimony shall be commenced; and

(B) identify a Commission investigator who shall conduct the investigation and the custodian to whom the transcript of such investigation shall be submitted.

●(7)

(A) Any civil investigative demand may be served by any Commission investigator at any place within the territorial jurisdiction of any court of the United States.

(B) Any such demand or any enforcement petition filed under this section may be served upon any person who is not found within the territorial jurisdiction of any court of the United States, in such manner as the Federal Rules of Civil Procedure prescribe for service in a foreign nation.

(C) To the extent that the courts of the United States have authority to assert jurisdiction over such person consistent with due process, the United States District Court for the District of Columbia shall have the same jurisdiction to take any action respecting compliance with this section by such person that such district court would have if such person were personally within the jurisdiction of such district court.

●(8) Service of any civil investigative demand or any enforcement petition filed under this section may be made upon a partnership, corporation, association, or other legal entity by-

(A) delivering a duly executed copy of such demand or petition to any partner, executive officer, managing agent, or general agent of such partnership, corporation, association, or other legal entity, or to any agent of such partnership, corporation, association, or other legal entity authorized by appointment or by law to receive service of process on behalf of such partnership, corporation, association, or other legal entity;

(B) delivering a duly executed copy of such demand or petition to the principal office or place of business of the partnership, corporation, association, or other legal entity to be served; or

(C) depositing a duly executed copy in the United States mails, by registered or certified mail, return receipt requested, duly addressed to such partnership, corporation, association, or other legal entity at its principal office or place of business.

●(9) Service of any civil investigative demand or of any enforcement petition filed under this section may be made upon any natural person by-

(A) delivering a duly executed copy of such demand or petition to the person to be served; or

(B) depositing a duly executed copy in the United States mails by registered or certified mail, return receipt requested, duly addressed to such person at his residence or principal office or place of business.

●(10) A verified return by the individual serving any civil investigative demand or any enforcement petition filed under this section setting forth the manner of such service shall be proof of such service. In the case of service by registered or certified mail, such return shall be accompanied by the return post office receipt of delivery of such demand or enforcement petition.

●(11) The production of documentary material in response to a civil investigative demand shall be made under a sworn certificate, in such form as the demand designates, by the person, if a natural person, to whom the demand is directed or, if not a natural person, by any person having knowledge of the facts and circumstances relating to such production, to the effect that all of the documentary material required by the demand and in the possession, custody, or control of the person to whom the demand is directed has been produced and made available to the custodian.

●(12) The submission of tangible things in response to a civil investigative demand shall be made under a sworn certificate, in such form as the demand designates, by the person to whom the demand is directed or, if not a natural person, by any person having knowledge of the facts and circumstances relating to such production, to the effect that all of the tangible things required by the demand and in the possession, custody, or control of the person to whom the demand is directed have been submitted to the custodian.

●(13) Each reporting requirement or question in a civil investigative demand shall be answered separately and fully in writing under oath, unless it is objected to, in which event the reasons for the objection shall be stated in lieu of an answer, and it shall be submitted under a sworn certificate, in such form as the demand designates, by the person, if a natural person, to whom the demand is directed or, if not a natural person, by any person responsible for answering each reporting requirement or question, to the effect that all information required by the demand and in the possession, custody, control, or knowledge of the person to whom the demand is directed has been submitted.

●(14)

> (A) Any Commission investigator before whom oral testimony is to be taken shall put the witness on oath or affirmation and shall personally, or by any individual acting under his direction and in his presence, record the testimony of the witness. The testimony shall be taken stenographically and transcribed. After the testimony is fully transcribed, the Commission investigator before whom the testimony is taken shall promptly transmit a copy of the transcript of the testimony to the custodian.

(B) Any Commission investigator before whom oral testimony is to be taken shall exclude from the place where the testimony is to be taken all other persons except the person giving the testimony, his attorney, the officer before whom the testimony is to be taken, and any stenographer taking such testimony.

(C) The oral testimony of any person taken pursuant to a civil investigative demand shall be taken in the judicial district of the United States in which such person resides, is found, or transacts business, or in such other place as may be agreed upon by the Commission investigator before whom the oral testimony of such person is to be taken and such person.

(D)

(i) Any person compelled to appear under a civil investigative demand for oral testimony pursuant to this section may be accompanied, represented, and advised by an attorney. The attorney may advise such person, in confidence, either upon the request of such person or upon the initiative of the attorney, with respect to any question asked of such person.

(ii) Such person or attorney may object on the record to any question, in whole or in part, and shall briefly state for the record the reason for the objection. An objection may properly be made, received, and entered upon the record when it is claimed that such person is entitled to refuse to answer the question on grounds of any constitutional or other legal right or privilege, including the privilege against self-incrimination. Such person shall not otherwise object to or refuse to answer any question, and shall not himself or through his attorney otherwise interrupt the oral examination. If such person refuses to answer any question, the Commission may petition the district court of the United States pursuant to this section for an order compelling such person to answer such question.

(iii) If such person refuses to answer any question on grounds of the privilege against self-incrimination, the testimony of such person may be compelled in accordance with the provisions of section 6004 of title 18.

(E)

(i) After the testimony of any witness is fully transcribed, the Commission investigator shall afford the witness (who may be accompanied by an attorney) a reasonable opportunity to examine the transcript. The transcript shall be read to or by the witness, unless such examination and reading are waived by the witness. Any changes in form or substance which the witness desires to make shall be entered and identified upon the transcript by the Commission investigator with a statement of the reasons given by the witness for making such changes. The transcript shall then be signed by the witness, unless the witness in writing waives the signing, is ill, cannot be found, or refuses to sign.

(ii) If the transcript is not signed by the witness during the 30-day period following the date upon which the witness is first afforded a reasonable opportunity to examine it, the Commission investigator shall sign the transcript and state on the record the fact of the waiver, illness, absence of the witness, or the refusal to sign, together with any reasons given for the failure to sign.

(F) The Commission investigator shall certify on the transcript that the witness was duly sworn by him and that the transcript is a true record of the testimony given by the witness, and the Commission investigator shall promptly deliver the transcript or send it by registered or certified mail to the custodian.

(G) The Commission investigator shall furnish a copy of the transcript (upon payment of reasonable charges for the transcription) to the witness only, except that the Commission may for good cause limit such witness to inspection of the official transcript of his testimony.

(H) Any witness appearing for the taking of oral testimony pursuant to a civil investigative demand shall be entitled to the same fees and mileage which are paid to witnesses in the district courts of the United States.

(d) Procedures for demand material

Materials received as a result of a civil investigative demand shall be subject to the procedures established in section 57b-2 of this title.

(e) Petition for enforcement

Whenever any person fails to comply with any civil investigative demand duly served upon him under this section, or whenever satisfactory copying or reproduction of material requested pursuant to the demand cannot be accomplished and such person refuses to surrender such material, the Commission, through such officers or attorneys as it may designate, may file, in the district court of the United States for any judicial district in which such person resides, is found, or transacts business, and serve upon such person, a petition for an order of such court for the enforcement of this section. All process of any court to which application may be made as provided in this subsection may be served in any judicial district.

(f) Petition for order modifying or setting aside demand

●(1) Not later than 20 days after the service of any civil investigative demand upon any person under subsection (c) of this section, or at any time before the return date specified in the demand, whichever period is shorter, or within such period exceeding 20 days after service or in excess of such return date as may be prescribed in writing, subsequent to service, by any Commission investigator named in the demand, such person may file with the Commission a petition for an order by the Commission modifying or setting aside the demand.

●(2) The time permitted for compliance with the demand in whole or in part, as deemed proper and ordered by the Commission, shall not run during the pendency of such petition at the Commission, except that such person shall comply with any portions of the demand not sought to be modified or set aside. Such petition shall specify each ground upon which the petitioner relies in seeking such relief, and may be based upon any failure of the demand to comply with the provisions of this section, or upon any constitutional or other legal right or privilege of such person.

(g) Custodial control of documentary material, tangible things, reports, etc.

At any time during which any custodian is in custody or control of any documentary material, tangible things, reports, answers to questions, or transcripts of oral testimony given by any person in compliance with any civil investigative demand, such person may file, in the district court of the United States for the judicial district within which the office of such custodian is situated, and serve upon such custodian, a petition for an order of such court requiring the performance by such custodian of any duty imposed upon him by this section or section 57b-2 of this title.

(h) Jurisdiction of court

Whenever any petition is filed in any district court of the United States under this section, such court shall have jurisdiction to hear and determine the matter so presented, and to enter such order or orders as may be required to carry into effect the provisions of this section. Any final order so entered shall be subject to appeal pursuant to section 1291 of title 28. Any disobedience of any final order entered under this section by any court shall be punished as a contempt of such court.

(i) Commission authority to issue subpoenas or make demand for information

Notwithstanding any other provision of law, the Commission shall have no authority to issue a subpoena or make a demand for information, under authority of this subchapter or any other provision of law, unless such subpoena or demand for information is signed by a Commissioner acting pursuant to a Commission resolution. The Commission shall not delegate the power conferred by this section to sign subpoenas or demands for information to any other person.

(j) Applicability of this section

The provisions of this section shall not-

•(1) apply to any proceeding under section 45(b) of this title, any

proceeding under section 11(b) of the Clayton Act (15 U.S.C. 21(b)), or any adjudicative proceeding under any other provision of law; or
●(2) apply to or affect the jurisdiction, duties, or powers of any agency of the Federal Government, other than the Commission, regardless of whether such jurisdiction, duties, or powers are derived in whole or in part, by reference to this subchapter.

57b-2. Confidentiality

(a) Definitions

For purposes of this section:

●(1) The term "material" means documentary material, tangible things, written reports or answers to questions, and transcripts of oral testimony.
●(2) The term "Federal agency" has the meaning given it in section 552(e) (FOOTNOTE 1) of title 5. (FOOTNOTE 1) See References in Text note below.

(b) Procedures respecting documents, tangible things, or transcripts of oral testimony received pursuant to compulsory process or investigation

●(1) With respect to any document, tangible thing, or transcript of oral testimony received by the Commission pursuant to compulsory process in an investigation, a purpose of which is to determine whether any person may have violated any provision of the laws administered by the Commission, the procedures established in paragraph (2) through paragraph (7) shall apply.
●(2)

(A) The Commission shall designate a duly authorized agent to serve as custodian of documentary material, tangible things, or written reports or answers to questions, and transcripts of oral testimony, and such additional duly authorized agents as the Commission shall determine from time to time to be necessary to serve as deputies to the custodian.
(B) Any person upon whom any demand for the production of documentary material has been duly served shall make such material available for inspection and copying or reproduction

to the custodian designated in such demand at the principal place of business of such person (or at such other place as such custodian and such person thereafter may agree or prescribe in writing or as the court may direct pursuant to section 57b-1(h) of this title) on the return date specified in such demand (or on such later date as such custodian may prescribe in writing). Such person may upon written agreement between such person and the custodian substitute copies for originals of all or any part of such material.

●(3)

(A) The custodian to whom any documentary material, tangible things, written reports or answers to questions, and transcripts of oral testimony are delivered shall take physical possession of such material, reports or answers, and transcripts, and shall be responsible for the use made of such material, reports or answers, and transcripts, and for the return of material, pursuant to the requirements of this section.

(B) The custodian may prepare such copies of the documentary material, written reports or answers to questions, and transcripts of oral testimony, and may make tangible things available, as may be required for official use by any duly authorized officer or employee of the Commission under regulations which shall be promulgated by the Commission. Notwithstanding subparagraph (C), such material, things, and transcripts may be used by any such officer or employee in connection with the taking of oral testimony under this section.

(C) Except as otherwise provided in this section, while in the possession of the custodian, no documentary material, tangible things, reports or answers to questions, and transcripts of oral testimony shall be available for examination by any individual other than a duly authorized officer or employee of the Commission without the consent of the person who produced the material, things, or transcripts. Nothing in this section is intended to prevent disclosure to either House of the Congress or to any committee or subcommittee of the Congress, except that the Commission immediately shall notify the owner or provider of any such information of a request for information designated as confidential by the owner or provider.

    (D) While in the possession of the custodian and under such reasonable terms and conditions as the Commission shall prescribe-
        (i) documentary material, tangible things, or written reports shall be available for examination by the person who produced the material, or by any duly authorized representative of such person; and
        (ii) answers to questions in writing and transcripts of oral testimony shall be available for examination by the person who produced the testimony or by his attorney.

●(4) Whenever the Commission has instituted a proceeding against a person, partnership, or corporation, the custodian may deliver to any officer or employee of the Commission documentary material, tangible things, written reports or answers to questions, and transcripts of oral testimony for official use in connection with such proceeding. Upon the completion of the proceeding, the officer or employee shall return to the custodian any such material so delivered which has not been received into the record of the proceeding.

●(5) If any documentary material, tangible things, written reports or answers to questions, and transcripts of oral testimony have been produced in the course of any investigation by any person pursuant to compulsory process and-
    (A) any proceeding arising out of the investigation has been completed; or
    (B) no proceeding in which the material may be used has been commenced within a reasonable time after completion of the examination and analysis of all such material and other information assembled in the course of the investigation; then the custodian shall, upon written request of the person who produced the material, return to the person any such material which has not been received into the record of any such proceeding (other than copies of such material made by the custodian pursuant to paragraph (3)(B)).

●(6) The custodian of any documentary material, written reports or answers to questions, and transcripts of oral testimony may deliver to any officers or employees of appropriate Federal law enforcement agencies, in response to a written request, copies of such material for use in connection with an investigation or proceeding under the jurisdiction of any such agency. The custodian of any tangible things may make such things available for inspection to such persons on the same basis. Such materials shall not be made available to any such agency until the custodian received certification of any officer of such agency that such information will be maintained in confidence and will be used only for official law enforcement purposes. Such documentary material, results of inspections of tangible things, written reports or answers to questions, and transcripts of oral testimony may be used by any officer or employee of such agency only in such manner and subject to such conditions as apply to the Commission under this section. The custodian may make such materials available to any State law enforcement agency upon the prior certification of any officer of such agency that such information will be maintained in confidence and will be used only for official law enforcement purposes.

●(7) In the event of the death, disability, or separation from service in the Commission of the custodian of any documentary material, tangible things, written reports or answers to questions, and transcripts of oral testimony produced under any demand issued under this subchapter, or the official relief of the custodian from responsibility for the custody and control of such material, the Commission promptly shall-

> (A) designate under paragraph (2)(A) another duly authorized agent to serve as custodian of such material; and
>
> (B) transmit in writing to the person who produced the material or testimony notice as to the identity and address of the successor so designated. Any successor designated under paragraph (2)(A) as a result of the requirements of this paragraph shall have (with regard to the material involved) all duties and responsibilities imposed by this section upon his predecessor in office with regard to such material, except that he shall not be held responsible for any default or dereliction which occurred before his designation.

(c) Information considered confidential

●(1) All information reported to or otherwise obtained by the Commission which is not subject to the requirements of subsection (b) of this section shall be considered confidential when so marked by the person supplying the information and shall not be disclosed, except in accordance with the procedures established in paragraph (2) and paragraph (3).

●(2) If the Commission determines that a document marked confidential by the person supplying it may be disclosed because it is not a trade secret or commercial or financial information which is obtained from any person and which is privileged or confidential, within the meaning of section 46(f) of this title, then the Commission shall notify such person in writing that the Commission intends to disclose the document at a date not less than 10 days after the date of receipt of notification.

●(3) Any person receiving such notification may, if he believes disclosure of the document would cause disclosure of a trade secret, or commercial or financial information which is obtained from any person and which is privileged or confidential, within the meaning of section 46(f) of this title, before the date set for release of the document, bring an action in the district court of the United States for the district within which the documents are located or in the United States District Court for the District of Columbia to restrain disclosure of the document. Any person receiving such notification may file with the appropriate district court or court of appeals of the United States, as appropriate, an application for a stay of disclosure. The documents shall not be disclosed until the court has ruled on the application for a stay.

(d) Particular disclosures allowed

●(1) The provisions of subsection (c) of this section shall not be construed to prohibit-

(A) the disclosure of information to either House of the Congress or to any committee or subcommittee of the Congress, except that the Commission immediately shall notify the owner or provider of any such information of a request for information designated as confidential by the owner or provider;

(B) the disclosure of the results of any investigation or study carried out or prepared by the Commission, except that no information shall be identified nor shall information be disclosed in such a manner as to disclose a trade secret of any person supplying the trade secret, or to disclose any commercial or financial information which is obtained from any person and which is privileged or confidential;

(C) the disclosure of relevant and material information in Commission adjudicative proceedings or in judicial proceedings to which the Commission is a party; or

(D) the disclosure to a Federal agency of disaggregated information obtained in accordance with section 3512 (FOOTNOTE 1) of title 44, except that the recipient agency shall use such disaggregated information for economic, statistical, or policymaking purposes only, and shall not disclose such information in an individually identifiable form.

●(2) Any disclosure of relevant and material information in Commission adjudicative proceedings or in judicial proceedings to which the Commission is a party shall be governed by the rules of the Commission for adjudicative proceedings or by court rules or orders, except that the rules of the Commission shall not be amended in a manner inconsistent with the purposes of this section.

(e) Effect on other statutory provisions limiting disclosure

Nothing in this section shall supersede any statutory provision which expressly prohibits or limits particular disclosures by the Commission, or which authorizes disclosures to any other Federal agency.

(f) Exemption from disclosure

Any material which is received by the Commission in any investigation, a purpose of which is to determine whether any person may have violated any provision of the laws administered by the Commission, and which is provided pursuant to any compulsory process under this subchapter or which is provided voluntarily in place of such compulsory process shall be exempt from disclosure under section 552 of title 5.

57b-3. Rulemaking process

(a) Definitions

For purposes of this section:

●(1) The term "rule" means any rule promulgated by the Commission under section 46 or section 57a of this title, except that such term does not include interpretive rules, rules involving Commission management or personnel, general statements of policy, or rules relating to Commission organization, procedure, or practice. Such term does not include any amendment to a rule unless the Commission-

> (A) estimates that such amendment will have an annual effect on the national economy of $100,000,000 or more;
>
> (B) estimates that such amendment will cause a substantial change in the cost or price of goods or services which are used extensively by particular industries, which are supplied extensively in particular geographic regions, or which are acquired in significant quantities by the Federal Government, or by State or local governments; or
>
> (C) otherwise determines that such amendment will have a significant impact upon persons subject to regulation under such amendment and upon consumers.

●(2) The term "rulemaking" means any Commission process for formulating or amending a rule.

(b) Notice of proposed rulemaking; regulatory analysis; contents; issuance

●(1) In any case in which the Commission publishes notice of a proposed rulemaking, the Commission shall issue a preliminary regulatory analysis relating to the proposed rule involved. Each preliminary regulatory analysis shall contain-

> (A) a concise statement of the need for, and the objectives of, the proposed rule;
>
> (B) a description of any reasonable alternatives to the proposed rule which may accomplish the stated objective of the rule in a manner consistent with applicable law; and
>
> (C) for the proposed rule, and for each of the alternatives described in the analysis, a preliminary analysis of the projected benefits and any adverse economic effects and any other effects, and of the effectiveness of the proposed rule and each alternative in meeting the stated objectives of the proposed rule.

●(2) In any case in which the Commission promulgates a final rule, the

Commission shall issue a final regulatory analysis relating to the final rule. Each final regulatory analysis shall contain-

(A) a concise statement of the need for, and the objectives of, the final rule;

(B) a description of any alternatives to the final rule which were considered by the Commission;

(C) an analysis of the projected benefits and any adverse economic effects and any other effects of the final rule;

(D) an explanation of the reasons for the determination of the Commission that the final rule will attain its objectives in a manner consistent with applicable law and the reasons the particular alternative was chosen; and

(E) a summary of any significant issues raised by the comments submitted during the public comment period in response to the preliminary regulatory analysis, and a summary of the assessment by the Commission of such issues.

●(3)

(A) In order to avoid duplication or waste, the Commission is authorized to

(i) consider a series of closely related rules as one rule for purposes of this subsection; and

(ii) whenever appropriate, incorporate any data or analysis contained in a regulatory analysis issued under this subsection in the statement of basis and purpose to accompany any rule promulgated under section 57a(a)(1)(B) of this title, and incorporate by reference in any preliminary or final regulatory analysis information contained in a notice of proposed rulemaking or a statement of basis and purpose.

(B) The Commission shall include, in each notice of proposed rulemaking and in each publication of a final rule, a statement of the manner in which the public may obtain copies of the preliminary and final regulatory analyses. The Commission may charge a reasonable fee for the copying and mailing of regulatory analyses. The regulatory analyses shall be furnished without charge or at a reduced charge if the Commission determines that waiver or reduction of the fee is in the public interest because furnishing the information primarily benefits the general public.

●(4) The Commission is authorized to delay the completion of any of the requirements established in this subsection by publishing in the Federal Register, not later than the date of publication of the final rule involved, a finding that the final rule is being promulgated in response to an emergency which makes timely compliance with the provisions of this subsection impracticable. Such publication shall include a statement of the reasons for such finding.

●(5) The requirements of this subsection shall not be construed to alter in any manner the substantive standards applicable to any action by the Commission, or the procedural standards otherwise applicable to such action.

(c) Judicial review

●(1) The contents and adequacy of any regulatory analysis prepared or issued by the Commission under this section, including the adequacy of any procedure involved in such preparation or issuance, shall not be subject to any judicial review in any court, except that a court, upon review of a rule pursuant to section 57a(e) of this title, may set aside such rule if the Commission has failed entirely to prepare a regulatory analysis.

●(2) Except as specified in paragraph (1), no Commission action may be invalidated, remanded, or otherwise affected by any court on account of any failure to comply with the requirements of this section.

●(3) The provisions of this subsection do not alter the substantive or procedural standards otherwise applicable to judicial review of any action by the Commission.

(d) Regulatory agenda; contents; publication dates in Federal Register

●(1) The Commission shall publish at least semiannually a regulatory agenda. Each regulatory agenda shall contain a list of rules which the Commission intends to propose or promulgate during the 12-month period following the publication of the agenda. On the first Monday in October of each year, the Commission shall publish in the Federal Register a schedule showing the dates during the current fiscal year on

481

which the semiannual regulatory agenda of the Commission will be published.

●(2) For each rule listed in a regulatory agenda, the Commission shall-
    (A) describe the rule;
    (B) state the objectives of and the legal basis for the rule; and
    (C) specify any dates established or anticipated by the Commission for taking action, including dates for advance notice of proposed rulemaking, notices of proposed rulemaking, and final action by the Commission.

●(3) Each regulatory agenda shall state the name, office address, and office telephone number of the Commission officer or employee responsible for responding to any inquiry relating to each rule listed.

●(4) The Commission shall not propose or promulgate a rule which was not listed on a regulatory agenda unless the Commission publishes with the rule an explanation of the reasons the rule was omitted from such agenda.

57b-4. Good faith reliance on actions of Board of Governors

(a) "Board of Governors" defined

For purposes of this section, the term "Board of Governors" means the Board of Governors of the Federal Reserve System.

(b) Use as defense

Notwithstanding any other provision of law, if-

    ●(1) any person, partnership, or corporation engages in any conduct or practice which allegedly constitutes a violation of any Federal law with respect to which the Board of Governors of the Federal Reserve System has rulemaking authority; and

    ●(2) such person, partnership, or corporation engaged in such conduct or practice in good faith reliance upon, and in conformity with, any rule, regulation, statement of interpretation, or statement of approval prescribed or issued by the Board of Governors under such Federal law; then such good faith reliance shall constitute a defense in any administrative or judicial proceeding commenced against such person, partnership, or corporation by the Commission under this subchapter or in any administrative or judicial proceeding commenced against such person, partnership, or corporation by the Attorney General of the United States, upon request made by the Commission, under any provision of law.

(c) Applicability of subsection (b)

The provisions of subsection (b) of this section shall apply regardless of whether any rule, regulation, statement of interpretation, or statement of approval prescribed or issued by the Board of Governors is amended, rescinded, or held to be invalid by judicial authority or any other authority after a person, partnership, or corporation has engaged in any conduct or practice in good faith reliance upon, and in conformity with, such rule, regulation, statement of interpretation, or statement of approval.

(d) Request for issuance of statement or interpretation concerning conduct or practice

If, in any case in which-

● (1) the Board of Governors has rulemaking authority with respect to any Federal law; and
● (2) the Commission is authorized to enforce the requirements of such Federal law; any person, partnership, or corporation submits a request to the Board of Governors for the issuance of any statement of interpretation or statement of approval relating to any conduct or practice of such person, partnership, or corporation which may be subject to the requirements of such Federal law, then the Board of Governors shall dispose of such request as soon as practicable after the receipt of such.

57b-5. Agricultural cooperatives

(a) The Commission shall not have any authority to conduct any study, investigation, or prosecution of any agricultural cooperative for any conduct which, because of the provisions of sections 291 and 292 of title 7, is not a violation of any of the antitrust Acts or this subchapter.

(b) The Commission shall not have any authority to conduct any study or investigation of any agricultural marketing orders.

57c. Authorization of appropriations

There are authorized to be appropriated to carry out the functions, powers, and duties of the Commission not to exceed $92,700,000 for fiscal year 1994; not to exceed $99,000,000 for fiscal year 1995; and not to exceed $102,000,000 for fiscal year 1996.

58. Short title

This subchapter may be cited as the "Federal Trade Commission Act."

Name Index

Name Index

Case Index

499

Subject Index